LET'S GO

www.letsgo.com

ITALY

researcher-writers
Julia Rooney
Alex Tomko
Elizabeth Weinbloom
William N. White

staff writers
Sophia Angelis
Juan Cantu
Rachel Granetz
Dorothy McLeod

research manager
Chris Kingston

editor
Bronwen Beseda O'Herin

managing editor
Marykate Jasper

D0097066

When in ROME

Hostels Alessandro

The best hostels in Rome

- Free Breakfast - Free Map
- Linen includ. - Central location
- A/C & lockers in all rooms
- Card key Access - Open for 24hrs
- Internet Access (PC & Wi-Fi)
- Large Common Room - No Curfew
- English Speaking Staff
- Free Pizza/Pasta Parties*
  (*Details on our website!)
- and MUCH MORE!

2010
LET'S GO recommends

info & on-line booking :

www.HostelsAlessandro.com

Wi-Fi In All Areas

Alessandro PALACE & BAR
Member of Europe's Famous Hostels

Via Vicenza 42
00185 Rome - Italy

EUROPE'S FAMOUS HOSTELS

Alessandro DOWNTOWN
Member of hostelling International

Via Carlo Cattaneo 23
00185 Rome - Italy

E-mail:
info@hotelsalessandro.com

Tel: +39/06-4461958

Fax: +39/06-49380534

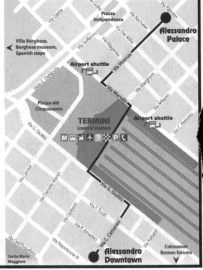

CONTENTS

RESEARCHER-WRITERS

JULIA ROONEY. This veteran of *Let's Go Italy 2009* demonstrated a prodigious knowledge of Italian culture that put her editors—and probably even a few locals—to shame. From trying (and failing) to sketch Marcus Aurelius's foot to devouring dangerous amounts of Roman gelato, Julia kept her cool with perfect prose and *perfetto italiano.*

ALEX TOMKO. Refusing to be worn down by Venice's antiquated structure, Alex somehow found time to train for a triathlon between afternoons visiting palatial hotels and nights wandering the streets in search of the perfect bar in Dorsoduro.

ELIZABETH WEINBLOOM. After the Dark Ages of grad school, Elizabeth went to Italy for *Let's Go* seeking her own Renaissance—and found it in the hallowed galleries of the Uffizi. After stressful encounters with Tuscan train schedules and angry San Gimignano nuns, Elizabeth resisted the temptation to settle down in Lucca and instead completed her route like a champ.

WILLIAM N. WHITE. An experienced sailor, William proved himself no ordinary 🚣**boat** nerd, displaying additional talents as a hiker, pizza critic, and—of course—star RW. While the beach bums around him soaked up the sun in Monterosso, William spent his time bringing subtle wit and a travel-savvy perspective to his research.

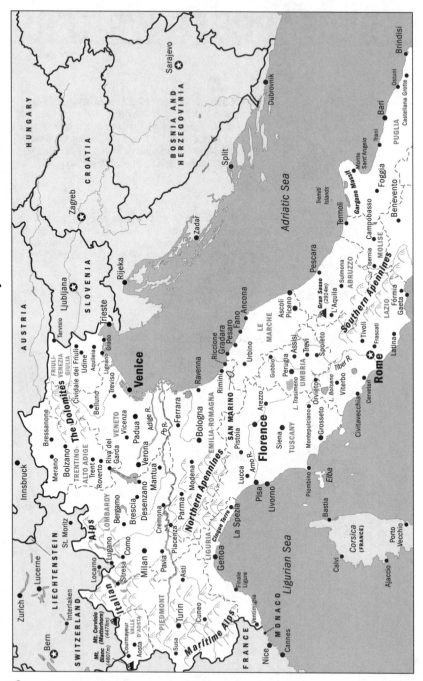

italy

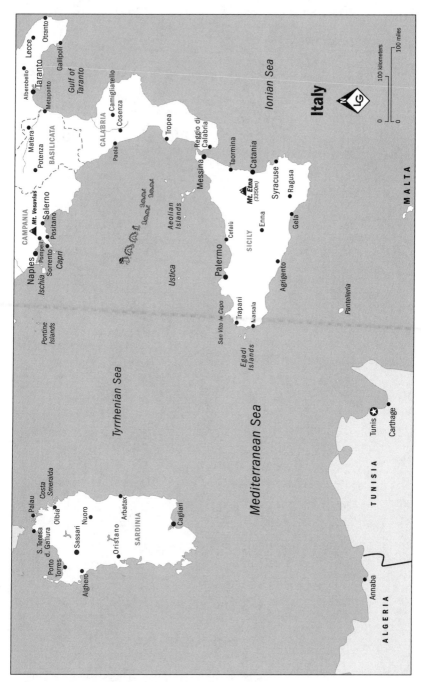

overivew map

DISCOVER

ITALY

For the home of the papacy, Italy sure knows how to do sensual pleasures right: stylish Vespas, intoxicating *vino*, vibrant *piazze*, and crispy pizzas covered in garden-fresh produce populate this country where *la dolce far niente* (literally, the sweetness of doing nothing) is a national pastime. While some travelers let Italy's quirks (supermarkets closed on Sunday and spotty A/C) impede their pursuit of *la dolce vita*, as a student traveler, you are uniquely situated to experience "the boot" in all its ridiculousness and sublimity. Striking out on your own, likely on a budget, you'll open yourself up to what someone who stays at the swankiest hotels and eats at all the five-star restaurants misses: making connections with the people and way of life of this chaotic wonderland. *Let's Go* researchers have reported being given copious amounts of free food, receiving unsolicited assistance, and sharing drinks with natives who were more than ready to help them navigate the caprices of a country where things we take for granted ("the customer is always right," street signs, etc.) are conspicuously absent. It's not like our researchers wear neon orange Let's Go T-shirts while they're traveling the country—they were treated this way because in their quests for the most divine scoop of gelato or the best-deal happy hour buffet, they reached out to the locals who know how much of the country's untainted energy can be found in its most affordable pleasures. You too can learn to see the beauty of Italy's sometimes befuddling customs, as getting acquainted with its people becomes as much a priority as taking in all its Renaissance art, Roman grandeur, and religious relics. Who knows? Maybe by the time you're ready to leave, some of those Italian oddities will be looking practically divine.

when to go

The number-one reason to study abroad in Italy is the opportunity to visit the country in the spring or fall, when the weather is mild and the tourist hordes have dwindled. If you end up enrolled at a university in one of the country's smaller cities like Bologna or Pisa, you'll have the added bonus of experiencing these college towns when nightlife is at its best, since in the summer the student crowd that fills bars and clubs is gone on vacation. However, if you can't figure out a good excuse to spend a semester in Italy and have already booked your tickets to Cabo for spring break, be prepared to deal with summer crowds and heat. In Rome and Florence, temperatures are known to climb into the mid-90s in low-humidity heat waves. Most Italians go on vacation in August, so follow their lead and find somewhere else to be during this month (Winnipeg, perhaps?).

You can expect cooler temperatures during the winter (colder in the north, where ski resorts capitalize on the snowfall). Many sights keep shorter winter hours, and some hotel and restaurant owners take vacation during this part of the year. When your wait to enter the Vatican is only 10min. and doesn't involve heatstroke, you'll be glad you chose to take on these minor inconveniences.

top five places be sacrilegious

5. MILAN'S DUOMO: In a salute to the city's fashion gods, don a Versace sheath dress and bare your shoulders under the soaring ceiling of Milan's central basilica.

4. VENICE: Be mischievous even when it's not Carnevale by placing a party hat on the head of every winged lion you see on April 25th, the feast day of the city's patron Saint Mark.

3. SIENA: Steal away St. Catherine's crucifix to see if this sacred object will bring your favored steed to victory in the town's famous *palio*.

2. NAPLES: Pooh-pooh Milanese refinement while toasting this gritty southern city with an ice-cold glass of local favorite *limoncello*.

1. VATICAN CITY: Disobey the guards in the Sistine Chapel and whisper sweet nothings into the ear of your traveling companion while pondering the fate depicted for you in Michelangelo's *Last Judgment*.

what to do

MONDO MANGIA

Yes, this is the land of pizza and pasta, but it's also where fresh, quality ingredients reign supreme. In this way, Italy is totally on-trend—perhaps even pre-trend, as it anticipated the whole locavore thing before it began. As you travel through the country, conduct your own informal study of the country's regional cuisines. In Rome, delight in the fresh produce of the fertile Lazio region and home-style cooking that wastes nothing (tripe, anyone?). In Venice, indulge in the fruits of the Adriatic as well as the wild game and mushrooms of the northern Italian mainland. In Florence, revel in Tuscan specialties like *panzanella* (a summer bread salad), *ribollita* (a soup made with seasonal veggies, beans, and bread), and *bistecca alla fiorentina* (grilled and seasoned T-bone steak). On the Amalfi Coast, gobble up unadulterated versions of the recognizable classic Italian dishes that have become staples of the American diet. Even if you can't splurge on a multi-course feast every night, you can still eat like royalty anywhere in the country if you know where to look. Hit up grocers for gourmet picnics, *fornaios* for sinfully affordable pizza, and *aperitivo* happy hours for assorted *antipasti* and the house wine. Is Treviso radicchio in season? You can bet you'll find it in the pasta dish you order in Venice, but don't count on finding it on the pizza you scarf down in Rome. So make like a cow and graze your way through this foodie paradise—you'll probably wish you had four stomachs, too.

- **GUSTO:** Stop by this combination *ristorante,* pizzeria, and *enoteca* during happy hour to fill up on a buffet of gourmet *antipasti* before a night out in the Piazza di Spagna. (Rome, p. 65.)

- **NAVE DE ORO:** This Venetian *enoteca* with multiple outposts invites you to fill up your empty bottles with any of the regional wines sold by the liter. (Venice, p. 197.)

- **ANTICA GELATERIA FIORENTINA:** Sample offbeat flavors of gelato like rosewater, cheesecake, and green tea—no need to limit yourself as one scoop of any variety costs only €1. (Florence, p. 303.)

- **CANTINA DI SCIACCHETRÀ:** Drop in for some refreshment at this wine shop as you hike the Cinque Terre. Take advantage of the free samples, and buy a bottle to enjoy on the beach. (Monterosso, p. 253.)

- **GINO SORBILLO:** Regardless of whether this place actually invented the calzone (as it claims), it surely seems capable of such a feat given its 21 scrumptious pizza varieties. (Naples, p. 394.)

WHERE REBIRTH WAS BORN

Italy contains a startling percentage of the western hemisphere's must-see works of art. Plan your time here wisely to avoid lines and crowds as best you can, and then get ready to marvel at the wonders of humanity. Men like Leonardo and Michelangelo who ushered in the humanistic spirit of the Renaissance had you in mind when they created the art that fills this country: they stretched the bounds of human expression to prove what we as a species were capable of doing, and the sense of excitement in their accomplishment that radiates from their work is contagious. Sure, Florence can start feeling like the Medici's giant Renaissance storage facility, but when it seems as if you just can't handle one more Madonna and Child, take a minute to dig a little deeper into what makes these artistic wonders so special. Escape the crowd in the Sistine Chapel as you imagine what it would be like to lie on your back, paint dripping down on your face, depicting something as epic as the creation of the world. Ponder what Venus might be thinking and feeling as she pulls tendrils of windswept hair about her in Botticelli's famous painting. Blow on the Bernini sculptures in the Galleria Borghese and see if they come to life. Take pleasure in all the vitality of these eternally captivating works of art.

- **UFFIZI GALLERY:** This is where you'll find Botticelli's biggies: *Birth of Venus, Allegory of Spring, Adoration of the Magi,* and *Slander.* Even if you don't get why these are touchstones of art history, you've got to admit that Venus is pretty damn sexy. (Florence, p. 289.)

- **VATICAN MUSEUMS:** All the goodies the Catholic church hauled in for itself during its rise as the arbiter of culture in the Western world. Resist the urge to race through these museums in order to reach the Sistine Chapel. (Rome, p. 50.)

- **GALLERIA DELL'ACCADEMIA:** Even more hot Florentine nudiness, this time in male form. Spend some time in this home of Michelangelo's *David* and a surprisingly informative musical instruments exhibit. (Florence, p. 295.)
- **PALAZZO DUCALE:** Get a feel for Venetian-style Renaissance opulence at this complex that once served as residence to the city's mayor. Don't miss hometown hero Tintoretto's *Paradise.* (Venice, p. 177.)

KICKIN' IT OLD SCHOOL WITH MARCUS AURELIUS ET AL.

Whether you can rattle off the succession of Roman emperors between Augustus and Hadrian at the tip of a hat or are the type who's right now wondering what makes Marcus Aurelius so special that he gets to go by two rather than the apparently standard single name, you've got to admit that the remarkably preserved arches, aqueducts, and amphitheaters of antiquity's sprawling Western empire add a certain something to the Italian landscape. Like all the Renaissance art and architecture, Roman ruins testify to humanity's impressive powers of creation. At the same time, they remind us that we, too, will one day be nothing more than the pitiful remnants of our society—a ragged Empire State Building surrounded by sleek, zippy hover-craft. As you marvel at the ingenuity and willpower behind the Romans' ambitious constructions, take a minute to ponder which of our modern-day monuments will make their way onto the sightseeing itineraries of the future. Perhaps consider what about Roman society and design makes this latter-day civilization so fascinating to us today. Watching the sun set on the city of Rome's Colosseum, don't be ashamed to feel a twinge of bittersweet melancholy. This is the magic of Roman ruins: the way they manage to evoke all that is eternal and noble in the human experience while simultaneously symbolizing our inevitable decay.

- **COLOSSEUM:** Yes, this is obvious, but that doesn't mean it shouldn't be included. Climb to the structure's upper tiers for a spectacular view of the Eternal City. (Rome, p. 35.)
- **NAPOLI SOTTERANEA:** Explore subterranean Naples' network of aqueducts originally built by the Greeks and then pimped out under Roman rule. (Naples, p. 390.)

student superlatives

- **MOST PROMISING FIXER-UPPER:** All that's needed is a few tons of marble and roughly 40,000 Christian slaves to bring the Baths of Diocletian (p. 55) back to their former glory.
- **MOST IN NEED OF STRAIGHTENING OUT:** Someone should really have a word with the Leaning Tower of Pisa's (p. 334) parents—that thing's been out of line for centuries.
- **BEST DRESSED:** The mannequins in Milan's designer stores (p. 140) beckon seductively as if to say, "All the cool kids are sporting €1000 hand-bags these days."
- **MOST ONE-OF-A-KIND:** Club Piccolo Mondo (p. 205) is Venice's only club, quite the rebel among all of the city's conformist canals and *palazzi.*
- **MOST LIKELY TO SUCCEED:** The enterprising Piazzale Michelangelo (p. 299) somehow managed to transcend its primary purpose as a parking lot, becoming a destination for millions of camera-toting tourists. If you've seen a photo of Florence, it was probably taken here.

- **POMPEII:** This petrified city is an archaeologist's paradise offering valuable insights into the way of life in the Roman Empire circa 79 CE. (Pompeii, p. 404.)

- **HERCULANEUM:** The little sib to Pompeii, this is another surprisingly intact ancient city. Take time to explore the town, which was allegedly founded by Hercules himself. (Herculaneum, p. 407.)

BEYOND TOURISM

Hate tourists? Then don't be one. Instead, travel to Italy as a student, volunteer, or salaried employee. It's hard to dread the first day of school when Rome is your campus and heaping bowls of pasta al dente and creamy gelato *alla fragola* make up your meal plan. Those with especial interests in art and architecture, archaeology and ancient civilizations, fashion design, or food and wine will find a wealth of study abroad programs that take advantage of Italy's particular resources in such areas. Indiana Jones wannabes can volunteer in archaeology work camps, and resumé-padders ought to consider interning in a Florentine architecture firm. Hippies might check out the World Wide Organization of Organic Farming (WWOOF) to find out about opportunities to get down-and-dirty on organic farms, and those with magical, bottomless carpetbags and umbrellas with talking-parrot handles should look into au pairing adorable Italian *bambini*.

Living as a non-tourist in Italy, you'll gain an interesting perspective on local culture as well as undeniable street cred. Plus, it's super-cool when you begin to blend in so well that American tourists bust out their broken Italian to ask you for directions. Not many people can call a foreign country their home-away-from-home, but as a student, volunteer, or worker in the city, you'll earn that privilege.

- **UNIVERSITÀ COMMERCIALE LUIGI BOCCONI:** Italy's first university to award a degree in economics is a haven for future i-bankers with a taste for the good life. (Milan, p. 460.)

- **STUDIO ART CENTERS INTERNATIONAL:** Enroll in a year-long program to receive a Post-Baccalaureate Certificate in art, art history, or art conservation—or just futz around the beautiful city during the summer. (Florence, p. 461.)

- **ARCHAEOSPAIN:** When you aren't clubbing at Monte Testaccio, come dig up the ruins of the "ancient pottery dump" left here by people of the first few centuries. (Rome, p. 462.)

- **PEGGY GUGGENHEIM COLLECTION:** Intern at this first-rate museum housed in a gorgeous *palazzo* and care for works by artistic superstars like Miró, Picasso, Dalí, and Magritte. (Venice, p. 465.)

- **COOK ITALY:** Take one of this company's crash courses in Italian regional cuisine to make your stay in Lucca or Bologna that much more delicious. (Bologna, p. 462.)

suggested itineraries

BEST OF ITALY IN 1 MONTH

Exploring the country as a whole, you'll get to sample all of Italy's culinary and cultural flavors. From the sophisticated north to the scrappy south, this is one tasty boot.

1. VENICE (3 DAYS): Begin your visit in Venice's most famous square, P. San Marco, and tour its majestic basilica. Duck into the Museo Correr to escape the tourist hordes, then grab lunch and do a little window shopping along Calle Larga XXII Marzo. Hit the Palazzo Ducale for hardcore Venetian history. If you want the full tourist experience, climb the Campanile for a pre-dinner stretch of the legs or shell out the money for a gondola ride to complete **day one.** Start your **second day** around Rialto Bridge, making sure to take in its market scene and considering a stop in the Palazzo Grassi. Continue on to Frari church in San Polo and check out the Tintoretto canvases in the Scuola Grande di San Rocco. After lunch, move on to Dorsoduro, *Let's Go's* favorite Venetian neighborhood. Tour the Peggy Guggenheim Collection, Santa Maria della Salute, and the Accademia. Consider rounding out your day with a vaporetto ride down the Grand Canal. On **day three,** explore the lagoon by vaporetto, stopping at Lido and Burano. Head to Santa Croce and fill your afternoon with Venice's Museum of Natural History. Eat an affordable meal in the neighborhood and wander back to see P. San Marco at night.

2. VERONA (1 DAY): Make a stop here en route to Milan to get your fill of Romeo and Juliet kitsch and catch an opera performance if you're visiting during the city's annual festival.

3. MILAN (3 DAYS): Start out your **first day** in P. del Duomo, the city's heart. Tour the square's majestic namesake structure and the nearby Pinacoteca Ambrosiana, where you can view Raphael's sketches for his *School of Athens.* Walk through the Galleria Vittorio Emanuele II, grabbing lunch on the way to La Scala. Take in the opera house's museum and the Museo Poldi Pezzoli, then return to P. del Duomo to grab delicious grub to go at Princi. Eat it while you wait for rush tickets at La Scala, then get ready to experience opera heaven. **Day two** is all about Castello Sforzesco, where you should spend the morning and make sure to check out the Museum of Ancient Art. Try the Chilli Chocolate gelato at Chocolat, then make your way to the Chiesa di Santa Maria delle Grazie. If you've bought a ticket months in advance, have fun viewing Leonardo's *Last Supper.* If not, consider joining a tour group that is scheduled to see the painting. Afterwards, peruse the Pinacoteca di Brera, the Museo Nazionale della Scienza e della Tecnologia "Da Vinci," and the Basilica di Sant'Ambrogio. Metro to the Navigli neighborhood for dinner at Big Pizza and dessert at Il Forno dei Navigli, then get ready to party the night away inside this student-friendly bar center. Nurse your hangover in the Giardini Pubblici on **day three,** devoting some time to the Galleria D'Arte Moderna. Move on to the Fashion District, where you should explore the Museo Bagatti Valsecchi before indulging in a little retail therapy (probably at D Magazine Outlet rather than Armani). Consider taking in a show at Piccolo Teatro Nuovo before you leave this stylish city.

4. TURIN (1 DAY): Don't miss the Mole Antonelliana, Palazzo dell'Accademia delle Scienze, or Rivetti Piaceri di Cioccolato.

5. CINQUE TERRE (2 DAYS): Devote your **first day** in this five-village beach area to a leisurely hike connecting the towns. On **day two,** linger in your favorite hill towns.

6. LUCCA (2 DAYS): Get ready for more relaxed sightseeing during your **first day** in this Tuscan escape. Perfect the art of doing nothing as you wander the city's walls, lounge in its *piazza,* and soak up the view from its towers. Dine at the only restaurant built in the walls and, if you're lucky, catch a summer opera or chamber music performance. Sleep in on **day two** and maybe drop into the Puccini Opera exhibit before heading to **Pisa,** where you can marvel at its lopsided tower. Catch the bus to the Marina di Pisa to soak up the sun as well as the *aperitivo* buffet at Sunset Cafe.

7. FLORENCE (4 DAYS): Head straight to the Duomo on your **first day,** taking time to explore the Baptistery of San Giovanni, the Campanile and Brunelleschi's dome, and the Museo Opera San Maria del Fiore. Spend the afternoon at the Uffizi (reserve in advance) and the Palazzo Vecchio. Begin **day two** viewing sculptures at the Bargello and Accademia. Get your fill of San Marco in the afternoon by visiting the Museo di San Marco and the Museum of the Opificio Delle Pietre Dure. **Day three** means more religion, with visits to the Basilica di Santa Croce and Synagogue of Florence. Wander around P. della Signoria, then turn north to Palazzo Medici Ricardi and the Basilica di San Lorenzo. On **day four,** cross the river to the Oltrarno neighborhood and spend the day at the Palazzo Pitti and Boboli Gardens. Catch sunset at the Piazzale Michelangelo before you move on to Siena.

8. SIENA (1 DAY): Explore the completely car-free center of this medieval town and pick your favorite of its 17 neighborhoods. Don't miss Il Campo or the cathedral.

9. ASSISI (1 DAY): If Assisi's lovely basilica doesn't inspire you to emulate the village's favorite saint, the views from this hilltop pilgrimage site certainly will.

10. ROME (7 DAYS): Start out strong, hitting the Colosseum, Roman Forum, and Velabrum in the morning, then moving on to Trastevere through the Isola Tiberina to check out Gianicolo Hill and the lovely Chiesa Di Santa Maria. End your **first day** with dinner at one of the neighborhood's homey trattorias before soaking up its vibrant nightlife. Make Vatican City your destination for **day two,** giving yourself enough time to thoroughly explore the Musei Vaticani and St. Peter's Basilica as well as the Sistine Chapel. For a comparatively low-key chaser, head to Castel Sant'Angelo before grabbing dinner. Cool off with some jazz at Fonclea and icy to complete the evening. Begin your **third day** at the Galleria Borghese (remember to reserve your ticket in advance), eating a picnic brunch in the gardens that surround the museum. Follow V. Veneto to Capuchin Crypt and Piazza Barberini. Try to erase the crypt's reminder of your mortality from your memory as you spend the rest of the day shopping and eating your way in the area around the Fontana di Trevi, Piazza di Spagna, and Piazza del Popolo. Make **day four** one of pilgrimage to Rome's best churches. Start with San Giovanni in Laterano, San Clemente, Santa Maria Maggiore, and San Pietro in Vincoli. Take a siesta, then head to Centro Storico for San Luigi dei Francesi and the Pantheon, an equally inspiring religious structure. Spend your **fifth day** in southern Rome, diving back into ancient history with a visit to the Circus Maximus. If you're ready for a walk, head to the Centrale Montemartini, or take the Metro to get there and then visit the Basilica di San Paolo Fuori le Mura. Return to Testaccio for excellent food and clubbing. Go even deeper south on **day six** and take a bus to the Appian Way where you can investigate the Catacombo San Sebastiano and San Callisto. On **day seven,** spend the morning rambling through the Baths of Diocletian, then head to P. del Popolo for lunch and pass the afternoon strolling down V. del Corso, making detours to check out Santa Maria del Popolo church and the Museo dell'Ara Pacis at your leisure. End at the Capitoline Hill for one final survey of the eternal city.

11. NAPLES (3 DAYS): Start **day one** at the Cappella San Severo to view Giuseppe Sanmartino's *Veiled Christ,* then tour Naples' dead-people-filled bowels. You'll want to try some of the city's famed pizza, so hit up Gino Sorbillo for a tasty pie. Escape the sun by exploring Naples' Museo Archeologico Nazionale. Get another taste of the Neopolitan specialty for dinner at Pizzeria Di Matteo, then shake what yo momma gave you at Tropicana. Make the trip to Castel Sant'Elmo on your **second day,** and fill up on some super-cheap eats at Friggitoria Vomero after spending your morning at the museum. Return to central Naples and the P. del Plebiscito for an afternoon at the Palazzo Reale. Rest your dogs at a nearby osteria or trattoria and investigate student ticket possibilities at Teatro di San Carlo. On **day three,** travel to Pompeii, Herculaneum, or both.

12. SORRENTO (2 DAYS): Spend **day one** recovering from the stretch of hardcore sightseeing while taking in the rays on Sorrento's beaches. Stay cool with a scoop from Primavera Gelateria. On your **second day,** ferry to the Isle of Capri.

13. POSITANO (1 DAY): Get outdoorsy on the Amalfi Coast, hiking the "Path of the Gods" in the morning and swimming in the pristine ocean all afternoon. Head home refreshed after an epic Italian adventure.

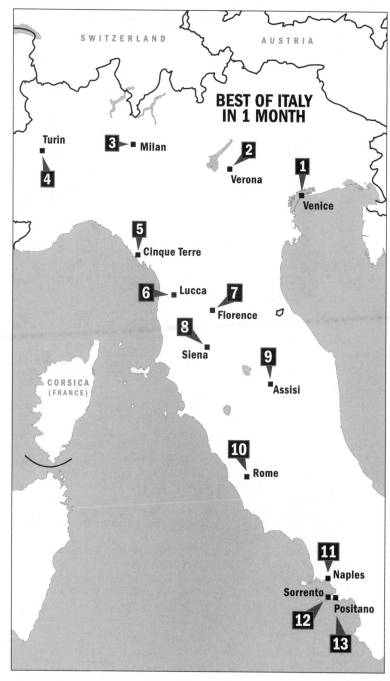

BEST OF ITALY
IN 1 MONTH

Turin

3 ■ Milan

2

■ Verona

1

■ Venice

5

■ Cinque Terre

6 ■ Lucca

7

■ Florence

8

■ Siena

9

■ Assisi

10

■ Rome

11

■ Naples

Sorrento

12

Positano

13

SWITZERLAND

AUSTRIA

CORSICA
(FRANCE)

VACATIONING ALFRESCO

Don't confine yourself to Italy's cities. Hikers and beach bums alike will be pleased to find that a trip to Italy doesn't have to involve the urban jungle.

1. TURIN (3 DAYS): Spend your time frolicking in the Alps adjacent to this city that played host to the **2006 Winter Olympics.** In the summer, golf in Sestriere.

2. CINQUE TERRE (4 DAYS): Spend your entire first day in Monterosso lounging on the beach. Next morning, take on the hike to Vernazza, where you'll be rewarded with a rugged castle. Hike the next stretch to Corniglia where you'll find good wine, views, and lodging. Catch sunrise and then onward-ho to Manarola. Spend the day swimming at this village's beach and stay for the night. For your final day in the Cinque Terre, hike the V. dell'Amore to Riomaggiore, then reacclimate to civilization, spending a day wandering through town.

3. LUCCA (2 DAYS): Enjoy the Tuscan hill-town beauty of this *Let's Go* favorite. Then, daytrip to Pisa, where you can take in the tower—and a beach.

4. CORTONA (1 DAY): Hike out to Eremo de le Celle, a 13th-century monastery built into the face of a mountain, and return to Cortona for blueberry pasta at Fufluns.

5. ISLE OF CAPRI (2 DAYS): Escape the isle's touristy areas and hike its trails. Devote day two to the gorgeous Grotta Azzurra.

6. SORRENTO (1 DAY): Explore this town's beaches and hiking trails.

7. POSITANO (2 DAYS): Whether you're ready to take on the 4hr. "Path of the Gods." or if secluded sunbathing is more your speed, you'll surely enjoy this coastal town.

8. AMALFI (3 DAYS): Give yourself a day at the beach, then a day to hike to **Ravello,** where lovely gardens and views await you. Take a third day for more beachiness. Relaxed yet?

DEBEACHERY

As is clear from the Italian Alfresco itinerary, this country is blessed with lots of oceanside oases. Get your fill of rustic villages in Cinque Terre, stylish urbanity in Venice, Rat Pack resorts in Capri, and beachy bliss on the Amalfi Coast.

1. NAPLES (3 DAYS): Begin your trip ready to take on this high-energy city. Get a sense for true Neapolitan culture at Spaggia Rotonda Diaz beach and enjoy the seaside views from the city's medieval Castel dell'Ovo.

2. ISLE OF CAPRI (2 DAYS): Lounge at the Grotta Azzurra, shop until you drop at P. Umberto, gorge on the giant treats at Pasticceria Gelateria San Nicola, and cough up the dough to rub shoulders with the rich and famous at Bye Bye Baby.

3. SORRENTO (2 DAYS): Drink *limoncello* on the beach and head out in the moonlight to join the gelato-lickers and cocktail-sippers on C. Italia.

4. POSITANO (1 DAY): The bikini was invented here, and no wonder: Positano's secluded Fornillo beach still retains the solitary beauty that drew John Steinbeck, Jack Kerouac, and Tennessee Williams to the town's shores.

5. AMALFI (2 DAYS): If Marina Grande is too crowded for your taste, head to the beaches at neighboring Atrani, where you might also consider staying if it's hard to find a budget accommodation in popular Amalfi.

6. RAVELLO (1 DAY): At least day trip here to take in the town's gardens, especially if you're around during its annual summer music festival.

7. PISA (1 DAY): Besides the famous tower, there's also a funky beach that merits a visit.

8. CINQUE TERRE (3 DAYS): Take one day to hike the trail and explore the towns—an afternoon break for a glass of wine in Corniglia is nice. Spend at least one day at the beach: Monterosso has by far the largest and most touristy, with dozens of lounge chair rental places and waterfront cafes. The more adventurous can escape civilization at Guvana Beach, off the trail. It's stunning, secluded, and, even better, clothing-optional.

9. VENICE (3 DAYS): End your coastal tour of Italy at its regal canal-veined city. If you're lucky, you'll be here during the hedonism of Carnevale, but even if you miss the festivities, there's no shortage of entertainment to be found. No beaches in the city proper, but P. San Marco and the Grand Canal offer all kinds of watery fun. Give yourself a day to explore the islands of the lagoon, particularly Lido, where you can enjoy free beaches such as Spiagge di Venezia. Hopefully you'll be ending this trip as bronzed as Apollo himself.

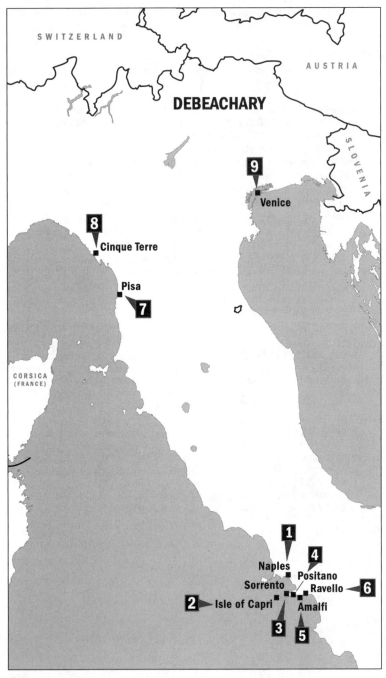

discover italy

SWITZERLAND

AUSTRIA

DEBEACHARY

SLOVENIA

9 ■ Venice

8 ■ Cinque Terre

Pisa ■ **7**

CORSICA
(FRANCE)

1

4

Naples ■

■ Positano

Sorrento ■ Ravello ■ **6**

2 ► Isle of Capri ■ Amalfi

3 **5**

how to use this book

CHAPTERS

In the next few pages, the travel coverage chapters—the meat of any *Let's Go* book—will begin. We throw you in at the deep end with Italy's most famous, and challenging city: **Rome.** Having thoroughly unsettled you, we'll then head north to the most cosmopolitan and classically Western World Italian cities: **Milan and Turin.** From there, we present to you northern Italy's most famous sinking city: **Venice.** Following that are three cities full of Shakespearean charm and really good food: **Padua, Verona, and Bologna.** Take a break from all the cities with **Cinque Terre,** northern Italy's premier seaside destination. From there we move to central Italy's greatest delights: the city of **Florence** and the provinces of **Tuscany and Umbria.** Finally, we go south to the **Bay of Naples,** finding a city possibly even more difficult than Rome and coastal towns on such steep inclines they might just slide into the Mediterranean.

But that's not all, folks. After that whirlwind tour around the peninsula, we also have a few extra chapters for you to peruse:

CHAPTER	DESCRIPTION
Discover Italy	Discover tells you what to do, when to do it, and where to go for it. The absolute coolest things about any destination get highlighted in this chapter at the front of all *Let's Go* books.
Essentials	Essentials contains the practical info you need before, during, and after your trip—visas, regional transportation, health and safety, phrasebooks, and more.
Italy 101	Italy 101 is just what it sounds like—a crash course in where you're traveling. This short chapter on Italian history and culture makes great reading on a long plane ride.
Beyond Tourism	As students ourselves, we at *Let's Go* encourage studying abroad, or going beyond tourism more generally, every chance we get. This chapter lists ideas for how to study, volunteer, or work abroad with other young travelers in Italy to got more out of your trip.

LISTINGS

Listings—a.k.a. reviews of individual establishments—constitute a majority of Let's Go coverage. Our Researcher-Writers list establishments in order from **best to worst value**—not necessarily quality. (Obviously a five-star hotel is nicer than a hostel, but it would probably be ranked lower because it's not as good a value.) Listings pack in a lot of information, but it's easy to digest if you know how they're constructed:

ESTABLISHMENT NAME ♥⊛ᕤ⊗⒫♈❄♨▼ type of establishment ❶
Address ☎phone number ◼website
Editorial review goes here.
� *Directions to the establishment.* **i** *Other practical information about the establishment, like age restrictions at a club or whether breakfast is included at a hostel.* ⑤ *Prices for goods or services.* ⏰ *Hours or schedules.*

ICONS

First things first: places and things that we absolutely love, sappily cherish, generally obsess over, and wholeheartedly endorse are denoted by the all-empowering ◪**Let's Go thumbs-up.** In addition, the icons scattered throughout a listing (as you saw in the sample above) can tell you a lot about an establishment. The following icons answer a series of yes-no questions about a place:

♥	Credit cards accepted	⊛	Cash only	ᕤ	Wheelchair-accessible
⊗	Not wheelchair-accessible	⒫	Internet access available	♈	Alcohol served
❄	Air-conditioned	♨	Outdoor seating available	▼	GLBT or GLBT-friendly

The rest are visual cues to help you navigate each listing:

☎	Phone numbers	🖥	Websites	🪧	Directions
i	Other hard info	$	Prices	⏰	Hours

OTHER USEFUL STUFF

Area codes for each destination appear opposite the name of the city and are denoted by the ☎ icon. When a city constitues its own chapter, its phone code appears in the orientation section in a box helpfully titled, "Call me!" Finally, in order to pack the book with as much information as possible, we have used a few **standard abbreviations.** You'll see these generally in addresses or directions, where Via becomes V., Viale becomes Vle., Piazza becomes P., and Corso becomes C. In Venice, if the directions begin "V:," it indicates a vaporetto stop.

PRICE DIVERSITY

A final set of icons corresponds to what we call our "price diversity" scale, which approximates how much money you can expect to spend at a given establishment. For **accommodations,** we base our range on the cheapest price for which a single traveler can stay for one night. For **food,** we estimate the average amount one traveler will spend in one sitting. The table below tells you what you'll *typically* find in Italy at the corresponding price range, but keep in mind that no system can allow for the quirks of individual establishments.

ACCOMMODATIONS	RANGE	WHAT YOU'RE LIKELY TO FIND
[1]	under €20	Generally a bed in a hostel dorm room or a campsite. Expect bunk beds and a shared bath. You may have to provide or rent towels and sheets.
[2]	€20-30	Upper-end hostels or decidedly lower-end hotels. If you get a private room in this range, chances are it will be tiny. It's unlikely you'll have a private bathroom, either.
[3]	€31-45	A small room with a private bath. Should have decent amenities, such as phone and TV.
[4]	€46-65	Should have bigger rooms than a [3], with more amenities or in a more convenient location. Breakfast probably included.
[5]	over €65	Large hotels or upscale chains. If it's a [5] and it doesn't have the perks you want (and more), you've paid too much.
FOOD	**RANGE**	**WHAT YOU'RE LIKELY TO FIND**
[1]	under €7	A wide variety of establishments, most commonly bakeries or *gelaterie.* Some of the cheapest pizzerias or cafes may squeeze into here. A [1] is unlikely to have table seating.
[2]	€7-15	Cheap restaurants or expensive cafes. Most ethnic eateries are a [2]. You should generally be able to sit down.
[3]	€16-25	A good-quality restaurant. Since you'll have the luxury of a waiter, tip will set you back a little extra.
[4]	€26-33	A fancy restaurant. Entrees tend to be heartier or more elaborate, but you're really paying for decor and ambience. Few restaurants in this range have a dress code, but some may look down on T-shirts and sandals.
[5]	over €33	We list very few [5]s, so if when we do, there's a reason—it's something fabulous, famous, or both. Slacks and dress shirts may be expected. Offers foreign-sounding food and a decent wine list. Don't order a PB and J.

ROME

Rome: the epitome of Italy, and its biggest enigma. It condenses every stereotype that plagues the country into one sprawling metropolis...and then rambles on another few kilometers and centuries to reverse them all. With neighborhoods off the map and streets too small to be mapped, this is a city as expansive as it is walkable, as global as it is local. And here's the biggest paradox of all: it's as young as it is old. And that doesn't mean Rome averages out to some middle-aged soccer mom. This city will blow your ears out with teenage gusto and shake its finger at you in codgerly reproval. Within its confines, crumbling bricks fight for space with candy-colored hotels, and centuries-old cobblestones shake to their bones as rubber tires roll over their weathered surface.

Good food, great art, and grand people—it's all here. But you could get these things in any Italian city (and honestly, Rome wouldn't win the prize in any of these categories). Instead, for every "quintessentially Italian" item you check off your list while here, Rome, challenging the tourists who come simply to make the rounds, will hit you with five more experiences that truly define the Italian character—and bend your preconceptions about what exactly that is. Don't expect to conquer Rome, especially not with a list. (Carthage tried to do it with an entire army and failed.)

Don't be fooled by the hundreds of postcards simplifying Rome's streets: the Eternal City is anything but picture perfect. Dirtier than Milan, bigger than Naples, and rougher than Florence, this is a city to be reckoned with. Rather than bowing to its tourists, it nods it head in recognition of them and marches on its way. Sometimes, like the speeding Vespas that only stop when you walk in front of them, Rome requires that you stand up to it. Are you ready for the challenge?

greatest hits

- **BUY ONE COUNTRY, GET ONE FREE.** Fed up with Italy? The Vatican City, small but magnificent, is still doing pretty well for itself (p. 22).
- **HOSTEL HEAVEN.** Rolling into Termini Station, you're on the brink of one of Europe's biggest concentrations of cheap beds (p. 31).
- **ANCIENT ANTIQUES.** The Colosseum is just the beginning of Ancient Rome's gifts to the modern city (p. 35).

student life

It's not only archaeology students who'll find something of interest in Rome. For a destination with such a prominent Ancient City, Rome is shockingly young, with a culture that's strongly influenced by its students and 20-something residents. The 147,000 students of Rome's **Sapienza University** give the city one of Europe's largest student bodies. Sapienza is based in the San Lorenzo neighborhood a little to the east of Termini Station. By a convenient coincidence, that puts it right next to tourists' main entrance point and the city's highest concentration of budget accommodations. If you're wondering where the young people stay, this area is the answer. In a remarkably unsurprising development, the combination of students and student travelers in Termini has transformed this area into one of the city's biggest nighttime destinations, with bars and clubs crowding the streets. Be aware that students aren't the only people around after dark: pickpockets love to operate here.

As much as Termini and San Lorenzo are the central student destinations, they're just the beginning in this diverse city. The **Centro Storico** may be full of Roman *piazze* and grand temples to the dead, but it also features extremely accessible bars that serve great *aperitivo* buffets each night. Try Drunken Ship if you've been away from a beer pong table for a little too long. To find international students, head across the Tiber to **Trastevere,** home of an American liberal arts college, John Cabot University. This is a favorite haunt of study abroad students, so come here and relax in Cafe Friends anytime between 7am and 2am. The southern neighborhoods of **Testaccio and Ostiense** are other great options. Or just chill at the Colosseum. Just because we're students doesn't mean we don't care about history, right? In Rome, though, with so much going on in the present, you just might forget to appreciate what the city is most famous for: its past.

orientation

call me!

The phone code for Rome is ☎06.

Rome is easily navigable on foot: every time you think you might be lost, another monument pops up and you're back on track. And when it's not a monument, it's a river, park, or ruin. Geographically (and perhaps metaphorically, as well), the best way to think of Rome is as a body: a few major arteries (some with significant blockage problems) will take you from region to region, while countless capillaries branch off into compact neighborhoods.

Starting from the ground up, **Termini** is definitely the foot: it gets trampled and does the trampling. As Rome's main intra- and intercity transportation hub, it is, not surprisingly, home to the highest number of budget accommodations in the city. The slightly quieter **San Lorenzo,** a few blocks east, teems with the students of Rome's largest university and the cheap food and clothing dives to match. With grid-like streets, this part of town is easy to navigate, though—like most feet—not too fun to look at. Sleep here and move on.

Two main streets, **Via Cavour** and **Via Nazionale,** are the legs leading in a straight shot up to the **Ancient City,** Rome's (once bloody) gut. Here, you'll find a lot of dirt (the **Fori Imperiali**), a traffic-light-less rotunda of zooming cars **(Piazza Venezia),** and unabashed Italian pride crowned in green horses (the gleaming white **Vittorio Emanuele II Monument**). This last landmark can be seen from virtually every elevated sight in Rome, making it a helpful edifice to recognize. From this busy center, the best way back out (and better out than in, we always say) is to take **Via del Quirinale,** which becomes **Via XX Settembre** as you head toward Termini: these wide boulevards are less trafficked and will lead you to the quieter region of **Via Nomentana** and its villas.

If you stay in the *centro,* **Via dei Fori Imperiali,** heading southeast, will take you past the **Roman Forum** and the **Colosseum,** where gladiators still reside, wearing plastic armor, feathered hats, and sandals. If you're more of a fashionista than those burly men, head northwest up **Via del Corso,** Rome's commerical mecca. Narrow and overcrowded with shopping bags, cars, and the owners of each, this is the city's busiest artery. It heads directly to **Piazza del Popolo** and is bordered on each side by those capillaries we spoke of earlier—Rome's most intricate web of tiny streets. Rather than trying to pinpoint your exact location on the map, orient yourself according to the major monuments: the **Trevi Fountain, Campo dei Fiori, Piazza Navona,** and the **Pantheon.** As might be expected, you can think of this cluster as Rome's heart, the **Centro Storico.** A more direct route through these flows up **Corso Vittorio Emanuele,** an artery that's slightly less clogged. If you do indulge Rome's heart condition and continue up V. del Corso, you'll hit the **Piazza di Spagna** region, a mini-Milan of clothing and commercialism.

At this point, it's time to mention the **Tiber River (Fiume Tevere),** the neck that separates Rome's body from its slightly less crazy head. Heading southwest on **Via Arenula** from C.Vittorio Emanuele, you'll pass through the **Jewish Ghetto** and cross either **Ponte Garibaldi** or **Isola Tiberina** into the residential **Trastevere.** The major destination across the river is (drumroll, please) **Vatican City.** From Trastevere, you'll have a pleasant walk up the river or through **Giancolo Hill** to reach the tiny city-state, which lies directly northeast of them. However, most people visiting the Vatican from Rome's center will take **Via Cola di Rienzo** from P. del Popolo. A grid of quiet streets leading to the Vatican offsets the crowds inside.

If you want to veer off Rome's central map, the areas south of the Roman Forum and Palatine Hill are worth exploring: **Aventine, Testaccio,** and **Ostiense** offer lots of good nightlife, food, residential streets, and a spattering of less-trafficked basilicas and museums. North of Piazza del Popolo, the refined and residential **Villa Borghese** and **Flaminio** await. Both are best attacked with a picnic basket and pair of shades.

ANCIENT CITY

With one of the highest camera-to-square-inch-of-sidewalk ratios in Rome, the Ancient City doesn't exactly feel "ancient" anymore. This vast stretch of tourist heaven, whose sights are the single reason many people come to Italy, is a stunning mix of old and new. For every ruin you'll see (and there are plenty), there's a plastic replica to match; for every nude statue, an overpriced sweatshirt to cover you up. And while you might have pecs rivaling those of the "gladiators" wandering around the Colosseum, you'll definitely need to put something on over those babies if you intend to enter any of the region's renowned churches. With so many sights worth seeing, it is all right for once to abandon your pride and surrender yourself to tourism in its full glory—photos with costumed gladiators, lines that only seem short compared to the 190m frieze on Trajan's column, and enough overpriced gelato to make even Augustus's purse feel a little empty. Kick off your flip-flops and don a pair of walking shoes to "hike" up the Palatine Hill, pick your way through the Roman Forum, or

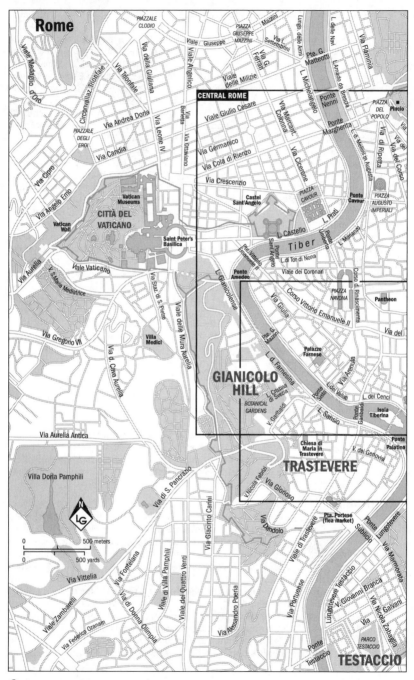

Rome

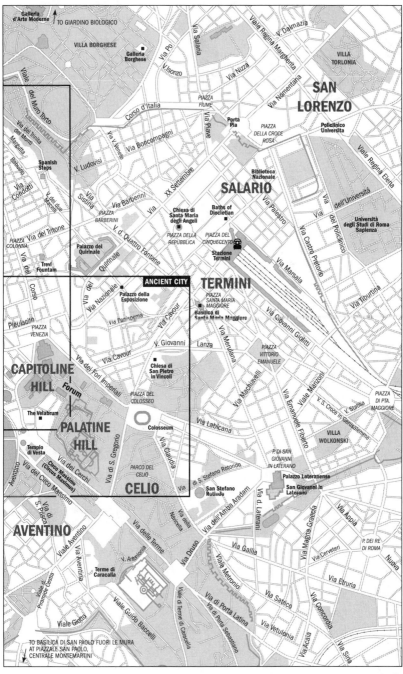

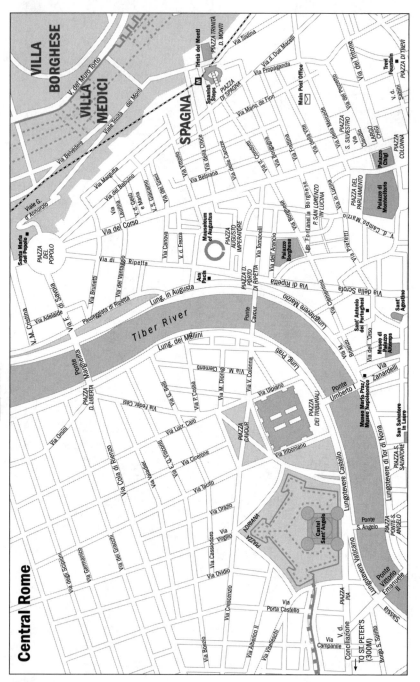

Central Rome

rome

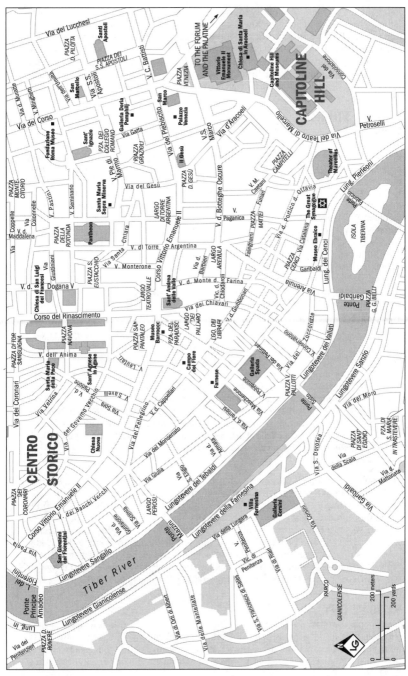

just get from one end of the City to the other—unlike most neighborhoods, which actually have an epicenter, the Ancient City is as scattered as some of its ruins. But don't worry, by the time you reach your destination—be it ruin or restaurant—you'll have forgotten the crowds and costs you endured to get there. Perhaps it's that feeling of traveling through time as you survey the remains of a civilization extinct for more than a millennium, or maybe it's the mouthwatering aroma of fresh-baked pizza dough that does it, but, whatever the cause, tourist travails pale in comparison to the pleasures of the Ancient City.

CENTRO STORICO

To the traveler who has paid one too many euros after waiting in one too many 4hr. lines, the Centro Storico offers a reprieve: nearly all of the churches, monuments, and *piazze* in this part of town are free of charge, and the only lines you'll be waiting in are the ones for overpriced gelato or food. With most of the main attractions compactly clustered on either side of **Corso Vittorio Emanuele,** this tangled web of streets is manageable in size, though not as easily navigable as a more grid-like pattern might be. Expect to get lost as *vias* suddenly split into numerous *vicolos,* so use the Corso as a departure point and the vibrant urban living rooms of **Campo dei Fiori** and **Piazza Navona** on either side as your major landmarks. Letting yourself get lost in the neighborhood's little alleyways might be the best way to approach the area, though; you'll find yourself effortlessly arriving at unassuming churches and monuments, only to realize that they're famous landmarks. The entire region seems to be in a constant state of entropy, with tourists bumping into each other as they dart from one photo opp to another in a part of town that is already high-energy even into the late-night hours.

PIAZZA DI SPAGNA

Rome has a 5th Avenue too, and this is it. Bordered by the overbearing **Via del Corso,** the grid-like streets surrounding the Spanish Steps are full of people shopping and goggling in front of windows at Rome's highest end stores. It's hard to find a well-priced meal or a respite from the congestion unless you make a return to nature along the Tiber River or in the Villa Borghese park, both of which cushion the tourist enclave. Also redeeming the area are some of the best sights in the city. As in the **Centro Storico,** many landmarks are outside and free to the public, so the only obstacle to an enjoyable experience will be the crowds. To avoid the capitalist onslaught, take a stroll on the elevated **Viale di Trinita dei Monti,** which offers the best view of P. di Spagna's madhouse as well as its artistic marvels.

JEWISH GHETTO

You could pass through the Jewish Ghetto and notice nothing more than a surprisingly quiet Friday evening and Saturday morning and slightly more ethnic cuisine than Rome's majority. Now occupying little more than a few streets near the Tiber River, this compact neighborhood was actually home to the first real community of Jews in Western Europe. Originally a true ghetto blocked off from the city proper with sturdy walls and plagued by an unfortunate tendency to flood, today it is a pleasant stretch of residential houses and excellent restaurants that dish up some of the best artichokes around. A low-key and less touristed area to meander through on the way to the nearby Centro Storico, the Jewish Ghetto may be small, but it is rich in history and flavor.

VATICAN CITY

The people-to-square-foot ratio is significantly cockeyed in this tiny state: an expected madhouse of crowds in the Vatican contrasts sharply with the mostly empty boulevards in the surrounding region of **Prati,** making any attempt to measure population density a joke. That's actually a good thing though—after forging through the crowds to pay a visit to the pope, you'll be able to wander effortlessly down the region's tree-lined streets, frequented by dog-walkers and the occasional lost tourist looking for a big dome (a.k.a. **St. Peter's**). If the concentration of plastic souvenirs, bright flags, and English menus isn't enough to indicate which of the two regions you're in, then the brick wall which physically separates Vatican City from Prati should give you a clue. Walk around outside its boundary on the Prati side, and you'll find surprisingly affordable hotels and casual trattorias scattered throughout fairly modern residential buildings colored in pastel greens and pinks. And for all this talk of the crowds in Vatican City, even when you make your way back into the pope's digs, the throng of people is more manageable than what you'll find in Central Rome. Maybe it's the gargantuan size of St. Peter's and its *piazza*, or perhaps people's religious consciences that check them, but somehow the tourist crush west of the Tiber and north of Trastevere is more diluted than you'd expect.

TRASTEVERE

Trastevere is to Rome what Brooklyn is to New York—overlooked by tourists, loved by locals, and removed from the metropolitan center while still being in the thick of things. Just across the Tiber River, this enclave of cobblestone streets and small *piazze* boasts some of the best nightlife Rome has to offer; it's as popular with international students at the nearby university as it is with neighborhood residents whose families have called Trastevere home for generations. Although you likely won't spend the night here, as there are few budget-friendly accommodations, dinner in Trastevere won't break the bank. Restaurants that have managed to escape the tourist bubble abound—just throw away your map, get a little lost, and make your way into one of the tasty and unpretentious homegrown establishments that fill the neighborhood. If you've had enough of monuments and ruins, take a walk in the lush gardens leading into Monteverde (which has the word for "green" in its name for a reason). You knew you weren't going to get through this book without reading that old saying, "When in Rome, do as the Romans do." Well, if living like a true Roman means making friendly Trastevere your home as well, following that well-worn adage can't do you wrong.

VILLA BORGHESE, PARIOLI, AND FLAMINIO

Who knew the Romans had a thing for palm trees and pastel-colored curlicues? In this city of cities, maybe it's a sign of a subconscious desire for some leisurely beach life. Even though there isn't a body of water for miles around (save a few famous fountains), the cool residents of Villa Borghese have done well for themselves—the expansive gardens that span most of the neighborhood are an oasis of greenery and shady streets that will make you wonder, "Who needs the beach anyway?" It's a good thing the grass inspires thoughts of picnics and light lunches, though—sit-down restaurants are expensive and harder to come by then you might expect. Even the businessmen who frequent the serene streets around **Via Po** have made panini rather than full-fledged *piatti* their lunch. Throw away your itinerary, lather on some sunblock, and spend the day strolling through the chill "Borghese bubble," whose pink houses make it feel like summer all year round.

TERMINI AND SAN LORENZO

Ask people if they saw the Vatican, the Colosseum, or any other number of famed sights on their last trip to Rome, and chances are they'll say no to at least one of them: with so much to take in, something's got to give. Ironic, then, that *everyone* passes through Termini, as mundane and unromantic as it is. It's the transportation capital of the capital city, after all. Too bad there isn't a beach around the block—there are enough hotels here to rival a resort town. Instead of a scenic vista or even a renowned Roman ruin, prepare yourself for a stifling stream of merchants, hotels, restaurants, dives, and, did we mention? . . . hotels. If you're arriving in Rome without a reservation, chances are you can find a last-minute budget option here, but even those who plan ahead often pick this bustling spot as their residence of choice. With prime access to the Metro, all major bus lines, some great nightlife (read: international student mania), and even a few sights of its own, no other part of Rome matches Termini in convenience. Our only advice: try to arrive by daylight. With a backpack, an unwieldy suitcase, and a long plane ride behind you, trekking around at night through the maze of people and advertisements that populate the area can provide not only a disheartening first impression of Rome, but also a somewhat dangerous one as well.

TESTACCIO AND OSTIENSE

Located south of the Colosseum, Testaccio and Ostiense are left off most tourist itineraries and are literally left off of Rome's central map. Take advantage of this relative anonymity and get lost in their quiet streets by day, making sure to save energy for their pulsing clubs at night. Composed of newer, residential housing and paved streets, these uncongested neighborhoods let you put away the guidebook for an afternoon (though studies have shown that copies of *Let's Go* double their lifespan if exposed to ample sunlight, so consider keeping yours out) and just wander a bit. The only lines in which you'll be waiting are those for Testaccio's clubs, some of the city's best despite their removed location. If, after a few nights, you've had enough of the good food and party scene, wander down and around the long **Via Ostiense** for sights that might not have brought you to Rome but that rival the Vatican in beauty and size. You may not come here with high expectations, but this will make the culinary, cultural, and clubbing surprises of these neighborhoods even more charming.

SOUTHERN ROME AND THE APPIAN WAY

Just because they're off the tourist map doesn't mean these parts of the city aren't worth at least a day of exploring—and we really do mean exploring—without an itinerary. The stretch of city below everything in your sightseeing schedule consists of quiet residential streets, enough churches to convert you to Catholicism, and, yes, more ruins of sorts. Though it takes a while to reach the more serene stretch of the Appian Way, once you do, you'll feel miles away from bustling Rome. The catacombs, though secluded (duh...they're underground), might remind you more of the city than you would expect—they can fill your guided-tour, hefty-entrance-fee, and historical-fact fixes. In the end, though, you'll want to meander through this region of Rome, popping into churches when you reach them and strolling along the Appian Way until your legs give out.

VIA NOMENTANA

V. Nomentana and the area surrounding it may be close to Termini, but they have little in common with that transit hub. Good restaurants, scenic and serene streets, great nightlife, and a truly residential feel make this a worthwhile area to explore on the way to Villa Borghese—or perhaps on a day of its own. Just outside the city center but still only a step away from the bustle of Termini, this lively strip of land deserves a place in the itinerary of anyone who wants to hit something a bit less touristy and a bit truer to Roman life.

accommodations

Finding lodging in Rome is not as daunting as it may seem, even though the tourist offices do not provide as extensive listings as those in other cities. Options range from cheap hostels to four-star hotels and a slew of places in between. Low season starts around November and goes until early March, with the lowest rates coming at the Christmas holiday. High season starts mid-March, peaks during April and May, and doesn't let up until October.

At bigger hotel chains and hostels, the best way to book is generally online, where you can get specific prices and sometimes promotional deals. If you ask in person, these types of establishments will usually refer you to their website (and are reluctant even to give price ranges) unless you're talking exact dates. Expect the most standard and comprehensive services at hotels, with a price to match. Better hostels have kitchens, no curfew, and services geared to students, such as maps, internet access, tours, and even bars. Smaller *pensioni*, bed and breakfasts, and *alberghi* (the Italian word for hotels) are often located within a larger building of apartments and thus may be harder to find without prior knowledge. Such establishments often offer fewer rooms and services but more availability during high season, even at the last minute. Disregard the rule for hotels and hostels at these lodging houses and make reservations in person. These are often more convenient for the proprietors and may get you a lower rate. Discounts are often given for longer stays and for payments made in cash.

Convents are another great option for female travelers who can deal with the early curfew and usually bare-minimum facilities. They are often more willing to accommodate longer-term stays. Men and those not eager to deal with the particular oddities of convent life can find apartment agencies scattered throughout the city. Be aware, however, that they are usually only helpful for buying or renting in the very long term (one year or more). For periods of one to six months, consult **Porta Portese** newspaper, sold at all *tabaccherie* for €1 (also available online at ▣www.portaportese.it) Other good online databases are **Easystanza** (▣*www.easystanza.it*) and ▣www.expatriates.com, an online community for foreigners in Rome. Also check out public places such as libraries, universities (John Cabot, American University in Rome and St. John's University), and even local cafes, which often post paper fliers advertising short-term rooms in shared apartments. In terms of convenience, residential feel, and cost, **Trastevere** (across the river), **Testaccio/Ostiense**, and **San Giovanni** (south of Termini) are ideal places to find your home away from home.

Termini is the best place, especially for travelers arriving by train, to find last-minute and conveniently-located accommodations. If you have not booked in advance, however, be wary of hotel scouts who will jump at the opportunity to advertise overpriced rooms late in the evening. Before booking, be sure to ask about services offered: some places charge for breakfast, A/C, internet, or, even worse, all three.

ANCIENT CITY

Home to some of the biggest monuments in Rome, the Ancient City is not the cheapest place to plant yourself during a visit to Italy's capital, though if you're willing to shell out at least €100 a night, you'll have more than enough four-star options to choose from. Never fear, however; plenty of bed and breakfasts and *pensioni* offer decent services at a much lower cost.

▨ CASA SANTA PUDENZIANA
V. Urbana 158

⊛⊗⁽ᵖ⁾⌂ CONVENT ❷
☎06 48 80 056

If you're of the female persuasion and don't mind a 10:30pm curfew *(12:30am on Sa)*, the quiet and spacious grounds of Casa Santa Pudenziana can provide you with a welcome relief from the more crowded (and somewhat pricier) hostels nearby. This convent's six-bed dorm, double, and single make for a small community of guests—and that's if there are no vacancies. Guests here often run into each other at breakfast, dinner, or throughout the day in the peaceful central garden. Library and chapel upstairs as well as clean common spaces with television, refrigerator, and microwave. Wi-Fi from nearby hotels floats through some parts of the convent, but *Let's Go* does not recommend relying on stolen Wi-Fi. No lockers or keys, so get ready to greet the friendly staff every time you buzz to get in.

⚑ ⓜA: Cavour. From V. Cavour, turn onto V. Urbana. *i* Women only. Breakfast included 7-9am; dinner 8pm, €10. ⑤ Dorms €22; singles €40; doubles €52. Inquire about discounts for longer stays. ◲ Strict curfew M-F 10:30pm, Sa 12:30am, Su 10:30pm.

STUDENT HOUSE
⊛ⓧ⁽ᵗ⁾ HOSTEL ❶

V. Merulana 117   ☎No phone—reserve online. ▣www.hostelworld.com

This small hostel does indeed feel like a house—the central reception area is more like a living room, complete with bookshelves, photos, TV, and colorful furniture than a place to check in and out. Student House's rooms consist of two six-bed co-ed dorms, so don't plan on making it your private getaway. The living spaces are sunny and equipped with bunks and mirrors. The hall bathrooms might not be convenient, but the small communal kitchen and free Wi-Fi are. Brush up on your Italian before you get here—the owner speaks no English.

⚑ ⓜA: Manzoni. From V. Emanuele Filberto, walk straight on V. Manzoni and make a right onto V. Merulana. *i* Reserve your space at ▣www.hostelworld.com. Set up check-in time in advance to avoid arriving when the owner is out. Towel rental €1. ⑤ Dorms €20.

HOTEL SAN DANIELE BUNDÌ
◗ⓧ⁽ᵗ⁾❄ HOTEL ❹

V. Cavour 295   ☎06 48 75 295 ▣www.hotelsandanielebundi.it

Neighboring establishments recommend Hotel Bundì for its simple rooms and accommodating staff. Although the hotel is small, its central location, competitive prices, and surprising tranquility make it a good bet. Rooms have Wi-Fi, air-conditioning, private bathrooms and TVs. Complimentary breakfast is an added perk.

⚑ ⓜA: Colosseum. From V. dei Fori Imperiali, make a right onto V. Cavour. Buzz at the doors and take Scale B to the 3rd fl. ⑤ Singles €65; doubles €85. ◲ Reception closes at 8pm.

prego

Prego. The word is like pizza: Italians have somehow found a way to top or dress it with anything; to have it in any context, at any time of day; and to make it hot, cold, or even lukewarm to match the occasion. Whatever the situation, it all flies:

- **"PREGO?"** The first thing you'll hear as you walk into a *pasticceria.* Translation: "How can I help you?" or "What do you want?" And they expect you to know, immediately. (Standing around asking prices doesn't fly too well.)

- **"PREGO!"** A favorite of the Sistine Chapel guards. Amid the clamor of docents shushing people and telling them not to take pictures, you hear the word muttered sternly, more like a reprimand than anything else. Translation: "Geez...thanks for being quiet after the 15th time I've told you to turn off your camera and shut your trap!"

- **"PREGO."** The sweetest version of them all, when it's just a simple statement, often following *"grazie."* After you buy a gelato or compliment someone, the recipient of your cash or flattery will often acknowledge his or her thanks by calmly uttering the word. Translation: "You're welcome" or "I'm honored."

- **"PREGO" (WITH OPTIONAL "!")** Actually used as the verb it is, this *prego* can mean "I pray." Now, Italians pray for all kinds of things—in religious contexts, in which case the exclamation mark probably isn't necessary, but also in more mundane or demanding contexts. It's often a favorite of cleaning ladies. Walking into a room full of strewn backpack contents, you might catch a despairing *"Pre-e-g-o-ooooo."*

rome

“reserve tours in Rome and the surrounding area”

Hotel San Pietrino

“located in a safe neighbourhood near Vatican City”

“a comfortable and relaxing environment”

“Bikes are available for rent”

“Internet connection is available in the rooms”

“situated on a quiet side-street so noise is not a problem”

“visit the historical center of Rome in two subway stops”

“listen to pleasant music or see a movie on demand”

“tourist information and free maps on arrival”

“five minute walk to St. Peter’s Square”

“Taxi and minibus reservation for the airports”

“experience the Italian style of having breakfast by having a cornetto and a cappuccino at a bar”

via Giovanni Bettolo,
43 00195 Rome
Tel. : +39 06 37 00 132
www.sanpietrino.it

PENSIONE ROSETTA 💳🚭📶❄ PENSIONE [4]

V. Cavour 295 ☎06 47 82 30 69 🖥www.rosettahotel.com

A friendly staff and clean, though spartan, rooms make Pensione Rosetta a convenient option for those who hope to roll out of bed and check out the Colosseum in their pajamas. Each of Rosetta’s 20 rooms have a private bathroom, a telephone, a TV, and air-conditioning; free Wi-Fi is available in public areas. The central courtyard provides a welcome respite from the busy V. Cavour.

 # [M]A: Colosseum. From V. dei Fori Imperiali, make a right onto V. Cavour. Buzz at the doors and take Scala B to the 1st fl. $ Singles €65; doubles €90; triples €105; quads €120.

CENTRO STORICO

The Centro Storico is not the cheapest place to stay, but hotels here often have a lot more character and offer better services than those found elsewhere. Reserve rooms well in advance and don’t expect them to be cheap.

👍 **ALBERGO DEL SOLE** 💵🚭📶❄ HOTEL [5]

V. del Biscione 76 ☎06 68 80 68 73 🖥www.solealbiscione.it

Especially well-furnished rooms with antique furniture, paintings, and curtains make this place feel more like a home than a hotel. Great common spaces, including a garden terrace and sitting rooms on each floor, give Albergo del Sole a lived-in quality. Knowledgeable staff are welcoming and straightforward.

 # Exit P. di Fiori onto V. del Biscione. ℹ Most rooms with A/C, otherwise with fan. Wi-Fi €1.50 per hr. $ Singles €70, with bath €110-125; doubles €100-105/€120-160. 🕐 Reception 24hr.

HOTEL SMERALDO 💳🚭📶❄ HOTEL [5]

Vicolo dei Chiodaroli 9 ☎06 68 75 929 🖥www.hotelsmeraldoroma.com

Somewhat tight rooms are clean and bright, sporting well-coordinated decor.

The gracious reception staff inspires confidence in guests by happily giving advice to travelers. There are no surprises here—rooms are well equipped and neatly kept.

⚐ From Campo dei Fiori, walk down V. dei Giubbonari, turn left onto V. dei Chiavari and right onto Vicolo dei Chiodaroli. *i* Breakfast included. All rooms have private bath. Wi-Fi €5 per hr. in common areas; public computer available. ⑤ Singles €70-110; doubles €90-145. ☒ Reception 24hr.

ALBERGO POMEZIO
⬤♿(•)❀ HOTEL ❺
V. dei Chiavari 13   ☎06 68 61 371

This hotel's fast-paced and assertive owner offers large and nicely decorated rooms with curtains and matching trimmings. Good services, including free Wi-Fi, for the location and price. The large breakfast room is one of the few common spaces for guests.

⚐ From Campo dei Fiori, walk down V. dei Giubbonari and turn left onto V. dei Chiavari. *i* All rooms have private bath. Free Wi-Fi. ⑤ Singles €70-100; doubles €100-140. Weekends tend to be more expensive.

PIAZZA DI SPAGNA

Staying in the Piazza di Spagna area is a pricey affair, and though you might be getting newer accommodations and slightly better services, you'll be surrounded by more crowds than are present in the Ancient City or Centro Storico. Boasting little nightlife to boot, this neighborhood is a better bet for older folks who want reliable services than for youth seeking value and fun.

▨ HOTEL PANDA
⬤⊗(•)❀ HOTEL ❹
V. della Croce 35   ☎06 67 80 179 ▣www.hotelpanda.it

Luckily (or not), there are no panda bears around, but you'll feel as warm and fuzzy as one of these bamboo-chomping cuties while staying at this small, family-run hotel. Simply decorated rooms come with A/C, Wi-Fi, and TV at a better price than the spiffier hotels down the street. Opt for a bigger room if you can, as the small ones really are small. Though there isn't much common space (read: narrow hallways and no breakfast room), the rooms are enough of a retreat for this shortfall to be inconsequential.

⚐ Ⓜ A: Spagna. From the Spanish Steps, take V. Condotti, turn right onto V. Belsiana and right onto V. della Croce. Hotel is on the 2nd fl. *i* Breakfast €5 at downstairs bar. A/C €6. Free Wi-Fi. ⑤ Singles €55-68, with bath €65-80; doubles €68-78/€85-108; triples €120-140. ☒ Reception 24hr.

DEPENDANCE ANAHI
⬤⊗(•)❀ HOTEL ❺
V. della Penna 22   ☎06 36 10 841 ▣hotellocarno.com

Though Dependance Anahi is an offshoot of the grander and more expensive Hotel Locarno, it still boasts a prime location and stellar services, if less history and pomp than its sister across the street. Mostly double rooms and two singles all have TV, A/C, private bath, minibar, and free Wi-Fi, and Art Nouveau detailing gives the place more flavor than your standard rooming house. Head across the street to enjoy a buffet breakfast in the quiet, vine-covered patio or relax in the palatial lounge rooms.

⚐ Ⓜ A: Flaminio. From P. del Popolo, exit near V. di Ripetta and immediately turn right onto V. Penna d'Oca. Across the street from Hotel Locarno; reception at V. della Penna 22. *i* Breakfast included. Bath, minibar, and safe ensuite. Free bike rental. Free Wi-Fi. ⑤ Singles €90-120; doubles €110-190. ☒ Reception 24hr.

HOTEL DE PETRIS
⬤⊗(•)❀ HOTEL ❺
V. Rasella 142   ☎06 48 19 626 ▣www.hoteldepetris.com

Not only are rooms equipped with all the basics—TV, A/C, free Wi-Fi, and minibar—but they're also especially elegant. Superior rooms are bigger than average and have hardwood floors and modern furniture, while the standards are less luxe. Expect no surprises from the rooms and reliable staff.

➡ ⓂA: Barberini. From P. Barberini, take V. del Tritone, turn left onto V. Boccaccio and left onto V. Rasella. i Breakfast included. All rooms have ensuite bath. Free Wi-Fi. $ Singles €94-136; doubles €113-171. Extra bed €46. ⏰ Reception 24hr.

DOMUS JULIA 💳🚭📶❄ HOTEL [4]

V. Rasella 32 ☎06 47 45 765 💻www.domusjulia.it

The friendly dog at Domus Julia makes up for the reception staff who can be a bit short of temper at times. The hotel's 18th-century building retains its historic look but brings itself up to the 21st century with all the expected comforts, including free internet. If you've gotten a bit bored of seeing Roman ruins, rent one of their bikes for free or even earn an extra euro by walking the dog. The breakfast room is a nice hangout even in the evening.

➡ ⓂA: Barberini. From P. Barberini, take V. del Tritone, turn left onto V. Boccaccio and left onto V. Rasella. i Breakfast included. All rooms have minibar and ensuite bath. Free Wi-Fi. $ Singles €60-100; doubles €78-180; triples €89-210. ⏰ Reception 24hr.

VATICAN CITY

When it comes to hotels, the area immediately around the Vatican is as overpriced as the pizza and souvenirs. However, the quieter streets nearer the river and Prati offer many affordable options, mostly small hotels within residential buildings. A nice area in which to stay due to its proximity to the sights and distance from the *centro*'s chaos, it may only be lacking in nightlife, which is (expectedly) quiet.

👍 **COLORS** 💳🚭📶❄ HOTEL, HOSTEL [1]

V. Boezio 31 ☎06 68 74 030 💻www.colorshotel.com

The rooms smell fresh like wood and look bright, as colors should. The boldly pigmented adornments of their 23 rooms help keep guests' stays comfortable, while the free Wi-Fi is simply convenient (and rare for this neighborhood). If the rainbow inside has you wanting some straight-up green, head to the rooftop terrace. One dormitory with five beds gives this hotel a hostel spirit. The room has A/C though, putting it miles beyond most hostels.

➡ ⓂA: Ottaviano. Walk down V. Ottaviano; turn left onto V. Cola di Rienzo and right onto V. Terenzio; at the intersection with V. Boezio. i Breakfast included at hotel; €7 in dorm. Common terrace, TV room, and mini-kitchen. Free Wi-Fi. $ Dorms €15-30; singles €30, with bath €50-80; doubles €70-100. ⏰ Reception 24hr.

HOTEL AL SAN PIETRO 💳🚭📶❄ HOTEL [3]

V. Giovanni Bettolo 43 ☎06 37 00 132 💻www.sanpietrino.it

Small green frogs (don't worry, they're ceramic) and the smell of flowers greet guests at this small hotel, located only 5min. from the Vatican museums. Though the rooms aren't particularly large, free Wi-Fi and staff that matches the upbeat decor make it a better deal than hotels advertised nearby. No breakfast, but there's an organic grocery store down the street.

➡ ⓂA: Ottaviano. Exit onto V. Barletta and turn left onto V. Bettolo. i Singles without bath. Free Wi-Fi. $ Singles €40-50; doubles €70-89; triples €115. ⏰ Reception 24hr.

HOTEL GIUGGIOLI 💳🚭📶❄ HOTEL [5]

V. Germanico 198, 2nd fl. ☎06 36 00 53 89 💻www.hotelgiuggioli.it

The silver accents and geometric furniture give this top-notch hotel a distinctly modern feel. Carpeted rooms are very clean and generously sized, though a bit dimly lit. If long lines at the Vatican aren't your thing, bike rental gives you another reason to travel elsewhere in the city. The lovely bar and kitchen area *(open 1-9pm)* feels more like an upscale restaurant then a hotel add-on.

➡ ⓂA: Lepanto. Walk down V. Ezio and turn right onto V. Germanico. i Breakfast included. All rooms have bath and minibar ensuite. Wi-Fi €1 per hr. $ Singles €70-110; doubles €80-130. Bike rental €12 per hr. ⏰ Reception 24hr.

MARTA GUEST HOUSE

Marta Guest House is situated in an elegant building in the Prati district, adjacent to Castel Sant'Angelo, just steps away from the VATICAN CITY, SPANISH STEPS, and PIAZZA NAVONA. Our beautiful rooms are spacious and lumiinous, with some of the furniture dating from the early 1900s. All have private bath, TV, safe and AC.

Come stay with us at Marta Guest House!

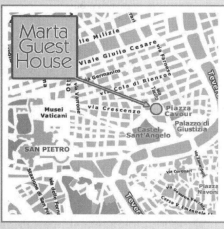

Singles ——— from 50 €

Doubles ——— from 70 €

Triples ——— from 90 €

phone : 39 06 6889 2992
fax : 39 06 6821 7574
email : martaguesthouse@iol.it

Book rooms online at:
http://marta.hotelinroma.com
http://www.martaguesthouse.com

HOTEL LADY

💧⊘(🕊) PENSIONE ❹

V. Germanico 198, 4th fl. ☎06 32 42 112 ▤www.hotelladyroma.it

Aesthetics trump amenities here: the old-fashioned charm of this former monastery is unfortunately accompanied by a lack of A/C and Wi-Fi. Still, the original wood-beamed ceilings and amber stained-glass windows create a comforting feel that most modern hotels can't replicate. Fans and antique wooden furniture that looks like it's been here for a century add to Hotel Lady's appeal. Rooms without bathrooms may be less convenient but are significantly bigger.

✡ Ⓜ*A: Lepanto. Walk down V. Ezio and turn right onto V. Germanico.* ℹ *Singles and triples with shared bath only. Internet room available.* Ⓢ *Singles €60; doubles €75, with bath €90; triples €120.* Ⓦ *Reception 24hr., but call about arrival time.*

A ROMA SAN PIETRO B AND B

💧⊘(🕊)✹ B AND B ❸

V. Crescenzio 85 ☎06 68 78 205 ▤www.ftraldi.it

Though it may not be quirkier than a hotel, this small bed and breakfast offers brightly colored (though somewhat blandly furnished) rooms with excellent perks: A/C, free Wi-Fi, and complimentary breakfast make it better than some hotels. Reserve in advance and schedule arrival time, as there are only five rooms and the owner might be out. Watch out for the dripping water in the courtyard.

✡ Ⓜ*A: Ottaviano. Walk down V. Ottaviano and turn left onto V. Crescenzio.* ℹ *Breakfast included. Free Wi-Fi.* Ⓢ *Singles €40-50; doubles €60-110; triples €70-140. Extra bed €10-25.* Ⓦ *Call to schedule arrival time.*

TERMINI AND SAN LORENZO

Termini abounds with hotels, hostels, bed and breakfasts, and *pensioni*. There's a roughly one-to-one ratio of extremely cheap to extremely overpriced options, so do research beforehand and try to book at least one week in advance, especially for summer stays. Although the proximity to Termini Station makes living here convenient, the area is not the safest place at night. Be wary of pickpockets and, if possible, avoid walking about in the late hours.

▨ M AND J PLACE HOSTEL

💧⊘(🕊)✹ HOSTEL ❷

V. Solferino 9 ☎06 44 62 802 ▤www.mejplacehostel.com

A prime location, helpful staff, and clean rooms grace this wonderful hostel. M and J Place boasts great common spaces (kitchen, balcony, and TV lounge) as well as a calm feel enhanced by rooms that are neat and not too crowded. Private rooms are more reminiscent of a hotel with A/C, computers, TV, and towels ensuite. The reception desk posts weekly events in the city, provides laptop rentals, lends books, offers printing and photocopying services, and has public computers in case you need to get organized. If you'd rather relax, head to the downstairs restaurant, bar, and club, which provide food all day, an *aperitivo* hour at 6pm, and a chance to dance at 11pm.

✡ Ⓜ*Termini. Walk down V. Marsala away from the station, and turn right onto V. Solferino.* ℹ *Breakfast included in some reservations; book online (€3 otherwise). Lockers outside room. Free luggage storage until 9pm. Towels €2. 1hr. free internet with booking; €2 per hr. or €5 per 4hr. thereafter. All-female dorms available.* Ⓢ *10-bed dorms €25; 8-bed €26; 6-bed €32-35; 4-bed €35-37.50. Singles €75; doubles €80-120; triples €150; quads €180.* Ⓦ *Reception 24hr. Restaurant/bar open daily 7am-late. Kitchen open 3-10pm.*

▨ ALESSANDRO DOWNTOWN

💧⊘(🕊) HOSTEL ❶

V. C. Cattaneo, 23 ☎06 44 34 01 47 ▤www.hostelsalessandro.com

This conveniently located hostel is a bit less party-hardy than its sister, the **Palace,** but it offers great services to backpackers and students. Large common spaces, communal kitchen, and dorms make it less cramped than nearby hostels, although bunk beds can bring down the comfort level of the largest dorms. Other than the midday cleaning which prevents you from resting in your room until after 3pm, Alessandro Downtown is ready to take care of you after a long day in the city.

*Ⓜ Termini. Take V. Giovanni Giolitti and turn left onto V. C. Cattaneo. **i** Breakfast included. Free pasta dinners M-F 7pm. 30min. Lockers ensuite; free luggage storage before 2pm. Towel rental. Book online 1 week in advance Apr-Aug. 30 min. free Wi-Fi daily; €2 per hr. thereafter. [$] 8-bed dorms €14-29; 6-bed €15-30; 4-bed (co-ed) with bath €19-40; doubles €50-53, with bath €55-110. ⏰ Reception 24hr. Rooms must be vacated 10am-3pm for cleaning.*

ALESSANDRO PALACE — HOSTEL ❶

V. Vicenza 42 ☎06 44 61 958 www.hostelsalessando.com

A historically decorated bar (check out the "frescoed" ceiling) turned modern (check out the speakers and TV!) makes this one of the most social hostels around. While the nightly pizza giveaway *(8:30pm)* goes fast, great happy hours and drink specials keep guests around all evening. A/C keeps the rooms bearable in the mid-July Roman heat, though big dorm size can make restful sleep difficult. Still, this is as close as a hostel gets to being a palace.

*Ⓜ Termini. Walk up V. Marsala away from the station and turn right onto V. Vicenza. **i** Breakfast included; free pizza daily Apr-July 8:30pm. Lockers ensuite. Fridges in some doubles. Reserve online at least 1 week in advance during high season. 30min. free Wi-Fi per day. All dorms have private bathroom. [$] 8-bed dorms €15-30; 6-bed €16-36; 4-bed €18-38, with bath €21-42. Doubles €55-115, with bath €65-130; triples €75-135/€81-147. ⏰ Reception 24hr. Free luggage storage before 3pm. Bar open daily 6pm-2am.*

THE YELLOW — HOSTEL ❶

V. Palestro 44 ☎06 49 38 26 82 www.the-yellow.com

This hostel isn't called "yellow" because it's scared, but because it's so darn happy. The perfect place for social butterflies, this establishment boasts a full bar (customers will likely spend more time here than in their somewhat small rooms) and over five floors of dorms as well as colored lights and funky posters in the hallways. Skype headsets, locks, and even laptops are conveniently available to rent or purchase at the reception desk. Come here for fun times...not to wake up at 6am for a hike to the Vatican.

*Ⓜ Termini. Take V. Milazzo away from the station and turn left onto V. Palestro. **i** Breakfast €2-10 at the bar next door. Lockers ensuite; free luggage storage before 1:30pm. €10 towel deposit. 30min. free internet per day on public computers. [$] 12-bed dorms €18-24; 7-bed €20-26; 6-bed €22-34; 4-bed €24-35. ⏰ Reception 24hr.*

LEGENDS HOSTEL — HOSTEL ❷

V. Curtatone 12 ☎06 44 70 32 17 www.legendshostel.com

This cramped but well-equipped hostel close to Termini brings in a mixed crowd of backpackers and older folk. There's little common space, and rooms are fairly distant from one other (some in a separate building). However, the small kitchen gives the place a sense of community, especially during delicious breakfasts and pasta dinners. The low-key staff is ready to assist you during your stay in Rome. Shared bathrooms can be a bit messy, but at least they come with soap.

*Ⓜ Termini. Walk up V. Marsala away from the station; turn right onto V. Gaeta and right onto V. Curtatone. Buzz and walk to 1st fl. **i** Breakfast included; free pasta M-F 7pm. Lockers ensuite. 5hr. free Wi-Fi; €1 per hr. thereafter. Public computers at reception desk. Fans in rooms. [$] 8-bed dorms €23-33; 6-bed €25-37; 5-bed €28-41; 4-bed €30-44. Triples €48-51; doubles €41-71. ⏰ Reception 24hr.*

FREEDOM TRAVELLER — HOSTEL ❶

V. Gaeta 23 ☎06 48 91 29 10 www.freedom-traveller.it

Freedom Traveller is a friendly and slightly less crowded hostel with the same great perks as nearby spots. Its sunny reception area and common spaces (TV room, backyard, and kitchen) immediately make you feel welcome. The first-floor location and proximity to Termini make it especially convenient for weary travelers.

➡ [M]*Termini. Take V. Marsala away from the station and turn right onto V. Gaeta.* ℹ *Free pizza and beer party Tu evenings. Free luggage storage until 2.30pm. All-female dorms available. Free Wi-Fi in common spaces and some rooms.* [$] *6- and 4-bed dorms €17-32; doubles €60-110; triples €75-135; quads €80-160.* ⏰ *Reception 24hr. Lockout 10:30am-2pm (except for private rooms). Quiet hours 11pm-8am. Communal kitchen open until 10:30pm.*

MOSAIC HOSTEL HOSTEL [2]

V. Carlo Cattaneo ☎06 44 70 45 92 💻www.hostelmosaic.com

Right below the busier **Alessandro Palace,** this similar hostel's reception boasts a comfy leather couch, warmly painted walls, and a helpful staff that immediately fosters a sense of home. Rooms that feel less utilitarian than those of your typical hostel (despite the requisite bunks) provide everything you need for a comfortable stay in Rome.

➡ [M]*Termini. Take V. Giovanni Giolitti and turn left onto V. Carlo Cattaneo. On the 2nd fl.* ℹ *Breakfast included; free pasta dinner M-F. Lockers ensuite; free luggage storage upon arrival. Towels €2. Kitchen access M-F. Female-only dorms available. Reserve online at least a week in advance. 30min. free Wi-Fi per day; €1 per hr. thereafter.* [$] *8-bed dorms €22; 6-bed €24; 5-bed €25; 4-bed €27.* ⏰ *Reception 24hr.*

CASA OLMATA HOSTEL [1]

V. dell'Olmata 36 ☎06 48 30 19 💻www.casaolmata.com

This quiet, well-kept, and cheerfully run hostel finds itself in a nicer region than most. Mixed 6-bed dorms, triples, doubles, and singles are a bit cramped, but wooden bunks and homey decorations (check out the old clocks and lace curtains in some rooms) provide a comfy, lived-in feel. Many rooms come with fully equipped ensuite kitchens, TV, fans, and private bath; others have access to a communal kitchen down the hall with microwave and fridge. It's definitely not a party hostel (quiet hours after midnight), but all the better for it.

➡ [M]*Termini. Walk toward P. Santa Maggiore and down V. Paolina. Turn left onto W. Quattro Cantoni and left onto V. Olmata.* ℹ *Breakfast included. Lockers in hallway and ensuite. 15min. free internet per day at public computer. Roof terrace. Free Wi-Fi.* [$] *Dorms €18-20; singles €38; doubles €56-58. Inquire about discounts for longer stays.* ⏰ *Reception 8am-2pm and 4pm-midnight.*

HOTEL PAPA GERMANO HOTEL [2]

V. Calatafimi 14/A ☎06 48 69 19 💻www.hotelpapagermano.com

Hopefully, Hotel Papa Germano's tacky decor will make you smile rather than judge, for if you write this place off too swiftly, you'll be missing out on its many great services. If the wallpaper doesn't make you grin, maybe the especially friendly reception or free Wi-Fi will. The modest rooms' TVs, A/C, and telephones make them good deals. The dormitory is an economical alternative that remains slightly nicer than hostel options.

➡ [M]*Termini. Take V. Marsala away from the train station, proceed straight as it becomes V. Volturno, and turn right onto the small V. Calatafimi.* ℹ *Breakfast included. 3 public computers.* [$] *Dorms €15-30; singles €30-60; doubles €40-95, with bath €50-120; triples €50-100/€60-140; quads €70-130/€80-150.* ⏰ *Reception 7am-midnight.*

BED AND BREAKFAST A CASA DI ZIA SERAFINA B AND B [4]

V. Filippo Turati 107 ☎06 44 66 458 💻www.casaserafina.it

A gracious host welcomes you to her four furnished and immaculately kept rooms off the bright central hallway of her apartment at this intimate bed and breakfast. A great deal amid most of Termini's less than charming accommodations, Signora Serafina's rooms are equipped with Wi-Fi, TVs, A/C, and cheerful decor. Chambers without bathrooms have access to a sparkling clean one in the hallway. Homemade breakfast cooked each morning by the signora herself.

➡ [M]*Termini. Walk down V. Ratazzi and turn left onto V. Filippo Turati. Buzz and proceed to 3rd fl. Call in advance to set up arrival time; guests are given a key to enter.* [$] *Doubles €70, with bath €80; triples €110.*

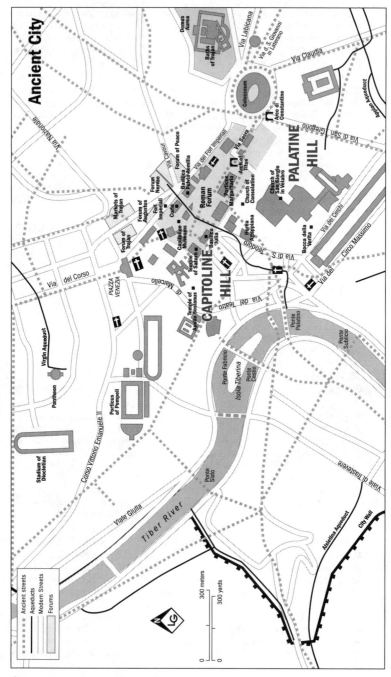

Ancient City

rome

Legend:
- Ancient streets
- Aqueducts
- Modern Streets
- Forums

Baths of Trajan
Domus Aurea
Via Labicana
Via d. S. Gioainni in Laterano
Via Claudia
Colosseum
Arco di Constantine
Appian Aqueduct
Forum of Peace
Via dei Fori Imperiali
Forum Nervia
Basilica Fulvia-Aemilia
Via Sacra
Arch of Titus
Portico Margaritaria
Church of Consolation
PALATINE HILL
Via di San Gregorio
Markets of Trajan
Forum of Augustus
Fori Imperiali
Curia
Roman Forum
Church of San Giorgio in Velabro
Via Nazionale
Via Cavour
Forum of Trajan
Capitoline Museums
Basilica Iulia
Temple of Saturn
Porta Aspiplana
Bocca della Verità
Via dei Cerchi
Via del Corso
PIAZZA VENEZIA
di Marcello
CAPITOLINE HILL
Via del S. Teodoro
Circo Massimo
Virgin Aqueduct
Temple of Apollo Sosianus
Via del Teatro
Ponte Paladino
Pantheon
Porticus of Pompeii
Ponte Fabricio
Isola Tiberina
Ponte Cestio
Ponte Sublicio
Stadium of Diocletian
Corso Vittorio Emanuele II
Ponte Sisto
Viale di Trastevere
Viale Giulia
Tiber River
Atsetina Aqueduct
City Wall

300 meters
300 yards
0

AFFITTACAMERE ARIES HOTEL ❹

V. XX Settembre 58/A ☎06 42 02 71 61 🖳www.affittacamerearies.com

The lovely owner might be reason enough to stay here—she'll be happy to offer you coffee upon arrival. A bit removed from the Termini cluster, this charming hotel decorated with flowers and frescoes offers six simple but spacious rooms. The stone floors and metal-framed beds might not be the warmest and fuzziest things around, but the accommodating service, friendly dog (which sometimes follows the owner around), and great amenities make up for it.

[M]Termini. Veer left toward P. della Repubblica, proceed onto V.V.E. Orlando, and turn right onto V. XX Settembre. Buzz and take Scala B to the 2nd fl. ℹ *Breakfast included. Free Wi-Fi.* $ *Singles €50; doubles €80; triples €105. Ask about a discount for longer stays.* ⏰ *Guests are given a key to enter, but reception essentially 24hr.*

sights

Do the sights of Rome even require an introduction? Like the extrovert who will shake your hand before you take your coat off, Rome's famous destinations have no trouble making themselves known: interrupting, side-tracking, and dragging out your itinerary before you even get started, they seem to beckon from every street corner and *piazza*. Don't worry—that's a good thing. If they were anything less than spectacular, the gargantuan number of must-sees in Rome would feel burdensome. Luckily, they *are* spectacular and, luckily again, fairly concentrated within the city. You'll run into about half of them by default. On your way to get gelato, for example, you'll come across a fountain that looks, to put it mildly, vaguely familiar. The sights you won't stumble upon while hunting for a good pizzeria can be tackled with a good pair of walking shoes, a whole lot of ambition, and an espresso to keep you going. Our suggestion: take at least one day without the guidebook or map and simply see where you end up. Chances are you'll hit a lot of those "must-sees" without even trying.

ANCIENT CITY

COLOSSEUM ANCIENT ROME

V. di San Gregorio, V. Cello Vibenna, and V. Nicola Salvi ☎06 39 96 77 00 🖳www.pierreci.it

A walk through the Colosseum provides an interesting mix of old and new—crumbling bricks and empty "cells" evoking the unfortunate ancients who once occupied them are juxtaposed against the vision of dozens of modern-day tourists who eagerly peer into the Colosseum's arena, a formerly sandy pit in which bloody (and sometimes not so bloody) combat took place. Perhaps the first thing you'll notice is the mix of architectural elements—admittedly, some of the more modern additions are attempts to keep this ancient structure from crumbling altogether. (You'll run into several construction workers assembling metal reinforcements on the ground level.) Contemporary alterations aside, the four types of architecture used to construct Rome's massive amphitheater are still evident, particularly on its northern side (the south side has been subjected to the looters of the city, who have been snatching the Colosseum's marble siding for themselves since the sixth century CE). The amphitheater's bottom tier, made of massive blocks of Travertine, was built the thickest. Its levels become lighter in both weight and appearance as you move upward. This visual "ranking" matched the organization of Roman spectators, who although given free admission, were assigned to seats in accordance with their social class. The emperor not only got VIP seating but also had the privilege of entering through the secret, "Passage of Commodus," an underground tunnel that protected him from the public. It would seem that gladiators and wild beasts were also granted this immunity (though likely for different reasons), as they too entered the Colosseum via winding corridors beneath the arena. Today, disintegrating walls and vaults covered in wooden planks are all that remain of the 15 original underground pathways. Of the 80 porticos dotting the arena's circumference, four were reserved for the emperor and the games' performers.

For the **◙best view** of the arena, climb to the upper tiers, where you can see the structure in its entirety—a massive 188m by 156m oval. Looking down, you'll get a feel for what it was like to witness the combats that took place in this arena. Most famously, this was the place where **gladiators,** men who could be anything from slaves to convicts to prisoners, to emperors (actually, the only one on record is Commodus, the emperor after whom the Colosseum is named) met for battle in the frenzy of the Roman games. Trained from the age of 17 and given rankings based on the number of fights they won, these combatants were seldom actually killed as they usually begged for mercy when defeat seemed imminent. It wasn't until the Middle Ages that massacre became the norm. Ranking had its own taxonomy, complete with scientific-sounding names (Retiarius, Oplomachus and Cruppellarius to name a few) and armor specific to the fighter's status. Check out the detailed costume and weaponry exhibits in display cases on the upper level. If you want to see the gladiator armor on something other than a stuffed mannequin, consider getting your picture taken with one of the costumed dudes accosting middle-aged women around the concession stands out front (usually €5). Probably bloodier than fights between the gladiators were those between wild animals, since back in ancient Rome there was no ASPCA watching out for the beasts used in executions and staged combat. Bones from some of the biggest animals, including the Libyan bears and giant ostriches, are also on display beside the armor.

While the arena takes center stage for most visitors, peer around the back side for a great view of the Arch of Constantine, the tree-lined V. San Gregorio, and the Roman Forum just across the way. **▧Tickets** to the Colosseum can be purchased at the Palatine Hill/Roman Forum entrance on V. San Gregorio. Head there midday, after the early morning frenzy, to avoid waiting in a 2hr. line at the Colosseum.

✦ Ⓜ️B: Colosseo or Ⓜ️Termini, then bus #75. *i*Ⓢ Tickets are purchased for entrance to the Colosseum, Palatine Hill, and the Roman Forum; 1 entrance per sight, used over the course of 2 days. €12, EU students ages 18-24 €7.50, EU citizens under 18 and over 65 free. Guided tour €4; audio tour €4.50; video guide €5.50. All available in English. ☑ Open daily 8:30am until 1hr. before sunset.

▧ **ARCO DI CONSTANTINE**　　　　　　　　　　ₕ ANCIENT ROME, MONUMENT
V. San Gregorio, South of the Colosseum near the Palatine Hill entrance.

Although most people only pass the Arch of Constantine on the way to the Colosseum or the Roman Forum across the street, its size and beauty are reason enough to seek it out. Towering an impressive 70 ft. over the V. San Gregorio, the arch stands in commemoration of Constantine's victory over Maxentius at the Battle of the Milvian Bridge in 312 CE. Despite the metal gates that prevent visitors from walking through the arch, those interested can take a closer look at the beautiful engravings and inscriptions depicting Constantine's battles and victories that etch the structure. The Romans, who seem awfully good at "borrowing" things (check out the torn-away marble sections of the Colosseum), continued the tradition here, decorating the side of the arch with medallions stolen from other monuments nearby. There's something to be said for kleptomania after all.

✦ Ⓜ️B: Colosseo or Ⓜ️Termini, then bus #75. Walk down V. San Gregorio from the Colosseum. Ⓢ Free.

A walk through the Roman Forum provides a pleasant (though somewhat bumpy) one-hour respite from the busy city just outside its gates, even if you don't know a bit of its history or read a single plaque. Chances are, though, you didn't pay €12 for a walk in the park. For that, try the **Domus Aurea.** To justify spending cash on ruins instead of gelato, consider picking up an audio tour that will at least clue you in to the history of a few of the sections you'll pass. There aren't many informational plaques along the way, so unless you're enough of a Latin scholar to understand the original inscriptions, your map (provided at the ticket office) and audio tour are the only things helping you tell your Tempios from your Basilicas.

Your route through the Roman Forum depends on the entrance you choose. Although the lines at this sight tend to be significantly shorter than those for the Colosseum, you can make them even shorter by coming in the mid- to late afternoon, when the early-morning crowds have died off. The free map of the Forum suggests that its main entrance is at V. Largo Ricci, though the lines may be shorter at V. San Gregorio.

Walking in, you will see a stunning view of the Forum, a plot of land used as a marketplace by the Greeks and Etruscans of the seventh and eighth centuries. Today, the area consists mostly of grassy and gravelly paths, crumbling temples, and a few reconstructed sights that contain most of the history of the place. The central area is lowest to the ground; as you move out, the pathways become more elevated. Because of this topographical fact, even those who don't purchase a ticket inside can get great views of the Forum's layout from the street.

Walk down **Via Sacra,** the oldest street in Rome, which runs through the center of the Forum. To the right, you'll find the remains of the **Basilica Fulvia-Aemilia,** originally built in 179 BCE by two Marcuses—Fulvia and Aemilia—but then renovated by the Aemilia family, perhaps as a mode of self-promotion. If you're having trouble finding the basilica, that's because it no longer exists—just the skeleton of a floor plan and some remains housed under a roof are still here. Step inside the **Curia,** originally the meeting place of the Senate, for a museum-like display of coins, columns, and recovered friezes that once decorated the basilica, including ☒**The Rape of the Sabine Women.** Outside again, you'll find the **Temple of Saturn** and the **Basilica Julia** flanking the sides of the central area. Duck into the tiny hut dedicated to Caesar, where flowers and photos add a bit of color to the dirt-covered area. The **Tempio di Romolo** on the left, with its massive green door, and the **Tempio di Antoninus and Faustina,** with beautiful pink and white columns guarding the entrance, are straight ahead. While the **Arch of Constantine** might have been free, you'll be glad you paid to see the **Arch of Titus,** built in 81 CE by Emperor Domitian to commemorate the victory over Jerusalem by his brother Titus. Although smaller than Constantine's, Titus's arch boasts a coffered archway and beautiful interior frieze depicting a hoard of horses, a menorah, and crowds of people after the victory that make it especially stunning. Further on, walk down the dirt paths of the **Severan Horrea** which are bordered by brick cell enclosures and excavation areas.

✦ Ⓜ*B: Colosseo or* Ⓜ*Termini, then bus #75. Enter at V. San Gregorio (near the Arch of Constantine), V. dei Fori Imperiali (halfway between Trajan's column and the Colosseum), or directly opposite the Colosseum. Entrance to the Forum is joint with that to the Palatine Hill, a neighboring sight.*
ⅈ *Tickets are purchased for entrance to the Colosseum, Palatine Hill, and the Roman Forum, 1 entrance per sight, used over the course of 2 days. €12, EU students ages 18-24 €7.50, EU citizens under 18 and over 65 free. Audio tour to the Forum €4, combined with the Palatine €6; available in English.* ☒ *Open daily 8:30am until 1hr. before sunset.*

The Palatine Hill, occupying the stretch of elevated land between V. dei Cerchi, V. di San Gregorio, and V. di San Teodoro, was once *the* place to live (even Cicero and Mark Antony had their homes here). Today, it consists mostly of grassy patches and ruined temples, though it still provides some of the best views of the city and the adjacent Roman Forum. At the very least, bring a camera, some water, and maybe a sandwich for a pleasant stroll through its grounds.

Entering at V. San Gregorio, you can either head right (which will lead you into the Roman Forum) or left (which will lead you to the Palatine Hill). The ascent up the hill is a bit steep and winding, but some convenient steps make getting to the top much easier and faster. On the left, you'll find the **Stadium and Severan Complex** whose huge territory was once used as a riding school. Immediately onward is the **Domus Augustana**. (Its lower floor is on the left, the upper on the right.) Cushioned between the *domus*'s remnants is the **Palatine Museum,** which houses a small collection of statues, tiles, busts, and other archaeological items from wealthy Roman households. *(Open daily 8am-4pm, 30 people per fl., 20min. at a time. Free.)* Next along your walk is the start of the **Domus Flavia,** a huge region which includes reception rooms, a peristyle, and the Nymphaeum, a space which houses an octagonal fountain that once covered the entire area and symbolized power but today is dried up. The **Casa di Livia,** sectioned between, was property of the Roman aristocracy during the first century BCE and today provides a welcome escape from the sun. Play a little "Theseus and the Minotaur" (a classic game for children circa 200 BCE), and walk through the surrounding labyrinth of dank tunnels containing placards that describe the area. The **Casa di Augustus** and the **Casa di Romolo** are immediately on the left, surrounded by tiny Romulean Huts. Most scenic of all are the ▓**Farnese Gardens,** which offer an unparalleled vista of the Roman Forum, the Colosseum, and Capitoline Hill. They're also a good place to stop for a picnic (which some travelers supplement with oranges from one of the nearby trees). Descend the stairs to check out the **Nymphaeum of the Rain,** a small cave with running water.

✢ ⓜB: Colosseo or ⓜTermini, then bus #75. Enter at V. San Gregorio (near the Arch of Constatine), V. dei Fori Imperiali (halfway between Trajan's column and the Colosseum), or directly opposite the Colosseum. Next to the Roman Forum. *i* Tickets are purchased for entrance to the Colosseum, Palatine Hill, and the Roman Forum, 1 entrance per sight, used over the course of 2 days. €12, EU students ages 18-24 €7.50, EU citizens under 18 and over 65 free. Audio tour to the Palatine Hill €4, combined with the Forum €6, available in English. ⌚ Open daily 8:30am until 1hr. before sunset.

FORI IMPERIALI   ♿ ANCIENT ROME
V. dei Fori Imperiali   ☎06 67 97 702

Walking down V. dei Fori Imperiali, it's impossible to miss—you guessed it— the Imperial Fora. Built in the 150 years after Caesar's reign, the four fora located here marked a new period of Roman dominance that ushered in a return to Hellenistic architecture. The open area enclosed by a colonnade to sequester the center from the surrounding, urban activity was the place where the business of the forum took place. This central region used for government affairs was topped off by a small temple decorated with friezes and paintings commissioned by the day's ruler to display his financial and political power. The first two fora were constructed by Caesar and Augustus, the next (christened the "Forum of Peace" to mark a calmer period in the empire's history) by Vespasian, and the last (called the Forum of Nerva) by Domitian. Down the way, you'll find the biggest forum of all, the **Forum of Trajan,** built between 107 and 113 CE.

In 1924, some of the land that once held the fora was paved over to make way for V. dei Fori's modern-day, less-than-regal central thoroughfare. Although the grounds themselves have been closed to the public for years, you can still admire them from the sidewalk, pick up a map of them at the tourist office and give yourself a tour, or explore them on a guided tour.

From the Colosseum, walk down V. dei Fori Imperiali. Ruins are on the right. i Call the tourist office for more information. $ Free. ⏰ Exhibition and info center open daily 9:30am-6:30pm.

DOMUS AUREA ♿ ANCIENT ROME, PARK

Vle. della Domus Aurea 1 (Colle Oppio Gardens) ☎06 39 96 7700

The expansive grounds of Domus Aurea sit between the Colosseum and busy V. Merulana. Shallow hills, patches of grass, and small children's playgrounds make a walk through this park a refreshing change of pace from the tourist crowds just next door. In the morning and early evening, the park is especially populated with dog walkers and joggers. Although you probably aren't here to see any monuments (by now, you might be eager to escape them), make sure to check out the **Trajan Baths,** which lie near the V. delle Terme di Traiano.

From the Colosseum, walk down V. Terme di Tito. Park is on the right and continues until V. Merulana $ Free. ⏰ Open daily 7am-9pm.

CHIESA DI SAN PIETRO IN VINCOLI ♿ CHURCH

P. di San Pietro in Vincoli, 4/a ☎06 97 844 950

Sitting atop a small hill just off V. Cavour, this fourth-century church houses Michelangelo's famous statue of Moses. After gazing at the bigger-than-life sculpture, take some time to admire the brightly colored frescoed ceilings and meander through the clean, white colonnade.

From V. Cavour turn onto V. S. Francis di Pacia and walk down V. Eudossiana. The church is on the left. i Fully covered legs and shoulders required. $ Free. ⏰ Open daily 8am-12:30pm, 3-6pm.

CIRCUS MAXIMUS ♿ ANCIENT ROME

It's only logical to pay a visit to the Circus Maximus after a long tour of the Colosseum and the Palatine Hill. While only a shadow of what it used to be (since it no longer exists and therefore actually can't cast a shadow), the Circus Maximus rounds out the key sights of your tour through Ancient Rome. At the end of V. di San Gregorio (near the P. di Porta Capena), this grassy plot of land was once Rome's largest stadium, home to more than 300,000 screaming Romans who came to watch the chariot races. Now, the fields only reach similar volumes during summer concerts and city celebrations, scheduled on a monthly basis. The best view of the long track is either from within the elevated Palatine Hill (where Emperor Augustus used to sit) or from the V. del Circo Massimo, which has fewer cars and is also slightly elevated (unlike the V. dei Cerchi). Other than tourists hoping to enjoy the view from these vantage points, dog walkers, joggers, and even some sunbathers come here to get away from the city congestion.

[M]B: Circo Massimo or bus #118. $ Free.

THE VELABRUM ♿ ANCIENT ROME

Amid all the nearby monuments boasting elevated views of the city, the Velabrum may feel a bit subterranean, but don't let that turn you off. The ruins in this valley blend into the surrounding neighborhood in a way that would be simply impossible for a structure the size of the Colosseum. You can approach the Velabrum from the waterfront (Ponte Palatino practically leads straight into it) or on V. Petroselli coming from the **Teatro di Marcello,** a round structure that looks remarkably like the Colosseum...perhaps because it was the model for Rome's most famous ruin. The **Portico d'Ottavia,** now only a skeleton of columns, sits at the corner of V. del Portico d'Ottavia, but the real star of the square is the **Chiesa di Santa Maria in Cosmedin,** a medieval church whose facade holds the famous **Bocca della Verità**. According to legend (and Gregory Peck in *Roman Holiday*), he who places his hand in the stone mouth will have it bitten off if he is a liar. Watch as dozens of people line up to prove their honesty or perhaps just have their picture taken.

✈ *From the Circo Massimo, walk down V. dei Cerchi until you reach P. S. Anastasia. The Velabrum and its sights are in the flat region at the base of the hill.* Ⓢ *Free.* Ⓒ *Church open daily 9:30am-5:50pm.*

CAPITOLINE HILL
Ⓧ PIAZZA, MUSEUM

Rome's small but magnificent capital sits nestled between the **Vittorio Emanuele II Monument** and the Roman Forum. From both these sights, views of the little Capitoline Hill are hard to miss. Coming up V. Arco di Settimio at the backside of the hill, you'll arrive at the **Piazza di Campidoglio,** designed by Michelangelo in 1536. At the center of the *piazza* sits an equestrian statue of **Marcus Aurelius**. It's actually a replica of the original, which you can view in a weatherproof chamber located in the Palazzo Nuovo. Still, this oft-photographed bronze statue is an impressive monument to one of Rome's more philosophically-inclined emperors. Piazza di Campidoglio. which is ringed by the **Capitoline Museums.** which hold a treasure trove of Roman and Greek sculpture as well as the oldest public collection of ancient art in the world. If you instead arrive at the *piazza* from V. del Teatro Marcello, you will be forced to climb a somewhat awkwardly slanted staircase. But get ready to be greeted by two symmetrical (and seductive) stone statues of a nude dude and his horse.

✈ *From V. dei Fori Imperiali, veer left towards the Monumento a Vittorio Emanuele II. Turn onto V. Teatro Marcello and head uphill* Ⓢ *Capitoline Museums €6.50, EU citizens age 18-25 €4.50, EU citizens under 18 and over 65 free. Audio tour €5. Available in English.* Ⓒ *Capitoline Museums open Tu-Su 9am-8pm. Ticket office closes 1hr. before museums close.*

CHIESA DI SANTA MARIA IN ARACOELI
Ⓧ CHURCH

While its exterior boasts nothing more than a dull wall of bricks, Chiesa di Santa Maria in Aracoeli's stunning pink-and-gold interior will reward those hardy enough to climb all 124 steps leading to its entrance. Built in the seventh century, this small church houses the **Bufalini Chapel** (to the right of the altar), decorated with Renaissance-era frescoes by Pinturicchio, and the even more entrancing **Cappella del San Bambino** (to the left of the altar), wallpapered with letters from sick children. Even if you don't spend much time in the church, take more than a minute to admire the exceptional view of the city from this vantage point. Five prominent domes dot the city's skyline, including the Dome of St. Peter's and, closest of all, the Cupola della Chiesa del Gesù. For an even better view of the city, consider taking the **Roma dal Cielo** elevator ride, which takes you up to the **Terrace of the Quadrigas.**

✈ *From Teatro Marcello, climb 124 steps to reach the church's perch.* ℹ *Fully covered shoulders and legs required.* Ⓢ *€7, ages 10-18 and over 65 €3.50.* Ⓒ *Open M-Th 9:30am-6:30pm, F-Su 9:30am-7:30pm. Last ticket sold 45min. before close.*

CENTRO STORICO

The Centro Storico abounds with sights that are as quintessentially Roman as pasta is Italian. Luckily, you won't have to pay or wait in line to see many of them, and their close proximity to one another makes it possible to visit all these sights in one rewarding afternoon.

▨ PANTHEON
ᗕ ANCIENT ROME

P. della Rotunda
☎06 68 30 02 30

Even without looking at your map, you're bound to stumble upon the Pantheon as you wander through the Centro Storico: signs pointing the way and crowds hovering outside will indicate that something great is coming. Corinthian columns and the large pediment atop give the edifice, which is currently under construction, the look of a Greek temple. Weighing an impressive 20 tons each, the bronze doors (originally plated in gold) leading into the Pantheon are enough to make visitors feel minuscule. Inside, the building's circular forum is full of people craning their necks to admire the perfect hemispherical dome (142 ft. in diameter and height) which, until Brunelleschi's Duomo in Florence, was the largest in the world. If you ever thought concrete was a poor man's material, think again. A mix of pumice, ash, sand, water, and chemical solidifiers, this material made the dome's casting possible by providing a viable alternative to the heavier stone blocks typically used. The coffered ceiling looks almost modern in form—a true geometrical abstraction—especially in contrast to the more traditional frescoes around it. Consider that the Pantheon's only source of light is the 27 ft. oculus at its center: over the course of the day, the beam of sun shining through it slowly moves along the temple's beautiful marble floor. (The best time to come, nevertheless, is on a rainy day, when water droplets flow directly through the central ring.) Notable for the architectural accomplishment of its design alone, the Pantheon is also a significant reflection of religious tolerance, dedicated to every god (of Ancient Rome, that is).

⇞ From P. Navona, follow signs for the Pantheon toward V. della Dogana Vecchia. $ Free. ⏰ Open M-Sa 8:30am-7:30pm, Su 9am-6pm.

★ CAMPO DEI FIORI — ♿☀ PIAZZA

Between P. Farnese and C. Vittorio Emanuele

Cushioned between stately Palazzo Farnese one block away and the busy C. Vittorio Emanuele, Campo dei Fiori is an enclosed world of its own where students, merchants, nighttime revelers, and performers make it their home. At its center, the somewhat ominous statue of a cloaked Giordano Bruno towers above the crowds. Aside from his imposing figure, street mimes clad in ridiculous garb are the only other even remotely statuesque shapes around. During the day, check out the market where merchants sell everything from 🍴**fish** to fresh produce to 🍷**alcohol** to clothes *(⏰M-Sa 7am-2:30pm)*. At night, the Campo is literally abuzz with the chatter of diners, while the clink of wine glasses and the thumping of a few disco-like clubs add to the jocular clatter of this happening center for city life.

⇞ From P. Navona, head towards C. Vittorio Emanuele and cut straight across to Campo dei Fiori. ℹ Watch your valuables at night. $ Free.

PIAZZA NAVONA — ♿☀ PIAZZA

Surrounded by V. di Santa Maria dell'Anima and C. del Rinascimento.

One of Rome's most picturesque *piazze*, Navona is right up there with the Colosseum and the Vatican in tourist popularity. Luckily for visitors, there's neither a 4hr. line nor a hefty admission price. Rather, the oval arena, originally a stadium built by Domitian in 86 CE, is full of tourists snapping pretty pictures, mimes performing at either end, artists selling trite watercolors, and musicians playing what sounds like the soundtrack of a Frank Sinatra film. This scene makes everything you heard about "classic Italy" seem true. Weave your way through the crowds—even grab a seat if you can—to take a closer look at Bernini's magnificent **Fontana dei Quattro Fiumi,** a massive stone sculpture that depicts four river gods, each representing a continent. The mix of masterfully cut rock and unadulterated, raw stone makes the figures and their "natural" environment especially convincing. The obelisk at the fountain's center may seem a bit out of place, but it actually mirrors many others scattered throughout the city. This one bears the mark of Pope Innocent X. Flanking the Fontana dei Quattro Fiumi, the less spectacular **Fontana di Nettuno** and **Fontana del Moro** draw significantly smaller crowds but provide good spots to take a seat and view the scene from afar.

⇞ Entrances into P. Navona at Palazzo Braschi, V. Agonale, V. di Sant'Agnese di Agone, and Corsia Agonale.

CHIESA DI SAN LUIGI DEI FRANCESI — [®] CHURCH

P. San Luigi dei Francesi 5 ☎06 68 82 71

From the exterior, this 16th-century church could easily be overlooked by pedestrians: its French facade is pretty unimpressive by Roman standards. Consequently, the surprise inside is even sweeter than it might have been. Three of Caravaggio's most impressive works, **The Calling of St. Matthew, St. Matthew and the Angel,** and **The Crucifixion,** grace the Contarelli Chapels in back. (If you're having difficulty finding them, it might be because they are not illuminated. Deposit €1 to light them up, or wait for someone else to step up.) Because they occupy the inner wall, it is slightly hard to get enough distance to view the paintings properly. However, these three works rival the private collection of Caravaggio's work held by the Galleria Borghese, so make sure to take them in as best you can. Their intense *chiaroscuro*, characterized by high contrast between light and dark, is characteristic of the religious and emotional meaning Caravaggio is famed for bringing out in his subjects.

From P. Navona, exit onto Corsia Agonale, turn left onto C. del Rinascimento and right onto V. Santa Giovanna d'Arco. $ Free. ⏰ Open M-W 10am-12:30pm and 4-7pm, Th 10am-12:30pm, F-Su 10am-12:30pm and 4-7pm.

VITTORIO EMANUELE II MONUMENT — [®] MONUMENT, MUSEUM

In P. Venezia ☎06 67 80 664; museum ☎06 67 93 526 💻www.risorgimento.it

The stunning Vittorio Emanuele II Monument towers—grandiose, theatrical, and triumphant—above P. Venezia. In fact, this flamboyant building remains a captivating presence. Even in far-away P. del Popolo, it towers in the distance down V. del Corso. The monument is affectionately (and a bit mockingly) referred to as "The Wedding Cake"—and justly so: its multiple tiers and pristine white facade look good enough to eat and garish enough to flaunt. Out front, huge Italian flags wave majestically as gladiators—or rather, plump men in metal garb—pose alongside confused tourists. Designed in 1884 and finally finished in 1927 by Mussolini, the huge building is as close as you can get to a giant megaphone that constantly yells out, "We are Italy! We are great!" The monument is best seen from P. Venezia or even from a few blocks away, but if you venture up its mighty steps, you'll find the **Museo del Risorgimento,** a slightly dull (and extremely dark) collection of artifacts tracing the course of Italian unification, inside. Though the museum is free, the view from outside is lighter, brighter, and more worth your time.

In P. Venezia. $ Free. ⏰ Monument open M-Th 9:30am-6:30pm, F-Su 9:30am-7:30pm. Museum open daily 9:30am-6:30pm.

PALAZZO VENEZIA — ♿ PALAZZO

V. del Plebiscito 118 ☎06 69 99 41; info and booking ☎06 32 810 💻www.galleriaborghese.it

In the northwest corner of P. Venezia, the Palazzo stands out as a result of its simple, brick facade rather than any particularly beautiful or ornate characteristic. As one of Rome's first Renaissance buildings, it certainly reflects an air of stateliness and grace, though it seems like a shy, quiet wallflower in comparison to the Vittorio Emanuele II Monument across the way. Though today it is not a site of governmental power, Mussolini once used it as his headquarters. The museum inside the Palazzo holds an impressive collection of documents, tapestries, paintings from the early Renaissance, and sculptures.

Across the way from Vittorio Emanuele II Monument, in P. Venezia. $ €4, EU citizens 18-25 €2, EU citizens under 18 and over 65 free. ⏰ Open Tu-Su 8:30am-7:30pm. Ticket office closes at 6:30pm.

PIAZZA DELLA ROTUNDA — ♿ PIAZZA

P. della Rotunda, right outside the Pantheon

The P. della Rotunda is either the *antipasto* or the *dolce* to your exploratory entree (which is the **Pantheon,** in case you haven't guessed). Before or after strolling under the beautiful dome of Rome's stately temple, crowds throng around the Egyptian obelisk crowning the center of this *piazza*. An 18th-century monument was created out of this obelisk when Clement XI "de-paganized" it by sticking a cross on top. The somewhat whimsical fountain in the square sports serpents and sharp-toothed heads that spew water from their mouths. The *piazze* surrounding this central spot are noticeably less crowded but contain some monuments of their own worth checking out. **Piazza della Minerva** features yet another obelisk sitting atop Bernini's elephant statues, whose figures supposedly represent the powerful "mind" needed to support the obelisks' wisdom. **P. di Sant'Eustachio** is full of small cafes and bars, including the famous **Sant'Eustachio Il Caffe** coffee den.

 # Outside the Pantheon. $ Free.

FONDAZIONE ROMA MUSEO — ♿ MUSEUM

V. del Corso 320 ☎06 67 86 209 🖳www.fondazioneromamuseo.it

Founded in 1999, this small museum is a place to remember due to its excellent selection of temporary art exhibits, lectures, and performances devoted to specific artists and periods in art history. Since the museum's opening, its curators have hosted approximately 30 shows in collaboration with other international museums, most recently a show devoted to Edward Hopper. The exhibitions here tend to present a retrospective of the artist's work alongside more interactive components as well as excellent commentary. Check their website for a full program of upcoming events.

 # From Palazzo Venezia, walk up V. del Corso for 7min. ℹ Rotating exhibits usually last at least 1 month; check online for updated information. Hours may vary according to each exhibition and its demand. $ €10; groups, under 26, and over 65 €8; under 6 free. ⏰ Open M 10am-6pm, Tu-Th 10am-8pm, F-Sa 10am-10pm, Su 10am-8pm. Ticket office closes 1hr. before museum.

PALAZZO DELLA ESPOSIZIONE — ♿ EXHIBITION SPACE

V. Nazionale 194 🖳www.palazzoesposizioni.it

The Palazzo della Esposizione is a cultural center devoted to curating art shows as well as housing performances, lectures, and events on a monthly basis. Its huge exhibition space is an excellent venue for the diversity of programs it offers. Most recently, it held a Giorgio De Chirico retrospective, tracing the origins and development of the 20th-century Italian artist in addition to his impact on modern art and Italy. Shows usually run for at least one month and are accompanied by supplementary lectures. Check online for a more detailed program of events.

 # From the Fori Imperiali, walk up V. Nazionale 7min. ℹ Check online for a program of upcoming shows; each usually lasts around 1 month. $ €12.50, under 25 and over 65 €10, disabled persons and under 6 free. Students €4 Tu-F. Free 1st W of the month 2-7pm. ⏰ Open Tu-Th 10am-8pm, F-Sa 10am-10:30pm, Su 10am-8pm. Last entry 1hr. before closing.

PIAZZA DI SPAGNA

★ PIAZZA DEL POPOLO — ♿ PIAZZA

At the end of V. del Corso

From the center of P. del Popolo, you can see the magnificent **Vittorio Emanuele II Monument** glowing (yes, it's so white, it glows) in the distance. Likewise, from the monument, a straight shot up V. del Corso has you gazing at this gigantic *piazza*, the "people's square," no ★**Communist connotation** intended. Despite the Corso's noise and crowds, this street is probably the best way to arrive at and appreciate the openness of the *piazza* which, for being so famous, is surprisingly uncongested. Perhaps it merely appears so thanks to its size and an oblong shape which makes its edges feel wider. At the center, the **Obelisk of Pharaoh Ramses II** stands triumphantly, attracting a few tourists to sit at its base. The ★**Santa Maria del Popolo** church is worth a visit, as it contains two Caravaggio masterpieces in the Capella Cerasi: *The Conversion of St. Paul* and *Crucifixion of St. Peter*, both of which are stunning examples of the artist's attention to *chiaroscuro* and the religious import this stylistic technique carried.

✦ ⓜA: Flaminio. ⓢ Church is free. ⏰ Church open M-Sa 7am-noon and 4-7pm, Su 8am-1:30pm and 4:30-7:30pm.

▨ MUSEO DELL'ARA PACIS
                                                        ♿ MUSEUM

At intersection of Lungotevere in Augusta and P. Porto di Ripetta   ☎06 06 08 🖳www.arapacis.it

This truly serene museum is a fitting space for its central monument, the **Ara Pacis.** The bare white walls and huge windows of the space reflect the peace of the monument, a frieze-covered enclosure constructed in 13 BCE to commemorate Augustus's victories throughout Spain and Gaul. Visitors can walk inside the structure to get a closer look at the 40m string of acanthus plant carved in the marble to represent renewal and unity under Augustus's Golden Age. On the outside, a mostly intact frieze of the ruler and his family reflects the tranquility of the period—the figures seem at ease, carved with an eye towards realism. Ironically, Augustus's body is chipped off in the procession and only his head remains. In the front of the museum, a row of busts including the head of Ottavia lie across from a reconstructed family tree. Check out the small model and accompanying map which shows the monument's original location in the context of Rome's current street layout. The area, now occupied by stores, restaurants, hotels, and, above all, tourists, was originally an open field where youth and soldiers used to compete in races and other athletic events. It's a shame that the only exercise going on now is the rush from shop to shop.

✦ ⓜA: Spagna. Take V. del Carrozze towards V. del Corso and proceed into P. Augusto Imperiale. ⓘ Audio tour available in English €3.50. ⓢ €6.50, EU citizens age 18-25 €4.50, EU citizens under 18 and over 65 free. ⏰ Open Tu-Su 9am-7pm. Last entry 1hr. before close.

TREVI FOUNTAIN
                                                         ♿ FOUNTAIN

Right beyond P. dell'Accademia di San Luca

The best time to see the fountain is at 4:30am, because it's probably the only hour where you'll be able to sit on one of the stone ledges without hearing the sounds of vendors selling overpriced trinkets and tourists snapping picture-perfect shots in the background. That's certainly the hour that Anita Ekberg, actress of Fellini's *La Dolce Vita*, came by when she took a dip in the fountain's gushing waters. (While you can make a late-night visit, don't follow her lead or you risk a steep fine.) Even if you don't make it during this empty hour, Nicolo Salvi's mix of masterfully cut rock and stone in the raw is phenomenal. Neptune, surrounded by the goddesses of abundance and good health as well as two brawny horsemen, is carved with exacting detail, while the environment in which he sits is realistic merely because it has been left untouched. As good as gelato may be, save your coins for the fountain: one will ensure a prompt return to Rome, two will bring you love in the Eternal City, and three will bring about your wedding.

✦ ⓜA: Barberini. Proceed down V. del Tritone and turn left onto V. Stamperia.

PIAZZA DI SPAGNA AND THE SPANISH STEPS
                             ⊛ MONUMENT, PIAZZA

P. di Spagna

In every sense, the P. di Spagna is a conglomeration of international roots—not only does it draw a global tourist crowd to its sandy-colored steps, but its history encompasses the Italians (who designed it), the British (who occupied it), the French (who financed it), and, oh yeah, the Spaniards (you've got this one). Built in 1723 as a way to connect the Piazza with the new **Trinita dei Monti** church above it, the magnificent steps now seem to be more of a hangout spot for tired shoppers, gelato eaters, and youth looking to avoid the expensive bar scene of this commercial neighborhood. The best view of the steps and Piazza is actually from the church's steps directly above—from there, you can get a better sense of

could you spare a million bucks?

If you've been to the Trevi fountain, then it's more than likely you've thrown a few coins in for good luck. What you probably don't know is that someone is making a living off of your spare change. **Roberto Cercelletta** has been taking money from the bottom of the fountain for the past 30 years, making upwards of US$150,000 a year in the process. The Roman and Italian courts have ruled that he is not stealing public money, and his activities are thus deemed legal. Almost every day, Cercelletta and his two minions slip on neon vests and enter the fountain in the early hours for 20-30min. to collect coins. The only day that he and his crew take a break is Sunday, when a local charity, Caritas, takes over the job, donating their findings to the poor. Caritas and other such organizations recently began protesting against Cercelletta's fishing. In counter-protest (warning: this story is about to get very real), Cercelletta climbed into the fountain numerous times and slashed his body with a knife, just to show that he is serious about his revenue stream, although apparently less so when it comes to his bloodstream. This all goes to show that if you can't find a job back home, you should go to Italy. Even the criminally insane can make a living in Rome.

their size while avoiding the cluster of people below. When you do make your way down, check out the **Fontana della Barcaccia,** built by Bernini the Elder before the steps were even constructed. The absurdly pink house and its two palm trees might remind you of leisurely beach life, but they actually commemorate the death of John Keats, who died there in 1821.

[M]A: Spagna.

TRINITA DEI MONTI — CHURCH

At the top of the Spanish Steps, at the intersection of V. Sistina and P. Trinita dei Monti

If you don't want to climb the steps just for the view, then this small church can give you an incentive. Built in 1502 and pillaged dozens of times, poor Trinita dei Monti has lost all of its original pieces but the transept above the highest altar. Check out the hand-drawn floor plan at the entrance to seek out some of the more famed frescoes gracing the chapels. Daniele da Volterra's *Descent from the Cross* was especially lauded by Poussin, and justly so—despite having undergone several restorations, it still brings a lot of color to the building's otherwise bleak walls.

[M]A: Spagna. Walk up the steps. $ Free. ⏰ Open daily 7am-noon and 4-7pm.

JEWISH GHETTO

The Jewish Ghetto consists of a few blocks just off Isola Tiberina. Come here for great food and a look back at one of the first Jewish communities in Western Europe.

THE GREAT SYNAGOGUE — ♿ SYNAGOGUE

Lungotevere dei Cenci and V. Catalana ☎06 68 40 06 61 💻www.museoebraico.roma.it

From afar, the Synagogue occupies a place in the Roman skyline right up there with many of the city's other, more famous cupolas. The Synagogue's beautiful, palm-tree-surrounded roof is distinct from the architecture and ruins that surround it, so stroll by to glimpse a different element of Rome's urban design. Construction of the Synagogue began in 1904 as part of an effort to revitalize and rebuild the Jewish Ghetto, which had for many decades suffered from flooding and unsanitary conditions. By 1904, the Synagogue, designed with a curious mix of Persian and Babylonian influences, had been completed. Its unique design

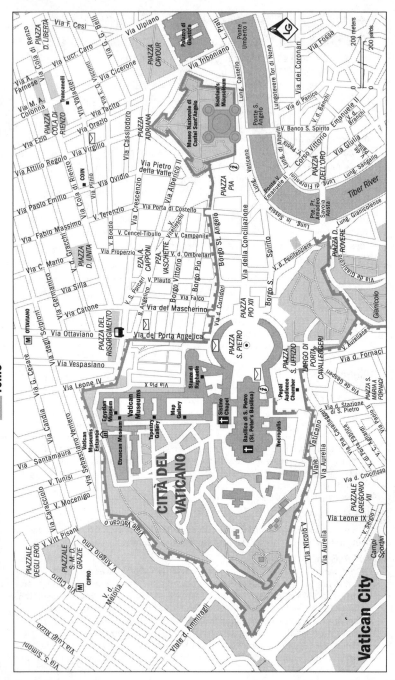

rome

Vatican City

was intended to make it stand apart from the city's many Catholic churches. Inside, highlights include a stunning mix of painted floral patterns by Annibale Brugnoli and Domenico Bruschi and an upper section of stained glass. Look up top for the small portion of clear glass commemorating a child who was killed in a 1982 plane crash.

At the corner of Lungotevere dei Cenci and V. Catalana. ℹ Open for services. $ Free.

PIAZZA MATTEI ♿ PIAZZA

Between V. dei Falegnami and V. dei Funari

The tiny P. Mattei is the center of the Jewish Ghetto, though today most of the neighborhood's culinary and social activity occurs on V. del Ottavio. Visit this *piazza* for a look at the **Fontana delle Tartarughe,** a 16th-century monument by Taddeo Landini that depicts four figures bearing tortoises and a strange basin atop their heads. The rest of the Piazza is composed of merchants and residential houses, save the **Chiesa di Sant'Angelo** in Pescheria, an unimposing eighth-century church named for its proximity to the fish market that once operated near Porta Ottavia. Though technically the center of the ghetto, this square feels more like a quiet respite from the busier streets nearby.

From the Area Sacra, walk down V. Arenula and turn left onto V. dei Falegnami; P. Mattei is on the right. ℹ The church cannot be entered due to repairs.

MUSEO EBRAICO ♿ MUSEUM

Lungotevere dei Cenci and V. Catalana ☎06 68 40 06 61 🖥www.museoebraico.roma.it

The Jewish Museum, located within the Synagogue, displays a comprehensive collection of Jewish artifacts tracing the history of Jews in Rome as far back as the 16th century. The collection, which includes textiles, silver pieces, ancient writings, and stone engravings, has been growing since 1960, the year of the museum's opening. Touring the museum is an informative supplement to a stroll through the nearby ghetto, which today retains most of its authenticity through its cuisine and residents.

From Ponte Garibaldi, turn right onto Lungotevere de Cenci and veer left toward the synagogue. $ €7, EU students €4, under 10 and handicapped persons free. Free guided tours of the Great Synagogue and the Spanish Synagogue available in English every hr. ⏰ Open June 16-Sept 15 M-Th 10am-6:15pm, F 10am-3:15pm, Su 10am-6:15pm; Sept 16-June 15 M-Th 10am-4:15pm, F 9am-1:15pm, Su 10am-4:15pm.

VATICAN CITY

More so than any other region of Rome, Vatican City fuses Roman history, artistic mastery, and Catholic ideology. As the administrative and spiritual headquarters of the Catholic Church, it has historically remained relatively independent from the rest of Rome, minting its own coins, using colorfully clad Swiss guards at its entrance, and running its own postal system. Expect some of the longest lines in the city but the greatest art to match, contained most notably in **St. Peter's Basilica** *(Basilica di San Pietro)* and the **Vatican Museums.**

St. Peter's Basilica and Environs

PIAZZA DI SAN PIETRO ♿ PIAZZA

At the end of V. della Concializione ☎06 69 81 662 🖥www.vaticanstate.va

There is no way to escape the arms of St. Peter—from the start of V. della Conciliazione they beckon pedestrians into the *piazza*, and once you've made your way inside, their embrace is enough to silence even the chattiest tourist in your group. If Bernini had seen this effect more than 400 years after the square's construction, he would have smiled. He intended the colonnade enclosing the *piazza*'s ovular area to symbolize the welcoming arms of the Catholic Church and greet tired pilgrims after a circuitous trek through the city. To enhance the vortex-like feel drawing people in, he designed the *piazza* in the form of an oval kissing a trapezoid. When standing at the square's center, you'll notice that this layout creates a perspective that makes the Basilica appear closer than it actually is. The row of 140 saints crowning the colonnade adds to the sense that the Basilica is pulling you inward. Stand at one of the round disks, and the quadruple rows of colonnades will seem to align themselves perfectly. Though it doesn't exactly compete with St. Peter's dome, the central obelisk (only 84 ft. tall) is at least a favorite with the pigeons, who often cluster at its base before perching on the saints' heads.

➔ Bus #23, 34, 40, 271, or 982 to P. Pia or bus #62 down V. della Conciliazione. ℹ The Pilgrim Tourist Office, to the left of the Basilica, has a multilingual staff, a gift shop, free bathrooms, a first-aid station, brochures, maps, currency exchange, and Vatican post boxes inside or nearby. Call the number or visit the website above for more info. $ Free. ⏰ Piazza open 24hr. Tourist Office open M-Sa 8:30am-6:15pm.

👍 ST. PETER'S BASILICA ♿ CHURCH

At the end of V. della Concializione ☎06 69 81 662 🖥www.saintpetersbasilica.org

If the Vatican's special post boxes aren't enough to remind you that you've entered another jurisdiction, then perhaps the airport-like security required before entering the Basilica will be. Though lines here don't get nearly as long as those for the **Vatican Museums** (see below), people are required to pass through scanned security before entering the church during visiting hours. Once you've cleared the metal detectors, head through any one of the colossal doors. You won't be able to use the **Porta Sancta** (last door on the right of the entrance porch) though: it's only opened during Holy Years.

Depending on the time of day, the church's interior appears in incredibly varied degrees of illumination—the ceilings are so high that on dark days the small windows near the Basilica's top do little to illuminate the nave. Immediately to the right, find Michelangelo's 👍**Pietà,** one of the most moving renderings of Mary and Jesus ever created. Since 1972, when a vandal attacked it with an axe, breaking Jesus's nose and Mary's hand, it has sat behind the bulletproof glass that slightly obscures the view even while it protects the precious piece of art. As you proceed onward, notice the strip of gold mosaics studded with Latin letters lining the perimeter of the nave and adding to the incredibly dogmatic and somewhat overbearing feel of the church.

Though it's hard to pinpoint the church's crowning element, Michelangelo's dome at least wins points for size—at a spectacular 138m in height and 42m in width, it remains the largest in the world. Directly below it, the somewhat ridiculous *baldacchino* (note the sculpted bumblebees buzzing around its twisting columns) marks the altar place used by the pope. The supposed tomb of St. Peter sits immediately below the altar. For a more complete story, visit the **Scavi Office** (see **St. Peter's Grave** listing), where you can sign up for an exclusive tour of the burial site.

Despite the hordes of people who frequent the Basilica each day, its size is enough to dwarf even the biggest crowds (60,000 and counting). Though most people come to the church as tourists, and the flash of cameras is nearly constant, consider participating in Mass, which is conducted before Bernini's bronze **Cathedra Petri** and lit from behind by glowing alabaster windows. If you're feeling really ambitious, it's even possible to hold your wedding in the Basilica, though the wait and price for the most famous church in the world could leave you eternally single. Only Catholics need apply.

ℹ Free guided tours in English leave from the Pilgrim Tourist Information Center. No shorts, mini-skirts or tank tops. For information on weddings visit 🖥www.saintpetersbasilica.org. $ Free. ⏰ Basilica open daily Apr-Sept 7am-7pm; Oct-Mar 7am-6:30pm. Tours in English Tu at 9:45am, Th-F at 9:45am. Mass M-F 8:30am, 10am, 11am, noon, and 5pm; Su and holidays 9am, 10:30am,

11:30am, 12:15pm, 1pm, 4pm, and 5:45pm. Vespers daily 5pm.

ST. PETER'S GRAVE (PRE-CONSTANTINIAN NECROPOLIS) 🚫📷🚫♿ TOMB

Office to the left of St. Peter's, tombs below Scavi Office ☎06 69 88 53 18

The beauty of St. Peter's Basilica draws crowds flocking to its doors, but the mystery of the saint and first pope's tomb has people flocking to the internet: the only way to pay his alleged remains a visit is to book a tour online well in advance of your desired day. If you finally get a spot, expect a claustrophobic walk through the tombs accompanied by explanations of the sight's historical and religious significance. The story goes that in about 330 CE, Roman Emperor Constantine constructed his first basilica directly over St. Peter's tomb. Over 1000 years later, the Renaissance basilica we see today was built in its place. The discovery of ancient ruins and a number of bones in 1939 had the Pope claiming that St. Peter's remains did in fact exist under the original altar. Though successive popes have affirmed the presence of the holy remains, many believe that the bones were removed during the Saracen pillaging of Rome in 849 CE. Don't expect to play Sherlock during the tour—just enjoy the sarcophagi, mosaics, and funerary inscriptions along the way.

➡ In the piazza. Instead of entering the Basilica, veer left and look for Swiss Guards dressed in stripes who will grant you access to the courtyard. The Scavi Office is on the courtyard's right side. ℹ The Necropolis can only be seen via a guided tour organized by the Scavi Office. Reservations must be made at least 1 day prior (but should be made as far in advance as possible, as much as 90 days). Pick up a reservation form at the office and hand deliver it or email. Do not call. Tours last 90min. and are available in English. Full-coverage attire required. No backpacks or bulky items. Must be at least 15 years old. $ €12. ⏰ Scavi Office open M-Sa 9am-5pm.

CUPOLA AND GROTTE VATICANE 🚫📷🚫♿ CHURCH

To the right of the Basilica 🖥www.vaticanstate.va/EN/Monuments/Saint_Peters_Basilica

If you haven't seen enough of Rome's sky or soil, consider the ascent up to St. Peter's Cupola or the descent into its *grotte* (underground caves). If you head skyward, get ready to be swept away: lose your breath climbing the 551 steps to the top (320 with the elevator), then have it stolen by the gasp-inducing view—one of the city's most spectacular panoramas and the only one in which St. Peter's doesn't steal the show as the biggest dome. A walk through the low-ceilinged tombs is eerie rather than breathtaking, as what feels like an endless collection of sarcophagi (including those of the last four popes) lines the stone passageways. Petri Apostoli's *sepolcro*, guarded by stone lions and protected behind glass, attracts the most attention, but don't miss the gold mosaics crowning Pius XI's final resting place.

➡ Walk to the last door on the right of the Basilica. In the courtyard, entrance to the Cupola is on the right, the Treasury on the left. ℹ Be prepared for at least 320 steps of climbing to the cupola, and a slightly claustrophobic setting in the Grotte. $ Cupola €5, with elevator €7. Grotte free. ⏰ Cupola and Grotte open daily Apr-Sept 8am-6pm; Oct-Mar 8am-5pm.

TREASURY 🚫♿ MUSEUM

In St. Peter's Basilica, to the left 🖥www.vaticanstate.va/EN/Monuments/Saint_Peters_Basilica

If St. Peter's Basilica's gold decorations aren't enough to dazzle you, then pay a visit to the Treasury, a small museum containing gifts bestowed upon the great pope's tomb. Goggle at the gold-and-silver-plated, gem-encrusted papal tiara, the intricate gold and silver embroidery on the Dalmatic of Charlemagne, and the several diamond, emerald, and ruby rings that are placed on St. Peter—his statue, that is—to commemorate Saints Peter and Paul Day every June 29th.

➡ Inside St. Peter's Basilica toward the left; look for the multilingual sign. ℹ No photography. $ €6, under 12 €4. ⏰ Treasury open daily Apr-Sept 8am-6:50pm; Oct-Mar 8am-5:50pm.

Other Vatican City Sights

◪ VATICAN MUSEUMS
◉⟨ MUSEUM

Entrance at Vle. Vaticano   ☎06 69 88 38 60 🖥www.museivaticani.va

After waiting in a 4hr. line, you should spend at least half as much time in the galleries themselves. Unfortunately, the lure of the Sistine Chapel (and frequent arrows pointing the way) pull people onward, creating a human stream with a very strong current. But you're not a ◪fish! Jump out and admire some of the more obscure treasures that are not only on display but comprise the building itself: stunning wall frescoes, floor mosaics, and even a **bronze double-helix ramp.** Check it out upon entering, as the intricate metalwork on the side is harder to see while on the stairs.

Maps, guidebooks, and audio tours will be for sale at the airport-like entrance where, yes, you are required to pass through scanned security. If this is your first time through these museums, forget the itinerary and just wander a bit, stopping at whatever piques your fancy. If you try to read and see everything in a guidebook, you will tire before getting even halfway through. Part of the pleasure is arriving at masterpieces unexpectedly.

After entering the complex, most people start in the **Museo Pio-Clementino,** which contains the world's greatest collection of antique sculptures, including the famous **Laocoon** in an octagonal courtyard. The sculpture, depicting a violent struggle between Laocoon and sea serpents as his sons try to rescue him, is a Greek masterpiece which awed even Michelangelo. Don't miss the **Stanza degli Animali,** filled with statues of roaring lions and more sedate donkeys. Look to your feet for an impressive mosaic floor of fruits, more animals, and abstract designs. The (relatively) small **Egyptian Museum** to the side generally attracts a smaller crowd; stop here if you need a spot to recuperate. Before heading upstairs, make sure to circumnavigate the ◪**Sala Rotonda,** a small room with unbelievable mosaics on the floor and a domed roof recalling the **Pantheon's** coffered ceiling and oculus.

Head directly upstairs to find the **Etruscan Museum,** which contains a daunting 18 rooms' worth of Etruscan artifacts, sarcophagi, and vases that offer a glimpse into Italy's earliest civilization. The **Candelabra Gallery** and dimly lit **Tapestry Gallery** are often treated as thoroughfares, but the **Map Gallery** is worth a stop. Huge frescoed maps of Italy line the walls and provide an eye into the country's diverse geographical regions. You can carry on via a shortcut to the Sistine Chapel from here, but if you can wait, meander through the **Stanza Sobieski,** with its strange mix of religious and military work, and then the **Stanze di Rafaele.** These four rooms, originally Julius II's apartments, were decorated by the great Raphael, and include the ◪**School of Athens** fresco on one large wall.

In no other collection would all the aforementioned works possibly be considered *precursors* to the main show. But you're in the Vatican Museum, and it's time for the main course. The ◪**Sistine Chapel** is undoubtedly the most sought out, crowded, and monumental part of the museum. Every few minutes, the guards shush the mass of people, reminding them not to take photos and ushering them onward. Minutes later, the chatter recommences, and a flash goes off. Expect an unpleasant experience in the way of people, but a remarkable one in the way of art. If craning your neck to see the ceiling becomes painful after a few minutes, imagine Michelangelo actually making the work—he painted the frescoes on a platform while bending backward and never recovered from the strain. Even those not versed in art history will recognize the famous **Creation of Adam,** one of nine panels depicting scenes from the story of Genesis. Occupying the entirety of the altar wall, the **Last Judgment** can be viewed with much less physical contortion. This huge fresco is, in a way, free of composition—it is a

rome

massive conglomeration of muscular figures, clouds, and land masses—but this adds to its uncontainable and inconceivable force. Though it can be difficult to focus on one area, look for the flayed human skin that hangs between heaven and hell, a self-portrait included by Michelangelo.

⇞ [M]A: Ottaviano. Head down V. Ottaviano, turn right onto V. dei Bastioni di Michelangelo, and follow the wall until you see the end of the line to the museums. Entrance is on Vle. Vaticano. ℹ A wheelchair-accessible itinerary is available, as are wheelchairs for rent. Call ☎06 698 81589 for info. $ €15, EU citizens ages 18-26 and 6-18 €8; under 6 free. Last Su of every month free. Entrance with guided and audio tours €31/€25. ⏰ Galleries open M-Sa and last Su of every month 9am-6pm. Last entry 2 hr. before close. Open Apr-July F 7-11pm for special viewing only; online reservation required, €4.

MUSEO NAZIONALE DI CASTEL SANT'ANGELO ❀♿ CASTLE, MUSEUM

Lungotevere Castello 50 ☎06 68 19 111 🖥www.castelsantangelo.com

If you thought all of Rome was basilicas and ruins, think again: that circular, brick structure on the river is a castle, complete with moat (okay, it's dried up) and torches (fine, they're electric). Originally built in the first century CE as a mausoleum for Hadrian and his family, it has since been converted from a tomb to a palace, castle, prison, and—finally—museum. A walk through the massive structure starts with the ascent up a 125m ramp whose dimly lit corridor is flanked by burial chambers. When you step into the light, note the central courtyard's crowning piece, the **Angel Statue** with rusted metal wings and a stone body designed by Raffaello da Montelupo. Floorplans of the castle's layout attempt to guide you through, but it's best to let yourself get lost in the staircases and rooms. If you can, make your way to the 🖼**Sala di Apollo,** a mostly white room with whimsical frescoes of part-human, part-animal beasts. Once you've toured the interior, take some time on the rooftop, where the panorama of Rome and view of the gleaming Sistine Chapel is one of the best in the city. The marble **Ponte Sant'Angelo** lined with statues by Bernini is best seen from this angle.

⇞ Bus #23, 34, 40, 271 or 982 to P. Pia. At the end of V. della Conciliazione and at the intersection with Ponte S. Angelo. $ €8.50, EU citizens ages 18-25 €6, EU citizens under 18 and over 65 free. Audio tour €4. ⏰ Open Tu-Su 9am-7:30pm. Ticket office closes 6:30pm.

PIAZZA CAVOUR ♿ PIAZZA

On the Lungotevere Castello

P. Cavour, cushioned between V. Triboniano and V. Ulpiano, is probably admired more from the heights of nearby monuments than from its center: most of the square's buildings are inaccessible to the public. The most imposing structure is Rome's **Supreme Court of Cassation,** where lawyers instead of lions determine the fate of those charged: there's no modern-day Colosseum here. The odd white structure on the left side is the **Chiese Valdese,** an evangelical church where the oldest existing group of non-Catholic Christians (the Waldensians) prior to the Reformation pray. If these two structures don't catch your eye from afar, then maybe the tall palms at the *piazza*'s center will, bringing you away from the gravity of St. Peter's and suggesting something a bit more playful.

⇞ From Castel Sant'Angelo, head down Lungotevere Castello away from St. Peter's Basilica. $ Free.

TRASTEVERE

Ahhh, Trastevere. With old cobblestone streets, hidden-away trattorias, and bustling nightlife, this oft-forgotten gem of a neighborhood is not one to miss. Even if you're only in Rome a few days, ditch some of those churches you had planned to visit and head across the Tiber to enjoy more intimate *piazze,* basilicas that rival their more-famous brethren on the other side of the river, and a tight-knit community proud of their unpretentious neighborhood. Cross the **Ponte Garibaldi** to make your way directly onto **Piazza G. Belli,** which holds the triumphant statue of poet Giuseppe Gioachino Belli. V. Trastevere runs through the neighborhood, and if not the most scenic of streets, it is still a reliable place to find cheap eats or clothes. To the left, most of the streets are fairly quiet but full of restaurants and small shops. By contrast, the right side of Trastevere contains most of the neighborhood's activity—turn right onto V. della Lungaretta to arrive at **Piazza di Sant'Apollonia** and the nearby **Piazza di Santa Maria in Trastevere.** Both are full of commotion and are more touristed than the rest of the neighborhood. Just at the end of the Ponte Sisto, **Piazza Trilussa** offers proximity to nightlife spots as well as scenic views of the river, making it particularly popular with students. **Piazza San Cosimato,** off of V. Luciano Manara, boasts an outdoor market selling fresh fruit, vegetables, and fish.

👍 ISOLA TIBERINA ♿ OPEN SPACE

With most of Rome's major sights located further "inland," tourists tend to forget about Rome's river, the Fiume Tevere, and the land out yonder. On your way to Trastevere, take the tiny **Ponte Fabriccio (a.k.a. the Ponte dei Quattro Capi),** which, in case you couldn't tell by its name, bears four stone heads, allegedly those of the architects who originally restored the bridge. You'll find yourself standing on Isola Tiberina, a small plot of land that, according to legend, is actually composed of the silt-covered bodily remains of Tarquin, an Etruscan ruler who was thrown in the river for raping the beautiful Lucretia. The island is only home to a few establishments, so most people only stay to check out the hard-to-pronounce **Fatebenefratelli Hospital,** which looks more like a church than a healing facility. If you want to stick around, head down the slope to the open expanse directly on the river. A few people might be fishing, but more will be **👍lying in the sun** on what is the closest thing Rome has to a beach.

⇆ From V. del Teatro Marcello, walk towards the water and onto Lungomare dei Pierleoni. Turn left and cross Ponte Fabricio. $ Free.

GIANICOLO HILL ♿ OPEN SPACE

While manmade monuments (or at least their remains) take center stage in Central Rome, those in Trastevere are rivaled by the neighborhood's natural wonders. The highest peak in this part of Rome, Gianicolo Hill, is a large expanse of land highlighted by the **Fonte Acqua Paola,** a fountain that marks the end of an aqueduct honoring Pope Paul V. While the crystal-blue pool of water and elaborate white facade above it are marvels of human design, the **👍surrounding landscape** really steals the show. If you continue up the winding (and steep) V. Garibaldi, you'll come to the site of what was once the **Porta San Pancrazio** (the main gate built around Gianicolo to protect Rome from raids), which, since the French raids in the late 1800s, has been replaced. It seems the French were not always known for raising the white flag...

⇆ From Fonte Aqua Paola, continue uphill, onto V. Aldo Fabrizi and enter the park. You will pass Monumento a Garibaldi on the pleasant walk. $ Free.

CHIESA DI SANTA MARIA IN TRASTEVERE ♿ CHURCH

P. Santa Maria in Trastevere ☎06 58 14 802

Located in the heart of Trastevere, this church is a tourist favorite, and for good reason: beautiful mosaics decorating the facade are matched by an equally stunning gold interior where more mosaics depicting Jesus, Mary, and a slew of other Biblical figures grace the apse. This *chiesa* was the first in Rome built exclusively for the Virgin Mary. The *piazza* out front is a lovely place to admire this Byzantine structure.

⇆ From Vle. Trastevere, turn right onto V. San Francesco a Ripa and walk 5min. until you get to the piazza. $ Free. ⏰ Open M-F 9am-5:30pm.

BOTANICAL GARDENS ♿ GARDENS

Largo Cristina di Svezia 23A. ☎06 49 91 71 07

The Botanical Gardens are located on the flat area of land adjacent to Giancolo

Hill. With over 3500 types of flora, ranging from bamboo in the Japanese garden to roses first grown in Rome during the Baroque Period, this oasis of green is a sharp contrast to most of Rome's drier and duller patches of natural land. Check out the **Garden for the Blind,** a star-shaped region with labels written in Braille.

⫟ Walk to the end of V. Corsini until you reach Largo Cristina di Svezia. Ⓢ *€4, ages 6-11 and over 59 €2.* Ⓒ *Open Tu-Su 9:30am-6:30pm. Closed in Aug.*

VILLA BORGHESE, PARIOLI, AND FLAMINIO

◪ VILLA BORGHESE
Park bordered by Vle. Trinita dei Monti and V. Porta Pinciana.

Ġ ⒴ GARDENS
☎06 32 16 564

The Villa Borghese sits north of Termini and provides a respite from the city's bustle. Mostly flat pathways cut through gardens, lawns, and various museums, including the **Galleria Borghese,** the **Museo Nazionale Etrusco di Villa Giulia,** and the **Galleria Nazionale d'Arte Moderna,** which actually sits right outside the park. Though most visitors choose to stroll or picnic in the park, there is also a bike rental stand just beyond the entrance of the Galleria Borghese.

⫟ Ⓜ A: Spagna or Flaminio. There are multiple entrances to the park: Porta Pinciana, Piazzale Flaminio, Vle. Belle Arti, V. Mercadante, and V. Pinciana. Ⓢ *Gardens free. Bike rental €10 per day or €4 per hr.* ▣*www.ascolbike.com.* Ⓒ *Gardens open daily Apr-Aug 7am-9pm; Sept 7am-8pm; Oct-Feb 7am-6pm; Mar 7am-8pm.*

GALLERIA BORGHESE
Piazzale del Museo Borghese 5

⫟Ġ MUSEUM
☎06 84 16 542 ▣www.galleriaborghese.it

While the beautiful gardens in which it sits are reason enough to make the trek up to this fabulous museum, the Galleria Borghese is a must-see while in Rome. Inside the villa, Cardinal Scipione's collection includes such standouts as Bernini's *David* and the dynamic *Apollo and Daphne,* Caravaggio's gruesome *David with the Head of Goliath,* and other masterpieces by Correggio, Raphael, Rubens, Titian, and Veronese. Note that reservations are required in advance of your visit to the galleria. They are easy to make over the phone or online, but you won't be able to wander in on a whim. On par with the Vatican museums and less crowded because of the required reservation, the Galleria Borghese is a true Roman gem.

⫟ Enter on V. Pinciana, near V. Isonzo. Proceed up Vle. dell'Uccelleria for about 5min. ⓘ *Reservations required; call* ☎*06 855 5952 or visit* ▣*www.ticketeria.it.* Ⓢ *€10.50, EU citizens ages 18-25 €7.25, EU citizens under 18 and over 65 €4. Tours €6, ages 9 and under free. 90min. audio tour (available in English) €5.* Ⓒ *Open Tu-Su 9am-7pm. Reservation phone line open M-F 9am-6pm, Sa 9am-1pm. Ticket office closes 30min. before museum. Guided tours available in English at 9:10am and 11:10am*

GALLERIA D'ARTE MODERNA
Vle. delle Belle Arti 131

⫟Ⓧ MUSEUM
☎06 32 29 81 ▣www.gnam.beniculturali.it

The Galleria d'Arte Moderna is not only a beautiful building but one that contains a superb collection of art dating from the past 200 years—certainly a relief to visitors who've spent days touring the sights of Ancient Rome. The museum's light-filled central room for greeting visitors offers an impressive display of works by Balla, Giacometti, Klee, Klimt, and Mondrian. Proceeding immediately ahead, you will reach the most contemporary of the rooms, which is crowned with a hanging sculpture by Calder and adorned with a number of white and black sculptural paintings by Castellani. The rest of the museum is well-organized by century and period, starting with works by Cezanne, Courbet, Degas, Manet, and Van Gogh and heading into the 20th century with a huge collection of Balla, Boccioni, De Chirico, Miró, Modigliani, and Morandi. Make sure to pass through famed modernist Marcel Duchamp's collection of ready-mades, including the famous Urinal.

From Vle. del Giardino in the Villa Borghese, veer right and exit the park onto Vle. delle Belle Arti. Museum is on the right. $ €8, EU citizens age 18-25 €4, ages under 18 and over 65 free. Audio tour (available in English) €4. ⏰ Open Tu-Su 8:30am-7:30pm. Ticket office closes at 7:15pm.

PINCIO — PANORAMIC VIEW

Near the park entrance off P. del Popolo.

Though the summit has a few sights of its own, the real motivation for climbing up this hill is the stunning vista of the P. del Popolo you will be able to view from its top. The most prominent monuments visible from the peak are the obelisk in the center of the *piazza*, the churches S. Maria dei Miracoli and S. Maria di Montesanto, and, looming in the distance, St. Peter's Basilica. Once you've absorbed the panorama, take some time to walk through the gardens and check out the **Idroconometro,** a clock powered by the water flowing through a group of fountains.

The fastest way to reach the top is from the steep ascent near P. del Popolo. A more scenic but slower route is through the Villa Borghese itself around V. Veneto. $ Free.

PIAZZA BARBERINI — ♿ PIAZZA

At the intersection of V. Tritone, V. Sistina, V. Barberini, and V. della Quattro Fontane

At the center of this especially busy *piazza* sit the lovely Fontana Tritone and Fontana delle Api, two Bernini fountains popular with pigeons and people. The *piazza* may not be the most restful spot, as loud cars constantly stream by, so consider heading inside to the **Palazzo Barberini** just down the street at V. delle Quattro Fontane 13, which holds the National Gallery of Arte Antica. Even if you don't venture inside, the courtyard's tall palm trees and the building's beautiful facade are worth a visit. At the Chiesa della Immacolata Concezione, the **Capuchin Crypt** *(V. Veneto 27 ☎06 48 71 185 💻www.cappucciniviaveneto.it.)* contains an awesome variety of human skulls and bones.

[M]A: Barberini. i Call ☎06 32 810 for information on booking palazzo. $ Piazza free. Palazzo €5, EU citizens age 18-25 €2.50, EU citizens under 18 and over 65 free. ⏰ Crypt open M-W 9am-noon and 3-6pm, F-Su 9am-noon and 3-6pm. Palazzo open Tu-Su 8:30am-7:30pm.

TERMINI AND SAN LORENZO

BASILICA DI SANTA MARIA MAGGIORE — ♿ CHURCH

In P. Esquilino — ☎06 69 88 68 02

It's a good thing the Basilica is so close to Termini, or the slew of cheap eats and hostels might be the only first impression visitors received of the area. Just a 5min. walk from the station, this fifth-century church is a stunning combination of Baroque and classic Roman design. With its white marble artifice and huge flight of stairs, the back of the church (close to V. Cavour) might be even more stunning than the front. Although the frescoes that line the side chapels are impressive, it's the gold-coffered ceiling and wide apse that really impress. Seriously, there's a lot of gold in here. If you aren't blinded by the shininess, the 14th-century mosaics covering the *loggia* and the large *baldacchino* at the altar are also beautiful. Adjoining the basilica is a small museum containing artifacts and artwork relating to the church's history, even though the basilica itself offers enough to see. Upon leaving, check out the beautiful indigo (violet, if you prefer) stained-glass window crowning the entrance.

[M]Termini. Turn right onto V. Giolitti and walk down V. Cavour. i Modest dress required. $ Basilica free. Museum €4, EU students and over 65 €2. Loggia €5/€3. Audio tour (available in English) €4. ⏰ Basilica open daily 7am-7pm. Museum open daily 9am-6pm.

CHIESA DI SANTA MARIA DEGLI ANGELI — ♿ CHURCH

P. della Repubblica — ☎06 48 80 812 💻www.santamariadegliangeliroma.it

At the crest of the expansive P. della Repubblica, this 16th-century church (Michelangelo's last, at age 86) is monumental, starting with its front doors; the façade is actually taken from the remains of Diocletian's hot baths, on which Pope Pius IV commissioned the church to be built. Half-sculpted and half-in-the-rough figures jut out of the huge doors; the bronze one on the left symbolizes the risen Christ. Throughout the interior, there are many similar statues left only partially completed. Inside, a small rotunda leads into an especially open interior whose design underwent many revisions before it was finally completed. The scarcity of seats makes it less crowded than most churches. A sundial, which leads from the east transept to the altar, was used by the Romans for centuries. Check out the schedule of sundial viewings or reserve a demonstration at the information desk.

🚏 Ⓜ Termini. Walk into the P. del Cinquecento and veer left toward V. Viminale. **i** *Sundial demonstrations should be reserved 2 days in advance, June 15-Sept 15. Call ☎06 48 70 749 for more information. ⏰ Open M-F 7am-6:30pm, Sa-Su 7am-7:30pm.*

BATHS OF DIOCLETIAN ⊗ MUSEUM, ANCIENT ROME

V. Enrico de Nicola 79 ☎06 39 96 77 00

In the heart of busy Termini, the Baths of Diocletian have weathered the city grime. Begun in 298 CE by Maximianus, brother of Diocletian, the baths took nearly 10 years—and more than 40,000 Christian slaves—to build. Upon completion, they were able to accommodate 3000 people in what ended up being much more than a mere "bath"—the Diocletian complex contained libraries, gardens, gallery spaces, gyms, and even brothels. Though the baths may no longer exist in the same state of glory, a visit to them is surely worth it.

🚏 Ⓜ Termini. Walk into P. dei Cinquecento; enter on V. Volturno. **i** *Part of the Museo Nazionale Romano group; buy 1 ticket for entrance to all 4 sights over 3 days. $ €7, EU students €3.50, EU citizens under 18 and over 65 free. ⏰ Open Tu-Su 9am-7:45pm.*

VIA XX SETTEMBRE ♿ STREET

Even though V. XX Settembre is mostly a functioning thoroughfare, a number of beautiful sights can be seen while walking along its length. The street merges into V. dei Quirinale on one end and V. Nomentana on the other. Between grabbing a bite and making your way to the next destination, check out the four obelisks built by the city in the 1700s to help define Rome's neighborhoods and improve traffic conditions. (Hard to believe that they needed improvement in a time that predated Vespas and the popularization of the car.) The best spot on XX Settembre from which to survey the scene is at V. delle Quattro Fontane, where you can see the monuments of **Via dei Quirinale,** the **Spanish Steps,** and **Santa Maria Maggiore.** Atop the P. San Bernardo sits the beautiful and seriously colossal **Fontana dell'Acqua Felice.**

🚏 Ⓜ Termini. Walk through P. della Repubblica until you reach V. XX Settembre. $ Free.

TESTACCIO AND OSTIENSE

👍 BASILICA DI SAN PAOLO FUORI LE MURA ♿ CHURCH

Piazzale San Paolo 1 ☎06 69 88 08 00 💻www.basilicasanpaolo.org

This is the light at the end of the tunnel, but unlike the kind you might see during a near-death experience, you should definitely make your way toward this light. After a 30min. walk down the empty-ish V. Ostiense, this magnificent basilica and its gold mosaics are the shining reward you've been waiting for. The second-largest church in Rome, the often overlooked Basilica di San Paolo Fuori le Mura shares extraterritorial status with the **Vatican, Santa Maria Maggiore,** and **San Giovanni in Laterano.** Though this sounds cool, it pretty much means that if you buy a stamp from the church's gift shop, you can only mail the letter in a post box on the premises. Historically, the basilica might be most famous for housing the body of St. Paul after his beheading, but for the aesthetically inclined, the gold mosaics both inside and out steal the show. Walking in from **Portico Gregoriano** on the side, the massive arch crowning the altar is like a gold crown consisting of mosaics that depict Christ giving the benediction to surrounding apostles. Around the perimeter, 200 portraits (and counting) of past popes will leave you wondering what is to be done when space runs out. The most stunning area of all, however, is the outside courtyard, where tall palm trees sway before the gold mosaic facade upon which an image of Christ, Peter, and Paul is depicted. Despite having been constructed after a 19th-century fire that damaged the building, this more contemporary work is just as compelling as the altarpiece inside.

The quiet cloister is worth seeing if the church's main mosaics aren't enough for you: its decorated columns are similar to those in San Giovanni. Before the trek back up V. Ostiense, head to the gift shop where you can buy holy sweets and papal alcohol to fortify yourself (€6.50-18).

🚇 Ⓜ B: Basilica San Paolo, or bus #23 to Ostiense/LGT S. Paolo stop. *i* Modest dress required. Ⓢ Basilica free. Cloister €4, reduced for students and groups. 1hr. guided visits available; reserve online. 🕐 Basilica open daily 7am-6:30pm.

🏛 CENTRALE MONTEMARTINI ●●Ⓧ MUSEUM

V. Ostiense 106 ☎06 42 88 88 88 🖥www.centralmontemartini.org

You might have believed that central Rome is *the* place for seeing old ruins juxtaposed with modern constructions, but the Eternal City is nothing compared to this museum. A relatively new addition to the **Musei Capitolini** family, this building—the first public electricity plant in the city—now houses an impressive collection of Roman statues, busts, and mosaics excavated during the early 1800s. Classical marble figures stand before gigantic engines and a 15m boiler, creating a peculiar tableau that combines the ancient and the modern. After wandering through the Sala Macchina on the first floor, check out the foot from the statue of **Fortuna Huiusce Diei**, a devotional piece from 101 BCE that originally stood an impressive 8m high. The foot itself is really more like 3—in length, that is. The sea-green **Sala Caldaie** has less modern machinery, but its floor is inlaid with a reconstructed mosaic that depicts a vicious hunting scene from the fourth century.

🚇 Ⓜ B: Ostiense. A 10min. walk down the V. Ostiense. Ⓢ €4.50, EU citizens age 18-25 €2.50, EU citizens under 18 and over 65 free. Combined ticket with Musei Capitolini €8.50/6.50. 🕐 Open Tu-Su 9am-7pm. Last entry 30min. before close.

CIMITERO ACATTOLICO PER GLI STRANIERI AND WAR CEMETERY ●& CEMETERY

War Cemetery on V. Nicola Zabaglia beside P. Vittorio Bottego ☎06 50 99 91

Cimitero Acattolico at V. Caio Cestio 6 ☎06 57 41 900 🖥www.protestantcemetery.it

We don't recommend making the trek to Ostiense for the sole purpose of seeing a cemetery, but after walking along mostly building-lined streets, these tree-filled and quiet spots are a peaceful retreat. From the outside, tall tamarind trees peek over the light pink wall of the Cimitero Acattolico, making the stroll down V. Caio Cestio all the more scenic. Inside, stray cats, more trees, and clusters of gravestones marking the death of non-Catholic foreigners compete for your attention. Notable names to look out for include John Keats (though instead of his name, the words "all that was mortal of a Young English Poet" are what you'll need to spot), Julis (son of Goethe), and Ⓢ**socialist** Antonio Gramsci. Across the street, the smaller and more refined War Cemetery is dedicated to the soldiers who died in WWII. A stone from Hadrian's Wall, the northernmost boundary of the Ancient Roman Empire, is marked to honor the soldiers.

🚇 Ⓜ A: Piramide. Walk through the Porta San Paolo and veer left. Ⓢ War cemetery free. Cimitero Acattolico €2 suggested donation. 🕐 War Cemetery open M-F 8am-3pm. Cimitero Acattolico open M-Sa 9am-5pm, Su 9am-1pm. Last entry 30min. before close.

Piazzale Ostiense and environs

Piazzale Ostiense is the geographical epicenter of the neighborhood, most accessible by public transportation and busier than the residential streets that surround it. At the *piazzale*'s center, a curious pyramid is surrounded by speedy Vespas and pedestrians who look up at its 27m peak. Built in the first century BCE after Gaius defeated Cleopatra and her army, the **Piramide di Caio Cestio** stands like the obelisks scattered throughout the city center—a gray duckling in a pool of white Roman classicism. Right beside it, the **Porta San Paolo** stands as a reminder of Rome's ancient days when the gateway linked the city to its most important port in Ostia. The hill of dirty green beyond it is **Monte Testaccio,** a landfill which has been accumulating old terra-cotta pots (known as *testae:* note the similarity to Testaccio in name) for centuries. Of the goods which were originally traded and deposited there, the only thing which you still might find here is wine—the base of the hill is surrounded by Testaccio's best nightclubs and bars.

☙ ⓜB: Piramide or bus #173 from Termini. ⓢ Free.

SOUTHERN ROME AND THE APPIAN WAY
The Appian Way and Environs

▣ **THE APPIAN WAY**   ♿ ANCIENT ROME
V. Appia Antica   ☎06 51 35 316 🖥www.parcoappiaantica.it

When you've had your way with Rome's busy *corsi*, it might be time to try the Appian on for size. Stretching 16km from Porta San Sebastiano to Frattocchie, it tends to be a little big for most people: walking itineraries generally end around the **Tomb of Cecilia Metella,** though the road extends another 5-6 mi. Don't expect that first stretch to be all dirt roads surrounded by fields and crumbling aqueducts. Since being paved over, the Appian Way has become, somewhat unfortunately, a modern-day reincarnation of its ancient self: a very busy road. That means you'll see your fair share of whizzing cars and walking tourists as you follow the street.

In the third century, V. Appia Antica—the main branch of the trail—extended about a mile from Porta Capena to Porta S. Sebastiano. Today that stretch has become V. delle Terme di Caracalla and V. di Porta San Sebastiano, and the true "Way" officially begins after you exit the **Aurelian walls.** At the time of its use, the ancient road served as the burial ground of the highest Romans and early Christians, since they were forbidden to keep their tombs within the city walls. Legends who actually walked the road included **Virgil, Saint Peter,** and **Spartacus,** each of whom left a trail of history behind him—in the case of Spartacus, a trail of bodies. If you plan on walking this stretch, keep in mind that its cobblestone ground practically shakes with buses and scooters zooming by, and there's little shoulder reserved for pedestrians. As the road merges into V. Appia Antica, the din doesn't stop until you reach the tourist office, where you'll need to make a decision about what roads to take. For the most scenic path, head up the slightly inclined road leading to San Callisto *(closed W)*, where you can see countryside and bushes of pink flowers from the elevated path. V. Appia Antica and V. Ardeatina on either side are traversed by buses.

The main attractions on this initial strip are the third-century catacombs, underground passageways full of bodies, sarcophagi, and paintings. For the more nature-inclined traveler, the true attractions will not start until after **Cecilia Metella,** where you can walk on the road's original paving stones and gaze at miles of unsullied land. If that sounds more appealing to you but you don't want to wander that far south, consider walking down V. della Caffarella (to the left of V. Appia Antica) and the pedestrian trails surrounding it instead of hitting the catacombs. (And at a hefty fee of €8 each, you'll be seeing fewer bones of the dead-person variety and more of the cash-monies kind by bypassing them completely.) Either way, bring yourself a picnic lunch to avoid a stop at the overpriced restaurants along the way.

➔ ⓂA: San Giovanni. Head through Porta San Giovanni and into the piazza. Take bus #218; to reach the info office, push the button after you turn left onto V. Appia Antica, right before Domine Quo Vadis. The bus continues up V. Ardeatina and drops you off near the S. Domitilla and S. Calisto Catacombs. Alternatively, take ⓂB: Circo Massimo or Piramide, then bus #118, which runs along V. Appia Antica to the S. Sebastiano Catacombs. If you want to walk, head down V. delle Terme di Caracalla from the Circo Massimo. At Piazzale Numa Pompilio, veer right onto V. di Porta S. Sebastiano, through the city wall and onto V. Appia Antica. ℹ Info office is located at V. Appia Antica 42, right before Domine Quo Vadis. It offers bike rental, free maps, historical pamphlets, a self-service bus ticket machine, and opportunities for activities along the way. For information on Archeobus tours leaving from Termini, call ☎800 281 281 or visit 🖥www.trambusopen.com. $ Road and park free. Bike rental €3 per hr., €10 per day. Archeobus taking you from Termini through the park with audio tour €10. ⏰ Info office open in summer M-Sa 9:30am-1:30pm and 2-5:30pm, Su 9:30am-5:30pm; in fall, winter, and spring M-Sa 9:30am-1:30pm and 2-4:30pm, Su 9:30am-4:30pm. Road is closed to cars on Su, making it the best day to walk the trail. Archeobus tours every 30min. 9:30am-4pm.

CATACOMBO DI SAN SEBASTIANO — ANCIENT ROME

V. Appia Antica 136 — ☎06 78 50 350 🖥www.catacombe.org

Though not quite as long as San Callisto, the 160,000 tombs making up San Sebastiano's catacombs give them a weighty status. Among the thousands of bodies, those of Saints Peter and Paul are perhaps most renowned, placed here during a harsh period of Christian persecution in the third century. Though the catacombs comprise four levels, only the second is accessible to tourist crowds—check out the symbols lining the wall. If you need something to take away as a souvenir, head to the gift shop for some jewelry reproductions.

➔ Bus #218 to stop near San Callisto and Santa Domitilla. Walk down V. Sette Chiese to V. Appia Antica and turn right. ℹ Catacombs accessible only on guided tours (available in English). Tours leave every 30min. from the ticket office. $ €8, ages 6-15 €5. ⏰ Open M-W 9am-noon and 2-5pm, F-Su 9am-noon and 2-5pm. Closed Nov 22-Dec 20.

BASILICA DI SAN SEBASTIANO — CHURCH

V. Appia Antica 136 — 🖥www.catacombe.org

One of the road's few respites that doesn't require a subterranean retreat, an entrance fee, and a tour guide to appreciate, the basilica, reflecting its somewhat modern restructuring (17th-century "modern," that is), is not as dark and ornate as some of Rome's more central churches but attracts a large crowd to admire its Bernini masterpiece, **Jesus Christ the Redeemer,** finished when the Baroque master had reached the ripe old age of 81. Look up to the ceiling for a magnificent wood relief of St. Sebastian pincushioned with arrows sticking out from his sides. It would seem that the Roman army had a pretty harsh "don't ask, don't tell" policy when it came to religious matters. Poor Captain Sebastian was shot with arrows and left to die after the military brass discovered that he was actually a Christian. When he managed to survive the barrage of projectiles, his persecutors resorted to the next best thing: death by clubbing.

➔ Bus #218 to stop near San Callisto and Santa Domitilla. Walk down V. Sette Chiese to V. Appia Antica and right. $ Free. ⏰ Open daily 8am-6pm.

CATACOMBO SAN CALLISTO — ANCIENT ROME

V. Appia Antica 110 — ☎06 51 30 15 80 🖥www.sdb.org

Twenty kilometers long and 20m deep, the Catacombs of San Callisto could be their *own* Appian Way. As Rome's oldest burial ground for Christians, the catacombs contain a mighty collection of corpses: 56 martyrs and 18 saints, many of whom were popes. If the thought of dead bodies isn't so aesthetically pleasing to you, check out the wall paintings which line the narrow passageways. There's a copy of *The Good Shepherd* at the entrance.

🚌 From P. di San Giovanni in Laterano, take bus #218 to Fosse Ardeatine. From Circo Massimo or Ostiense, take bus #118 to Catacombe di San Callisto. ℹ Catacombs accessible only on guided tours (available in English). Tours leave every 30min. from the ticket office. $ €8, ages 6-15 €5. ⏰ Open Mar-Jan M-Tu 9am-noon and 2-5pm, Th-Su 9am-noon and 2-5pm.

PORTA SAN SEBASTIANO AND MUSEO DELLA MURA ⊗ MUSEUM, ANCIENT ROME

V. di Porta San Sebastiano 18 ☎06 70 47 52 84 💻www.museodellemuraroma.it

At the end of the car-crammed path leading to the start of the Appian Way, this massive archway, the largest and best-preserved of the original Aurelian walls, remains. You've survived the cars and can now enjoy the small museum inside, but back in the third century, invaders would meet their death here. After being trapped inside, they would be massacred by archers. While the museum is intriguing, the scenic view offered from its terrace is a particular highlight if you expect to spend the rest of the afternoon in underground catacombs.

🚌 Bus #218. Get off at intersection of V. Mura Latine and V. Appia Antica. $ €3, EU citizens ages 18-25 €1.50, under 18 and over 65 free. ⏰ Open Tu-Su 9am-2pm. Last entry 30min. before close.

DOMINE QUO VADIS? ⊗ CHURCH

At the intersection of V. Appia Antica and V. Ardeatina ☎06 51 20 441 💻www.catacombe.org

Even its questioning name reflects the speculation that surrounds this tiny church. Supposedly, Christ's **footprints** are set in stone up the middle aisle, though San Sebastiano down the way claims the same novelty. (Sounds like something we've heard before at the Vatican.) The church's name derives from the question St. Peter asked Christ when he feared the Lord was fleeing Rome. Christ replied he was returning to the city to be crucified. St. Peter was eventually dealt that very same fate, though he requested to be hung upside down, not believing himself enough of his master's equal to meet death in the same way. Though speculation surrounds the footprints, the tourist office's brochures indicate that this church is winning the debate.

🚌 Bus #218. $ Free. ⏰ Open in summer M-Sa 8am-7:30pm, Su 8:15am-7:40pm; in winter M-Sa 8am-6:30pm, Su 8:15am-6:45pm.

Other Sights

👍 BASILICA DI SAN GIOVANNI IN LATERANO ⊗ CHURCH

P. San Giovanni in Laterano 4 ☎06 69 88 64 33

Practically off the radar in central Rome, San Giovanni in Laterano is hardly something to be overlooked. Before St. Peter's became such a hot spot, this massive basilica was the home of the papacy and today shares its extraterritoriality (along with **San Paolo Fuori della Mure**). If you're approaching from the side door near V. Merulana, note the beautiful frescoed ceiling on the outside portico. From the main entrance, the doors, moved from the Roman Senate House in the Roman Forum, attract a bigger crowd. Big windows and a white mosaic floor make the nave feel lighter than that of St. Peter's (though the lack of huge crowds also helps). The dynamic statues of apostles glaring down from their elevated position make you feel just as small and inconsequential, however. At the nave's end, you might hear the chink of coins being thrown into the crypt of **Pope Martin V.** The most striking (and fortunate) difference between San Giovanni and St. Peter's is the accessibility of the gold *baldacchino*, which can be viewed up close and completely circled. Decorated by **Giotto,** this canopy of state and its "roof" painted in blue sky and gold stars provide reason enough to make the trip to Laterano.

✈ Ⓜ️A: San Giovanni or bus #16 from Termini. ⓘ *For information about the Museo della Basilica, call ☎06 69 88 64 09.* Ⓢ *Basilica free. Cloister €2, students €1. Museo della Basilica €1. Audio tour €5.* 🕐 *Basilica open daily 7am-6:30pm. Cloister open daily 9am-6pm. Museo della Basilica open M-F 9:30am-6:15pm, Sa 9:30am-6pm.*

🏛 CHIESA DI SAN CLEMENTE   ⊗ CHURCH
P. San Clemente   ☎06 77 40 021 📧www.basilicasanclemente.com

Without knowing anything factual about this small church, you can still appreciate its unique layout, frescoes, and mosaics, all of which trump some basilicas twice its size. Masses, conducted in Italian, are held in the church's nave, curiously enclosed by an intricately engraved stone wall. The church's wooden pews face each other, adding to the intimacy of the service, and golden mosaics bordered by an aquamarine strip and 12 sheep are as beautiful as they are didactic. Near the back, the 🏛**Chapel of Santa Caterina** is decorated with Masolino's delicate 15th-century frescoes—their interplay of rendered and flat forms keeps you staring. Though the art on the wall is enough to satiate the eye, head down to the fourth-century lower basilica for some history to satisfy your intellectual tummy. The underground area now consists of a labyrinth of passageways, built to support the basilica above. The remains of original frescoes might take more effort to discern than the brighter ones upstairs, but they evoke more curiosity.

✈ Ⓜ️*B: Colosseo or bus #85 or 87.* Ⓢ *Basilica free. Excavations €5, students €3.50.* 🕐 *Basilica open M-Sa 9am-12:30pm and 3-6pm, Su 10am-12:30pm and 3-6pm. Lower basilica and excavations open M-Sa 9am-12:30pm and 3-6pm, Su noon-6pm. Last entry 20min. before close.*

CHIESA DEI SANTI GIOVANNI E PAOLO   ⊛⊗ CHURCH
P. San Giovanni e Paolo   ☎06 70 45 45 44 📧www.caseromane.it

Dusty meets very bright and sparkly at Chiesa dei Santi Giovanni e Paolo. The facade is nothing to gawk at, but the crystal chandeliers adorning this 12th-century basilica make one wonder whether this is a palace or a site of religious worship. Head back to the **Case Romane,** where even richer decoration—this time slightly more traditional—graces the foundation for the original fifth-century church. Beautiful wall paintings can also be found depicting Roman life as it was carried out between the third and 12th centuries. Surprisingly, things look like they were nicer back then than they were bloody.

✈ Ⓜ️*B: Colosseo. From the Colosseum, take V. Claudia and turn right onto V. di San Paolo della Croce. The basilica is in the courtyard, while the Case Romane entrance is to its left, through the archway.* Ⓢ *€6, reduced €4, under 12 free.* 🕐 *Open daily 8:30am-noon and 3:30-6:30pm. Office of the church open M-Th 9-11:30am and 4-6pm, Sa 9-11:30am and 4-6pm. Case Romano open M 10am-1pm and 3-6pm, Th-Su 10am-1pm and 3-6pm.*

CHIESA DEI SANTI QUATTRO CORONATI   ⊗ CHURCH
V. dei Santissimi Quattro Coronati 20

Up a steep hill, this small church's peaceful interior makes the trek well worth it. From the austere courtyard, turn right to reach the 13th-century **cloister:** after ringing the bell, you'll be met by a nun requesting a €1 donation before letting you into the grounds. If the simplicity of the cloister has you seeking something a bit flashier, head to the **chapel,** where a bright 13th-century fresco depicts the life of Constantine. Inside the basilica itself, more paintings line the altar and give some life to the otherwise quite dark interior. The church feels like a retreat from the busy city because that's what it was meant to be: over 800 years ago, it served as a refuge for popes under siege thanks to its strategic location near the Lateran Palace.

✈ Ⓜ️*B: Colosseo. Head up V. Labicana, turn right onto V. dei Normanni, and walk up the steep hill of V. dei Santissimi Quattro Coronati.* ⓘ *Ring bell to enter cloister and a nun will let you in.* Ⓢ *Basilica free. Cloister requested donation €1.* 🕐 *Basilica and cloister open M-Sa 6:15am-8pm, Su*

6:45am-12:30pm and 3-7:30pm. Chapel open M-Sa 9am-noon and 4:30-6pm, Su 9-10:40am and 4-5:45pm. Crypt open M-F; ask at cloister for admittance.

VIA NOMENTANA

V. Nomentana is a sight in itself, even if you don't hit any real "sights" along the walk. Lined with beautiful houses (that were ironically once used as farms), it is worth an afternoon stroll if you want to get out of the busy city center.

🔲 PORTA PIA   ♿ MONUMENT
Piazzale Porta Pia

The magnificent Porta Pia marks the end of **Via XX Settembre** and the start of **Via Nomentana,** a tree-lined street that leads out of the city center. Michelangelo was commissioned by Pope Pius IV to construct this gate to replace the Porta Nomentana, which was not accessible at the time. There is much debate about the degree to which Michelangelo's plan was altered, especially because he died shortly before the gate's completion. Today, Porta Pia marks the end of Termini and the beginning of the more residential zones beyond. At the center, a statue of La Patria di Bersaglieri presides over an ideal spot in which one can admire the *piazza* or grab a lunch break.

🏵 Ⓜ*A: Repubblica. Turn right onto V. XX Settembre and proceed straight until you reach the Porta Pia; after that, the street becomes V. Nomentana.* Ⓢ *Free.*

VILLA TORLONIA   ♿ MUSEUM
V. Nomentana 70   ☎06 06 08 🖥www.museivillatorlonia.it

The Villa Torlonia is a beautiful complex of buildings and park grounds, originally owned by the wealthy Pamphilj family and used as a farm. It wasn't until Giovanni Torlonia acquired the farm that the villa came to resemble a palace rather than an agricultural ground. In 1925, Mussolini co-opted the property, paying a grand total of one lira (the equivalent of about a penny) to the Torlonia family. Since its abandonment in 1943, the house and park grounds have undergone drastic changes and are now open to the public as a group of museums. The Casino Nobile is perhaps the most prominent of the buildings and was the primary home of the family, making it the most ornate and expansive building of the complex's trio. The Casina delle Civette is renowned for its Art Deco work and stunning stained-glass windows, while the Casino dei Principi contains gorgeous mosaic floors and amazing marble reliefs on the doors. Even if you don't venture into the museums, a walk in the park is more than pleasant.

🏵 *From Piazzale Porta Pia, walk about 10min. down V. Nomentana.* ℹ *For tickets or reservations call* ☎*06 06 08 from 9am-9pm.* Ⓢ *Casina delle Civette €3, EU citiznes age 18-25 €1.50. Casino Nobile and show €7/5; Casino Nobile, Casina della Civette, Casino dei Principi, and show €9/5.50. EU citizens under 18 and over 65 free.* 🕙 *Open from 1st-last Sa in Mar and 1st-last Sa in Oct 9am-5:30pm; from last Su in Oct-Sept 30 9am-7pm; from last Su in Oct-Feb 28 9am-4:30pm. Ticket booth closes 45min. before museum closing.*

MAUSOLEUM OF COSTANZA   ⊗ CHURCH
V. Nomentana 349   ☎06 86 20 54 56

This mosaic-covered fourth-century church was named after Constantine's daughter and built as a mausoleum after her conversion to Christianity. It was later transformed into a baptistery and then church, which is what it functions as today for viewers who make the effort to see it. Inside, beautiful mosaics, especially over the upper domes, tell early Christian stories in elaborate layouts of animals and other earthy designs.

🏵 Ⓜ*Termini. Either walk 2km down V. Nomentana or take the #36 bus.* Ⓢ *Free.* 🕙 *Open M 9am-noon, Tu-Sa 9am-noon and 4-6pm, Su 4-6pm.*

food

If Italy is the king of fine food, then Rome is its crown jewel. The sheer number of trattorias, cafes, *alimentari* (local grocery stores), *osterie, tavole calde* (cafeterias), pizzerias, and *gelaterie* is enough reason to be overwhelmed without even picking up your fork. With so many options, it's tempting to simply settle for the most convenient—but don't. Always head away from the blocks immediately surrounding major sights: food here is overpriced and usually not well made. Avoid "tourist menus" with bright photos illustrating the plates and English translations. Restaurants with nonstop hours (no midday closing) are often those that cater to tourists rather than locals. When there seems to be no high-quality, cheap meal around, look for *panifici* (bakeries) or supermarkets where you can always pick up fresh breads or pastries to tide you over. Be aware that sitting at a table (instead of at the *banca*—bar) will knock up the bill as much as €2. Bread and water doesn't come with your meal either, but to make up for the extra €5 euro you'll be shelling out, a tip is not usually expected of customers.

Roman menus usually contain *primi* ranging from classics—*spaghetti alla carbonara* anyone?—to more Roman specialties. Local favorites, particularly during the summer when the ingredients are in season, include *carciofi alla giudia* (deep-fried artichokes) and *fiori di zucca* (stuffed, fried zucchini flowers). Though a Roman might find it hard to believe you could ever tire of the city's cuisine, cravings for ethnic food can be satisfied by one of Rome's African or Middle Eastern eateries. You might also try sampling the fare at establishments that focus on vegetarian food. Despite Rome's size and variety, however, certain cuisines remain woefully underrepresented—the few Chinese, Japanese, and Indian restaurants in the city tend to be overpriced and may differ markedly from what you'd find in the rest of the Western (or for that matter, the Eastern) world.

ANCIENT CITY

It's a shame that eating's necessary. Well, not really, but since everyone has to do it—and nearly everyone in Rome comes to the Ancient City—restaurants in this region are often overcrowded and overpriced. For the best deals, avoid places closest to the sights and meander down some of the quieter streets.

👍 PIZZERIA DA MILVIO — 🚫💳🚫♿ PIZZERIA ❶

V. dei Serpenti 7 — ☎06 48 93 01 45

A sign that reads, "40 Types of Pizze e Pane," hangs above this pizzeria's bright red walls, a little reminder to passersby that this is the spot for variety, convenience, and flavor. Architecture students crowd the casual stools in back for simple *primi* like *pomodoro con riso (€5)* and *secondi (€6)* served from hot trays. Up front, the friendly servers cut dozens of thin-crust pizzas into slices sold by weight. Be ready to eat on the go; lunch is the busiest hour.

⇄ From V. Cavour, turn onto V. dei Serpenti and walk 2min. Ⓢ Primi €5; secondi €6. Pizza €0.80-1.40 per etto. ⏰ Open daily 7am-midnight.

👍 LA CUCCUMA — 💳♿⛅ RISTORANTE ❶

V. Merulana 221 — ☎06 77 20 13 61

Even if you're not sitting at their outdoor tables, La Cuccuma's warmly colored walls, arched ceilings, and airy interior will make you feel like you're in the warm Roman sun. The €9 fixed meal *(primi, secondi, contorni, and bread)* is hard to beat with huge portions. Still, this restaurant threatens to outdo itself, selling thin-crust pizza by the kilo to hungry students looking for a meal on the go. Generous slices loaded with toppings will set you back less than €4.

⇄ ⓂA: Vittorio Emanuele. Walk down V. d Statuto, and turn right onto V. Merulana. Ⓢ Pizza

€8-12.90 per kg. ⏰ *Open daily 11am-midnight.*

ANTICA BIRRERIA PERONI 💳♿🍸 RISTORANTE, DELI [2]

V. San Marcello 19 ☎06 67 95 310 💻www.anticabirreriaperoni.net

Pizza and panini may abound in Rome, but far harder to come by are the German-Italian plates Antica Birreria Peroni has been making for over 100 years. This popular establishment's tiny interior feels a bit like an old-fashioned candy shop—albeit, a candy shop filled with adults instead of children and beer instead of sweets. It is constantly teeming with customers ordering takeout plates like grilled pork sausage *(€4)* or the smoked pork with sauerkraut *(€10)*. Four types of beer on tap go for as little as €3 to wash down the wurstel *(€6.50-13)*. Be ready to stand or scramble for one of the few stools at the bar.

⇄ *From the Vittorio Emanuele monument, turn right on V. Cesare Battisti, left into P. dei Santissimi Apostoli, and walk 2 blocks down.* $ *Primi €5-7; secondi €4-19. Buffet €3.50-6.50.* ⏰ *Open M-Sa noon-midnight.*

LA TAVERNA DA TONINO E LUCIA 🚫💳♿🍸 RISTORANTE [3]

V. Madonna dei Monti 79 ☎06 47 45 325

You'll feel like you're in some Italian *madre*'s home as soon as you walk into this local favorite: mouthwatering aromas, a view into the kitchen, and a cork-lined wall full of pictures and lights give La Taverna da Tonino e Lucia its cozy feel. Tight quarters may just have you becoming *amici* with your neighbors at the next table by meal's end, but that's par for the course here where the regulars already know each other. The small menu's limited selection is actually a blessing in disguise—the plates are so good that a bigger selection might make choosing impossible. Try the veal rolls with tomato sauce or the specially recommended *paglia ai funghi*.

⇄ *[M]B: Cavour. Walk down V. Cavour towards the Fori Imperiali, turn right onto V. dei Serpenti and left onto V. Madonna dei Monti.* $ *Pasta €8, meat €9-13.* ⏰ *Open M-Sa noon-2:30pm, 7-10:30pm.*

LA CARBONARA 💳🚭🍸 RISTORANTE [3]

V. Panisperna 214 ☎06 48 25 176 💻www.lacarbonara.it

The wall of handwritten comments and the massive collection of wine corks beside it should give you an idea of how long this standby has been around (try over 100 years). Despite its history and fame, La Carbonara has remained well priced and down to earth—just read some of the comments made by customers and family members as you gobble down classics like *carciofi alla giuldia* (fried artichoke) and *cacio e pepe* (cheese and black pepper). If you like what you get (and you surely will), don't hesitate to scribble your own sweet nothings on the wall. Just try to compose something a bit more poetic than the graffiti on your hostel bunk bed.

⇄ *From S. Maria Maggiore, walk 5min. down V. Panisperna.* $ *Primi €6-9; secondi €9-15.* ⏰ *Open M-Sa 12:30pm-2:30pm and 7pm-11pm.*

IL GELATONE 🚫💳🚭 GELATERIA [1]

V. dei Serpenti 28 ☎06 48 20 187

Il Gelatone deserves every bit of its name: the suffix "*one*," which means big, translates to plentiful scoops and an expansive selection of flavors. Twenty-eight types of sorbet, more than 30 creamier *gelati*, and four flavors of yogurt make ordering hard—it's a good thing even small cones *(€2)* come with a choice of three flavors. To make matters better (or worse, if you have a hard time making up your mind), you can top off your frosty delight with anything from meringue to pistachio to fresh fruit, whipped cream, and chocolate.

⇄ *From the Fori Imperiali, walk up V. Cavour and make a left onto V. dei Serpenti.* $ *Cones or cups €2-4.* ⏰ *Open daily 10am-10pm.*

CENTRO STORICO

Catering to hungry tourists, restaurants in the Centro Storico tend to be overpriced. Your best bet for a quick meal is to head to a *panificio, pasticerria,* or pizzeria and eat your grub in a nearby *piazza*. For a sit-down meal, try to wander down narrow and out-of-the way streets rather than stay in more central regions.

■ DAR FILETTARO A SANTA BARBARA ●&♥♨ FISH ❶

Largo dei Librari 88 ☎06 68 64 018

We're glad that some places never change. Despite its fame and hordes of customers—families and fancily clad couples alike—Dar Filettaro a Santa Barbara has remained reliably excellent. The *piazza* fills with the sound of chatter from those who dine and those in line. The unadorned interior gets even louder with the sound of happy customers. It won't be hard to make an order: the one-sheet menu features only salad, *antipasti*, and the classic fried cod fillet. Plus, nearly everything is €5, so feel free to leave your calculator at home. Draft beer *(€2.50 per pint)* and wine might make the wait seem shorter. Once you've eaten at this simple eatery, you'll be convinced that patience is a virtue, or at least the path to a good meal.

₮ *From Campo dei Fiori, walk down V. dei Giubbonari and turn left onto the tiny Largo dei Librari.* ⑤ *Salads, antipasti, and fried fish €5. Desserts €0.50-3.50. Beer €2.50-4.50.* ◘ *Open M-Sa 5:30-11:30pm.*

■ FORNO MARCO ROSCIOLI ✎⊗ BAKERY ❷

V. dei Chiavari ☎06 68 64 045 ▣www.anticofornoroscioli.com

If you can find a stool at this bakery, grocery, and fresh food "deli," grab it, or else you'll be forced to eat standing at one of the beer barrel tables outside (which frankly, isn't too bad an option). Most people grab a slice of something to go—a strip of thin-crust pizza or *kranz*, a flaky, twisted roll with almonds and raisins. But the best deals are Forno's fresh plates of *primi*, like its cold rice salad and hot tomato gnocchi, which customers order at the counter according to portion size as they stealthily nab one of the coveted stools. At only €5-7 a plate, Forno's prices beat those of any restaurant around.

₮ *From Campo dei Fiori, walk down V. dei Giubbonari and turn left onto V. dei Chiavari.* ⑤ *Primi €5-7. Pizza €9.50-18 per kg. Strudel €1.80 per etto.* ◘ *Open M-Sa 7am-8pm.*

GELATERIA DEL TEATRO ✎⊗❄ GELATERIA ❶

V. di San Simone 70 ☎06 45 47 880

Ever wondered what makes Italian gelato so darn good? Well, much like Willy Wonka, the friendly owners here offer customers a peek into the magic makings of their product—and it really is a *teatro*-tastic experience watching fruit and milk get churned into creamy perfection. The result of Gelateria Del Teatro's alchemy? Over 40 flavors of truly unique gelato, and the owners pride themselves on individually developing each one. After the show, indulge in varieties like garden sage with raspberry, lemon cheese cake, or ricotta, fig, and almond, which, if you hadn't seen it made, would seem like the result of some superhuman culinary feats.

₮ *From P. Navona, turn left onto V. dei Coronari and look for the tiny V. di San Simone on the left.* ⓘ *Free tours offered for groups; call (or unwrap a golden ticket) to reserve a spot. Credit cards accepted for purchases over €20.* ⑤ *Cones and cups €2-8.* ◘ *Open daily noon-midnight.*

PIZZERIA DA BAFFETTO ●&♥♨ PIZZERIA ❷

V. del Governo Vecchio 114 ☎06 68 61 617

At Pizzeria da Baffetto, the doors stay sealed and the menu stays hidden until the server lets you in. When the doors do open, a cloud of warm, pizza-infused air slips out to tempt the many eager patrons waiting in line. The service here

rome

may be brusque, but that's because they need a Soup Nazi demeanor to control the crowds waiting for a table. This pizzeria cooks up some of the best pizza in the city, served in a no-frills, packed dining room. While you're in line, check out the drawings and letters plastered on the restaurant's window by loving customers—a decorating motif that seems to double as a tactic to keep you from seeing inside.

➜ From P. Navona, exit onto P. Pasquina and continue as it becomes V. del Governo Vecchio. ℹ *Long waits and no reservations; arrive early if you want a table.* $ *Pizza €5-9.* ⏰ *Open M-W 6:30pm-12:30am, Th-Su 6:30pm-12:30am.*

CUL DE SAC
💳♿🍸⛅ RISTORANTE [2]

P. Pasquino 73 ☎06 68 80 10 94

When it's so close to Rome's most famous *piazza* (P. Navona), it's surprising that Cul de Sac's fresh mix of international flavors is the only touristy thing about the place. Though Roman classics abound, the "international thing" seems to be catching on: try the *escargots alla bourguignonne (€6.60),* an order of *baba ghanoush (€6.20),* or a cup of hot chocolate made with cocoa from Ghana, Ecuador, Venezuela, and Trinidad. The cool marble bar up front is surrounded by hundreds of wine bottles to pair with the dishes on the diverse menu (written in four languages). Wooden benches and the vine-decorated walls and floors create a laid-back, picnic feel.

➜ From P. Navona, walk onto P. Pasquino. $ *Primi €7.10-8.90; secondi €6.70-9.80. Desserts €4.30.* ⏰ *Open daily noon-4pm and 6pm-12:30am.*

PIZZERIA TAVOLA CALDA
💳♿ PIZZERIA [2]

C. Vittorio Emanuele II 186/188 ☎06 68 80 62 29

Haphazard and playful decor creates a relaxed vibe in which to gobble down some really fine food. Though pizza is sold by the slice, the best deal is to order a "sort of" round pie and cheap beer *(€2)* and eat at one of the colorful tables. Classic *primi*, changed daily and priced by portion size, are dished up from behind the counter. As casual and fun as the guys who work here, this place is "lunch on the go"—just at a table.

➜ From Campo dei Fiori, head towards C. Vittorio Emanuele II. $ *Round pizza €3.50-6, by the slice €9-14 per kg. Primi €4; secondi €5.50. Beer €2-3.* ⏰ *Open daily 10am-10pm.*

IL CORALLO
💳♿🍸⛅ RISTORANTE [4]

V. del Corallo 10/11 ☎06 68 30 77 03

Even on a warm night, every table inside Il Corallo will be full, and the outside patio will have filled up long ago. The warm aroma is enough to draw you in the first time, and the generous portions will hook you for good. Their seafood specialties, like the creamy stock-fish mousse or pasta with orange and crab *(€13),* offer creative twists on classics. Sandy-colored brick and dark wooden rafters give the place a cozy, tavern-y feel.

➜ From P. Navona, exit onto V. di Sant'Agnese di Agone; continue as it becomes V. di Tor Millina, and veer left looking for V. del Corallo. $ *Primi €10-13; secondi €15-22. Pizza €5-10.* ⏰ *Open daily noon-3:30pm and 7pm-1am.*

PIAZZA DI SPAGNA

Between Prada, the Spanish Steps, and the teems of tourists frequenting both, it might be hard to find a tasty and economical bite midday. For lunch, try heading to *panifici* (bakeries) or pizzerias and eating on the *piazze.* For dinner, veer onto smaller streets for better quality and service, even if it will cost you a bit more.

👍 GUSTO
💳♿🍸⛅ RISTORANTE, BAR [3]

V. della Frezza 23 and P. Augusto Imperatore 9 ☎06 32 26 273 💻www.gusto.it

The difference between good taste and bad is as clear as black and white—and by taste we mean flavor *and* style. Black-clad waiters whisk around Gusto's white, brick interior that's divided between a wine lounge and a sit-down restaurant opening onto P. Augusto Imperatore. Tall mirrors make the place feel even bigger than it is, but petite tables near the bar bring it back to life-size for you and your date. On the *piazza* side of things, your best bet is one of the stellar pizzas cranked out of their open brick oven. The real action (and the best deal), however, is to be found at the bar during nightly happy hours: Gusto's buffet of gourmet treats like vegetable couscous and curious black-bread *tramezzini* is better than a sit-down meal. If it weren't for the accompanying cocktails, you'd swear your mom was feeding you right out of her kitchen.

 # Directly across from Mausoleo Augusto on the piazza or, from P. del Popolo, exit onto V. di Ripetta and turn left onto V. della Frezza. i Happy hour buffet with drink €10. Pizzeria and restaurant are on piazza side; enoteca is on V. della Frezza side. $ Primi €10; secondi €10-18.50. Pizza €6-9.50. Beer €3-5.50. Wine €4.50-12. Cocktails €9. ⏰ Open daily 10am-2am. Happy hour daily 6-9pm.

FRASCHETTERIA BRUNETTI — RISTORANTE ❷

V. Angelo Brunetti 25b — ☎06 32 14 103 www.fraschetteriabrunetti.it

Save your messiness for a melting gelato after dinner—there'll be no greasy pizza fingers or spaghetti mishaps here. Instead, Fraschetteria Brunetti focuses primarily on baked pasta dishes, including 11 types of lasagna in varieties that you won't find anywhere else; try the rich gorgonzola and walnut. Covered in handwritten notes from loyal patrons, this place is legit, managing to avoid jacked-up prices and watered-down cuisine despite its proximity to the sights.

 # [M]A: Flaminio. From P. del Popolo, exit onto V. di Ripetta and turn right onto V. Angelo Brunetti. i Fixed lunch of entree, coffee, and drink €7.50. $ Primi €8. Panini €3.50. Cocktails €4. ⏰ Open M-Sa 11am-midnight, but may close earlier or later depending on the crowd.

CAMBI — PIZZERIA, BAKERY ❶

V. del Leoncino 30 — ☎06 68 78 081

Better than a cheapo pizzeria and cheaper than a sit-down restaurant. The mix of salty and sweet scents perfuming the area has most folks starting with a loaded slice of pizza and following it up with a €1 fruit torte. But don't overlook their real specialties: unleavened bread (hard bread lightly doused in oil) and *crostata* (cookies filled with chocolate or fruit). When you see tourists paying three times the price down the street, your meal will taste even better.

 # From Ara Pacis/Mausoleo Augusto, walk down V. Tomacelli and turn right onto V. Leoncino. i No seating. Only vegetable oil used. Also sells basic groceries. $ Cookies €0.80, €33 per kg. Panini €3.50. Pizza €7.50-15 per kg. Crostatine €11. ⏰ Open M-Sa 8am-8pm.

BAR SAN MARCELLO — CAFE ❶

V. D. San Marcello 37-8 — ☎06 69 92 33 15

Don't let the curt service turn you off from this small *tavola calda*, a lunchtime favorite among local workers. The ratio of Italians to tourists means you won't hear much English as you munch on fresh pasta salads, grilled fish, or panini. Take advantage of the linguistic discrepancy: with the **Trevi Fountain** right around the corner, you can easily get your full share of English chatter for the day just a short walk away.

 # From Palazzo Venezia, take V. del Corso; turn right onto V. Santissimi Apostoli and left onto V. di San Marcello. i Takeout available. Limited seating in back. $ Panini €3.50-4. Primi €4-5. ⏰ Open daily 6am-5:30pm.

NATURIST CLUB — RISTORANTE, VEGETARIAN ❸

V. della Vita 14, 4th fl. — ☎06 67 92 509

Like its street name, this restaurant is all about *"la vita"*—that is, saving a few *vite* by serving up an entirely macrobiotic menu. Climb up four well-worn flights of stairs (which might be part of the health kick) to enjoy totally atypical Roman fare like ravioli stuffed with creamy tofu and pesto *(€8)* or seitan escalope with grilled vegetables *(€9)*. Despite their exotic twists, dishes here taste like they might have been made at any one of the trattorias down the street. Those skeptical of macrobiotic food might find that this place changes their mind.

☞ *Directly off V. del Corso around P. San Lorenzo in Lucina; turn right onto V. della Vita from V. del Corso and look for #14. Buzz and walk to 4th fl.* *i* *90% organic and totally macrobiotic; fish is the only non-vegetarian option.* ⑤ *Primi €8-9; secondi €9-11. Fixed vegetarian meal €14; lunch/dinner combo €8-10/€20-25. Organic wine €12-16 per bottle.* ⌚ *Open M-F 12:30-3pm and 7-10:30pm.*

F.LLI FABBI
♥♿♀ DELI ②

V. della Croce 27-28
☎06 67 90 612 ▣www.fabbi.it

Save your euro for Dolce and Gabbana down the street, and get your real *dolce* on the cheap at this corner deli. A few slices of their *prosciutto di parma* and *mozzarella di bufala* along with some homemade pesto (all sold by weight) make the perfect snack to be enjoyed in the *piazza* down the way. If all that food has inspired your inner chef, pick up some homemade ravioli or gnocchi and a bottle of imported olive oil for the stove. The store also sells grocery staples like milk and beer.

☞ ⓜA: Spagna. Walk down V. della Croce. ⑤ *Homemade pasta €8.80-22 per kg. Cheese €8.95-23 per kg. Smoked meats €14.30-27.30 per kg.* ⌚ *Open M-Sa 8am-7:40pm.*

JEWISH GHETTO

Though the Jewish Ghetto is one of the smaller neighborhoods in Rome, it is rich in fine cuisine and character. Most restaurants are on V. del Portico d'Ottavia, and while not exactly cheap, they are a great alternative to classic Italian fare if that's all you've been eating. Most are kosher and closed early Friday through Saturday.

▨ ANTICO FORNO DEL GHETTO
🅔🅑 BAKERY, GROCERY ①

P. Costaguti 31
☎06 68 80 30 12

You don't have to resort to a slice of pizza in order to avoid the overpriced plates of a sit-down restaurant: grab a loaf of to-die-for bread, a few slices of smoked meat, and a hunk of cheese at this family-run neighborhood staple instead. Locals flock to the small store to buy anything from fresh pasta to cookies and milk to a hot slice of flatbread or focaccia topped with veggies.

☞ *From Ponte Garibaldi, walk down V. Arenula, turn right onto V. di Santa Maria del Pianto and into P. Costaguti.* *i* *Only pizza and bread guaranteed kosher. Cheese, bread, cookies, and meat sold by lb.* ⑤ *Pizza and focaccia €1.20-2 per piece, €7.70-9.70 per kg.* ⌚ *Open M-F 7:45am-2:30pm and 5-8pm, Sa-Su 7:45am-1pm.*

LA TAVERNA DEL GHETTO
♥♿♨ KOSHER ④

V. del Portico d'Ottavia 7/b-8
☎06 68 80 97 71 ▣www.latavernadelghetto.com

The small dining area out front might have you thinking that this is an intimate cafe with Middle Eastern music and delicious food to match. But head around the block, and you'll see that this popular spot opens up into an expansive dining space that can play host to bigger parties and more festive dining. The first kosher restaurant in Rome, La Taverna del Ghetto is an expert in the classics: *baccalà* (fried catfish), *fiori di zucca*, and any variation of artichoke. Soy-based desserts are dairy-free and pleasantly mild after an otherwise heavy meal.

☞ *From Teatro Marcello, walk down V. del Piscaro and veer right as it becomes V. del Portico d'Ottavia.* *i* *Strictly kosher.* ⑤ *Primi €11.50; secondi €15.90-19.50.* ⌚ *Open M-Th noon-11pm, F noon-4pm, Sa 9-11pm, Su noon-11pm.*

PASTICCERIA BOCCIONE LIMENTANI
🅔♿ BAKERY ②

V. Portico D'Ottavio 1
☎06 68 78 637

This tiny, unadorned *pasticceria* doesn't need the cuteness factor to promote itself: its small assortment of baked goods is strong enough to bring customers running, no advertisements needed. Only about four products are made here—

freshly baked tortes and a range of biscottini with nuts and fruits—so all you have to do is know what you want, order, and enjoy.

➡ Right on the corner of V. Portico D'Ottavio; look for numbers, as it's practically unmarked. 💲 Cookies around €18 per kg. Tortes €18-22 each. ⏰ Open M-Th 7:30am-7:30pm, F 7:30am-3:30pm, Su 7:30am-7:30pm.

KOHSER BISTROT CAFE — CAFE, KOSHER ❸

V. Santa Maria del Pianto 68/69 ☎06 68 64 398

This cheerful and brightly lit cafe doubles as an early evening spot for cocktails and an anytime spot for delicious kosher food. Picnic-like wooden tables on the street are often full of locals munching on finger food with their wine or enjoying fuller plates like curry chicken with artichokes. The modern interior has a full bar and a few shelves with packaged food items for sale.

➡ From Ponte Garibaldi, walk up V. Arenula and turn right onto V. Santa Maria del Pianto. 💲 Primi €9-11; secondi €8-9. Beer and wine €6-7. Cocktails €7-8. ⏰ Open M-Th 9am-9pm, F 9am-sundown, Su 9am-9pm. Aperitivo happy hour 5-9pm.

PANE VINO E SAN DANIELE — RISTORANTE, ENOTECA ❸

P. Mattei 16 ☎06 68 77 147 💻www.panevinospa.it

You won't see the classic *primi* and *secondi* format at this dark and diverse *enoteca* and restaurant. Instead, the menu features plates with regal names like the *piatto del re* (a large plate of raw prosciutto) or *la duca*. All the food and wine on the menu hails from the San Daniele region, and there is an ample selection of polenta plates as well as *sformato*, an egg-based casserole stuffed with vegetables, cheese, and meat. Sea-green walls and dark wooden tables scattered throughout the low-ceilinged, dimly lit space create a grandiose but quirky feel.

➡ In P. Mattei. 💲 Salads €7-8.50. Sformati €9.50. Wine €4-7.50 per glass. ⏰ Open M-Sa 9:30am-2am. Kitchen closes at 10:30pm.

VATICAN CITY

The longest line in Rome eventually becomes a hungry crowd. The selection of neighborhood trattorias and small stores that lines the quieter streets outside the Vatican walls won't disappoint, but the bright English menus and beckoning waiters closer to the museums will.

CACIO E PEPE — RISTORANTE ❸

V. Avezzana 11 ☎06 32 17 268 💻www.cacioepeperistorante.com

If you're in the area (and by that, we mean as far as 1 mi. away), it will be well worth your time to trek to this true trattoria. Welcoming owner Gianni will personally seat you and make sure your *cacio e pepe* (fresh egg pasta topped with oil, grated cheese, and black pepper) is everything it should be: big, flavorful, and perfectly *al dente*. Its popularity with locals instead of tourists has kept the vibe casual and the service as good as the food—and that's saying a lot.

➡ [M]A: Lepanto. From Metro, walk up V. Lepanto (away from the Vatican), turn right on Vle. delle Millizie and left onto V. Avezzana, a 5min. walk. 💲 Primi €8; secondi €9-10. ⏰ Open M-F 12:30-3pm and 7:30-11:30pm, Sa 12:30-3pm.

OLD BRIDGE GELATERIA — GELATERIA ❶

V. Bastioni di Michelangelo 3/5 ☎06 38 72 30 26 💻www.gelateriaoldbridge.com

Gelato so sinfully good you might need to visit the Vatican just to confess it. Despite being practically on the doorstep of the most touristed sight in the city, this hole-in-the-wall *gelateria* has thankfully remained just that. It's tiny and unadorned yet amazingly good. Beware: lines may rival those of St. Peter's, but the size of your order (huge) will make the wait worthwhile.

➡ Off P. Risorgimento and across the street from the line to the Vatican Museums. 💲 Cones €1.50-3; cups €3-4. ⏰ Open M 3pm-2am, Tu-Su 9am-2am.

FA BIO

⊛♿❄ CAFE, ORGANIC ❶

V. Germanico 43 ☎06 64 52 58 10 ▣www.fa-bio.com

If you're going to pay €4 for a panino, it may as well be organic, right? And if all that pizza and gelato have you craving something green, then Fa Bio will be your Eden. Just walking in, you'll be refreshed by the smell of blended smoothies and fresh salads alone. Organic pie (€1.50), hearty tofu salads (€4.50), and bread that is, for once, not white, are enough to sustain you for a full afternoon of sightseeing. If you still need a pick-me-up after the 4hr. waits, re-energize with "L'energizzante," a potent shake of milk, pear, ginger, and cacao.

✚ ⓂA: Ottaviano. Walk down V. Ottaviano and turn left onto V. Germanico. *i* All food organic. ⑤ Panini €4. Salads €4.50. Cookies €0.50-1. Fruit juices and smoothies €3.50. ⌚ Open in summer M-Sa 9am-8pm; in winter M-Sa 9am-5pm.

FABBRICA MARRONS GLACES GIULIANI

⊛♿❄ CIOCCOLATERIA ❷

V. Paolo Emilio 67 ☎06 32 43 548 ▣www.marronglaces.it

This is the kind of place you visit first for yourself, second to do some gift-shopping for friends back home, and third...for yourself again. The shop's old school '40s feel adds to the delight of ordering your sweet confections from the family owners. Their specialties—*marron glacés* (candied chestnuts) and chocolate—are the perfect match of sweet and rich. Though they may not survive a boxed trip home to your folks, the candied fruits are stellar—shiny and big as crown jewels.

✚ ⓂA: Lepanto. Take Vle. Giulio Cesare toward the Vatican and turn left onto V. Paolo Emilio. ⑤ Marron Glacés €3.50 per etto. Candied fruit €4.50 per etto. Chocolates €4.50 per etto. ⌚ Open in summer M-Sa 8:30am-1pm and 3:30pm-7:30pm; in winter M-Sa 8:30am-8pm, Su 9am-1pm.

FORNO TACIO

⊛⊗ BAKERY ❶

V. Tacito 20 ☎06 32 35 133

If melting gelato is making your hands sticky, try a warm pastry from this local bakery and grocer. Their waffle-shaped *ferratelle* cookies (€15 per kg) are mild and crispy, while their flaky *fiocchetti* twists are a lighter alternative to the standard croissant (€0.85). To slow the sugar rush, excellent pizza (less greasy and better priced than the standard slice) and bread are great taken hot or cold.

✚ ⓂA: Lepanto. Walk down V. Ezio and continue straight as it becomes V. Tacito. *i* Also sells basic groceries. No seating. ⑤ Pizza €7-13 per kg. Cookies €9.50 per kg. Fruit and cream tarts €1.50 each. ⌚ Open M-F 8am-2pm and 5-8pm, Su 8am-2pm and 5-8pm.

WINE BAR DE' PENITENZIERI

⊛⊗♈ CAFE, BAR ❸

V. dei Penitenzieri 16/A ☎06 68 75 350

Before hitting the inescapable nest of pizzerias surrounding the Vatican, grab a bite at this small but hugely popular lunch spot. The stand-up bar makes it easy to munch on a panino (€4-5) and sip your cappuccino (€0.90-2.50) without having to pay for table service. A rotating list of classics—mostly pastas and salads—is reserved for those who nab a seat in the adjoining room. If you don't want real sustenance, have a cocktail instead. Hey, you're not in St. Peter's yet.

✚ From St. Peter's, take V. della Conciliazione toward the river, turn right onto V. dei Cavalieri del San Sepolcro, and keep straight as it becomes V. Penitenzieri. ⑤ Primi and meat-and-cheese plates €10. Panini €4-5. Beer €3-4.50. Wine €3.50-4. Cocktails €6. ⌚ Open M-Sa 6am-8:30pm.

L'ARCHETTO

⊛⊗♨ PIZZERIA ❷

V. Germanico 105 ☎06 32 31 163

Tired of the same old pizza toppings and overpriced slices? Order one in the round from a menu that trumps the regular list. Try L'Archetto's namesake specialty with cooked mozzarella, arugula, sausage, and peppers or, for a smaller bite, an order of bruschetta (€1.50-2.80). Though the setting might not be anything special, their lunch special—€8 *primo* with a choice of soup—makes the

food . vatican city

pizzeria popular with the economically minded and hungry midday crowd.

 # [M]A: Ottaviano. Walk V. Ottaviano toward the Vatican and turn left onto V. Germanico. i Primi served only at lunch. $ Bruschette €1.50-2.80. Pizza €3.50-8. Primi with soup €8. ⏰ Open daily 12:30-3pm and 7pm-midnight.

TRASTEVERE

There are plenty of dining options in Trastevere, whether you want a luxurious sit-down meal, a bite on the go, or something in between. While the *piazze* are full of great choices, explore smaller side streets for some of the harder-to-find gems.

LA RENELLA — PIZZERIA, BAKERY 1

V. del Politeama 27 — ☎06 58 17 265

La Renella is as close to a true neighborhood eatery as you're likely to find, with locals coming here at all hours of the day for everything from their morning bread to lunchtime pizza to after-dinner cookies. The handwritten menu looks like it hasn't changed for years, but with Roman classics like the *fiori di zucchini* (huge orange zucchini flowers topped with anchovies and cheese), why should it? The wall is covered in flyers for local events, apartments for rent, and job offerings, so if you're not in the mood to eat, at least come in to browse through the neighborhood happenings. You may not walk away having found a new apartment, but in all likelihood, you'll have succumbed to the tempting call of La Renella's marmalade-and-chocolate *fagotini* cookies *(€14 per kg).*

 # From P. Trilussa, walk down V. della Renella; the front entrance is here, but there's also a back entrance on V. del Politeama. $ Pizza €5-12 per kg, sweet tortes and crostate €10-18 per kg, biscotti €10-16 per kg. ⏰ Open daily 7am-10pm (closing time can be variable).

SIVEN — PIZZERIA, DELI 1

V. San Francesco a Ripa 137 — ☎06 58 97 110

There's hardly a moment of the day when someone isn't entering or exiting this tiny spot, where cheap pizza and hot pasta *primi* are sold by weight. Lasagna, gnocchi, eggplant parmigiano, and calzones would make meals on their own, but most people come away with a few slices of thin-crust pizza, loaded with all the standards—think zucchini, potatoes, mushrooms, or steak. There's nowhere to sit and the service is fast, so be ready to eat on the go. And make sure you know what you want, or you'll just get in the way of the regulars behind you.

 # From Vle. Trastevere, turn right onto V. San Francesco a Ripa. $ Pasta €0.75-0.80 per etto, calzones €2.50, pizza €1-1.30 per etto. ⏰ Open M-Sa 9am-10pm.

LE FATE — RISTORANTE 3

Vle. Trastevere 130 — ☎06 58 00 971 www.lefaterestaurant.it

Inspired by the fable of Aurora, this festive restaurant has taken on the themes of love and solidarity in both its ambience and the quality of its food. The warmly lit dining area has the feel of a woodland cottage, with a bookshelf of cookbooks in the corner, twinkling star lights, and a string of vines covering the wall. All ingredients come from Lazio, so you can expect especially fresh plates; the homemade gnocchi with steak, cream, spinach, and ricotta is as rich in flavor as Princess Aurora was in gold. Students who aren't blessed with riches like the fairytale heroine should take advantage of the €10 meal, complete with bruschetta, pasta, dessert, and a glass of wine. Just say the magic word (or show your student ID).

 # About 15min. down Vle. Trastevere from P. G. Belli. i Free Wi-Fi. Inquire about cooking classes and apartment rentals for students. $ Primi €10-13; secondi €12-25. ⏰ Open daily 6-11pm.

PIZZERIA DA SIMONE — PIZZERIA, DELI 1

V. Giacinto Carini 50 — ☎06 58 14 980

After a long trek up to Ponte Acqua Paola and the surrounding gardens, there's no better way to replenish yourself than with a hot slice of Da Simone's pizza.

rome

Pies topped with anything from shrimp to the more classic sun-dried tomatoes and *mozzarella di bufala* go for about €1.50-4 per slice. Down the counter, you'll find freshly made pasta dishes, steamed vegetables *(€12-16.90 per kg)*, and huge legs of chicken *(€3)* that are filling enough to be a complete dinner. If you're hoping to grab dinner here, be ready to take your food and make a picnic of it in the park, as there's no seating.

➡ From the Porta San Pancrazio on Giancolo Hill, walk downhill on V. Giancinto Carini for about 7min. $ Pizza €6.96-16.90 per kg. ⏰ Open M-Sa 7am-8pm.

CASETTA DI TRASTEVERE
⊛♿🍸⛺ RISTORANTE [2]

P. de Renzi, 31/32 ☎06 58 00 158

Inside is like outside at this budget-friendly restaurant. A hanging clothesline, painted Italian facade and terra-cotta rooftop transform the spacious interior of Casetta di Trastevere into just what its name implies—a *casetta*, or little house. Upstairs, a banquet-size table serves especially large groups, but downstairs, smaller clusters of students consistently fill the tables. With the cheapest pizza in town *(marinara pie €3)*, this little house is a very, very, very fine house, allowing you to save your euros for Trastevere's teeming nightlife just down the street.

➡ From S. Maria in Trastevere, walk down V. di Piede until you hit V. della Pelliccia. P. de Renzi is just beyond. $ Pizza €3-6. Primi €5-8; secondi €5-16; dessert €3-5. ⏰ Open daily noon-11:30pm.

BISCOTTIFICIO ARTIGIANO
⊛♿ BAKERY [1]

V. della Luce 21 ☎06 58 03 926

With piles on piles of freshly baked cookies, this place seems more like a factory than a humble bakery. With no seats or decorations to speak of, Biscottificio Artigiano's success rests solely on its scrumptious cookies and ever-growing reputation. (Note the wall of newspaper clippings.) Try the paper-thin *stracetti*—a slightly sweet cookie made from nuts and eggs. Family-run for over a century, this bakery cooks with recipes that are like no one else's in Rome.

➡ From P. Sonnino, take V. Giulio Cesare Santini and turn left on V. della Luce. $ Most cookies €7.5-16 per kg. Rustic and fruit tortes €15. ⏰ Open M-Sa 8am-8pm and Su 9:30am-2pm.

HOSTARIA DAR BUTTERO
💳♿🍸 RISTORANTE [3]

V. della Lungaretta 156 ☎06 58 00 517

Amid hanging tools, framed sketches and paintings, dangling lamps, and polaroid snapshots, you'll find classic Roman cuisine at this popular local lunchtime spot. The eclectic decor speaks to the owner's time spent collecting artwork and furniture throughout Italy, the fruits of which have been assembled into a cozy nest of a restaurant. Specialties of the house include *Rigatoni alla Buttero*, a rich dish of pancetta, mushrooms, and tomatoes covered in parmesan and butter *(€8)*. If your eyes need a break from the impressive array of objects inside, head to the peaceful indoor garden that is covered in vines.

➡ From P. San Sonnino, turn left onto V. della Lungaretta. $ Pizza (evenings only) €5-7. Primi €6-10; secondi €7-15. ⏰ Open M-Sa noon-3pm and 7-11pm.

AI SPAGHETTARI
💳♿🍸⛺ RISTORANTE [4]

P. San Cosimato 57/60 ☎06 58 00 450 💻www.aispaghettari.it

With photos of Alberto Sordi and Al Pacino lining the walls, this place is obviously loved by at least a few Italians. Since 1896, Ai Spaghettari has served a hearty mix of meat and seafood on its casual patio overlooking the small *piazza*. Don't fill up on the huge selection of *bruschette (€2.50-4)* before you try the restaurant's classic "Ai Spaghettari" pizza, which is topped with tuna, arugula, balls of fresh cheese, and tomato *(€9)*. Rivaling the menu, huge barrels of wine just inside the building make this a viable alternative for late-night drinks.

➡ From Vle. Trastevere, turn right onto V. San Francesco a Ripa and then left onto V. Natale d. Grande until you reach P. San Cosimato; veer right on the piazza. $ Primi €8.70-10.50; secondi

€13.50-18.50. Pizza €6.50-9.50. ⏰ Open M-Tu 5pm-12:30am and W-Su noon-12:30am.

IL GALEONE CORSETTI
🍴♿♄❄♨ SEAFOOD ❺

P. San Cosimato 27   ☎06 58 09 009 📧www.corsettigaleone.it

A galleon-turned-cruise ship, this elegant restaurant serves seafood in style. Jazz, stripped white wood, and waiters in matching uniforms give the place an upscale, though relaxed, feel. The *spaghetti alla corsetti (seafood in white sauce; €16)* comes highly recommended when paired with one of over 100 wines hailing from Trentino Alto-Adige, Campania, and everywhere in between.

⚑ From Vle. Trastevere, turn right onto V. San Francesco a Ripa, and left onto V. Natale d. Grande until you reach P. San Cosimato; restaurant is on the center-left side of the piazza. ⓢ Primi and secondi €11-50. ⏰ Open daily noon-3:30pm and 7:30pm-midnight.

VIN ALLEGRO
🍴♿（ʔ）♄♨ RISTORANTE, ENOTECA ❸

P. Giuditta Tavani Sonnino   ☎06 58 95 802 📧www.vinallegro.it

"Eat and drink in happiness" is the motto here. A bottle of wine tops each of the tiny tables both inside and out on the vine-covered patio, but there are 18 pages worth of options and bookshelves full of bottles if the one on your table isn't enough. While a full dinner menu ensures that you're not drinking on an empty tank, recommended wine pairings all the way through dessert will keep you feeling just fine as live jazz and blues start around 10pm.

⚑ From P. Sidney Sonnino, walk down V. Gustavo Modern and turn left onto P. Giuditta Tavani Arquati. ℹ Full buffet with drink €7 during happy hour. Free Wi-Fi. ⓢ Primi and secondi €7-15. Shots €4. Wine €5-15. Cocktails €7. ⏰ Open daily 11am-2am. Happy hour 5-9pm.

VILLA BORGHESE, PARIOLI, AND FLAMINIO

Food in this area is best eaten away from the dinner table. In other words, because it is primarily a residential area surrounded by park, eating out tends to be pricey. Your best bet is to pack a picnic beforehand and eat it in one of the lovely gardens.

STAROCIA LUNCH BAR
🍴♿♄♨ CAFE ❶

V. Sicilia 121   ☎06 48 84 986

Pop into this bustling, modern cafe after a stroll in the Villa Borghese. Chic white decor and a small patio out front distinguish it from other food bars offering the same, standard fare. Fresh (and huge) panini, pasta, cocktails, and coffee are surprisingly well-priced given Starocia's hip vibe. Especially popular with the lunch crowd, though its evening happy hour buffet for only €4 (€6 with wine) means you'll probably make it your dinner spot.

⚑ Walking south on V. Po (away from the Villa Borghese), make a right onto V. Sicilia. ℹ Happy hour buffet €4, with wine €6. ⓢ Pasta and secondi €4-7. Tramezzini and panini €1.80-3. Coffee €0.80-1.80. Cocktails €4.50-5.50. ⏰ Open M-Sa 5:15am-9:30pm. Happy hour M-Sa 6pm.

BUBI'S
🍴♿♄♨ RISTORANTE ❹

V. G.V. Gravina 7-9   ☎06 32 60 05 10 📧www.bubis.it

The small menu and serene pistachio walls of this elegant restaurant cater to diners with refined taste. Terrace seating behind a wall of leaves is great for a more intimate meal and makes you feel far removed from the busy V. Flaminia. Though specializing in classic Roman cuisine, the restaurant serves entrees like *straccetti di pollo* with curry and Canadian rice as well as a range of gourmet hamburgers that add a little bit of international flare.

⚑ Ⓜ A: Flaminio or tram #19 to Belle Arti. Walk up V. Flaminio from the Metro for about 5min. and turn left onto V. Giovanni Vincenzo Gravina. ⓢ Primi €9-12; secondi €12-18. Panini €12-14. ⏰ Open M-Sa 12:30-3pm and 8-11pm.

TREE BAR
🍴♿♄♨ CAFE ❷

V. Flaminia 226   ☎06 32 65 27 54

If you're in the park and want to feast somewhere besides a picnic bench, this classy lunch bar does the trick. The white pebbles, glass "walls," and wooden decor (even the lanterns are made of wood, but try to banish those thoughts of potential fire hazard from your mind) make you feel like you're at a vacation house and should be sunbathing by the pool. But save that for outside—the art magazines, chic bar, and plush green couches inside create an upscale vibe. Healthy entrees and finger foods are listed on the chalkboard menu, which is posted on a column in the center of the room.

➜ ⓂB: Flaminio. Walk about 25min. up V. Flaminia. Or tram #2 to Belle Arti. Ⓢ Primi and secondi €6-16. ⏰ Open M 6pm-2am, Tu-Su 10:30am-2am.

IL MARGUTTA RISTORANTE
💳🚭🍸❄ VEGETARIAN ❸

V. Margutta ☎06 32 65 05 77 🖥www.ilmargutta.it

Vegetarians, rejoice! (Even vegans can let out a shout of joy.) The expansive interior of this meatless restaurant, accented by tall potted plants to match the green cuisine, creates a surprisingly sophisticated feel. Black circular booths mixed with small, orange tables welcome both bigger parties and couples. Those tired of traditional pasta can feast on refreshing plates like buckwheat noodles topped with strawberries, asparagus, and gorgonzola. For a protein kick, try the seitan escalope with lemon and Cartizze sauce. Though a single entree will probably fill you up, full tasting menus are offered for those who can't get enough. The Sunday festivity brunch features a huge buffet with live music *(€25)*.

➜ ⓂA: Flaminio. From Piazzale Flaminia, walk into P. del Popolo and veer left onto V. del Babuino. Proceed 5min. and turn left onto the small alley street, V. Margutta. Ⓢ Primi €10-12; secondi €11-14. Lunch buffet €12-18. ⏰ Open daily 12:30-3:30pm and 7:30-11:30pm.

TERMINI AND SAN LORENZO

Termini and its surrounding region are dominated by restaurants representing both extremes of the price range: cheap eats and over-priced tourist menus catering to hungry travelers. Avoid restaurants immediately surrounding the station and head into some side streets for higher quality options. Hostel dwellers with kitchen access should make the huge **SMA grocery store** *(⏰ Open M-Sa 8am-9pm, Su 8:30am-8:30pm)* located downstairs next to the Coin store on V. Esquilino, right on the corner of P. Santa Maria Maggiore, their friend. There's also an **indoor market** filled with merchants selling fish, meat, fruit, vegetables, and various canned goods at V. Giolitti 271/A *(alternative entrance on V. Principe Amadeo 188 ⏰ Open M 5am-3pm, Tu 5am-5pm, W-Th 5am-3pm, F-Sa 5am-5pm)*.

👍 ANTICA PIZZERIA DE ROMA
🚭♿❄ PIZZERIA ❶

V. XX Settembre 41 ☎06 48 74 624 🖥www.mcmab.net

Businessmen may take home a big paycheck, but that doesn't mean they don't like bargains when they see them: midday, this tiny pizzeria is full of men in suits, munching some of the best-priced and freshest pizza in the neighborhood. Though this pizzeria offers the same standard fare that infiltrates all of Rome (thin-crust pizza sold by weight), watching the workers cut, weigh, and serve up fresh pies like a science (or whip out an individual one in less than 10min.) is a real pleasure—and you haven't even taken your first bite. Once you do, you'll be ready to join the businessmen every day.

➜ From P. della Repubblica, walk down Vittorio Emanuele Orlando and turn right onto V. XX Settembre. Proceed 7min. Ⓢ Individual pizzas €2.20-5.50, €0.70-2 per etto. ⏰ Open daily 8am-9:30pm.

PASTICCERIA STRABBIONI ROMA
🚭♿🍸☀ CAFE, PASTICCERIA ❷

V. Servio Tullio 2a-2b ☎06 48 73 965

Not much has changed at Strabbioni since it opened in 1888: not the hand-painted flowers gracing the ceiling or the old-fashioned lamps, and definitely not the good service and food. (While *Let's Go* might not have been around in 1888, we're pretty sure this place would have merited a listing in *Let's Go Grand Tour 1889*.) The second-oldest bar of its type still in Rome, this is the place where locals come for a cheap lunch (*primi* classics are written daily on a chalkboard outside), a freshly baked pastry, or even an afternoon mixed drink. At only €3.50-4 a drink, how can you resist? Enjoy a specialty like the *budino di riso*, a small rice pudding cake, in the casual seating outside or while standing at the wooden bar as you chat with the staff.

From Porta Pia, walk down V. XX Settembre and make a right onto V. Servio Tullio. $ Primi €6-7; secondi €8. Pastries €0.80-3. ⏰ Open M-Sa 7am-8pm.

FASSINO — CAFE, GELATERIA ❷

V. Bergamo 24 ☎06 85 49 117

The folks at Fassino will have you know gelato isn't just a summer thing. Their famous *Brivido Caldo* reinvents the favorite frozen treat, sticking a cookie in its middle and turning it into a hot delight topped off with whipped cream. If it's a winter month, try their richest flavor, the *cioccolato* with brandy and cream. If it's summer, their original *cioccarancio* (dark chocolate and orange) is to die for. After the sugar rush (or before, if you're one of those people who's been brainwashed into the dessert-after-dinner rule), settle down for a savory crepe, which the Sicilian owner makes with no butter fat—only extra virgin olive oil—for a lighter taste. Though their fixed lunch meal *(a crepe, drink, dessert, and coffee; €8.50)* is a steal, consider coming in the evening when a classical pianist plays until the customers leave.

From the end of V. XX Settembre, turn left onto V. Piave and walk until you hit P. Fiume. Turn right onto V. Bergamo. i Live music M-W, F, Su 10pm-closing. $ Gelato €1.50-3. Brivido Caldo €3 (winter only). Cocktails €4.50-5. ⏰ Open M-F 9:30am-1am, Sa 3:30pm-1am, Su 9:30am-1:30pm and 3:30pm-1am.

RISTORANTE DA GIOVANNI — RISTORANTE ❸

V. A Salandra 1 ☎06 48 59 50

A hand-written menu, shelf of old typewriters, and even a hanging carcass greet customers at this subterranean trattoria. Don't worry: the meat is dangling in the kitchen, ensuring that your entree will be that much fresher. With only a few windows near the ceiling and a wood-lined interior, this family-run Roman restaurant oozes with dark warmth that matches its classic dishes. You've seen it written dozens of times at numerous establishments, but you'll never get tired of Da Giovanni's *cacio e pepe*, which they've been making for over 50 years.

From P. della Repubblica, walk up V. Vittorio Emanuele Orlando and turn right onto V. XX Settembre. Walk 5min. and turn left onto V. M Pagano; veer left onto V. Antonio Salandra. $ Primi €5.50-6.50; secondi €4.50-12. ⏰ Open M-Sa noon-3pm and 7-10:30pm.

RISTORANTE AFRICA — AFRICAN ❸

V. Gaeta 26-28 ☎06 49 41 077

The area around Termini abounds with cheap, international dives, but this African restaurant distinguishes itself with better-quality food and a more welcoming decor. The friendly staff will be happy to recommend a dish to the customer ignorant of African cuisine or Italian, but English translations provide ample assistance. Vegetarians can finally feast on something other than pasta: the *aliccia* is a healthy dish of puréed vegetables simmered in onion and herb sauce and served with traditional African bread *(€9)*. Bright orange walls, carved wooden seats, and African sculptures bring you out of Italy, at least for the hour you're here to eat.

[M]Termini. Walk in the direction of P. del Cinquecento and turn right onto V. Gaeta. $ Appetizers €3-4; entrees €9-12. ⏰ Open M-Sa 8am-midnight

TESTACCIO AND OSTIENSE

Testaccio is known among Roman residents as one of the best spots for high-quality, well-priced food. Its location farther from the sights means it evades the tourist crowds of the city center. Whether you want an upscale restaurant or a cheaper trattoria, you won't have any trouble finding it here.

👍 IL NOVECENTO
💳🚭🍸 RISTORANTE [3]

V. dei Conciatori 10 ☎06 57 25 04 45 💻www.9cento.com

Fresh. Homemade. Family-run. You've heard these adjectives used all too often to describe Italian cuisine, but here, they actually come to life. Watch the owner's son roll out pasta dough, cut it into *tagliatelle*, and dump it into boiling water before it ends up on your plate topped with their own pesto *(€9)*. If pasta isn't your thing, then how about pizza or roasted meat—again, you can see both sliced and diced minutes before you eat them. Though the wood-lined rooms up front are especially cozy, try to grab a table in the huge dining room in back so you can take in all the kitchen action.

➡ [M]B: Piramide. Walk down V. Ostiense and make a right onto V. dei Conciatori. $ Primi €8-10; secondi €12-18. Pizzas €5-9 (only at dinner). ⏰ Open M-F 12:30-2:30pm and 7:30-11pm, Sa-Su 7:30-11pm.

👍 FARINANDO
💳🚭 PIZZERIA, PANIFICIO [2]

V. Lucca della Robbia 30 ☎06 57 50 674

At Farinando, you can get top-notch pizza by the kilo or pie, huge calzones, and anything from cookies to fruit tarts without having to pay for expensive table service or retreat to a park bench. Stock up before hitting the long V. Ostiense for some sightseeing.

➡ [M]B: Piramide. Walk up V. Marmorata; turn left onto V. Galvani and right onto V. Lucca della Robbia. $ Calzones €3. Whole pizzas €4-7, €7-18 per kg. ⏰ Open M-Th 7:30am-2pm and 4:30-8:30pm, F 7:30am-9pm, Sa 5-9pm.

LA MAISON DE L'ENTRECÔTE
🚭♿🍸☀ RISTORANTE, ENOTECA [3]

P. Gazometro 1 ☎06 57 43 091 💻www.lamaisondelentrecote.it

You don't need a plane ride or a time machine if you want to return to bohemian Paris: just retreat to Le Maison's dim downstairs, where stained-glass lamps and slow music put you at ease. The small menu lets you pair classic French dishes like cheesy onion soup *(€7)* with Italian staples. Try their *crema* gelato topped with Grand Marnier. Check out the antique mirror and the 10% discounted menu scribbled atop it, then check yourself to see if your cheeks are pink like Moulin Rouge from the wine you've been sipping.

➡ [M]B: Ostiense. Walk down V. Marmorata away from Piramide for 5min. and turn right onto P. Gazometro. $ Primi €7-10. Salads €5-7. Meats €9-14. Beer €4. Cocktails €6. Wine by the bottle €12-16. ⏰ Open Tu-Th 1-3pm and 8pm-midnight, F-Sa 8pm-midnight.

OSTERIA DEGLI AMICI
💳♿🍸❄ RISTORANTE [3]

V. Nicola Zabaglia 25 ☎06 57 81 466 💻www.osteriadegliamici.info

Besides the excellent cheese-topped pasta dishes, there's nothing cheesy about this place. Enjoy hot saffron risotto sprinkled with smoked Scamorza cheese and drizzled in balsamic vinegar while downing a glass of their stellar wine (whose cork might get added to the gigantic collection up front). If the relaxed setting makes you want to linger, split a spicy chocolate souffle—almost as hot as the entrees—with your *amico*, who's hopefully bringing the heat as well.

➡ [M]B: Piramide. Walk up V. Marmorata; turn right onto V. Luigi Vanvitelli and left onto V. Nicola Zabaglia. $ Primi €7-9; secondi €12-16. ⏰ Open W-Su 12:30-3pm and 7:30pm-midnight.

L'OASI DI BIRRA
💳♿🍸 RISTORANTE [2]

P. Testaccio 40 ☎06 57 46 122

Most liquor menus round off their selection at a few pages, but this two-floor mecca of food and alcohol has six pages devoted to Belgian beer *alone.* It requires a book to catalogue the rest of their international collection, which also includes wine, grappa, rum, and whiskey. The floor-to-ceiling bottles (both upstairs and down) probably make up less than 10% of their actual collection. The best way to tackle the menu is to order a bottle for the table (some upwards of €200) and match it up with a few six- or eight-variety plates of *salumi*, cheese, or bruschetta which come in nearly as many combinations as the alcohol. If you're bad at making decisions, drop in during happy hour when you can endlessly sample the goods for only €10 at the *aperitivo* buffet.

[M]B: Piramide. Walk up V. Marmorata and turn left onto P. Testaccio. ***i*** *Also carries a small selection of bottled food products.* Ⓢ *Bruschette €8. Salumi and formaggi plates of 6-8 types €16-19. Draft beer €4-10. Wine €12-200+ per bottle.* ⏰ *Open M-Sa 4:30pm-12:30am, Su 7:30pm-12:30am. Happy hour 5-8:30pm.*

FELICE A TESTACCIO RISTORANTE ❸

V. Mastro Giorgio 29 ☎06 57 46 800 www.feliceatestaccio.com

*Sunday, Monday, happy days...*except replace happy with *felice* and make that *every day* at this place. Part of a rotating selection of seven entrees each day, the plates here are among the freshest and best in Testaccio. If you're picky, choose your day wisely: Friday is particularly fish heavy (and consequently more expensive), while Wednesday might be a good day for vegetarians given that it's the day they serve up their special rigatoni pasta and Roman broccoli *(only in season; €10).* You can count on finding an assortment of Roman standards—prepared far above the standard—which are made daily and are the only things served on Sunday.

[M]B: Piramide. Walk up V. Marmorata; turn left onto V. Galvani and right onto V. Mastro Giorgio. Ⓢ *Primi €8-10; secondi €13-22.* ⏰ *Open M-Sa 12:30-2:45pm and 8-11:30pm, Su 12:30-2:45pm.*

CACIO E COCCI RISTORANTE ❸

V. del Gazometro 36 ☎06 57 46 419

In case you didn't know you were in an *hostaria*, there's a 5 ft. sign hanging on the yellow walls reminding you where you are. Cacio e Cocci has been making traditional Roman dishes since 1944; pick up a menu and you'll see a 1960 (the year the sign was inaugurated) shot of the restaurant and its proud mother. Since then, specialties like the ricotta ravioli with oranges *(€10)* and fresh fish plates like spaghetti with clams, zucchini, and saffron keep locals streaming in. Though it could be a casual dinner spot, the best deal is the €9 lunch menu, which includes a *contorno*, *primo*, water, and coffee.

[M]B: Ostiense. Walk down V. Ostiense; turn right onto V. dei Magazzini Generali and immediately left onto V. del Gazometro. Ⓢ *Primi €7.50-11; secondi €9-16.* ⏰ *Open M-Sa noon-3pm and 7-11:30pm.*

LINARI CAFE ❶

V. Nicola Zabaglia 9 ☎06 57 82 358 www.pasticcerialinari.it

If you closed your eyes, the sound of clinking plates and busy counter orders might have you thinking you were in an American diner. In fact, with its small tables, counter stools, and sunny feel, Linari isn't far off. Instead of ordering a banana split or sundae, you'd be best off indulging in homemade gelato atop apple strudel or perhaps one of the fresh-made, heavenly pralines *(€5 per etto).* Nab a table at breakfast or lunch or stand at the bar Frank Sinatra style while sipping on a happy hour cocktail *(€4).*

[M]B: Piramide. Walk up V. Marmorata; turn right onto V. Luigi Vanvitelli and left onto V. Nicola Zabaglia. ***i*** *Seating only at breakfast and lunch. Happy hour buffet with drink €6.* Ⓢ *Gelato €2-2.50. Primi €4.50-5. Pizza €12 per kg. Pastries €18-20 per kg.* ⏰ *Open M 6:30am-9:30pm, W-Su 6:30am-9:30pm. Happy hour 6-9pm.*

nightlife

Don't spend all your euros and energy at the museums—Rome's nightlife is varied and vast, giving you a whole other itinerary to attack after the guards go home and the cats come out to prowl the ruins. Generally, you'll be able to find whatever nightlife you're into, though each neighborhood has its own flavor and characteristic selection. The only areas where your nights might end a bit early are, unsurprisingly, Vatican City and the region near Villa Borghese.

d-squared

Drinking and dining are two of Italy's most famous attractions. For all the great cuisine on offer, however, sit-down meals in Italy can equal time and money. If you're looking to save on both those fronts while indulging your stomach and liver (livers *want* alcohol, right?), the Italians are have something to help you out: the *aperitivo* happy hour. This works as follows. Anytime after 5:30pm, most places put out a buffet spread containing anything from finger food to *primi*, into which customers are free to dive after purchasing a drink. Though you don't get the service of a sit-down meal, the food is often extremely fresh and well-made, the vibe is casual, and the value unbeatable: as much food as you want and well-priced cocktails for under €10. The only thing to prevent you from loading up your plate with refill after refill is pride. After your fifth trip back to the food table in the course of two hours, you'll probably realize you don't have too much of that.

Enoteche (wine bars, often with *aperitivi*) are scattered throughout the city but are especially prevalent in the **Ancient City** and **Centro Storico.** They generally cater to an older crowd seeking high-quality drinks and low-key conversation.

Irish pubs and American-style bars populate **Trastevere,** busy *corsi* (Vittorio Emanuele, V. del Corso, V. Nazionale, etc.), and the area around **Termini.** They often have weekly specials (karaoke and quiz nights) and air sporting events. Note that "bar" in Italy generally refers to a cafe where you can buy alcoholic beverages but that is mostly a daytime spot for food. Cocktail bars and lounges are called "American bars." More upscale lounges are common in the area around **Piazza di Spagna,** where they're about all you'll find.

The ragers in your party should head to **Testaccio,** known for some of the best discos in the city, most of which are conveniently clustered around the base of Monte Testaccio. If you're up for the trek, take a night bus to **Ostia,** Rome's closest beach, and enjoy plenty of opportunities for dancing and lounging on the sand as the morning sun rises. Go with a group, though, as the long stretches between discos tend to be isolated at odd hours.

Speaking of beaches, many clubs migrate to the sandy shore starting in late May and continuing through August. Check out **Gilda on the Beach** (*Lungomare di Ponente 11 in Fregene* ☎*06 66 56 06 49*).

While indoor venues such as bars, clubs, and discos can provide a fun setting for your evening pursuits, they expectedly rake up a large bill: cover fees and pricey cocktails may have you broke after a few nights. As an alternative, head to **Campo dei Fiori, Piazza Santa Maria in Trastevere, Piazza Colonna** (outside the Pantheon), or the **Spanish Steps** for an inevitably large crowd (even on a "tame" Tuesday), impromptu live performances, and an evening before some of Rome's greatest monuments without the constant flash of photos. (It's okay to snap your camera during the day, but you'd just be the lame tourist at night.) Alcohol by the bottle is surprisingly cheap at the supermarket and drinking outside is as common as smoking, for better or worse. Crack open a Peroni or a bottle of wine and make your own nightlife on the *piazza*. A note to the overzealous, underage American tourist, however: getting wasted is not looked upon favorably by the Italian populace. Drinking is as much a part of the culture as eating, so there's little sense in overdoing it on a single night. Hopefully, you'll grow out of the beer pong, pub crawl, and open-bar phase after one night of trying each.

ANCIENT CITY

Nightlife in the Ancient City is confined mostly to Irish pubs, upscale wine bars, and small cafes open until the late hours. While there's nothing like walking down a cobblestone street after a few glasses of wine, if you're looking for young, pumping clubs, head elsewhere.

ICE CLUB

CLUB, BAR

V. Madonna dei Monti 18/19 ☎06 97 84 55 81 www.iceclubroma.it

Gelato isn't the only way to cool off from the hot Roman sun: enter Ice Club, the only bar in Italy made entirely of ice. For €15, you get a silver cloak, a pair of gloves, and one free drink at what may be Rome's (literally) coolest spot, an ice tube of colored lights, pulsing music, and stellar drinks. Vodka goes down smooth as, you guessed it, ice and not only because it's served in an ice cup: with over 40 flavors ranging from strawberries and cream to chocolate, you'll never know you're drinking your liquor straight. Clearly, this is how the place keeps its clientele, since after a few shots, it's hard to tell that the temperature is below freezing.

From the Fori Imperiali, turn right onto V. Madonna dei Monti. i M, W-F, and Su drop by between 6-9pm and get in free after 11pm. Open bar Tu €15. Buy 1 shot, get 4 free Th. Credit cards accepted for cover. Cash only at the bar (because credit cards would just be impractical in that weather). $ Cover €15; includes 1 drink. Shots €2.50. Straight vodka €7. Cocktails €8. Ice luge €10. Open daily 6pm-2am.

SCHOLAR'S LOUNGE

BAR

V. del Plebiscito 101/b ☎06 69 20 22 08 www.scholarsloungerome.com

There'll be no scholars reading here: with nine TVs (including two that are over 5 ft. wide) and over 250 kinds of whiskey (the biggest collection in Italy), they're probably dancing on the table. Don't bother bringing your Italian phrasebook, because the Irish bartenders, huge Irish flag hanging over the bar, and steady stream of Irish dishes *(beef in Guinness stew, €9.50)* make this a bit of Dublin on the Tiber. Although you can keep it cheap at only €3.50 for a pint of beer, those looking for a splurge should check out the whiskey list: a shot of Jameson Rarest Vintage Reserve goes for a whopping €133.50. Ask to see their private collection, which might as well be at a museum.

From P. Venezia, follow V. del Plebiscito to just where it intersects V. del Corso. i Live music Th-F. Karaoke on Tu and Su. $ Pints €3.50-5.50. Cocktails €7.50-9.50, €5 during the day. Student specials: long drinks €4.50, shots €1. Open daily 11am-3:30am. Happy hour until 8pm.

LIBRERIA CAFÉ

CAFE

V. degli Zingari 36 ☎33 97 22 46 22

Libreria's "business card" is a bookmark, just in case you want to remember the address—or perhaps the page number—where you left off. You'll find yourself in relaxed company at this bohemian cafe, accoutered with draped cloths, antique couches, votive candles, lamps that might as well have come from a Lewis Carroll novel, and, of course, walls of books by Karl Marx, Victor Hugo, Freud, and any number of Italian authors. Check out the coffered ceiling of the stone "den" downstairs, which, surprisingly, is brighter, if a bit musty. Smooth jazz playing in the background will feel even smoother after a glass of one of the 47 varieties of wine *(€5)* offered. If you do, in fact, want to read, try a cup of tea instead, hailing from Russia, Japan, or even South Africa *(€5)*.

🔔 ⓂB: Cavour. From V. Cavour, turn right onto P. degli Zingari and left onto V. degli Zingari. ⑤ Beer €3-5. Wine €5. Cocktails €5-6. Appetizers €6-10. 🕐 Open M 6pm-2am and W-Su 6pm-2am. Aperitivo buffet 7-9pm, €8.

STUDIO 33 LE BAIN

🏄👪♿🍸❄ CLUB

V. delle Botteghe Oscure 33   ☎06 68 65 673 🖥www.studiolebain.it

If the Roman gods ever came down to earth, they might choose this grandiose spot to make their landing. Elegant white tables and fresh flowers juxtaposed beside playful neon paintings and suave gold cushions should clue you in to the mixed crowd which comes here—both sophisticated adults looking for fine food and younger *ragazze* seeking pumping tunes. During the day, full breakfast and brunch are served in the creamy-colored central hall. Starting at 7pm, crowds cluster around one of two bars for aperitifs *(€7)*, cocktails *(€7)*, and conversation. *Dopo cena*, expect a louder and more experimental mix during the week.

🔔 From C. Vittorio Emanuele, turn right onto P. del Gesu; head down V. Celsa, then turn left onto V. d. Botteghe Oscure. ⑤ Cocktails €10. Primi €10-16; secondi €15-18. Buffet lunch €10. 🕐 Open daily 7am-2am.

CAVOUR 313

🏄👪🍸 ENOTECA

V. Cavour 313   ☎06 67 54 96

The 100 varieties of wine, savory plates, and numerous awards honoring Cavour 313's classy offerings make it the spot of choice for those whose idea of a night out consists of fine food and even finer wine. The wine collection, conveniently on file up front in good library fashion, hails from all over Italy, as do *golosità* plates like the Calabrian—a mix of hot salami, sun-dried tomatoes with herbs, and olives. For something to offset the salty offerings, try a bit of gorgonzola cheese with honey and sweet marsala wine *(€8)*. Cozy wooden booths can make your dining experience not only more private, but also less noisy.

🔔 Midway up V. Cavour coming from V. dei Fori Imperiali ⑤ Wine €3.50-8. Mixed cheese plates €8-12, meat plates €8-10. 🕐 Open M-Sa 12:30-2:45pm and 7:30pm-12:30am.

CENTRO STORICO

The Centro Storico might be old, but it packs in a young crowd at night. One of the best places to find bars and clubs, both in terms of location and quality, this area remains fairly safe after sunset due to its bustle at most hours. If you don't feel like heading inside, check out the Campo dei Fiori, where many spend the evening enjoying the outdoor scenery.

📍 DRUNKEN SHIP

🏄👪🍸❄♨ BAR, CLUB

Campo dei Fiori 20/21   ☎06 68 30 05 35 🖥www.drunkenship.com

Wait, is this the campo or the campus? Walking into Drunken Ship, you may very well think you're back at college, as it comes complete with nightly beer pong, TVs airing sports games, a DJ spinning Top 40 tunes, and a raucous crowd of students ready to enjoy it all. Great weekly specials, including Wednesday night power hours and Pitcher Night Thursdays *(€10)*, make this one of the most popular spots for young internationals aching for some university-style fun.

🔔 In Campo dei Fiori. *i* M-Th half-price drinks for women until 11pm, Tu buy-1-get-1-free until 11pm; check online for more specials. Student discounts. Happy hour pint of wine with free buffet €4. ⑤ Shots €3-6. Long drinks €6. Cocktails €7. 🕐 Open M-Th 3pm-2am, F-Sa 10am-2am, Su 3pm-2am. Happy hour M-F 4-8pm.

📍 SOCIETE LUTECE

🏄👪🍸♨ BAR

P. di Montevecchio 17   ☎06 68 30 14 72

The total opposite of an American-college-student-ridden bar, Societe Lutece

nightlife · centro storico

attracts an artsy late 20s to early 40s crowd. Homemade bags made from recycled material hang from the ceiling, and the menu is a fabric-covered panel of wood into which prices are etched. To complete the natural feel, all food and drinks are organic or locally produced. If you're hunting for high-quality and low-stress nightlife, how could you look any further than this place's nut colada *(€8)?*

➡ From P. Navona, exit and turn left onto V. Coronari; continue and make a sharp left onto V. Montevecchio. ℹ Happy hour drinks with free buffet €8. $ Beer €5. Wine €6. Cocktails €8. ⏰ Open Tu-Su 6pm-2am. Aperitivo 6:30-10pm.

MOOD
💳🚭🍸❄ CLUB

C. Vittorio Emanuele 205 ☎329 06 42 240

It may be painted entirely silver, but it meets the golden standard as far as Roman discos go. Room after room in Mood's cavernous downstairs lets guests choose between lounging or dancing. But with the stereo blaring Top 40 early on and drinks flowing generously (student specials abound), most people will be up on the floor by the time 1am rolls around. Because it's downstairs, the Centro Storico's 2am norm for closing may as well not exist.

➡ Near Campo dei Fiori. ℹ Americans get in free. 2 drinks for €10 or open bar €15 until 1am. €2 shots for ladies. Student specials; show ID. $ Cocktails €10. ⏰ Open daily 11pm-4am.

FLUID
💳🚭🍸❄ BAR, CLUB

V. del Governo Vecchio 46 ☎06 68 32 361 🖥www.fluideventi.com

Fluid seems to be working a "natural" theme—though the fake tree branches, caged rocks, and faux ice cube stools don't exactly scream "crunchy granola." With a lounge early in the evening and an upbeat DJ set later in the night, this is the place to come for post-dinner drinks and company. The drink menu, which is essentially a book of cocktails, features unorthodox mixes, like the cinnamon red: a smoothie of *cannella rossa* liqueur, yogurt, *crema di limone*, and whipped cream *(€7.50).*

➡ From P. Navona, exit onto P. Pasquina and continue as it becomes V. del Governo Vecchio. ℹ DJ nightly. Aperitivo drink and buffet €7.50. $ Beer €5-6. Cocktails €7.50. ⏰ Open daily 6pm-2am. Aperitivo hour 6-10pm.

ARISTOCAMPO
💳♿🍸☀ BAR

P. Campo dei Fiori

On the doorstep of Campo dei Fiori, this fast-paced bar gets crowded early thanks to its better-than-average *aperitivo* buffet. Pumping music pulses from the small bar inside, but most of the action is on the patio where nearly every stool is occupied. Great panini—good for carni-, herbi-, and omnivores—satisfies those late night cravings wrought by yet another cocktail.

➡ In Campo dei Fiori. ℹ Aperitivo drink and buffet €5. $ Beer €5-6. Cocktails €7. Panini €4-5. Salads €8. ⏰ Open daily noon-2am. Aperitivo hour 6-8pm.

ANIMA
💳🚭🍸❄ CLUB, BAR

V. di Santa Maria dell'Anima 57

Anima's copper entrance leads into a dim lounge, complete with black lights, low couches, and two bars. Lounge music plays in the early evening as a mixed crowd of students and 20-somethings wander in. Starting around midnight, the dance floor heats up with house and commercial tunes spinning until the wee hours. Head up the tiny spiral staircase if you want to step off the floor and people-watch from above.

➡ From P. Navona, turn left onto V. di Santa Maria della'Anima. ℹ Ladies' night 2-for-1 drinks on M. Open bar Th and Su. Happy hour beer €2.50, Cocktails €4.50. $ Beer €4-5. Cocktails €6, €10 after midnight. ⏰ Open daily 7pm-4am. Happy hour 7-10pm.

ABBEY THEATRE
🏷♿📶🍸 IRISH PUB

V. del Governo Vecchio 51/53 ☎06 68 61 341 💻www.abbey-rome.com

A traditional Irish pub where you can get your fair share of bar food, soccer, (American football?!), and great drinks—try a "mixed beer" special like the hard cider and grenadine *(€5.50)*. The wooden interior is huge but fills up quickly during big games. Comedy nights (in English) cater particularly to an international crowd, but monthly specials like an open mike and a night of live Irish music bring everyone from expats to locals.

‡ From P. Navona, exit onto P. Pasquina and continue as it becomes V. del Governo Vecchio. $ Shots €4-6.50. Beer €5.50-6. Cocktails €7. ⏰ Open daily noon-2am. Happy hour noon-8pm.

PIAZZA DI SPAGNA

There's a reason the Spanish Steps are so popular at night, and it's not their beauty (though that's a definite perk). Young travelers seeking nightlife in this neighborhood would rather lounge on the steps than pay €15 for drinks and light music at a lounge nearby. There's no reason to stay in this neighborhood for a night out, unless you like walking down empty streets of closed boutiques or rubbing shoulders with businessmen and the patrons of five-star hotels.

ANTICA ENOTECA DI V. DELLA CROCE
🏷♿🍸⛅ ENOTECA

V. della Croce 76b ☎06 67 90 896

Escape the pretentiousness of the surrounding snazzy bars and head to this old-fashioned *enoteca* for a drink and a meal. The airy feel set by tall ceilings and rustic arches is refreshing compared to nearby places. A plate of homemade pasta with duck sauce and a glass of wine will cost you less than €15 and can be enjoyed in comfort at the long bar or a small side table. Unfortunately, there's no happy hour, but that just means you can enjoy €5 draft pints at 3pm.

‡ [M]A: Spagna. From the Spanish Steps, walk down V. della Croce. $ Wine €4-10 per glass (also available by the bottle). Beer €5. Cocktails €8. Primi €8-9; secondi €12-16. ⏰ Open daily 11am-1am.

GILDA
🏷🚭🍸❄ CLUB

V. Mario dè Fiori 97 ☎06 67 84 838 💻www.gildabar.it

We don't think the gold walls and chichi leather couches are a coincidence—dress sharply and prepare to schmooze with Rome's elite (or those with aspirations). One of the city's most famous discos, this upscale spot caters to an exclusive crowd wanting only the best cocktails and music. Pay for a table or rent a private room while you sip that martini and wait for the dance floor to fill up with stylishly-clad clubbers. Colored lights, multiple stereos, and ceilings rivaling St. Peter's in height don't disappoint. Our advice: if you make it here, just forget that "budget" thing and resign yourself to weeping in the morning.

‡ [M]A: Spagna. From the Spanish Steps, walk down V. Condotti and turn left onto V. Mario de Fiori. ℹ Disco open from Sept to mid-June; moves to the beach at Ostia during the summer. Happy hour buffet with drink €8. $ €20-30 for a table, includes 1 drink. Cocktails €15. ⏰ Disco open Sept-June Th-Su midnight-4am. Restaurant open daily from noon. Happy hour 5-9pm.

TRASTEVERE

Trastevere is home to some of the best nightlife in the city—student and otherwise. Whether you want a small bar, a classy lounge, or somewhere where you can move around a bit, make the trek over the river and get ready for a late night.

FRENI E FRIZIONI
🏷♿🍸⛅ BAR

V. del Politeama 4-6 ☎06 45 49 74 99 💻www.freniefrizioni.com

To find this place, don't look for a street number: turn your head skyward until you spy a jam-packed bar. Located just up the stairs off V. del Politeama, Freni e Frizioni has essentially created its own *piazza*. (And you thought only high

Roman authorities could do that.) The white interior, decorated with art work and bookshelves, feels more like a living room than a lounge. The extensive bar is only a precursor to the *aperitivo* room in back—a dining table to rival that of the Last Supper's, constantly replenished with fresh entrees served directly from the pots they were cooked in, awaits you. Check out the "shelf" of wooden drawers bearing foreign words, upon which international dips like Tzatiki and *salsa tonnata* are served. The outside *piazza* is possibly even more popular than the interior and is perfect for literally "looking down" on the world.

✂ *From P. Trilussa, head down the tiny V. del Politeama and look for the steps (and the crowd) on the left.* **i** *Happy hour €6-10.* Ⓢ *Wine €6. Cocktails €7-8.* ☼ *Open daily 6:30pm-2am. Aperitivo happy hour 6:30-10:30pm.*

✉ CAFE FRIENDS
P. Trilussa 34

🍽&ᵗ⁽ᵗ⁾ᵗᵗ CAFE, BAR, CLUB
☎06 58 16 111 ▦www.cafefriends.it

Like good friends (well, even mere acquaintances) should, the servers here know your name. Locals and international students alike crowd this hip cafe-lounge at all hours of the day. Fully decked out with a swanky silver bar, stylish cartooned walls, and spacious indoor and patio seating, Cafe Friends caters to more American tastes: a full breakfast is served daily 8:30am-12:30pm. But abandon those early-morning ways for the more typically Italian *aperitivo* mixed-drink buffet, served nightly 7-10pm *(€6-8)*, which draws the biggest crowd. The special Friends drinks, like the "Zombie" *(rum, Jamaicano, cherry brandy, orange juice, and lime; €6.50)* will keep you going to music that blasts all the way into the early evening and gets cranked even louder on the weekends.

✂ *From Ponte Sisto, head into P. Trilussa.* **i** *Free Wi-Fi.* Ⓢ *Beer €3.50-5. Martinis €7. Cocktails €8. 15% discount for international students with ID.* ☼ *Open M-Sa 7am-2am, Su 6:30pm-2am.*

PEPATO
V. del Politeama 8

🍽&ᵗᵗ BAR
☎06 58 33 52 54

Follow the illuminated red Pepato sign into this dim haven of drinks and music, where predominantly black decor sets a sophisticated vibe. Sleek black stools line the silver bar where young staff serve Pepato specials like the "Royal," a powerful mix of Absolut Peppar, peach vodka, and champagne *(€7)*. Although there are plenty of couches and tucked-away corners for sitting, rock and house tunes blaring on the stereo will probably have you moving before the night is out. The wooden patio outside offers some reprieve from the pulsing interior, reminding you that you are on a historic, cobblestone street in a good ol' Catholic city.

✂ *From Ponte Sisto, turn left onto Lungotevere Raffaello Sanzio; head down the stairs in the piazza on the right, and make a left.* Ⓢ *Shots €3. Beer €4-7. Wine €5-7. Cocktails €6.* ☼ *Open Tu-Su 6:30pm-1am. Aperitivo buffet with drinks 6:30-10pm, €10.*

GOOD CAFFE
V. di San Dorotea 8/9

🍽&ᵗ⁽ᵗ⁾ᵗᵗ CAFE, BAR
☎06 97 27 79 79 ▦www.goodcaffe.it

Alcohol really finds a home here—a refrigerator full of white wine, a bookshelf full of red, and an armoire of liquor make the place especially homey. Of course, the twinkling lights, colorful chandeliers, and festive red walls don't take away from the comfy feel. Most customers come for casual conversation over drinks, but live jazz and blues Monday and Thursday and a DJ on weekend nights make Good Caffe a better-than-good place to check out any night.

✂ *From P. San G. de Matha, take V. di San Dorotea as it veers left.* **i** *Free Wi-Fi.* Ⓢ *Beer on tap €4.50-7. Cocktails €8.* ☼ *Open daily 8am-2am. Happy hour aperitivo 7-9pm, €5 with wine, €8 with cocktails.*

BEIGE
V. Politeama 13-14

🍽&ᵗ❋ BAR
☎06 58 33 06 86 ▦www.beigeroma.com

Somehow swanky black and white decor equals...Beige? Distinguishing itself from some of the more low-key establishments nearby with its plush stools, modern black arches, and dark green lounge, Beige caters to a sophisticated crowd all evening long. Its 12+ page menu, organized solely into pre- and post-dinner beverages, gives a drink to match nearly every hour until 2am. Mellow music and plenty of seats.

✦ *From Ponte Sisto, turn left onto Lungotevere Raffaello Sanzio, head down the stairs in the piazza on the right, and make a left.* ⑤ *Cocktails €8.* ⏰ *Open Tu-Su 7:30pm-2am. Aperitivo happy hour 7:30pm-10:30pm.*

BACCANALE
✦ ఈ ♈ ⌂ BAR

V. della Lungaretta 81   ☎06 45 44 82 68

While many places down the way may tout classier decor, none can approach Baccanale's prices or spirit. Bacchus would indeed be proud. The dark interior is made more colorful by dozens of alcohol flags and posters, an entire row of Aperol and Bacardi lining the wall, and a display of currency donated by the teems of international students that have visited over the years. Though their famous mojitos go for only €5, if you're with a crowd, you might consider ordering a pitcher for a mere €15 or 2L of Peroni for €18. Pop and R and B during the evening keep the crowds young.

✦*From Vle. Trastevere, turn right onto V. della Lungaretta.* ⑤ *Drafts €3.50-5. Cocktails €5-7.* ⏰ *Open Tu-Su 9:30am-2am.*

MA CHE SIETE VENUTI A FÀ
◉ఈ ♈ BAR

V. Benedetta 25

Cocktails? Wine? Forget it all. Ma Che Siete Venuti A Fà's 16 taps and keg-lined interior will make you fall in love with beer—and only beer—all over again; even the lamps are made from recycled beer bottles. There is no "special" because, according to the friendly owner, they're all special; check out the chalkboard menu up front to order one of their constantly changing international brews. Customers can either retreat to what is essentially a wooden box in back or spill out onto the street as crowds accumulate in the early evening. Quiet music and tight quarters make casual conversation with *amici* about the only thing possible.

✦ *From P. Trilussa, turn right onto V. Benedetta.* ⑤ *Bottled beer €3.50-5, draft €4-6.* ⏰ *Open daily 3pm-2am.*

NY.LON
✦ఈ ♈ ⌂ BAR

Lungotevere Raffaello Sanzio 8b   ☎06 58 34 06 92 ▣www.nylonroma.it

If its name indicates anything, NY.LON will seem somewhat like a hip downtown loft in NY—exposed white brick, sky-high ceilings, and a slightly raw but modern feel. The red-lit bar and matching couches fill up around 7pm for a happy hour of fresh *aperitivo* and drinks (*€10 nightly until 10:30pm*). Thursdays, a live band sets up camp downstairs. The slightly quieter upstairs gives customers even more options.

✦ *From Ponte Garibaldi, turn right onto L. Raffaello Sanzio and walk 5min.* ⑤ *Beer and wine €6. Cocktails €8.* ⏰ *Open M 7pm-2am, W-Su 7pm-2am.*

CANTINA PARADISO
✦ఈ ⑽❄⌂ CAFE, BAR

V. San Francesco a Ripa 73   ☎06 58 99 799

It really is a little paradise here—stripped wooden tables topped with tiny lamps, red chandeliers and roses, cowprint stools, and purple beach chairs make for an unusual mix of rustic and couture. A lounge, wine bar, and cafe all in one, customers come to work (*free Wi-Fi*), dine (*vegetarian buffet €5, with drink €7*), or kick back for a mixed drink on the outside patio where you'll find a bit of beach and a bit of "cozy."

✦ *From P. San Sonnino, walk down Vle. Trastevere and turn left onto V. San Francesco a Ripa.* ⑤ *Beer €4. Wine €5. Cocktails €8-10.* ⏰ *Open daily noon-2am. Aperitivo buffet 6-9pm.*

D. J. BAR
Vicolo del Cinque 60

◉◐&Ⴠ CLUB, BAR
☎338 85 98 578

Who ever said size matters? Although the tiny upstairs occupies just barely a
street corner, this place packs a big punch with its loud music, colored lights,
and over 100 types of cocktails. Cool black-and-white wallpaper decorates the
upstairs, and a DJ blaring commercial tunes pumps up the crowd. The swanky
green bar with lit-up Red Bulls fills up around 10pm, while the bigger arena
downstairs gets crowded when people start wanting to dance.

✈ *From Santa Maria in Trastevere, veer into P. San Egidio and turn right onto Vicolo del Cinque.* Ⓢ
Shots €3. Beer €5. Cocktails €7. ⓏⒾ *Open daily 5pm-2am. Happy hour F-Sa 7-10pm.*

ENOTECA TRASTEVERE
V. della Lungaretta 86

◐&Ⴠ♨ ENOTECA
☎06 58 85 659 ▣www.enotecatrastevere.it

A quote by Oscar Wilde hangs on one of Enoteca Trastevere's stripped brick
walls: "Life is too short to drink mediocre wine." Enoteca Trastevere ensures
that you won't: bookshelves filled with bottle after bottle treat customers to only
the best. Though you can choose from one of their standby varieties, check out
the weekly special menu (with dessert suggestions to match) on your little table.
Indeed, it's hard to resist ordering a *limoncello* custard cake to go with your
glass *(€5)* when the dessert case is right in sight. If the old-fashioned interior
feels a bit dim for you, head outside to the comfy couches shaded by umbrellas
and plants.

✈ *From Largo San G. de Matha, turn right onto V. della Lungaretta.* Ⓢ *Hard liquor €3.50-6.50.*
Wine €3.5-10. Cocktails €6.50-8. Desserts €5-7. Ⓩ *Open M-Th noon-1am, F-Sa noon-2am, Su*
noon-1am. Happy hour M-F 6-8:30pm.

TERMINI AND SAN LORENZO

There are plenty of bars surrounding Termini, most of them close to hostels and thus
especially popular with students. If you plan on staying out late, travel with a group
and watch your purse. Stay away from the station as much as possible.

AI TRE SCALINI
V. Panisperna 251

◐⊗⊗((ŋ))Ⴠ CAFE, ENOTECA
☎06 48 90 74 95

Look down V. Panisperna and you'll see two things: a hanging curtain of vines
and a crowd of people. The *sorridenti* customers at this socially-conscious *eno-*
teca and cafe often spill out onto the street, wine glass in hand. Inside, the giant
blackboard menu features only locally grown and seasonally harvested products
hailing from Lazio. Their *bufala con miele di tartufo (€6)* is especially good. The
beverage selection is just as sustainable, including organic and hand-cultivated
wines (the Sangiovese was made by prison inmates); the restaurant also refuses to sell bottled mineral water. Blues in the background, frescoed walls, tiny
tables, and dim lights make this the perfect spot for casual conversation, a game
of chess (check out their antique set), or some Roman history catch-up (their
mini bookshelf should help). Before leaving, make sure to sign the guestbook,
which has more than four years of scribbles in it, and check out the *piscina*
(male toilet), where vintage photos of nude women tastefully decorate the wall.

✈ *From the intersection of V. XIV Maggio and V. Nazionale (near Trajan's column), walk up V. Pa-*
nisperna. Ⓘ *Free Wi-Fi. 10% discount at lunch hours.* Ⓢ *Beer on tap €3-5. Wine €3.50-6 per*
glass, €11-70 per bottle. Sfizi (bite-sized appetizers) €2.50-3; primi €3-8. Ⓩ *Open M-F noon-1am,*
Sa-Su 6pm-1am. Aperitivo hour 6-9pm.

YELLOW BAR
V. Palestro 40

◐&Ⴠ♨ CAFE, BAR
☎06 49 38 26 82 ▣www.the-yellow.com

Feeling a bit homesick for college, or perhaps just your home country? Whatever
locale you have a hankering for, the international folks at Yellow Bar are sure
to cure your case of the blues. Next door to its hopping hostel, this bar caters

to a mixed crowd of travelers and students who come for cheap drinks, relaxed music, and good company. Order one of their special cocktails like the ⬛**Chuck Norris Roundhouse Kick to the Face Crazy Shot** (don't ask what's in it—just drink up) before heading downstairs to the beer pong room, fully equipped with two regulation-size tables and an official list of house rules. If you have to sit out a couple of rounds, be sure to scribble something on the white brick already covered in both lewd and lovely comments from past travelers. After the long night (or, shall we say, early morning), there's nothing like a "full American Breakfast" to get your day going—or perhaps prepare you for a nap.

✚ Ⓜ*Termini. From V. Marsala, near track 1, walk down V. Marghera and then turn left onto V. Palestro.* ***i*** *Pub quiz on W €5. Open bar on F €15.* Ⓢ *Cocktails €8. Beer pong pitchers €14.50. Happy hour spirits €2.50; wine €1.50.* 🕐 *Open daily 7:30am-2am. Kitchen open 7:30am-noon. Happy hour 3-9pm.*

TWINS

⬤⊗ ☂ ❄ BAR, CLUB

V. Giolitti 67 ☎366 13 58 140 or 06 48 24 932 ▪www.twinbar.com

Flashing lights, loud music, and red walls set a lively stage for the international crowd that packs Twins every night. Located just outside of Termini's station, this club is as busy as the street outside. The front bars cater to those seeking more of a lounge, while the back room and its private outdoor courtyard pack it in with loud beats and dancing. Nightly themes ranging from Brazilian to house music keep the crowd mixed. One of the stops on a €20 pub crawl featuring two long drinks at each club (check website for details). Though it's easy to get carried away here, keep your wits about you and your wallet close to your body Termini Station is known for pickpockets.

✚ Ⓜ*Termini. Right outside of station.* ***i*** *Latin night on Tu. Brazilian night on Th House/Commercial most other nights.* Ⓢ *Beer €3.50-5. Cocktails €8. Primi €7-13; secondi €12-23.* 🕐 *Open daily 6am-2am. Happy hour 5-7pm.*

DRUID'S DEN

⬤♿ ☂ ⟋ IRISH PUB

V. San Martino ai Monti 28 ☎06 48 90 47 81 ▪www.druidspubrome.com

Wait, we're in Italy? You'd never know it in this green-lit Irish pub, the second oldest in the country. The brick walls are lined with memorabilia from the owner's frequent trips back home, an assortment ranging from flags to wooden place-name placards. Popular mostly with Italians and expats in the neighborhood, this is the place to come for quality drinks against a backdrop of national soccer games (though they've been known to take homesick American requests for baseball) or traditional live Irish music, depending on the night.

✚ Ⓜ*B: Cavour. Walk down V. Giovanni and veer left onto V. San Martino ai Monti.* ***i*** *Live music F-Sa around 10pm.* Ⓢ *Special whiskeys €4-5. Cocktails €4.50. Drafts €5.50. Happy hour prices about €1 less.* 🕐 *Open daily 5pm-2am. Happy hour 5-8:30pm.*

L'ISOLA CHE NON C'È

⬤♿ (⟋) ☂ ⟋ LIBRERIA

V. San Martino ai Monti 7/A ☎06 48 82 134

Lavender walls and a sleek wooden catwalk lined with books and bottles make up the little *isola* that, according to its name, "is not here." (Maybe that's because it's a paradise?) Books are only a starting point for discussion, an excuse for intellectual folk to gather over good wine and food. Occasional lectures on environmental concerns and live music on select nights provide other reasons to pop by this place and see what's going on. While classically Italian in its low-key style, Isola's tiny menu is a bit spunkier, with specials like smoked swordfish and pineapple or vegetarian delights like tabbouleh with zucchini.

✚ Ⓜ*B: Cavour. Walk down V. Giovanni and veer left onto V. San Martino ai Monti.* ***i*** *Free Wi-Fi. Live music most Th and Sa. Free buffet with purchase of a drink.* Ⓢ *Wine and beer €3-5. Cocktails €4-8. Primi €7-11.* 🕐 *Open M-Th 11am-midnight, F-Sa 11am-2am.*

THE FIDDLER'S ELBOW IRISH PUB

V. dell'Olmata 43 ☎06 48 72 110 www.thefiddlerselbow.com

So, what exactly is a "fiddler's elbow"? A musician might say it's a sore elbow caused from the up-and-down motion of playing the fiddle, but a good Irishman will tell you it's actually the result of raising beer flask to mouth so often that the elbow stiffens. They're more prone to the latter injury here, the oldest Irish pub in Rome, which has been liquoring up The Eternal City since 1976. Renowned in the neighborhood for its family history, congenial company, and great drinks, this pub brings in everyone from the backpacker to the neighborhood expat to the sophisticated businessman stopping in after a day's work. The wooden interior is speckled with objects from the Emerald isle and full of loud conversation. Locals love playing piano on open-mike night.

[M]Termini. Walk toward P. Santa Maggiore and then down V. Paolina. Turn left onto W. Quattro Cantoni and left onto V. Olmata. i Open mike Th at 10pm. Pool and dart room in back. $ Beer €5-5.50, €4-4.50 during happy hour. Open daily 5pm-2am. Happy hour 5-8:30pm.

OLD STATION PUB AND CLUB CAFE, CLUB

P. Santa Maria Maggiore ☎06 47 46 612 www.oldstationmusicpub.it

You'd never know that beneath the old-fashioned cafe upstairs a raucous party of 20-somethings is raging. Come here for gelato, panini, and coffee with your parents; come for body shots, cocktails, and dancing until 4am with your friends. Beats ranging from reggae to house to R and B spin every night in the wooden "den" downstairs, where people either dance or lounge in one of the three rooms. Check out their website for themed parties and special events.

On the corner of P. Santa Maria Maggiore. i Karaoke on W. $ Cover €10; includes 2 drinks. Shots €3-4. Beer €5-6. Cocktails €8. Cafe open daily 7am-11pm. Bar and club open daily 9pm-4am.

CHARITY CAFE JAZZ CLUB BAR, JAZZ CLUB

V. Panisperna 68 ☎06 47 82 58 81 www.charitycafe.it

Though the long black benches are lined up like pews, you won't hear any classical choir here—only exceptional live jazz, all night, every night. The terra-cotta walls are covered with pictures of famed musicians as well as scribbles from past customers singing their praise. Great, well-priced drinks during happy hour make the jazz sound even smoother.

From the intersection of V. XIV Maggio and V. Nazionale (near Trajan's column), walk up V. Panisperna. i Check their monthly calendar for a schedule of nightly shows. $ Beer €6-7, during happy hour €3.50-4.50. Cocktails €8/4.50. Open in summer M-Sa 6pm-2am; in winter daily 6pm-2am. Happy hour daily 6-9pm.

TESTACCIO AND OSTIENSE

Off Rome's central map, Testaccio and Ostiense cater to in-the-know partygoers: locals who've sought out the best clubs and the savvy tourists or students who've sought out the locals. The strip of clubs, restaurants, and lounges surrounding **Via di Monte Testaccio** begs to be explored, though as the evening rolls on longer lines make it harder to gain admission. The streets closer to the train station tend to have smaller, low-key establishments that stay open late, an option if you don't feel like heavy-duty clubbing.

CONTE STACCIO BAR, CONCERT VENUE

V. di Monte Testaccio 65/b ☎06 57 28 97 12 www.myspace.com/contestaccio

If bumping and grinding to DJ'd music isn't your thing, then you'll probably love Conte Staccio. Live music ranging from indie rock to electro-funk draws a mixed crowd of internationals and not-so-mainstream students and locals. Two rooms—one with a stage, the other with tables for late-night nibbles—give you the option to enjoy the music from afar or rock out up close, though the

rome

smallish quarters mean that the huge stereos might blow your ears out before long, regardless of room. Head to the outdoor steps if you need a break from the music, but chances are the crowd outside will be just as packed.

♬ ⓂB: Piramide. Walk up V. Marmorata towards the river, turn left onto V. Galvani ,and veer left onto V. di Monte Testaccio. Ⓢ Beer €2.50-5. Wine €3-5. Cocktails €6-7. Pasta €8. Secondi €10. ⓩ Open daily 8pm-5am. Restaurant 8pm-3am. Music 11pm-5am.

🏴 AKAB   ➤&♥❀♨ CLUB
V. di Monte Testaccio 69   ☎06 57 25 05 85 🖥www.akabcave.com

It's hard to tell what's inside and what's out at Akab, where the switch is so subtle that you don't know if your feeling is a cool summer breeze or some powerful A/C. During the summer most of the action starts in the central room, as live bands warm up the crowd and customers load up at the blue-lit bar staffed by buff bartenders. When the DJ starts, head back to room after room of dimly lit lounges and dance halls that, with ramps and flashing lights galore, feel somewhat like a psychedelic amusement park for adults. During the winter, the neon-colored upstairs lounge opens to accommodate the crowds. Though the cover and drinks cost a pretty penny, you'll be paying for one of Testaccio's hottest clubs and crowds.

♬ ⓂB: Piramide. Walk up V. Marmorata towards the river, turn left onto V. Galvani, and veer left onto V. di Monte Testaccio. ⓘ Beer €5 on Tu. Electronic on Tu. House on Th. Rock on F. Commercial and house on Sa. Ⓢ Cover €10-20 on F-Sa includes 1 drink. Cocktails and beer €10. ⓩ Open Tu 11:30pm-4:30am, Th-Sa 11:30pm-4:30am.

COYOTE   ➤⊗♥&♨ BAR, CLUB
V. di Monte Testaccio 48/B   ☎340 24 45 874 🖥www.coyotebar.it

Cowboys might ride off into the sinking western sun, but night visitors at Coyote will wander home as the sun rises in the east. Get here early to avoid Colosseum-sized lines and an entrance fee to match. Once inside, ascend the curving ramp to a huge outdoor patio where beer flows generously under green and red lights. Once the clock strikes midnight, what started out as a casual cocktail bar becomes a full-fledged disco spinning house, Latin, and Top 40 tunes. The wooden floors give the place an extra bounce as the stereo cranks up and the crowds begin to move. If you're sober enough before leaving, check out the trail of American license plates lining the wall—last time we checked, the eastern seaboard was heavily outweighed by the wild west and the sultry south. New Yorkers, donate a plate, please?

♬ ⓂB: Piramide. Walk up V. Marmorata toward the river, turn left onto V. Galvani, and veer left onto V. di Monte Testaccio. ⓘ No food—hit Top Five downstairs if you get hungry. Ⓢ Cover €10 F-Sa after midnight. Beer and wine €5. Cocktails €8. ⓩ Open daily 9pm-5am. Bar 9pm-midnight. Disco midnight-5am.

ON THE ROX   ➤&♥ BAR
V. Galvani 54   ☎06 45 49 29 75

The lively crowd that frequents this huge lounge still "rox" out big time, even if the place isn't technically a club. Rustic arches offset by twinkling chandeliers give the place a spunky vibe that matches its nightly mix of students and locals. Pop music plays in the background, but the real buzz comes from conversation and the cheers of customers watching sports on the flatscreen TVs. With great nightly specials, even Tu becomes an ideal day for a night out.

♬ ⓂB: Piramide. Walk up V. Marmorata toward the river and turn left onto V. Galvani. ⓘ Pitcher night on M, €10. Buy 1 get 1 free on W. Ladies' night 2-for-1 cocktails on Th. Live music 4 nights per week in the winter. Student special long drinks €5. Happy hour buffet €7. Ⓢ Shots €2.50. Beer €4. Cocktails €6. Food €6-8. ⓩ Open M-W 6pm-4am, Th-Su 6pm-5am. Happy hour 6-10pm.

nightlife · testaccio and ostiense

LA CASA DELLA PACE

◉⊗❣⌂ CULTURAL CENTER, CONCERT VENUE

V. di Monte Testaccio 22 ☎329 54 66 296 ▣www.myspace.com/bigbang

More than a nightlife haven for artsy and intellectual folks, this "House of Peace" holds multicultural events, art exhibitions, and live music performances throughout the year. In the evening, join a truly mixed crowd on any of the floors as live music ranging from reggae to electro-funk plays on the stripped-wood dance floor. Multiple adjoining rooms, including the upstairs gallery space, slowly fill up with beer sippers, conversationalists, performers, and artists. Drop by Friday or Saturday for La Casa's "Big Bang" nights or check online for a schedule of upcoming events. Be sure to try out the ▧**mosaic-tiled bathroom,** which rivals some of Rome's greatest—bathrooms, that is.

⚑ Ⓜ*B: Piramide. Walk up V. Marmorata towards the river, turn left onto V. Galvani, and veer left onto V. di Monte Testaccio.* *i* *€7 membership card required to enter; buy at the desk, and reuse for all events.* Ⓢ *Shots €2.50. Beer €2.50-4. Cocktails €6.* ☼ *Open M-Th 3-10pm, F-Sa 10pm-5am, Su 3-10pm.*

CARUSO

◐⊗❣❋ CLUB, LATIN

V. di Monte Testaccio 36 ☎06 57 45 019 ▣www.carusocafe.com

Move your hips to merengue rather than the same old pop mix. The distinctive orange glow in this club's cluster of dance rooms will warm you up for dancing; cool (though slightly pricey) drinks and strong A/C will cool you down when things get too hot. Plenty of tables and padded chairs sit beside rather random Buddha sculptures, so take this opportunity to lounge next to the big enlightened guy. Live bands take the small stage when the DJ steps down.

⚑ Ⓜ*B: Piramide. Walk up V. Marmorata toward the river, turn left onto V. Galvani, and veer left onto V. di Monte Testaccio.* *i* *Live and DJ'd Latin music.* Ⓢ *Cover Su-Th €8; F-Sa €10; includes 1st drink. Beer €6. Cocktails €6-11.* ☼ *Open M-Th 11pm-2am, F-Sa 11pm-4am, Su 11pm-2am.*

VIA NOMENTANA

V. Nomentana is near the cluster of hostels surrounding Termini, making it a great option for students wanting to venture a bit further. Good bars and discotecas which open and close seasonally are always popping up. Many of the winter clubs close once summer hits and students at Erasmus go home, so bars are generally a more sure-fire option throughout the year.

▧ BOEME

◐⊗❣❋ CLUB

V. Velletri 13 ☎06 84 12 212 ▣www.boeme.it

An expansive downstairs disco lined entirely in black and white stripes and funky flowered wallpaper brings in a happening crowd on the weekends. Multiple platforms for dancing, flashing lights, a sound system blaring house and Top 40 hits, a huge bar, and neon accents create a psychedelic experience for partiers willing to drop a few euros.

⚑ *From P. Fiume, walk up V. Nizza and turn left onto V. Velletri.* Ⓢ *Cover €15-20; includes 1st drink. Drinks €10.* ☼ *Open F-Sa 11pm-5am.*

NEW AGE CAFE

◉♿❣⌂ BAR, CAFE

V. Nizza 23

Whether it's 3am or 3pm, this corner cafe will have music playing and beverages of some sort flowing. The extensive menu features everything from 7am eggs and panini to an extensive buffet of complimentary appetizers during their nightly happy hour. Lounge on the outdoor patio, climb the spiral staircase to the mini balcony up top, or grab a stool at the bar while you sip your mixed drink or cappuccino. This little island in the middle of the city is made for relaxation at midday or drinks at midnight. Even if the caffeine doesn't pick you up, the upbeat, commercial tunes playing from dawn to...dawn certainly will.

⚑ *From P. Fiume, walk down V. Nizza.* Ⓢ *Shots €2.30. Draft beer €3.50-5; L €12. Cocktails €6.50. Lunch panini and primi €3-5.* ☼ *Open daily 7am-4:30am. Aperitivo bar 6:30-9:30pm.*

rome

arts and culture

"Arts and culture?" you ask. "Isn't that Rome, *itself*?" Psshh. Well, yes, Renaissance paintings, archaeological ruins, and Catholic churches do count. But aside from these antiquated lures, Rome offers an entertainment scene that makes it much more than a city of yore. Soccer games might not quite compare to man-fights-lion spectacles, but with hundreds of screaming Italians around, it comes close. If you need more ideas, check Rome's city website (🖳*www.060608.it*) for a schedule of upcoming events ranging from live music to festivals. Other good resources are *Romac'è* (🖳*www.romace.it*) and 🖳www.aguestinrome.com. Or just wander the streets scouting out advertisements and flyers, which are nearly as common as ruins. In Rome, it's definitely possible to experience "arts and culture" in places where an alarm won't go off when you get too close.

JAZZ

Unfortunately, most jazz places close during the summer months, either re-opening in September or heading outdoors. **Alexanderplatz Jazz Club,** one of Rome's most popular of its kind and Italy's oldest, shuts its doors mid-June and hosts a spectacular program of outdoor performances at the Villa Celimontana. (☎*06 58 33 57 81; call M-F 9:30am-5:30pm ⚐ Ⓜ️B: Colosseo. Concerts at V. della Navicella. ⓘ Ticket sales at V. della Navicella start at 7:30pm. 🕔 Doors open at 9pm; shows start at 10:10pm.)* At other times of the year, Alexanderplatz can be found at V. Ostia 9. (☎*06 58 33 57 81 9:30am-2pm, ☎06 39 74 21 71 6pm on. Ⓢ Monthly card €10, yearly €30. 🕔 Open 8pm-2am; concerts at 10pm.)* For a current schedule of other jazz events check out 🖳www.romace.it, 🖳www.romajazz.com, or 🖳www.casajazz.it.

▩ FONCLEA ●●⊗⊘🍸 VATICAN CITY

V. Crescenzio 82A ☎06 68 96 302 🖳www.fonclea.it

Crowds linger on the street and trickle down the steps into this den of live jazz and food. Amid hanging skis and teapots, nightly performers pay homage to anything from swing to The Beatles. Munch on chips and guacamole during the *aperitivo* hour while trumpeters and saxophonists warm up their lips. Drinks and food are a bit overpriced, but with music this good, who's thinking of eating?

⚐ Ⓜ️A: Ottaviano. From P. Risorgimento, head away from the Vatican on V. Cresenzio. Ⓢ Cover F-Sa €6. Beer €7. Cocktails €10. 🕔 Open from mid-Sept to mid-June M-Th 7pm-2am, F-Sa 7pm-3am, Su 7pm-2am. Music at 9:30pm. Aperitivo buffet 7-8:30pm.

CHARITY CAFE JAZZ CLUB ●⊗⊘🍸✳ TERMINI

V. Panisperna 68 ☎06 47 82 58 81 🖳www.charitycafe.it

Charity's a rarity in that it's open year-round.

⚐ Ⓜ️B: Cavour. From the intersection of V. XIV Maggio and V. Nazionale (near Trajan's column), walk up V. Panisperna. Ⓢ Beer €6-7. Cocktails from €8. 🕔 Open in summer M-Sa 6pm-2am; in fall, winter, and spring daily 6pm-2am.

BIG MAMA ●●♿🍸 TRASTEVERE

Vicolo San Francesco a Ripa 18 ☎06 58 12 551 🖳www.bigmama.it

She's not just a "Mama"—when it comes to the blues, she's a *big* mama. Nightly concerts by aspiring and well-known performers including jazz and blues guitarist Scott Henderson and rock singer-songwriter Elliott Murphy make this self-proclaimed "House of Blues" a place for all kinds of musical fare.

⚐ Bus #75 or 170 or tram #8. From P. Garibaldi, walk down Vle. Trastevere, turn left onto V. San Francesco a Ripa, and veer right onto the tiny vicolo. Ⓢ Year-long membership card (€14) or monthly card (€8) grants free admission to most shows. A few big shows require an additional ticket fee. 🕔 Open daily from late Sept to late May 9pm-1:30am. Music at 10:30pm.

CLASSICAL MUSIC AND OPERA

TEATRO DELL'OPERA

🎫♿ TERMINI

P. Beniamino Gigli 7 ☎06 48 16 02 55 or 06 48 17 003 🖥www.operaroma.it

Once you've caught a glimpse of the 6m chandelier and frescoes by **Annibale Brugnoli** gracing this four-tier theater, you'll be happy you shelled out the extra euro even if arias, pirouettes, and musical overtures aren't exactly your thing. If you really did just come for the opera and ballet, you might consider Teatro dell'Opera's affiliated newer and less ornate **Teatro Nazionale** across the street, which has cheaper tickets. From June 30 to early fall, additional performances are held outdoors at the **Baths of Caracalla** *(Terme di Caracalla)*.

 # [M]A: Repubblica. Walk down V. Nazionale, then turn left onto V. Firenze and left onto V. del Viminale. i 2nd location (Teatro Nazionale) at V. del Viminale 51. Tickets can also be bought online at 🖥www.amitsrl.it. $ At Teatro dell'Opera opera €17-130, ballet €11-65; at Teatro Nazionale opera €30, ballet €20. Students and over 65 receive 25% discount. Check website for last-minute tickets with 25% discount. ⏰ Regular box office open Tu-Sa 9am-5pm, Su 9am-1:30pm, and 1hr. before performance-15min. after its start. Box office for Baths of Caracalla open Tu-Sa 10am-4pm, Su 9am-1:30pm.

ACCADEMIA NAZIONALE DI SANTA CECILIA

🎫 VILLA BORGHESE

Vle. Pietro de Coubertin 30 ☎06 80 82 058; ☎06 89 29 82 for tickets 🖥www.santacecilia.it

Founded in 1585 as a conservatory, the Accademia is now both a place of training for aspiring and renowned musicians and a professional symphonic orchestra. Past conductors have included **Debussy, Strauss, Stravinsky,** and **Toscanini.** Concerts are held in three massive halls located in the Parco della Musica near Flaminio, so if you're as much into the great outdoors as you are into music, this is the perfect venue.

 # [M]A: Flaminio and then tram #2 to P. Euclide. Or take the special line "M" from Termini (every 15min. starting at 5pm) to Auditorium. Last bus after last performance. i Box office at Largo Luciano Berio 3. $ Tickets €18-47. ⏰ Box office open daily 11am-8pm.

TEATRO FLAIANO

🎫🚭 CENTRO STORICO

V. Santo Stefano del Cacco 15 ☎06 67 96 496 🖥www.piccolalirica.com

Contemporary and innovative takes on traditional opera give this small theater

culture on the tiber

One hardly needs a map to arrive at a *piazza* or historical sight while in Rome: the streets are as dotted with churches and statues as they are with *gelaterie*. A real reason to take out the map again is to navigate a 450m section of the Tiber River, which, since 2005, has been the site of a different type of *piazza*. "Piazza Tevere," a straight strip of water between Ponte Sisto and Ponte Mazzini, has become a nexus of contemporary art installations ranging from projected animations inspired by Roman history to live music and performances.

Each year, the project ("Teverterno") brings together an international group of artists to create public pieces that deal with modern-day cultural and environmental concerns. Envisioned as a way to revitalize the Tiber, which had for many years been a forgotten resource for Romans and tourists, Teverterno provides a refreshing chance to see current work in a setting other than a museum or gallery. Everyone loves a fresco, but larger-than-life projections of the historic she-wolf on the river's embankment walls are hard to beat. For more information and a schedule of installations, visit 🖥www.tevereterno.it.

a definite edge on other companies. Shows are kept short—around 90min.—and highlight particularly melodramatic moments of already melodramatic works, including *Tosca* and *Carmen* in recent seasons. If you don't want to sit through three hours of arias, the productions' brevity and creative interpretations will certainly please.

✂ *Tram #8. From V. Corso Vittorio Emanuele II, turn left onto V. del Gesu and right onto V. Santo Stefano del Cacco.* Ⓢ *Tickets €44-60.* ⌚ *Box office open Tu-Sa 3-7pm; general office open Tu-Sa 11am-7pm. Shows at 8pm.*

ROCK AND POP

Live music can be heard throughout the city. ▧www.060608.it is a great resource for information on upcoming shows.

ROMA INCONTRA IL MONDO
Villa Ada at V. di Ponte Salario

✒ VILLA BORGHESE, PARIOLI, FLAMINIO
☎06 41 73 47 12 ▧www.villaada.org

This venue hosts an eclectic mix of rock, reggae, folk, and ethnic music at the large outdoor grounds of Villa Ada, near the Villa Borghese. Most of the acts are international performers on tour, many hailing from as nearby (if you can call it that) as Africa to as far away as Australia. Recent ones include Habib Koite and Bamada (Mali), Luciano (Jamaica), and local Christina Dona.

✂ ⓂA: Flaminio, then Ferrovie Urbane bound for Civitacastellana; get off at Campi Sportivi. Enter the park at Vle. della Moschea and veer right down the winding V. di Ponte Salario. Ⓢ Tickets €5-15. ⌚ Concerts from mid-June to early Aug. Concert area opens at 8pm; concerts start at 10pm and usually last until 2am.

FIESTA
Ippodrome delle Capanelle, V. Áppia Nuova 1245

✒ SOUTHERN ROME
☎348 88 89 950 ▧www.fiesta.it

This huge concert venue complete with restaurant, bar, disco, and lounge area features popular Latin performers most nights of the week. The festival wouldn't be complete without crowds in the thousands and so much dancing that your hips will start to feel like those of an octogenarian. Big names include Don Omar, La India, Los 4, and the legendary **Ricky Martin.**

✂ Bus #664 to Colli Albani or ⓂA: Cinecittà and then bus #654 down V. delle Capanelle. *i* Buy tickets online at ▧www.greenticket.it or ▧www.ticketone.it or in person at concert venue. Ⓢ Tickets €10-35. Weekday performances usually cheaper than weekends. ⌚ Concerts June-Aug at 9:30pm. Concert venue open for ticket sale M-Th 8:30pm-1am, F-Sa 8:30pm-2am, Su 8:30pm-1am.

SPECTATOR SPORTS

STADIO OLIMPICO
V. del Foro Italico 1

 OUTSKIRTS
▧www.asroma.it, www.sslazio.it

Soccer matches—the favorite game of the Romans since their gladiator days—are held here. The stadium serves as the battleground for **A.S. Roma** and **S.S. Lazio.** The easiest way to tell them apart is by color (red and sky blue, respectively). Tickets aren't easy to come by: check the spots below or ask around.

✂ ⓂA: Ottaviano. Then take bus #32 to Piazzale della Farnesina. *i* Tickets can be purchased at the stadium, online at sites like ▧www.listicket.it, or at various ticketing spots around the city such as Lazio Point (V. Farini 34/36 ☎06 48 26 688). Ⓢ Tickets €20-80. ⌚ Most matches Sept-May Su afternoons. Lazio Point box office open daily 9pm-1am and 2:30-6pm.

shopping

When it comes to shopping, it would be significantly easier to make a list of what Rome *doesn't* have than what it does. Fashionista, artista, or "intelligista," you won't leave Rome unsatisfied, though your pocketbook might be significantly lighter. European chains like **United Colors of Benetton, Tezenis, Motivi,** and even **H and M** speckle the city. Those with a taste for high fashion should head to the Piazza di Spagna region, Rome's equivalent of Fifth Ave., which is home to the regular gamut of designer stores: **D and G, Valentino,** and **Prada,** to name a few. Smaller (though no less costly) boutiques dominate the Centro Storico. Major thoroughfares like V. del Corso, C. Cavour, V. Nazionale, and V. Cola di Rienzo abound with cheap clothing stores touting a similar collection of tight, teeny-bopper glitz and fare that comes unattached to a brand name. The regions around Termini, Vle. Trastevere, and the Vatican contain a fair number of street vendors selling shoes, lingerie, dresses, and sunglasses, usually for under €15. Established open-air markets will have a bigger selection.

DEPARTMENT STORES

Everyone needs a department store to stock the basics, whether that means Gucci underwear at discounted prices or jeans and a sweater to cover up at the Vatican. Expect to find everything from makeup to household products to entire clothing wardrobes at most stores.

LA RINASCENTE   ✦⊗❈ PIAZZA DI SPAGNA
P. Colonna 195/199   ☎06 67 84 209 ▪www.rinascente.it
Glamorous, big, and well stocked, La Rinascente allows you to save a couple of euro by offering those coveted designer brands from around the block on V. dei Condotti on their discounted clothes racks. A good selection of makeup and accessories on the first floor makes way for clothing upstairs and down. With

rome

spagna stores

It's not Milan. It's not Paris. It's Rome—and that's no small thing. The area around Piazza di Spagna has all the glitz you might want—ice-cold stores with ice-cold staff hovering about making sure you don't paw through their precious items. You'd think you were in another museum or something. Here's where to find the priciest and snobbiest of stores:

- **DOLCE AND GABBANA.** (*P. di Spagna 94* ☎*06 69 38 08 70* ▪*www.dolcegabbana.it* ◷ *Open M-Sa 10:30am-7:30pm, Su 10:30am-2:30pm and 3:30-7:30pm.*)

- **EMPORIO ARMANI.** (*V. del Babuino 140* ☎*06 32 21 581* ▪*www.giorgioarmani.com* ◷ *Open M-Sa 10am-7pm.*)

- **GUCCI.** (*V. Condotti 8* ☎*06 679 0405* ▪*www.gucci.com* ◷ *Open M-Sa 10am-7:30pm, Su 10am-7pm.*)

- **PRADA.** (*V. Condotti 92/95* ☎*06 679 0897* ▪*www.prada.com* ◷ *Open M-F 10am-7:30pm, Sa 10am-8pm, Su 10am-7:30pm.*)

- **VALENTINO.** (*V. del Babuino 61 and V. dei Condotti 15* ☎*06 36 00 19 06 and* ☎*06 67 39 420* ▪*www.valentino.com* ◷ *Open daily 10am-7pm.*)

- **VERSACE.** (*V. Bocca di Leone 26/27* ☎*06 67 80 521* ▪*www.versace.com* ◷ *Open M-Sa 10am-7pm, Su 2pm-7pm.*)

the designer selection of lingerie, you could be spending three times the money on one third the material. The store also has a tax refund office.

✈ *Bus #116.* ✪ *Open daily 10am-9pm.*

COIN
●&❄ VATICAN CITY

V. Cola di Rienzo 173 ☎06 36 00 42 98 ▇www.coin.it

With a generous selection of everything you might need in both designer and basic varieties, COIN is a good place to come for hours of rack-sorting, bargain-hunting, euro-dropping, and, if that line at the Vatican has left you in need of a restroom, peeing.

✈ Ⓜ*A: Ottaviano. Head down V. Ottaviano and turn onto V. Cola di Rienzo from P. Risorgimento.* ✪ *Open M-Sa 10am-8pm, Su 10:30am-8pm.*

UPIM
●&❄ TERMINI

V. Gioberti 64 ☎06 44 65 579 ▇www.upim.it

Come here to dress your house rather than your bod. A well-priced selection of furniture, cookware, bedding, and toys outdoes the basic clothing, most of which is seasonal. Dress up the simple lines of the store's garments with some makeup, which has taken over the first floor in full force.

✈ *Near Termini, across from Basilica Santa Maria Maggiore.* ✪ *Open M-Sa 9am-8:30pm, Su 9:30am-8:30pm.*

OVIESSE
●&❄ TRASTEVERE

Vle. Trastevere 62 ☎06 58 33 36 33 ▇www.oviesse.com

Oviesse stocks a somewhat small collection of cheap, seasonal clothes for women and men: it's nothing special, but hey, you're wearing something, right? You might smell better than you look—the adjoining perfumerie's collection is comparable in size. There are also plenty of clothes for children and babies in case their fashion is more important than yours. Custom tailoring available.

✈ *Tram #8 down Vle. Trastevere.* ⓘ *Huge BILLA supermarket downstairs with great prices.* ✪ *Open M-Sa 8:30am-8pm, Su 9:30am-1:30pm and 4-8pm.*

OUTDOOR MARKETS

One of the few things that tourists and locals appreciate with equal enthusiasm are Rome's outdoor markets. You can find real bargains if you're willing to rifle through the crowds and stacks. With early hours on both their opening and closing ends, make sure you set that alarm. It's best to stick to official markets rather than take on merchants who set up shop individually. The fine for buying fake designer products rests on the buyer, not the seller, and can reach into the hundreds of thousands of euro.

▨ PORTA PORTESE
◉& TRASTEVERE

From P. di Porta Portese to P. Ippolito Nievo ▇www.portaportesemarket.it

The legs of this U-shaped market seem to extend forever and are of markedly different qualities. The longer V. Portuense is occupied by clones—vendors selling the same selection of cheap garments, toiletries, furniture, plastic jewelry, and shoes. We're talking 2m stacks of €2 clothes. If you're not exhausted by the madhouse (reminiscent of the hustling crowds of the Vatican Museums), make it to the antiques section where cooler treasures reside: old comic books, records, jewelry, and furniture.

✈ *Bus #40 to Largo Argentina and tram #8.* ✪ *Open Su 7am-2:30pm.*

MERCATO DI VIA SANNIO
◉& SOUTHERN ROME

V. Sannio ☎06 06 08

Cheap doesn't have to mean mass-produced and homogenous. Head here early to be the first of many to dig through mostly used clothes and items. A refreshing change from the ubiquitous street merchants spattering Rome, this large market

is the outdoor equivalent of a New York thrift store. Hipsters rejoice.
➜ Ⓜ A: San Giovanni. ⏰ Open M-Sa 9am-1:30pm.

CAMPO DEI FIORI — CENTRO STORICO

Campo dei Fiori

Thank God there's a place to buy fresh fruit and vegetables in the middle of overpriced trattorias: the lively Campo makes a great lunch spot if you don't mind the crowds. Giving as much flavor to the *piazza* during the day as bars give it at night, the market's open stalls vend cheap clothing, produce, fish, and even alcohol—no need to head to San Marino to pick up some absinthe.

➜ Bus #116 or tram #8. ⏰ Open M-Sa 7am-2:30pm.

MERCATO DELLE STAMPE — PIAZZA DI SPAGNA

Largo della Fontanella di Borghese

The small *piazza* and academic assortment of goods keep this market more manageable than most others in Rome—after all, how rowdy can a crowd get around a stack of books? Older crowds weave through the stalls, where you can find a curious selection of used books, old prints, and other dusty articles.

➜ Bus #224 or 913 to P. Imperatore or bus #492, 116, or 81. ⏰ Open M-Sa 9:30am-6pm.

essentials

PRACTICALITIES

- **TOURIST OFFICES: Comune di Roma** is Rome's official source for tourist information. Green **P.I.T. Info booths** are located throughout the city around most major sights. English-speaking staff provide limited information on hotel accommodations and events around the city, though plenty of free brochures and a city map are available. The booths also sell bus and Metro maps and the **Roma Pass** *(P.I.T. booth locations include V. Giovanni Giolitti 34 in Termini, P. Sidney Sonnino in Trastevere, and V. dei Fori Imperiali ☎06 06 08 for main info center; check online for individual booth numbers 🖳www.turismoroma.it, 🖳www.060608.com ⏰ Most locations open daily 9:30am-7pm; Termini location open 8am-8:30pm.)* **Enjoy Rome** has only 2 offices but provides much more comprehensive services, including tour bookings, information on bike and scooter rental, city maps, accommodations advice, and general orientation tips. They also publish a free city guide, *Enjoy Rome,* which details extensive information on transportation, city monuments and museums, suggested eating and entertainment, and daytrips. *(Main branch at V. Marghera 8A; 2nd office in P. San Pietro ☎06 44 56 890 🖳www.enjoyrome.com ➜ From Termini, walk down V. Marghera. ⏰ Both locations open M-F 8:30am-6pm, Sa 8:30am-2pm.)*
- **CURRENCY EXCHANGE AND BANKS: Money exchange** services are especially abundant near Termini and major sights but tend to have high rates. **Western Unions** are also readily available. *(⏰ Most banks open M-F 8:30am-1:30pm and 2:30-5pm.)*
- **LUGGAGE STORAGE: Termini Luggage Deposit.** *(☎06 47 44 777 🖳www.grandistazioni.it ➜ In Termini, below Track 24 in the Ala Termini wing. ℹ Takes bags of up to 20kg each for 5 days max. Cash only. $ €4 for 1st 5hr., €0.60 per hr. for 6th-12th hr., €0.20 per hr. thereafter. ⏰ Open daily 6am-11:50pm.)*
- **LOST PROPERTY: La Polizia Municipale** holds property a few days after it is lost; check the closest branch to where you lost your item. After that point, all lost property is sent to **Oggetti Smarriti,** run by the Comune di Roma. To retrieve an item, you must present a valid form of ID, a statement describing the lost item, and a cash payment of €2.97. *(Circonvallazione Ostiense 191 ☎06 67 69 3214 🖳www.060608.*

it or email oggettismarriti@comune.roma.it with questions ⇟ Ⓜ*B: Piramide or* Ⓜ*B: Garbatella.* ⏰ *Open M 8:30am-1pm, Tu 8:30am-1pm and 3-5pm, W 8:30am-1pm, Th 8:30am-5pm, F 8:30am-1pm.)* For property lost on Ⓜ**A lines:** *(P. dei Cinquecento* ☎*06 48 74 309* ⏰ *Open M 9:30am-12:30pm, W 9:30am-12:30pm, F 9:30am-12:30pm.)* Ⓜ**B lines:** *(Circonvallazione Ostiense 191* ☎*06 67 69 32 14* ⏰ *Open M-F 9am-1pm.)*

- **GLBT RESOURCES:** The Comune di Roma publishes a free guide to gay life in Rome, *AZ Gay*, with listings for gay-friendly restaurants, hotels, clubs, and bars. Pick one up at any P.I.T. Point. **ARCI-GAY** is a resource for homosexuality awareness, offering free courses, medical, legal, and psychological counseling, and advice on gay-friendly establishments in the city. *(V. Zabaglia 14* ☎*06 64 50 11 02;* ☎*800 71 37 13 for helpline* 🖳*www.arcigayroma.it* ⇟ Ⓜ*B: Piramide. Walk up V. Marmorata and turn right onto V. Alessandro Volta; it's at the intersection with V. Zabaglia.* ℹ *ARCI-GAY cards allow access to all events and services run by the program throughout Italy; €15 (valid 1 year).* ⏰ *Open M-Sa 4-8pm. Helpline open M 4-8pm, W-Th 4-8pm, Sa 4-8pm. Welcome Groups Th 6:15-9pm, Young People Groups F 6:30-9pm.)*

EMERGENCY!

- **POLICE: Police Headquarters.** *(V. San Vitale 15* ☎*06 46 86* ⇟ Ⓜ*A: Repubblica.)* **Carabinieri** have offices at V. Mentana 6 *(*☎*06 58 59 62 00* ⇟ *Near Termini.)* and P. Venezia (☎06 67 58 28 00). **City Police** *(P. del Collegio Romano 3* ☎*06 69 01 21).*
- **CRISIS LINES: Rape Crisis Line: Centro Anti-Violenza** provides legal, psychological, and medical counseling for women of all nationalities. *(V. di Torre Spaccata 157, V. di Villa Pamphili 100* ☎*06 23 26 90 49;* ☎*06 58 10 926* 🖳*www.differenzadonna.it* ⏰ *Phone lines open 24hr.)* **Samaritans** provides psychological counseling on the phone in many languages; call for in-person guidance. *(*☎*800 86 00 22* 🖳*www.samaritansonlus.org* ⏰ *Line operating daily 1-10pm.)*
- **LATE-NIGHT PHARMACIES: Farmacia della Stazione** is by Termini Station. *(P. dei Cinquecento 49/51* ☎*06 48 80 019* ⏰ *Open 24hr.)* **Farmacia Internazionale** is toward the Centro Storico. *(P. Barberini 49* ☎*06 48 25 456* ⇟ Ⓜ*A: Barberini.* ⏰ *Open 24hr.)* **Farmacia Doricchi** is toward the Villa Borghese. *(V. XX Settembre 47* ☎*06 48 73 880* ⏰ *Open 24hr.)* **Brienza** is near the Vatican City. *(P. del Risorgimento 44* ☎*06 39 73 81 86* ⏰ *Open 24hr.)*
- **HOSPITALS/MEDICAL SERVICES: Policlinico Umberto I** is Rome's largest public hospital. *(Vle. del Policlinico 155* ☎*06 44 62 341* 🖳*www.policlinicoumberto1.it* ⇟ Ⓜ*B: Policlinico or bus #649 to Policlinico.* Ⓢ *Emergency treatment free. Non-emergencies €25-50.* ⏰ *Open 24hr.* **International Medical Center** is a private hospital and clinic. *(V. Firenze 47* ☎*06 48 82 371* 🖳*www.imc84.com* ⇟ Ⓜ*A: Repubblica.* ℹ *Prescriptions filled. Call ahead for appointments.* ⏰ *Open M-F 9a-8pm.)* **Rome-American Hospital.** *(V. Emilio Longoni 69* ☎*06 22 551 for emergencies,* ☎*06 22 55 290 for appointments* 🖳*www.rah.it* ⇟ *Well to the east of the city; consider taking a cab. To get a little closer, take bus #409 from Tiburtina to Piazzale Prenestina or tram #14 from Termini.* ℹ *English-speaking. Private emergency and laboratory services include HIV testing.* ⏰ *Call-line for appointments. open M-F 8am-8pm, Sa 8am-2pm. Hospital open 24hr. for emergency care.)*

GETTING THERE

By Plane

DA VINCI INTERNATIONAL AIRPORT (FIUMICINO; FCO)

30km southwest of the city ☎06 65 951

Commonly known as Fiumicino, Da Vinci International Airport oversees most international flights. If you're arriving in Rome from a different continent, you'll almost certainly land here, as it's serviced by most carriers. To get from the airport—which is located right on the Mediterranean coast—to central Rome, take the **Leonardo Express** train to **Termini Station.** After leaving customs, follow signs to the **Stazione Trenitalia/Railway Station,** where you can buy a train ticket at an automated machine or from the ticket office. (Ⓢ €14. Ⓣ 32min., every 30min. 6:47am-11:37pm.) The **Sabina-Fiumicino Line (FR1)** will take you to **Trastevere Station** and other Roman suburbs. (Ⓢ €8. Ⓣ 20-45min., every 15min. 5:57am-11:27pm.) Visit ▣www.trenitalia.it to check specific times. Don't buy a ticket from individuals who approach you, as they may be scammers. If you arrive late, you will have to use an automated machine. Before boarding the train, make sure to validate the ticket in a yellow box on the platform; failure to do so may result in a fine of €50-100. If you need to get to or from Fiumicino before 6:30am or after 11:30pm, the easiest option is to catch a **taxi.** For destinations in Central Rome, you'll be charged a flat rate of €40, which should include baggage and up to four passengers. Check with the driver before departing.

ROME CIAMPINO AIRPORT (CIA)

15km southeast of the city ☎06 65 951

Ciampino is the rapidly growing airport serviced by ▣budget airlines like Ryanair and EasyJet. There are no trains connecting the airport to the city center, but various options for getting into Rome from Ciampino exist. The **SIT Bus Shuttle** (☎06 59 23 507 ▣www.sitbusshuttle.it Ⓢ €4. Ⓣ 40min., every 45-60min. 7:45am-11:15pm.) and **Terravision Shuttle** (☎06 97 61 06 32 ▣www.terravision.eu Ⓢ €4. Ⓣ 40min.; every 20-50min., depending on time of day, 8:15am-12:15am.) both run from the airport to V. Marsala, outside Termini Station. For easy access to the Rome Metro, the **COTRAL bus** runs to Rome's Ⓜ A: Anagnina station. (Ⓢ €1.20. Ⓣ 30min., every 40min. 6am-10:40pm.)

By Train

All **Trenitalia** trains run through **Termini Station,** the main transport hub in central Rome. International and overnight trains also run to Termini. City buses #C2, H, M, 36, 38, 40, 64, 86, 90, 92, 105, 170, 175, 217, 310, 714, and 910 stop outside in the P. del Cinquecento. The station is open 5:30am-midnight; if you are arriving in Rome outside of this time frame, you will likely arrive in **Stazione Tiburtina** or **Stazione Ostiense,** both of which connect to Termini by the night bus #175.

Trains run to and from **Florence** (Ⓢ €16.10-44. Ⓣ 1½ -4hr., 52 per day, 5:57am-8:15pm.), **Venice** (Ⓢ €42.50-73.50. Ⓣ 4-7hr., 17 per day, 6:45am-8pm.), **Milan** (Ⓢ €46-89. Ⓣ 3-8hr., 33 per day, 6:45am-11:04pm.), **Naples** (Ⓢ €10.50-44. Ⓣ 1-3hr., 50 per day, 4:52am-9:39pm.), and **Bologna.** (Ⓢ €36-58. Ⓣ 2-4 hr., 42 per day, 6:15am-8:15pm.)

GETTING AROUND

Rome's public transportation system is run by **ATAC.** (☎06 57 003 ▣www.atac.roma.it Ⓣ Open M-Sa 8am-8pm.) It consists of the **Metro, buses,** and **trams,** which service the city center and outskirts, as well as various **Ferrovie urbane** and **Ferrovie metropolitane,** which service more distant suburbs including Ostia Lido, Tivoli, Fregene, and Viterbo. Transit tickets are valid for any of these lines and can be bought at *tabacherrie* throughout the city, at some bars, and from self-service machines or ticket windows at major stations including Termini, Ostiense, and Trastevere. A **BIT** (integrated time ticket; €1) is valid for 1¼hr. after validation and allows unlimited bus travel plus one Metro ride within that time frame; it is generally the most economical choice. A **BIG** (integrated daily ticket; €4) is valid until midnight on the day of validation and allows unlimited bus and Metro use. The **BTI** (integrated tourist ticket; €11) grants unrestricted access for three days after validation. The **CIS** (integrated weekly ticket; €16) grants unrestricted access for seven days after validation. Tickets **must be validated** at Metro station turnstiles and stamping machines on buses and trams.

rome

Below are some Roman bus routes that connect the sights and regions you're most likely to frequent.

- **#64:** Termini, P. Venezia, C. Vittorio Emanuele, P. Navona, Campo dei Fiori, Pantheon, Castel Sant'Angelo/St. Peter's Basilica.
- **#40:** Same as 64, but runs express.
- **H:** Termini, V. Nazionale, P. Venezia, V. Arenula, Trastevere.
- **#116:** V. Veneto, P. Barberini, P. di Spagna, C. Rinascimento, Campo dei Fiori, P. Farnese, St. Peter's.
- **#170:** Termini, V. Nazionale, P. Venezia, Testaccio, EUR.
- **#175:** Termini, V. dei Tritone, V. del Corso, Jewish Ghetto, Ostiense.
- **#492:** Tiburtina, Termini, P. Venezia, P. Cavour, P. Risorgimento.
- **#23:** P. Clodio, P. Risorgimento, Lungotevere, Punto Garibaldi, Basilica di San Paolo.

Night Buses run from 12:30-5:30am on the ½hr., mostly out of Termini and P. Venezia:

- **#78N:** Piazzale Clodio, Piazzale Flaminio, P. Venezia, Termini.
- **#40N:** Metro B route.
- **#29N:** Piazzale Ostiense, Trastevere, Vatican, San Lorenzo, Colosseo, Piazzale Ostiense.
- **#80N:** Route of train from Roma to Ostia Lido.

By Bus

The best way to get around the city other than by walking is by bus: dozens of routes service the entire city center as well as outskirts. **Bus stops** are marked by yellow poles and display a route map for all lines that pass through the stop. For a few useful bus lines, see **Rome Bus Routes.**

By Metro

Rome's **Metro** system consists of two lines: Ⓜ A, which runs from Battistini to Anagnina (hitting P. di Spagna and S. Giovanni), and Ⓜ B, which runs from Laurentina to Rebibbida (hitting the Colosseum, Ostiense, and southern Rome); they intersect only at **Termini Station.** While the Metro is fast, it does not service many regions of the city and is better used for getting across long distances than between neighborhoods. Stations throughout the city are underground and marked by poles with a red square and white M. Tickets are validated at turnstiles upon entering the station.

By Tram

Electric trams make many stops but are still an efficient means of getting around. A few useful lines include **tram #3** *(Trastevere, Piramide, Aventine, P. San Giovanni, Villa Borghese, P. Thorwaldsen),* **tram #8** *(Trastevere to Largo Argentina),* and **tram #19** *(Ottaviano, Villa Borghese, San Lorenzo, Prenestina, P. dei Gerani).*

By Bike

ATAC runs **Bikesharing** *(☎06 57 03 🖳www.bikesharing.roma.it).* Purchase a card at any ATAC ticket office. *(⚷ Ⓜ A: Anagnina, Spagna, Lepanto, Ottaviano, Cornelia, Battistini or Ⓜ B: Termini, Laurentina, EUR Fermi, or Ponte Mammolo. ⌚ Open M-Sa 7am-8pm, Su 8am-8pm.)* Bikes can be

essentials · getting around

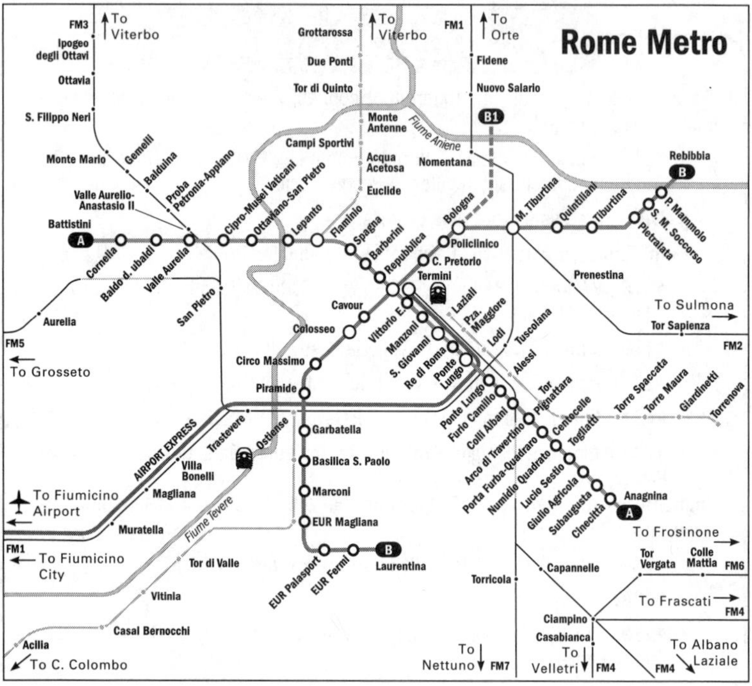

parked at 19 stations around the city. Cards are rechargeable. *($ €5 initial charge, €0.50 per 30min. thereafter. ⏰ Bikes available for a max. 24hr. at a time.)* Plenty of companies also rent bikes, including **Bici and Baci** and **Eco Move Rent** (see **By Scooter**).

By Scooter

Rome is truly a city of scooters. Depending on the vehicle, prices range from €35-85 per day. A helmet (required by law) and insurance are usually included. **Bici and Baci** rents bikes and scooters. *(V. del Viminale 5 ☎06 48 28 443 💻www.bicibaci.com ⏰ Open daily 8am-7pm.)* **Treno e Scooter Rent** also rents scooters with lock and chain included. *(Stazione Roma Termini ☎06 48 90 58 23 💻www.trenoescooter.com ⏰ Open daily 9am-2pm and 4-7pm.)* **Eco Move Rent** rents scooters, Vespas, and bikes, lock included. *(V. Varese 48/50 ☎06 44 70 45 18 💻www.ecomoverent.com ⏰ Open daily 8:30am-7:30pm.)*

By Taxi

Given the scope of Rome's bus system, taxis should only be reserved for desperate or time-sensitive affairs. Legally, you may not "hail" a cab on the street—either call **RadioTaxi** *(☎06 66 45)* or head to a taxi point (near most major sights) where drivers wait for customers. Ride only in yellow or white cars and look for a meter or settle on a price before the ride. **Rate 1** is charged for rides within the center. *($ €0.78 per km.)* **Rate 2** is applied to rides outside. *($ €1.29 per km.)* Though it's hard to tell what rate is being applied, write down the license number if the cost seems especially high. A tip is not expected.

MILAN AND TURIN

While vaunted Rome may have been the center of influence in the ancient Italian peninsula, the North—Milan and Turin in particular—has been the most important commercial influence on modern-day Italy. In 1860, at the time of the country's unification, Turin held the seat of royalty. In the mid-20th century, Milan, Turin, and Genoa formed the triangle of the nation's industrial might. And today, Milan serves as the country's financial clearinghouse. For centuries, the power and funds that keep the country running have passed through these two cities.

With such riches comes an unmatched cultural sophistication. Milan has seen opera flourish at La Scala, and the high art form thrives in Turin as well. Contemporary art collections in both cities grow alongside the Baroque Italian works that have called Milan and Turin home for centuries. Milan sets international trends, while Turin offers what is quite possibly the country's best nightlife and certainly its best chocolate. Beat that, Rome. *Your* sweet concoction will melt away in the summer's stifling heat, while Turin's, well, it'll only get a little mushy.

Known for their high standards of living, both metropolises pride themselves on cleanliness and efficiency. Indeed, Northern Italy can seem like a completely different animal than the country's southern reaches. However, for all of these northern cities' relative order, they also know how to live a little when the time is right: Milan's fine dining and Turin's extensive cafe scene keep the locals happy and well fed. With good food and drink, high culture and style, and business sense and wealth, Milan and Turin don't need ancient history to earn their cosmopolitan credentials. In more ways than one it's abundantly clear: the Milan and Turin of today are thriving cities with impeccable pedigrees.

greatest hits

- **FAST FASHION.** Find just about every single designer brand you've ever heard of, all within a few blocks in Milan's Fashion District (p. 140).

- **SAVORING SAVOY.** Turin was Italy's first capital and has an often overlooked history as the seat of the House of Savoy. See their palaces and the Savoy Gallery, holding their prodigious collection of art (p. 150).

- **DANCE THE NIGHT AWAY.** Both cities have great nightlife, but Milan's Navigli district is the first place you should check out (p. 132).

It's hard to go wrong with these two northern cities if you're looking for great student life. The biggest problem may be trying to decide how to split your time between the two of them. In Milan, the Navigli area is a fantastic place to spend time. Nightlife is great across the city, but the student focus is very much on this area. Located just south of Bocconi University, Navigli is full of bars that are in turn full of young people on most nights. The profusion of young people creates a more laid-back atmosphere than in the uptight clubs in the north of the city. Hit the *aperitivo* buffets to grab a cheap meal as well. A little further west, Turin makes a great accompaniment to Milan's always hip scene, with the whole city just a little less self-conscious than what you'll find in most of Milan. The nightlife here rages in a free and less serious way, so you can spend a little less time worrying about your outfit and a little more time having fun. The bars lining the River Po, particularly on Murazzi del Po are an excellent destination. Try Murphy's Pub if you're looking for study-abroad students, particularly of the English-speaking variety. It is, after all, a British-themed pub. The University of Turin itself is very central, and the influence of its large student body seems to infiltrate this fun and lively town, where a young traveler can easily find a great place to hang out.

milan *milano* ☎02

An intersection of fashion and finance, Milan is a city whose residents are ready to proclaim their pride in the sophisticated metropolis they call home. Italy's moral capital is the antithesis of the chaotic south. Citizens speak in a refined dialect, the government officials actually work, and even the scooters stop for red lights. Although the cost of living is high and traffic can be a nightmare, the spires of the city's intricately carved **Duomo,** the echoing notes of the renowned **La Scala** theater, and the gleaming boutiques of the **Fashion District,** where casually parallel parking a cherry-red Ferrari is no big deal, help prove the Milanese's point: this is a truly cultured town. But in addition to its role as a national and global trendsetter, Milan plays an essential part in the Italian economy, home as it is to rubber giant Pirelli and scores of banks, hedge funds, and other GDP-boosting institutions that remain mysterious to the layperson. While the city's dark-suited bankers walk its streets with a clear purpose, meandering tourists can find many artistic treasures that remain less known. Leonardo's *Last Supper*, one of the world's best-known paintings, is here, as are the collections at the **Pinoteca di Brera** and **Pinoteca Ambrosiana,** both filled with priceless Italian art dating from the Renaissance to the 20th century. Today, however, the city's most famous export may be its championship soccer teams, Inter and AC Milan. When they face off twice annually, the entire city comes to a halt as all eyes follow the match. Hearts pound with every pass and goal, and screams erupt at the sight of each yellow card. The city has everything that's to be expected from a world-class metropolis—wealth, culture, sport, and more—all carried off with that cosmopolitan, stylish élan of which the Vespa-driving, street-smart Milanese are so proud.

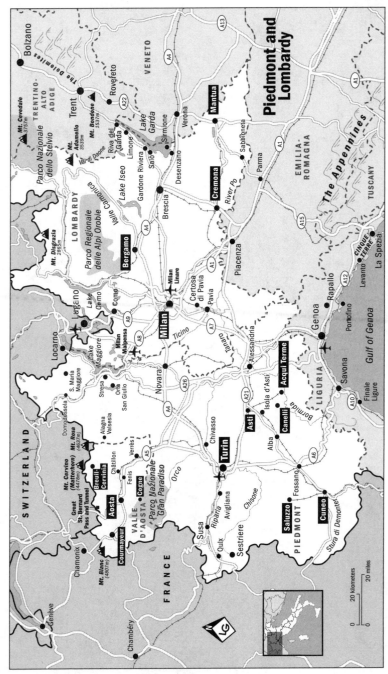

Piedmont and Lombardy

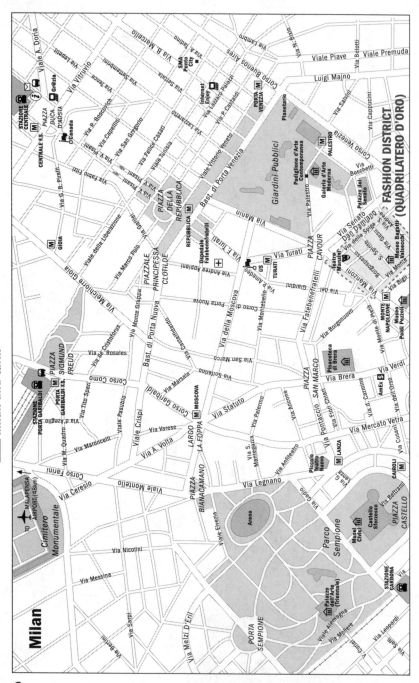

milan and turin

Milan

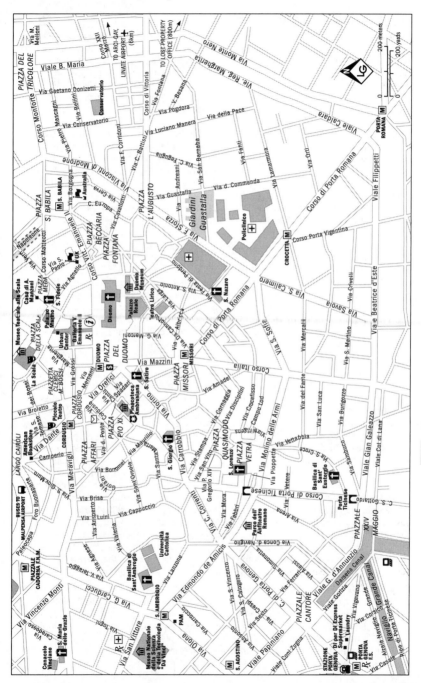

milan

ORIENTATION

On a map, Milan's city center resembles the web made by a rather loopy spider—it's a series of concentric circles connected to one another by an erratic array of thin roadways and broad boulevards whose names change as frequently as their direction. The heart of the city is the **Duomo**, which marks the center of nearly all maps. The city's tourist and business districts surround four squares: **Piazza del Duomo,** at the meeting point of V. Orefici, V. Mazzini, and C. Vittorio Emanuele II; **Largo Cairoli** and **Piazza Castello,** in front of **Castello Sforzesco; Piazza Cordusio,** connected to P. Castello by V. Dante and to P. Duomo by V. Orefici; and **Piazza San Babila,** where C. Vittorio Emanuele II meets V. Monte Napoleone, marking the entrance to the **Fashion District.** All four squares are stops on the Ⓜ1 (red), which makes a sweeping "U" through the *centro*. Past P. San Babila, the name changing begins, as C. Vittorio Emanuele II becomes C. Venezia, shooting to the northeast past the **Giardini Pubblici,** then becoming C. Buenos Aires and continuing to the *pensione* (cheap hotel) district near **Stazione Centrale,** Milan's primary train station and intercity transit hub. The station is located at the intersection of V. Pirelli, Vle. Doria, and V. Pisani in **Piazza Duca d'Aosta.** To the west along V. Pirelli is **Stazione Porta Garibaldi,** another important train terminal, and the **Cimitero Monumentale.**

For a quick tour of major sights, follow V. Pisani toward the *centro* as it becomes V. Turati past the US Consulate. Then trace V. Manzoni through the Fashion District and into **Piazza della Scala,** home of the world's most famous opera house—the fat lady singing, too. **Galleria Vittorio Emanuele II** connects this square to the Duomo. From the city's famous landmark, follow V. Orefici to V. Dante and **Parco Sempione,** one of Milan's two principal parks (the other is the Giardini Pubblici) and the residence of the 14th-century fortress of the Castello Sforzesco. Southwards from the Duomo, V. Torino leads to the shopping and nightlife strip of **Corso di Porta Ticinese** and the boozy canals of the **Navigli.**

Piazza del Duomo

Sitting in the heart of downtown *centro*, the Duomo is the geographical and spiritual center of Milan. It is also the city's tourist hub, from which many tours make their start. Consequently, this neighborhood is characterized by overpriced chain restaurants and souvenir stalls. Home to a number of museums, it is also a base camp for scammers who surprise unsuspecting foreigners. In P. del Duomo, watch out for those who offer to "give" you a bracelet or "let" you feed the pigeons with their birdseed. In reality, they expect something (namely, 💰moolah) in return. Beneath the plaza, **Fermata Duomo** is one of the underground's busiest stations and has a connection between the 1 (red) and 3 (yellow) lines. Northeast of the *piazza* to the northeast, international banks and luxury hotels draw a more suited-up crowd. To the northwest along **Via Dante** is **Castello Sforzesco,** the city's other primary tourist attraction. More affordable accommodations can be found along **Via Manzini** (becoming C. Italia), which stretches to the south. **Via Torino** heads southwest, linking up with **Corso di Porta Ticinese** in an area that contains many more authentic restaurants and bars. Except for these main thoroughfares, the street "grid" is more like a deformed spiderweb, with few streets extending in a straight line for more than a few blocks, making a map critical for any successful exploration of this neighborhood.

Fashion District

Perhaps not coincidentally, Milan's most elegant area, once called the **Quadrilatero d'Oro,** is located right in the middle of everything—all the more convenient for the Bentley chauffeurs and Ferrari-driving executives who have places to be and people to see. From here, the Duomo is to the southwest, the Brera district is to the west, and the Giardini Pubblici is to the northeast. **Via Monte Napoleone,** a street of brand-name shops with elaborate window displays and equally extravagant price tags, connects **Corso Vittorio Emanuele II** and **Piazza San Babila** (Ⓜ1: San Babila) in the south to **Via Manzoni** (Ⓜ3: Montenapoleone), home of Armani, in the north. Branching off from V. Monte Napoleone, the District's main thoroughfare, several smaller roads lead to the pedestrian-only, cobblestoned **Via della Spiga,** home to lesser-known names but equally high prices, even in the specialty stores selling silk baby bibs and Italian leather dog collars. V. della Spiga leads to **Piazza Cavour** and the famous gate that traditionally marked the entrance to the land of wealth within this chichi part of the city.

Giardini Pubblici

The neighborhoods near Giardini Pubblici connect the Porta Venezia area and the public gardens themselves to Stazione Centrale. Many hotels can be founds near the station and along the main roads of **Corso Buenos Aires** and **Viale Tunisia.** V. Torriani leads from the heart of the neighborhood towards the train terminal. The gardens are bordered by **Corso Venezia** to the east, **Via Palestro** to the south, **Via Manin** to the west, and **Bastioni di Porta Venezia** to the north. Along the streets parallel to the edge of Giardini Pubblici, including V. Castaldi, take your pick of the dozens of quaint cafes and bars that seem to fill every intersection. The area's primary Metro station, ⓂPorta Venezia, is located on C. Buenos Aires at P. S. F. Romano, a maze of traffic and trams that can't be missed.

Castello Sforzesco

This part of Milan contains an eclectic mix of neighborhoods and attractions, ranging from a major tourist center and transportation hub to upscale apartments and the artsy neighborhood of Brera. At the center of it all is the castle, which—like the Duomo—is surrounded by hawkers toting their wares to tourists. Largo Cairoli and V. Dante from the Castello to Duomo are full of touristy restaurants with high prices and food that doesn't merit the cost. To the east is the Brera district with its famous art museum; this area proves especially appealing to art students who enjoy perusing its vintage shops. To the west, upscale, brand-name stores; high-class residences; and da Vinci's *Last Supper* can be found on C. Magenta. To the south, V. Carducci leads to the **Basilica di Sant'Ambrogio,** while north of the castle is a large park where city dwellers relax and wander on summer days.

Navigli

The Navigli area is a triangle bounded by two waterways, the Naviglio Grande to the northwest and the Naviglio Pavese to the east, though the area's many bars and restaurants spread a few blocks beyond. The canals meet at P. le XXIV Maggio, which is marked by a traffic circle and stone monument. ⓂPorta Genova, the nearest Metro stop, is located a few blocks west of the *piazza* on V. Vigevano. The picturesque **Ripa di Porta Ticenese** runs along Naviglio Grande, while **Via Ascanio Sforza,** Navigli's main nightlife drag, sits on the east side of Naviglio Pavarese. Many car- and pedestrian-friendly bridges cross the canals, but not at every intersection. Most nightlife hot spots are on V. Ascanio Sforza, north of where it is crossed by the tree-lined V. Liguria/V. Tibaldi, though some restaurants and hotels can be found on V. Ascanio Sforza to the south of the intersection. Beware when crossing this thoroughfare, especially the motorcycle and bus lane in the center that sometimes appears empty just before vehicles round the bend at high speed. Following this advice should help you to avoid the hair-raising experience of one hapless *Let's Go* Researcher-Writer, to whom this book might have been dedicated if the cyclist hurtling toward him on V. Liguria had not possessed lightning-quick reflexes and equally responsive brakes. Just another example of us here at *Let's Go* risking life and limb in pursuit of the information you hold in this guidebook... or just making all the mistakes in advance so that you don't have to deal with them yourself.

City Outskirts

While it seems at first that most of Milan's attractions are packed within the city center, many cultural heavyweights and affordable accommodations can be found farther afield. Because of Milan's extensive Metro and tram system, most outskirts are easily accessible from the *centro*. Northwards, **Corso Garibaldi** leads to the lively nightlife street of **Corso Como** and the vast **Cimitero Monumentale,** resting place of many Italian luminaries. Northwest of the city is the wealthy **Fiera** neighborhood, home to Milan's business expos as well as less affluent residential areas around Ⓜ**Lotto** and Ⓜ**QT8.** Soccer fans will swoon when they see the **San Siro** stadium complex, home to Milan's famous soccer teams. To the southwest, V. Washington has a number of inexpensive hotels and shops. **Piazza Buonarotti** is packed with cafes, as is **Porta Romana** to the southeast. More affordable accommodations are east of the city in the mostly residential areas around **Corso Independenza.** Some areas are seedy, especially near Stazione Centrale, where travelers should be careful walking alone late at night.

---

a question of morality

Some Italian cities boast of their raging nightlife. Others of their centuries-old ruins, stunning Renaissance frescoes, or hell, even the shape of their pasta. Milan's residents, however, seem to be courting a different kind of tourist crowd: namely, the pious. For reasons that are at best quaintly misguided, and at worst impossibly illogical, Milan calls itself Italy's "Moral Capital." Try getting that printed on your souvenir shot glass.

The actual origins of this title are rather obscure. Certainly, like most Italian towns, Milan has a long history of religiosity. It was the Edict of Milan, signed by Emperor Constantine in 313 CE, that protected Christians from persecution at the hands of the Romans, while the Milan Duomo, in addition to being one of the city's best examples of Gothic architecture, is also the fourth-largest cathedral in the world. But Milan's inhabitants are emphatic that it being a Moral Capital means something more than churches or proclamations. It's in the intangibles, we hear.

And really, why should we be skeptical? Milan is the undisputed center of Italian finance. And nothing reeks of morality like Italian financial dealings. And Milan is also one of the world's most fashionable cities, exhibiting all that is good and virtuous in the world of stilettos and shoulder bags. Just behind that famous Duomo is Galleria Vittorio Emanuele, reputed to be the world's oldest shopping mall, and the stomping ground of only the most pious holders of Visa Gold.

But there is, perhaps, one thing in Milan absolutely above moral reproach. As the hometown of legendary composer Giuseppe Verdi and the glorious opera house of La Scala, Milan has a musical history that is sacred indeed.

ACCOMMODATIONS

As you would expect in any large city, Milan's accommodations run the gamut, though the publicly posted star rating can give you a pretty good indication of what to expect from an establishment. One star means you'll get a bed and bath but not much else; five means the doorman will probably take more interest in polishing the Bentley parked out front than in an approaching backpacker. A few youth hostels can be found scattered around the city, and some are very conveniently located in quiet residential areas just a short Metro ride from the *centro*. A number of quality one-star hotels surround the **Giardini Pubblici** and lie to the southeast of Porta Venezia as well as along **Via Giorgio Washington.** International chains are clustered closer to the city center, where budget accommodations can be hard to come by. But even in one of the world's most fashionable cities, there are still unfashionable lodgings to be found. The area just south and east of Stazione Centrale is littered with *pensioni* and one-star hotels, many quite cheap but also bare-boned.

Piazza del Duomo

Checkbooks out, please. The Duomo area is Milan's tourist hub and home to many luxury hotels, but because of their prime location, even the few budget hotels tend to charge steep rates. At these properties, there tends to be a wide swing between prices for the high and low seasons. We recommend you stay somewhere else and take advantage of Milan's public transit systems.

HOTEL ALISEO
♨⊗((ŋ)) HOTEL ❸

C. Italia 6 ☎02 86 45 01 56 ▦www.hotelaliseo.it

Things may get a little cozy if you decide to bring that new friend from the bar (or church—who are we to judge?) back to your thin single bed at this hotel. Then again, maybe that's the idea. The marble staircase makes it ever so slightly more like the Ritz.

✦ Ⓜ3: Missori. Hotel is directly across from the exit on C. Italia. ⑤ Singles €40-80; doubles €50-110; triples €80-130.

HOTEL VECCHIA
♨⊗⚥✿ HOTEL ❹

V. Borromei 4 ☎02 87 50 42 ▦www.hotelvecchiamilano.it

It might take a compass and sextant to find this place that's located on a quieter back lane, but the extra navigation effort is worth it. A comfy, wood-paneled lobby and breakfast room greet guests, and a whimsical spiral staircase above the front desk leads to generously sized double rooms upstairs.

✦ Ⓜ1: Codusio. Follow V. Cordusio, which becomes V. Boccheto and then V. Podone. At P. Borromeo, turn right. ⑤ Singles €50-70; doubles €70-90; triples €90-110.

Fashion District

The heart of the Fashion District might as well be called Five Star City. Trust us: it's not just the handbags that are expensive. A short walk (or a two-stop Metro trip) away from this stylish money vacuum are a couple of comfortable and at least somewhat affordable accommodations.

HOTEL CASA MIA
♨⊗((ŋ))✿ HOTEL ❹

Vle. Vittorio Veneto 30 ☎02 65 75 249 ▦www.casamiahotel.it

Sadly, this small, nicely decked-out hotel is not your home, despite the name. But that might be a good thing because with its location a 10min. walk from the Fashion District and Milan's *centro*, the rent would probably be sky-high. Better to enjoy the views of P. Repubblica through the large windows of someone else's yellow-walled breakfast area—the perfect sunny place to watch the world go by over a newspaper and cappuccino—and daydream that your home were as classy as this one.

✦ Ⓜ3: Repubblica. Hotel is on the corner of the piazza. *i* Breakfast included. ⑤ Singles €50-65; doubles €70-90; triples €100-120. ⌚ Reception 24hr.

WINDSOR HOTEL
♨♿((ŋ))✿ HOTEL ❺

V. Galileo Galilei 2 ☎02 63 46 ▦www.hotelwindsormilan.com

Snobby doormen at the Fashion District hotels have you seeing red? Take a short walk here, where red is the color of choice on the carpets and linens but won't be in your vision. Windsor has all the comforts of a newly refurbished hotel removed from the hubbub. With remarkably affordable prices during the low season, it's the little extras like fitness center admission and a daily newspaper that make this hotel stand out. Huge variation in prices between low- and high-season rooms, so check ahead of time.

✦ Ⓜ3: Repubblica. Follow Vle. Monte Santo for 1 block and turn right onto V. Galileo Galilei. *i*

Free Wi-Fi. [S] Singles €65-170; doubles €90-230; triples €150-280.

Giardini Pubblici

The area between Stazione Centrale and the Giardini Pubblici is packed with hotels, some of them cheap and seedy, others with a doorman and concierge. Many hotels occupy floors of apartment buildings, but despite their unorthodox arrangement, these represent some of the best (and most hidden) travel deals.

👍 HOTEL EVA AND HOTEL ARNO — 💳🚭📶 HOTEL [2]

V. Lazzaretto 17, 4th fl. ☎02 67 06 093 💻www.hotelevamilano.com or www.hotelarno.com.

Friendly staff and clean, comfortable rooms make this quirky dual-hotel setup (the two are across the hall, and share a reception) a good choice for budget travelers. No record of whether Eva and Arno are Facebook official.

➜ [M]1: Porta Venezia. Follow V. Castati, then turn right onto V. Lazzaretto. Ring bell. ℹ Free Wi-Fi. Free luggage storage. [S] Singles €30-45; doubles €50-100; triples €65-90. ⏰ Reception 24hr.

HOTEL KENNEDY — 💳🚭📶 HOTEL [3]

Vle. Tunisia 6, 6th fl. ☎02 29 40 09 34 💻www.kennedyhotel.it

Stacked on top of Hotel San Tomasso, Hotel Kennedy steals the view of Milan with its large windows and quaint balconies.

➜ [M]1: Porta Venezia. ℹ Free luggage storage. Small pets allowed. [S] Singles €35-80; doubles €50-150; triples €66-160; quads €80-200.

HOTEL ITALIA E NAZIONALE — 💳🚭📶🍸 HOTEL [3]

V. Vitruvio 44/46 ☎02 66 93 826 💻nazionaleeitalia@tiscalinet.it

Despite the slight smell of smoke in some rooms, the prices at this establishment—including breakfast and in-room TV—are hard to beat in central Milan.

➜ [M]2/3: Centrale FS. ℹ There are several steps up to the elevator entrance. [S] Singles €35-55; doubles €55-95; triples €110-120.

HOTEL BAGLIORI — 💳♿📶🍸⛅ HOTEL [4]

V. Boscovich 43 ☎02 29 52 68 84 💻www.hotelbagliori.com

The idyllic front garden might have been plucked straight out of Versailles and the breakfast room stolen from a country club. Conveniently located and excellently appointed, the Bagliori would make the builders of its centuries-old villa location proud.

➜ [M]1: Lima. Follow C. Buenos Aires south to V. Boscovich. ℹ Wi-Fi €10 per 24hr. [S] Singles €50-180; doubles €130-250. Significant web discounts.

HOTEL SAN TOMASO — 💳🚭📶 HOTEL [1]

V. le Tunisia 6, 4th fl. ☎02 29 51 47 47 💻www.hotelsantomaso.com

The rooms are clean, but plastic vines on white walls provide the only decoration at this thimble-sized hotel. More importantly, hotel staff do not necessarily speak English, making booking a room here somewhat difficult. Check out Hotel Kennedy upstairs for a one-stop comparison.

➜ [M]1: Porta Venezia. [S] Dorms €20; singles €35-85; doubles €50-95; triples €70-120; quads €80-165.

Castello Sforzesco

Like the Duomo, the neighborhoods around Castello Sforzesco offer very few inexpensive hotels. Milan is a wealthy city, and staying right in its center is going to take a bit of change.

HOTEL PANIZZA — 💳🚭📶 HOTEL [2]

V. Panizza 5 ☎02 46 90 604 💻www.hotelpanizza.it

Don't get discouraged walking down the street: we're not sure why this small and simple hotel decides to hide itself with only a small plaque announcing its presence, but it is indeed ready and waiting for your patronage. Inside, stained glass on the guestroom doors recalls Milan's Duomo. Since the hotel is on the far end of the neighborhood and remains a fair walk from the city's main sights, you may need a reminder of what the city's major landmark looks like if you're staying here.

✈ ⓜ1: Conciliazione. Follow V. Porta Vercellina and turn right onto V. Biffi and again onto V. Panizza at the piazza. **i** No ensuite bathrooms. ⓢ Dorms €25-27; singles €30-45; doubles €45-90; triples €65-120; quads €75-150. ⓩ Reception 24hr.

HOTEL LANCASTER
V. Abbondio Sangiorgio 16

●◆⊗⟨⟨ᵖ⟩⟩⟨⟨ꟼ⟩⟩⟨⟨ᶜ⟩⟩ ❄ HOTEL ❻

☎02 34 47 05 ▣www.hotellancaster.it

Everything's bigger on this side of the park, but we mean that in the most politically correct way, of course. The elegant Hotel Lancaster offers relatively enormous rooms, gigantic beds, and humongous showers. Classically decorated, the rooms feature minibars and satellite TV, while the breakfast area and lobby downstairs provide comfortable places to relax.

✈ ⓜ1/2: Cardona F.N. Take tram #19 towards Ospedale Sacco and get off at P. Giovanni XXIII. Follow V. Savoia to V. Sangiorgio. **i** Breakfast included. Wi-Fi €3.50 per 24hr. ⓢ Singles €65-130; doubles €90-230; triples €130-300.

parking problems

Walking around Milan, it's probably a good idea to do your best to avoid the cars whipping around the city's streets. What is almost impossible to avoid, however, is the remarkable quantity of cars parked on the sidewalk, grass, or even right in the middle of a crosswalk. After a while you might end up thinking, "Can't you just find a real spot?"

But apparently that's not the way in Italy, where the sidewalks pockmarked by moped kickstands would put a New York City pothole to shame. Milan's government seems not to have helped matters much when, in 2008, they implemented a London-like congestion charge for cars in the city center. Nice neighborhoods—names have been withheld to protect the innocent—near the border of the toll zone have become virtual used-car lots during the work day. All that beautiful green space in the middle of the city's boulevards? No more.

This seems like kind of a failure for what was supposed to be a decidedly green initiative. Maybe the consolation is that the scaled-down cars the Milanese drive are fuel-efficient: tiny Smart Cars, zippy Fiats, and, well, mini Mini Coopers. But that only makes it easier for them to squeeze onto the sidewalk, park on corners, and generally drive pedestrians nuts.

milan • accommodations

Navigli
Known for its student crowd but less touristy than other areas of the city, the Navigli is not overflowing with places to stay. Bed and breakfasts can be a good option on the canals, but for cheap hotels, one must look slightly farther afield.

🏨 OSTELLO LA CORDATA
V. Burigozzo 11

●◆ᾔ⟨⟨ᵖ⟩⟩ HOSTEL ❷

☎02 58 30 35 98 ▣www.ostellolacordata.com

Home to a lively, international backpacking crowd headed for the disco lights of the Navigli district, Ostello La Cordata has a party-hostel reputation. However, this doesn't stop penny-pinching older European men and school groups from calling it their home-away-from-home. Insider tip: if asked, choose the top bunk. It's not high off the ground, and the lower bunk has little headroom.

✈ ⓜ3: Missori. From P. Missori take tram #15 two stops to Italia S. Luca; continue in the same direction for 1 block and turn right onto V. Burigozzo. Entrance around the corner on V. Aurispa. **i**

Free internet and Wi-Fi. ⑤ Dorms €21-25; singles €50-70; doubles €70-100; triples €90-120; quads €110-140. ⌚ Reception 2:30pm-1pm. Lockout 11am-2:30pm.

RIPA DEL NAVIGLIO
⮎((ᵞ))❄ B AND B ❺

Ripa de Porta Ticinese 71, 4th fl. ☎02 89 69 33 43 💻www.ripadelnaviglio.it

The red blankets and cozy double beds make this bed and breakfast ripe for romance. Want to impress that cute Italian girl? Take her here—with a flowered balcony overlooking the rooftops and an airy breakfast room in sunburst colors, Ripa del Naviglio is a hidden oasis.

⚑ Ⓜ2: Porta Genova. Walk down V. Casale. Cross the footbridge and turn right. *i* Flatscreen TV and refrigerator ensuite. Free Wi-Fi. Only 3 rooms. ⑤ Doubles €110, can sometimes be negotiated lower for stays over 3 days. Uses PayPal.

HOTEL MERCURIO
⮎Ⓧ((ᵞ)) HOTEL ❸

V. A. Sforza 73 ☎02 84 66 774 💻www.hotelmercurio.net

Is that parked Vespa a prop? It might seem that way, as the coral-walled, palm-lined courtyard leading into Hotel Mercurio looks too classically Italian to be true. You'll find 19 spare—but more than adequate—rooms inside the hotel, each with an ensuite bathroom.

⚑ Walk east on V. Liguria, turn right onto V. Sforza. *i* Breakfast included. TV ensuite. Free Wi-Fi. Twin beds available. ⑤ Singles €30-100; doubles €50-200; triples €75-250. ⌚ Reception 24hr.

LA VIGNETTA HOTEL
⮎Ⓧ((ᵞ))❄ HOTEL ❹

V. Pietro Custodi 2 💻www.lavignettahotel.it

Near the Navigli's central *piazza*, this hotel features fresh rooms, including some that span two stories. Room prices vary widely based on availability and time of year, so find out which end of the range you'll be on before booking. At the lower end, this is a good deal; at the upper end, you could probably do better elsewhere to save your money for Navigli's clubs.

⚑ Ⓜ2: Porta Genova. *i* Satellite TV in rooms. Internet. Dogs welcome. ⑤ Singles €50-90; doubles €70-120; triples €90-160. Occasional web specials.

ART HOTEL NAVIGLI
⮎♿((ᵞ))☗❄ HOTEL ❺

V. Angelo Fumagalli 4 ☎02 89 41 05 30 💻www.arthotelnavigli.com

Perhaps the hotel nearest to the action, this newly renovated property boasts an intimate garden. Its modern bar, though an attractive place to grab a nightcap, stays quiet due to the nightlife that draws guests away from the hotel and into the nearby streets.

⚑ Ⓜ2: Porta Genova. Follow V. Valenzia across the Navigli Grande. Turn left across the bridge and V. A. Fumagalli is on the right. *i* "Superior" rooms have undergone recent renovation, while "classic" rooms have not. ⑤ Singles €75-135; doubles €110-160; triples €135-195. Occasional web specials.

City Outskirts

Outside of the *centro*, accommodations vary widely in both price and quality. The area east of Stazione Centrale has some of the cheapest *pensione*, though these are often located on seedy streets. To the southeast are inexpensive rooms in less questionable surroundings. **Via Giorgio Washington**, to the west, offers a wide range of options, from international brands to simple rooming houses where your motto may be, "only sleep." The few youth hostels Milan can boast are generally located near out-of-the-way Metro stops along with three- and four-star hotels, especially near the Fiera area—but be warned that rates jump drastically during the fall exhibition season.

🌣 ZEBRA HOSTEL
⮎Ⓧ((ᵞ)) HOSTEL ❷

Vle. Regina Margherita 9 ☎02 87 23 66 83 💻www.zebrahostel.it

Fortunately, the zebra theme is muted, and there are no tacky striped walls to keep you awake at night. But staying up late must be seriously fun in this new, clean hostel's gigantic common room which features the regular—a TV and foosball table—and the awesome—classic arcade games! Breakfast is served in the homey kitchen, where the young backpacker clientele gathers to drink the 24hr. coffee supply.

⚲ Ⓜ3: Crocetta. Take V. A. Lamarmora to V. Margherita, and turn left. Hostel is up the stairs and to the left. *i* Breakfast included. Bike rental available. Free Wi-Fi and internet access in common room. Ⓢ Dorms €24-26; singles €35; doubles €30-32. €4 linen deposit. ☒ Reception 24hr.

▨ POP HOUSE
◉⊗⒨⌂ HOTEL ❸

V. Menabrea 13 ☎335 80 56 883 🖳www.pophouse-milano.com

Welcome to the Pop House, where a cell phone is your doorman, a computer your concierge, and you're the room service. The three fashion industry workers who run this simple, modern spot are often off around the globe, but they're available to open the door from a thousand miles away thanks to high-tech gadgetry. Inside both the two-room "loft" and three-room "house" are comfortable lounge areas with compact kitchens. Small spiral staircases connect the ground floor to the sleek, stone-walled bathrooms and bright bedrooms—plus a rooftop terrace.

⚲ Ⓜ3: Maciachini. Follow V. Menabrea 2 blocks. Ⓢ Singles €35-50; doubles €50-70; triples €60-75. ☒ No reception; call on arrival.

MISTER BEEM
◉⊗⒨ HOSTEL ❶

V. Goldoni 84 ☎380 46 72 253

Though the doorknob may be falling off the front door, this hostel is located in a safe and quiet residential area southeast of the city center. If you have an allergy to flowers—tacky paintings of sunflowers, that is—the orange-colored common room might make you want to sneeze, but the simple bedrooms and free breakfast (with Nutella!) keep traveling students coming back.

⚲ Ⓜ1: Porta Venezia. Take tram #5 or 33, in direction of Ortica or Limbrate, to P. Savoia. Continue walking in the same direction 4 blocks and turn right onto V. Cicognara. Make a left onto V. Goldoni. *i* Breakfast included. Free Wi-Fi. Ⓢ Dorms €18-23. ☒ Lockout 11am-1:30pm.

HOTEL BRASIL
⬥⊗ HOTEL ❸

V. G. Modena 20, 4th fl. ☎02 70 10 22 76 🖳www.hotelbrasilmilano.com

Descisions, decisions, decisions. Hotel Brasil offers a myriad of different room setups at varying prices. All are brightly colored with an abundance of natural light in the high-up floor of an apartment building southeast of C. Venezia. Even though bags of linens are sometimes left in the hallway, guests in every room receive the same basic hospitality from the helpful staff.

⚲ Ⓜ1: Palestro. From C. Venezia, turn right onto V. Salvini, which becomes V. Vitali. Make a slight left at V. de Bernardi, which becomes V. Belloti. Walk 5 blocks and turn right onto V. Modena. *i* Small breakfast buffet €3. Ⓢ Singles €35-45; doubles €40-55; triples €50-65; quads €65-80.

HOTEL CALAIS
◉⊗⒨ HOTEL ❹

V. Washington 26 ☎02 46 94 760 🖳www.hotelcalaismilano.com

Even given the two world clocks set to Havana and Moscow in the hotel's lobby, we won't pass judgment on the owner's political leanings.What we can say is that he (and his little dog, too!) is helpful and runs a quirky establishment—guestroom walls painted with turquoise waves to mimic the breaking surf of *La Manche* and all.

⚲ Ⓜ1: Wagner. From the large traffic circle, follow V. Washington to the south. Ⓢ Singles €50-65; doubles €65-80; triples €85-100.

OSTELLO A.I.G. PIERO ROTTA (HI)
⬥⊗⒨⌣ HOSTEL ❶

Vle. Salmoiraghi at V. Calliano ☎02 39 26 70 95 🖳ostellomilano.it

Comparing this hostel to an aging supermodel probably gives it a little too much credit—or too much insult to supermodels—but it's certainly ready for some plastic surgery. Built in the 1950s, this large, 400-bed hostel has dark hallways and aging bathrooms, but recently began a major renovation.

✚ Ⓜ1: QT8. *When facing park after exiting station, follow V. Salmoirghi to the right.* Ⓢ *6-bed dorms €22; private rooms €25. €5 cash key deposit required.* ⌚ *Lockout 10am-2pm.*

SIGHTS

Is this a city without a history? An *Italian* city without a history, at that? Of course not, though compared to Rome, Venice, and Florence, Milan can sometimes seem rather without roots. With a city center that's grown up around the 14th-century **Duomo**, Milan does indeed have a robust past of politics, art, and culture that is revealed in its sights. **Castello Sforzesco,** just a few blocks from the Duomo, is one of the most imposing edifices in the city, and today, it's full of engaging museums. Other art museums in the *centro* fill the ornate, gilded halls of Renaissance *palazzi*, and the **Pinacoteca di Brera** is recognized as one of the world's finest collections of Italian paintings. Classical ruins exist in the city, too, particularly at the many gates that define its geography. Then there are the modern marvels—the stadium at **San Siro** and the **Pirelli Tower**—which tell a history of a city that has grown to become a *capitale* of both business and culture.

Piazza del Duomo

Ascending from the Metro and catching a first glimpse of the Duomo's immense sculpted facade is simply breathtaking. This kind of aesthetic elation, however, draws thousands of tourists to the *piazza*. There are also lots of grungy, gray pigeons, but it seems unlikely that they are drawn to the square for exactly the same reason. After touring the cathedral's interior, move away from the Duomo to some of the many other less crowded attractions nearby. In addition to the many existing attractions, a new museum of 20th-century art, the **Museo Novecento,** opened November 2010 on the Piazza del Duomo.

DUOMO   ♿ CHURCH
P. del Duomo   ☎02 72 02 33 75 ◙www.duomomilano.it

The second-largest Catholic cathedral in the world, the Duomo takes up the largest spot in the hearts of Milan's residents. With a construction spanning from 1386 to the 1900s, the building juxtaposes an Italian Gothic style with Baroque architectural elements added at the order of Archbishop Borromeo, who sought to show solidarity with Rome during the Protestant Revolution. **Giacomo de Medici's tomb,** inspired by the work of Michelangelo, is inside. The rooftop, accessible by elevator or stairs, offers one of Milan's best vistas. The nearby **Museo del Duomo** remains closed for renovation but normally houses paintings, tapestries, and artifacts dating back to the cathedral's construction. Remember that the Duomo is the most popular tourist stop in Milan, so there can occasionally be lines at the security checkpoint, especially from late morning to midday. It's worth the wait, even if you have to stave off pilgrims and camera-toting tourists.

✚ Ⓜ1: Duomo. *i Modest dress code strictly enforced.* Ⓢ *Free. Rooftop elevator €8. Stairs €5.* ⌚ *Open daily 7am-7pm. Roof open daily Feb 16-Nov 14 9am-10pm.*

PINACOTECA AMBROSIANA   ♿ MUSEUM
P. Pio XI 2   ☎02 80 69 21 ◙www.ambrosiana.it

When a gallery's halls themselves count as art, how much more spectacular does that make the works they house? It's a fair question at this museum just blocks from the Duomo. The palatial rooms of the Ambrosiana feature walls of vibrant colors and molded ceilings in gold leaf, while the building is graced by a cavernous library and a spiraling rotunda watched over by Roman statuettes above. The masterworks on the walls include the first Italian still-life, Caravaggio's *Basket of Fruit*. Raphael's expansive sketch of the **School of Athens** fills an entire wall in a room darkened for preservation. Tibaldi, Crespi, Breugel, and

Bril are among the dozens of other notable painters whose works have ended up in this Milanese museum.

♯ Ⓜ1: Duomo. Follow V. Spadari off V. Torino, and turn left onto V. Cantu. Ⓢ €8, under 18 and over 65 €5. 🕐 Open Tu-Su 9am-7pm. Last entry ½hr. before close.

MUSEO POLDI PEZZOLI
●& MUSEUM

V. Manzoni 12   ☎02 78 08 72 🖳www.museopoldipezzoli.it

Enter the home of one of Milan's most storied collectors, Gian Giacomo Poldi Pezzoli. His broad collection includes a number of famous Italian works, including Botticelli's *Madonna* and Pollaiuolo's *Portait of a Young Woman*. Works by some Flemish and Northern European painters, including Brueghel the younger, are on display as well. Jewelry, furniture, and timepieces round out this *palazzo*'s marvelous trove of *objets d'art*. Stop by Gian Giacomo's study (in which he spent his final hours) at the far end of the upper floor to see stained-glass windows, his china collection, and some marble statuettes. Downstairs, the collection of European armor, displayed in a dark castle-like room, has a thrillingly ominous tone. The free audio tour enriches the experience inside the museum by offering insight not only into the history of the paintings but also into the collecting habits of Gian Giacomo himself. If you're an incredibly lazy person (or if you're reading this book at home rather than in Milan, you super-traveler you), the entire collection can be viewed on the museum's website; you can listen to the audio tour there, too. It's just like getting guided through the museum, except your feet don't get tired and you can do it in your underwear.

♯ Ⓜ1/3: Duomo. Follow V. Manzoni past La Scala. *i* Audio tour included with admission. Ⓢ €8, students and seniors €5.50, ages under 10 free. 🕐 Open M 10am-6pm, W-Su 10am-6pm.

MUSEO TEATRALE ALLA SCALA
●⊗❋ MUSEUM

P. della Scala   ☎02 88 79 24 73 🖳www.teatroallascala.org

It's unclear if there's a joke in Italy to match the American "How do you get to Carnegie Hall?", but there sure could be—and La Scala would be the punchline destination. This theater may be opera's most acclaimed venue, and it possesses a storied past to match its reputation. The theater's museum explores that past in detail through a series of small, lavishly designed rooms on an upper floor of the building. For opera devotees or the completely uninitiated, the glimpse into La Scala's main hall (with its famous chandelier that, believe it or not, has never fallen) is stunning. The museum itself adds context, with displays from historic posters to musical instruments to a plaster cast of Toscanini's hand. Note that tour groups crowd the space easily, so the earlier you can visit here, the better. For information on performances, see **Opera and Ballet.**

♯ Ⓜ1/3: Duomo. Pass through the Galleria to P. della Scala. Entrance to museum is on the left side of the building. *i* No theater viewing when productions are in progress. Ⓢ €5. 🕐 Open daily 9am-12:30pm and 1:30-5:30pm.

MILAN URBAN CENTER
& EXHIBIT

Galleria Vittorio Emanuele 11/12   ☎02 88 45 68 06 🖳www.comune.milano.it/urbancenter

Quiz time! The World's Fair stopped being held after which of the following: (A.) That one in Paris where they built the Eiffel Tower (B.) That one in Chicago when they built the Ferris Wheel or (C.) That one in New York where they built that globe and the weird UFO things that the alien tries to escape from in *Men in Black*. Correct answer: none of the above! The World's Fair continues, and Milan is hosting the next one, in 2015. One of the themes will be sustainable urban development, and the community is showing its stuff early with this exhibition space, which has displayed models of skyscrapers and soccer stadiums from around the world.

♯ Ⓜ1/3: Duomo. In Galleria Vittorio Emanuele, near P. Scala. Ⓢ Free. 🕐 Open M-F 9am-6pm.

milan . sights

GALLERIA VITTORIO EMANUELE II

                                                       ⛫ ARCHITECTURE

P. del Duomo

Welcome to what may be the world's first shopping mall. But as they say, oft-imitated, never duplicated, and no suburban teen hangout can match the Galleria in intricacy and expense. After construction, its 48m glass and iron cupola was considered a radical feat of engineering. As the light streams in, the array of glass above this five-story arcade of offices, restaurants, and overpriced shops is still a marvelous sight. Before electricity, a miniature train circled high above the pedestrians, keeping candles lit along the glass. Today, the closest thing to whimsy is the juxtaposition of an American fast food chain with Milan's finest cuisine.

   ✈ Ⓜ1/3: Duomo. To the left when facing the Duomo. Ⓢ Free (entry at least).

MUSEO DI MILANO

                                                       ⛫ MUSEUM

V. Sant'Andrea 6   ☎02 88 46 41 75 ▣www.museodimilano.mi.it

Think you know Milan like the back of your hand? Not a chance, for while you may have a vague memory of what your hand looked like when you were five, you certainly have very little idea of what Milan resembled back in the 19th century. Head back in Milan's history at this municipal museum, which displays a remarkable number of paintings of Milan dating back decades and centuries. One focus is the construction of the Duomo, which unfolded over hundreds of years, revealed in just a few rooms of cityscapes. And to show that Milan still hasn't gone out of style, the museum also displays historical fashions and military uniforms once worn by the city's denizens.

   ✈ Ⓜ1: San Babila. Follow V. Bagutta. Turn right onto V. Sant'Andrea. Museum is up the stairs on the far side of the courtyard. Ⓢ Free. Ⓣ Open Tu-Su 9am-1pm and 2-5:30pm.

PALAZZO REALE

                                                    ✦⛫ EXHIBITION

P. del Duomo 12   ☎02 88 451 ▣www.comune.milano.it/palazzoreale

Once the home of Milanese royalty, this expansive mansion now boasts a royally confusing schedule of hours and exhibits. The building, designed by **Giuseppe Piermarini** of La Scala fame, also served as a town hall during its illustrious history but now plays host to an ever-rotating collection of exhibitions, sometimes up to five simultaneously.

   ✈ Ⓜ1/3: Duomo. To right when facing the Duomo. Ⓢ About €8, varying by exhibition. Ⓣ Open M 2:30-7:30pm, Tu-W 9:30am-7:30pm, Th 9:30am-10:30pm, F 9:30am-7:30pm, Sa 9:30am-10:30pm, Su 9:30am-7:30pm.

MUSEO MESSINA

                                                       ⊗ MUSEUM

V. San Sisto 4/a   ☎02 86 45 30 05

Located in a former church restored by the artist, every inch of this small gallery is filled with sculptures by **Francesco Messina,** one of Milan's best known 20th-century artists. Focusing on nudes and horses in terra cotta and bronze, Messina also added color to his rather beige sculpting repertoire by creating lighthearted pastel sketches which adorn the walls.

   ✈ Ⓜ1/3: Duomo. Follow V. Torino and take hard right onto V. San Sisto. Ⓢ Free. Ⓣ Open Tu-Sa 2-6pm.

Fashion District

While the most significant monuments of the Fashion District are the stores themselves, the side streets hold some unique, less frequented museums to explore.

▦ MUSEO BAGATTI VALSECCHI

                                                    ✦⊗ MUSEUM

V. Gesu 5   ☎02 76 00 61 32 ▣www.museobagattivalsecchi.org

This stunningly preserved 19th-century *palazzo* has no business calling itself a museum—it's more like a time machine. Built to appear several centuries older than it actually is, this former home of brothers Fausto and Giuseppe Bagatti

Valsecchi is full of Renaissance artwork and artifacts, including paintings by **Giovanni Bellini.** The building's artistic holdings are supplemented by an even greater number of Renaissance-style furniture pieces built in the 1800s. Every ceiling is ornately patterned, every cabinet handcrafted, and every modern convenience cleverly hidden. Though the house had running hot and cold water—advanced technology even for the latter part of the 19th century—its shower is an imposing marble edifice meant to evoke baths of yore. As jealousy-inducing as this tub may be, the most impressive room must be the arms gallery, which is full of breastplates, helmets, swords, and spears worn in battle all over Europe during the Renaissance era.

✦ Ⓜ3: Montenapoleone. Walk down V. Monte Napoleone and turn left onto V. Gesu. Ⓢ €8, students and over 65 €4. €4 for all on W. ◷ Open Tu-Sa 1-5:45pm.

FERRARI STORE
✦♿❅ STORE

P. del Liberty 8 ☎02 78 15 02 💻www.ferrari.com

Yes, it sells things. But this bright, screaming-red shrine to Italy's most famous automobile contains many artifacts of the storied brand that will interest even those who can't afford to buy the genuine Formula 1 engine block (€48,000). Given the price tag, you're probably better off taking a look at it in the showroom than admiring it in your own home. There's also a complete race car, and visitors can even see the undercarriage from the level below thanks to a useful glass floor. Many models of unique Ferraris, including a speedboat created by the automaker, are on display—and for sale—as well. Those who really want to take something home can purchase a teddy bear *(from €14)* or a shirt *(€60).*

✦ Ⓜ1: San Babila. Walk down C. Vittorio Emanuele II until you see P. Liberty to your right. Ⓢ Free. Products not so much. ◷ Open daily 10am-7pm.

MUSEO DELLA PERMANENTE
♿ MUSEUM

V. Filippo Turati 34 ☎02 65 99 803 💻www.lapermanente.it

While a tale of warring art curators in chainmail and berets might be more likely to catch a Hollywood screenwriter's eye, this museum is the result of a longtime collaboration between two once-independent societies that started working together in 1881. The object of interest at La Permanente is not its ownership, but its small and important collection of contemporary artwork, ranging from the colorful, movement-based cityscape of Emilio Tadini to the simple and thought-provoking splatters of Giulio Turcato's *Itinerari.*

✦ Ⓜ3: Turati. Follow V. Turati north 1 block. Ⓢ Free. ◷ Open Tu-Su 10am-1pm and 2:30-6:30pm.

Giardini Pubblici

If you feel as if you're running low on oxygen in Milan's treeless concrete jungle, here's your neighborhood. This human-friendly element does wonders for the brain, too, which is appropriate since some of Milan's lesser-known but still valuable museums and cultural institutions can be found in the Giardini Publicci area.

🖼 GIARDINI PUBBLICI
♿ GARDENS

C. Venezia at Bastioni di Porta Vinezia ☎02 67 06 093

More than just a park and namesake to the neighborhood, the Giardini Publicci brings a swath of green to a city in which all streets feel walled in by buildings and most foliage is confined to private interior courtyards. Designed in 1786 by **Giuseppe Piermarini** to be an Italian version of an English public garden, the garden was finalized in its current form for the World's Fair of 1871. Milan's main park is a popular spot among the city's residents who come here to walk their dogs, lie in the sun, or simply wander amidst the garden's shady ponds, open lawns, and mossy cliffside trails. (Just don't remind them that the Italians imitated the *English* when they designed this *giardini.*) Look for the outdoor bar with foosball *(open daily 8am-7pm)* near V. Palestro. For children, there are bumper cars—perfect practice for a future life driving on Italian roads *(€2, 6 rides for €10)*—and a carousel *(€1.50, 8 rides for €10)*.

✈ Ⓜ1: Porta Venezia or Palestro. Ⓢ Free. ☾ Open June-Aug 6:30am-11:30pm, Sept 6:30am-11pm, Oct 6:30am-9pm, Nov-Dec 6:30am-8pm, Jan-Feb 6:30am-8pm, March-April 6:30am-9pm, May 6:30am-10pm. Bumper cars open daily in summer 9:30am-7pm.

GALLERIA D'ARTE MODERNA
                                                ♿ MUSEUM

V. Palestro 16   ☏02 88 44 59 47 🖥www.gam-milano.com

Located in the historic Villa Reale—whose ornate ballrooms-turned-galleries are nearly a sight unto themselves—this gallery on the fringe of the Giardini Pubblici features a vast array of modern Italian art focusing on the 18th and 19th centuries. Among the best-known artists represented here are the Post-Impressionist **Paul Gauguin** and the Futurist **Giacomo Balla.** Over the years, many wealthy residents of Milan have donated or loaned their private collections to the museum, ensuring that it represents local taste as well as international flair.

✈ Ⓜ1: Porta Venezia. Ⓢ Free. ☾ Tu-Su 9am-1pm and 2pm-5:30pm.

MUSEO STORIA NATURALE
                                         ♨♿ MUSEUM

C. Venezia 55   ☏02 88 46 33 37 🖥www.comune.milano.it/museostorianaturale

Sure, from a scientific perspective, it's nice to start off, as the Museo Storia Naturale does, from the beginning—however many millions of years ago that may be. We're sure minerals and gemstones are cool, too. But to get to the really neato stuff, follow the footprints on the floor that lead to Hall 8, home of the 🦖**T-Rex.** He's joined by pliosaurs (fish ancestors of amphibians) who hang from the ceiling as well as other palentological specimens. The museum also houses exhibits on the history of humans, galleries of exotic animals, and stuffed dioramas of the creatures of Italy. There's also a free academic library in the building.

✈ Ⓜ1: Palestro. Ⓢ €3, students, Milan residents, and over 65 €1.50. ☾ Open Tu-Su 9:30am-5:30pm. Last entry 1/2hr. before close. Library open M-F 9:30am-12:20pm and 1:30-4:50pm.

PLANETARIO
                                            ♨♿ MUSEUM

C. Venezia 57   ☏02 88 46 33 40 🖥www.comune.milano.it/planetario

Visitors don't come to Milan for stargazing; the light pollution in Italy's second-largest city makes it hard to distinguish Mars from a large jet plane. What Milan does offer, however, is a planetarium where you can go on a tour of the universe after you've toured Italy's moral capital. The 80-year-old octagonal building, designed to recall Rome's Pantheon, features the image of a 1930s-era Milanese skyline at the base of its projection screen (notice any modern-day landmarks that are missing?) and also houses a small collection of meteorites, which can be viewed even when shows are not in session.

✈ Ⓜ1: Palestro. Ⓢ €3. Students, Milan residents and over 65 €1.50. ☾ Schedule varies month to month, but shows generally occur Tu, Th 9pm and Sa-Su 3pm and 4:30pm. Full schedule available online.

PADIGLEONE D'ARTE CONTEMPORANEA
                                           ♥♿ MUSEUM

V. Palestro 16   ☏02 76 00 90 85 🖥www.comune.milano.it/pac

Home to rotating exhibits of 20th-century art, the Padiglione d'Arte Contemporanea (PAC) complements its older and more well-known neighbor, the Galleria d'Arte Moderna. Focused on work that looks to the future, the museum has hosted previous exhibits that have included unique installation pieces. Exhibits change about every two months.

✈ Ⓜ1: Palestro. Ⓢ €6. Students, ages 6-14, and over 65 €4. 5 and under free. ☾ Open M 2:30-7:30pm, Tu-W 9:30am-7:00pm, Th 9:30am-10:30pm, F-Su 9:30am-7pm. Last entry 6:30pm, 9:30pm on Th.

Castello Sforzesco

Welcome to Milan's tourist district, part two. The Castello is a hub for many visitors, hawkers, and museums, but the surrounding area, with less trodden ground, hides a few extraordinary gems.

maximian luxury

Milan is famous for many things: its fashionable denizens, who walk the sidewalk as they would a runway; its financial dealings, which make it the hub of Italy's economy; and even its champion soccer teams. Unlike many places in Italy, however, it's not known for once being the capital of the Roman Empire.

Hold on a sec. Wasn't Rome the capital, you ask? Well, no, not under Emperor Maximian, who, in 286 CE, decided that Milan, with its perfect climate and beautiful pastoral setting, would be the ideal place to reside. And where the emperor goes, of course, the administration follows, resulting in a sprawling (for the time—today it stretches over a few city blocks) imperial district within the city.

And where the emperor lives, too, no expense is spared. The ruins on V. Brisa, about 1km from Castello Sforzesco, once held the emperor's stately residence. The floorplan revealed by the remaining brickwork is evidence of a circular main room, from which a dome probably rose, giving Maximian lots of natural light as he lounged, chewing on grapes while being fanned by his servants. He also had the most high-tech architectural accessory of the day: central heating. This luxury fit for an emperor was created by the circulation of warm air in a space beneath the floors, remnants of which are still there today.

Although the Roman court eventually moved on, this building was used by genteel Milanese citizens through the fifth century. Evidently, however, Attila the Hun—who conquered Milan in 452—had little use for such refinement. Sometime over the next few centuries, the building was destroyed, not to be seen again until nearly 1000 years after the Huns' wrath.

For a full primer on Milan's ancient past, head to the city's **Museo Civico Archeologico.** *(C. Magenta 15 ☎02 86 45 00 11 ⚓ Ⓜ1: Lotto. From P. Lotto, a long walk down V. le Caprili, which becomes Piazzale del Sport. Enter through gate 14. Ⓢ Museum €7, under 18 and over 65 €5. Museum and tour €12.50/€10. ⚏ Open daily 10am-5pm. Sometimes varies on gamedays and during special events.)* It's conveniently close to Maximian's deteriorated digs.

▣ CASTELLO SFORZESCO

⚓♿ CASTLE, MUSEUM

P. Castello ☎02 88 46 37 00 🖥www.milanocastello.it

Visiting Castello Sforzesco is just like being in a toy shop: A castle! With a moat! And gates that crash down! And coats of arms! And knights in shining armor! And princesses! And museums of ancient art and Egypt and prehistory and decorative arts and musical instruments! (OK, so maybe not all of us had ancient art museums at our local toy store.) Really, Milan's dominant fortress, constructed in 1368 to defend the city, is way better than a toy box. Leonardo's studio could once be found within the castle, which today pays tribute to him and many other artists in its ▣**Museum of Ancient Art,** where Leonardo's frescoes cover the ceiling. Also worth a look are the Museum of Musical Instruments and the Museum of Decorative Art, which showcases distinctive Italian furnishings from throughout the ages as well as Murano glass.

✦ Ⓜ1: Cairoli. Ⓢ *Grounds free. All-museum pass €3, students and seniors €1.50.* Ⓒ *Castle grounds open daily Apr-Oct 7am-7pm; Nov-Mar 7am-6pm. Museums open Tu-Su 9am-5:30pm.*

CHIESA DI SANTA MARIA DELLE GRAZIE AND CENACOLO VINCIANO ✦⚭ CHURCH
P. Santa Maria delle Grazie 2 ☎02 89 42 11 46 ▧www.cenacolovinciano.org

Leonardo's *The Last Supper* is one of the world's most famous paintings and— unlike another famous da Vinci masterpiece—it isn't surrounded by hundreds or thousands of gawkers. Due to the fragility of the painting, which was restored and returned to public display in 1999, groups of only 25 are granted 15min. slots in which to view the painting. Still, as any economist will tell you, this limited supply creates a significant shortage of tickets, so book ahead (☎02 92 80 03 60). Batches of six-week's worth of tickets are released unannounced so as to thwart tour groups that buy up these scarce commodities as soon as they are available. For those lucky enough to gain admission, impressive, colorful frescoes grace the walls and archways of the church's Gothic nave.

✦ Ⓜ1: Conciliazione or Ⓜ3: Cardona. *From P. Conciliazione, take V. Boccacio and then turn right onto V. Ruffini for 2 blocks.* ⓘ *Many tickets for the Last Supper are bought up by tour companies months in advance, so be sure to reserve early online.* Ⓢ *Church free. Refectory €6.50, EU residents 18-25 €3.25, EU residents under 18 or over 65 free. Reservation fee €1.50.* Ⓒ *Church open daily 7am-noon and 3-7pm. Refectory open Tu-Su 8am-7:30pm; last entry 6:45pm.*

PINACOTECA DI BRERA ✦⚭ MUSEUM
V. Brera 28 ☎02 72 26 31 ▧www.brera.beniculturali.it

"I'm naked!" screamed the nude from her canvas. But not because her shapely painted figure was bare—she was used to that already—but because her frame, that beautiful, ornate, golden frame, had been unceremoniously removed. Now, from the other side of the glass wall, all the world could see the painting in its birthday suit. One of the Pinacoteca di Brera's most unique aspects is that, within a glass enclosed cube in Gallery 14, conservators work on paintings, providing a glimpse into how art museums keep their priceless works fresh. Founded for the private study of art students, this art museum also includes highlights such as Raphael's *Marriage of the Virgin* and Caravaggio's *Supper at Emmaus* in addition to numerous other works spanning from the 14th to 20th centuries. To experience how today's art is made, wander the halls of the ground floor where academy students sculpt and paint between classes.

✦ Ⓜ2: Lanza or Ⓜ3: Montenapoleone. *Walk down V. Pontaccio and turn right onto V. Brera. Or from La Scala, walk up V. Verdi until it becomes V. Brera.* ⓘ *Visitors with disabilities enter V. Fiori Oscuri 2.* Ⓢ *€5, EU citizens under 18 or over 65 free.* Ⓒ *Open Tu-Su 8:30am-7:30pm. Last entry 45min. before close.*

MUSEO NAZIONALE DELLA SCIENZA E DELLA TECNOLOGIA "DA VINCI"
✦⚭ MUSEUM
21 V. San Vittore ☎02 48 55 51 ▧www.museoscienza.org

No automobiles here, but there *are* planes, trains, ships, and a submarine—some designed by Italy's most famous inventor and the museum's namesake, whose sketches have been reconstructed in 3D so kids can try to make that outrageous whirlybird fly. Youngsters will also love pushing the buttons in the robotics section and climbing up to the many impressive vehicles on display, including four trains and a full-rigged naval ship. While kids swarm about the museum's entrance on weekends, the wide, open water- and air-transport exhibits offer more space and quiet.

✦ Ⓜ2: Sant'Ambrogio. Ⓢ *€8, under 18 and students with ID €6. Submarine tours additional €8.* Ⓒ *Open Tu-F 9:30am-5pm, Sa-Su 9:30am-6:30pm.*

BASILICA DI SANT'AMBROGIO

⊕ & CHURCH

P. Sant'Ambrogio 15

☎02 86 45 08 95

Soaring domes of golden mosaics. Towering arches with intricate brickwork. Two towers that totally don't match—and quite a few skeletons. Indeed, walk up the right side of this church's nave and into the crypt beneath the altar to see the entombed bodies of several saints and martyrs, dressed up in what you might call their centuries-old Sunday best. Despite being considered one of the most important examples of Lombard Romanesque design, Sant'Ambrogio's architecture is far from perfect. A long-running feud between two groups—canons and monks—each of whom controlled one side of the church, left the lopsided bell-towers that remain today. Though the monks, on the right, might have seemed to draw the short straw (err, steeple), their structure was completed in the 9th century CE, while the canons, beginning work in 1128, took nearly 1000 years longer to build theirs.

⚡ Ⓜ2: Sant'Ambrogio. Walk up V. Carducci; the church wall rises on the right. Ⓢ Church free. Museum of mosaics and artifacts €2, students €1. Ⓣ Church open daily 7:30am-12:30pm and 2:30-7pm. Mosaics open daily 9:30-11:45am and 2:30-6pm.

Navigli

Landlubber no more! Even a fear of water shouldn't stop visitors from enjoying a cruise through Navigli—the **Navigli Boat Tour** (⚡Ⓧ Alzaia Naviglio Grande 4 ☎02 33 22 73 36 🖳www.naviglilombardi.it ⚡ Ⓜ2: Porta Genova. Ⓢ €12, over 60 €10, under 8 €8, under 3 free. Ⓣ Open F-Su; 7 55min. trips per day 10:15am-6:15pm.) never goes more than a few feet from each shore. Navigate the neighborhood's canals as 16th-century merchants might have, minus the pimp-tastic hat plumage (and with the addition of two outboard motors). Tours highlight the church of **San Cristoforo**, the Darsena canal, and the Conchetta area. Plan ahead, as tours often sell out.

⧄ BASILICA DI SAN LORENZO MAGGIORE AND LORENZO COLUMNS

& CHURCH

C. di Porta Ticinese 39

☎02 89 40 41 29 🖳www.sanlorenzomaggiore.com

Up, up, and away is the feeling as San Lorenzo's soaring dome draws eyes to the heavens. Its gold-plated altar and organ make for another holy feast for the eyes. The columns outside the building are the most significant Roman ruin remaining in Milan and act not only as a historical reminder but as a social gathering spot. The basilica itself also has historic relevance, as its round floorplan became a symbol of the circle's perfection during the Renaissance.

⚡ Ⓜ1: San Ambrogio. Follow V. de Amicis. Ⓢ Free. Ⓣ Open daily 7:30am-12:30pm and 2:30-6:45pm.

TICINESE CITY GATE

& ARCHITECTURE

P. XXIV Maggio

Originally part of a wall built to protect Milan in the 1100s, today this gate is wide open to the onslaught of cars, scooters, and trams that invade the city. As the only gate from the period remaining in the city, Ticinese is an impressive survivor. Today, a countercultural scene can be found making its weekend home under the gate's arches, with impromptu concerts filling the Friday night air, bars sprouting from the back of parked VW buses, and ⧄**communist** rallies bringing out the *carabinieri*.

⚡ Ⓜ2: Porta Genova. Ⓢ Free.

City Outskirts

While Milan's monuments are concentrated in the city center, beyond this area a number of museums whose scope stretches past the classical art and history found near the Duomo await. From sports to modern sculpture and poster art, there's much to explore beyond Milan's ring roads.

milan · sights

CIMITERO MONUMENTALE ♿ CEMETERY

Piazzale Cimitero Monumentale ☎02 88 46 56 00 💻www.monumentale.net

Imagine Arlington Cemetery in Virginia, with its rows of even, identical gravestones. Then imagine the exact opposite. That's Cimitero Monumentale, whose often gaudy mausoleums and sculpted headstones offer an everlasting image of the departed. Famed conductor Toscanini makes this graveyard his final resting place. Try to spot his tomb, which was designed for his son who died at the age of four. It's pockmarked with scars left from the World War II bombs that battered Milan. When the tomb was recently restored, the holes were left as a reminder of Toscanini's staunch resistance to Mussolini's regime. For a time, the cemetery was also home to the body of Eva Peron, the Argentine political icon who was buried secretly, under a pseudonym to protect her remains from a hostile regime. Today, the vast landscape makes for a quiet and refreshing walk in the shade—if you can avoid the meandering tour groups of senior citizens.

🚏 Ⓜ2: Porta Garibaldi. Walk parallel to the tracks and under the overpass. Cross V. Farini to the cemetery parking lot. $ Free. ⏰ Open Tu-Su 8am-6pm.

FONDAZIONE ARNALDO POMODORO 🎫♿ MUSEUM

V. Solari 35 ☎02 89 07 53 94 💻www.fondazionearnaldopomodoro.it

Founded in 1999 to showcase the work of Italian sculptor Pomodoro, this large, warehouse-like museum southwest of the city now focuses on giving a first chance to a number of young, up-and-coming artists who work in three-dimensional mediums. Nevertheless, it is the striking and disconcerting bronze reliefs of Pomodoro, characterized by the forceful explosion of their geometric patterns, that make the first impression. The gallery has a permanent collection of 28 Pomodoros (you know you're a legit artist when people use your name as a concrete noun), including an outdoor obelisk, which rotates through the exhibition space regularly. Beyond these pieces, the collection sitting under towering skylights can be both enthralling and confusing. Though the exhibitions change frequently, shows tend to include contemporary installation pieces ranging from inflatable sculptures to clothing collections.

🚏 Ⓜ2: Sant'Agostino. Take tram #14 to Solari/Stendhal. $ €8, students €5. ⏰ Open W-Th 11am-6pm, F 11am-10pm, Sa-Su 11am-6pm.

MUSEO AND TOUR SAN SIRO 🎫♿ MUSEUM, SOCCER

V. dei Piccolomini 5 ☎02 40 42 432 💻www.sansirotour.com

Located inside the stadium that is home to the AC Milan and Inter Milan soccer teams (see **San Siro**), this museum traces the history of both clubs through displays of everything from posters to jerseys to vintage noisemakers. Tour the stadium—including behind-the-scenes areas and the locker rooms of the professional clubs—on which construction began in the 1920s. It has since been expanded to seat nearly 85,000 people. Those who fill the stadium climb up corkscrew-like ramps and sit under a roof of bubbles for the chance to see local football heroes duel on the pitch hundreds of feet below. Needless to say, the original architects would never recognize their creation. Inside the museum, visitors can pose next to life-size statues of 24 of the greatest players from both clubs—almost as good as seeing them in person from the nosebleeds.

🚏 Ⓜ1: Lotto. From P. Lotto, a long walk down V. le Caprili, which becomes Piazzale del Sport. Enter through gate 14. $ Museum €7, under 18 and over 65 €5. Museum and tour €12.50/10. ⏰ Open daily 10am-5pm. Sometimes varies on gamedays and during special events.

PIRELLI TOWER ♿ TOWER

P. Duca d'Aosta 3

If the Duomo is the elegant symbol of Milan's heart and soul, the Pirelli tower is the manifestation of its industrial brawn and economic prosperity. Upon orders from Alberto Pirelli, president of the famous tire company, construction began in 1956. Soon the 30-story tower was the tallest building in Italy. Architecturally, it was definitive as well, with tapered edges rather than a flat face. Eventually sold to the Region of Lombardy, the building continues to be used as a government headquarters while maintaining its historic name. Today, it is one of the city's best known buildings. The municipal planetarium built in 1930—long before the Pirelli Tower was imagined—features a dated skyline along the inside of its dome. One of the questions most frequently posed to docents at the planetarium is: where is the tower?

� Ⓜ2/3: Centrale F.S. 𝒊 Interior not open to the public. Ⓢ Free.

GALLERIA CAMPARI
                                             ⟁ MUSEUM

Vle. Gramsci 161, Sesto San Giovanni   ☎02 62 251 🖳www.campari.com

If an elementary school group can visit an alcohol museum, it must be good. Or it must not really be about alcohol. The Galleria Campari, while still not particularly child-friendly, is a *really* good alcohol museum. Located in Campari's historic factory and showcasing the history of the famous Italian aperitif, the gallery is, in effect, an exhibit of 20th-century graphic art and advertising. Filled with video screens displaying television ads and vintage poster art, the gallery is more than just a shameless self-promotion. Look for caricatures of celebrities such as Greta Garbo and Charlie Chaplin holding tight to their favorite beverage (guess) on the walls. Notable graphic artists represented in the Campari catalogue include **Bruno Murari,** some of whose work for Campari is displayed in New York's MoMA, and **Marcello Dudovich,** the recognized master of early 20th-century Italian publicity posters.

✠ Ⓜ1: Sesto Maggio F.S. Purchase an "Urban+1/2 Zone" ticket for €1.55. From the station, turn left. Ⓢ Free. 🕐 Open Tu 10am-1pm and 2-6:30pm, Th-F 10am-1pm and 2-6:30pm. Guided viewings at 10am, 11:30am, 2pm, 3:30pm, and 5pm.

BENI CULTURALI CAPPUCCINI MUSEO
                                             ⊗ MUSEUM

V. Kramer 5   ☎02 77 12 23 21 🖳www.bccmuseum.org

Commemorating the history of the Cappuccini Order of monks—related to Franciscans, not coffee—who once held broad influence in Lombardy, this museum is full of delicately painted Christian symbols and religious artifacts from the 1800s and earlier. A fascinating diorama presents the Porta Venezia area of Milan as it appeared hundreds of years ago. The only part of the original layout that remains today is the central church now located off Vle. Tunisia and surrounded by walls.

✠ Ⓜ1: Palestro. From C. Venezia, take V. Salvini, which becomes V. Vitali and then V. de Bernard and V. Belloti. Turn right onto V. Kramer. 𝒊 Most informational signs are in Italian only. Ⓢ Free; donations encouraged. 🕐 Open Tu-W 3-6:30pm, Th 10am-6:30pm, F 3-6:30pm, Sa-Su 10am-6:30pm.

FOOD

There's much to be had from Milan's culinary scene, from slices of pizza enjoyed while sitting on the sidewalk to fine dining in the city's venerable sit-down, button-up establishments. Starting the night off right is easy with happy hour *aperitivo* buffets offered by many bars, especially near the Navigli—all-you-can-eat spreads of breads, pasta, meats, and cheeses come included with the purchase of one drink. Sadly overlooked most everywhere except inside the city's ring road, Milanese cuisine with its risotto and *cottoletta alla milanese* (breaded veal cutlet) is still served up in a number of quaint trattorias. Often hard to find in Italy, ethnic cuisines from Argentina to Eritrea and beyond take center stage in some neighborhoods, particularly around **Giardini Pubblici.** The bottom line of Milan's dining scene, especially near the tourist attractions: if it feels like it was too easy to find, it probably was. Hop on the metro, get away from the Duomo, and see what your fork can find.

Piazza del Duomo

When it's time to sit down and eat after your sightseeing, identify the touristy spots on the Piazza del Duomo—then steer clear. A better bet is to venture down a few side streets, where there are a number of great, inexpensive options. If price is no obstacle, check out famous **Savini** *(Galleria V. Emanuele II ☎02 72 00 34 33 💻www.savinimilano.it)*, where a hamburger will set you back only €22.

👍 PRINCI

🍴🍸 BAKERY, PIZZERIA [1]

V. Speronari 6 ☎02 87 47 97 💻www.princi.it

Restaurant idea lab, circa the foundation of Princi: "Hey, I've got an idea! Let's put an Italian bread shop into an Egyptian tomb!" In such a manner, this dimly lit, sandstone-walled bakery might have been conceived. Regardless, as much as the place feels like the inside of King Tut's post-death pad, no tomb was ever this tasty. The bakery is not nearly as silent as a mausoleum, either. The hubbub of locals swarming the counter can be intimidating to tourists unfamiliar with the place, but to order a tasty pizza slice *(€3.50-5)* or pastry *(€1-4)*, just be assertive and push through the throngs to reach the counter.

➜ [M]1/3: Duomo. Take V. Torino and make first left. $ Primi and secondi €5-10. 🕐 Open daily 7am-8pm.

PIZZA AND FRIENDS

💳♿🍸 PIZZERIA [2]

V. F. Baracchini 9 ☎02 87 23 81 33 💻www.pizzaandfriends.com

If you believe the names of its dishes, this place should cost a fortune. Luckily, it doesn't. The "St. Tropez" *(tomato, mozzarella, tuna, leek, and basil; €9)* ain't nearly as expensive as the vacation destination it's named after, and the "Rockefeller" *(mozzarella di bufala, truffles, egg yolk, arugula, and parmesan; €12)* doesn't require the bank account of America's famous oil tycoon. The greatest part? These pizza pies taste like a million bucks.

➜ [M]3: Missori. From P. Missori, follow V. M. Gonzaga. At P. Diaz, turn right onto V. Baracchini. $ Pizzas €5.50-12; sandwiches €5-6.50. 🕐 Open daily 11:30am-1am.

GROM

💳♿ GELATERIA [1]

V. Santa Margherita 16 ☎02 80 58 10 41 💻www.grom.it

This place's gelato is so good that they have to hide it. While other establishments have mounds of the stuff on display, at Grom, only the privileged few get a chance to see the masterpiece frozen treats that servers keep covered under American-style tin lids. Unfortunately for some customers (but perfect for those with squirrel-like sensibilities), nut flavors seem to be a specialty, as pistachio and hazelnut are favorites.

➜ [M]1/3: Duomo. Pass through the Galleria to P. Scala. Follow V. San Margherita to the right. $ Gelato €2.50-3.50. 🕐 Open M-Th noon-11pm, F-Sa noon-midnight, Su noon-11pm.

3CAFE

💳♿🍸❄ ARGENTINIAN [2]

C. di Porta Ticinese 1 ☎02 45 49 60 85 💻www.3cafe.it

In Milan, a place of refined taste and class, it seems practically vulgar to put a picture of a big, juicy, hunking piece of meat in your window. But that's just how 3Cafe adorns itself, and this method seems to work, as the restaurant draws people in for steaks prepared in a way that you just can't get at an Italian *ristorante*. The best deals are at lunch: steak, fries or salad, dessert, red wine, and coffee for €15.

➜ [M]2: Sant'Ambrogio. Follow V. de Amicis and turn left onto C. di Porta Ticinese. $ Primi €6; secondi €7.50. 🕐 Open M-Sa noon-3pm and 7:30-11:30pm.

FRATELLI LA BUFALA

💳🚭🍸❄ RISTORANTE, BUFFALO [2]

C. di Porta Ticinese 16 ☎02 83 76 529 💻www.fratellilabufala.com

Yes, *mozzarella di bufala* is one of Italy's most famous cheeses. But no, it's not the focus at this family-gathering spot. The star of the show at this Argentinian kitchen is the buffalo of the *meat* variety—the horned animal that may be just as hard to milk as it is to kill. Not to worry though; all that nasty killing stuff has been dealt with in advance, so you can enjoy your buffalo burger (€16) or buffalo meat pizza *senza attenzione*.

✚ Ⓜ2: Sant'Ambrogio. Follow V. de Amicis and turn left onto C. di Porta Ticinese. Ⓢ Pizza €5.50-10. ☾ Open daily 12:30-3pm and 7:30pm-midnight.

LA RINASCENTE
⌖ ♿ FOOD COURT ❶

V. San Raffaele 2, 7th fl. ☏02 88 52 471 ▣www.rinascente.com

So many options, so little time! This multifaceted food court on the top floor of a well-known Milanese department store not only sells gourmet chocolate, chives, and cheeses, but also serves up deals that lead even students to take the high-speed elevator ride to the building's roof. Sushi (€2.50-€7.50) is among the favorites here, while the best value for meals can be found in Juice Bar's lunch special of water and coffee with panini (€8) or salad (€10).

✚ Ⓜ1/3: Duomo. On the left side of the Duomo. Take elevator just inside the door. Ⓢ Varies by outlet. Entrees €5-15. ☾ Open daily 9am-midnight.

RONCHI 78
⌖⊘⌖ RISTORANTE ❸

V. San Maurilio 7 ☏02 86 72 95 ▣www.ronchi78.it

Things must get a bit noisy at this back-lane establishment. Otherwise, why would Ronchi 78 post a sign that asks customers to "avoid noises outside?" With acoustic musicians performing nightly and a lively neighborhood crowd milling about, some ambient sound is to be expected. At lunch, the food served in the homey upstairs or cavernous brick cellar is remarkably affordable, with *primi* and *secondi* offerings from €7 that include vegetables and sides served from bowls on the bar.

✚ Ⓜ1/3: Duomo. Take V. Torino; turn right onto V. Maurillo. Ⓢ Salads €7. Dinner primi and secondi €9-18. ☾ Open M-Sa 8am-midnight.

PECK
⌖⊘ CAFE ❷

V. Spadari 9 ☏02 80 23 161 ▣www.peck.it

Stepping into Peck is like entering an elegant food "shoppe" of yore and taking a trip back in time. Black-tied waiters and high-hatted butchers can dish up any food imaginable, including prepared dishes from the back counter that can be combined at your whim to form a gourmet meal. Visit the upstairs cafe for fine sandwiches on a budget.

✚ Ⓜ1/3: Duomo. Follow V. Torino and take first right. Ⓢ Prepared foods from €4. Sandwiches €6. ☾ Open M 3:30-7:30pm, Tu-F 9:15am-7:30pm, Sa 8:45am-7:30pm.

Fashion District

Restaurant options can be limited within the central shopping zone of the Fashion District, and much of what's there is overpriced fare aimed at tourists or fashionistas. Try going south of **Piazza San Babila** or to the nearby parts of the Brera district for some better values.

▨ BREK
⌖♿⌖❄ BUFFET ❶

Piazzetta Giordano 1 ☏02 76 02 33 79 ▣www.brek.com

Grab and go is not the motto here. This is fast food Fashion District style, so the buttoned-up throngs take their meal on china from the buffet and walk down the wide, grand staircase to eat. Typical Italian entrees like lasagna and pizza accompany sides ranging from meat and cheese plates to chocolate cake and tiramisu, meaning this eatery offers whatever flavor—and calorie level—the diner desires.

✚ Ⓜ1: San Babila. From P. San Babila, walk through the arcade named "Galleria San Babila" to Piazzetta Giordano. ⓘ Don't spend your money on the bottled water–tap water and glasses are available in the seating area. Ⓢ Salads €3-4. Pizza slices €3-4. Primi €4-6. ☾ Open daily noon-3pm and 6:30-10:30pm.

milan · food

BIANCO LATTE 🏷♿📶❄ CAFE, GELATERIA [2]

V. Turati 30 ☎02 62 08 61 77 🖥www.biancolattemilano.it

This *gelateria* puts the California Milk Processor Board to shame. The people at Bianco Latte (literally, "White Milk") claim they strive to keep everything pure, simple, and homey by focusing on the wonders of dairy. No need for "Got Milk" ads with that kind of philosophy. In the form of smooth, cool gelato in an array of nutty and sweet flavors, their dairy is something to moo over. Before the afternoon ice cream rush, businesspeople flood the cafe's front room for a coffee and pastry *(€1)* during the morning cappuccino rush. Also serves lunch and dinner plates, like the *latteria*, with three cheeses and salad *(€10)*.

➡ *[M]3: Turati. Head north a ½-block.* [$] *Gelato €2.50-4.* ⏰ *Open M 7:30am-7:30pm, Tu-F 7:30am-midnight, Sa-Su 8am-midnight.*

CAFE VECCHIA BRERA 🏷🚭🍸 CAFE [2]

V. dell'Orso 20 ☎02 86 46 16 95 🖥www.creperiavecchiabrera.it

Crepes and beer. What's not to love? Even better, this casual establishment claims to offer an entire "world" of different and exotic brews *(€3-15)*, and the bar has the bottles and taps to prove it. No matter which brew you choose, combine that cool golden beverage and a steaming golden crepe *(€5-7)* piled high with chocolate, fruit, and whipped cream—or meat or vegetables, if you prefer—there's no way to lose (a few pounds).

➡ *[M]1: Cairoli. From Largo Cairoli, follow V. Cusani until it becomes V. dell'Orso just before the cafe.* [$] *Cover €1. Crepes €5-7. Sandwiches €7-8.* ⏰ *Open M-Sa 7am-2am, Su 11am-2am.*

ARMANI/NOBU 🏷♿🍸❄ ASIAN [3]

V. Gastone Pisoni 1 ☎02 62 31 26 45 🖥www.armaninobu.it

Frugal diners won't believe their eyes when they see the prices on this menu. You're not being deceived by the darkroom-like orange light: it's surprisingly affordable, especially considering the famous names on the marquee and the price tags in the boutique next door. Dishes from the "Nobu Specialties" *(€8-16)* are among the best deals, while sushi rolls *(€6-12)* are also satisfying to both the palate and the wallet. Only in the menu's last few pages do the digits start to tick upwards.

➡ *[M]3: Montenapoleone. Exit towards "V. Montenapoleone" and Armani is in front of you. Restaurant entrance at back right side of building.* [$] *Nobu Specialties €8-16. Entrees €23-35.* ⏰ *Open daily noon-2:30pm and 7:30-11:30pm. Bar open noon-3pm and 7:30pm-midnight.*

RISTORANTE BAGUTTA 🏷🚭🍸❄ RISTORANTE [5]

V. Bagutta 14 ☎02 76 00 27 67 🖥www.bagutta.it

Nothing is constant here at this restaurant, which breaks out of the Lombard mold to take its influence from the far away fields of Tuscany. The menu changes with the season, the day's shopping, and, quite possibly, the whim of the talented chef. The one thing that does not change is the restaurant's location on a small, stoned street behind V. Monte Napleone where, since 1924, visitors from all over the world have joined Milan's elite to enjoy some of the finest cuisine around.

➡ *[M]1: San Babila. From the piazza, head toward V. Monte Napoleone and turn right onto V. Bagutta.* [$] *Primi €13-17; secondi €22-32.* ⏰ *Open M-Sa noon-3pm and 7pm-midnight.*

Giardini Pubblici

The streets surrounding Giardini Pubblici offer an (eventually welcome) respite from the Italian fare that dominates the city. Locals—who are adamant about cooking their own homegrown recipes—come to this neighborhood for its selection of cuisines from Asia, Africa, and even the Americas. (And, no, we don't mean the United States.) For more ethnic cuisine without breaking the bank, purchase Indian staples at **Krishna Indian Bazaar.** *(🏷 V. P. Castaldi 35. ☎02 20 24 04 51. ⏰ Open M-Sa 10am-10pm.)* There's also an **Unes Supermarket.** *(🏷 V. Spallanzani 10. ☎02 29 51 95 76. ⏰ Open daily 8am-9pm.)*

CASATI 19

🍴⊗❄ RISTORANTE ❸

V. F. Casati 19   ☎02 29 40 29 94 ■www.ristorantepizzeriacasati19.it

This family-run establishment has gotten a reputation as Giardini Pubblici's go-to neighborhood *ristorante*. Its pizzas, including the featured "Casati 19" with artichokes and cured beef (€7.50), are always filling.

🍴 Ⓜ1: Porta Venezia. Ⓢ Cover €1.50. Primi and secondi €8-16. 🕐 Open Tu-Su noon-3pm and 7-11pm.

RISTORANTE ASMARA

🍴⊗❄ ERITREAN ❸

V. L. Palazzi 5   ☎02 89 07 37 98 ■www.ristoranteasmara.it

Prepare your taste buds before entering this African establishment that features spicy food beneath Eritrean flags and portraits of tribesmen. Use your 🖐hands to scoop up *zighini* with meat and vegetables into a flatbread (€10). Vegetarian options are also available.

🍴 Ⓜ1: Porta Venezia. Ⓢ Cover €1.60. Appetizers €4-5.50; entrees €8-10. 🕐 Open M-Tu 10:30am-3:30pm and 6pm-midnight, W 6pm-midnight, Thu-Su 10:30am-3:30pm and 6pm-midnight.

L'OSTERIA DEL TRENO

🍴⊗❄🛋 RISTORANTE ❶

V. San Gregorio 46/48   ☎02 67 00 479 ■www.osteriadeltreno.it

Step right up to this cozy self-service restaurant, where locals gather at lunchtime to catch up with friends and meet for work dates with colleagues. While you might resent the feeling of stepping back into your high school cafeteria as you order your food from the little old woman at the kitchen window, we doubt your high school served up dishes this tasty. The menu changes daily, but you can count on a number of pasta and meat options—and no mystery meat.

🍴 Ⓜ2/3: Centrale F.S. Ⓢ Primi €4.50; secondi €6.50. 🕐 Open M-F 10am-7pm and 8:30pm-12:20am, Sa noon-7pm and 8:30pm-12:20am, Su 10am-1pm and 7pm-12:30am. Lunch service begins at 12:30pm.

RISTORANTE INDIANO NEW DELHI

🍴⊗❄ INDIAN ❸

V. Tadino 1   ☎02 29 53 64 48 ■www.ristorantenewdelhi.it

Spaghetti, pizza, gelato: so old hat, right? Though these Italian staples may not have tired your taste buds yet, the Milanese who can expertly prepare them in their own kitchens turn to the bright orange awning at Ristorante Indiano New Delhi for something they *don't* know how to prepare: the best Indian food in the neighborhood. If you're feeling particularly native, join the crowd and chow down on a fresh-cooked samosa, enjoy one of New Delhi's lunch specials (vegetarian €8, with meat €9), or sample from the Indian-style antipasti (€3.50-6).

🍴 Ⓜ1: Porta Venezia. Ⓢ Tandoori and curry dishes €11-14. 🕐 Open daily 11am-4pm and 6pm-midnight.

AZZURRA GRILL

🍴⊗❄ SEAFOOD ❸

V. San Gregorio 11   ☎02 29 40 61 15

The deep blue sea is pretty far from Milan, but fresh fish still come in daily at this grill. At Azzura, you can sample all of the ocean's bounty in pastas, cooked as main dishes, and on pizzas. Try the thin sliced swordfish (€13) or Azzurra's signature pizza, which is topped with tomatoes and seafood (€9).

🍴 Ⓜ1: Porta Venezia. Ⓢ Primi €7-12. Seafood dishes €11-19. 🕐 Open daily 7-11pm.

PANIFICIO LAGO

🍴⊗ BAKERY ❶

V. F. Casati 24, at V. Lazzaretto   ☎02 66 98 73 99 ■www.panificio-lago.it

Panificio Lago provides a midday carbo-boost for skateboarding middle schoolers, cane-carrying grandparents, and everyone in between. With the opportunity to buy focaccia (€1-4) by the kilo at this mouth-watering *fornaio*, you'll be considering the anti-Atkins diet as you dive into this great deal.

🍴 Ⓜ1: Porta Venezia. Ⓢ Pastries €1-3. 🕐 Open M-F 7:15am-2pm and 4-7pm, Sa 7:15am-2pm.

milan • food

IL PANINO GIUSTO 🍴 SANDWICHES ❷

V. Malpighi 3 ☎02 29 40 92 97 🖳www.paninogiusto.it

For a hearty and simple panino or a unique and elaborate one, head to this sandwich shop where the wide variety of options aims to satisfy the craving of any passerby. Il Panino Giusto also serves more expensive entrees but shouldn't as hardly anyone ever orders them. Avoid the overpriced soda pop; instead, cough up the extra half-euro for something much more worth it, and get yourself an oat soda.

 # [M]1: Porta Venezia. From P. S. F. Romana, follow V. Melzo to V. Malpighi. $ Sandwiches €4.50-7. Entrees €8-19. ⏰ Open daily noon-1am.

Castello Sforzesco

As is the case with the Duomo, restaurants within sight of the Castello Sforzesco are designed to catch tourists who don't know where else to eat. These establishments leech as much as they can out of these unsuspecting victims, serving food that is overpriced and often marginally edible. Try **Corso Magenta** and some parts of the Brera district instead.

CHOCOLAT 🍴 GELATERIA ❶

V. Boccaccio 9 ☎02 48 00 16 35 🖳www.chocolatmilano.it

Six different flavors of gelato, and that's just counting those of the chocolate variety? Say what? You'll find that this *gelateria* not only earns its name but goes beyond the call of duty, serving up white chocolate, coffee, nougat, and fruit flavors as well. Locals say that the unique, spicy Chilli Chocolate flavor is a must-have. When you take in the cakes, pastries, and candy bars all with—you guessed it—chocolate that fill this sugar-fiend's delight, you have a place that would make even Willy Wonka die of joy (or maybe just a sugar high).

 # [M]1/2: Cardona F. N. $ Gelato €2.50-3.50. ⏰ Open M-F 7:30am-midnight, Sa 8am-midnight, Su 10am-midnight.

JAMAICA BAR 🍴 CAFE ❷

32 V. Brera ☎02 87 67 23 🖳www.jamaicabar.it

Don't visit this Brera establishment for a serving of modesty—it's not on the menu at this historic cafe that's played host to a line of important artists, writers, and even Nobel prize winners. What is on sale here is Milan's culinary classic, *cottaletta alla milanese*, a fried veal cutlet served with risotto *(€14.50)*. Even as its neighborhood has gentrified, Jamaica stays close to its roots by showcasing up-and-coming local artists on its walls.

 # [M]1: Lanza. Take V. Tivoli, which becomes V. Pantaccio. Turn right onto V. Brera. $ Panini €5-6. Antipasti €5-7. Pizza €7-9. ⏰ Open daily 9am-2am. Closed Su for 5 weeks in July and Aug.

ATMOSFERA 🍴 RISTORANTE ❺

P. Castello, corner V. Beltrami ☎800 80 81 81 🖳www.atm-mi.it

Public transportation is generally not associated with the high life. The two trams that compose ATMosfera, however, seek to put the class back in coach. Milan's Transit Authority has duly restored two decades-old trams and now runs them as restaurants—literally. These eateries travel around the city as you dine. There's no gum stuck on the floor here, just gold trim and wood paneling. If only every Milan tram was like this, the ride back to your hostel would be so much more agreeable.

 # [M]1: Cairoli. i Reservations required. 3 menus: meat, fish, or vegetarian. $ €65. ⏰ Departs Tu-Su 8pm. Trip lasts about 2½hr.

PASTICCERIA MARCHESI 🍴 BAKERY ❶

V. Santa Maria alla Porta 11/A ☎02 87 67 30 🖳www.pasticceriamarchesi.it

Ouch! Our sweet tooth is aching just looking at this place's pastel-colored frosted cakes and chocolate delights laid out to tempt the weak of will. For most of us, (we assume, perhaps incorrectly, that most are strong enough to resist the sugary pull) an exquisite pastry and coffee will do. Dozens of local office workers swarm the bar for this morning pick-me-up.

⇄ [M]1: Cairoli. Follow V. San G. Sul Moro to intersection with C. Magenta. $ Pastries €2-5. ⏰ Open Tu-Sa 8am-8pm, Su 8am-1pm.

DA VINCI LA PIZZA — 💳 🚭 🍸 ❄ PIZZERIA ❷

V. San Prospero 4 — ☎02 87 57 74

As the inventor of so many modern technological achievements, da Vinci himself would no doubt be pleased with how technology improves the service at this lunch-only spot near V. Dante. After waiters take orders on handheld computers, golden-crusted pizza is whisked to the table at the speed of light, or just a pinch slower. Try Da Vinci's namesake slice, with tomato, mozzarella, broccoli, and spicy salami *(€6)*.

⇄ [M]1: Cordusio. Walk up V. Dante and turn right onto V. San Prospero. $ Cover €0.50. Pizza €4-7. Salads €8-10. ⏰ Open M-Sa 10am-3:30pm.

OSTERIA 29 — 💳 🚭 🍸 RISTORANTE ❷

C. Magenta 29 — ☎02 86 93 069 💻www.osteriaal29.com

This low-key *ristorante* offers classic Italian dishes at delightfully low prices. Served in a homey room with exposed wood beams and walls playfully decorated with items like a pitchfork and wine barrel, traditional Italian fare like spaghetti with a rich Neapolitan sauce never tasted so good.

⇄ [M]1/2: Cardona F.N. Follow V. Carducci. Turn left at C. Magenta. $ Antipasti €7-9; primi €5-6.50. Pizza €5.50-12. ⏰ Open M-F noon-2:30pm and 7:15-11pm, Sa noon-2:30pm.

AL TEATRO CAFE — 💳 ♿ 🍸 ❄ ⛅ CAFE ❶

C. Garibaldi 16 — ☎02 06 42 22

Aaaand, action! The bartender moves in from stage right, the patrons fill the seats stage left. They enter quickly, eagerly sitting themselves in the director's chairs out front. They've gathered for the lunch specials consisting of water, coffee, and *primi (€7)* or *secondi (€9)* at this bustling cafe. They'll eat and leave, and more will fill in for *aperitivo* in the evening. That's when the bartender pulls a bottle of bubbly from the shelves behind him. Aaaand, pop! The evening begins.

⇄ [M]2: Lanza. Take V. Pontaccio away from the castle and turn left onto C. Garibaldi. $ Panini €4. Primi €5; secondi €7. Happy hour aperitivo buffet €7. ⏰ Open daily 10am-2am. Happy hour 7-9pm.

Navigli

Put simply, the Navigli is known for what goes on after dinner—the dancing and drinking, not the chatting and chewing. Nevertheless, the neighborhood also has many dining options, as quick and inexpensive spots abound. Many bars also serve happy hour buffets. A full service **Simply Market** supermarket with a notable alcohol aisle is located at V. le Tibaldi 7. *(☎02 83 23 918 💻www.simplymarket.it ⏰ M-Sa 8:30am-9pm.)* For a kick, check out the bottom of Simply's receipt, where you'll find a helpful euro-to-lire conversion—just in case you have some old Italian currency whose value you want to assess. In P. XXIV Maggio, the **Mercato Communale** *(⏰ Open M-Sa; hours vary)* sells fresh fruits and vegetables.

BIG PIZZA: DA NOI 2 — 💳 ♿ 🍸 ⛅ PIZZERIA ❶

V. Giosue Borsi 1 — ☎02 83 95 677 💻www.danoi2.com

The name is no lie. These pizzas are big—bigger than the plate, bigger than a New-York-style slice, maybe bigger even than the Big Apple itself. Get your belly ready for these thin-crust puppies, especially if you order the signature pizza and pasta, a carb-lover's idea of heaven that is literally a large pizza pie with pasta on top *(€9.50)*.

⇄ [M]2: Porta Genova. $ Cover €1.50. Pizza €6.50-8.50. ⏰ Open M-Sa noon-2:30pm and 7pm-midnight. Sometimes stays open later on weekends, depending on crowds.

IL FORNO DEI NAVIGLI

🍴⊗ BAKERY ❶

Alzaia Pavese 2

☎02 83 23 372

Lots of kids dream of having a house made of candy. This house is made of sugary, golden pastry, fresh from the oven and stretching from wall to wall. Try a bagel to see if Milan's version compares with New York's.

✦ Ⓜ2: Porta Genova. *i* *Also sells breads.* Ⓢ *Pastries €0.50-6. Sold by the kg.* ☒ *Open M-Sa 7am-2pm and 6pm-1am, Su 6pm-1am.*

GHIRERIA GRECA

🍴♿♀ GREEK ❶

Ripa di Porta Ticinese 13

☎02 58 10 70 40

Take a quick trip across the Adriatic—or at least the Naviglio Grande—to stop at this quick and scrumptious Greek sandwich shop that provides a satisfying alternative to nighttime bar food.

✦ Ⓜ2: Porta Genova. Ⓢ *Entrees €6-13.* ☒ *Open M-F noon-2:30pm and 6pm-2pm, Sa noon-3am, Su noon-2pm.*

RUGANTO

🍴♨♀ RISTORANTE ❸

V. Fabbrini 1.

☎02 89 42 14 04

Ah, *Italia*. Pasta and pizza on the *piazza*, and in the shadow of ancient Roman columns to wit. Here, the cuisine is classic Italian, made as it should be.

✦ Ⓜ2: Sant'Ambrogio. Walk down V. Edmondo de Amicis, turn right onto C. Porta Ticinese. Ⓢ *Beer €4-5. Pizza €6-12. Primi and secondi €9-20.* ☒ *Open daily 12:30-3pm and 7:30pm-midnight.*

City Outskirts

If picking out the needle of a good restaurant in the haystack of touristy cafes near the Duomo was tough, just try to sort through the restaurants of an entire city connected only by subway lines. The best of the best in Milan's hinterlands aren't necessarily near one another, but the search just adds to the reward. The outskirts' best restaurants tend to be clustered near major *piazze*, where residents seek good cuisine near their apartment-style homes.

CHOCO CULT

🍴⊗♀❄ GELATERIA, BAKERY ❶

V. Buonarroti 7

☎02 48 02 73 19 🖥www.chococult.it

You don't have to drink the Kool-Aid, but you do have to lick the gelato to join this semi-secret sorbet society located in one of the many lively squares outside of Milan's city center. Both an early-morning coffee stop and a refreshing afternoon ice cream stand, this establishment actually makes most of its revenues from the sale of hard chocolate (*€50-200 per kg*). Luckily, its chocolate-making skills are also put to good use in all of its other delicacies.

✦ Ⓜ1: Wagner. Ⓢ *Gelato €2.50-3.50. Coffee and espresso €1-3.* ☒ *Open daily 7am-midnight.*

AMERICAN DONUTS

🍴⊗❄ CAFE, AMERICAN ❶

V. Sirtori 4

☎02 89 05 77 79 🖥www.americandonut.it

Oh beautiful, for sprinkle skies, and amber rings of dough! In fact, such a soundtrack might be the last touch missing from this clever diner that certainly doesn't take itself too seriously—Old Glory graces everything from the coffee mugs to the servers' aprons. For a breakfast on the go, grab a doughnut (*€1.80*), or take on a more leisurely and fattening American meal and enjoy a burger or fried chicken (*€7-10*).

✦ Ⓜ1: Porta Venezia. From P. Romana, take V. Melzo and turn right onto V. Malpighi, then a quick left onto V. Sirtori. Ⓢ *Cookies and muffins €1.50. Sandwiches €3-4.50.* ☒ *Open M-F 7:30am-7:30pm, Sa 8:30am-7:30pm, Su 9am-7pm. Brunch served Sa-Su 10am-4pm.*

PICHANAS

🍴⊗♀❄ BRAZILIAN ❸

Piazzale Lotto 14

☎02 39 21 44 08 🖥www.pichanas.com

If you're on the one-meal-a-day diet but not really feeling it, here's the place for you. One meal is all you will need after Pichana's gigantic buffet of meat, pastas,

milan and turin

and vegetable side dishes. The dinner buffet *(€40)* is accompanied by live Latin music and features 20 appetizers and 12 different meats, but the real deal is the smaller lunch *(€15)* with two to three meats served with water, wine, and coffee.

✦ Ⓜ1: Lotto. On the circle in Hotel Oro Blu. ⑤ Lunch €15; dinner €40. ☒ Open daily 12:30-3pm and 8pm-2am. Will sometimes stay open later than officially stated.

CAFE CAPOVERDE
♥ �• ♀ ♨ RISTORANTE ❷

V. Leoncavallo 16 ☎02 26 82 04 30 ■www.capoverde.com

Bring your hiking boots for the long trek from Stazione Centrale to this foliage-filled establishment—after hiking through a forest of apartment houses and office parks, you'll finally get to connect with nature just inside the restaurant gates. That's because, in addition to its culinarily capable cafe, Capoverde is a working greenhouse where flowers, cacti, and maybe even fungi abound. At night, things can get lively during the happy hour *aperitivo (€9)*.

✦ Ⓜ1/2: Loreto. A 20min. walk along V. Costa, which becomes V. Leoncavallo. *i* Gluten-free dishes available. ⑤ Pizza €10. Primi €11-13. ☒ Open M-Th 12:30-2:30pm and 6pm-midnight, F 12:30-2:30pm and 6pm-1am, Sa 12:30-2:30pm and 6pm-2am, Su 6pm-midnight. Happy hour daily 6:30-9pm.

LA CANTINA DI MANUELA
♥ ⊗ ♀ ♨ ❄ RISTORANTE ❸

V. Procaccini 41 ☎02 34 52 034 ■www.lacantinadimanuela.it

Wine bottles for sale hang on the wall at this intimate brasserie, which claims to focus first and foremost on that most sacred art of drinking *vino*. Small-batch Italian vintages and well-known brands are all available from behind the bar. In the kitchen, dishes range from risottos to fish and beef filets, and many courses feature wine-based sauces.

✦ Ⓜ2: Garibaldi F.S. Walk alongside the tracks on V. Sturzo, then continue in front of the cemetery building to V. Procaccini on the other side of the piazza. ⑤ Antipasti and primi €8-10; secondi €19-22. ☒ Open M-Sa 11:30am-3pm and 6:30pm-2am.

SQUARE BAR
♥ �• ♀ ♨ CAFE ❷

V. Buonarroti 5 ☎02 43 71 50

You can get a simple and scrumptious square meal for not much dough at this easy cafe, which draws groups of students and older women alike to sit at its outdoor area on a sunny afternoon. A wide selection of 14 different sandwiches *(€4.50)* plus daily changing *primi* and *secondi (€5-8)* keep regulars coming back to their patio seating every time the weather permits.

✦ Ⓜ1: Wagner. ⑤ Wraps €5. Coffee €1-2. ☒ Open daily 6am-11pm.

DON JUANITO
♥ ⊗ ♀ ❄ STEAKHOUSE ❸

C. di Porta Vigentina 33 ☎02 58 43 12 17 ■www.donjuanito.it

Come for the sizzling red meat or the tongue-meltingly good chocolate desserts. This place serves both in a bright South American atmosphere where Spanish—not English—is the second language on the menu.

✦ Ⓜ3: Crocetta. Head south on C. Vigentina. ⑤ Steaks €16-24. Desserts €8. ☒ Open M-Sa 11:30am-3:30pm and 6-11pm.

NIGHTLIFE

In terms of sheer variety, very few places on earth can rival Milan when it comes to nightlife—and there are plenty of locals eager to rave about their city's vibrant after-hours scene. **Corso Como** is home to the city's most exclusive and expensive clubs, where mere mortals can mingle with models and football stars, provided their attire passes the judgment of the big man with the earpiece and clipboard. Dozens of small bars with big (and inexpensive) *aperitivo* buffets line the canals of the **Navigli** area, drawing students and young people to the neighborhood in droves. Beyond these hubs, the nightlife spokes stretch to all edges of the city, throughout which both local bars and international clubs are scattered. **Largo Cairoli** is home to two popular outdoor dance venues, while the region east of **Corso Buenos Aires** is home to much of the city's GLBT scene. **Corso di Porta Ticinese,** north of the Navigli, draws students and locals who bring their chilled concoctions outdoors to—where else?—a church courtyard in the shadow of ancient ruins for a laid-back block party unlike any other.

Piazza del Duomo

Nightlife on P. del Duomo is pretty much the same as the daylife: a lot of tourists gawking at the pile of intricate stonework that is the Duomo and Galleria Vittore Emanuele. While there are some good times to be found in the surrounding streets, venture 5min. down V. Torino to C. di Porta Ticinese for a more lively scene.

👍 TASCA

💳🚭🍸 ENOTECA

C. di Porta Ticinese 14 ☎02 83 76 915 💻www.iltasca.it

In vino, veritas, the saying goes. Does that translate into Spanish? After several glasses of wine from this lively spot, there are more than a few people—inhibitions erased—who are willing to tell the whole truth to any passerby who will listen. Inside, the owners focus on Spanish cuisine, fixing up tapas as they take a few sips of Chardonnay themselves.

⇄ Ⓜ2: Sant'Ambrogio. Follow V. de Amicis and make a left onto C. di Porta Ticinese. $ White wine €5-6, red €5-9. Tapas €5-10. ⏰ Open M-Sa 12:30pm-1:30am.

BAR STRAF

💳♿🍸❄ BAR

V. San Raffaele 3 ☎02 80 50 81 💻www.straf.it

Straf is different. As is not the case for many other Milanese bars, the drinking hordes who take over the streets surrounding the hip hotel in which this bar is housed meet little resistance from trams and automobiles because Straf's street is shut to traffic most hours of the day. Capitalizing on this felicitous situation, the super-mod establishment provides cube-like red seats outside in the evenings, so the crush of patrons can rest their weary bottoms (though not their livers) while downing cocktails and champagne.

⇄ Ⓜ1/3: Duomo. Walk to the left of the cathedral and take the 1st left. $ Cocktails €10. Dishes $12-15. ⏰ Open M-F 9am-midnight, Sa-Su 11am-midnight. Happy hour 6-10pm.

CUORE

💳🚭🍸 BAR

V. Gian Giacomo Mora 3 ☎02 58 10 51 26 💻www.cuoremilano.it

Interesting fact: in Italy, certain liquor licenses prohibit dancing, as places are supposed to be bars not clubs. Cuore is a bar, but some travelers report getting their illicit dance on here, even though busting out your interpretation of The Robot is technically illegal after 11pm in the small dance floor brought to life by a pumping DJ set.

⇄ Ⓜ1/3: Duomo. Follow V. Torino to C. Porta Ticinese, and turn right onto V. G. G. Mora before the columns. $ Beer €5. Cocktails €7-8. ⏰ Open daily 6pm-2am.

LOGU

💵🚭🍸⛅ BAR

V. Urbano III at corner of C. Porta Ticinese ☎02 94 30 23 69

From this well-located corner bar, you can see the world pass by, though you certainly won't be able to hear it. Two DJs in the lineup most nights mean the beat of electronic, house, rap, and even Brazilian music will be drowning out the sounds of the street. A remarkably affordable happy hour *(€5)* keeps young grads swaying to the music from dusk until (practically) dawn.

⇄ Ⓜ1/3: Duomo. Follow V. Torino to C. Porta Ticinese. $ Beer €3.50-6. Cocktails €5-7. ⏰ Open daily 8am-2am. Happy hour 7-9pm.

THE FOOTBALL ENGLISH PUB

💳🚭🍸❄ BAR

V. Valpetrosa 5 ☎02 86 44 64 💻www.thefootballenglishpub.com

In the window you'll spot a cheeky gravestone for Bayern Munich, one of Inter Milan's most formidable football opponents, engraved with the score of its defeat by the local favorite. No doubt this place went wild when that Milanese victory took place. With dozens of beers on tap and more than a few TVs on which to catch all the matches, this is a pub that would make any Englishman proud, even if the beer is served cold (thank God). Oh, and the English probably wouldn't like the Italy-only cheering sections.

🍴 Ⓜ1/3: Duomo. Follow V. Torino, then take a right onto V. Valpetrosa. *i* Accent not required. Ⓢ Beer €3-5. Cocktails €6.50. Ⓒ Open M-Th noon-3pm and 6:30pm-1am, F noon-3pm and 6:30pm-2am, Sa 1pm-2am, Su 3-10pm.

Fashion District

When it comes down to it, the Fashion District is really a business area, a fact that becomes clear once the shops close and the professionals working above leave their desks. The neighborhood's nightlife follows the trend: it's muted and happens early on. In fact, some of the best people-watching may be in the shop windows of V. Monte Napoleone, where salespeople and installers dance a late-night tango with their mannequins as they rush to get new displays in place.

CARUSO FUORI RESTAURANT AND BAR
🍴 ♿ ⛾ ❄ ⛄ BAR

Piazzetta Croce Rossa
☎02 72 31 41

Young professionals leaving work and looking for a place to roll up their sleeves and nurse a cocktail head for the shadow of one of the district's most buttoned up fashion houses. Armani sits next door to this buzzing cafe, from which workers in various states of undress (no, this doesn't go beyond a partially unbuttoned shirt or loosened tie) flow into the *piazza*. *Let's Go* does not recommend undoing more than three buttons at happy hour.

🍴 Ⓜ3: Montenapoleone. Ⓢ Beer €8. Happy hour cocktail €10. Ⓒ Open M 12:30-5:30pm, Tu-Sa 12:30-2:30pm and 6:30-10pm. Happy hour Tu-Sa 6:30-10pm.

DOLCE AND GABBANA MARTINI BAR
🍴 ⊗ ᵍ⟨ⁱ⟩ ⛾ ❄ ⛄ BAR

C. Venezia 15
☎02 76 01 11 54 🖥www.dolcegabbana.it

Here, in the supposed epitome of hip, this sleek black and white bar of a fashion designer's dream (complete with a modish glass ceiling) brings the reality of downtown nightlife home. Alive and hopping for an early evening *aperitivo* buffet of olives, meats, and cheeses (€10), this place closes by 10pm. Make it before the doors lock shut, though, and waiters in skinny ties will happily serve you one of their many specialized martinis (€10-20).

🍴 Ⓜ1: San Babila. Follow C. Venezia ½ block from the piazza. Ⓢ Cocktails €7-20. Salads €1. Meat dishes €12-18. Ⓒ Open daily 7:30am-10pm.

Giardini Pubblici

Nightlife is possibly the only category where "crowded" isn't a dirty word. In the summer months at Giardini Pubblici's tiny bars, it's not just the buildings themselves that fill up, but the sidewalks, too, as patrons march to their next mixed drink.

🏆 ATOMIC BAR
⊛ ⊗ ⛾ BAR

V. Casati 24
☎02 89 05 91 69 🖥www.atomicbar.it

Thirsty students recline beneath Pop Art murals as their overstuffed and well-worn space-age chairs burst at the seams. Students don't stay seated for too long, however, as the dance floor heats up to beats spun by a different DJ every night of the week (starting at 11pm).

🍴 Ⓜ1: Porta Venezia. *i* Reservations recommended. Ⓢ Cocktails €10, €8 during happy hour. Ⓒ Open daily 7pm-2am. Happy hour 7-10pm.

L'ELEPHANT
🍴 ⊗ ⛾ ❄ ▼ BAR

V. Melzo 22
☎02 29 51 87 68 🖥www.lelephant.it

Small groups of men and a few women recline on couches and chitchat at L'Elephant, one of Milan's oldest hangouts for the GLBT community. The buttoned, plastic-feeling faux-leather on the walls makes the whole place seem a little like the couches that sit off to one side, but the palms overhead and pink

milan · nightlife

boas draped about will remind you where you are.

☝ Ⓜ1: Porta Venezia. Follow V. Melzo from P. Romana. Ⓢ Cocktails €5-8. Happy hour €6. 🕐 Open Tu-Su 6:30pm-2am. Happy hour 6:30-9:30pm.

MONO
☝♿🍸 BAR

V. Lecco 6 ☎33 94 81 02 64 ✉www.myspace.com/monomilano

Hipsters in fedoras mingle outside this über-retro corner bar. Definitely a hipster bar, Mono is full of molded plastic chairs, dim lamps and an old-school radio and record player.

☝ Ⓜ1: Porta Venezia. Ⓢ Cocktails €8. 🕐 Open Tu 6:30pm-1am, W-Th 6:30pm-1:30am, F-Sa 6:30pm-2am, Su 6:30pm-1am.

Castello Sforzesco

Home to one of Milan's most student-friendly clubs, the area around Castello Sforzesco is otherwise full of quieter bars and lounges, some of which cater to an older crowd. Still, this area can offer an enjoyable, if more chill, night on the town.

📷 OLD FASHION CAFE
☝♿🍸 CLUB

Vle. Emilio Alemagna 6 ☎02 80 56 231 ✉www.oldfashion.it

If you're under 30, this is the place to see and be seen in Milan—everyone you know will probably be here on Friday, and Tuesdays could bring some familiar faces too. If you're over 30, you'll probably be driven crazy within 100m of the place when your ears first catch the sappy pop songs mixed in with bass beat. In summer, dancing on the outdoor dance floor takes center stage, as well-dressed clubgoers fill couches and line up at bars on its fringes under the trees.

☝ Ⓜ1/2: Cardona F. N. Walk up V. Paleocapa next to the station and turn slight right onto Vle. Alemagna before the bridge. Club is to the left of Palazzo dell'Arte along a cobblestone path. 𝑖 Su appetizer buffet included in cover. Ⓢ Cover €10; sometimes higher for men and lower for women. 🕐 Open M-Tu 10:30pm-4:30am, W 10:30pm-4am, Th-Sa 10:30pm-4:30am, Su 11am-4pm and 7pm-midnight.

BAR MAGENTA
☝⊗(ຖ)🍸 BAR

V. Carducci 13 ☎02 26 82 04 30 ✉www.barmagenta.it

This quiet bar offers a vast menu of sandwiches in addition to big-screen TVs that showcase all the big games from the wide world of sports. Come on the day of a match for a packed house; other times, Magenta is a place to relax with a drink, a friend, and an eye for the world passing by. Live rock and blues (starting at 10pm) brings up the tempo on Friday night.

☝ Ⓜ1/2: Cardona. A short walk down V. Carducci to C. Magenta. 𝑖 Free Wi-Fi. Ⓢ Beer €4-6. Cocktails €8. 🕐 Open daily 9am-2am. Happy hour 6-9pm.

IL PATUSCINO
☝⊗🍸❄ PIANO BAR

V. Madonnina 19 ☎02 72 09 53 34 ✉www.asdfkl;

A student walks into a bar. Ouch! Fortunately at Il Patuscino, the pain is mitigated quickly by the very strong drinks and welcoming attitude of the slightly older patrons. It only takes two stiff cocktails to get everyone lining up for Wednesday night karaoke or swinging to the beat of nightly live music (starting at 11pm). While the musician plays a piano, his computer helps create the effect of any instrument imaginable.

☝ Ⓜ2: Lanza. From V. Tivoli, make a right onto V. Mercato and then a quick left onto Fiori Chiari. V. Madonnina is to the right. Ⓢ All drinks €10. 🕐 Open Tu-Su 9pm-3am.

Navigli

Around 2pm each afternoon, the bars along V. A. Sfarza start to shed their armor. Rolling up their graffiti-stained grates one by one, proprietors slowly transform the avenue from a slightly seedy thoroughfare into a lively destination. Students on a budget frequent this nightlife hot spot to chow down on the *aperitivo* buffets during happy hour then hit up one of the clubs for DJs and live music. Later on, many clubgoers leave the bars and take their drinks, moving to a packed outdoor hangout

milan and turin

by the Lorenzo columns—on a church *piazza*—off C. di Porta Ticinese.

🏛 LE TROTTOIR
♦⊗♥⌂ CLUB

P. XXIV Maggio 1 ☎02 83 78 166 💻www.letrottoir.it

This ever-crowded club attracts all comers with live nightly music (11pm-3am) ranging from rock and pop to reggae and soul. Upstairs, where a DJ spins (Th-Sa 11pm-3am), a rotating art exhibit showcases alternative—and sometimes raunchy—pieces. If the art is too hot and heavy for your taste, park yourself outside in one of the comfy seats on the deck.

♯ Ⓜ2: Porta Genova. Located in P. XXIV Maggio as its own island in a sea of roads. i Concert schedule online. Ⓢ Cover €8, with table service €9. Beer €6-7. Cocktails €8. Pizza and sandwiches €6-8. ☑ Open daily 11am-3pm.

SCIMMIE
♦⊗♥⌂ BAR, RISTORANTE

V. Sforza 49 ☎02 89 40 28 74 💻www.scimmie.it

A more grown-up crowd gives way to youngsters as the night flies by at this multifaceted establishment that features a ristorante, club, floating pizzeria, and wine bar as well as a very expensive first drink *(€10).*

♯ Ⓜ2: Porta Genova. i Concert schedule online. Ⓢ 1st drink €10. Cocktails €4-9. Primi €8-10; secondi €18-20. ☑ Open daily 7pm-2:30am. Live music begins 11pm.

TAXI BLUES
♦⌂♥⌂ BAR

V. Bocconi 6 ☎02 58 31 52 46 💻www.taximilanoblues.it

Local students enticed by Taxi Blues' €6-7 *aperitivo* (though vegetarians might want to steer clear on Friday, when sushi is served) sink into plush, white leather couches in this psychedelic wonderland of a bar. Visit on Wednesday Brazilian nights, when the shimmering ceiling quakes to the beats of a popular South American DJ.

♯ Ⓜ3: Porta Romana. Follow Vle. Sabotino to Vle. Bligny. i DJ on F-Sa. Also serves breakfast and lunch. Ⓢ Beer €5. Cocktails €7. ☑ Open daily 7am-2am. Happy hour 6:30-9:30pm.

SPRITZ NAVIGLI
⊛⌂♥ BAR

Ripa di Porta Ticenese 9 ☎02 83 39 01 92 💻www.spritz-navigli.it

A big sliced orange—and crowd of waiting 20-somethings—marks the entrance to this student favorite known for its varied and scrumptious happy hour food.

♯ Ⓜ2: Porta Genova. Ⓢ Happy hour buffet €8. ☑ Open daily 6pm-2am. Happy hour 6-10pm.

SPAZIO MOVIDA COCKTAIL BAR
♦⌂((·))♥⌂ BAR

V. Sforza 41 ☎02 58 10 20 43 💻www.spaziomovida.it

Don't forget to pop your collar and wear your sunglasses inside this trendy (read: Eurotrash) establishment, which features a popular *aperitivo* and serves food all night long.

♯ Ⓜ2: Porta Genova. i Free Wi-Fi. Ⓢ Cocktails €7. Aperitivo buffet with mixed drink €8, with beer or wine €7. ☑ Open daily 6pm-2am. Happy hour 6-9pm.

CAPE TOWN CAFE
♦⌂♥⌂ BAR

V. Vigevano 3 ☎02 89 40 30 53

It's unclear whether the jovial staff at this round-the-clock establishment ever have time to sleep, but they do draw a crowd. Don't mind the traffic—the huge throngs eventually spill so far into the street that cars have to drive on the other side of the road outside this classic, wood-paneled cafe.

♯ Ⓜ2: Porta Genova. i Also serves breakfast and lunch. Ⓢ Beer €3.50-5. Hard liquor and cocktails €7. Sandwiches €5. Drink prices lower during the day. ☑ Open daily 7am-2pm. Happy hour 6:30-8:30pm.

LA VINERIA
♦⌂♥ ENOTECA

V. Casale 4 ☎02 83 24 24 40 💻www.la-vineria.it

I do not like wine from a box; I will not drink it with some lox. So said Boozy the

Fox, the character unfairly axed from Dr. Seuss's classic *Green Eggs and Ham*. Well, Boozy would feel right at home at La Vineria, where you'll find vats and vats of wine, and none of it in boxes. This enoteca sells wines in bulk, both to take home and to party with on the sidewalk at night. Slightly quieter than the rest of V. Sforza, this is a good place to have a relaxed conversation.

✸ Ⓜ2: Porta Genova. *i* Also sells bulk olive oil. Ⓢ Wine by the bottle €5, by the glass €1. Ⓒ May-Oct M 4pm-midnight, Tu-Sa 10am-1:30pm and 4pm-midnight; Nov-Apr M 4-8pm, Tu-Sa 10am-1:30pm and 4-8pm.

SLICE

✦●⊗Ⴤ✳ BAR

V. A. Sforza 9

☎02 58 10 53 66

A man with a clipboard stands outside most nights to keep the crowds at bay. Local students say it's worth the wait to get to the happy hour buffet *(€8)* and bar—if you can find your way through Slice's dimly lit interior.

✸ Ⓜ2: Porta Genova. Ⓢ Beer €5. Cocktails €7. Ⓒ Open daily 6pm-2:15am. Happy hour 6-10pm.

City Outskirts

Areas outside of Milan's *centro* feature some of its best known clubs as well as a few exotic outliers. █**Corso Como,** north of the Duomo near Porta Garibaldi, showcases the city's world-renowned nightlife. It also plays host to an informal fashion show as well-dressed out-and-abouts strut the street on weekend nights. East of **Corso Buenos Aires** and **Stazione Centrale** are a number of bars popular with locals. You'll also find much of the city's GLBT scene here. To the south and west are a number of scattered clubs and bars, the more suburban of which can be hard to find.

█ ONDANOMALA

✦●ㅎ Ⴤ⚄ CLUB

V. Lampugnano 109

☎393 33 60 025 █www.ondanolmala.it

The only thing missing is the limbo. Actually, we'd be lying if we said we missed that. Here, in a trendy club tucked behind a housing development, there's sand between the toes and bamboo on the bar, even in the center of northern Italy. On weekends, hundreds of people pack the sandy main room and seven private areas ranging from the crimson-draped "Arabian" room to poolside cabanas which can be reserved—champagne and fruit baskets included. Live music and DJs keep the tempo high most nights.

✸ Ⓜ1: Uruguay. About a 15min. walk. From V. Croce, turn left onto V. Omodeo. Turn right at V. Montale, which becomes V. Lampugnano. *i* Reservations recommended. Ⓢ First drink €7-15, depending on day of the week; afterward cocktails €7. Ⓒ Open May-Sept Tu-Su 6pm-3am; Oct-Dec Th-Su 6pm-3am; Feb-Apr Th-Su 6pm-3am. Happy hour 6-10pm.

ATMOSPHERE SOUL JAZZ

●●⊗Ⴤ⚄ BAR, JAZZ CLUB

V. Sidoli 24

☎335 69 42 059 █www.atmospheresouljazz.com

There's live music every night—if the employee banging drumsticks on the bartop counts as live music. Otherwise, Friday and Saturday are the evenings to come for live jazz, soul, and "funky" blues. The crowds arrive later in the evening to sip drinks named after their favorite musicians *(€6)*, like the peach-flavored B.B. King, and to enjoy the low wicker patio couches while gazing through the window to the red lava lamp inside.

✸ Ⓜ1: Porta Venezia. Take tram #5 or 33 in direction of Ortica or Limbrate to Piazza Savoia. Continue walking in the same direction 5 blocks. The bar is on the right before Piazzale Susa. Ⓢ Beer €3-4. Cocktails €6. Happy hour €6. Ⓒ Open daily 6pm-2am. Happy hour 6-10pm.

HOLLYWOOD

✦●⊗Ⴤ✳ CLUB

C. Como 15

☎02 65 98 996 █www.discotecahollywood.com

The spotlight is on at this celeb-filled club, among the most elite in Milan. Man or woman, the dress code here isn't just elegant but "dress to impress" if you want to make it past the ropes into the blue-tinted lobby. Got this far? Pat yourself on the back and, while your hand's there, reach for your wallet and get ready to pay for the red-carpet treatment. Tuesday's Erasmus night is packed with students seeking half-price admission and the attraction of deafening bass in a strobe-lit basement that not any old dorm room can provide.

✣ Ⓜ2: Garibaldi F.S. Exit the station to the right, follow Vle. Sturzo and turn right onto C. Como. *i* Dress code is described as "elegant." Some female travelers report being able to get in for free earlier in the evening. Ⓢ Cover €20-25. Cocktails €10. Ⓩ Open Tu-Sa 11pm-5am.

BLANCO ✇⊗℆⚶ BAR
V. Morgagni 2 ☎02 29 40 52 84 💻www.blancomilano.com

Wearing sunglasses inside might be cool all over Milan, but Blanco's blindingly white interior virtually requires it. Fortunately, the majority of patrons at Blanco's well-known happy hour flow into the street, where the pulsating beat can be heard (and felt) over the din of hundreds of voices.

✣ Ⓜ1: Porta Venezia. Head north on C. Buenos Aires, until making a right at V. Stoppani. At the park, Blanco is across and to the left. Ⓢ Cocktails €8. Ⓩ Open M-Sa 6:30am-2am.

LOOLAPALOOSA ✇க℀℆⚶ CAFE, CLUB
C. Como 15 ☎02 65 55 693 💻www.loolapaloosa.com

Looks can be deceiving, and here they sure are. Quiet cafe by day becomes crazy party by night—and no DJ is even required. Dancing fills the front room of this lounge and takes over any surface it can find, even the bar top.

✣ Ⓜ2: Garibaldi F.S. Exit the station to the right, follow Vle. Sturzo and turn right onto C. Como. Ⓢ Cover from €6. Cocktails €6-8. Ⓩ Open M-F noon-5:30pm and 11:30pm-4am, Sa-Su 6:30pm-5:30am.

MILANO ✇க CLUB
V. Procaccini 37 ☎02 34 93 00 10 💻www.mastmilano.it

Sit down, relax, and stay awhile—just don't put your dirty shoes on that ottoman! The comforts of this living-room-like bar may lull some patrons into thinking they've returned home, but most nights, it's hard to get too comfortable since you'll likely be enjoying the club's popular *aperitivo* bar with a few hundred of your less-than-close friends. Designed with a vast terrace and airy lounge by one of Milan's best-known club owners, Milano was created to be the epitome of easygoing Italian nightlife.

✣ Ⓜ2: Garibaldi F. S. Walk alongside the tracks on V. Sturzo, then continue in front of the cemetery building to V. Procaccini on the other side of the p. Ⓢ Cocktails €8. Ⓩ Open M-Sa 6pm-2am. Happy hour 6-10pm.

RADETZKY ✇⊗℆⚶ CAFE, BAR
C. Garibaldi 105 ☎02 65 72 645 💻www.radetsky.it

A cool, young crowd loudly takes to the streets for happy hour at this classic European cafe before dispersing to nearby nightclubs. They leave with bellies satisfied by the classic Italian *aperitivo* dishes offered here. Inside, jovial bartenders keep older patrons' wine glasses (and, very likely, their own shot glasses) full and the conversation flowing until late in the evening.

✣ Ⓜ2: Moscova. Ⓢ Cocktails €8. Ⓩ Open daily 7am-2am.

ARTS AND CULTURE 🎎

If there's anything all of Milan's residents can agree on, it's that they're *cultured*. Whether this equates to an appreciation for the sculpted spires of the Duomo, the delicate colors of Renaissance paintings, or the beat of the latest hard rock band, it's clear that the Milanese are indeed knowledgeable when it comes to matters of art. The landscape of their cosmopolitan city reflects the refinement of its citizens. Theaters and concert venues, from the storied **La Scala** to the critically acclaimed **Piccolo Teatro,** are all over the city. Classical music is a pastime of many, even those who couldn't tell you the difference between a violin and a viola. Yet Milan's residents also demonstrate their city's cultural pride in another way—one that, to say the least, doesn't display quite so much refinement. The city's raucous soccer celebrations can fill city streets with banners and horns. From famous paintings to hooligans' facepaint, Milan has it all.

Opera and Ballet

In addition to all its other "capital city" distinctions, Milan has a reputation for being one of the world's opera and ballet centers. That reputation is largely due to one famous theater, but a few others around the city make the scene more diverse.

TEATRO ALLA SCALA
P. della Scala

♿ PIAZZA DEL DUOMO

☎02 72 00 37 44 ■www.teatroallascala.org

They say it's not over until the fat lady sings. Similarly, no opera can be complete without having been performed at La Scala, the world's preeminent venue. Patrons awaiting each performance sit on the edge of their seats in the theater's beautiful, cavernous red and gold hall. Even after the enormous crystal chandelier dims, the beauty of the place remains palpable, as the opera house's stunning acoustics and unparalleled audience enthusiasm make seeing a show at La Scala a treat for audience members as far removed from the stage as the highest balcony. Opera season runs from December to July and September to November, overlapping with the ballet season. The theater also occasionally hosts symphony concerts, typically in December and March.

✦ Ⓜ1/3: Duomo. Pass through the Galleria to P. della Scala. *i* Dress code: jacket and tie for men, appropriate attire for women. Ⓢ Ticket prices vary widely depending on performance. Any remaining tickets sold at a 25% discount 2hr. before the performance; student discounts available. ☒ Box office open daily noon-6pm in Ⓜ1: Duomo, and at theater 2hr. before performances. Theater closed Aug.

TEATRO SAN BABILA
C. Venezia 2/A

♿ FASHION DISTRICT

☎02 79 54 69 ■www.teatrosanbabila.it

There are very few in Milan who want to compete with La Scala at its bread and butter, the opera. Teatro San Babila is one of the rare theaters that at least attempts. But far from aiming to usurp its better known counterpart, it seeks to put on productions of lesser known scores, often *opera buffa*, or comedies, complementing La Scala's repertoire of well-known works.

✦ Ⓜ1: San Babila. Ⓢ Tickets €24-34. ☒ Box office open M-F 10am-1pm and 2-6pm, Sa 11am-1pm and 2:30-6:30pm, Su 2-6pm.

Classical Music

For the traditionally inclined listener, Milan certainly offers a world beyond **La Scala.** Violas, violins, harps, and timpani can come out of the orchestra pit and take the stage in their own right at these concert venues.

CONSERVATORIO DI MUSICA GIUSEPPE VERDI
V. Conservatorio 12

♿❋ FASHION DISTRICT

☎02 76 21 101 ■www.consmilano.it

There's pretty much always some sort of music emanating from this school. Stop by any time to hear repetitive drum rolls or piano scales drifting from the windows above. For something a bit more polished, the Conservatory's theater hosts various classical ensembles on a regular basis. Summer concert series in the courtyard.

✦ Ⓜ1: San Babila. Take V. Monforte and turn left onto V. Conservatorio. *i* Aside from posters outside its entrance, the Conservatory itself offers little information on concerts by outside groups. Consult a publication from the tourist office for more info. Ⓢ Tickets free-€25. ☒ Student concerts W 6:30pm except in summer.

AUDITORIUM DI MILANO
Largo Gustav Mahler

♿❋ OUTSKIRTS

☎02 83 38 91 ■www.laverdi.org

Milan's Symphony Orchestra—known colloquially as "La Verdi"—fills this hall to capacity with audience members and the moving notes of its namesake's pieces.

Of course, Verdi isn't the only composer this group has the privilege of playing: as the premiere symphony in Milan, it performs a repertoire that spans as wide a catalogue as classical music itself.

🏛 ⓜ2: Romolo. Take V. Liguria heading east, then turn left onto V. Torcelli. *i* Tickets also available at tourist office. Ⓢ Tickets €13-40, students €10-25. ⓩ Open Tu-Su 2:30-7pm.

Theater and Film

When you start reading the theater listings in the local paper, it begins to feel like many theaters double as fashion boutiques in this city. While *Let's Go* did not conduct a formal count, we're confident this is not in fact the case, but regardless, there's more than enough drama and film to fill up an entire stay in the city. On Tuesday nights, hit up **Arcobaleno Film Center** (Vle. Tunisia 11 }02 29 53 63 68 ▣www.cinenauta.it) for first-run English-language movies.

🎭 PICCOLO TEATRO
● ⅁ CASTELLO SFORZESCO

V. Rovello 2 and Largo Greppi 1   ☎848 80 03 04 ▣www.piccoloteatro.org

Meet the little engine that could, the *piccolo* theater that almost singlehandedly brought drama to Milan, starting with its founding in a converted cinema in 1924. Since then, its appeal and fame have grown, to the point where an entirely new stage was added, and the company now frequently runs two plays simultaneously. From cultural extravaganzas on the large stage at Teatro Strehler to Shakespeare in the intimate setting of Teatro Grassi, this company (perhaps no longer quite so *piccolo*) has managed to do it all.

🏛 To Teatro Grassi, ⓜ1: Cordusio. Walk toward the castle 1 block and turn right onto V. Rovello. To Teatro Strehler, ⓜ2: Lanza. Ⓢ Tickets €20-32, student discounts available. ⓩ Open M-Sa 9:45am-6:45pm, Su 1-6:30pm.

Sports
🔲

Not just a city of spectators (though there are plenty of people tuning in for each soccer match), Milan is an active community whose parks and recreation facilities are alive with runners and athletes of all kinds. Join the locals at city-run sports complex **Lido di Milano.** (Piazzale Lotto 15 ☎02 39 27 91 ▣www.comune.milano.it 🏛 ⓜ1: Lotto. Just off P. Lotto on V. Diomede. Ⓢ €4.50-5.50. ⓩ Open M-F 9am-11pm, Sa-Su 9am-8pm.)

🎭 STADIO GIUSEPPE MEAZZA, SAN SIRO
● ⅁ ✿ OUTSKIRTS

V. dei Piccolomini 5   ☎02 48 70 71 23 ▣www.acmilan.com and www.inter.it

There's just one thing that all Milanese can be said to take too seriously: soccer. With two world-renowned squads occupying the same city—and stadium—every single citizen has picked a side. For nine months of the year, they hang banners, wear jerseys, and scream their heads off at the television over all things *calcio*. Not surprisingly, then, matches in this 85,000-seat complex are raucous affairs, especially when the city's two teams, AC Milan and Inter, go head-to-head twice a year. Tickets can be hard to come by, so buy them early.

🏛 ⓜ1: Lotto. From P. Lotto, a long walk down Vle. Caprili, which becomes Piazzale del Spor. *i* Tickets can be purchased at local banks—AC Milan at Intesa San Paolo and Inter at Banca Populare di Milano, both of which have many locations throughout the city. Ⓢ Tickets €7-135. ⓩ Most games Sept-June Su afternoon.

IDROSCALO
● ⅁ OUTSKIRTS

V. Circonvallazione Idroscalo 29   ☎02 70 20 09 02 ▣www.idroscalo.info

Who says Milan isn't on the Riviera? At this human-made lake, you can sail, water ski, wakeboard, or just lie on the beach and bask in the glorious sunshine as it reflects off the water. Only a few minutes from the city center, it has all the hallmarks of a beach resort, except for, well, any waves.

🏛 ⓜ:1 San Babila. Take bus #76 to Linate Airport and bus #183 from the airport to Idroscalo. Bus #183 runs only in summer. *i* Watersports run by independent organizations. Ⓢ Free. Water skiing €18 per 1hr., €35 per day. ⓩ Open daily June 5-Sept 15 7am-9pm; Sept 16-June 4 7am-5pm.

milan · arts and culture

gameday in milan

Today, it's gameday in Milan. It's not the Super Bowl, not the Olympics, not even the World Cup Finals. Today, it's the *Derby della Madonnina*.

On this day in Milan, the colors of Italy aren't green, white, and red. They're red and black or blue and black, the jersey colors of AC Milan and Inter Milan, the primary soccer clubs of Italy's financial capital. It's a rivalry that consumes the city's populace far beyond the stadium's 80,074 lucky ticket holders. Here are the top three factors to consider when choosing who to support:

- **ARE YOU A SCREWDRIVER OR A BRAGGART?** Traditionally, the two teams have been associated with certain social groups in the city: the working class cheered wildly for AC Milan, while the bourgeoisie clapped reservedly for Inter. Taking after the great Italian wordsmiths like Dante (OK, perhaps with less eloquence) the two factions have taken to naming the other side's fans. AC fans were named after that handy metal tool—"For what else are these people?" asked the captains of industry from their palazzos—while Inter fans become boasters, for their tendency to brag about their team.

- **WHICH DO YOU PREFER, THE SERPENT OR THE DEVIL?** Seems like a tough choice, eh? Clad in red and black—and disliked by enough Italians for it to stick—AC Milan has acquired the nickname of "the devils." A fiery, pointy-tailed little man even once joined the team's badge after the flag of Milan got a little too boring. (It's since been removed.) The serpent of Inter is a more Milanese symbol, representing the historical rulers of the city going back to the Holy Roman Empire. Why they chose such a slimy character, no one knows, but Inter claims to embrace its heritage like no other.

- **WHO'D YA LIKE? DUBYA OR ROCKEFELLER?** Or, at least, their Italian counterparts? In addition to his official and unofficial posts of prime minister, media mogul, and Italy's chief womanizer, Silvio Berlusconi is the proud owner of AC Milan. Despite his conservative roots, Berlusconi has managed to get along with the working man just long enough to turn AC into the fifth most valuable football franchise in the world. Heck, he even wrote their official song—imagine an American politician popular enough to do that. Inter, by contrast, is the crown jewel of Massimo Moratti, an oil tycoon who sits to the left of Berlusconi (on the political spectrum, of course. We doubt they go anywhere near each other on gameday.)

SHOPPING

If any city can claim its designer fashions are worth their astronomical pricetags, it's Milan. That's because clothes really do make the man (or woman) in this world center of fashion. Particularly after the semiannual shows held here, wealthy disciples of the current season flock to **Via Montenapoleone** and the surrounding environs to buy up the newest style of suit or handbag in one of the street's temples to Armani, Cavalli, Prada, and more. Mere mortals follow in their footsteps, but usually just to gawk at the glittering jewels and flowing fabrics in store windows. Designer wear can also be glimpsed on the fashionistas who strut down the sports-car-lined sidewalk as if it were their runway. To get your hands on reasonably priced designer items, you'll first need to wait (there's nothing cheap in season) and then head to one of the designer **outlets** located outside the city center.

Students and young people frequent the city's charming **vintage stores** as well, filling their bags with delicate and decades-old first-rate designers in addition to less pedigreed but nonetheless comfortable garments. An even wider cross section of the community comes out to paw through the wares at the city's many open-air markets, where some clothes can cost just pennies (no guarantee they'll survive two trips through the washer though) and good finds waiting to be discovered hide on stall racks. No matter where they shop, however, the Milanese have a knack for finding just the right style and wearing it well.

Clothes

Dress isn't taken lightly in this city where even sneakers can be a vital fashion accessory, but high style need not be expensive. There are discount stores all over town, though some locals say the best outlet deals are actually in Switzerland at Fox Town *(☎+41 (0)848 82 88 88 💻www.foxtown.ch)*, a 40min. bus ride away. *(Contact Zani Viaggi ☎02 86 71 31 💻www.zaniviaggi.it $ Round trip €20.)*

Looking to Buy

D MAGAZINE OUTLET — 💳♿ FASHION DISTRICT

V. Monte Napoleone 6 — ☎02 76 00 60 27 💻www.dmagazine.it

Quite possibly the only store in sight without a brand name attached, this shop hides its deals—up to 90% off original prices—behind a small door and up a long hallway. Brand-conscious, time-saving deal hunters can check the computer monitor outside to see if their brand and size are in stock. Otherwise, rummage through the over-packed shelves where for once the clothes aren't made to sit on pedestals like works of art. Don't let the casual display fool you, though. That amazing 90% discount may still leave a €300 price tag.

🚏 [M]3: Montenapoleone. $ Men's and women's apparel from €30. ⏰ Open daily 9:30am-7:45pm.

IL SALVAGENTE — 💳⊗ OUTSKIRTS

V. Fratelli Bronzetti 16 — ☎02 76 11 03 28 💻www.salvagentemilano.it

The long list of designers on sale here reads like a Fashion District phonebook. The walk to get here is just as long, and it feels even longer when you're toting two handfuls of bags. For those hardy individuals who want a huge selection and aren't too picky about the latest and greatest styles, the walk to Salvagente will be a piece of cake.

🚏 [M]1: San Babila. The walk is straight but long. Alternatively, take bus #54 or 61 to C. Indipendenza/V. Bronzetti. $ Men's and women's clothing from €20. ⏰ Open M 3-7pm, Tu-Sa 10am-7pm.

NORTH SAILS SPORTSWEAR — 💳♿ GIARDINI PUBBLICI

C. Buenos Aires 10 — ☎02 20 24 17 40 💻www.northsails-sportswear.com

Sailor Chic is the style at this beachy boutique named after a North American maker of another expensive fabric...actual sails (yes, for boats). Notwithstanding the fact that Milan is rather far from any real navigable water, the brand, with its light polos and sporty swimsuits, is popular for those sunny afternoons when residents feel like sitting back, popping their collars, and imagining that the sidewalk cafe is the deck of a nice, big yacht. We're right there with you, wistful landlubbers.

🚏 [M]1: Porta Venezia. $ Men's swimwear €50. Polos €90. Dresses €140. ⏰ Open M-Sa 9:30am-7:30pm.

BORDERLINE — 💳⊗ PIAZZA DEL DUOMO

V. Gian Giacomo Mora 12 — ☎02 36 51 18 46 💻www.youneedthisshit.com

The window display is screaming, "You need this shit!" So is the website URL. Clearly this store isn't subtle, but compared to the self-important shopping palaces of the Fashion District, it's a breath of fresh air. Screenprinted T-shirt designs ranging from Warhol-esque Campbell's Soup cans to a life-size ribcage running down the shirt's chest are dreamed up by local artists and hand-printed in the basement of the shop.

✢ ⓜ1: Duomo. Walk or take tram #3 down V. Torino to C. Porta Ticinese. Turn right onto V. Mora. ⓢ Shirts €35. ⓚ Open daily 11am-2pm and 3-7:30pm.

Just Looking...

A quick tour of the famous fashion houses that line **Via Monte Napoleone.**

ARMANI
V. Manzoni 31

✦ᴕ ⴲ ❁ FASHION DISTRICT
☎02 72 31 86 00 ◻www.armani.com

After gazing in the dark, tinted windows and walking past the black-clad guard into this lacquered and mirrored temple to fashion, one might begin to wonder: where are all the clothes? Each shelf bears only a few items, all looking as if they were pinned into perfect postion by the designer himself (he does live around the corner, you know.) It's all right, though: there are few customers who could afford to buy more than one article of clothing here anyhow.

✢ ⓜ3: Montenapoleone. ⓘ Cafe inside. ⓢ T-shirts €96. Get the idea? ⓚ Open M-W 10:30am-7:30pm, Th-F 10:30am-9pm, Sa 10:30am-7:30pm, Su 2:30-7:30pm

PRADA
V. Monte Napoleone 6-8

✦⊗❁ FASHION DISTRICT
☎02 77 71 771 ◻www.prada.com

The first thing you see when you walk inside Prada's flagship store? Purses and handbags neatly arranged on different blocks. And what can you put in handbags? Jackets and dresses and shoes and sunglasses and perfumes and anything else that Prada makes. How convenient. There's only one thing that's likely to be coming out of the handbag, though, and that's a credit card.

✢ ⓜ1: San Babila. Walk up V. Monte Napoleone. ⓢ Handbags €200-2000+. ⓚ Open M-Sa 10am-7:30pm, Su 11am-7pm.

VERSACE
V. Monte Napoleone 11

✦⊗❁ FASHION DISTRICT
☎02 76 01 12 71 ◻www.versace.com

Can anyone say "in your face?" While other stores along the refined row have well-decorated, classic window displays, Versace lets its windows explode with pulsating neon. The show is irresistible to passersby who wander into the store to gawk at low-cut dresses and shimmering, tight-fitting shirts. A select few even walk out with a brand new style.

✢ ⓜ1: San Babila. ⓢ Men's and women's apparel from €350. ⓚ Open M-Sa 10am-7pm, Su 11am-6pm.

SALVATORE FERRAGAMO
V. Monte Napoleone 3 and V. Monte Napoleone 20/4
◻www.ferragamo.com

✦⊗❁ FASHION DISTRICT
☎02 76 00 00 54 and 02 76 00 66 60

F is for Ferragamo, but it's also for fun! The famous maker of silk and leather products—though the couturier has branched far beyond both—offers at least one stop on the Monte Napoleone train that isn't too serious. Other than on shoe leather, the color black is not to be found in this boutique, and in a hallmark of the brand, many of the men's ties and women's scarves feature dandy little critters and cartoons, from astronauts to zebras and anything in between.

✢ ⓜ1: San Babila. ⓢ Ties €110. Women's apparel from €200. ⓚ Open M-Sa 10am-7:30pm, Su 11am-7pm.

Jewelry

▧ L'ARTE DEL MORO
Inside ⓜ1: Cairoli

✦ᴕ CASTELLO SFORZESCO
☎02 45 47 17 55

This treasure is buried, but it shouldn't take a pirate to find it. The owners of this unique, underground shop keep their store and workshop within a Metro station rather than on the surface alongside dozens of fashionable boutiques. All the simple and inexpensive bead designs are produced in-house at a desk visible through the front windows, but that doesn't mean the necklaces and bracelets lack for sparkling color or elegant composition.

[M]1: Cairoli. $ Earrings €5-15. Necklaces €15-100. ⏰ Open M 2-7:15pm, Tu-Th 9am-7:15pm, F 9am-noon and 3-7:15pm, Sa 2-7:15pm.

J. RIVIERE — FASHION DISTRICT

V. Brera 2 — ☎02 72 02 38 02 www.riviere.it

Jewelry designer James Riviere has his own shop in Milan's Fashion District, where he displays hundreds of pieces. For someone whose work sits in the Louvre museum and the pope's personal jewelry collection, however, a fancy store in a fancier neighborhood probably feels like a bit of a letdown. It's no letdown for those who aren't international religious figures, though, as a trip by the store's windows and a look at the colorful, playfully designed pieces will reveal why Riviere's jewels have become conversation pieces the world over.

[M]1: Cairoli. Take V. Cusani, which becomes V. dell'Orso. Store is at the corner of V. Brera. $ From €250. ⏰ Open daily 10am-2pm and 3-7pm.

Department Stores

Milan is far from a department-store type of town. Beyond **La Rinascente,** the store primarily favored by fashionable Milanese, most large retail establishments offer comfortable but inexpensive clothes that lack the all-important brand names the city's citizens covet.

LA RINASCENTE — PIAZZA DEL DUOMO

V. Santa Radegonda 3 — ☎02 88 521 www.rinascente.it

A department store? How utterly last century. So might some anticipate the Milanese reaction to these shopping blocks. But they'd be wrong so long as the department store in question is La Rinascente, a seven-story palace of designer labels just like those found on V. Monte Napoleone. Located in the heart of the city next to the Duomo, La Rinascente is also home to a popular **food court** on its top floor. Good cuisine tops fashion and jewelry any day.

[M]1: Duomo. $ Men's and women's apparel from €50. ⏰ Open M-Th 9:30am-9pm, F-Sa 9:30am-10pm, Su 10am-9pm.

COIN — OUTSKIRTS

C. Vercelli, 30-32 — ☎02 43 99 00 01 www.coin.it

Similar to La Rinascente in size and scope, Coin holds its high fashions within an unfortunate, brown, warehouse-looking building on one of the city's overlooked shopping rows, C. Vercelli.

[M]1: Pagano: Take V. Pagano south and turn left onto C. Vercelli. $ Men's and women's apparel from €50. ⏰ Open M-F 10am-7:30pm, Sa 10am-8pm, Su 10am-1pm and 3-7:30pm.

Markets

While street vendors try to press their faux-designer bags upon naive tourists every day around the city's major sights, locals do flock to the lively weekend outdoor markets.

MERCATONE DELL'ANTIQUARIO, NAVIGLIO GRANDE — NAVIGLI

Alzaia Naviglio Grande — ☎02 89 40 99 71 www.navigliogrande.mi.it

Locals call it Milan's most comprehensive and highest quality market. Unlike many sales around the city, the Navigli's occurs only once at the end of each month. Make a day out of it with a leisurely brunch at one of the neighborhood's many bakeries or bars followed by an afternoon sifting though the labyrinth of stalls.

[M]1: Porta Genova. $ Prices vary widely. ⏰ Open last Su of every month 9am-6pm. Closed July.

FESTIVAL PARK

V. Puglie   ☎02 29 00 68 29 ▣www.festivalpark.it

Step right up and fulfill all your outdoor-market dreams. Including a farmers' market, secondhand clothing, antiques, and crafts displays, this vast vacant lot—it's hard to fairly call the space a park—fills up every weekend with junk dealers and bargain hunters. Take the time to dig around: you can find some steals if you're dedicated enough to hunt them down.

⛎ Ⓜ3: *Corvetto. Take bus #84 to Apulia-Cook.* ⓢ *Prices vary widely.* ⏰ *Open Su 8am-5pm.*

FIERA DI SENIGALLA

⚂♿ NAVIGLI

Alzaia Naviglio Grande at V. Valenza, and surrounding streets   ▣www.fieradisinigaglia.it

Despite being founded in the early 1800s, this weekly market doesn't show its age—except for the fact that vinyl records are still on sale. (No, grandma, it's *mp3*, not *LP*.) Though clothing and antique stalls are represented, this fair retains a cultural bent, with artwork, ethnic crafts, and books for sale in addition to music and collectables.

⛎ Ⓜ2: *Porta Genova. Turn right out of the station and walk along the tracks until reaching the canal.* ⓢ *Prices vary widely.* ⏰ *Open Sa 8am-6pm.*

Antiques and Vintage Clothing

As most Milan residents will tell you, vintage is the way to go. When the elites are done with their designer labels, they liquidate the assets by selling them back—cash goes to the rich, and affordable fashions to the frugal.

▧ CAVALLI E NASTRI

✍⚂ FASHION DISTRICT, PIAZZA DEL DUOMO

V. Brera 2, V. Gian Giacomo Mora 3 and 12   ☎02 72 00 04 49 ▣www.cavallienastri.it

When they get sick of the poodle-in-my-purse parade on V. Monte Napoleone, the fashionistas join the wannabes here for both bargains and collectables. From first-line dresses of many well known brands to nameless but stylish skirts and jeans, the line-up available at Cavalli e Nastri has fashion students referring their less well-dressed friends here—and visiting to shop for themselves as well. The stores on V. Gian Giacomo Moro, especially, offer wide selections of everything from Looney Tunes and Hogwarts T-shirts to designer fashions.

⛎ *Brera store:* Ⓜ1: *Cairoli. Follow V. Cusani, which becomes V. dell'Orso, to V. Brera and turn left. V. Mora stores:* Ⓜ1: *Duomo. Walk or take tram #3 down V. Torino to C. Porta Ticinese. Turn right onto V. Mora.* ⓘ *Alternative contacts* ☎02 97 38 26 29 *or* 02 89 40 94 52. ⓢ *Men's shirts from €25; ties from €10. Women's dresses from €50.* ⏰ *Open M 3-7:30pm, Tu-Sa 10:30am-7:30pm. Closed 2 weeks in Aug.*

▧ HUMANA VINTAGE

✍⚂ PIAZZA DEL DUOMO

V. Cappellari 3   ☎02 72 08 06 06 ▣www.humanaitalia.org

Shoppers—even when they're groups of friends roaming the mall in packs—have a tendency to get caught up in themselves. Something about the overwhelming desire to look good and all the mirrors reminding them how close to (or far from) that goal they are. At Humana, buyers can look good and give back, as all proceeds help fund the group's development projects in developing countries around the globe.

⛎ Ⓜ1: *Duomo. From V. Mazzini, take the 1st left at V. Dogana. Store is at the corner of V. Cappellari.* ⓢ *Men's and women's shirts €18. Dresses €40.* ⏰ *Open M 2:30-7:30pm, Tu-Sa 10:30am-7:30pm.*

ESSENTIALS

Practicalities

- **TOURIST OFFICES: Informazioni Accoglienza Turistica** is Milan's central tourist office. It publishes *Hello Milano,* which offers information in English on events and nightlife, and the monthly *Milanomese,* which has a comprehensive listing of events and exhibitions in Italian and English. Tour operators keep desks here as well, and the office has helpful English-speaking representatives. (*P. Duomo 19A* ☎02 77 40

43 43 💻www.visitamilano.it 🪧 Next to the pharmacy, on the left when facing the cathedral, and down the stairs or elevator. ⏰ Open M-Sa 8:45am-1pm and 2-6pm, Su 9am-1pm and 2-5pm.) **Stazione Central Branch** *(☎02 77 40 43 18/19 🪧 Directly across from the tracks.)*

- **TOURS: Autostradale,** with a sales desk in the tourist office, operates hop-on, hop-off sightseeing city tours that circle the *centro*. Taped commentary available in English. 3hr. tours *(€55)* depart P. Duomo at 9:30am and include admission to Leonardo's *The Last Supper*. Walking tours *(€20-30)* including the Duomo, Galleria Vittorio Emanuele II, and La Scala or Castello Sforzesco depart daily at 10am and 11:30am. *(☎02 33 91 07 94 💻www.autostradale.it)*
- **CONSULATES: Australia.** *(V. Borgogna 2, 3rd fl. ☎02 77 67 41 💻www.italy.embassy.gov.au 🪧 [M]1: San Babila. ⏰ Open M-Th 8:30am-1pm and 1:30-5pm, F 8:30am-1pm. Appointments recommended.)* **Canada.** *(V. Vittor Pisani 19 ☎02 67 581 💻www.canada.it 🪧 [M]2/3: Centrale F.S. ⏰ Open M-F 9am-noon.)* **New Zealand.** *(V. Terraggio 17 ☎02 72 17 00 01 💻www.nzembassy.com/italy 🪧 [M]1/2: Cardona F.N. ⏰ Open M-Sa 8:30am-noon and 1:30-5:30pm.)* **UK.** *(V. S. Paolo 7 ☎02 72 30 01 💻www.britain.it 🪧 [M]1/3:Duomo. ⏰ Open M-F 8am-noon and 1-4pm.)* **US.** *(V. Principe Amedeo 2/10 ☎02 29 03 51 💻www.milan.usconsulate.gov 🪧 [M]3: Turati. ⏰ Open M-F 8:30am-noon.)*
- **CURRENCY EXCHANGE:** Banks and **ATMs** are abundant. *(⏰ Most banks open M-F 8:30am-1:30pm and 3-4pm.)* **Western Union** located in Stazione Centrale. *(⏰ Open daily 9am-7:45pm.)* **American Express** *(V. Larga 4 ☎02 72 10 40 10 🪧 Near the Duomo. ⏰ Open M-F 9am-5:30pm.)*
- **LUGGAGE STORAGE: Stazione Centrale.** *($ 1st 5hr. €4. Each additional hr. up to 12hr. 6 cents per hr. After 12hr. 20 cents per hr. ⏰ Open daily 6am-11:50pm.)*
- **GLBT RESOURCES: ARCI-GAY "Centro D'Iniziativa Gay."** *(V. Bezzeca 3 ☎02 54 12 22 25 💻www.arcigaymilano.org ⏰ Open M-F 3-8pm.)*
- **DISABLED SERVICES: AIAS Milano Onlus.** *(V. Paolo Mantegazza 10 ☎02 33 02 021 💻www.aiasmilano.it)*
- **POST OFFICES:** *(P. Cordusio 4 ☎02 72 48 21 26 🪧 Near P. Duomo. ℹ Currency exchange and ATM. ⏰ Open M-F 8am-7pm, Sa 8:30am-noon.)*
- **POSTAL CODE:** 20100

Emergency!

- **POLICE:** *(In P. Cesare Beccaria, near Duomo ☎02 77 271)*
- **LATE-NIGHT PHARMACIES:** These can be found in **Stazione Centrale** *(☎02 66 90 735)* and **Stazione Porta Garibaldi** *(☎02 29 06 32 62)*. Most other pharmacies post after-hours rotations.
- **HOSPITALS/MEDICAL SERVICES: Ospedale Fatebenefratelli** *(C. Porta Nouva 23 ☎02 63 631)* and **Ospedale Maggiore di Milano.** *(V. Francesco Sforza 35 ☎02 55 031 🪧 5min. from Duomo on inner ring road.)* **Ospedale Niguarda Ca'Grande** is in the north of the city *(P. Ospedale Maggiore 3 ☎02 64 441)*.

Getting There

By Plane

Milan is served by three primary airports.

MALPENSA AIRPORT (MXP)

48km northwest of the city ☎02 23 23 23 💻www.sea-aeroportimilano.it

Shuttles run to the right side of Stazione Centrale *(☎02 58 58 31 85 💻www.malpen-*

sashuttle.it ($ *€7.50, round-trip €12.* ⏰ *Trip lasts 50min., departs every 20min. daily to airport 5am-9:30pm; to Stazione Centrale 6:20am-12:15am.)* Malpensa Express **train** departs Cardona Station, a.k.a. Stazione Nord. *($ €11, round-trip €17.* ⏰ *Trip lasts 40min., departs every 30min. daily to airport 5:50am-8:20pm; to Stazione Nord 6:45am-9:45pm.)*

LINATE AIRPORT (LIN)

7km east of the city ☎02 23 23 23 💻www.sea-aeroportimilano.it

Serves domestic, European, and some intercontinental flights. Starfly buses *(☎02 58 58 72 37)* run to Stazione Centrale. *($ €5.* ⏰ *Trip lasts 20min.; departs every 30min. daily to airport 5:40am-9:35pm, to Stazione Centrale 6:05am-11:35pm.)* City bus #73 runs to the downtown San Babila Metro station *(€1).*

ORIO AL SERIO AIRPORT (BGY)

Bergamo, 58km northeast of the city ☎035 32 63 23 💻www.sacbo.it

With **budget airlines,** there's always a compromise that's gotta be made. And that compromise is location. So, though Bergamo might be a completely different city, it provides a cheap option for arriving in Milan. Airlines that fly here include RyanAir and Wizz. Inconvenience is greatly reduced by the shuttle bus that runs to Stazione Centrale. *($ €7.90.* ⏰ *1hr.; departs every 30min.; to airport 4am-11:30pm, to Milan 4:30am-1am.)* General information, including a link to transport workers' strike calendar, can be found at the above number and website.

By Train

Milan's main train station—Italy's second busiest—is **Stazione Centrale.** *(☎89 20 21 ⌖ Northeast of the city center in P. Duca d'Aosta.)* It serves most **Trenitalia** trains, including high-speed *Frecciarossa (Eurostar)* lines. The ticket office on the ground floor is open daily 5:45am-10:45pm. The Trenitalia information booth located in the ticket office is open daily 7am-9pm. Trains to **Florence** *($ Eurostar €52, regional trains €27.50.* ⏰ *Eurostar 2hr., departs every hr. 5:45am-8:15pm. Regional train 3hr., departs every 3hr. 6:50am-8:15pm.)*; **Rome** *($ Eurostar €89, regional trains €46.* ⏰ *Eurostar 3½hr., more than once an hr. 5:45am-9pm. Regional train 6½hr., every 3hr. 6:50am-11:30pm.)*; **Turin** *($ €9.55.* ⏰ *2hr., every hr. 5:15am-12:15am.)*; **Venice** *($ €30.* ⏰ *2hr., every hr., 6:35am-9pm.)*; and numerous local destinations.

Milan has several other, smaller stations on its periphery. The most significant of these is **Cardona-Stazione Nord** *(☎199 15 11 52),* hub for **Ferrovie Nord,** northern Italy's regional train company. **Malpensa Express** also departs from Cardona station (see **By Plane**). **Stazione Porta Garibaldi** is a primary commuter station serving local destinations. Milan's oldest train station, **Porta Genova,** is slowly being phased out of the network, so you probably won't need to worry about it.

By Bus

Airport buses depart from the southeast side of Stazione Centrale, with signs for times and prices posted outside. Tickets are available onboard. Most intercity buses depart from the town's periphery. **Autostradale** departs from [M]1: Lampugnano and Stazione Porta Garibaldi. Other companies depart from P. Castello near Stazione Nord *([M]1: Cairoli).* Bus service is available to many towns, including **Turin** and basically anywhere you could (and couldn't) care about in Lombardy, in addition to some places beyond.

Getting Around

By Public Transportation

We still can't tell if Milan's subway trains slowly slide backwards as people board because the operators find it amusing or because these trains aren't as advanced as we're led to believe. Regardless, Milan's extensive and efficient transit network is the pride of the city. The [M]**Metropolitana Milanese** underground system runs from 6am-midnight and is the quickest and most useful branch of public transit, covering most areas in the city proper. **Line 1** (red) streches from the suburbs of Sesto northeast of the city (Sesto 1 Maggio F.S.) to the exposition centers of **Rho-Fiera** in the northwest and to **Bisceglie** in the southwest. **Line 2** (green) links Milan's three

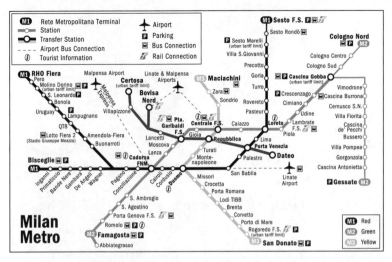

Milan Metro

Legend:
M1 Rete Metropolitana Terminal
○ Station
◉ Transfer Station
- - - Airport Bus Connection
ⓘ Tourist Information
✈ Airport
P Parking
🚌 Bus Connection
🚆 Rail Connection

M1 Red
M2 Green
M3 Yellow

primary train stations—**Cardona F.N.**, **Garibaldi F.S.**, and **Centrale F.S.**—while spanning from **Cologno Nord** and **Gessate** in the east to **Abbiategrasso** in the west. It crosses Ⓜ1 at **Cardona** and **Loreto**. **Line 3** (yellow) runs south from the up-and-coming neighborhoods near **Maciachini** to **San Donato**, crossing Ⓜ2 at **Stazione Centrale** and Ⓜ1 at **Duomo**.

The subway's reach is not all-encompassing, so beyond its range a system of **trams** and buses connects Metro stations to the less accessible parts of the city. Trams #29/30 circle the city's outer ring road, while bus #94 circles the inner road. Ask for a map at an **ATM Point** (for Azienda Trasporti Milanese) located in the Duomo, Stazione Centrale, and Cardona stations as well as others. Tickets (Ⓢ €1.) are good for Metro, trams, and buses for a period of 1hr. after validation; €3 buys a 24hr. pass, and €5.50 gets 48hr. Evening tickets (Ⓢ €1.80) are valid after 8pm until close on the day validated. Tickets are available at machines in the stations, newstands, tobacconists, and the ATM Points. When boarding a tram or bus, make sure to **validate** your ticket in the red machines; inspectors frequently stop passengers to check tickets, and fines are steep. For late-night travel, ATM operates a **Radiobus** service (☎02 48 03 48 03), which will pick up passengers holding valid ATM tickets anywhere in the city for a €2 surcharge (€1.50 if purchased in advance from the locations above), from 8pm-2am.

By Cab

White taxis are omnipresent in the city, and cab stands in major *piazze* usually have cabs day and night. Otherwise, call one of the three major companies: **Autoradio Taxi** (☎02 85 85), **Taxi Blue** (☎02 40 40), or **RadioTaxi** (☎02 69 69).

By Bike

Milan's environmental movement has made bike rental virtually obsolete. Instead, try bike sharing. The new **bikeMi** (☎800 80 81 81 🖥www.bikemi.it) program has installed dozens of pick-up and drop-off locations where locals and visitors can check out bikes and leave them at their destination. These are sprinkled throughout the city and its outskirts. (Ⓢ *Daily subscriptions €2.50, weekly €6, plus fees of €0.50 per 30min. after 1st 30min. up to 2hr. maximum. After 2hr., fines of €2 per hr. apply.*) Really want a bike of your own? Rental shops do exist, but will require a €100 security deposit and ID. One rental company is **AWS**. (*V. Ponte Seveso 33 ☎02 67 07 21 45 🖥www.awsbici.com Ⓢ €11 per day for 1st 3 days, €2.60 per day thereafter; 1 month €80.*)

milan · essentials

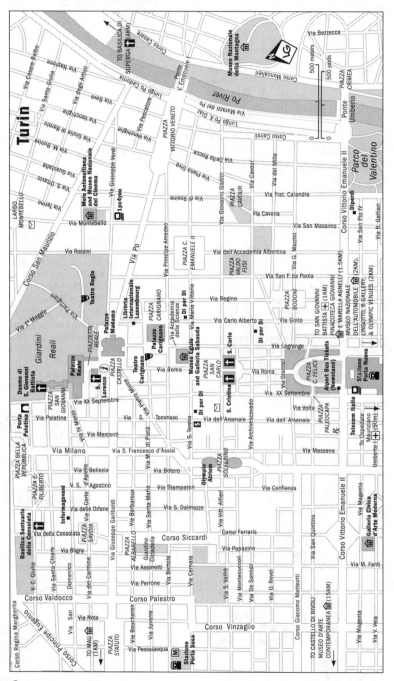

milan and turin

Turin

turin *torino* ☎011

The ⚡**2006 Winter Olympics** put "Torino" on the map—literally. The confusion over which name to use, the hard English "Turin" or the smooth, rythmic Italian has heightened since the city insisted on its native tongue back when it got the games. Regardless of which name it goes by, the often overshadowed northern city is universally admired now that it's had a chance to show off its many wonders. One of the greenest big cities in Italy, with vast public parks, the river Po, the hills beyond, and tree-lined boulevards blazed by Napoleon, Turin can in some ways feel more French than Italian in character. Espresso is *caffé*, the downtown is filled with royal history, and isolated *castelli* dot the hillsides surrounding the city. The seat of the wealthy Savoy king up until the mid-1900s, Turin became the first capital of the unified Italy in 1860 while its resident dynasty became the new nation's monarchs.

Though it has long since lost the title of Italian capital and the remaining Savoys are desperately clinging to their title in the current republic, culturally, Turin remains impressive. It is a showcase of contemporary art masterpieces, and its theater and music offerings rival those of Milan, the country's larger and more famous northern city. In many ways, Turin, with its rich history and quiet, beautiful neighborhoods, surpasses its fashionable neighbor.

ORIENTATION

Geographically, there are really two Turins. On the left bank of the **River Po,** there's a dense Neoclassical city and a street grid with—gasp—right angles at nearly every corner. On the right bank, there's an Alpine village, with roads winding up the mountainside and castle-like homes clinging to the slopes. The city's spiritual center is found in **Piazza Castello,** the square east of the river and home to many museums and sights. To reach the charming **Quadrilatero Romana,** follow V. Garibaldi and turn right onto V. San Agostino. C. Regina Margherita runs just north of the Castello, passing through P. della Repubblica, the site of a major outdoor market, to the east. V. Po runs from P. Castello to the long plaza of **Piazza Vittorio Veneto,** a major nightlife destination in addition to the riverbanks themselves, and then across the river to the Basilica di Gran Madre di Dio. V. Roma, the major shopping street, runs south from the castle to **Stazione Porta Nuova,** the point of arrival for most travelers. In front of Porta Nuova, **Corso Vittorio Emanuele II** runs west toward the river past a number of pubs and pizza joints, crossing the water at Ponte Umberto I and leading to the leafy residential neighborhoods of the hills. From C. Emanuele, V. Nizza runs south alongside the railroad tracks through an area filled with cheap hotels and onward to the revitalizing area of **Lingotto,** site of a former Fiat factory that has now been transformed into a mall and art galleries.

ACCOMMODATIONS

Turin's budget accommodations consist of a wide variety of hostels, hotels, and B and Bs that can suit anyone's tastes, but there's seemingly no rhyme or reason to the layout of these many properties. Many new hotels opened in the city center for the Olympic Games, while the city's hostels are located mainly on the periphery in all directions, from the green hills east of the Po to the low-rise, industrial area near **Stazione Dora.** Some budget hotels are clustered near **Stazione Porta Nuova.** Family-run B and Bs, which offer some of the most comfortable and convenient lodging, can be found in the city's nicest residential neighborhoods near the attractions of **P. Castello.**

▨ OPEN 011   ✈ઙ(ᵗ) HOSTEL ❶
C. Venezia 11   ☎011 25 05 35 ▣www.openzero11.it

We like to call the owners of this hostel "giant-friendly." Not even a 7 ft. ogre would hit his head here, for this hostel has high ceilings and no bunk-beds in its 34 gleaming rooms, each of which has a bathroom inside. With a grand staircase and comfortable (if somewhat worn) seating in the common areas, plus a bar, restaurant, and terrace, Open 011 offers ample space to spread out and relax.

➡ From Porta Nuova, take bus #52 (67 on Su) to V. Chiesa della Salute. Turn right at the next intersection and then left onto C. Venezia. Or 5min. walk from Stazione Dora. ℹ Wi-Fi €1 per 30min., €3 per 2hr. Breakfast included. Key deposit €5. $ 3- to 4-bed dorms €18; singles €31; doubles €44. ⏰ Reception 24hr.

HOTEL CAMPIDOGLIO 💳♿📶❄ HOTEL, HOSTEL [2]

V. Corio 11 ☎011 77 65 808 💻www.hotelcampidoglio.it

Located down an alley "paved" with grass and smoothed stones, this place truly earns the seemingly contradictory title of "luxury hostel." While many of its hotel rooms have had modern renovations and look damn good as a result, the dorm rooms retain their unfortunate pink floral wallpaper. Regardless of the decor, all rooms have soft mattresses, bedside tables, and are bunk-free.

➡ Take tram #9 toward Stampala and get off at the Ospedale Maria Vittoria stop. After exiting, turn around and make the 1st right onto V. Cibrario, then turn left onto V. Corio. ℹ Breakfast included. Free Wi-Fi and computer. $ 3- to 4-bed dorms €22-24; singles €35-40, with bath €50-55; doubles €52-57/€65-70. ⏰ Reception 24hr.

OSTELLO TORINO (HI) 💳🚭📶 HOSTEL [1]

V. Alby 1 ☎011 66 02 939 💻www.ostellotorino.it

It's quite possible that this hostel was constructed to mimic the mountain it sits on, for after a steep hike to get here, travelers face steeper spiral stairs to their rooms. Luckily, the staff is warm and helpful and some of the cozy rooms feature impressive views of the city and river below.

➡ From Porta Nuova, take bus #52 (64 on Su) to Lanza stop at V. Crimea. Follow the "Ostello" signs to C. Lanza and then up steep, winding V. Gatti. ℹ Breakfast included. Locket key deposit €10, towel rental €1. Wi-Fi €0.50 per 30min. $ 3- to 8-bed dorms €15; doubles €35, with bath €40; triples €51; quads €68. ⏰ Reception 7am-12:30pm and 3-11pm. Lockout 10am-3pm. Curfew 11pm; ask for key if staying out later.

HOTEL ALPI RESORT 💳🚭📶❄ HOTEL [4]

V. Alfonso Bonafous 5, 3rd fl. ☎011 81 29 677 💻www.hotelalpiresort.it

First off, one note: this hotel is no more in the Alps than any part of Turin. It's still got a great location, though, one block from the city's bustling nightlife hub. With spacious rooms, free internet, flatscreen TVs, and breakfast served all morning long, there's little not to like once you've stepped out of the classic wood paneled elevator in this restored apartment building.

➡ Just off P. Vittorio Veneto. ℹ Breakfast included. Free Ethernet in rooms. $ Singles €50-65; doubles €69-85; triples €89-120. ⏰ Reception 24hr.

ALBERGO AZALEA 💳🚭 HOTEL [3]

V. Mercanti 16 ☎011 53 81 15 💻www.hotelazalea.it

Whether you're watching a football game or playing poker, Albergo Azalea's spacious common room that overlooks a bright courtyard provides the perfect venue for enjoying the company of others (and the TV). The hotel has 10 meticulously clean and brightly colored rooms in an apartment building just minutes from the heart of Torino's *centro*.

➡ 100m from P. Castello. Take V. Pietro Micca from the piazza's southwest corner, and turn right onto V. Mercanti. $ Singles €40-55; doubles €55-70; triples €75-80; quads €85-90. ⏰ No reception; call ahead.

FORESTERIA DEGLI ARTISTI 🚫💳🚭❄ B AND B [4]

V. degli Artisti 15 ☎011 83 77 85 💻www.foresteriadegliartisti.it

Sharing its street with frame workshops and graphic designers, this charming B

and B lives up to its name. The kind husband-and-wife owners greet their guests personally. From the pink courtyard and antique furniture to modern rooms and DVD collection, the family will provide everything you need for a comfortable stay.
From P. Castello, walk along V. Verdi and turn left at V. Sant'Ottavio, then right onto V. degli Artisti. Ring bell for "Coss Noire," then walk to 2nd door on the left and ring again. **i** *Reserve ahead. Closed several weeks in July.* $ *Singles €60; doubles €90; addtional bed €30.* ⏰ *No reception; call ahead.*

SIGHTS

MOLE ANTONELLIANA — MUSEUM

V. Montebello 20 ☎011 81 38 560 www.museocinema.it

Once the world's tallest structure built from traditional masonry (read: brick) as its construction neared completion in the 1880s (before the builders added some concrete—brilliant), the Mole Antonelliana is at the very least Turin's highest structure, dominating its otherwise pedestrian skyline. The tower, begun as a synagogue in the 1830s but soon after purchased by the city of Turin, has gained fame today by virtue of gracing the euro two-cent coin. Home to the **Museo Nazionale de Cinema,** the Mole holds the distinction of being the world's tallest museum. It also holds a panoramic elevator, a glass box that is not for the faint of heart or the fearful of heights: suspended only by cable, it rises straight through the building's towering atrium known as **Temple Hall.** Those prepared to battle a little vertigo are able to enjoy a magnificent view of the city and surrounding hills. On the museum's second floor, visitors can recline on red lounges and watch movies on towering screens or experience firsthand a number of film's most famous genres by meandering through the rooms along the hall's periphery—a mad scientist's lab, Wild West saloon, and romantic love nest among them. On the first level, an interactive exhibit of the physics and development of photography and cinema is highlighted by examples of some of the first crazy machines that made pictures move. A movie-poster-covered suspended staircase circles upward from Temple Hall.
From P. Castello, walk east on V. Giuseppe Verdi and turn left onto V. Montebello. $ *Museum €7, students and over 65 €5. Elevator €5/3.50.* ⏰ *Museum open Tu-F 9am-8pm, Sa 9am-11pm, Su 9am-8pm. Last entry 1hr. before close. Elevator open Tu-F 10am-8pm, Sa 10am-11pm, Su 10am-8pm.*

tourin' card

Boy, does Turin have a deal for you! The biggest steal in the city is the **Torino+Piemonte Card** *($ 48hr. €20, 7-days €35),* which provides free entrance to all the museums and monuments in Turin and Piedmont, rides on public transportation (except underground), access to the hop-on, hop-off TurismoBus Torino, the panoramic lift in the Mole, the Sassi-Superga cable car, and the boats for river navigation on the Po, as well as discounts on guided tours and shows. The card is available at any Turismo Torino info point and at most hotels.

PALAZZO DELL'ACCADEMIA DELLE SCIENZE — MUSEUM

V. Accademia delle Scienze 6 ☎011 44 06 903 www.museoegizio.it

It's not King Tut's tomb, but this *palazzo* is still the final resting place of some well-known Egyptian royalty. The first Egyptian collection outside of Cairo, Turin's **Museo Egizio** consists of many artifacts that were acquired in the Italian Archaeological Mission of 1903-1937, which was responsible for the acquisition of thousands of artifacts currently on display. The staff of Kha inlaid with bronze as well as *sarcophgi* from his tomb fill the museum's first rooms. The most impressive item on display is the Temple of Ellesiya, a full-sized temple of carved stones praising the gods. Hieroglyphics are translated for the benefit of mere mortals. Upstairs in the same building is the **Galeria Sabuda,** the Savoy Gallery, which houses the art collections that were once kept for the personal enjoyment of the Palazzo Reale and Palazzo Carignano's residents. Renowned for its 14th- to 18th-century Flemish and Dutch paintings, the museum also contains works by Rembrandt and other noted artists.

➜ 2 blocks from P. Castello. ℹ Alternative contact ☎011 564 1791 and website 💻www.artito.arti.beniculturali.it. $ Egypt museum €7.50, students 18-25 €3.50. Savoy Gallery €4/2. ⏰ Egypt museum open Tu-Su 8:30am-7:30pm. Last entry 1hr. before close. Savoy Gallery open Tu 8:30am-2pm, W 2-7:30pm, Th 10am-7:30pm, F-Su 8:30am-2pm.

CATTEDRALE DI SAN GIOVANNI AND CHIESA DI SAN LORENZO ♿ CHURCH

V. Palazzo di Città 4 ☎011 43 61 540 (Cattedrale di San Giovanni) ☎011 43 61 527 (San Lorenzo) 💻www.sanlorenzo.torino.it.

The ★**Holy Shroud of Turin,** one of the holiest and most enigmatic relics in all of Christianity, is kept in the Turin cathedral's **Capella della Santa Sindone.** Said to be Jesus's burial cloth and bearing a faint image of his face, the 3 by 14 ft. cloth itself is available for viewing by tourists only a few weeks every 25 years—the most recent exhibit was 2010, so book now for 2035. Operators are standing by! While the shroud has been held in the cathedral since 1694, nowadays, casual visitors will only be able to see its full-size reproduction in Chiesa di San Lorenzo, which served as a temporary home to the shroud before the cathedral was completed in the 15th century. But sadly even this image pretty much resembles one found anywhere in the world with a good search engine. A negative image shows more detail, including the face of a man with a fractured nose and broken cheek. Also of interest in Chiesa di San Lorenzo is the Baroque architecture of Guarino Guarini, particularly the soaring dome with its eight-pointed star evoking the Islamic design Guarini so admired. His intricate Baroque facade was never built, because Savoy rulers insisted that buildings on the *piazza* share a uniform design.

➜ To Cattedrale di San Giovanni from P. Castello, take V. Palazzo di Citta 1 block and turn left onto V. XX Settembre. San Lorenzo's entrance is on P. Castello, in front of and to the left when facing the Palazzo Reale gates. ℹ Modest dress required. $ Free. ⏰ Cattedrale di San Giovanni open M-Sa 7am-noon and 3-7pm, Su 8am-noon and 3-7pm. San Lorenzo M-F 7:30am-noon and 4-7pm, Sa 7:30am-noon and 3-7:15pm, Su 9am-1pm and 3-7:15pm.

PALAZZO REALE 🎧♿ TOWER, MUSEUM

Piazzetta Reale ☎011 43 61 455 💻www.ambienteto.arti.benculturali.it

The Princes of Savoy's residence for more than 200 years, since 1865, the Palazzo Reale has been as much a relic representing a time that predates Italy's current republic. Designed as part of an effort by Ascanio Vittozzi to revitalize the Savoy capital in the late 1500s, it is the most central of the *"Crown of Delitie,"* a ring of Piedmont castles that became a UNESCO World Heritage Site in 1997. The Palazzo Reale has over 300 rooms, many unfurnished. Thirty of them are featured on a guided tour that is the only way to see the palace's interior. The tour visits the throne room and king and queen's apartments, plus the private rooms of Umberto II of Savoy, the last of the dynastic rulers. The gardens behind the residence were designed by André Le Nôtrê, famous for the gardens at Versailles, but have been dramatically reduced in size and elegance.

➜ On P. Castello. ℹ Guided tour in Italian with available English audio tour. Call or check website for dates of the occasional and popular tours of the royal kitchens. $ €6.50, students €3.50. Gardens free. ⏰ Open Tu-Su 8:30am-6:20pm. Required guided tour lasts 1hr., departs every 30min. Gardens open daily 9am-1hr. before sunset.

ARMERIA REALE ⊛♿ MUSEUM

P. Castello 191 ☎011 54 38 89 💻www.ambienteto.arti.beniculturali.it

Shimmering, shining, certainly not rusting, the collection of swords, daggers, and armor in this small but densely packed museum looks as ready for battle as it must have when the weapons were forged hundreds of years ago. Knights on horses (plus a samurai, who must've made a long trip) stand ready to gallop out and defend the Savoy kingdom, while jeweled swords given as gifts to the Savoys by diplomats from India and Turkey are on display as well.

🪧 In the right wing of Palazzo Reale, outside of the gates and behind the Castello. ℹ Handicapped patrons must enter at Palazzo Reale; call ahead. $ €4, students €2, under 18 and over 65 free. Handicapped patrons and 1 guest free. Students studying related subjects such as military history and architecture can sometimes enter free. ⏰ Open Tu-Su 9am-7pm. Hours subject to change.

PINACOTECA GIOVANNI E MARELLA AGNELLI ⊛♿ MUSEUM

V. Nizza 230 ☎011 00 62 713 💻www.pinacoteca-agnelli.it

This tiny jewel box of a museum sits in a glass house atop a former Fiat factory south of Turin's city center, and it has just 26 paintings in its permanent collection, but many of these works are the creations of the 20th century's foremost artists, including Picasso and Matisse. The Pinacoteca also holds groups of significant 18th- and 19th-century works. The seven Matisses on display here are separated by 20 years of the painter's life. As a result, they demonstrate the notable development in his vibrant, simplified style over the course of his career.

🪧 Take bus #1 or 18 to Lingotto. Entrance is on the 1st fl. of the 8 Gallery mall, through the museum bookshop. ℹ Hosts 2 temporary exhibits per year. $ €4, students and ages over 65 €2.50. ⏰ Open Tu-Su 10am-7pm. Last entry 45min. before close.

CHIESA SAN FILIPPO NERI ⊛ CHURCH

V. Maria Vittoria 5 ☎011 53 84 56 💻www.sanfilippotorino.it

Lacking a relic to brag about, Turin's largest church is not its most famous. Chiesa San Filippo Neri hasn't needed the leftover fingernails of a long-dead saint to solidify its position as Turin's spiritual center, however. The current church building was designed by Antonio Bettino, and its construction was nearly complete when, in 1706, the violence of the Siege of Turin caused the church's dome to collapse. The new church built by Filippo Juvarra remains today. A beautiful space with few pews and a white sculpted ceiling, the *chiesa* feels almost like a monumental ballroom (hopefully that's not a blasphemous comparison). The towering altar, designed by Michelangelo Garove (Mickey G. to his friends, not to be confused with the Mike B. of Sistine Chapel fame) and Melchiore Galleani, represents the history of the Savoy in dark stone and gold.

🪧 Just south of P. Castello. Take V. Accademia delle Scienze for 3 blocks; church is to the left. $ Free. ⏰ Open M-F 8am-7pm, Sa 8am-noon and 5:30-7pm, Su 10am-noon.

CASTELLO DI RIVOLI MUSEO D'ARTE CONTEMPORANEA ⊛♿ MUSEUM

P. Mafalda di Savoia, Rivoli ☎011 95 65 222 💻www.castellodirivoli.org

It takes a trip to reach this museum, but remember that time isn't money. At any rate, the collection of contemporary art—none of it older than the 1950s—held in this expansive Savoy residence 22km from Turin is well worth the time spent getting to it. The huge, vaulted rooms have been used as canvas for many sculptors including Sol Lewitt, whose 1992 *Panels and Towers* was designed specifically for installation at the museum. Other important artists represented in the museum include Bruce Nauman and Claes Oldenburg.

🪧 22km outside Turin. Take bus #36 or 66 from Turin, or Ⓜ Paradiso and then bus #36 to Rivoli. Inquire at the bus station about the direct shuttle bus. $ €6.50, students and ages over 64 €3.50 ⏰ Open Tu-Th 10am-5pm, F-Su 10am-9pm.

BASILICA DI SUPERGA 💳⃠♿⃠ CHURCH

Superga Hill ☎011 89 97 456 💻www.basilicadisuperga.com

"The most enchanting position in the world." That's how the famous modernist architect Le Corbusier described the site of this basilica perched on a summit 672m above sea level. The view from the summit is spectacular in all directions (when the sky is clear), with Turin and the Alps beyond in clear focus.

⇆ Tram #15 to Stazione Sassi, then bus #79 or a cable railway for an 18min. ride uphill. $ Cable car €4 round-trip, €5.50 on Sa-Su. Basilica free. Royal tombs and royal apartment €4, students €3. Dome €3/2. ⏰ Cable car open M 9am-noon and 2-8pm, W-F 9am-noon and 2-8pm, Sa-Su 9am-8pm. Returns on the ½hr. Basilica open M-Sa 9am-noon and 3-6pm, Su 12:45-6pm. Tombs and Royal Apartment open daily 9:30am-7:30pm; 30min. guided tour in Italian required with translation available. Dome open M-F 10am-6pm, Sa 10am-7pm, Su 12:45-7pm.

PALAZZO MADAMA 💳♿⃠ PALAZZO

P. Castello ☎011 44 33 501 💻www.palazzomadamatorino.it

The *palazzo* that anchors P. Castello, and all of Turin for that matter, has a fascinating archaeology. Suffice it to say that its been renovated more times than Bob Villa's own home. What began as a Roman gate became a dark, brick medieval castle, then was refinished—on one side only—as a Baroque palace. A visit just inside the palace gates reveals this history at the free medieval courtyard, but a trip inside allows visitors to see the towers and structures first hand. Oh, and as an added bonus, the palace is full of an enormous collection of Baroque paintings, golden artifacts, and mosaics on four floors.

⇆ The "Castello" of P. Castello. $ €7.50, students under 25 €6. ⏰ Open Tu-F and Su 10am-6pm, Sa 10am-8pm.

PARCO DEL VALENTINO 💳♿ PARK

Vle. Virgilio 107 ☎011 44 31 701 💻www.borgomedivaletorino.it

Italy's first public park, Parco del Valentino surrounds the French-style **Castello del Valentino** which now houses Torino University's architecture faculty and is not typically open to the public. What is open, of course, is the theme-park version—a mini reproduction of a castle in the Piedmont style intended to show life as it might have been in 15th-century Turin. Built for an 1884 exposition, the **Boro e Rocca Medivale** also houses a crafts market on a replica village street.

⇆ Castle and park along the Po, at the end of C. Vittorio Emanuele. $ Village free. Castle €5, students €4. ⏰ Village open Ap-Oct daily 9am-8pm; Nov-Mar daily 9am-7pm. Castle open Tu-Su 10am-6pm; last entry 45min. before close. 30min. guided tour.

THE GREAT OUTDOORS ⛰

Turin city proper wasn't the only thing onstage at the 🏅**2006 Winter Olympic Games;** the majestic white-capped Alps beyond also got their fair share of TV time. While they made an occasional pretty backdrop for the TV cameras in town for the Games, they have always been woven into the fabric of Torinese life. The **Via Lattea** ski area *(☎0122 79 94 11 💻www.vialattea.it)*, or "Milky Way," hosted Olympic Alpine and cross-country skiing and ski jumping events. Visitors to Turin can bust out their less Olympian ski poles on its over 400km of skiable runs, 80 of which have snowmaking capabilities. The resort runs more than 80 lifts from a number of villages *(Lift tickets about €34)*. The village of **Sestriere,** just 17km from the French border, hosted Alpine skiing at the Games and got most of the press attention. No surprise, as it was home to the mountainside media village. It also has Europe's highest 18-hole golf course in the summer months, a 4828 yd., par-65 course with stunning mountain vistas. Teeing off here, gullible golfers will come to believe that hundred-foot drop-offs make for great hazards (*☎012 27 62 43 in summer months 💻www.vialattea.it/it/show/102/Il Club ⏰ Open June-Sept.)* The resort most convenient to and popular among Turin residents is **Sauze d'Oulx,** once a destination for the city's aristocracy. In 2006, it was the place for freestyle ski events—those are the intense acrobatic runs. Saul d'Oulx and Sestriere combined have 30 lifts. Though the slopes from the games remain, keep in mind that there's not much "style," free or otherwise, in going for the triple jump (to impress the boy or girl in the cute goggles) if you land flat on your face. On the other hand, that could be a strategy to meet a hunky ski patroller. Sadem has buses to Sauze d'Oulx and Sestriere in winter (☎011 30 00 611 ■www.sadem.it).

Farther away, outside of the long Olympic reach, is **Alagna** (☎0163 92 29 22 ■www.freerideparadise.it) in the Monte Rosa region. This place is known for its 1200m vertical drop, expert-only trails, and wide open *pistes* that allow skiiers to chart their own path down (Ⓢ *Lift tickets €36, discounts for seniors*). Knowledgeable skiers and boarders call it amazing, but those in over their heads will probably find that riding down on their butt isn't all that fun. Nearby is the lower-altitude **Wold** area designed for youngsters and beginners (*1 trip down €3, daily pass €20*).

The Piedmont Region tourism office (☎011 43 21 504 ■www.piemontefeel.it) in Turin provides abundant information about planning a ski trip in the area.

FOOD

The Savoys first drank *cioccolato* in the 1600s, and since then, it's been all chocolate all the time in the ex-capital city that's home to the famous ▨**Nutella** and **Ferrero Rocher** brands. The city's illustrious but quirky history is responsible for some of the sweet substance's attributes too, as Napoleon's restriction on its importation during his occupation of the city led to the creation of what is now Turin's most famous gelato flavor: a hazelnut substitute known as *gianduia*. Beyond chocolate, Piedmont's cuisine has little international stature. Even within the city, food is focused around cafes and bars rather than elaborate sit-down restaurants. Where it's available, Piedmontese food blends northern Italian cooking with French influences: here, Italy's favorite olive oil is replaced by butter, an ingredient whose qualities have been exploited to their fullest by the French.

While the city's relatively nondescript nosh may seem overpriced, the drink is both divine and affordable. Three of Italy's best wines—**Barolo, Barbaresco,** and **Barbera**—are available for a relative pittance in Turin, as the grapes from which they are fermented grow well in the region's fog. Maximize your moolah and buy your groceries at one of the **Di per Di** supermarkets (*Including V. S. Massimo 43* ☒ *Open M-Tu 8:30am-1:30pm and 3:30-7:30pm, W 8:30am-1:30pm, Th-Sa 8:30am-1:30pm and 3:30-7:30pm*) throughout the city, then buy up bottles of the local *rosso* to send home.

▨ **EATALY** ❤⛓♈❄⛄ MARKET ❷

V. Nizza 224 ☎011 19 50 68 11 ■www.eataly.it

Toto, I don't think we're in Turin any more. We've just walked into a veritable town of its own. It really feels that way, as dozens of house-like stores set up shop under this market's tremendous glass skylights. With outlets serving gelato, pizza, pasta, meat, cheese, and more, plus a full gourmet grocery and wine shop, the 10,000-square-foot facility that is Eataly could practically take a half-day of sightseeing on its own. If you don't have that much time, at least stop by the meat-and-cheese stations for a quick sample plate. And despite its name, Eataly even stocks some American brands. Also offers cooking classes by guest chefs, available in English by group reservation.

⚑ *Take bus #1, 18, or 35 to Lingotto.* Ⓢ *Sweets €3-4.50. Meat dishes €10.* ☒ *Open daily 10am-10:30pm. Meat and fish restaurants open daily 10am-3:30pm and 5:30-10:30pm.*

▨ **AGNOLOTTI AND FRIENDS** ❤⛓♈❄⛄ RISTORANTE ❸

P. Corpus Domini 18/b ☎011 43 38 792 ■www.agnolottiandfriends.it

Somehow hidden just blocks from P. Castello, Agnolotti and Friends finds itself shrouded in peacefulness in the midst of the bustling downtown. Its pedestrian-only *piazza* location allows patrons to sit outside and enjoy the Piedmont region in more ways than one—*agnolottti*, a beef- and vegetable-stuffed ravioli that is the restaurant's specialty, is a signature Piedmont dish.

Take V. Palazzo della Citta 2 blocks from P. Castello. $ Appetizers €7.50. Agnolotti €12. ⏰ Open daily 12:30-3pm and 8pm-midnight.

IL PUNTO VERDE VEGETARIAN ❷

V. San Massimo 17 ☎011 88 55 43 💻www.il-punto-verde.it

Where do you go to eat when you don't want meat? Heading toward the university's always a good bet—that whole "liberal bastion" thing—and doing so will lead weary vegetarian travelers right to Il Punto Verde's €5 student lunch menu and vast array of options, including vegan dishes. At night, live a little larger with the expansive €27 *prix-fixe* menu, including an *antipasti* buffet and entrees.

Off V. Po, near P. Carlo Emanuele II. $ Cover €1.80. Primi and secondi €8. ⏰ Open M-F 12:30-2:30pm and 7-10:30pm, Sa 7-10:30pm.

CAFFÉ CIOCCOLATERIA AL BICERIN CAFE ❶

P. della Consolata 5 ☎011 43 69 325 💻www.bicerin.it

Count Chocula is wondering why he didn't think of this. Coffee, cream, and chocolate together in a glass mug that permits the layers of goodness to be revealed in all their glory. Call this delightful confection Bicerin *(€5)*. First served here in 1763, the drink's habitat has expanded throughout Piedmont and beyond. Nietzsche, Dumas, and Puccini loved to sip the creamy concoction at this cafe, and so will travelers today.

Take C. Regina Margherita through P. della Repubblica, then turn left onto V. del Orfane and right onto the small piazza. $ Bicerin cake €4.50. ⏰ Open M-Tu 8:30am-7:30pm, Th-F 8:30am-7:30pm, Sa-Su 8:30am-1pm and 3:30-7:30pm.

LE VITEL ETONNE CAFE ❸

V. San Francesco da Paola 4 ☎011 81 24 621 💻www.leviteletonne.com

Wine comes straight from the cellar at this rustic-looking spot—in fact, parched diners can descend to drink their *vino* right beside the barrels, an option that becomes popular in the evenings when the seats on the ground floor are full. Pair wine and cheese with your drink for €5 or dine on one of the dishes from a menu of Italian staples that changes daily depending on the chef's whim and what's fresh in season *(€8-10)*.

A short walk from P. Castello. Follow V. Po and turn right at V. Paola. $ Wine €3. ⏰ Open daily Tu-Sa 10:30am-1am, Su 10:30am-3:30pm.

CAFE GELATERIA FIORIO CAFE, GELATERIA ❶

V. Po 8 ☎011 81 73 225 💻www.fioriocafegelateria.com

In 1821, students allegedly gathered here to plot a poisoning of the Savoy king. Today, students flock to this cafe for its inexpensive, gourmet lunch buffet, but now they're joined by throngs and throngs of tourists who gawk with their cameras to see the red-velvet restaurant where Melville and Twain once spent their afternoons overseas. Plus, tourists are people too, and therefore they want gelato.

Just off P. Castello. $ Gelato €2-3. Lunch buffet €7-9. ⏰ Open M-Th 7am-1am, F-Sa 7am-2am, Su 7am-1am.

STARS AND ROSES RISTORANTE ❷

V. Paleocapa 2 ☎011 51 62 052

It's easy to miss the unimposing entrance to this traditional Italian pizzeria and restaurant, but once you've stepped inside, it'll be hard to forget. The walls are a showcase for murals in the colors of an elementary school art class—dark was not in the painter's vocabulary. The food is filling, with pizzas and typical Piedmont pasta dishes leading off the menu.

Directly across from Porta Nuova, off the left side of P. Carlo Felice. $ Pizza €5-9.50. Primi and secondi €10-16. ⏰ Open daily 7:15pm-12:30am.

NIGHTLIFE

It's hard to tell when *Torino* sleeps—things are happening every night of the week. From the pounding bass of dance clubs, to quiet wine bars and even calmer cafes, Turin offers something for just about every taste. **I Murazzi,** a long boardwalk between Ponte Vittorio Emanuele I and Ponte Umberto along the west bank of the Po, is unquestionably the epicenter of nighttime revelry. It's packed with dance clubs and bars with live music and DJs, many of which charge no cover (though some distribute consumption cards that must be stamped and returned and will expect you to pay exorbitant lost card fees). Go south of Ponte Umberto to drink under the leaves of **Parco Valentino,** which has many bars and clubs in addition to a real-life castle. To the west of the city center is the historic **Quadrilatero Romana,** known for its quieter set of bars and less dance-heavy scene. Even this part of town spontaneously erupts into full-on parties some weekend nights, however. Foreign students and expats flock to the English pubs and wine bars along C. Vittorio Emanuele II near Porta Romana.

OLÉ MADRID

⊛⊗℃♨ BAR

V. Murazzi del Po 5 ☎338 58 02 884

Spanish theme? Rather unclear where that comes from. But one thing's for sure: strutting in on a Saturday night in a sombrero would be rather inconvenient, as the dance floor is packed with students swaying to the rhythms of the club's duo of local DJs and getting to the bar is difficult even with a head of normal size. On weekdays, similar crowds are often drawn by the all-night drink specials, including two beers for €5.

♯ *On the banks of the Po. From Porta Nuova, walk or take tram #9 or bus #34, 52, or 67 to C. Massimo d'Azeglio. Walk to the bridge and down the ramps to the left.* Ⓢ *Shots €2. Beer €4. Cocktails €6.* Ⓘ *Open M-Th 9:30pm-3am, F-Sa 9:30pm-5am, Su 9:30pm-3am. Happy hour specials M-Th and Su.*

SIX NATIONS MURPHY'S PUB

✦⊗℃♨ BAR

C. Vittorio Emanuele II 28 ☎011 88 72 55 ▣www.sixnations.it

Come for the English, stay for the pints. Even when no football match is on the big screen (and especially if one is), this pub draws British expats and international students looking for a place to speak their mother tongue. The selection of seven unusual brews on tap keeps the visitors happy, while classic non-Italian dishes like the Six Nations burger *(€9)* provide many a welcome respite from the pasta and pizza of the world outside.

♯ *On C. Vittorio Emanuele, to right when exiting Porta Nuova.* Ⓢ *Beer €3-5. Cocktails €5.50* Ⓘ *Open daily 6pm-3am.*

TUBE

⊛⊗℃♨ BAR

P. Emanuel Filiberto 10/a ☎011 19 86 46 96 ▣www.tube-torino.com

In creating this place, the owners tended not to "mind the gap" between London and Mexico. Patrons nibble on tortilla chips and drink Coronas in a small, psychedelic, and rainbow-colored bar covered in subway maps blown up to epic proportions. The kitchen stays open late, meaning that the action here—even for dinner—doesn't start until the evening is nearly done.

♯ *From Porta Nuova, take bus #52 to Santa Chiara. Then turn right onto V. Santa Chiara and then left onto V. Sant'Agostino to reach the piazza.* Ⓢ *Beer €4. Cocktails €6.50. Tacos €5.* Ⓘ *Open Tu-Th 7pm-2am, F-Sa 7pm-3am, Su 7pm-2am. Kitchen closes 90min. before bar.*

FLUIDO

✦⊗℃♨ CLUB

Vle. Umberto Cagni 7 ☎011 66 94 557 ▣www.fluido.to

Everything in Fluido flows down from the natural amphitheater, really a large grassy depression, that serves as its late-night seating bowl. Live music fills this happening spot outside the club's front doors with beach ball-bouncing students and hipsters.

turin · nightlife

On the banks of the Po. $ Shots €3. Cocktails €6. Open Tu-W 10am-2am, Th 10am-3am, F-Sa 10am-4am, Su 10am-1:30am.

LOBELIX II BAR

P. Vittorio Veneto ☎347 43 50 050 www.lobelix.it

The owners of Lobelix II found a novel way to help people navigate their way through the crowds of young professionals and students waiting for the bar—they opened a walk-up window accessible from the sidewalk. Though patrons who sit outdoors at one of the abundant tables will miss the glowing red bar, they'll be right in the middle of the camaraderie that unites the throngs who sit in the *piazza* on warm evenings.

In P. Vittorio Veneto, on the far left side when facing the river. Reachable from P. Castello by tram #15 or 16 and bus #55 or 56. $ Cocktails €5. Open daily 6:30pm-2am.

ARTS AND CULTURE

Turin isn't one to brag, but it's got a notable cultural heritage. Having kings around tends to do that, and in Turin's case, the royal influence led to the development of a particularly rich theater scene which has continued off and on to this day. In more recent years, sports have arisen as another source of civic pride. For an updated listing of events, ask at the tourist office (which publishes one every three months) or visit www.turismotorino.org. Turin's daily newspaper *La Stampa* also publishes a weekly cultural listing (in Italian) on Thursdays.

TORINO SOTTERRANEA MUSIC

V. Murazzi del Po ☎011 76 51 687 www.htsmusica.com

They say the bands are unheralded, underrated, and most certainly unsigned. They call them "underground." But there's only one event where they actually perform below street level: Torino Sotteranea. Putting on weekly music events in the summer, this festival brings local bands to fill the stone caverns of Il Murazzi with harmonies and young concertgoers. From high schoolers to recent college graduates, hundreds of young people flock to get in the door at what has become as much a social event as a music exposition. Of course, the bar inside doesn't scare anyone away either.

*From P. Castello take tram #15 or 16 and bus #55 or 56 to P. Vittorio Veneto. **i** Venue at Il Murazzi varies by concert; call or check online. $ Tickets €25. 8 shows in summer, usually beginning between 9 and 11pm.*

milan and turin

STADIO OLIMPICO AND OLYMPIC VENUES SPORTS

V. Filadelfia 82-88 ☎011 32 71 302 www.juventus.com or www.torinofc.it

Nothing, not royalty, not chocolate, not even those ever-reliable Fiats, has made Turin prouder than hosting the 2006 Winter **Olympic Games,** which brought unprecedented attention to a city that often takes a back seat to its national neighbors. With the games also came a construction spree south of the city center. The fruits of that labor, the Olympic Village and venues, stand today. The **Olympic Arch** towers over the railroad tracks, an olympic-sized lipstick mark on the sky. The shining metal box of the **Palasport Olimpico,** Italy's largest indoor arena and the former home to Olympic ice hockey, now primarily plays host to concerts. Passion was the theme of the games, and the passion that they embodied did not disappear when the Olympic flame was extinguished. It lives on in another venue: **Stadio Olimpico,** also known as Stadio Comunale di Piemonte, home to Turin's soccer teams **Juventus** and **Torino F.C.** As with many Italian cities, one team—Juve—has a large international following while the other draws the wild cheers of local fans. The teams are preparing to get a divorce (Juventus wasn't a good sharer and is building a stadium of its own), but the Torinese passion for sport persists.

Take bus #4 or 63 south to the Filadelfia stop. $ Soccer tickets €12-120. Most matches

Su afternoon, Sept-June.

TEATRO REGIO
◆⑤ OPERA, BALLET

P. Castello 215 ☎011 88 15 241 🖳www.teatroregio.torino.it

At one time, Teatro Regio, more than any princely palace or basilica on a hill, was the pride of the Savoy kingdom, a gilded symbol of total splendor in the heart of the capital. But when the theater burned to the ground in 1936, opera for some time became irrelevant in Turin. Today, it's back stronger than ever, even if it no longer serves a king or contains a royal box. Behind the geometric, sculpted bronze gates of Teatro Regio's modern building, an artistic masterpiece designed in 1973, the theater stages an annual season of 12 shows from October through June. Its work focuses primarily on opera, including Verdi and Wagner, but ballet shows are also on the schedule for 2011.

⚑ *In P. Castello, to the right of Palazzo Reale.* ⑤ *€48-80. 20% discount for ages under 30.* ⟰ *Box office open Tu-F 10:30am-6pm, Sa 10:30am-4pm.*

SHOPPING

Turin's shopping options can't match the luxury boutiques of Milan, but for more realistic buyers, the city has a wide array of choices. Stroll down **Via Roma** from P. Castello to window-shop in the brand-name stores that line the route. For a more hectic atmosphere but much lower prices, the markets in **Piazza della Repubblica** are a good option.

🍫 RIVETTI PIACERI DI CIOCCOLATO
◆⊗ CHOCOLATE

V. Monte di Pieta 15/b ☎011 50 69 280 🖳www.piaceridicioccolato.it

If Turin is a chocolate capital of the world, call this the prime minister's residence. The best and brightest chocolates in town are served from a glass case or in small, individually wrapped bags that make it just too easy to walk out and munch on that gift you had intended to give to Mom.

⚑ *Take V. Roma out of P. Castello and turn right onto V. Monte di Pieta.* ⑤ *Chocolates from €40 per kg. Small bag of wrapped chocolates €4. Chocolate spreads from €3.60.* ⟰ *Open Tu-F 9:45am-1pm and 3:30-7pm, Sa 9:45am-12:30pm and 4-7pm.*

PIAZZA REPUBBLICA MARKET
◉⑤ MARKET

P. della Repubblica

It claims to be Europe's largest open-air market. Lacking data and being too engrossed in the mass of people and stalls to pull out our tape measure, *Let's Go* declines to dispute the claim. Regardless of the market's size, it's possible to find pretty much anything here, especially on Saturdays. From a dozen farms-full of vegetables and meats to shirts to soccer jerseys to detergent or shampoo, the array here is a dream-come-true for budget-conscious one-stop shoppers.

⚑ *In P. della Repubblica.* ⑤ *Prices vary widely. Shirts from €4, jeans from €7. Fruits and vegetables from €1.* ⟰ *Open M-Sa 8am-3pm.*

ESSENTIALS

Practicalities

- **TOURIST OFFICES: Turismo Torino** has helpful staff who speak English, French, German, and Spanish (oh, and Italian, too). They offer an excellent map of Turin and its transit system as well as info on museums, cafes, and tours. (*P. Castello 161* ☎011 53 51 81 🖳*www.turismotorino.org* ⚑ *At the intersection of P. Castello and V. Garibaldi.* **ⁱ** *Also has an info booth at Porta Nuova, opposite platform 11.* ⟰ *Open daily 9am-7pm.*)

- **CURRENCY EXCHANGE:** (*In Porta Nuova* ⟰ *Open M 8am-8pm, Tu 10am-5:30pm, W-Sa 8am-8pm, Su 10am-5:30pm.*) Otherwise try banks, most with **24hr. ATMs** which are easy to find in the *centro*. (⟰ *Generally open M-F 8:20am-1:20pm and 2:20-4:20pm.*)

- **LAUNDROMATS: Lavasciuga Laundrettes and Internet Points** are located throughout the city. Check website for complete list (🖳*www.lavasciuga.torino.it*).

turin • essentials

- **POST OFFICES:** *(V. Paulo Sacchi 2* ☎*011 56 68 411* ***i*** *Fax and money transfer available.* 🕐 *Open M-F 8:30am-7pm, Sa 8:30am-1pm.)*

Emergency!

- **LATE-NIGHT PHARMACIES: Farmacia Porta Nuova.** *(V. Paulo Sacchi 4* ☎*011 51 75 237* 🚶 *Exit Porta Nuova to the left.* ***i*** *Pharmacies post after-hours rotation, available at* ▪️*www.farmapiemonte.org.* 🕐 *Open daily 8am-7:30pm.)*

- **HOSPITALS/MEDICAL SERVICES: San Giovanni Batista,** commonly known as Molinette *(C. Bramante 88-90* ☎*011 63 31 633* ▪️*www.molinette.piemonte.it)*, **Maria Adelaide** *(V. Zuretti 29* ☎*011 69 33 111* ▪️*www.cto.to.it)*, **Mauriziano Umberto I** *(Largo Turati 62* ☎*011 50 81 111).*

Getting There

By Plane

Caselle Airport *(*▪️*www.aeroportoditorino.it)*, 20km from the city, serves European destinations. From Porta Nuova, take the blue Sadem buses to "Caselle Airport" via Porta Susa. *(*☎*011 22 72 022* Ⓢ *€5.50.* 🕐 *30min.)* Buses depart frequently to airport *(5:15am-11:15pm)* and to the city *(6:05am-12:05am).* Buy tickets in bars and newstands right outside the station or onboard *(€0.50 surcharge).* Train to the airport departs from Stazione Dora *(*Ⓢ *€3.40.* 🕐 *20min., every 30min.)* to the airport 5:04am-11:09pm and to Turin 5:05am-9:45pm. The DoraFly bus connects Stazione Dora to Porta Susa and the underground line, or take tram #10 from Porta Susa or buses #46 or 49.

By Train

Stazione Porta Nuova *(*☎*89 20 21 or* ☎*011 66 53 098)*, on C.Vittorio Emanuele II, is the main hub. **Luggage storage** is to the left when facing the platforms. *(*Ⓢ *First 5hr. €4, hours 6-12 €0.60 per hr., after 12hr. €0.20 per hr.* 🕐 *Open daily 6am-10pm.)* Trains to: **Genoa** *(*Ⓢ *€9.10.* 🕐 *2hr., departs every hr. 5:20am-10:25pm.)*; **Milan** *(*Ⓢ *€9.55.* 🕐 *2hr., departs every hr. 4:50am-10:50pm.)*; **Rome** *(*Ⓢ *From €41.* 🕐 *6-7hr., 9 per day 6:37am-9:55pm.)*; **Venice.** *(*Ⓢ *From €35.* 🕐 *5hr., departs every hr. 4:50am-10:50pm.)* Turin's **Stazione Porta Susa** is one stop toward Milan and has TGV trains to **Paris** via **Lyon.** *(*Ⓢ *Around €95.* 🕐 *5-6hr.; 8:11am, 9:40am, 5:35pm, 7:05pm, 9:18pm.)*

By Bus

If, for some reason, you hate trains, buses are a slower and barely cheaper option for getting to Turin. Intercity buses run out of **Autostazione Terminal Bus.** *(C. Vittorio Emanuele II 131/H* ☎*011 43 38 100* 🚶 *From Porta Nuova, take tram #9 or 15 5 stops.* 🕐 *Ticket office open daily 6:30am-1pm and 2-7pm.)* **Sadem** *(*☎*011 300 0611)* buses run to **Milan.** *(*Ⓢ *€8.70.* 🕐 *2hr., departs every hr.)*

Getting Around

By Public Transportation

Buy tickets at *tabaccherie*, newsstands, or bars. Buses run daily 5am-1am; some routes stop at midnight. Friday through Saturday, a few special "Night Buster" routes run until 5am, so if you're paying attention, you'll realize that means there's 24hr. service. *(*Ⓢ *70min. tickets to city buses and trams €1, 1-day tickets €3.50, weekly passes €9.50.)*

The underground, automatic **Metro** (whoa—no driver!) is less useful for seeing the city and, because it is still under construction, can be unreliable. Tickets *(€1)* are single-use only, but valid for 70min. on other forms of transport. Get a public transit map that include all bus and tram routes from the tourist office.

Alternatives

Taxis can be found throughout the city or phoned for service *(*☎*011 57 37 or* ☎*011 57 30).* For **Bike Rental,** try **Tourinbike.** *(V. Fiochetto 39* ☎*011 57 93 314* ▪️*www.tourinbike.com* ***i*** *Also offers guided bike tours.* Ⓢ *€10 per 4hr., €15 per day, discounts for multiple days.)*

VENICE

On any given day, the number of tourists in Venice—20 million annually—constitutes a larger percentage of the city's population than do locals—all 60,000 of them. This has given the city an unfairly reductive reputation as a tourist hub whose beauty and charm have been eviscerated by camera-toting yokels without an appreciation for anything outside a good photo op. Though you're certain to encounter the neon fanny pack crowd in the major squares, churches, museums, and monuments, if you let yourself escape down any one of Venice's many labyrinthine side streets, you'll discover traces of Venice's glorious past preserved in dilapidated *palazzi*, beautiful syncretic architecture hinting at Eastern influences, and street signs written in the vanishing Venetian dialect. Moreover, you'll find a vibrant and resilient local culture impervious to the tourist onslaught. Characterized by an incredible performance art and music scene, some of Italy's best seafood, bustling docks where local artisans still repair boats by hand, and numerous schools dedicated to building upon Venice's artistic legacy in the modern era, this hardy spirit makes modern Venice a joy to explore. This collection of 117 islands in a lagoon of the Adriatic Sea is famously both a difficult city to know and an easy city to love, but if you're not afraid to step off the beaten path, you'll come to appreciate the subtleties of the Venetian character that can't be discovered on a gondola ride or captured in a postcard.

greatest hits

- **MARK OF GREATNESS.** P. San Marco may be Venice's most (fanny-)packed piazza, but its awe-inspiring buildings and views fully justify braving the crowds (p. 179).

- **LOSE YOURSELF.** Wander the winding walkways of Dorsoduro. Given the city's bizarre street system, it's pretty easy to get lost anywhere. In this neighborhood, though, it's a pleasure (p. 161).

- **ESCAPE THE CITY.** And pay a visit to Lido, Venice's beach resort. Just take a vaporetto across the lagoon and you can lounge on the shore of the Adriatic (p. 189).

student life

For all its many charms, Venice is not a city with a vibrant student scene. You're far more likely to run into another tourist group than a frat party. One exception can be found in the neighborhoods of San Polo and Dorsoduro, thanks to **Ca' Foscari University,** which is located on the border between the two *sestiere* and brings in the city's most lively youth culture. Dorsoduro is home to easily the greatest concentration of bars in the city as well as Venice's only true club. That being said, this isn't really a student city, though if you look hard and get to know people, you'll find that there's plenty of entertainment to be had, and not just in churches or museums. Try heading to Lista di Spagna in Cannaregio to experience locals lounging around on a piazza drinking wine through the evening, a chilled-out but certainly pleasurable way to enjoy this city.

orientation

Venice's historical center is composed of six main *sestieri* (neighborhoods). Often divided along vague boundaries, the neighborhoods each consist of several islands. **San Marco** is at the geographic center of the city, across the Grand Canal from **San Polo** and **Santa Croce. Cannaregio** lies to San Marco's north and **Castello** to its northeast, while **Dorsoduro** marks the city's southern edge. Outside of the city proper, a set of numerous islands including Giudecca, Lido, Murano, and Burano are not to be forgotten.

call me!

The phone code for Venice is ☎041.

SAN MARCO

While walking along the quiet canals of Venice's residental neighborhoods, it's easy to forget that the city is populated by just as many tourists as full-time residents. Cross over to San Marco, and that fact hits you with full force—dozens of museums, upscale hotels, designer stores, art galleries, and, of course, thousands upon thousands of tourists. The crisis of conscience most travelers undergo when planning their time in Venice is usually this: "How much time should I spend in San Marco?" Because let's be honest—as crowded and expensive as San Marco is—the neighborhood is popular for good reason. The museums and sights here are as impressive as you'll find anywhere in Europe, and the tourist industry has brought world-class shopping, hotels, and cuisine to the area, particularly to the region closest to **Piazza San Marco.** Travelers who want to spend just a couple days in Venice but want to see all of the city's typical postcard attractions should look for a budget hotel on the fringes of the neighborhood. This won't put you more than a 10min. walk from either the Rialto Bridge or P. San Marco. Be forewarned, however, that San Marco is conspicuously less residential than any other neighborhood in Venice—if you're in a section that isn't currently overrun by tourists, it's likely to seem a bit abandoned or even post-apocalyptic.

CANNAREGIO

Cannaregio is one of Venice's largest neighborhoods, and for travelers willing to step off the beaten path, it offers a great opportunity to see a less touristy side of Venice than is on display in places like San Marco. Most hotels are located on the eastern and western edges of the neighborhood (by the Rialto Bridge and train station, respectively) in areas with a fair amount of tourist traffic, but the beauty of Cannaregio is that you're never more than 10min. away from both the liveliest, most crowded *piazze* and the quiet residential neighborhoods that are more representative of typical Venetian life.

SAN POLO

San Polo is the smallest of Venice's six neighborhoods, but its location in the heart of the city makes it a prime tourist destination. The **Rialto Bridge** markets and **Frari** basilica are among San Polo's highlights. Many tourists also favor the neighborhood for shopping, both for souvenirs and upscale clothing, and dining, as San Polo's concentration of high-quality restaurants sets the city standard. Surprisingly, despite the heavy tourist traffic, there are relatively few hotels. However, those that are available tend to be reasonably priced affairs with good access to the city's points of interest. Despite the neighborhood's small size, it's surprisingly easy to get lost, especially if you think that the signs reading "San Marco" are actually leading you toward the square—in many cases, they're not. Your best bet is use a map and stick to wider streets with more tourists. If you try to take shortcuts, you'll probably end up walking in circles.

SANTA CROCE

Although a small neighborhood by Venetian standards, Santa Croce is incredibly diverse and easily accessible from western Cannaregio, San Polo, and Dorsoduro. **Piazzale Roma,** the main stop for most buses and taxis coming into Venice, is located in Santa Croce and defines the character of the neighborhood's western side. Restaurants and hotels around this transportation hub tend to be of a generic international style, so visitors to Santa Croce who see only this section of the neighborhood will leave unimpressed. The small area near San Polo, however, offers some of the best restaurants and hotels in Venice at exceptionally reasonable prices. From the main street of **Salizada San Pantalon,** the sights of Cannaregio as well as the restaurants and nightlife of Dorsoduro are easily accessible. The Rialto Bridge and P. San Marco are a ways off, but the vaporetti run frequently. For travelers willing to trek a bit in order to reach Venice's main sights, Santa Croce can serve as a budget-friendly base camp.

🗝DORSODURO

As neighborhoods go, Dorsoduro is a *Let's Go* favorite. Unlike some of the other *sestiere*, Dorsoduro possesses the ideal combination of awesome local flavor, proximity to major sights, great nightlife, and exceptional restaurants. Granted, if you want to stay in Dorsoduro, you'll probably pay 25% more than you would for a comparable room in Santa Croce or Cannaregio, but, as in most Italian cities, with a little luck and a little haggling you can still end up with a bargain. Moreover, the intersection of San Polo, Santa Croce, and Dorsoduro is the heart of Venice. From here, or just about anywhere else in Dorsoduro, you shouldn't be more than a few minutes from some of Venice's best museums. You also won't have to struggle too much to make it back to your hotel after a night out. Dorsoduro has its fill of unique side streets but remains an easily navigable neighborhood (at least by Venetian standards), with more incredible restaurants, fabulous art galleries, and cool shops than any other district in Venice. Whether you stay in Dorsoduro or not, do not make the mistake of relegating the neighborhood to the bottom of your itinerary—there is no better way to experience Venice than by wandering through Dorsoduro, *sans* map, in a day spent getting lost in the neighborhood's winding roads and alleyways.

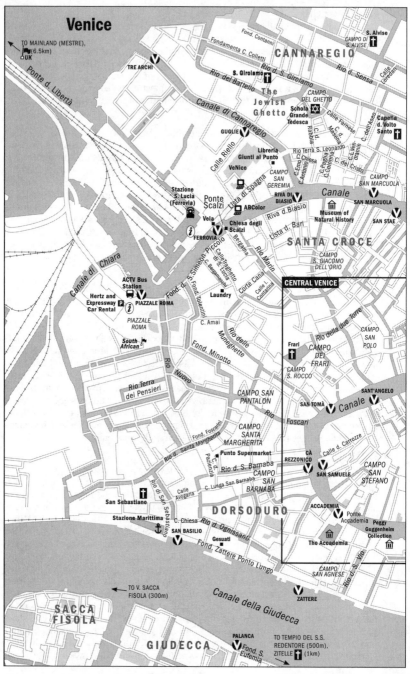

Venice

TO MAINLAND (MESTRE),
(6.5km)
UK

Ponte d. Libertà

CANNAREGIO

Fond. Contanni

Fondamenta C. Colletti

Rio d. S. Girolamo

Rio d. Sensa

Calle Loredan

TRE ARCHI

S. Girolamo

Rio del Battello

CAMPO DI S. ALVISE

S. Alvise

The Jewish Ghetto

CAMPO DEL GHETTO

Calle Lorense

Canale di Cannaregio

Schola Grande Tedesca

Calle Farnese

C. d. Messana

C. dell'Aseo

Capella d. Volto Santo

GUGLIE

Libreria Giunti al Punto

C. d. Rabbia

Rio Terra S. Leonardo

C. Chiesa Cantoni

C. Erno Tron

C. Paglia

C. Goldoni

C. del Cristo

C. L. Venidrin

Calle Riello

VeNice

CAMPO SAN GEREMIA

CAMPO SAN MARCUOLA

Stazione S. Lucia (Ferrovia)

Ponte Scalzi

Lista di Spagna

ABColor

RIVA DI BIASIO

Canale

SAN MARCUOLA

Vela

Riva d. Biasio

Museum of Natural History

SAN STAE

Chiesa degli Scalzi

FERROVIA

Riva d. Bari

Lista d. Bari

SANTA CROCE

Calleragheto di S. Lucia

C. Bergama

Bergama

Rio Marin

CAMPO S. GIACOMO DELL'ORIO

Fond. d. S. Simeon Piccolo

C. Bergamaschi

Corte Canal

Calle L. Contarina

CENTRAL VENICE

ACTV Bus Station

PIAZZALE ROMA

Laundry

Rio della due Torre

CAMPO SAN POLO

Hertz and Expressway Car Rental

PIAZZALE ROMA

C. Amai

Rio delle Muneghette

Frari

CAMPO DEI FRARI

South African

Fond. Minotto

CAMPO S. ROCCO

Rio Nuovo

Rio Terra dei Pensieri

CAMPO SAN PANTALON

Rio Foscari

SAN TOMÀ

Canale

SANT'ANGELO

Fond. Foscarini

CAMPO SANTA MARGHERITA

Rio d. Santa Margherita

Punto Supermarket

C. d. Pazienza

Rio d. S. Barnaba

CAMPO SAN BARNABA

C. Lunga San Barnaba

CA' REZZONICO

Calle d. Carrozze

SAN SAMUELE

CAMPO SAN STEFANO

Calle Avogaria

San Sebastiano

DORSODURO

ACCADEMIA

Ponte Accademia

Peggy Guggenheim Collection

Stazione Marittima

Rio di San Sebastiano

C. Chiesa

Rio d'Ognissanti

Gesuati

The Accademia

SAN BASILIO

Fond. Zattere Ponto Lungo

CAMPO SAN AGNESE

Rio d. S. Via

TO V. SACCA FISOLA (300m)

ZATTERE

SACCA FISOLA

Canale della Giudecca

PALANCA

Fond. S. Eufemia

GIUDECCA

TO TEMPIO DEL S.S. REDENTORE (500m), ZITELLE (1km)

orientation

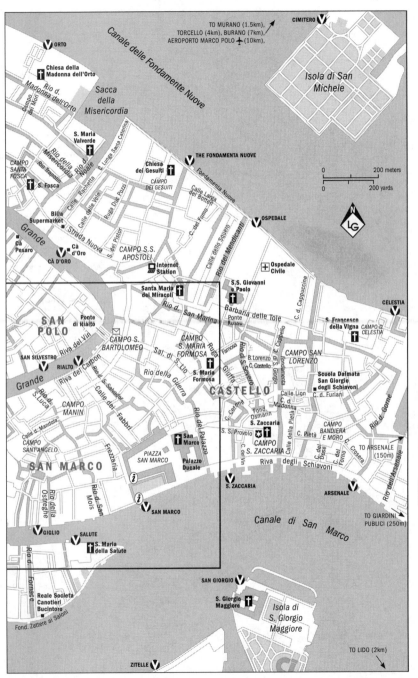

TO MURANO (1.5km),
TORCELLO (4km), BURANO (7km),
AEROPORTO MARCO POLO ✈ (10km),

CIMITERO

Isola di San Michele

ORTO

Chiesa della Madonna dell'Orto

Canale delle Fondamente Nuove

Sacca della Misericordia

S. Maria Valverde

THE FONDAMENTA NUOVE

Rio d. Madonna dell'Orto

Rio d. Noale

Calle Lunga Santa Caterina

Chiesa dei Gesuiti

CAMPO DEI GESUITI

CAMPO SANTA FOSCA

S. Fosca

Fondamenta Nuove

Rio della Misericordia

Rio Trapolin

Calle Racheta

Calle delle Vele

OSPEDALE

Billa Supermarket

Cà Grande

Cà Pesaro

Strada Nuova

Calle del Pistor

Ruga Due Pozzi

Calle Larga dei Botteri

Calle dello Squero

Cà d'Oro

CÀ D'ORO

CAMPO S.S. APOSTOLI

Internet Station

Rio dei Mendicanti

Ospedale Civile

C. d. Cappuccine

Santa Maria del Miracoli

S.S. Giovanni e Paolo

Rio d. San Marina

Barbaria delle Tole

Ponte Rosso

S. Francesco della Vigna

CELESTIA

CAMPO D. CELESTIA

SAN POLO

Ponte di Rialto

CAMPO S. BARTOLOMEO

CAMPO S. MARIA FORMOSA

Ruga Giuffa

Salizada Famosa

Rio d. S. Severo

Fondamenta

CAMPO SAN LORENZO

SAN SILVESTRO

RIALTO

Riva del Vin

Riva del Carbon

Sal. di S.to Lio

S. Maria Formosa

B. Lorenzo C. Castello

Scuola Dalmata San Giorgio degli Schiavoni

Grande

Rio di S. Luca

Rio di S. Salvador

Rio della Guerra

CASTELLO

Calle Lion

C. d. Furlani

C. d. Madonna

CAMPO MANIN

Calle dei Fabbri

Rio del Palazzo

C. Corona

Rio d. Gorne

Rio di Gorne

Calle d. Mandola

Fond. Osmarin

C. della Pietà

Fond. d. Dose

CAMPO SANT'ANGELO

Frezzaria

PIAZZA SAN MARCO

San Marco

S. Zaccaria

S.S. Provolo

CAMPO S. ZACCARIA

CAMPO BANDIERA E MORO

TO ARSENALE (150m)

SAN MARCO

Rio della Ostreghe

Rio di San Moisè

Palazzo Ducale

C. del Vin

C. del Dose

C. del Forno

C. Crosera

Rio dell'Arsenale

S. ZACCARIA

Riva degli Schiavoni

ARSENALE

GIGLIO

SALUTE

S. Maria della Salute

Canale di San Marco

TO GIARDINI PUBLICI (250m)

Rio d. Fornace

Reale Società Canotieri Bucintoro

Fond. Zattere ai Saloni

SAN GIORGIO

S. Giorgio Maggiore

Isola di S. Giorgio Maggiore

TO LIDO (2km)

ZITELLE

0   200 meters
0   200 yards

orientation · dorsoduro

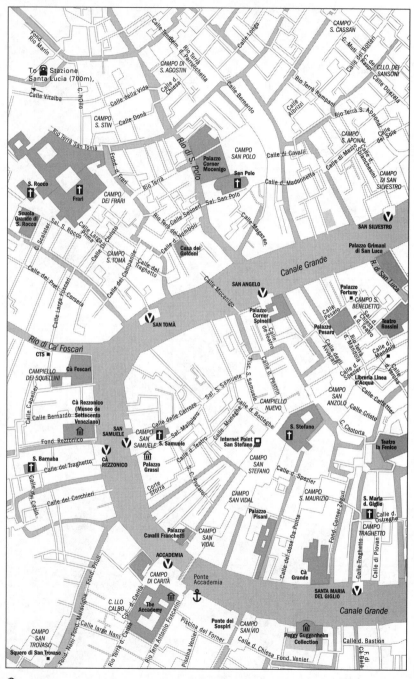

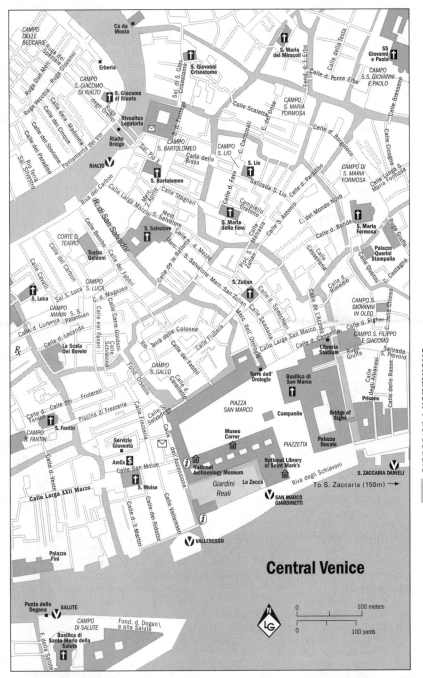

Central Venice

CAMPO DELLE BECCARIE

Cà da Mosta

Erberia

CAMPO S. GIACOMO DI RIALTO

S. Giacomo di Rialeto

Ruga Due Mori

Ruga dei Spezieri

Ruga Giovanni

Ruga Vecchia

Calle della Madonna

Ruga dei Oresi

Calle dei Cinque

Calle del Stormone

Sal. Pio X

Calle del Paradiso

Rio Terra S. Silvestro

Rivoaltus Legatoria

Rialto Bridge

RIALTO

S. Bartolomeo

CAMPO S. BARTOLOMEO

Riva del Carbon

Riva del Ferro

Rio di San Salvador

Calle Larga Mazzini

CORTE D. TEATRO

Teatro Goldoni

Calle del Carbon

Calle dei Fabbri

Calle Cavalli

S. Luca

Sal S. Luca

CAMPO S. LUCA

CAMPO MANIN

S.S. Paternian

Calle d. Cortesia

Calle d. Locanda

La Scala Del Bovolo

R.

S. Gioy. Crisostomo

S. Giovanni Crisostomo

Sal. d. S. Gioy. Crisostomo

S. Maria dei Miracoli

Calle d. Erbe

Fond. d. Ponte Erbe

Calle della Testa

SS Giovanni e Paolo

CAMPO S.S. GIOVANNI E PAOLO

Calle Bressana

Calle Scaletta

CAMPO S. MARIA FORMOSA

Calle d. Borgoloco

Calle Cicogna

Calle Longa S. Maria Formosa

CAMPO S. LIO

S. Lio

Calle della Bissa

Calle d. Fava

Salizada S. Lio

Calle d. Paradiso

CAMPO DI S. MARIA FORMOSA

Campiello Oratorio

S. Maria della Fava

Merc. 2 Aprile

Merc. d. Mezzo

Calle Stagneri

Merc. S. Salvatore

Calle d. Malvasia

Calle S. Antonio

C. dei Mondo Novo

Calle d. Bande

S. Maria Formosa

Ruga Giuffa

Palazzo Querini Stampalla

Calle Querini

C. Castagna

S. Salvatore

Mere de le Balloni

Merc. di S. Salvatore Marz.

San Zulian

C. d. Carampani

Calle Scavezza

Calle Cassellaria

Calle d. Rimedio

Calle d. Chiesa

Calle Benho

Calle dei Fabbri

C. d. Magazen

Calle dei Fuseri

Calle Goldoni

Calle Schiavine

Rio Terra delle Colonne

Calle Fiubera

Calle dei Fabbri

Calle d. Bonho

S. Zulian

Calle Larga San Marco

Calle dell'Orologio

Calle Specchieri

Calle Larga San Marco

Calle d. Angeli

CAMPO S. GIOVANNI IN OLEO

Calle d. Stagneri

CAMPO S. FILIPPO E GIACOMO

Salizada S. Provolo

Ruga Giuffa

Calle d. Albanesi

Calle delle Rasse

Libreria Studium

Torre dell' Orologio

Basilica di San Marco

Prisons

Calle d. Canonico

CAMPO S. GALLO

Calle d. Frutaroli

Calle d. Fenice

S. Fantin

CAMPO S. FANTIN

Calle S. Servadego

Calle Frezzeria

Calle d. Ascensione

Piscina di Frezzeria

Fond. Orseolo

Calle Caballetto

PIAZZA SAN MARCO

Campanile

Bridge of Sighs

Museo Correr

PIAZZETTA

Palazzo Ducale

Servizie Gioventù

AmEx

Calle San Moise

S. Moise

National Archaeology Museum

National Library of Saint Mark's

La Zecca

Riva degli Schiavoni

S. ZACCARIA DANIELI

To S. Zaccaria (150m) →

Calle Larga XXII Marzo

Calle d. Veste

Calle d. Ridotto

Giardini Reali

SAN MARCO GIARDINETTI

Calle d. 3 Martiri

Calle Vallaresso

VALLERESSO

Palazzo Fini

Punta della Dogana

SALUTE

CAMPO DI SALUTE

Fond. d. Dogan a alla Salute

Basilica di Santa Maria della Salute

F. della Salute

N

LG

0   100 meters

0   100 yards

CASTELLO

With proximity to two of Venice's prime tourist destinations, the Rialto Bridge and P. San Marco, Castello is in many ways a less expensive alternative to San Marco. If you know where to look, you can find great hotels and restaurants at much more competitive prices. While Castello tends to get a lot of spillover tourist traffic from San Marco, the farther north and east you go, the more apparent Castello's charming, quaint local character becomes. Since Venice lacks traditional streets, neighborhoods can change from block to block. This is especially evident here, where crowded, loud, and overdeveloped thoroughfares suddenly give way to quiet and scenic sidestreets. If you have a few days in Venice, it's certainly worth exploring this neighborhood, including its eastern portion; however, there are few notable sights, and it's easy to get lost. Though residents proudly proclaim that eastern Castello represents the true, vanishing Venice, visitors will find the west more to their liking, with excellent restaurants and easy access to the rest of the city.

accommodations

Though Venice has very few hostels, there are dozens upon dozens of great budget hotels throughout the city that are typically worth the extra cost. Save money by requesting a room with a shared bathroom. Your bedroom will be private (and typically with its own sink), but you will share a shower and toilet with the other people on your floor. Since most small hotels offering Wi-Fi, A/C, or wheelchair-accessibility only have a limited number of rooms with these features, particular requests for room selection should be made ahead by phone or email. Booking in advance can also help you find a lower rate. Nightly rates almost always include breakfast, which can range from some toast and coffee to an extravagant affair.

Even if you're trying to book last-minute during the high season, you should be able to find affordable, quality options. Hotels dot the sidewalks, so walk around and talk to the managers of a few different establishments before paying for a room. Don't be afraid to negotiate prices; offering to pay in cash sometimes helps travelers finagle a lower rate.

If you want to sleep right by Venice's major sights or in a room with views of the Grand Canal, it'll cost you. Most travelers, however, will probably find the minor inconvenience of being a few minutes removed from the hot spots worth the few dozen euro they save nightly by staying at one of Venice's numerous budget accommodations.

SAN MARCO

Unlike most other Venetian neighborhoods, which are home to primarily 1- and 2-star hotels, San Marco is packed with establishments of the 4- and 5-star variety whose luxury is exceeded only by the amount you'll have to drop to book one of their rooms. Still, there are bargains to be had, particularly if you're willing to stay on the western side of the neighborhood, farther from the **Rialto Bridge** and **Piazza San Marco.** If your main priority is proximity to these sights, you ought to consider a hotel in Castello, which can end up being both closer to the main attractions of San Marco and less expensive than a hotel that claims a San Marco address.

⧉ NOVECENTO   ⬥⊗(•)❄ HOTEL
Calle del Dose 2683   ☎041 52 12 145 🖳www.novecento.biz

Incorporating South and East Asian design influences, trendy Novecento sets the standard for boutique hotels in Venice. With excellent lounge areas, top-notch rooms (each with its own unique design theme), and access to a nearby fitness club free of charge, Novecento offers amenities and a quality of service unmatched by the vast majority of budget hotels in Venice.

➜ *V: Santa Maria del Giglio. Walk north approximately 45sec.; hotel is on the right.* ℹ *Breakfast included.* $ *Singles €100-130; doubles €160-260; triples €180-300.*

👍 HOTEL CASANOVA
💳♿ HOTEL [5]

Frezzeria 1284 ☎041 52 06 855 💻www.hotelcasanova.it

Approximately 1min. away from P. San Marco, Hotel Casanova is an incredible value for the area. Though you'll have to contend with chaos on the narrow street below from dawn until dusk, you can't get much closer to Venice's main attractions. With Hotel Casanova's exceptional accommodations, the largest and most comfortable you'll find anywhere in Venice in this price range, you get convenience without sacrificing quality.

➜ *Exit the southwest corner of P. San Marco, opposite Basilica di San Marco, and take first right onto Frezzeria; the hotel is less than 1min. ahead on the right.* ℹ *Breakfast included.* $ *Singles €70-120; doubles €90-170; triples €120-200; quads €150-230.*

RESIDENZA SAN MAURIZIO
💳🚭❄ HOTEL [4]

Campo San Maurizio 2624 ☎041 52 89 712 💻www.residenzasanmaurizio.com

A 5-7min. walk from P. San Marco but only 3-4min. from Dorsoduro, Residenza San Mauricio is at an ideal location for travelers who want to see the museums of

approximations

Enrico Fermi—physicist, quantum theorist, statistician. Italian.

Fermi had one of the greatest scientific minds of the 20th century, but spending time in Italy is enough to make you question his method of informal approximation. Basically, Fermi argued that one could accurately estimate the answers to complex problems by appropriately analyzing their necessary factors and assumptions. Fermi's theory has clearly been taken to heart by the people of Italy, because everyone here approximates. Everything. All the time. And, sadly, not always as well as Fermi did.

Directions tend to be kind of dicey approximations—we're pretty sure that over 75% of hotels in Venice claim to be within 5min. walking distance of the Rialto Bridge. Wi-Fi availability is also a source of wild estimation. If a hotel advertises wireless internet access, what they really mean is that they have some *approximation* of Wi-Fi—even if it's only in the lobby and working roughly 3hr. per day. Most restaurants and hotels boast of their A/C, which they definitely have...at least in one room. But it might not be working this week.

There are perks to this system of guesstimation as well. In the states, we tend to think of prices as set in stone, but here, they are simply estimates—estimates that can be recalculated based on how charming a shop owner finds you. The approximation of opening and closing times also tends to work out well: in Venice, you'll never have a restaurant door closed on you because you arrived 5min. after business was supposed to end. Also, if you sleep past check-out time, don't sweat it—as long as you exit your room *approximately* on time.

To strung-out, type-"A" Americans, the blurry lines of Venetian approximation can be frustrating to no end. If you, like *Let's Go* researchers, make a habit of hanging around in hotel lobbies, you'll see plenty of arguments between managers and customers over technicalities to which the customer adheres rigidly and the proprietor, well, not so much. Venice is a wonderful city with a lot to be appreciated, but to most enjoy the city, it's best to quickly learn how to chill out and take things as they come. And trust that they will turn out right...more or less.

Dorsoduro, spend time around the P. San Marco, and see the sights of the Rialto Bridge. Located down a quiet alley off Campo San Maurizio, the hotel offers some of the lowest prices you'll find in San Marco, and it doesn't compromise the quality of its rooms. It also has a thoroughly competent website, which people looking to book online will quickly discover is uncommon among Venetian hotels.

➡ V: Santa Maria del Giglio. Walk north, pass 1 bridge on the left, turn left onto the 2nd bridge, and cross consecutive bridges; the hotel is less than 1min. away on the right. ***i*** *Breakfast included.* *Ⓢ Singles €55-85; doubles €85-110; triples €80-130; quads €100-155.*

HOTEL ASTORIA

💳♿📶❄ HOTEL [4]

Calle Fiubera 951 ☎041 52 25 381 💻www.hotelastoriavenezia.it

A small, modest hotel on a crowded street near P. San Marco, Hotel Astoria offers some of the best rates you'll find anywhere in Venice, making it a truly exceptional value for the San Marco area. Though less roomy and perhaps not as extravagantly decorated as some hotels nearby, Hotel Astoria boasts Wi-Fi included in your room cost, an elevator, and several other amenities that make it thoroughly practical.

➡ From P. San Marco, walk beneath the St. Mark's Clock Tower and turn left onto Calle Fiubera; the hotel is less than 1min. ahead on the right. ***i*** *Breakfast included. Free Wi-Fi.* *Ⓢ Singles €45-125; doubles €105-190; suites €180-280.*

CANNAREGIO

Cannaregio has some of the best budget hotels in Venice, particularly on the western islands near the train station. Luckily, the rest of the traveling world hasn't caught on yet, and even if you're arriving in Venice without a reservation during the busy season, Cannaregio has many top-notch accommodations that can be booked at reasonable rates. The neighborhood itself is mostly residential and has a more laid-back vibe than other areas of Venice.

✓ HOTEL SILVA ARIEL

💳♿❄ HOTEL [4]

Calle della Masena 1391/A ☎041 72 93 26 💻www.arielsilva.it

If you're able to negotiate a good price with the manager, Hotel Silva Ariel is one of the best values you'll find in all of Venice. A couple blocks removed from the more tourist-laden area around Campo San Geremia, this beautiful and remarkably spacious hotel sits relatively close to almost anything you would want to see in Cannaregio.

➡ Left from the train station, then 5min. walk over Guglie Bridge and left onto Calle della Masena. ***i*** *Breakfast included.* *Ⓢ Singles €55-75; doubles €80-100.*

✓ HOTEL BERNARDI SEMENZATO

💳🚭📶❄ HOTEL [2]

Calle dell'Oca 4366 ☎041 52 27 257 💻www.hotelbernardi.com

Lots of hotels on the eastern side of Cannaregio are overpriced and poorly maintained, but Hotel Bernardi bucks the trend by offering great rooms at ridiculously low prices (well, for Venice at least). The singles without private bathrooms can get uncomfortably warm during the summer, but the free Wi-Fi more than makes up for this minor discomfort.

➡ From Campo SS. Apostoli, head north on Salizada Pistor and take the 1st left. ***i*** *Breakfast included. Free Wi-Fi.* *Ⓢ Singles €30-35; doubles €54-78.*

HOTEL ROSSI

💳🚭📶❄ HOTEL [3]

Lista di Spagna 262 ☎041 71 51 64 💻www.hotelrossi.ve.it

Just a few steps off Lista di Spagna, Hotel Rossi's peaceful setting seems miles (kilometers?) away from Cannaregio's more active center. Next to one of the neighborhood's nicest gardens, this hotel has reasonably large rooms, air conditioning, and understated classic Italian decor—all of which make it popular with middle-aged tourists, but perhaps less so with students scared away by the high Wi-Fi fee *(€14 per 24hr.)*.

➜ *Walk 3min. from the train station, then turn left down a side street immediately before Campo San Geremia.* ℹ *Breakfast included.* $ *Singles €45-72; doubles €80-95.*

HOTEL STELLA ALPINA HOTEL ❺

Calle Priuli 99/D ☎041 52 45 274 🖥www.hotel-stellaalpina.com

If you've been on the road for a while and the thought of another night spent in a sleeping sack is making you wish you'd stayed home and taken that summer job at Taco Bell, look no further than Hotel Stella Alpina, which offers budget-friendly luxury to the tired traveler. From the classic, almost formal, furnishings in the lobby to the modern decor in the dining room and bedrooms, this hotel's ambience certainly tops that of your local fast food franchise. But you'll have totally forgotten about your lost opportunity in the food service industry once you've laid yourself down in one of the hotel's air-conditioned rooms on the most comfortable bed you might ever find. Just make sure to get the job next summer to pay for this splurge...

➜ *From train station, turn left at the 1st st. past Calle Carmelitani and walk for about 1.5min.* ℹ *Breakfast included. Discount for booking ahead online.* $ *Singles €70-90; doubles €75-105.*

ALBERGO CASA BOCCASSINI HOTEL ❹

Calle Volto 5295 ☎041 52 29 892 🖥www.hotelboccassini.com

You could walk right past Albergo Casa Boccassini and never know it was there, nestled as it is in an unassuming residential area removed from Cannaregio's major thoroughfares. However, you'd be missing one of this neighborhood's little-known all-stars. Casa Boccassini's comfortably-sized and thoughtfully decorated rooms seem well priced (especially if you haggle down the rate), but the true standouts of this inconspicuous hotel are its gorgeous garden and the delightful indoor and outdoor seating you can enjoy while eating your compli mentary breakfast.

➜ *Coming from Fondamenta Nuove along Calle del Fumo, turn right at the 1st st. past Calle Larga dei Boteri.* ℹ *Breakfast included* $ *High-season singles €70, low-season €50.*

HOTEL TINTORETTO HOTEL ❹

S. Fosca 2316 ☎041 72 17 91 🖥www.hoteltintoretto.com

Hotel Tintoretto is a great hotel—if you can book it for the right price. Located right off Strada Nova in a section of Cannaregio that has relatively few budget hotels but is close to everything else in the neighborhood, this is an exceptionally clean, comfortable place to stay. Call ahead to find out about prices and attempt to bargain your way to a better deal, because if you can get a room toward the lower half of Tintoretto's spectrum, especially during the busy season, you'll be taking advantage of one of Cannaregio's sweetest deals.

➜ *Strada Nova, about 12min. from train station and 10min. from Rialto Bridge.* ℹ *Breakfast included.* $ *Singles €41-150; doubles €74-210.*

HOTEL SAN GEREMIA HOTEL ❹

Campo San Geremia 290 ☎041 52 42 342 🖥www.sangeremiahotel.com

Located directly on Campo San Geremia, this is a solid pick for students looking to be as close as possible to the busier sections of Cannaregio as well as the neighborhood's most exciting nightlife. The hotel itself is fairly typical for the area; however, its exceptionally helpful staff and competitive prices set it apart from rival establishments.

➜ *From train station, follow Lista di Spagna until reaching Campo S. Geremia.* ℹ *Breakfast included.* $ *Singles €50-70; doubles €70-90.*

HOTEL AL VAGON HOTEL ❸

Cannaregio 5619 ☎041 52 86 861 🖥www.hotelalvagon.com

If you have a burning desire to be on the eastern side of Cannaregio closer to Rialto Bridge, check out Hotel Al Vagon. It offers clean, spacious rooms at much better rates than most hotels in the area. As is the case with many of the hotels listed here, calling ahead and trying to figure out the logistics of your stay before you arrive could get you a significantly lower quote on your room.

Along Strada Nova eastward, cross the 1st bridge past Ca' d'Oro and turn left. i Breakfast included. $ Singles €30-70; doubles €50-120.

HOTEL MARTE E BIASIN — HOTEL ❷

Ponte delle Guglie 338 ☎041 71 63 51 www.hotelmarteebiasin.com

Hotel Marte e Biasin, located in two separate buildings divided by a canal, has more personality than just about any other hotel you'll find in Cannaregio—maybe even in all of Venice. The managers are charmingly upfront and take pride in running a tight ship, so the rooms are always well kept. However, all the Harry Potter fans who wonder what life was like under the staircase of Number 4, Privet Drive should take a look at the hotel's tiny single bedrooms with shared bath to get a sense of the boy wizard's plight. Despite the cramped and spartan quality of some of its rooms, Hotel Marte e Biasin is a great option for travelers trying to save some money in an expensive city. Whether you're paying in Galleons or euros, this hotel's prices can't be beaten.

From train station along Lista di Spagna, turn left immediately before bridge. i Breakfast included. $ Singles €25-85; doubles €40-100. 5% student discount.

SAN POLO

Though San Polo is home to relatively few hotels and hostels, the ones that are here offer a central location at double-take rates.

ALBERGO GUERRATO — PENSIONE ❹

Calle drio la Scimia 240/A ☎041 52 85 927 www.pensioneguerrato.it

Located in an 800-year-old *palazzo* just steps away from the Rialto Bridge, Albergo Guerrato offers competitive rates on some of the most desirable rooms in Venice. Characterized by simple but neat aesthetics that focus less on excessive decoration and more on comfort, they're perfectly suited to hard-living travelers.

From the Rialto Bridge, continue west and turn onto the 3rd street on the right; the hotel is shortly ahead on the right. i Breakfast included. $ Doubles €95-140; triples €120-155; quads €185; quints €195.

A VENICE MUSEUM — HOSTEL ❷

Calle del Traghetto 2812 ☎340 73 57 468

The owners of A Venice Museum, one of the very few true youth hostels in Venice, are so committed to running a fun, vibrant, engaging, and social establishment that they've banned everyone over 40 (not a joke—check the age requirements). The price is unbelievable, you can do laundry on-site (an indescribably huge perk given the lack of laundromats in Venice), and the hostel hosts dinner every night for only €3. If you're the type who doesn't mind waiting for the shower and loves to party with loud music until late at night, you're sure to have a blast here.

V: San Tomà. Go straight, make the 1st right, take the next right, and then take the next right. The hostel is not conspicuously advertised; look for a dark green door with several doorbells. Ring the one that says "Museum" for entrance to the hostel. i Breakfast included. Sheets €5 per night; towels €2. Dinner €3. Under 40 only. $ Dorms €28-35.

LOCANDO CA' SAN POLO — HOTEL ❹

Calle Saoneri de la Malvasia 2697 ☎041 24 40 331 www.casanpolo.it

If you want luxurious accommodations in Venice without spending all your money at once, do you (a) seduce a rich Venetian heiress, (b) sneak into Palazzo Ducale and take up residence in the Doge's Apartments, or (c) stay here? Ca' San Polo is by far the most legal, moral, and plausible of these three options. With study desks, blackout curtains, comfortable king-size beds, and beautiful views of the neighborhood from the third-floor terrace and dining area, this hotel proves that budget and luxury are not mutually exclusive.

➜ V: San Tomà. Continue north toward Frari, turn right, continue across the bridge, turn right, and take the 1st left; the hotel is ahead on the right. Signs indicate the direction toward the hotel. ℹ Breakfast included. Ⓢ Doubles €80-110; triples €100-120; quads €140-180.

HOTEL ALEX 💳🚭 HOTEL ❸

Frari 2606 ☎041 52 31 341 💻www.hotelalexinvenice.com

A small family hotel just across the bridge from the Frari, Hotel Alex prides itself on offering clean, quiet, and comfortable rooms. Though students may feel out of place in the family atmosphere, quads that go for €20 per person per night make hosteling look like a crummy deal. Consider booking in advance to request a room with a balcony overlooking the street.

➜ V: San Tomà. Continue north toward Frari, turn right, continue across the bridge, turn right, and turn left; the hotel is ahead on the left. ℹ Breakfast included. Ⓢ Singles €35-56; doubles €40-120; triples €60-162; quads €80-200.

LOCANDA POSTE VECIE 💳🚭 HOTEL ❸

Pescheria Rialto 1612 ☎041 71 82 44 💻www.locandapostevecie.com

Close to the Rialto Bridge, Locanda Poste Vecie is right in the heart of one of Venice's most crowded and lively districts, but with comfortable rooms decorated in traditional Venetian style, it manages to maintain a serene ambience. Consult its website before booking, as it offers frequent discounts and promotions online.

➜ From the Rialto Bridge, continue straight for about 200m through Campo De Le Becarie and take the 2nd right after the Campo. The hotel is on the right. ℹ Breakfast included. Ⓢ Doubles €70-130; triples €90-160; quads €110-190.

HOTEL IRIS 💳🚭📶 HOTEL ❸

V. San Polo 2910/A ☎041 52 22 882 💻www.irishotel.com

Located right at the intersection of Dorsoduro and San Polo and just steps away from the vaporetto, Hotel Iris offers convenient access to all of Venice's neighborhoods in addition to peaceful, comfortable rooms in one of Venice's most scenic areas. Prices vary frequently and tend to spike on weekends, so be sure to book well in advance.

➜ V: San Tomà. Walk straight until reaching a T intersection, turn left, continue to the canal, and turn right; the hotel is ahead on the right. ℹ Breakfast included. Ⓢ Singles €40-100; doubles €70-120; triples €120-180; quads €160-240.

SANTA CROCE

Although Santa Croce isn't known for its budget accommodations, you can find a room at the right price to make the neighborhood your home-away-from-home. Santa Croce is centrally located, with San Marco and the Rialto Bridge just minutes away and the nightlife in Dorsoduro easily accessible. At the same time, the neighborhood enjoys wide, quiet streets that aren't overrun with tourists. It's best to stay away from its western side, as you're more likely to discover good deals in the eastern section.

👍 ALBERGO AI TOLENTINI 💳🚭📶 HOTEL ❹

Santa Croce 197/G ☎041 27 59 140 💻www.albergoaitolentini.com

Albergo ai Tolentini is a small hotel without many different options accommodations-wise, but what it does have is exceptional. Start with what are in all likelihood the largest double rooms you'll find for less than €100 in Venice, decorated in an elaborate Venetian style and featuring private baths. Add on the hotel's convenient location, which is about as central as you can get in Venice, and you've got the makings of one very serviceable little hotel.

➜ Follow Piazzale Roma east, cross consecutive bridges, turn left, and continue along canal for 3-4min. before turning right away from Hotel Sofitel. Continue for 2min.; hotel is on the left. ℹ Breakfast included. Ⓢ Doubles €85-115.

ALBERGO CASA PERON 💳🚭 HOTEL [3]

Salizzada San Pantalon 84 ☎041 71 00 21 💻www.casaperon.com

A small, family-owned hotel with tons of personality, Albergo Casa Peron is worth the time to book in advance. A prime location on one of Santa Croce's main streets put this hotel in our good graces from the outset, but Albergo Casa Peron scores extra points with *Let's Go* for its supremely cool owner and the pet parrot who helps oversee the hotel from his shoulder.

⇄ Follow Piazzale Roma east, cross consecutive bridges, and continue for approximately 2min. ⓘ Breakfast included. $ Singles €30-90; doubles €50-100; triples €80-130.

PENSIONE DA IVANO 💳♿ PENSIONE [3]

Santa Croce 373 ☎041 52 46 648 💻www.daivanovenezia.it

Close to Piazzale Roma, Pensione da Ivano possesses a peaceful location, despite being a bit out of the way. The spacious, well-decorated rooms are only brightened by the friendly presence of their dedicated manager, who has owned the *pensione* and nearby Caffé Las Ramblas for the past 37 years. Feel free to chat him up, as he loves to talk with travelers about his city.

⇄ East from Piazzale Roma, turn right at the 1st canal you see and turn right onto Sestiere Santa Croce. Go to Caffé Las Ramblas, where you can be redirected to the pensione (4min. away). ⓘ Breakfast included. $ Rooms €45-100.

HOTEL FALIER 💳♿📶❄ HOTEL [5]

Salizada San Pantalon 130 ☎041 71 08 82 💻www.hotelfalier.com

Most of the hotels in the Santa Croce area are rather pricey, but Hotel Falier bridges the gap between luxury and budget fairly well. The price of a single room is as far from inexpensive as Venice is from Sicily, but the doubles are a good value compared to some of the luxury hotels in the neighborhood, without any compromise in quality. You won't be cheated the extra bucks you're shelling out: the hotel's phenomenal location is accompanied by an excellent dining room, a desk manager fluent in English, a lovely balcony, and other subtle pleasantries.

⇄ Follow Piazzale Roma east, cross consecutive bridges, and continue for approximately 2min. ⓘ Breakfast included. $ Singles €100-150; doubles €120-170.

DORSODURO

Finding a good hotel at the right price can be a bit tricky in Dorsoduro, but if you're patient and willing to put in a little bit of legwork calling places or checking their websites, you should be able to find a solid rate on a great hotel in the heart of Venice's best neighborhood.

👍 **HOTEL MESSNER** 💳♿📶❄ HOTEL [5]

Fondamenta di Cà Bala 216/217 ☎041 52 27 443 💻www.hotelmessner.it

Described by its owner as "three hotels in one," Hotel Messner offers one-, two-, and three-star accommodations—great for budget travelers who want to save money but still have the flexibility to choose their room's amenities. Regardless of star ranking, most rooms are brightened by floor-to-ceiling windows that prove a blessing in the humid Venetian summer.

⇄ V: Zattere. Turn right, walk 4-5min., turn left onto Fondamenta di Cà Bala and continue for about a min. Reception is approximately 1min. past the hotel in Ristorante Messner. ⓘ Breakfast included. $ Singles €70-105; doubles €95-160; triples €135-180; quads €150-200.

👍 **HOTEL ALLA SALUTE** 💳♿📶 HOTEL [3]

Fondamenta di Cà Bala 222 ☎041 52 35 404 💻www.hotelsalute.com

A lot of hotels in Venice overdo the whole Venetian theme, making you feel as if you're trapped in an antique dealer's storage facility. Hotel alla Salute, by contrast, presents a simple, modern take on Venetian aesthetics with some of the least cluttered and most beautiful hotel rooms in the city. Given the hotel's prime location and generous breakfast buffet, staying here is quite a deal.

➡ *V: Zattere. Turn right, walk 4-5min., turn left onto Fondamenta di Cà Bala and continue for about 2min.* ℹ *Breakfast included.* Ⓢ *Doubles €64-95; family rooms (fit 3-5) €75-135.*

HOTEL AMERICAN 💳♿📶❄ HOTEL [4]

San Vio 628 ☎041 52 04 733 💻www.hotelamerican.com

If you can book Hotel American anywhere at the bottom of their price range, we strongly advise you to do so. In addition to its old-world-hotel regal air, the American possesses all the amenities you could possibly want from a budget hotel.

➡ *V: Zattere. Turn right, walk 3-4min., turn left onto San Vio and continue for just over 1min.* ℹ *Breakfast included.* Ⓢ *Singles €60-230; doubles €80-370; suite €150-460. Extra bed €20-70.*

CA' SAN TROVASO 💳♿❄ HOTEL [5]

Fondamente delle Romite ☎041 27 71 146 💻www.casantrovaso.com

Ca' San Trovaso, one of the few hotels in Venice that is honest about how far it is from major sights, has recently undergone renovations that make it a gem of a budget hotel in Dorsoduro. One huge plus to staying at Ca' San Trovaso is access to the rooftop solarium, which provides excellent views of the city as well as space to relax.

➡ *V: Zattere. Turn right, take the 1st possible left, cross the bridge, turn left, cross the bridge immediately ahead, turn immediately right; the hotel is just ahead to the left.* ℹ *Breakfast included.* Ⓢ *Singles €75-100; doubles €80-145; triples €90-160.*

ANTICA LOCANDA MONTIN 💳🚭 B AND B [4]

Fondamenta Eremite 1147 ☎041 52 25 151 💻www.locandamontin.com

Although it is less than 2min. from each of Dorsoduro's two biggest streets, Antica Locanda Montin feels removed from these heavily trafficked areas. This is a small inn that lacks some of the conveniences available at large hotels, but it makes up for this inadequacy with a quaint small-town ambience and excellent values on exceptionally comfortable rooms.

➡ *V: Zattere. Turn right, take the first possible left, cross the bridge, turn left, turn immediately right, and the hotel is shortly ahead on the left.* ℹ *Breakfast included.* Ⓢ *Singles €50-70; doubles €130-160.*

HOTEL GALLERIA 💳🚭 HOTEL [4]

Campo de la Carità 878 ☎041 52 32 489 💻www.hotelgalleria.it

A small boutique hotel located near the Accademia, this establishment replicates the Accademia's formidable, faded-glory sort of charm with gorgeous rooms that were clearly designed with an eye towards quality rather than economy. Though perhaps less meticulously run than hotels with larger tourist volume, you're unlikely to find more spectacular rooms in this price range, particularly with a location so close to San Marco and the major galleries of Dorsoduro.

➡ *From the Ponte dell'Academia, facing the Accademia, turn right and walk for approximately 1min. The hotel is on the right.* ℹ *Breakfast included.* Ⓢ *Singles €65-86; doubles €110-160.*

ALBERGO HOTEL ANTICO CAPON 💻🚭📶❄ HOTEL [2]

Campo San Margherita 3004 ☎041 52 85 292 💻www.anticocapon.altervista.org

Hotel Antico Capon's location is both a blessing and a curse. If you're planning to hit the hay every night at 9pm to get up early and see Venice, you'll probably be frustrated with the constant din of Campo San Margherita, Dorsoduro's prime nightlife spot, echoing throughout the square. On the other hand, if you want to party every night you're in the city but don't want to navigate winding streets back to your hotel in the wee hours of the morning, Antico Capon might be your best bet. The rooms here are cheap for a reason: they're tiny.

➡ *Opposite the northeast corner of the square.* ℹ *Breakfast included.* Ⓢ *Doubles €45-95; triples €60-75; quads €120.*

CASTELLO

Castello is bursting at the seams with overpriced hotels looking to exploit tourists who mistakenly believe they just have to be within a 5min. walk of the Rialto Bridge and P. San Marco. Hidden among these flashy establishments, however, are a good number of hotels that are accessible to the major sights but manage to maintain the quiet neighborhood ambience that makes Venice so charming. Hotel prices tend to fluctuate more in Castello than in most neighborhoods, so it's worth calling around to see the best available rates. Keep in mind that if you stay in the northern section of Castello, you'll have a much easier time getting to Cannaregio and San Polo, whereas if you stay in the southern or western section you'll have better access to San Marco, Dorsoduro, and all vaporetto lines.

LA RESIDENZA ◆⊗(ᵗ) HOTEL ❹

Campo Bandiera e Moro 3608 ☎041 52 85 315 ▣www.venicelaresidenza.com

Every hotel in Venice wants to claim that it is located in a former palace, but at La Residenza, you can tell that they aren't lying. The regal decor, stately reception area, and magnificently decorated guest rooms evoke a sense of Venice's extravagant mercantile history. Although this is far from the typical budget hotel, staying here provides a uniquely Venetian experience.

✈ *From P. San Marco, walk towards the water, turn left, and cross 4 bridges; then turn left and continue to Campo Bandiera e Moro.* ℹ *Breakfast included. Free Wi-Fi.* Ⓢ *Singles €50-110; doubles €60-200. Extra bed €35.*

THE GUESTHOUSE TAVERNA SAN LIO ◆⊗(ᵗ)❄ B AND B ❹

Salizada San Lio 5547 ☎041 27 77 06 69 ▣www.tavernasanlio.com

Staying in Venice on a budget means forgoing a lot of luxuries that might be taken for granted in American hotels, but if you book a room at the Guesthouse Taverna San Lio at the right time, you can get an incredible room that feels authentically Venetian yet still includes Wi-Fi, A/C, a private bathroom—creature comforts certainly not enjoyed by the city's Renaissance residents—and, perhaps most importantly, a mouth-watering breakfast. The hotel also boasts excellent proximity to both the Rialto Bridge and P. San Marco in an area that is lively with local color.

✈ *From Rialto Bridge, go east along Salizada San Lio for 3-4min.; hotel is on the right.* ℹ *Breakfast included. Free Wi-Fi.* Ⓢ *Doubles €70-150; triples €100-180; quads €130-200.*

FORESTERIA VALDESE ◆♿ HOTEL, HOSTEL ❷

Palazzo Cavagnis 5170 ☎041 52 86 797 ▣www.foresteriavenezia.it

One of the few places in Venice to get a shared dormitory room more typical of a hostel, Foresteria Valdese is an oasis of value in a sea of €90-per-person, one-star hotels. The hotel is run by a Protestant church that maintains the house in which the hotel is located. While the reservation system can be tricky, especially for dorms, Foresteria Valdese offers both a unique experience and a great deal in Venice.

✈ *From Campo Santa Maria Formosa, take Calle Larga Santa Maria Forma; Foresteria Valdese is immediately across the 1st bridge.* ℹ *Breakfast included.* Ⓢ *Dorms €23-29; doubles €78-96; triples €90-111; quads €114-144.*

ALBERGO DONI ◆⊗ HOTEL ❹

Calle del Vin 4656 ☎041 52 25 267 ▣www.albergodoni.it

Rooms at the low end of the price range here are an absolute steal. Although you'll pay for proximity to P. San Marco with heavy tourist traffic and some street noise, the hotel's 17th-century building features spacious rooms, excellent antique furniture, and even some breathtaking ceiling frescoes.

✈ *From P. San Marco, walk toward the water, turn left, and cross 2 bridges; take the 1st left and walk 30sec.* ℹ *Breakfast included.* Ⓢ *Singles €50-65; doubles €60-120.*

under the sea

Traveling to Venice is a wayfarer's dream: great food, incredible history, and beautiful architecture. But sometimes visiting the city can feel a bit like being a boatswain on the post-iceberg Titanic because, like the Titanic, Venice is sinking. Over the past century, Venice has sunk about 1 ft. and is predicted to sink by as much as another 20 in. during the next 50 years. That might not sound like much, but seeing P. San Marco, the most famous landmark in Venice, underwater during the highest tides of the year has the locals feeling a bit seasick. The evidence of the city's watery fate is evident everywhere—stairways that a couple centuries ago led to perfectly functional docks are now covered by several feet of water.

Novel solutions ranging from constructing moveable dams to pumping water into the foundations of the city have been proposed, but Venetians are far from reaching consensus. A $4 billion project to construct mobile inflatable flood barriers is underway, but it has met with opposition from some who contend it will destroy the natural ecology of the lagoon and actually make flooding worse. Whether a radical solution is achieved or the city continues to rely on the duct-tape approach of fixings things as they break, you'll likely share the locals' concern when you realize that the street you're walking on right now could be the place you bring your kids for a swim in 20 years' time.

HOTEL CANADA VENEZIA ➥⑧⑴⑴※ HOTEL ❹

Salizada San Lio ☎041 52 29 912 ◨www.canadavenice.com

Set back a bit from the more hectic and heavily trafficked areas of Castello, Hotel Canada Venezia, situated in an area far from the cacophony of tourists that echoes throughout the area around P. San Marco, might be more popular with older travelers than students. It does, however, merit a look from anyone desiring one of the more upscale budget hotels in Castello.

⚑ *From Rialto Bridge, walk east across Campo S. Bartolomeo, cross a bridge, and then continue for less than 1min.; the hotel is on the left.* 𝒊 *Breakfast included. Free Wi-Fi.* ⑤ *Singles €65-129; doubles €85-165; triples €110-199; quads €140-254.*

OUTSKIRTS

By staying in the outskirts, you can upgrade your digs on the cheap or go even more bargain-basement than is possible in the *centro*. Lido is loaded with hotels that are less expensive than their Venetian counterparts, and ⛺camping on the islands or the Italian mainland is a popular alternative for even more saving. While camping might conjure up images of improvised tents and fishing for dinner, Italians campsites offer RV-park luxury, with fully furnished trailers or at least fairly decent permanent tents.

▨ OSTELLO DI VENEZIA (HI) ➥⑧⑴⑴※ HOSTEL ❷

Fondamenta Zitelle 86 ☎041 52 38 211 ◨www.hostelvenice.com

Ostello Venezia sets the standard for hostels in Venice. With 260 beds, a restaurant, common room, bar, and state-of-the-art facilities, it's an incredible value. Located in Giudecca, it's not too far from Dorsoduro or San Marco. Groups can often book rooms in advance, but outside of those cases, dorms are strictly divided by gender. For those apprehensive about leaving their belongings unattended in a room with a dozen other people, the hostel provides free private lockers with keys and padlocks. Though having to use the vaporetto system can be a bit of a hassle, the hostel's great facilities and efficient and helpful staff more than make up for any inconvenience caused by its out-of-the-way location.

accommodations · outskirts

V: Zitelle, turn right and continue for less than 1min. The hostel is on the left. i Breakfast included. €3 daily surcharge for those without YHA membership. Wi-Fi €2.50 per 12hr., internet terminals €3 per hr. $ Dorms €22. ⏰ Lockout 10am-1:30pm.

CAMPEGGIO SAN NICOLÒ

CAMPING ❶

V. dei Sanmichieli 14 ☎041 52 67 415 www.campingsannicolo.com

Lido's only major camping site, Campeggio San Nicolò is a great budget option. Though the site is removed from Lido's major vaporetto stops, bike rentals make the island extremely accessible. Tents offer reasonable short-term accommodations, and campers are surprisingly nice given the cost per person. This kind of camping is an interesting and uniquely European experience—something worth trying before you leave Italy (though not cool enough to be attempted when rain is in the forecast).

From dock Lido San Nicolò, turn right, and continue north for about 5min. There will be signs indicating the direction of the camp site. i Laundry €3. Parking €2. Bike rental €7. $ Prices vary depending on what exactly you're looking for, but will probably cost about €18 per person per night.

CAMPING JOLLY

CAMPING ❶

V. Giuseppe de Marchi 7 ☎041 92 03 12 www.ecvacanze.it

This is a place to stay if you want to *say* you came to Venice but actually spend your whole trip partying on the Italian mainland. It takes about 45min. to get from Camping Jolly to Venice proper, so don't pop your tent here if you want to be in the city. Instead, come here for the nice pool, awesome bar, tons of backpackers, and a DJ who seems to love Kanye West. Lots of people think that traveling is a lost art in the age of the internet, but dancing to **Thriller** with backpackers from Japan, some hair-metal fans from Germany, and a pair of Italian bartenders is a great reminder of what it can be when done right.

There are several ways to get to Camping Jolly. The best route from Venice is to take bus #6 from the train station toward Marghera, get off at V. Paleocapa, turn onto V. Beccaria, and continue for about 10min. until you reach V. Della Fonte. Turn right onto V. Della Fonte and continue until the street ends. You'll see an outdoor park/sports complex. Follow the walkway along the park until you reach an underpass. Go through the underpass, and you will emerge at Camping Jolly. $ 1- to 3-person tents €12.50; bungalows (up to 3 people) €39-58.50; casa mobile (up to 4 people) €60-79; chalet (up to 5 people) €84-116.

LOCANDA AL SOFFIADOR

HOTEL ❹

Vle. Bressagio 1 ☎041 73 94 30 www.venicehotel.it

For those who want a traditional hotel with relatively easy access to Venice but also hope to spend more time exploring the islands of the northern lagoon, Locanda Al Soffiador offers an ideal location. In a great spot on Murano, an island with enough shopping, studios, and history to keep glass aficionados occupied for days, the hotel is just over 20min. from the Venetian "mainland" (if it's possible to apply that term to a collection of islands). It boasts great proximity to the rest of the northern lagoon as well. The hotel itself is beautiful, well-maintained, and much less expensive than comparable hotels in Venice.

V: Faro, walk straight ahead along the island's main street; the hotel is about 3min. ahead on the right. i Breakfast included. $ Singles €50-60; doubles €60-90; triples €80-130.

sights

An incredible number of churches, museums, palaces, and historic sights line Venice's canals—you could easily spend a month in the city and still be stumbling across new places to check out on a daily basis. If you're planning to spend any time sightseeing here, you should seriously consider purchasing the **Rolling Venice Card** (available at any IAT/VAT Tourist office for €4), a tourist pass for visitors to the city between the ages of 14 and 29 which provides unlimited use of ACTV public transit, free admission to the Civic Museums of Venice, free admission to the churches that are a member of the Chorus Pass collective, reduced admission at any number of other sights, and discounts at various hotels and restaurants.

a chorus of churches

For a small city, Venice sure has a lot of churches—a lot of very memorable ones that are worth your time, too. Most of them charge €3 for entry, though, which might make you ask if they're worth your money. Eliminate this calculation, however, with the Chorus Pass, which can be purchased for €10 and grants unlimited entry to participating churches (there are 18 of them) for a year. Buy it at participating churches and then feel free to wander in and out as much as you wish: it won't cost you another cent (unless the collection plate comes around).

SAN MARCO

It's easy to be overwhelmed by the number of sights in San Marco. In fact, before you even head out into the wider neighborhood, it's easy to be overwhelmed by the number of sights in **Piazza San Marco** alone. In the *piazza*, the two main attractions, **Basilica di San Marco** and **Palazzo Ducale**, are found easily enough, but several other sights of great interest are often overlooked by visitors. In the wider *sestiere* closer to **Rialto Bridge**, for example, attractions like the excellent **Palazzo Grassi** await. Perhaps most importantly, before braving this area be sure to meditate for a couple of minutes, have a glass of Venetian wine, pop a couple of Xanax, or do whatever else is necessary to prepare yourself for the jostling, shoving, elbowing, shouting, and general rudeness that crops up as inevitably in the heart of *La Serenissima* as it does in any overcrowded tourist area. Once you've done that, you'll be ready to experience one of the densest concentrations of spectacular sights in the whole of Europe.

PALAZZO DUCALE ❧♿ PALAZZO, MUSEUM

P. San Marco 1   ☎041 27 15 911 ▧www.museicivicuveneziani.it

This massive palace that served as the residence of Venice's pseudo-monarchical mayor and the seat of his government throughout most of Venetian history is, perhaps, the best showcase of Venetian history, art, and architecture you'll find in a single building. Unfortunately, it has lost much of its character in recent years as it has increasingly sought to traffic as many visitors as possible through its exhibits with the most minimal inconvenience. Unlike the serene **Accademia** or **Guggenheim Museum,** where it's possible to move leisurely through the galleries and follow no particular path, the Palazzo Ducale poses challenges to those who would like to meander through its halls, as numerous guided tours block hallways and crowd some of the museum's most famous attractions. For the best way to see the Palazzo, rent a handheld audio tour *(€5)* or stop by the the museum shop to purchase a guide before you enter. Then, proceed at your own pace. While there are many bottlenecks in some of the more famous rooms, where guides tend to linger, if you time things well, you should be able to evade clusters of tourists while still managing to see everything. And there is a remarkable amount to see, from Sansovino's statues in the courtyard to Veronese's *Rape of Europa*.

Every room open to the public is worth visiting, and *Let's Go* recommends allowing yourself to wander through the Palazzo, spending more time in the rooms that are of particular interest to you. If you decide to go all-in and read about the history of every room, you could easily spend 4hr. in the place, but in any case, budget at least 90min. for your visit. No visit to the Palazzo Ducale can be complete without seeing Tintoretto's *Paradise*, an impossibly massive oil painting with strongly religious themes that gives the **Great Council Room** an ominous, foreboding air. The numerous exhibitions in the **Doge's Apartments,** including the Doge's private libraries and dining room, should prove fascinating to anyone with an interest in Venetian history or high culture. Surprisingly, one of the least crowded sections of the palace is the area containing the **Bridge of Sighs** and prisons, which constitute an extensive labyrinth throughout the lower eastern side of the palace and provide stark contrast to the opulence and majesty of the floors above.

⚑ *Entrance to the Palazzo Ducale is along the waterfront.* Ⓢ *Apr 1-Oct 31 €13, EU citizens ages 18-25, ages 6-14, over 65, and holders of the Rolling Venice card €7.50; Nov 1-Mar 31 €12/6.50.* ⚅ *Open daily June-Oct 8:30am-6:30pm; Nov-March 9am-6pm; Apr-May 9am-7pm. Ticket office closes 1hr. before museum.*

▨ BASILICA DI SAN MARCO   ⊛⊛ CHURCH
P. San Marco   ☎041 27 08 311 ▣www.basilicasanmarco.it

This basilica is maybe the top "can't miss" sight in all of Venice, and not just because admission is free. Lines to the Basilica are often long, but don't be deterred. Visitors rarely spend more than 15min. inside the Basilica, so even if you're behind a few hundred people, it shouldn't take more than a wait of 20min. or so for you to enter what is universally considered the most impressive church in Venice. If you're planning a day in P. San Marco, either go to the Basilica first thing in the morning before it is crowded or mid-afternoon when light streams in through the windows and provides some of the most striking natural illumination you'll find anywhere in the world.

Even before you enter the church, you cannot help but be struck by its size and intricate design. Spend a few minutes admiring the Basilica's facade, overlooked by far too many visitors. It is every bit as impressive as the inside's soaring domes, marble inlay, and gorgeous golden mosaics that acquire an eerie life-like quality in the proper lighting. The majesty of the church is a testament to the history of Venice, as the Basilica di San Marco dates back to the origins of the city. Founded in the ninth century by two Venetian merchants who daringly stole St. Mark's remains from the city of Alexandria and smuggled them past Arab officials by hiding them in a case of pork meat, the church was originally a much smaller, more modest wooden building that suffered serious damage during a fire in the 11th century. Venice, emerging as a powerful city state, dedicated substantial time, effort, and funding to the construction of the new Basilica di San Marco, which was further embellished as the Republic of Venice rose in stature. Today, it stands more or less as it was completed in the 17th century. The church's interior is clearly the product of the various cultural influences that have affected the Venetian identity, seamlessly incorporating Byzantine, Roman, and Northern European influences into an interior that is simultaneously ostentatious in its gilded excess and mysterious in the dark, rich detail of its altars and mosaics.

Though admission to the Basilica is free, those interested in further exploration of the remarkable building's history will have to pay extra to see its three affiliated sights: the Pala d'Oro, treasury, and St. Mark's Museum. Anyone intrigued by the Byzantine influences in the Basilica should take a few minutes to appreciate the **Pala d'Oro,** an altar retable that is widely regarded as one of the most spectacular intact examples of Byzantine artwork. A visual history of the life of Saint Mark, the Pala d'Oro was meticulously designed with thousands of precious gemstones adorning what is certainly one of the most breathtaking pieces of religious artwork you'll see anywhere in Italy. The **treasury** houses various precious objects of religious significance, a collection that anyone with an interest in the history of the Basilica will enjoy exploring even if it includes a small fraction of the number of artifacts it featured prior to the Napoleonic invasions. **St. Mark's Museum** helps to contextualize the Basilica and is a great primer in Venetian history for anyone with a short stop in Venice. Nevertheless, visiting the museum isn't essential to appreciating the astounding beauty of the Basilica, which is the main attraction here.

✦ Entrance on east side of P. San Marco, north of Palazzo Ducale. *i* Modest dress required—no bare shoulders or revealing skirts or shorts. Ⓢ Basilica free. St. Mark's Museum €4. Pala d'Oro €2. Treasury €3. All prices reduced 50% for groups of 15 or more. Ⓩ Basilica open Easter-Nov M-Sa 9:45am-5pm, Su 2-5pm; Nov-Easter M-Sa 9:45am-5pm, Su 2-4pm. Pala d'Oro and treasury open Easter-Nov M-Sa 9:45am-5pm, Su 2-5pm; Nov-Easter M-Sa 9:45am-4pm, Su 2-4pm. Museum open daily 9:45am-4:45pm.

▨ PALAZZO GRASSI
♥⛭ MUSEUM

Campo San Samuele 3231　　　　　☎041 52 31 680 🖥www.palazzograssi.it

A highbrow museum of contemporary art that's not afraid to laugh at itself, Palazzo Grassi is at once entertaining and refreshing. Sponsored by François Pinault and affiliated with the **Punta della Dogana** museum in Dorsoduro, Palazzo Grassi features artwork in numerous media from prominent contemporary artists such as **Matthew Day Jackson, Oy Twobly,** and **Jeff Koons.** The Palazzo's signature piece is a series of canvases that constitute a visual interpretation of events in Japanese history. Created by Takashi Murakami over the course of six years, the work was initiated at the behest of Pinault for installation specifically in this gallery. Even if you aren't familiar with modern art, there are enough pieces in enough media here that something is bound to interest, challenge, or even just amuse you. Unlike other sights in Venice, Palazzo Grassi doesn't shy away from self-parody. This is exemplified in Rob Pruitt's "101 Artistic Ideas," a work featured in the Mapping the Studio exhibition. Some of Pruitt's ideas have been put into practice throughout the museum. You might think you've seen every imaginable take on the Renaissance fresco after a few days in Venice, but until you've seen Idea #72 ("Put 🔳googly eyes on things") put in practice on a priceless 17th-century mural, you really don't know what you're missing. Palazzo Grassi's sense of humor makes its collections more accessible to those with a casual interest in artwork, as do the frequent events that the museum hosts to introduce visitors to prominent artists and the artistic process. Such events seek to contradict, defy, and critique notions about art while maintaining a certain levity that gives the museum its welcoming, cheeky character.

✦ Follow the signs to Palazzo Grassi from anywhere in San Marco. If coming from the Rialto Bridge, continue along the streets running parallel to the Grand Canal, staying near the Canal, until you see signs directing you toward Palazzo Grassi. Palazzo Grassi is also immediately adjacent to vaporetto stops S. Samuele (line 2) and S. Angelo (line 1). Ⓢ €15, with affiliated Punta della Dogana in Dorsoduro €20. Ⓩ Open M 10am-7pm, W-Su 10am-7pm. Last entry 1hr. before close.

PIAZZA SAN MARCO
⛭ PIAZZA

P. San Marco

Indisputably the most important square in Venice and home to many of the city's most important historical and cultural attractions, P. San Marco is a study in contrasts. Chaotic despite its spectacular views of Venice's serene lagoon, this dignified, historical home of Venetian government is now overrun by tour groups of texting teenagers and foreigners who chase pigeons for amusement. In this way, P. San Marco encapsulates both the best and worst of Venice. When you stand in the square, you're only moments from the **Basilica di San Marco,** the **Campanile,** the **Palazzo Ducale, Saint Mark's Clock Tower,** and almost half a dozen notable museums. You're also just a few steps away from Venice's most upscale shopping and dining establishments, which draw visitors from all over the world. Though not without its high-end attractions, the Piazza has mass appeal as well, with occasional street performers, numerous salesmen offering knock-off designer goods, gelato galore, and the infamous pigeons who have given rise to an industry of their own. Shrewd locals sell stale bread to tourists who want to feed the birds. The **boldest** (or dumbest) of these avian-loving visitors cover themselves in bread so as to attract dozens of the flying scourge to roost on them. (Why anyone would want pigeons sitting on their shoulders is a mystery.) It takes a rare disposition to appreciate the Piazza at its chaotic midsummer peak—particularly after the arduous trip into the city, the square's crush of people can be quite overwhelming. It is best to visit early in the morning or late at night, when the Piazza evokes memories of a time before Venice had become one of the world's tourist capitals. In recent years, the Piazza has been known to flood at high tide, so when you are ready to soak up San Marco's old-world glamor, make sure to leave those new Ferragamo pumps you just bought at home.

⇞ This is possibly the only place in Venice that isn't hard to find. $ Free.

CAMPANILE ♿ TOWER

P. San Marco ☎041 27 08 311 🖥www.basilicasanmarco.it

One of the most prominent buildings in P. San Marco, the Campanile is undeniably the dominant fixture of the Venetian skyline—so much so that in 1997, a group of separatists advocating the political division of Italy decided to storm the tower to proclaim their message from its heights. The incident, which marked the 200-year anniversary of the end of the Venetian Republic, is one of the tower's few claims to legitimate historical significance, since the original (completed in 1514) spontaneously collapsed in 1902. Remarkably, given the size and central location of the tower, no one was killed during the collapse, and the reconstruction of the tower was completed a decade later. The Campanile has a fully functioning elevator capable of taking over two dozen people to the top of the tower, from which you can enjoy fantastic views of the city. Unfortunately, it's a complete tourist trap, since access to the lift costs €8 and usually requires a substantial wait. Most visitors, at least those without a political message to proclaim from the heights of the tower, will likely be content to admire the simple brick structure of the Campanile from ground level.

⇞ In P. San Marco. $ Entrance and lift access €8. ⏰ Open daily July-Sept 9am-9pm; Oct 9am-7pm; Nov-Easter 9:30am-3:45pm; Easter-June 9am-7pm.

FONDAZIONE DI VENEZIA: FOTOGRAFIA ITALIANA ♿❄ MUSEUM

P. San Marco 71/C ☎041 22 01 215 🖥www.fondazionedivenezia.org

A small photography museum featuring seasonal exhibits that change frequently, the Fondazione di Venezia's museum of Italian photography is a great addition to P. San Marco. Unlike the other museums in the square, which can become frustratingly expansive and unapproachable after several hours of staring at the similar-looking artifacts that fill each of them, the Italian Photography museum is distinguished by a smaller, selective collection of works presented in an engaging and informative manner. As the name of the museum implies, the Fondazione di Venezia has set up a retrospective on the history of Italian photography, from its late 19th-century influences to its more modern forms. The museum can be thoroughly explored in under an hour and offers greater context and perspective within which to consider the works featured in Venice's other art museums, including both of François Pinault's museums and **The Guggenheim Collection** in Dorsoduro.

⚔ *The southwest corner of P. San Marco, opposite the entrance to Museo Correr.* Ⓢ *€5, under 14 and over 65 free.* ☑ *Open M 10am-6pm, W-Su 10am-6pm.*

TORRE DELL'OROLOGIO-ST. MARK'S CLOCK TOWER ●⊗ CLOCKTOWER
P. San Marco ☎848 08 20 00 🖳www.museicivicivenezieani.it
Also known as the Moors' Clock Tower, the Torre dell'Orologio was constructed as a symbol of Venice's wealth, scientific prowess, and artistic skill when the Republic of Venice was near the height of its power. The clock tower, which has undergone little alteration since the beginning of the 16th century, is less impressive than the nearby **Basilica di San Marco** and **Campanile** in terms of sheer size, but its expert artistry rivals any of Venice's more famous sights. Thousands of tourists pass beneath the clock tower each day without knowing that tours of the structure are available. These are run through the Civic Museums of Venice, though visits require prior booking. Many rave about the tour, which features a history of the building as well as views of the clock tower's inner workings, but during peak months, tours may fill up weeks in advance. In addition to a reservation, you'll have to be in good physical condition to navigate the tower's narrow corridors.

⚔ *The north end of P. San Marco.* 𝒊 *Prior booking required.* Ⓢ *€12, ages 6-14 and over 65, students 15-25, and holders of the Rolling Venice card or Museum Pass from the Venice Civic Museums €7.* ☑ *Tours available in English M-W at 10am and 11am, Th-Su at 2pm and 3pm.*

MUSEO CORRER ●♿♍❋ MUSEUM
P. San Marco 52 ☎041 24 05 211 🖳www.museicivicivenezieani.it
The largest and most impressive of the three museums affiliated with the **Palazzo Ducale,** the Museo Correr exhibits artifacts from the history of Venice in an informative and compelling presentation that offers a refreshing change of pace from the rest of P. San Marco. Though the museum is one of Venice's finest, it's rarely crowded, especially in comparison with the nearby **Basilica** and Palazzo Ducale. Designed to entertain both serious history buffs and tourists seeking shelter from Venice's midsummer heat, the Museo Correr features a different theme relating to the history of Venice in each room, resulting in a surprisingly novel and effective presentation. For the visitor who has no particular interest in ▥**medieval coinage,** for example, it's easy to bypass the exhibit on that particular subject and continue on to rooms focused on cartography, military history, or any other aspect of Venice's illustrious past. The museum's second floor contains a substantial gallery of medieval and early Renaissance artwork, a boon for sightseers on a tight schedule who would like to visit the **Accademia** but might not have sufficient time to do so. If you're planning to visit the Palazzo Ducale, carve out some time for the Museo Correr, as it offers perhaps the most engaging history of Venice you'll find anywhere in the city.

⚔ *Entrance in southwest corner of P. San Marco.* Ⓢ *May-Sept €13, students and seniors €7.50; Nov-Apr €12/€6.50. Free admission with a ticket from the Palazzo Ducale. Pass to all Civic Museums €18/€12.* ☑ *Open daily Apr-Oct 9am-7pm; Nov-Mar 9am-5pm. Last entry 1hr. before close.*

NATIONAL ARCHAEOLOGY MUSEUM ●♿♍ MUSEUM
P. San Marco 52 ☎041 24 05 211 🖳www.museicivicivenezieani.it
Founded in the mid-16th century, the National Archaeology Museum features mostly ancient Roman and Greek artifacts that were regarded as historically significant even at the time of the museum's founding. Unlike most other museums in Venice, which rarely contain any objects predating the city's founding, the National Archaeology Museum has numerous objects in its collection that are over two millennia old. Though the Archaeology Museum is not as well organized as the **Museo Correr,** and many of the artifacts are presented without information

to help put them in a historical context, there are still a few items that make the museum well worth a visit. Several Rosetta Stone-esque tablets engraved in Latin and Greek script and fragments of huge statues erected at the height of the Roman Empire's power throughout the Mediterranean are of especial interest.

Entrance in southwest corner of P. San Marco. $ May-Sept €13, students and seniors €7.50; Nov-Apr €12/€6.50. Free admission with a ticket from the Palazzo Ducale. Pass to all Civic Museums €18/€12. 🕐 Open daily Apr-Oct 9am-7pm; Nov-Mar 9am-5pm. Last entry 1hr. before close.

NATIONAL LIBRARY OF SAINT MARK'S — MUSEUM, LIBRARY

P. San Marco 52 ☎041 24 05 211 🖥www.museicivicivenezianі.ite

Also known as the Marciana Library, the National Library of Saint Mark's was founded in the mid-16th century and moved to the western wing of the Palazzo Ducale after the fall of Napoleon. One of the best-preserved collections of original texts and manuscripts from the early Renaissance period, the Marciana Library currently houses over one million books, including tens of thousands of manuscripts and original texts, several drafts of Cavalli's operas, and foundational translations of the Bible. Though the section of the library open to public viewing is relatively small, its incredible design, a testament to the importance of the library for the Venetian state, and the thousands of books shelved within the main section of the library will awe both bibliophiles and the barely literate.

Entrance in southwest corner of P. San Marco. $ May-Sept €13, students and seniors €7.50; Nov-Apr €12/€6.50. Free admission with a ticket from the Palazzo Ducale. Pass to all Civic Museums €18/€12. 🕐 Open daily Apr-Oct 9am-7pm; Nov-Mar 9am-5pm. Last entry 1hr. before close. Free tours of the library available in English every Su (except the 4th Su of each month) at 10am, noon, and 2pm.

PALAZZO CAVALLI FRANCHETTI — PALAZZO, MUSEUM

Campo Santo Stefano 2842 ☎041 53 34 420 🖥www.vivaticket.it

Right across the bridge from the **Accademia** in the Instituto Veneto di Scienze Lettere ed Arti, Palazzo Cavalli Franchetti hosts frequent art exhibitions often featuring the work of 19th- and 20th-century Venetian artists. Exhibitions typically run for several months at a time, and though the artists, movements, and artistic forms vary, the quality of the exhibits remains consistently excellent. Exhibitions tend to be relatively small and rarely feature more than a few dozen works, so a visit to Palazzo Cavalli Franchetti doesn't take an inordinate amount of time. Nonetheless, a visit will often provide greater insight into the work of a particular artist or movement featured in other Venetian museums. The Palazzo, though located in San Marco, is just moments away from the Accademia and an excellent place to visit as part of an art museum day featuring the three major Dorsoduro collections. When visiting the museum, be sure to dedicate at least a few minutes to admiring the *palazzo* itself, which is impressively maintained and features gorgeous frescoes as well as statuary that is almost as impressive as the artwork you'll find in the museum.

Across the Ponte dell'Accademia from the Accademia. $ €9. 🕐 Open daily 10am-6pm. Last entry 30min. before close. Hours may vary depending on exhibitions featured.

CANNAREGIO

To get the most out of Cannaregio, take the locals' advice and treat your stay here as an opportunity to experience the real Venetian lifestyle rather than as a time for sight-seeing. Most of the notable attractions in the neighborhood are churches which hold architectural as well as religious interest, but the two can't-miss destinations in Cannaregio are the Ca' d'Oro and the Jewish Ghetto.

CA' D'ORO — MUSEUM

Strada Nova 3932 ☎041 52 00 345 🖥www.cadoro.org

A truly Venetian institution, this palace of a few centuries ago now houses one of the most impressive art collections in the region. Comprising works dating from the city's earliest days, the museum's assortment of art is surprisingly extensive, easily meriting a visit of 2 or 3hr. The ex-*palazzo*'s architecture rivals the art for splendor, as do the views of Venice (perhaps the best you'll find) from the museum's balconies. All of these aesthetic delights make the somewhat pricey tickets (€6.50) well worth the expense, even if you're not that into art. Plus, you'll be able to tell your parents of at least one high-culture experience you had while you were in Italy. Ah, *la dolce vita.*

✾ Going east on Strada Nova, find the Ca' d'Oro on the right immediately before reaching Calle della Testa. *i* Bookshop and Loggias only accessible by staircase. Ⓢ €6.50, EU citizens 18-25 €3.25, EU citizens under 18 and over 65 free. ⏰ Open M 8:15am-2pm, Tu-Su 8:15am-7:15pm. Last entry 30min. before close.

THE JEWISH GHETTO
    ♿ NEIGHBORHOOD
Around Campo di Ghetto Nuovo   ☎041 71 50 12 🖳www.moked.it/jewishvenice

Stepping into Venice's Jewish Ghetto, the first neighborhood in the world to bear a title that has now become so ubiquitous that suburban teens questionably use it to describe their two-year-old cell phones, will give you a taste of what this part of the city was like a few centuries ago. Much of the ghetto's original architecture has been preserved, including several **synagogues.** Although you'll be able to see the buildings of Venice's past, don't expect to witness any Shylock-ian angst—unlike residents who lived here in the 16th century, today's inhabitants of the ghetto are not forced here by government edict. The area remains uniquely Jewish, however, with strong Israeli and Italian-Jewish influences. Many of the signs in this section of Cannaregio are written in Hebrew as well as Italian.

✾ Across the Guglie Bridge going northeast, turn left onto Fondamenta Pescheria, walk 1 block and turn onto Ghetto Vecchio.

CHIESA DEI GESUITI
    ⊗ CHURCH
Campo dei Gesuiti

Duck into Chiesa dei Gesuiti and be rewarded by the impressive art it contains, including an original work by Titian. Gesuiti was built later (by Venetian standards) than many other churches in Cannaregio, so a visit here will give you a sense of what was hip and happenin' back in the 18th century. Cannaregio's streets are dotted with churches, but if you only have time for one holy encounter, make a beeline for Gesuiti.

✾ From Sestiere Cannaregio, going east, turn right onto Campo del Gesuiti. ⏰ Open M-Sa 10am-noon and 4-6pm.

THE FONDAMENTA NUOVE
    ♿ STREET
Northeast Cannaregio

If the tourist hordes of Strada Nova turn you off from Venice's longest street, the broad walkways and cool sea breezes of Fondamenta Nuove should provide a refreshing respite to enjoy excellent views of neighboring islands, most prominently San Michele. The street runs along the northernmost part of Cannaregio, and with several vaporetto stops scattered along its path, Fondamenta Nuove is always busily trafficked, though never excessively. The Fondamenta Nuove is lined by excellent and sometimes expensive restaurants as well as some of the best gelato shops in Cannaregio, so consider treating your stomach and psyche to this pleasant promenade.

✾ Take Calle Larga from Strada Nova to Fondamenta Nuove.

SAN POLO

Though a small neighborhood, San Polo has several sights that are well worth visiting. In addition to the **Rialto Bridge** and the area immediately surrounding it, several nearby churches and museums count among Venice's most rewarding destinations.

🏛 RIALTO BRIDGE

Over the Grand Canal

Even before the Rialto Bridge, or *Ponte di Rialto*, was built in 1591, its site at the intersection of four of Venice's six *sestiere* (San Marco, Cannaregio, San Polo, and Castello, to be precise) served as a major point of transfer among Venice's islands. In the 12th century, construction began on a series of bridges to accommodate pedestrian traffic across the **Grand Canal,** but as trade in the Republic of Venice continued to expand, the need for a permanent structure that wouldn't interfere with **boat traffic** became apparent. Though numerous famous Italian artists of the day were considered, ultimately **Antonio da Ponte** directed the project, deciding on the controversial stone construction that has become a Venetian trademark. The bridge today stands in essentially the same form in which da Ponte designed it, with three lanes of pedestrian traffic divided by two narrow lanes of shops, and it continues to be a center of shopping and dining for Venetian locals and tourists. With glass shops, stores stocked with souvenirs, athletic apparel sellers, trendy boutiques, and *haute couture*, the shopping options on the Rialto Bridge offer something for almost anyone. Those who grow tired of browsing should enjoy the vantage point from the bridge's high point, which affords the city's best view of the Grand Canal. Facing north, you'll be able to see some of Venice's best-preserved *palazzi*, while facing south you're sure to be graced with breathtaking visions of the San Marco and San Polo waterfront and gondolas docked along the canal. Those seeking the perfect picture of the bridge should head south on San Marco from the Rialto Bridge, cross two smaller waterfront bridges, and then take a snapshot that captures Rialto's entire span.

🎏 *From anywhere in the city, follow the bright yellow signs that say Per Rialto and you will eventually make it to the bridge.*

the grand canal

The best introduction to the city of Venice may be a ride along the Grand Canal, the 4km waterway that is the main thoroughfare for most of Venice's **boat traffic.** Though many tourists opt to experience the canal via gondola ride, most budget travelers making their way through Italy in smaller groups will find the cost of such a trip, even with the most reasonably priced gondoliers, a bit steep. A much-overlooked option is to hop on the vaporetto Line 2 *(€6.50 per ride)* with a guidebook and take in some of the major sights of Venice from there. Granted, your watery carriage can get a bit crowded, and locals making their way to and from work aren't likely to be enthusiastic about conspicuous tourists in their presence, but if you get on mid-morning when it's not too busy, you'll be able to both admire the facades of Venice's gorgeous *palazzi* with ease and familiarize yourself with the city, for a fraction of what it would cost you to do so on a gondola ride. Whatever transport you opt for, you shouldn't miss an opportunity to see the city from its unique waterways. Since most of Venice's main attractions are located either along the banks of the Grand Canal or the lagoon, standing on *terra firma,* you just can't gain the same appreciation for the majesty of this maritime city as you can when floating on its waters.

venice

🏛 FRARI

🚶♿ CHURCH

Campo dei Frari 3072   ☎041 52 22 637 🖥www.basilicadeifrari.it

From the outside, Basilica di Santa Maria Gloriosa dei Frari might look like it belongs more in the industrial section of **Giudecca** than in the pantheon of Venice's great churches, but if you make it inside this rough, foreboding brick structure you'll be awestruck by one of the city's largest and most spectacular churches. Second only to the **Basilica di San Marco** in size, the Frari houses numerous notable works by famous artists such as **Bellini** and **Titian** as well as remarkably well-preserved wooden seating that once cradled the bottoms of Venetian nobility and several spectacular mausoleums dedicated to the church's early patrons. The church is large enough to have several smaller rooms that function as museums of the church history and house frescoes, stonework, and historical golden artifacts. Unlike most churches in Venice, which can take just a couple of minutes for the typical tourist to enjoy, it can take an hour to fully appreciate the artistic subtleties of the Frari. The numerous altars are all masterpieces in their own rights, while the mausoleums are a spectacular display of Venice's artistic prowess as well as the egotism and incredible wealth that characterized the city's elite throughout most of its history. Though the church is a spectacular sight to visit at any time of day, try to make it near opening or closing, when there are fewer tour groups around. At these times, every footstep that hits the church's stone floor can be heard echoing under its towering arches, and its serene beauty can be best appreciated.

⚑ *V: Campo San Tomà. Proceed straight until you reach a T intersection, turn right, make the 1st left, and continue to the square; the entrance to the church is immediately ahead.* ⓢ *€2.50, with Chorus Pass free. Audio tour €2.* ⏲ *Open M-Sa 9am-6pm, Su 1-6pm.*

SCUOLA GRANDE DI SAN ROCCO   ⚐⊗ MUSEUM

Campo di San Rocco 3054   ☎041 52 34 864 ▪www.scuolagrandesanrocco.it

Home to some of Tintoretto's greatest works as well as canvases by **Titian**, Scuola Grande di San Rocco is not as extensive as many other galleries in Venice, but its works are every bit as impressive. Originally designed as a place for laypersons of the Catholic faith to meet and promote various acts of religious piety, the Scuola has been preserved primarily as an art museum, and though the displays are small, the collection is well-organized and quite accessible to visitors. Anyone who has spent hours craning their necks to admire paintings on the ceilings of Venetian museums, *palazzi*, and churches will appreciate the mirrors provided for examining Tintoretto's magnificent religious scenes painted on the second-floor ceiling. ⚑ *From Campo dei Frari, walk to the west end of the church, turn right, and follow the signs north toward San Rocco. The school is on the left.* ⓢ *€7, students €5, under 18 €3.* ⏲ *Open daily 9:30am-5:30pm. Last entry 30min. before close.*

CAMPO SAN POLO   ♿ PIAZZA

Campo San Polo

As Venice's second-largest public square—you may have heard of the largest, **Piazza San Marco**—Campo San Polo is the default winner of the award for largest Venetian square that doesn't spend half its time under a flood of seawater or tourist traffic. It's also home to some of the city's most important events, including outdoor concerts, screenings for the **Venice Film Festival,** and numerous pre-Lenten festivities during Carnevale. During major events, the square is transformed from a quiet, open space housing a few street vendors and gelato stands into the Venetian equivalent of an amphitheater, packed with tourists and locals enjoying some of the best partying Venice has to offer. Events hosted in Campo San Polo tend to be well-publicized and draw crowds from the Veneto mainland as well as many international arrivals.

Even if there aren't any major events going on in Campo San Polo while you're visiting Venice, this historic square deserves a visit. Formerly the site of bullfights and religious services, the square is now quiet most days and home to several small restaurants and cafes. It's worth spending some time looking

sights • san polo

at San Polo's historic buildings, including the **Palazzo Tiepolo Passi,** a 16th-century palace that has been converted into a hotel, and the **Chiesa di San Polo,** which houses several works by **Giovanni Tiepolo.**

🚶 From the Rialto Bridge, walk through the markets along Ruga dei Oresi, turn left onto Rughetta del Ravano, continue for approximately 4min., and you'll arrive at Campo San Polo.

SANTA CROCE

👍 MUSEUM OF NATURAL HISTORY — 💳♿ MUSEUM

Santa Croce 1730 ☎041 27 50 206 💻www.museicivicivenezianі.it

Venice's Museum of Natural History is one of those rare museums that can be as much fun for adults as it is for children. Unlike many Venetian museums, which house great collections that are presented devoid of context in empty *palazzi*, the Museum of Natural History almost seems like a museum of modern art when you first enter. Fossils hewn into simulated archeological sites rather than housed in glass cases successfully draw the visitor more into the museum experience. Rooms detailing the history of earlier life forms build up the ambience with judicious use of theatrical lighting, while the quiet primordial soundtrack is as entertaining on its own as anything the museum houses. A full visit to the museum takes 30-60min. and may take even less time for visitors who aren't able to read Italian, since information about the exhibits is displayed in only the one language.

🚶 V: San Stae. Continue down Salizada San Stae, make the 1st right that leads to a bridge, continue straight across 2 bridges, then make the 2nd possible right, and continue until you reach the museum. It will be difficult to find, but if you follow the signs to Fontego dei Turchi, you will get there. $ €4.50, students ages 15-25, ages 6-14, over 65, and holders of the Rolling Venice Card €3, under 6 and holders of the Civic Museums pass free. ⏰ Open W 9am-5pm, Sa-Su 10am-6pm. Last entry 1hr. before close.

CA' PESARO — 💳♿ MUSEUM

Santa Croce 2070 ☎041 72 11 27 💻www.museicivicivenezianі.it

Though in most cities Ca' Pesaro would be deserving of a 👍**thumbpick,** the otherwise spectacular museum is just one of many impressive modern and contemporary art collections in Venice. This museum features an interesting mix of paintings and sculpture—mostly from the late 19th and early 20th centuries—that chronicles the development of modern art as a transnational movement. As one of Venice's more famous art museums, Ca' Pesaro has the added advantage of hosting frequent temporary exhibitions, which generally feature pieces from the mid- to late 19th century and tend to be more lowbrow, general-interest affairs than the more esoteric exhibits in its permanent collection. Even those left unimpressed by the art can still marvel at the *palazzo*'s intact ceilings, which far too many visitors miss completely. Others may explore the second floor's gallery of East Asian artwork. Though this exhibit is not nearly as well-presented as the first floor's modern art gallery, the assemblage of Japanese ornamental weaponry accompanied by informational videos about the extensive decorating process is far different from anything else you'll find in Venice.

🚶 V: San Stae. Exit the church square left (facing away from the Grand Canal), cross the 1st bridge possible, continue straight, make the 1st possible left, and you should see the entrance to the museum. There will also be signs indicating the direction toward the museum. $ €6.50, students ages 15-25, ages 6-14, over 65, and holders of the Rolling Venice Card €4, under 6 and holders of the Civic Museums pass free. ⏰ Open Tu-Su Apr-Oct 10am-6pm; Nov-Mar 10am-5pm. Last entry 1hr. before close.

DORSODURO

👍 THE PEGGY GUGGENHEIM COLLECTION — 💳♿ MUSEUM

Dorsoduro 704 ☎041 24 05 411 💻www.guggenheim.org

When you walk into a museum and the first room features works by Miró,

Picasso, Dalí, and Magritte, you know it's exceptional. The Peggy Guggenheim Collection is a great museum to visit, both for art aficionados and for those who think of karate-kicking turtles when they hear the names of Leonardo, Michelangelo, Donatello, and Raphael. The collection is a relatively small one that includes notable works from almost every major movement of the late 19th and early 20th centuries. It comprises works that notable traveler Guggenheim collected during her lifetime, and thus contains pieces that hail from all over Europe and the Americas. Her assortment of artwork emphasizes the international character of art produced during this period while retaining a certain Venetian flair: a substantial number of works are by Venetian and Italian artists. Even if you have no interest in artwork, the *palazzo* itself is well worth the price of admission. Its immaculately maintained gardens and house make it one of the most beautiful *palazzi* in all of Venice.

✦ From Santa Maria della Salute, follow the signs west towards the Guggenheim Museum for approximately 4min. ⑤ €12, students €7, seniors €10. ⌚ Open M 10am-6pm, W-Su 10am-6pm. Last entry 5:45pm.

▨ BASILICA DI SANTA MARIA DELLA SALUTE   ⊛ CHURCH
Campo della Salute   ☎041 52 25 558

Don't make the mistake of contenting yourself with views of Santa Maria della Salute across the water from P. San Marco. While the vision of the sun setting behind the church is incredible, the sanctuary itself is just as impressive—and equally free to enjoy. Santa Maria della Salute, built between 1631 and 1687, was intended to be an homage to the Virgin Mary, who many Venetians believed was capable of protecting them from the ravages of the plague. Since 1629 marked the last great outbreak of the plague in Venice, it is unclear whether the church's construction did anything to end the spread of the disease. Regardless, the church stands today as an architectural and aesthetic wonder, with its innovative dome remaining perhaps the most recognizable sight in Venice. Paintings by Tintoretto and Titian highlight the interior of the church, which also features numerous statues, arches, columns, and altars that have led some to call Santa Maria della Salute the most beautiful church in Venice.

✦ From the Ponte dell'Accademia, turn left and continue to the eastern tip of Dorsoduro (approximately 6-8min.). ⌚ Open daily 9am-noon and 3-5:30pm.

PUNTA DELLA DOGANA   ✦♿❄ MUSEUM
Fondamenta della Dogana alla Salute 2   ☎041 52 31 680 ▤www.palazzograssi.it

A new museum by the über-chic François Pinault, the Punta della Dogana-Palazzo Grassi complex is an absolute must-see for anyone with an interest in contemporary art. Simultaneously more interactive, more accessible, and more intimidating than any conventional art museum, Punta della Dogana features artwork that is visceral, graphic, and that blurs the distinctions between low and high art—even in a country famed for its Renaissance celebration of the human form, you'd be hard-pressed to find a museum with more phallic representations. A great complement to the collection of earlier works found in the Accademia and the assortment of modernist art featured in the Guggenheim, Punta della Dogana's collection of contemporary art is one of the most impressive in Italy. Due to the combined entry fee, it is especially worth seeing if you also plan to check out the **Palazzo Grassi** in San Marco.

✦ From the Ponte dell'Accademia, turn left and continue to the eastern tip of Dorsoduro for 6-8min. ⑤ €15, with affiliated Palazzo Grassi in San Marco €20. ⌚ Open M 10am-7pm, W-Su 10am-7pm. Last entry 1hr. before close.

THE ACCADEMIA   ✦♿ MUSEUM
Campo della Carità   ☎041 52 00 345 ▤www.gallerieaccademia.org

Venice's premier museum for pre-19th-century art, the Accademia is currently

sights · dorsoduro

undergoing extensive renovations that limit the number of visitors it can accommodate daily. These renovations have also changed the museum layout, but the Accademia still remains chock-full of important Italian art. Unlike the **Peggy Guggenheim Collection** or **Punta della Dogana**, which feature relatively few works, the Accademia is home to a substantial collection that will likely leave most casual visitors overwhelmed. Nonetheless, there are several truly awe-inspiring works to be found in its hallways, and there is perhaps no better place than the Accademia to enjoy Venice from an artistic perspective, as many of the works featured represent scenes and sights that will be familiar to travelers who have already spent a few days in the city.

⇄ Immediately across the Ponte dell'Accademia from San Marco. $ €6.50, EU citizens 18-25 €3.25, EU citizens under 18 and over 65 free. ⏰ Open M 8:15am-2pm, Tu-Su 8:15am-7:15pm.

GESUATI ⊗ CHURCH

Fondamenta delle Zattere ai Gesuati 917 ☎041 27 50 462 💻www.chorusvenezia.org

One of Venice's more modern churches, the Gesuati church (also known as Santa Maria del Rosario) was not completed until 1755 and thus reflects a more modern, majestic style than many others within the city. The altars, ceilings, and beautiful natural lighting distinguish Gesuati from other Venetian churches. Its highlights include paintings by Tintoretto and Tiepolo, which make spending a half hour or longer wandering Gesuati's nave very easy to do. You spent enough money to make it to Venice—don't get miserly over the €2.50 entrance fee like so many other tourists. There's no need to resign yourself to pressing your face against the entryway window for 20sec.—drop the cash and enjoy one of Venice's most beautiful churches.

⇄ V: Zattere. Directly across from stop. $ €2.50, with Chorus Pass free. ⏰ Open M-Sa 10am-5pm, Su 1-5pm.

PONTE DELL'ACCADEMIA ⊗ BRIDGE

Over the Grand Canal

Perhaps the most underappreciated bridge in Venice, the Ponte dell'Accademia, though quaint when compared with the Rialto Bridge's grandeur, is not without its own unique charm. While many locals would have preferred a stone bridge over the Ponte's wooden construction, this design choice has made it a less conspicuous (and therefore less-touristed) sight—a welcome step back from the mercantile overcrowding that makes the Rialto nearly impossible to navigate on busy days. With better views of the Grand Canal than perhaps any other bridge in the city, access to **San Marco** that avoids its busy eponymous *piazza*, and quieter cafes, Ponte dell'Accademia is absolutely worth seeing.

⇄ V: Zattere. Turn right, make the 1st possible left, and continue past the Accademia to the end of the street at the Grand Canal, where the bridge is located. $ Free.

SAN SEBASTIANO ⊗ CHURCH

Campo San Sebastiano ☎041 27 50 462 💻www.chorusvenezia.org

Before you visit Venice, it might be a good idea to make a long list of churches you want to see. There are a lot. If you are an art aficionado, put this one, perhaps the city's brightest and most colorful, pretty high up. San Sebastiano is home to *History of Esther*, one of Paolo Veronese's most famous works. Despite maintaining the monochromatic, plain facade typical of most Venetian churches, San Sebastiano has an interior decked out with beautiful and historically significant paintings which are as much of a draw as the building itself. In other respects, the edifice is quite similar to the other churches that populate nearly every street corner of the floating city.

⇄ Walk east along Fondamenta delle Zattere until it ends; go right, continue past 1 bridge, and turn left onto the 2nd bridge. $ €2.50, with Chorus Pass free. ⏰ Open M-Sa 10am-5pm, Su 1-5pm.

islands of the lagoon

The islands in the lagoon surrounding Venice are often given short shrift by travelers on tight schedules, but they have played a vital role in Venetian history and remain fascinating to this day. If you have a couple of hours of free time and the foresight to plot a good vaporetto route from island to island, you can visit a half-dozen of them with relative ease. The one thing shared by the islands is their ability to retain distinct identities. The major islands remain strikingly different from one another and proud of their independent cultural and historical legacies. Some are strongly provincial and have generally eschewed economic diversification, while others have maintained a strong sense of local community despite being subject to change and turmoil. Many are still virtually uninhabited. Visitors tend to have mixed feeling about the islands of the Venetian Lagoon, some considering them not worth the time or trouble, others maintaining that the islands are the main reason to visit the city. If you want a complete overview of the city of Venice, get on a 🚤 **boat** and explore the myriad opportunities the lagoon offers.

🏖 LIDO

Once the world's most popular beach resort, Lido is largely forgotten by the 20 million travelers who visit Venice annually. Though the island's beautiful and historic hotels still fill up each summer, it's now a quiet counterpart to the city center rather than the main draw for international travelers. As a result, visitors to the island can enjoy scenic bike rides along the coastline, strolls along gorgeous tree-lined streets, and sun-bathing spots on one of its eastern coast's pristine (if occasionally crowded) beaches—all without too much trouble. Since the vaporetto #1 line regularly makes stops at the island, and frequent ferries run from Piazzale Roma, the seeming wall between Lido and the city center is more of a psychological barrier than anything else. If you're in San Marco or eastern Castello, you can easily make a quick 3hr. trip to Lido and see a lot of the island without difficulty.

GRAND VIALE

♿ PROMENADE

Grand Vle.

This famous promenade cuts from eastern Lido—with its majestic hotels and fine restaurants—to the western portion of the island, where you'll find miles of sandy shoreline, gorgeous beach resorts, and the glamorous theaters and hotels that support Lido's annual film festival. A walk along the Grand Viale can take as little as 15min. or as long as several hours, depending on how intent you are on enjoying the sights. Since Lido was largely uninhabited until the 20th century, it lacks the grandly historic character that distinguishes Venice, but you'd never mistake it for a Hawaiian or Caribbean resort community. Walking along the Grand Viale, you'll experience Lido as a resort town worthy of an F. Scott Fitzgerald novel, with beautiful hotels that feature towering columns, breathtaking mosaic facades, and a spectacularly anachronistic sense of Old World aristocracy. If you make it to the eastern side of the island and turn right onto Lungomare Gabriele D'Annuzio, you'll see what may be Lido's most impressive sight, the grandiose and slightly preposterous **Grand Hotel des Bains** (the setting of Thomas Mann's novella *Death in Venice*), which still annually hosts the most impressive gathering of celebrities this side of Cannes during Venice's own film festival.

🚶 *From dock Santa Maria Elizabetta, walk straight ahead. The Grand Viale runs east-west.*

sights • lido

SPIAGGE DI VENEZIA

BEACH

Piazzale Ravà ☎041 52 61 249 www.veneziaspiagge.it

With hotels limiting access to a lot of the prime stretches of **beach** in Lido, just spending a day on the shore can end up costing over €50 per person simply for chairs, umbrellas, and towels. Spiagge di Venezia—which manages two popular stretches of beach in Lido—is the more budget-conscious option if you want to soak up the sun without spending too much cash. You could certainly rack up the charges with food, drinks, a changing room, and umbrella and chair, but none of these are necessary to enjoy Lido's magnificent sandy expanses and pristine waters.

From dock Lido San Nicolò, go east on V. Giannantonio Selva for 6-8min. and you'll reach the Spiagge. $ Beach free. Umbrella and chair €12. Private changing room €23. Open daily 9am-7pm.

GIUDECCA

Giudecca, technically a part of Dorsoduro but separated from the neighborhood by the Giudecca Canal, is the most easily accessible of the lagoon islands, as the vaporetto #2 line zigzags the Giudecca Canal and makes several stops on the island. A €2 ticket for crossing the Giudecca canal supposedly exists, but the vaporetto operators *Let's Go* spoke with said they didn't care if we hopped on for one stop free of charge. Thanks, guys! In recent years there has been talk of constructing a tunnel between Dorsoduro and Giudecca, but it appears no such plans will be implemented in the foreseeable future. Giudecca seems to have a rather cyclical history. It was first inhabited by wealthy families who claimed a preference for large estates with gardens but were really being pressured to leave the city due to political controversy. The lack of large-scale residential development on the island later made Giudecca the center of the city's early 20th-century industrial boom, and for a time, the island produced the vast majority of commercial boats used in the city. After WWII, Giudecca lacked viable industry and fell into disrepair but is completing the cycle again with the development of upscale housing and hotels. Though Giudecca is coming back into fashion, its industrial history remains an influence: the island's most prominent landmark and one of Venice's most prestigious hotels, **The Molino Stucky Hilton,** is located in a former granary and flourmill which retains a sternly industrial exterior despite its interior's refinement and elegance.

IL REDENTORE

CHURCH

Campo S.S. Redentore 195 ☎041 27 50 462 www.chorusvenezia.org

One of Venice's most celebrated churches, Il Redentore is by far the biggest attraction on Giudecca. The church, which was constructed to give thanks for divine deliverance from the plague (perhaps a bit prematurely) in 1577, is considered one of **Andrea Palladio's** greatest works, displaying his acute awareness of proportion in architectural design. Inside the church, paintings from some of the city's greatest artists, including **Saraceni, Veronese,** and **Tintoretto** hang, underscoring the prominence of the church in Venetian society. So highly regarded was Palladio's masterpiece that it gave rise to its own festival, the **Festa del Redentore,** which began as an annual political procession from the **Doge's Palace** to the church and, though now largely devoid of religious sentiment, continues to be celebrated every third weekend in July.

Take vaporetto line #2 to Redentore; the church is immediately ahead. $ €2.50, with Chorus Pass free. Elevator to campanile €4. Open M-Sa 10am-5pm. Last entry 15min. before close.

MURANO

Known colloquially as "The Glass Island," Murano is one of the largest lagoon islands and has been the center of Venice's glass industry since the 13th century, when concerns about the possibility of fires in the city center led politicians to ban glass production. Of course, safety concerns never stopped enterprising Venetians from *selling* the glass anywhere, and buyers of the stuff are everywhere (see **Venetian Glass and Lace**). Nevertheless, Murano remains the glass headquarters of Venice. Though the large brick buildings, open kilns, and occasional abandoned workshops give the island a slightly gritty industrial feel, it also features a few beautiful tree-shaded streets with glass shops displaying the work of the island's top artisans. If you spend more than a few minutes exploring Murano, you're almost certain to find a *fornace* in operation where you can see some of the world's most talented artisans practicing their craft. If you're lucky, you might even find a studio that lets visitors try their hand at glass blowing. Travel times to Murano vary, but expect to spend at least 30min. getting there by vaporetto lines #41, 42, or LN, which are generally the most accessible options.

MUSEO DEL VETRO — 🎟 🚫♿ MUSEUM

Fondamenta Giustinian 8 — ☎041 73 95 86 💻www.museicivicivenezani.it

Anyone with enough interest in artisan glass to visit Murano shouldn't leave without checking out the Museo del Vetro, which traces the development of Murano's glass industry from its earliest stages to the present day. The museum features several exceptional pieces, both contemporary and historical, that reflect the ways in which glass has been historically used both practically and aesthetically. Though the collection is impressive, the real draw is the wing dedicated to glass production that gives an overview of how different glasses are made and the minerals that are used to give the material its different colors and textures. Don't miss the museum garden and its fascinating artifacts.

➡ V: Museo (accessible by lines R, 41, 42, N, and DM). Follow the signs to the museum. $ €6.50, students ages 15-25, ages 4-14 and over 65, and Rolling Venice Card holders €4. Admission included in Civic Museums Pass. ⏰ Open daily Apr-Oct 10am-6pm; Nov-Mar 10am-5pm. Last entry 30min. before close.

BASILICA DI SANTA MARIA E SAN DONATO — ♿ CHURCH

Calle San Donato 11 — ☎041 73 90 56

A unique church, Murano's Basilica contrasts sharply with the Renaissance architecture that you'll find throughout Venice and Italy as a whole. With distinct Byzantine influences in its exterior, elaborate arches, and strong geometric patterns, the Basilica embodies Eastern influences that have profoundly shaped the development of Venetian culture and society. The floors within the church, comprised of thousands upon thousands of jewel-like tiles, are incredibly intricate and some of the city's most breathtaking mosaics. What really sets the church apart, though, are the two displays near the altar. The first, a giant glass cross that symbolizes Murano's pride in its local industry, outshines practically every other glass trinket you'll find on the island. The second, probably Venice's most unusual church display, is a collection of bones reputed to be the remains of a **dragon** killed by the church's namesake, Saint Donatus of Arezzo. The bones, which are over 1m long each, have never been definitively identified and remain a source of wild speculation.

➡ V: Museo (accessible by lines R, 41, 42, N, and DM). Walk past the museum along the canal for about 2min.; the church is ahead on the left. $ Free. ⏰ Open daily 8am-7pm.

BURANO

Burano—about an hour away from Venice by vaporetto lines LN and N—is a relatively small island best known for its handmade lace production and fishing industry. Visitors to Burano almost inevitably stop in Murano first, since that island is on the way from Venice, and are consistently surprised at the contrast between the two. Whereas Murano is populated by brick and stone buildings and is almost as devoid of vegetation as Venice, Burano boasts several large parks, lots of open space, and famously colorful houses. Originally, at least according to legend, the fishermen of the island painted their homes ostentatious shades of blue, pink, red, green, yellow, and orange so that each could readily identify his home from a distance when returning to the island, and the fantastically colorful homes have evolved into a Burano trademark. While this tradition is now somewhat obsolete given technological improvements in nautical navigation, lace production in Burano continues in much the same fashion that it has for centuries. Though you can shop for Burano-style lace in Venice (see **Venetian Glass and Lace**), Burano itself is the best place to find a wide selection of lace goods that are guaranteed to be handmade. Be forewarned, however, that the lace production process is labor-intensive, and that labor will be reflected in the price of pretty much anything you buy. Even if you're not shopping for lace, it's still absolutely worth paying a visit to Burano. An hour or two of wandering will bring you to the beautiful **Church of San Martino** and its infamous leaning campanile; the **Lace Museum** *(P. Galuppi 187 ☎041 73 00 34),* which is returning in 2011 after an almost year-long sabbatical; and some of the most beautiful and whimsical buildings in all of Venice.

TORCELLO

Accessible by vaporetto line N and a ferry (T) from Burano, Torcello isn't the easiest island to get to but definitely rewards those who make the effort. Though the island—the first settlement in the lagoon—was once home to over 20,000 people, from the 12th to the 15th centuries it was largely abandoned as the lagoon surrounding it became a swamp. Torcello is now home to only a few dozen people managing a couple of restaurants, a hotel, and the scant attractions that bring tourists to the island. Walking around this bit of land can be a surreal experience; it's hard to comprehend that this largely abandoned and overgrown island once was home to the largest population center of the Venetian Republic. So few relics remain.

CATHEDRAL OF SANTA MARIA ASSUNTA ⊘ ⊘ CHURCH

Isola di Torcello ☎041 27 02 464

Founded over 13 centuries ago, the Cathedral of Santa Maria Assunta offers a strong reminder of the thriving community that once existed on Torcello. It's definitely not worth making the trip all the way out to Torcello just for this small church, but as an example of the eclecticism in Venice's early places of worship, its mosaics and incredible rendering of the Last Judgment are engaging. The campanile, once abandoned, is again in operation and affords the best view of the northern lagoon you'll find anywhere. Also affiliated with the cathedral are the smaller churches of **Santa Fosca** and **Museo di Torcello,** both of which are sure to fascinate any visitors intrigued by the strange history of Venice's abandoned island.

⇄ From the island's only vaporetto stop, follow the path to the island's only substantial settlement. It's a 7-10min. walk; just look for the tower in the distance. $ Church €4. Campanile €4. Both €7.50. ⏰ Open daily Mar-Oct 10:30am-6pm; Nov-Feb 10am-5pm.

food

As you might expect in a city visited by over 20,000,000 tourists each year, Venice has no shortage of restaurants. Almost all are receptive to international travelers and offer English-language menus and service, particularly those where the tourist industry is centered.

Since visitors to Venice range from international celebrities to student backpackers, most restaurants try to accommodate all tastes and budgets. Even in the most upscale Venetian restaurants, you should typically be able to get a pizza for less than €10.

That being said, a few restaurants in prime locations bank on being able to overcharge hungry tourists who don't have the energy to look beyond the first place they see. Avoid suffering a less-than-memorable *and* expensive meal and do a bit of comparison shopping before settling on an eatery. Also take note of whether you should expect a service charge. These should be written on the menu of most establishments that have one. While common, the service charge can come as an unpleasant surprise.

Most restaurants in Venice serve food typical of the Veneto region, which shouldn't offer any particular surprises for travelers familiar with the basics of Italian cuisine. Risotto, beans, and polenta are particularly popular here. Menus tend to be rather

grocery greatness: part 1

Since pretty much every hotel in Venice is "breakfast included," but most are about as liberal with croissants and cereal as they are with Wi-Fi, expect your morning sustenance to consist of little more than a roll with Nutella (maybe some orange juice if the management is feeling magnanimous). At a grocery store, however, you can get fresh fruit and bread, both more substantial than what most hotels offer for breakfast. Plus, purchasing them at the grocery store means you don't have to get up at 8:30am.

When grocery shopping in Venice, you have two options: supermarkets or smaller local stores. Here are the pros and cons of supermarkets.

PROS

1) Supermarkets tend to have a greater selection. Back home, this probably means more choice and better value. In Venice, this means getting to laugh at absurd products like Durex Jeans, a brand of condom whose marketers apparently failed to consider the uncomfortable implications of comparing their particular product to another with the texture of denim.

2) The music. America brought the world Isis, MC Hammer, and Michael Jackson, but you have to travel halfway around the world to hear music of that quality blasting in a supermarket.

3) Many Italian supermarkets stock incredible fresh baked goods, Italian cheeses, and more kinds of sliced deli meat than you knew existed. This can quickly become a "con" if going home looking like Marlon Brando in the mid-'90s isn't part of your travel plans.

CONS

1) Really, really long check-out lines. If you're buying a six-pack of Birra Moretti, expect it to be a three-pack, at best, by the time you get out.

2) You shouldn't even try to speak English with the check-out-counter employees, who don't appreciate delays while trying to keep lines manageable. If you do make the attempt, they will probably look at you with about as much contempt as they would if you had just propositioned them with a box of Durex Jeans.

3) Familiar brands aren't always what they seem. You might think you can guess what the Italian on your box of soap means, but you'll be playing with fire. Don't make the same mistake as one *Let's Go* researcher, who spent two weeks washing his hair with what turned out to be women's body wash. You, too, could reap the benefits of delightful added volume, but the extra scent might be a bit overbearing...

food

seafood-heavy, but pasta, chicken, and steak are also fairly standard offerings. Pizza, of course, is a staple of almost every dining establishment. Since the tradition of eating cat in Northern Italy has been banned, there shouldn't be anything too troubling on the menu for English-speaking tourists, with the possible exceptions of squid-ink pasta *(nero di seppia)* and **horse** meat *(cavallo)*, which aren't too common. For students really looking to save time and money, sandwich shops, snack bars, kebab shops, and small pizzerias often offer decent and reasonably filling meals, including a drink, for less than €6.

SAN MARCO

Like most things in San Marco, dining tends to be expensive and upscale. You'll find some of Venice's best restaurants here, but they tend to be some of the priciest as well. Despite this trend, there are a surprising number of restaurants that offer great values, particularly if you're willing to trek a couple blocks away from P. San Marco and the Rialto Bridge.

🏛 TRATTORIA PIZZERIA AI FABBRI ⬢♿♥❀ TRATTORIA, PIZZERIA ❸
Calle dei Fabbri 4717 ☎041 52 08 085

An eclectic pizzeria that cooks up more than just your conventional margherita and *quattro formaggi* varieties, Pizzeria Ai Fabbri is distinguished by a high degree of culinary creativity, evident in their unusual appetizers (including sumptuous duck dumplings) and wide selection of side dishes that wouldn't find their way onto a typical Venetian menu. Though a flatscreen TV by the entrance tuned into news or soccer matches gives the restaurant a bit of a bar-like feel, those who would prefer a quiet meal in the back dining room can enjoy the same excellent menu in a more serene setting.

🍴 *Go through the St. Mark's Clock Tower, turn left, continue to Calle dei Fabbri, and continue for 2-3min.; the restaurant is on the right.* ⓢ *Entrees €7.50-23.* 🕐 *Open daily 11am-midnight.*

🏛 BISTROT DE VENISE ⬢♿♥❀🍴 RISTORANTE ❹
Calle dei Fabbri ☎041 52 36 651 ▣www.bistrotdevenise.com

With an innovative menu that features historic recipes citing origins in the 16th century (which appears to be when the restaurant won its first award, given the incredible number of honors it has since racked up), Bistrot de Venise specializes in traditional Venetian food prepared to the absolute highest standard. Though the sticker shock might dissuade some budget travelers, if you want a world-class meal in San Marco, you won't find anything nearly this good for anything less.

🍴 *Go through the St. Mark's Clock Tower, turn left, continue to Calle dei Fabbri, and continue for about 2min.; the restaurant is on the right.* ⓢ *Entrees €18-28.* 🕐 *Open M-Th noon-3pm and 7pm-midnight, F-Sa noon-3pm and 7pm-1am, Su noon-3pm and 7pm-midnight.*

RISTORANTE NOEMI ⬢♿♥❀🍴 RISTORANTE ❺
Calle dei Fabbri 912 ☎041 52 25 238 ▣www.ristorantenoemi.com

For those of you craving a steak or some veal after weeks spent subsisting on a carb-heavy Italian diet, Ristorante Noemi should make its way onto your radar, as it is reputed to serve up some of the best grilled food in Venice. Affiliated with the upscale Hotel Noemi but catering to a clientele that goes beyond the hotel's guests, this restaurant offers high-quality traditional Venetian food at respectable prices, especially if you manage to avoid the temptation to order the menu's highest-priced items.

🍴 *Go through the St. Mark's Clock Tower, turn left, continue to Calle dei Fabbri, and continue 2min.; the restaurant is on the right.* ⓢ *Entrees €8-34.* 🕐 *Open daily 11:30am-midnight.*

ACQUA PAZZA ⬢♿♥❀🍴 SEAFOOD ❺
Campo San Angelo 3808 ☎041 27 70 688 ▣www.veniceacquapazza.it

Acqua Pazza, roughly translated as "Crazy Waters," is both the name and the motif of this fine restaurant near San Marco's two modern art museums. Featuring excellent seafood and bizarre, though amusing, aquatically inspired decor—Acqua Pazza is just as sweet as it is salty—its €12 house desserts are some of the best confections Venice has to offer.

⇄ From Teatro La Fenice, continue northwest on Calle de la Verona for less than 2min., take the 1st left after crossing a bridge, take the next right, and take the next left; the restaurant is in Campo San Angelo. ℹ Men are required to wear long pants to dinner. Ⓢ Entrees €18-35. ⏰ Open daily noon-3pm and 7pm-11pm.

BAR MIO
💳♿🍸 SNACK BAR [1]

Frezzeria 1176

If you're feeling bold, try to claim a spot at Venice's most heavily trafficked snack bar. You'll be rewarded with a sandwich crisped to perfection—though never overheated—at a pleasantly low price. You're unlikely to see any other tourists in Bar Mio, but that doesn't mean the place is starving for business. The incredibly efficient employees don't have a moment's rest from opening to close, as locals constantly stream in for first-class coffee and sandwiches.

⇄ Exit the southwest corner of P. San Marco, opposite Basilica di San Marco, and take 1st right onto Frezzeria; the restaurant is less than 1min. ahead on the right. Ⓢ Sandwiches €4.50-7. ⏰ Open daily 6:30am-9pm.

RISTORANTE ANIMA BELLA
💳♿🍸 RISTORANTE [3]

Calle Fiubera 956 ☎041 52 27 486

A quirky and small restaurant that bills itself as a combination *ristorante*, pizzeria, and grill, Anima Bella is more reminiscent of the dining room in a typical Italian villa than a tourist-filled restaurant in San Marco. Since Anima Bella tends to focus on relatively few dishes prepared exceptionally well, you could order anything off the menu without regretting it. However, while everything here is prepared with care, you could eat ravioli for weeks in Venice and find none that match the quality you'll get at Anima Bella.

⇄ Exit P. San Marco beneath St. Mark's Clock Tower, take 1st possible left onto a street with a bridge and cross the bridge; the restaurant is on the right. Ⓢ Entrees €8-20. ⏰ Open daily 11am-10pm.

RISTORANTE AL COLOMBO
💳♿🍸❄⛱ RISTORANTE [5]

Corte del Teatro 4619 ☎041 52 22 627 💻www.alcolombo.com

Many upscale restaurants in San Marco offer similar menu items at equal prices, but none can match Ristorante Al Colombo's excellent patio, jovial service, and delightful Chateaubriand. Unlike many fine restaurants in San Marco whose excessive formality pushes them to the point of dourness, Ristorante Al Colombo isn't afraid to have a bit of fun. Case in point: the spectacular centerpieces arranged around national team soccer balls that one *Let's Go* researcher witnessed while visiting at the peak of World Cup fever.

⇄ From the Rialto Bridge, turn right and continue along Riva del Carbon for approximately 2min.; turn right onto Calle del Carbona and continue for 1min.; the restaurant is in the square. Ⓢ Entrees €16-45. ⏰ Open daily noon-midnight.

CANNAREGIO

As many great places as there are to eat in Cannaregio, there are just as many mediocre and touristy options. Stay away from the main streets and menus targeting out-of-towners, and you'll find some of the best cuisine Venice has to offer.

✔ RISTORANTE CASA BONITA
💳♿🍸⛱ RISTORANTE [3]

Fondamenta S. Giobbe 492 ☎041 52 46 164

One of the trickiest things about eating in Venice is that almost every restaurant claims to be authentically Venetian and displays a mouth-watering menu—then you walk in and realize that there are more Germans than Italians in the house. Casa Bonita is the rare Venetian restaurant that is both accessible from the main thoroughfares and genuinely Venetian. Often packed throughout the day, this restaurant caters to local tastes with excellent food in generous portions for a reasonable price. The canal-side outdoor seating is excellent, and the bar gives you any number of excuses to stay at your table and people-watch after your meal.

➜ From the train station, turn left and walk 5min. down Lista de Spagna. Immediately before Guglie Bridge, turn left and continue for 4min. $ Entrees €12-18. 🕐 Open Tu-Su 10am-3pm and 5:30pm-1am.

OSTERIA BOCCADORO VENEZIA 💳♿🍸🔔 RISTORANTE [5]

Campo Widmann 5405/A ☎041 52 11 021 💻www.boccadorovenezia.it

Unlike your typical Venetian restaurant, Osteria Boccadoro Venezia offers an haute-cuisine reinterpretation of the region's traditional foods. Although Osteria Boccadoro's prices may seem excessive, rest assured that its food merits the cost. The restaurant's minimalist, modern aesthetic might not match up to your standard idea of what a fine Venetian restaurant looks like, but in sacrificing a bit of tradition, this *osteria* has foregone nothing in terms of stomach-pleasing fare, winning over discerning locals and tourists alike with its quality dishes.

➜ Halfway along Calle Widmann. $ Entrees €20-28. 🕐 Open Tu-Su noon-2:30pm and 7-10:30pm.

TRATTORIA STORICA 💳♿🍸🔔 RISTORANTE [3]

Ponte dei Gesuiti 4858 ☎041 52 85 266 💻www.trattoriastorica.it

Trattoria Storica is an upscale, family-operated Venetian restaurant with exceptionally friendly service and great food. An excellent choice for anyone looking to savor a longer meal in a quieter section of Cannaregio, Storica offers generous portions that make for a very filling dinner, though you might consider splitting one of their dishes for lunch with a fellow traveler. With a helpful English-language menu, the restaurant does a great job welcoming foreigners without compromising its Venetian character.

➜ Exiting the Gesuiti to Campo dei Gesuiti, turn left and cross the bridge; Storica is on the left. $ Entrees €16-22 . 🕐 Open daily 11am-4pm and 7pm-midnight.

GAM GAM 🥦♿ KOSHER [3]

Canale di Cannaregio 1122 ☎041 71 52 84

Perhaps the premier kosher restaurant for the more-than 1000 Jewish residents of Venice, Gam Gam brings together traditional Italian kosher cooking (and if that phrase sounds like an oxymoron to you, you really should try out Gam Gam), Venetian cuisine, and newer Israeli culinary influences in a menu unlike any other you'll find in Venice. Although almost all of Gam Gam's patrons are Orthodox or Conservative Jews, this restaurant is also a great place for gentiles to experience Venice's small but remarkably vibrant Jewish community. Just make sure to call in advance, since the restaurant occasionally hosts private functions. That's not necessarily a reason to avoid the place, however, since if you look Jewish, you might just get invited in to sample some free food, as was one *Let's Go* Researcher-Writer. Also worth checking out is the affiliated dessert shop just a couple storefronts north.

➜ From Campo S. Geremia, cross the Guglie Bridge and turn left. $ Entrees €8-15. 🕐Open M-Th noon-10pm, F noon-4pm, Su noon-10pm.

PASTICCERIA MARTINI 🥦🚭🔔 BAKERY [1]

Rio Terà San Leonardo 1302 ☎041 71 73 75

At first glance, Pasticceria Martini is a lot like other pastry shops in Cannaregio, but once you try one of their croissants, you'll realize why so many residents pass by a half-dozen other pastry shops on their way here. The pastries (made fresh several times daily) are excellent, and several of their coffee options (including coffee with ginseng) are wildly popular. You can stop in here for a quick and tasty breakfast or lunch, but just try to resist walking away with a fat sack of Martini's mini-pastries, all sold by weight.

Just past the Guglie Bridge going North. $ Pastries €1. Coffee €1.50. Open daily 6am-9pm.

OSTERIA L'ORTO DEI MORI RISTORANTE ❹

Campo dei Mori ☎041 52 43 677

The best dining option near **Madonna dell'Orto,** Osteria L'Orto Dei Mori combines classic and modern aspects of Venetian identity remarkably well with its trendy-yet-traditional style. Its patio on the Campo dei Mori offers great views of one of the most architecturally fascinating squares in Cannaregio, and the tasteful, earth-tone colors of the dining room make eating inside an appealing option as well. An excellent choice for dinner, this restaurant is the perfect place a leisurely meal—at least, you'll feel that way until the check arrives.

Directly across the bridge from the Church Madonna dell'Orto. $ Entrees €14-23. Open M 12:30-3:30pm and 7pm-midnight, W-Su 12:30-3:30pm and 7pm-midnight.

NAVE DE ORO ENOTECA ❶

Rio Terà San Leonardo 1370 ☎041 71 96 95

Essential for any traveler seeking lots of alcohol for little money, the Nave De

grocery greatness: part 2

Since we've unloaded all our cheap jokes at the expense of supermarkets, it's now time to do exactly the same for local grocery stores. These are everywhere and range from small convenience stores to bakeries and *gelaterie* that also stock basic grocery items.

CONS

1) They're never open. You thought supermarkets had limited hours? Getting an audience with your local grocer is about as difficult as getting one with the pope.

2) Expiration dates can be dicey. Definitely remember that they're marked the European way–Day/Month/Year, not Month/Day/Year. You don't want to forget that when you're getting milk for your cereal, as some of us have found out the hard way.

3) These stores are small, and Italian customer service involves much more observation of customers than actual servicing of them. Expect uncomfortable moments.

PROS

1) Whereas chain stores tend to have set selections to keep up with their competitors, local stores are able to feature more variety in accordance with their owners' tastes. In most cases, this means more absinthe–a lot more.

2) They're a surprisingly good place to watch soccer matches. Sure, it might take 45min. to find someone willing to ring up your bottle of water and croissant, but if you're here, you're probably on vacation anyway–just enjoy the snapshot of Italian culture.

3) The owners tend to be really friendly, and if you're willing to chat, you're sure to get tips on some hidden Venetian gems, such as restaurants and cafes you would otherwise never visit. This can be problematic if one of these "hidden gems" happens to be a grandniece who just so happens to be your age ("You are about 30 years?"), speaks English "very good," and the owner would just love to introduce her to you.

Oro in Cannaregio is one of six locations in Venice where wine is sold by the liter and "BYOB" stands for bring your own (empty) bottle. Provided you have €2 and an empty bottle of any kind (yes, even an old water bottle will do), you can get a liter of one of the surprisingly good regional wines offered by the friendly and knowledgeable staff. Welcome to Venice—you know you're in Europe when the wine is less expensive than the water.

East of the Guglie Bridge along Rio Terà San Leonardo. [$] Wine €1.70-2.20 per L. ⏰ Open M-Sa 8am-1pm and 4:30-7:30pm.

SAN POLO

Along the Grand Canal, San Polo suffers from the same generic tourist cuisine that you'll find near all of Venice's sightseeing destinations, but if you manage to get away from the main drag around the Rialto a little bit, you'll be rewarded with the unique specialties and terrific ambience of Venice's best small restaurants.

ANTICO FORNO — PIZZERIA 2

Ruga Rialto 970/973 ☎041 52 04 110

Let's Go's top recommendation for pizza in Venice, Antico Forno makes standard pies with top-quality ingredients as well as adventurous vegetarian options (olives, a variety of peppers, feta cheese, etc.) and deep-dish pizza that will put anything from Chicago to shame. The price might seem a bit high for single slices, but a large piece of their perfectly crisped and seasoned deep-dish pizza is substantial enough to serve as a meal.

From Rialto Bridge, go straight ahead to Ruga Rialto and turn left onto Ruga Rialto; Antico Forno is ahead on the right. [$] Slices €2-3.50. ⏰ Open daily 11am-10pm.

CIOCCOLATERIA VIZIOVIRTÙ — CIOCCOLATERIA 1

Calle Balbi 2898 ☎041 27 50 149 www.viziovirtu.com

Venice's premiere chocolatier, Cioccolateria VizioVirtù crafts an incredible selection of creative, delicious, and (unfortunately) expensive chocolates in-house daily. While VizioVirtù does an excellent job with staples such as pralines, truffles, and baked goods, its mastery of the fine art of confectionery is best on display in its unconventional chocolates, including ones spiced up with red pepper, and replica Venetian masks that make great, site-specific gifts.

V: San Tomà. Walk straight until you reach a T intersection and turn left; the shop is on the right. [$] Various chocolate creations €1-2.50. ⏰ Open daily 10am-7:30pm.

OSTERIA NARANZARIA — RISTORANTE 4

Naranzaria 130 ☎041 72 41 035 www.naranzaria.it

Osteria Naranzaria is a trendy, international-style restaurant and lounge with a menu as diverse as its clientele. Without completely abandoning its Venetian roots, the restaurant takes risks, dishing up unusual items such as fresh sushi, supposedly the best of its kind available in the city. Naranzaria also tends to serve smaller portions, so it's a great place to have a light lunch by Rialto Bridge or enjoy some sushi and drinks before heading out for the night.

From Rialto Bridge, walk past San Giacomo, turn right, and cross the square; the restaurant is directly ahead. [$] Entrees €7-18. Sushi 10 pieces for €15. ⏰ Open Tu-Su noon-2am.

BIRRARIA LA CORTE — RISTORANTE 3

Campo San Polo 2168 ☎041 27 50 570 www.birrarialacorte.it

The top restaurant in Campo San Polo, Birraria la Corte boasts a pretty adventurous repertoire without abandoning the staples of every Italian menu. Two unconventional entrees it has perfected include buffalo steaks and chicken curry, both of which go great with any number of the imported beers the restaurant has on tap.

From the Rialto Bridge, walk through the markets along Ruga dei Oresi, turn left onto Rughetta del Ravano, continue for approximately 4min., and cross the square; the restaurant is in the northwest corner. [$] Entrees €6.50-19. ⏰ Open daily noon-2:30pm and 7-10:30pm.

MURO VENEZIA FRARI

♥⛄♥❀♨⛄ RISTORANTE ❹

Rio Terà dei Frari 2604

☎041 52 45 310 ■www.murovenezia.com

Muro Venezia eschews the dry, regal ambience typical of most fine Venetian restaurants in favor of a more cutting-edge aesthetic. This preference for the avant-garde is also on display in the restaurant's creative interpretations of classic Venetian recipes, including one of the most incredible vegetable risottos you'll ever have. If you like the feel here, you should check out the bar owned and operated by the same people near the Rialto Bridge, **Muro Venezia Rialto.**

⫶ *From Campo dei Frari, cross a bridge to the east, turn right, continue for 30sec. to the end of the street, and turn left.* Ⓢ *Entrees €7-25.* Ⓞ *Open M-W 11am-1am, F-Su 11am-1am. Kitchen open noon-3pm and 7-10:30pm.*

SANTA CROCE

If you're looking to get a meal in Santa Croce, stay toward the east side of the neighborhood. You can walk around the western end for half an hour without finding anything worthwhile, but if you stick to the eastern side, especially immediately southeast of Piazzale Roma, you'll discover a lot of small, personality-filled neighborhood restaurants that offer great values for budget travelers.

▨ RISTORANTE RIBOT

♥⛄♥⛄ RISTORANTE ❸

Fondamenta Minotto 158

☎041 52 42 486

Venice is an incredible culinary city, but Ristorante Ribot manages to stand out, with exceptional food at real-world prices. The restaurant pays tribute to the best of traditional Venice—regional cuisine, excellent Italian wines, and a beautiful patio garden—but keeps it fresh with an innovative kitchen, modern design, and live music three to four times a week. It's tough to find better food anywhere in Venice, let alone at comparable prices.

⫶ *Follow Piazzale Roma east, cross consecutive bridges, and continue for approximately 2min.* Ⓢ *Entrees €8-14.* Ⓞ *Open daily noon-2:30pm and 7-10:30pm.*

▨ PANIFICO BAROZZI

❀⛄ BAKERY, GROCERY STORE ❶

Salizada San Pantalon 86/A

☎041 71 02 33

One of the trickiest things about Venetian pastries is that, from a window shopper's perspective, every store's baked goods look practically identical. Sadly, looks can be deceiving, meaning that identical-looking cookies can in fact vary in quality from barely palatable to incredibly delicious. Panifico Barozzi's pastries, however, taste as scrumptious as they appear. With an impressive number of different delicacies to sample and the added bonus of a small grocery store (surprisingly tough to find in most neighborhoods) stocked with inexpensive and convenient snacks, this is a one-stop shopping experience you can't miss.

⫶ *Follow Piazzale Roma east, cross consecutive bridges, and continue for approximately 3min.* Ⓢ *Pastries €1-2.* Ⓞ *Open daily 6am-7:30pm*

ANTICO GAFARO

♥⛄♥⛄ RISTORANTE, PIZZERIA ❸

Salizada San Pantalon 116/A

☎041 52 42 823

A traditional restaurant with excellent pastas (especially lasagna) and serviceable pizzas, Antico Garafo is so perfectly Venetian that it could pass for a movie set. With the gorgeous backdrop of a canal frequented by quiet boats and some of the neighborhood's most beautiful buildings, this restaurant is a great place to relax and enjoy a long meal.

⫶ *Follow Piazzale Roma east, cross consecutive bridges, and continue for approximately 3min.* Ⓢ *Entrees €8-22.* Ⓞ *Open daily 11:30am-11:30pm.*

AGLI AMICI

♥⛄♥⛄ SNACK BAR, RISTORANTE ❸

Sestiere Santa Croce 189

☎041 52 41 309

With impressive omelettes and a great selection of cheeses, Agli Amici is a welcome anomaly in Venice, where breakfast usually consists of nothing more than tea and toast. Although the seafood options are a bit expensive, everything else here is of solid value, making this restaurant a quick but hearty lunch stop.

☂ *Follow Piazzale Roma east, cross consecutive bridges, immediately turn left, and continue for 1½min.* Ⓢ *Entrees €6-20.* Ⓩ *Open daily 8am-7:30pm.*

LAS RAMBLAS
●&♈♨ CAFE ❸

Santa Croce 373 ☎041 52 46 648

Inspired by Barcelona's famous pedestrian street, Las Ramblas does not quite recreate the famous Catalan circus feel: its tranquil atmosphere is a far cry from the street-performing madness of its namesake. Nevertheless, the restaurant serves delicious food at reasonable prices that are, rain or shine, far better than most restaurants you'll find around Piazzale Roma. It's worth waiting for a sunny day, however, to appreciate the restaurant's beautiful patio.

☂ *Following Piazzale Roma east, turn right at the 1st bridge you see; continue for 30sec.; turn right again and continue for 30sec.* Ⓢ *Entrees €8-20.* Ⓩ *Open daily 9:30am-11pm.*

TRATTORIA IN CAMPIEO
●&♈♨ RISTORANTE ❸

Campieo Mosca 24 ☎041 71 10 61

A step back from Salizada San Pantalon, Trattoria in Campieo has Campieo Mosca almost entirely to itself and uses this space to full effect, offering a great outdoor setting in which to enjoy a tasty Venetian meal. Although the food is excellent, be forewarned that portions tend to run on the small side. Consider stopping here for a light lunch unless you don't mind lightening your wallet considerably.

☂ *Follow Piazzale Roma east, cross consecutive bridges, continue for approximately 3min., and turn right into Campieo Mosca.* Ⓢ *Entrees €10-22.* Ⓩ *Open daily noon-3pm and 6-10:30pm.*

ALIBABA KEBAB
●& KEBAB, PIZZERIA ❶

Salizada San Pantalon ☎041 52 45 272

Anyone staying in Venice for an extended period of time should seriously consider trying some sort of kebab, one of Venice's major ethnic foods. Alibaba Kebab offers pretty exceptional and authentic kebab at a reasonable price and in one of the nicest kebab restaurants you'll find in the city. Alibaba also serves pizzas, but seeing how there's a pizzeria on every corner, you might as well take the opportunity to try something a little different.

☂ *Follow Piazzale Roma east, cross consecutive bridges, and continue for approximately 5min.* Ⓢ *Pizza €1.50. Kebab €4.* Ⓩ *Open daily 11am-3pm and 5:30-9:30pm.*

DORSODURO

Most of the nice restaurants in Dorsoduro tend toward the expensive side, but the neighborhood also offers some of the best cafes and pizzerias in the city, which makes the area appealing to travelers on a budget.

🔖 RISTORANTE LINEADOMBRA
●&♈♨ RISTORANTE ❺

Ponte dell'Umiltà ☎041 24 11 881 ▤www.ristorantelineadombra.com

Probably not the type of restaurant most budget travelers can afford to eat at more than once per trip, but if you're prepared to spring for an expensive meal, you won't find a restaurant that takes its work more seriously than Ristorante Lineadombra. The food is reputed to be some of Venice's best and is served in a beautiful, modern restaurant aesthetically similar to the nearby **Punta della Dogana** in its minimalist sensibility. Since you're going to pay a premium anywhere you eat along Zattere, you might as well go all-out and enjoy a truly excellent meal.

☂ *V: Zattere. Turn right and continue for 6-7min. The restaurant is on the left, with patio seating on the right.* Ⓢ *Entrees €21-35.* Ⓩ *Open daily noon-3pm and 7-10:30pm.*

🔖 SUZIE CAFE
●&♈ CAFE ❷

Dorsoduro 1527 ☎041 52 27 502 ▤www.suziecafevenice.com

With tons of classic-rock memorabilia, highlighted by a sweet guitar boasting half a dozen signatures on its body, Suzie Cafe distinguishes itself from other snack bars and cafes with both great food and high-personality decor. You could spend weeks in Venice without finding a better place to sit down and enjoy an €8 meal.

🍴 *V: Zattere. Turn left; walk 5-7min. to end of Zattere, turn right, and continue for 2-3min.; the snack bar is in the corner of a square.* Ⓢ *Sandwiches and light meals €4-11.* 🕗 *Open M-Th 7am-8pm, F 7am-1am.*

RISTORANTE AI GONDOLIERI
🍴⊗🍸 RISTORANTE ❹

San Vio 366   ☎041 52 86 396 🖥www.aigondolieri.com

An upscale restaurant that is famous for its catering, having hosted multiple events for the nearby Guggenheim Museum, Ristorante Ai Gondolieri is a great place to take a date after a day of visiting art galleries. Although Ai Gondolieri can be expensive, especially if you order a bottle off of their extensive wine list, the quality is proportionate to the price.

🍴 *From Santa Maria della Salute, walk east towards the Guggenheim, past the museum; when you reach the bend in the canal, the restaurant will be immediately across the water.* Ⓢ *Entrees €11.50-32.* 🕗 *Open M noon-3:30pm and 7-10:30pm, W-Su noon-3:30pm and 7-10:30pm.*

IL DOGE
🍴♿ GELATERIA ❷

Campo San Margherita 3058   ☎041 52 34 607

Sure, there are gelato places on pretty much every street corner in Venice, but Il Doge is unique. It doesn't use syrups or artificial flavors in its ice cream, opting instead for fresh ingredients that make for a better taste and texture. And, although the quality is high, the prices are among the lowest you'll find in a Venetian *gelateria*. With a few unique flavors that defy description, Il Doge has quickly helped at least one *Let's Go* researcher fatten up.

🍴 *The southwest corner of Campo San Margherita.* Ⓢ *1 scoop €1.20, 2 scoops €2, 3 scoops €2.80.* 🕗 *Open daily noon-11pm.*

PIZZA AL TAGLIO
🍴♿🍸 PIZZERIA ❷

Sacca de la Toletta 1309   ☎041 52 36 518

The Pizza Academy diploma on the wall doesn't lie—the owner of this shop knows how to cook up some serious pizzas and sandwiches. Unlike the bland, flat, lukewarm stuff you'll find at many pizzerias, Pizza Al Taglio's pizza and sandwiches are fresh, filling, and delicious. The nutella calzones *(€1.50)* are sure to make your day but ruin your diet.

🍴 *From the Accademia, go east, turn left at the 1st canal you meet, and turn right at the 1st bridge ahead on the left; continue straight for 2-3min.* Ⓢ *Slices of pizza €2. Sandwiches €3. Calzones €3.* 🕗 *Open daily 10:30am-10:30pm.*

RISTORANTE CANTINONE STORICO
🍴♿🍸🛏 RISTORANTE ❸

Fondamenta di Ca' Bragadin 660/661   ☎041 52 39 577

Situated between the Guggenheim and Accademia, Ristorante Cantinone Storico is the rare Dorsoduro restaurant that offers great Venetian cuisine in a relaxed setting at prices more commonly seen in the back roads of Cannaregio and the eastern reaches of Castello. Stop here for a long lunch break between visits to the neighborhood's museums.

🍴 *V: Zattere. Turn right, walk 3-4min., and turn left onto Fondamenta Bragadin. Continue for 2-3min.; the restaurant is on the right.* Ⓢ *Entrees €10-24.* 🕗 *Open daily 12:30-5:30pm and 7:30-10:30pm.*

CASTELLO

Since Castello is so close to P. San Marco, it gets a lot of tourist traffic, and restaurants with well-priced cuisine tend to be few and far between. There are quite a few good restaurants in Castello, but they're typically a bit pricier than comparable restaurants in other neighborhoods. In a lot of cases, you're going to have to compromise either on quality (and opt for a cheap restaurant) or convenience (and trek out to Cannaregio or eastern Castello), or just be prepared to pay a bit more than you otherwise might.

👍 TAVERNA SAN LIO 💳♿🍸🌳 RISTORANTE [4]

Salizada San Lio 5547 ☎041 27 70 669 💻www.tavernasanlio.com

One of the best restaurants you'll find in all of Venice, Taverna San Lio serves an incredible Venetian menu with a bit of international flair. Reflecting the owner's eclectic taste, both the decor and the cuisine are strongly Venetian but reflect the city's increasingly cosmopolitan identity. If the quality of the food isn't enough to turn heads, the bright colors of the walls will catch your attention.

➔ From Rialto Bridge, go east along Salizada San Lio for 3-4min.; restaurant is on the right. $ Entrees €12-26. ⏰ Open M noon-11pm, W-Su noon-11pm.

RISTORANTE AI BARBACANI 💳🚭🍸 RISTORANTE [3]

Calle del Paradiso 5746 ☎041 52 10 234 💻www.ristoranteaibarbacani.com

Far and away the most impressive restaurant in the area around Santa Maria Formosa, Ristorante ai Barbacani boasts an excellent Venetian menu, extensive wine list, subtle, yet elegant Venetian decor, and gorgeous floor to ceiling windows that open on to a canal trafficked by gondoliers and kayakers. If you're looking to impress a date, consider calling ahead to reserve the table for two closest to the window near the bridge.

➔ From Campo Santa Maria Formosa, immediately across westernmost bridge off the square. $ Entrees €9-20. ⏰ Open daily noon-2:30pm and 6-10:30pm.

CIP CIAP 🥡🚭🍸 PIZZERIA [1]

Calle del Mondo Novo 5799/A ☎041 52 36 621

You'll be hard pressed to find pizza of this quality for a better price in Venice. The calzones and pizza are made fresh several times daily and then cooked to order. Budget travelers weary of the sensibly-sized portions found in most Venetian restaurants may find themselves suffering a stomachache after gorging themselves on Cip Ciap's cheap pies.

➔ Immediately across bridge to Calle del Mondo Novo from S. Maria Formosa. $ Calzones €3. Pizza €1.50 per slice. ⏰ Open M 9am-9pm, W-Su 9am-9pm.

RISTORANTE AL COVO 💳♿🍸🌳 RISTORANTE [4]

Campiello della Pescaria 3968 ☎041 52 23 812 💻www.ristorantealcovo.com

From the outside, there isn't anything too striking about Ristorante al Covo, but this modest restaurant offers the most incredible Venetian cuisine in Castello, if not the entire city. Though pricey for budget travelers, a €25 meal here is an absolute steal when compared to other restaurants of comparable quality.

➔ East from P. San Marco, cross 4 bridges and turn left onto the last street before the 5th bridge going east. $ Entrees €16-29. ⏰ Open daily 12:45-3:30pm and 7:30-midnight.

TRATTORIA DA NINO 💳♿🍸🌳 RISTORANTE [3]

San Zaccaria 4668 ☎041 52 35 886 💻www.trattoriadanino.com

Though Trattoria da Nino doesn't exactly give off a traditional Venetian vibe, the menu is authentic Italian done well. The patio seating is excellent, and the restaurant itself has a great, relaxed ambience and exceptionally friendly staff.

➔ From P. San Marco, walk south toward water, turn left, cross 2 bridges, make the 1st left, and walk about 1min.; the restaurant is on the left. $ Entrees €10-22. ⏰ Open daily 11:30am-10:30pm.

nightlife

For all of its fascinating history, awe-inspiring architecture, and delightful cuisine, the one thing that Venice desperately lacks is nightlife. Whereas the ubiquity of historic *palazzi*, excellent seafood, and lovely hotels in Venice means you could find them while blindfolded, if you head out in search of a random bar you'll likely end up heading home an hour later with nothing more than a kebab to show for it. Stick to the major hot spots listed here, and you'll have a lot more success. Additionally, be prepared for a much more laid-back bar scene than that of most major Italian cities. You're not going to find much dancing or serious partying, but there are a couple great places to sit back, enjoy a few drinks, and appreciate Venice at night. **Campo San Margherita** in Dorsoduro is the city's biggest nightlife hub, and that whole neighborhood is the place to be after 9pm. Crime in Venice is less of a concern than it is almost anywhere else in Italy, but use common sense: don't carry too much cash or walk alone at night, and you will probably be fine.

SAN MARCO

After tourists head out for dinner at around 7pm, the bells of the Campanile stop chiming every few minutes, and pigeons and seagulls are left to drift aimlessly in the sky as the tourists who fed them bread during the day disappear. It is at this time of day that P. San Marco is at its finest.

After the beauty of the early evening, things get slower and duller. Dozens of places market themselves as "bars," but that term is more likely to denote a light-fare restaurant that serves alcohol than a nightlife hot spot. There are certainly a couple of places worth visiting, but since San Marco caters to the city's typical tourist, expect to see a lot more middle-aged couples holding hands and a lot fewer students downing body shots.

BACARO LOUNGE BAR
💳♿🍸❄ BAR

Sestiere San Marco 1345 ☎041 29 60 687

An ultra-chic minimalist bar just steps away from P. San Marco, Bacaro Lounge is one of the few establishments in San Marco that caters to the young and fashionable post-dinner crowd. Whereas most bars here are filled with middle-aged tourists rocking fanny packs and visors, Bacaro Lounge recalls the scene at an exclusive club in Manhattan or LA. With an understated playlist, sleek lounge set-up conducive to free conversation and mingling, and an extensive list of wine and cocktails, Bacaro Lounge is clearly the hottest place to be after dark in San Marco.

🚏 Exit the southwest corner of P. San Marco, opposite Basilica di San Marco; the bar is shortly ahead on the left. $ Drinks €3.50-13. ⏰ Open daily until 2am.

RISTORANTE GRAN CAFFÉ QUADRI
💳♿🍸☀ CAFE

P. San Marco 121 ☎041 52 22 105 💻www.quadrivenice.com

Caffé Quadri isn't a bar or club, and the tone tends more toward refinement than debauchery, with a string quartet dressed in formalwear setting the soundtrack. Sipping one of their excellent drinks (the wine list is unbeatable, and the coffee is reputedly some of Venice's best) to the tune of the strings playing in the background, you'll experience P. San Marco as it ought to be, showcased in the lovely setting provided by this cafe.

🚏 In the northwest corner of P. San Marco. $ Drinks €3-8. Dessert €3-7. ⏰ Open daily until 12:30am.

GRAND CANAL RESTAURANT AND BAR
💳♿🍸☀ HOTEL BAR

Calle Vallaresso 1332 ☎041 52 00 211 💻www.hotelmonaco.it

A welcoming hotel bar, the Grand Canal Restaurant and Bar in upscale Hotel Monaco manages to avoid pretension and cultivate a clientele that stretches beyond the hotel's guest list. The wine list is exceptionally good, the bar has comfortable seating, and the dock opens into a nice summer breeze and excellent views across the water to **Basilica di Santa Maria della Salute**.

✪ *From P. San Marco, walk towards the water, turn right, and continue for 2min.; Hotel Monaco is at the end of the street.* Ⓢ *Drinks €4-10.* ☾ *Open daily until midnight.*

CANNAREGIO

People don't travel to Cannaregio for its nightlife, but anyone can enjoy sitting outside with a good bottle of wine or a couple scoops of gelato while taking in this low-key neighborhood's nighttime scene. The natives here are generally more receptive to out-of-town visitors than are the residents of Venice's more popular destinations, probably because Cannaregio remains free of the floods of gondola-searching tourists that fill places like P. San Marco. Cannaregio's decidedly more intimate Campo San Marco on Lista di Spagna is a particularly pleasant place to while away the night hours, as Venetian locals and tourists socialize in restaurants and on benches well into the evening.

CASINO MUNICIPALE DI VENEZIA: CA' VENDRAMIN CALERGI ✪♿✿❀ CASINO
Cannaregio 2040   ☎041 52 97 111 ▣www.casinovenezia.it

One of the first things you might notice after getting off the plane at VCE is that Venice takes its gambling seriously—even the baggage carousels have a roulette-wheel theme, sponsored by the (in)famous Venetian Municipal Casino. While serious gamblers might want to head straight to Lido where the historic casino's main branch still operates, the Cannaregio location should be fun for anyone who just wants to play (or count) some cards and have a few drinks.

✪ *Going east on Strada Nova, take the 1st left past Calle Vendramin.* ℹ *Male guests should wear formal jackets.* Ⓢ *Entry €5, guests at some hotels get in free. Ask at your reception desk.* ☾ *Open M-Th 3pm-2:30am, F-Sa 3pm-3am, Su 3pm-2:30am.*

THE IRISH PUB VENEZIA ✪♿✿ BAR
Cannaregio 3847   ☎041 52 81 439 ▣www.theirishpubvenezia.com

A friendly crowd of boisterous locals and rowdy tourists brings The Irish Pub Venezia some of the best nightlife in the neighborhood. The drinks are strong and the bar is crowded, but patrons tend to be jovial and are happy to strike up a conversation on Venice, politics, or just about any other subject at the drop of a hat. Loud music and the pub's proximity to the late-night restaurant Neapolis Kebab keep it hopping long into the evening, even on weekdays.

✪ *Just off Strada Nova, on the left going east.* Ⓢ *Drinks €3-6. Snacks €6-12.* ☾ *Open daily until 1:30am.*

SAN POLO

Nightlife-wise, San Polo is second only to Dorsoduro. The area around the **Rialto Bridge** in particular is home to some of Venice's best bars, popular with both Venetian locals and tourists.

▨ JAZZ CLUB 900 ✪♿✿ JAZZ CLUB
San Polo 900   ☎041 52 26 565 ▣www.jazz900.com

Just down Ruga Rialto from the bars near the Rialto Bridge, Jazz Club 900 is a live-music hot spot. With shows up to several times each week, top-notch pizza, and reasonable prices on bottles, glasses, and pitchers of beer, this venue can be a chill hangout or a lively music bar, depending on what groups the club is hosting.

✪ *From the Rialto Bridge, continue straight, turn left onto Ruga Rialto, continue for 2min., and turn right: it's ahead on the left. Signs lead to the jazz club.* Ⓢ *Drinks €2.50-5. Pizza €6-11.* ☾ *Open Tu-Su 11:30am-4pm and 7pm-2am.*

MURO VENEZIA RIALTO ✪♿✿❀ BAR
Campo Bella Vienna Rialto 222   ☎041 24 12 339 ▣www.murovenezia.com

With chic metal-and-dark-leather decor reminiscent of trendy bars in downtown

Manhattan, Muro Venezia Rialto is one of Venice's most popular drinking spots for travelers and locals in their mid-20s. A bit more upscale than most other bars around the Rialto Bridge, Muro Venezia keeps the music low and emphasizes its lounge ambience.

From Rialto Bridge, continue straight ahead for less than 2min., and turn right; the bar is on the left. $ Drinks €3-7. ⏰ Open M-Sa 9am-3:30pm and 4pm-1:30am, Su 4pm-1:30am.

ANCÒRA VENEZIA

BAR

Rialto 120 ☎041 52 07 066 www.ancoravenezia.it

One of Venice's most popular (and crowded) bars, Ancòra complements the subtle Asian and modernist aesthetics of its decor with some of the most universally lauded bartenders in the city. If the bar is overly crowded, grab a drink to enjoy outside in Campo di San Giacometto.

From the Rialto Bridge, continue straight; Ancòra is the last bar on the right side of the Campo di San Giacometto. $ Drinks €3-6.50. ⏰ Open M-Sa 9:30am-2am.

SANTA CROCE

In a city not known for its nightlife, Santa Croce is about the last place you'd want to go for an evening out. Unlike some other neighborhoods with at least a few bars and restaurants open late, Santa Croce offers only a couple of places that keep the home-fires burning after midnight.

BAR AL CARCAN

BAR [3]

Salizada San Pantalon ☎041 71 32 36

While most of Santa Croce shuts down around 11pm (even on weekends), Bar Al Carcan stays crowded well into the night with tourists and locals alike looking to get a quick nightcap or enjoy a few drinks on the patio. The bar is small and fairly popular, though never overcrowded, and offers cheap drinks and good music.

Follow Piazzale Roma east, cross consecutive bridges, and continue for approximately 2min. $ Drinks €3-6. ⏰ Open until 1am most days during the summer.

DORSODURO

Dorsoduro has far and away the best nightlife of any neighborhood in Venice. Though there are dozens of bars and clubs, the vast majority of them are concentrated around **Campo San Margherita,** which is located just minutes away from Santa Croce and San Polo. As there isn't any action to be found on the island's western and southern edges, your best bet is to barhop near this vibrant campo. "Night"life in Dorsoduro begins before sunset during the summer, and the infamous **Club Piccolo Mondo** keeps it going almost until daybreak. So if you're looking for some bacchanalian revelry in the surprisingly sober city of Venice, Dorsoduro is the place to go.

CLUB PICCOLO MONDO

CLUB

Accademia Dorsoduro 1056 ☎041 52 00 371 www.piccolomondo.biz

The definitive epicenter of Venetian nightlife, Club Piccolo Mondo puts most other bars in the city to shame. Small and down a dark side street near the Accademia, it might not impress from the outside, but if its world-class bar, excellent music, chill lounge areas, and awesome dance floor are enough to draw Mick Jagger and Naomi Campbell, they should be able to earn your patronage, even with the steep cover charge *(€10).* The club prides itself on the diversity of its clientele, which ranges from students to middle-aged patrons and includes locals as well as tourists, so anyone should feel welcome here. A lot of visitors opt to start the night at another bar before coming to Club Piccolo Mondo, due to the place's expensive drinks. As a result, things usually don't get too crazy until after midnight.

From Ponte Accademia, facing the Accademia, turn right; continue onto the 1st street directly ahead (running parallel to the Grand Canal); continue for approximately 2min.; club is on the right. $ Cover €10. Drinks €9-12. ⏰ Open daily 11pm-4am.

VENICE JAZZ CLUB

JAZZ CLUB

Ponte dei Pugni/Fondamenta del Squero 3102 ☎041 52 32 056 www.venicejazzclub.com

The Venice Jazz Club is a great place to begin a night out in Dorsoduro. While most bars are still in restaurant mode, this club is serving drinks to the tune of excellent music. It tends to attract an international crowd of 20-somethings and empty out once concerts end, despite technically remaining open. Given that it's the premier spot for live jazz music in Venice, perhaps this focus on the jams is to be expected.

From Campo San Margherita, walk towards Campo San Barnaba; turn right immediately before the bridge; the club is just ahead on the right. $ Cover €20; includes one drink. Drinks €5-10. Appetizers €5-15. ⏰ Opens daily at 7pm. Concerts start at 9pm and usually last about 2hr.

MADIGAN'S PUB

IRISH PUB

Campo San Margherita 3053/A

Madigan's Pub seeks to replicate the ambience of an Irish pub and does so to great effect, creating the loudest, rowdiest bar in Campo San Margherita and maybe in all of Venice. On weekend nights, the pub is packed, both inside and on the patio, with international patrons drinking beers, taking shots, and shouting to old (and new) friends over the bar's deafening music.

At the southwest end of the Campo San Margherita. $ Drinks €4-8. ⏰ Open daily until 1:30am.

MARGARET DUCHAMP

BAR

Campo San Margherita 3019 ☎041 52 86 255

One of the biggest bars in Venice and a Dorsoduro institution, Margaret Duchamp is the most prominent watering hole in Campo San Margherita. Though the bar typically plays jazz or pop, the music isn't overwhelmingly loud, making this an excellent place for a few hours of chill time spent enjoying some of the best cocktails in Venice.

At the southwest end of the Campo San Margherita. $ Drinks €3.50-9. ⏰ Open daily 9am-2am.

ORANGE RESTAURANT AND CHAMPAGNE LOUNGE

BAR

Campo Santa Margherita 3054/A ☎041 52 34 740 www.orangebar.it

With an excellent patio, comfortable lounge furniture, and an awesome terrace looking out over Campo San Margherita, Orange Restaurant and Champagne Lounge has a more refined ambience than other Venetian bars. It might not get as crazy as some Dorsoduro hot spots, but make no mistake: with a wine list featuring over 60 Italian vintages and 20 imports, mega-screen TVs, and a top-notch bartender, Orange is a choice place for a night out.

At the southwest end of the Campo San Margherita. $ Drinks €4.50-12. ⏰ Open daily 10am-2am.

BISTROT AI DO DRAGHI

BAR

Campo San Margherita ☎041 52 89 731

More bohemian than most bars in Campo San Margherita, Bistrot Ai Do **Draghi** tends to draw grungier travelers than the other bars in the square. In fact, this place is so full of such when-did-you-last-shower travelers that it's a surprise there isn't a stack of backpacks in the corner. The bar itself has an exceptionally relaxed and social character, with conversation rather than music constituting the dominant background noise.

The northeast corner of Campo San Margherita. $ Drinks €1.50-6. ⏰ Open M-Tu 7:30am-2am, Th-Su 7:30am-2am.

BLUES CAFE

BAR

Crosera San Pantalon ☎348 24 06 444

Like most bars east of Campo San Margherita, Blues Cafe has a calm, sophisticated vibe that draws patrons in their late 20s and early 30s. Unlike a lot of other bars, Blues Cafe keeps the good times rolling well into the evening every night of the week, especially when there is live music. *Let's Go* gives Blues Cafe bonus points for musical diversity, as it spins jazz, pop, and the best old-school hip hop playlist this side of the South Bronx.

 # From Campo San Margherita, go west, and cross the 1st bridge you come to; continue across the square; the bar is on the 1st cross street you come to. $ Drinks €4-10. ⏰ Open M-F 10am-2am, Sa-Su 3pm-2am.

IMAGINA CAFE
💶♿🍸☁ CAFE, BAR

Campo San Margherita 3126 ☎041 24 10 625 🖥www.imaginacafe.it

Part art gallery, part cafe, and part bar, Imagina Cafe is a favorite hangout of the Venetian *intelligentsia*. With awesome white, leather couches, consistently changing artwork, and sophisticated drinks, Imagina Cafe is a great place for stimulating conversation about the latest exhibit in François Pinault's **Punta della Dogana** contemporary art museum, but probably not the best bar if you want to get crunk or hear Miley Cyrus's latest hit.

 # The southwest end of the Campo San Margherita, near Ponte dei Pugni. $ Drinks €2-8. ⏰ Open Tu-Su 8am-2am.

CAFFE BAR AI ARTISTI
💶♿🍸☁ CAFE, BAR

Campo San Barnaba 2771 ☎39 68 01 35

If you want to grab a bite to eat before calling it a night or heading to **Club Piccolo Mondo,** but don't want to be the one person eating a full meal in a bar with 200 people sipping on cocktails, Caffe Bar Ai Artisti is a great stop. With exceptionally good food, a strong drink selection, a bumping playlist, and proximity to both Campo San Margherita and Club Piccolo Mondo, Caffe Bar Ai Artisti is an excellent place to hang out, for 20min.—or 4hr.

 # From Campo San Margherita, continue along Rio Terà Canal, cross the bridge, and enter Campo San Barnaba. $ Drinks €3.50-8. Food €8-16. ⏰ Open M-F 7am-2am, Sa 8am-2am, Su 9am-2am.

IMPRONTA CAFE
💶♿🍸 CAFE, BAR

Crosera San Pantalon 3815 ☎041 27 50 386

Whether you go earlier in the evening, when the cafe is almost always packed, or late at night, when it has a much quieter, intimate atmosphere, you're sure to appreciate Impronta Cafe's sleek aesthetics, extensive bar options, and nifty dessert menu. A great place to take a date after a night out or to cool down after some serious barhopping, this bar and cafe offers a serene and more sensible alternative to much of Dorsoduro's nighttime action.

 # From Campo San Margherita, go west, and cross the 1st bridge you come to; continue across the square; the club is on the 1st cross street you come to. $ Drinks €2.50-6. Snacks and desserts €3-8. ⏰ Open M-Sa 7am-2am.

CASTELLO

A great place to sit outside at a cafe and relax well into the night, Castello isn't particularly notable for its nightclub scene. However, its good number of bars and cafes still draw large crowds during the summer. Most nightlife hotspots are along the waterfront that marks the southern boundary of the neighborhood, but there are a couple of places worth checking out further north close to the Rialto Bridge as well as on the eastern side of Castello.

★ TAVERNA L'OLANDESE VOLANTE
⊛♿🍸 BAR

Castello 5658 ☎041 52 89 349

Blasting reggae beats until 2am, Taverna L'Olandese Volante is one of the most popular bars in the neighborhood. It seems to have wide appeal, drawing tourists, locals, students, and middle-aged customers to its great selection of beers on tap, prime location in one of Castello's best squares, and thoroughly impressive (and surprising) reggae playlist. Excellent, mahn.

From Rialto Bridge, walk east toward Salizada San Lio; continue along Salizada San Lio, then turn left at T-intersection at end of street; the bar is shortly before the 1st canal. $ Drinks €2.50-6. Snacks €5-12. ⏰ Open Sa-Su until 2am in high season.

BAR VERDE SNACK BAR

Calle de le Rasse 4525 ☎041 52 37 094

Bar Verde isn't an overwhelmingly unique establishment, but it's a great place to grab a couple of drinks and something quick to eat late at night near P. San Marco in Castello. The bar is frequented mainly by tourists staying at hotels in the area, so your neighbor at the bar may run the gamut from a budget traveler sipping inexpensive beer to a middle-aged couple stepping out for some late-night gelato.

From P. San Marco, walk south toward water, turn left, cross 1 bridge, turn left onto 2nd street on the left, and continue for about 2min. $ Drinks €3-6. Gelato €1.50-4. Snacks €6-12. ⏰ Open Sa-Su until 2am in high season.

CAFFE INTERNAZIONALE CAFE, BAR

Riva degli Schiavoni 4183 ☎041 52 36 047

A great place to grab coffee or beer and maybe a quick snack right along the water, Caffe Internazionale is distinguished by an excellent patio with incredible views of the canals. This is a convenient stop at which to refuel before catching the vaporetto home after a long night in Castello or San Marco, and the nearby docks serve as an intriguing vantage point for people-watching the party boats and luxurious yachts that constantly drift past.

From P. San Marco, walk south toward water; turn left and continue for 2-3min., crossing 2 bridges; the bar is on the left. $ Drinks €2-5. Snacks €5-10. ⏰ Open Sa-Su until 1:30am in high season.

BAR METROPOLE HOTEL BAR

Riva degli Schiavoni 4149 ☎041 52 05 044

Probably as close as most budget travelers will get to the opulent hotel in which this establishment is housed, the elegant yet intimate bar at the Metropole is a great place to get some of the most expertly mixed drinks in Venice. While you might be breaking the bank (there are particularly tempting options for doing so on their wine list), you're paying for quality. The high-class ambience is also well worth the cost.

From P. San Marco, walk south toward water; turn left and continue for 3-4min., crossing 3 bridges; the bar is on the left. $ Drinks €5-12. ⏰ Open Sa-Su until 2am in high season.

ARCO BALENTO SNACK BAR

Castello 3977 ☎041 52 29 940

Popular with locals, Arco Balento is a great bar for grabbing a table and splitting a few rounds with friends. (Even) quieter and less flashy than the rest of Castello's nightlife, Arco Balento remains a good destination due to its strong drink selection and neighborhood vibe.

From P. San Marco, walk south toward water, turn left, and walk 5-6min., crossing 4 bridges. Then turn left on 3rd street after 4th bridge. $ Drinks €3-6. Snacks €6-14. ⏰ Open until 2am.

OSTERIA AL GARANGHÈLO RISTORANTE

V. Giuseppe Garibaldi 1621 ☎041 52 04 967 www.garanghelo.com

The restaurant officially closes at midnight, but this is Italy, where no one cares about such technicalities. On summer nights, especially weekends, Osteria al Garanghèlo has customers coming in well into the night. The restaurant feels more like a nighttime destination than other late-night restaurants in Castello, with loud Italian music, enthusiastic conversation, and a lot of energy.

From P. San Marco, walk south toward water, turn left, and continue for 7-10min. $ Drinks €4-6. Entrees €7-13. ⏰ Open M until midnight, W-Su until midnight.

arts and culture

At the height of its power during the Italian Renaissance, the Venetian Republic was one of the centers of artistic and cultural innovation, and the profound legacy of the Renaissance is evident in the architecture, music, painting, and theater that so many tourists flock to Venice to enjoy. Things have been changing quickly, though, and particularly in recent years, Venice has begun to incorporate more contemporary and modern influences in its creative scene. As a result, you'll find an incredible diversity of artistic and cultural experiences here, from the classical to the avant-garde and from the expensive to the remarkably affordable.

ORCHESTRAL MUSIC

INTERPRETI VENEZIANI - CHIESA DI SAN VIDAL — ♿ SAN MARCO

Campo San Vidal 2862/B ☎041 27 70 561 www.interpretiveneziani.com

Held in the beautiful San Vidal Church in San Marco, Interpreti Veneziani's concert series has garnered the acclaim of the most discerning critics and is regarded by many as the best orchestral music in Venice. While many churches host concerts that are more casual and better suited for those who feel like they should listen to this kind of music but don't really understand it, Interpreti Veneziani caters to serious aficionados, and their concerts are much more akin to a performance at La Fenice than your typical church choir.

Immediately across the bridge from the Ponte dell'Accademia. $ Tickets are usually €40.

FRARI CONCERT SEASON - BASILICA DEI FRARI — ♿ SAN POLO

Campo dei Frari 3072 ☎041 52 22 637

Famous for its organ, which serves as the centerpiece of many concerts, Basilica dei Frari keeps things a bit less formal than some of the other orchestral events in the city but no less praiseworthy. Concerts here tend to be less predictable than those at other venues, since the church often welcomes guest choirs (and offers reduced ticket prices for the occasion), but the venue is in high demand, meaning that performances are invariably of the highest quality.

V: Campo San Tomà. Proceed straight until you reach a T intersection; turn right, make the 1st left, and continue to the square; the entrance to the church is immediately ahead. $ Tickets €18.

THEATER

TEATRO LA FENICE — ♿ 🍸 SAN MARCO

Campo San Fantin 1965 ☎041 78 65 11 www.teatrolafenice.it

Venice's most versatile and prestigious venue, Teatro La Fenice is the place to go if you can only see one musical or theatrical performance during your stay. The theater itself is a remarkable building, having earned its name (The Phoenix) after rising from the ashes of three separate fires, and it's worth the price of admission just to experience the space on the night of a show. However, La Fenice is more than just a beautiful building. Its world-class acoustics draw some of the globe's top musical and theatrical talent. If you opt for the least expensive seats, you might find your view obscured, but regardless of where you're sitting, the performances here are unforgettable.

Exit the southwest corner of P. San Marco, take the 1st right onto Frezzeria, continue for 3-4min., following the turn left in Frezzeria as the road becomes Calle del Frutariol, and turn left at Calle de la Verona; the theater is shortly ahead on the right. $ Ticket prices depend on quality of seats and type of show. Opera €10-180, concerts €10-60, ballet €10-100. Tours €7, students under 26, over 65, and holders of the Rolling Venice Card €5. ⏰ Showtimes vary, with performances most weekday evenings and weekend afternoons and evenings. Open for tours daily 9:30am-6pm.

TEATRO GOLDONI ♿ 🍸 SAN MARCO

Calle dei Fabbri 4650 ☎041 24 02 011 💻www.teatrostabileveneto.it

Named after **Carlo Goldoni**, one of Venice's most influential playwrights, the Teatro Goldoni offers perhaps a greater variety of theatrical performances than any other venue in the city. The theater hosts numerous different performances over the course of a season, ranging from conventional European dramas to more contemporary works that present new and challenging perspectives on the art of theater. With its notable acoustics, Teatro Goldoni is also a fine place to take in musical performances.

From Rialto Bridge, turn right onto Riva del Carbon, continue for 3-4min., and turn right onto Calle dei Fabbri; the theater is shortly ahead on the left. $ *Prices vary according to seating and shows; contact box office for up-to-date information.*

TEATRO FONDAMENTA NUOVE ♿ CANNAREGIO

Fondamenta Nuove 5013 ☎041 52 24 498 💻www.teatrofondamentanuove.it

A smaller venue that often hosts less conventional and more avant-garde performances than Venice's best-known theaters, Teatro Fondamenta Nuove is the favorite of many locals and quickly endears itself to tourists who see its shows. Visitors who want to see artistically innovative performances with challenging content would be wise to check out Fondamenta Nuove's programming. The theater also hosts frequent musical performances, so be sure to look up their website for the upcoming schedule.

From Ca' d'Oro, turn left onto Strada Nova, then right onto Corte Longa Santa Caterina; continue for 5-7min., then turn left onto Fondamenta Nuove. i *Tickets can be purchased online or by telephone and picked up at the theater before the show begins, or purchased at Venice tourism offices.* $ *Prices vary according to seatings and shows; contact box office for up-to-date information.*

FESTIVALS

Venice is home to two of the premier arts festivals in Europe, the Venice Biennale and the Venice Film Festival. Although Venice is a popular tourist destination year-round, the number of visitors spikes during these two events as art and film aficionados flock to the city.

gondolas

Probably the most recognizable (and cliché) symbol of Venice, the gondola once filled the city's canals, serving as the city's main mode of water transportation. They were decorated with brilliant colors and designs that rivaled the extravagance of the famed Venetian Carnevale masks, but the city put the kibosh on the artistic arms race in the 16th century and mandated black as the standard color. In the centuries that followed, the gondola eventually fell out of favor as more efficient means of aquatic transportation became available, but several hundred still remain for the enjoyment of tourists. To prevent unsanctioned price-gouging, legal standard rates *(€80 for 40min. and up to 6 people, €40 for each additional 20min., 25% price increase for night tours)* have been established for gondola rides. Some gondoliers manage to circumvent these by charging for add-ons such as tours, singing, or other amusements. The gondola is certainly a Venetian novelty and many travelers will feel that their trip is incomplete without a ride in one, but budget travelers unwilling to shell out more for a 40min. ride than they're spending on the night's accommodations can hop on the *traghetti* for a much abbreviated, more goal-oriented (getting from one side of the Grand Canal to the other) version of the same experience. It's €0.50, and comes without the funny hats and singing (usually).

LA BIENNALE DI VENEZIA

Ca' Giustinian, San Marco 1364/A ☎041 52 18 711 ▣www.labiennale.org

First held as a relatively small art exhibition in 1895, the Venice Biennale has sky-rocketed into one of the world's most celebrated festivals of contemporary artwork. Though war, politics, and changes in the artistic community intervened to dramatically restructure the festival several times during the 20th century, it continues to attract some of the world's most talented and original artists. The festival is organized around 30 national pavilions that display contemporary artwork from the sponsor countries but also incorporates various special exhibitions. Critics laud the national pavilion format of presentation, which encourages expression of each participating nation's unique perspectives on contemporary artwork and makes visiting the Biennale as culturally informative as it is aesthetically challenging. While the Biennale is held only once every two years (that is, after all, what the name boils down to), it has become such a popular event that it has given rise to other festivals including the **International Architecture Exhibition** and **International Festival of Contemporary Music,** which have run for 12 and 54 years, respectively. The Biennale is held in years ending with an odd number (so 2011 is in luck), while the other festivals are typically held during years ending in an even number.

☞ *In the Giarddini Pubblici in Castello. Vaporetto line #1, 2, 41, 42, 51, 52, or N. ☒ June 4-Nov 27 2011. Odd-numbered years only.*

VENICE FILM FESTIVAL

Ca' Giustinian, San Marco 1364/A ☎041 52 18 711 ▣www.labiennale.org

Venice is home to the world's oldest film festival, which was first held in 1932 and continues to draw thousands of artists, actors, directors, and film critics to the city each fall for film screenings and celebrations of Italian and international cinema. The festival, held on Lido, has endured political turmoil (which saw Mussolini Cups awarded as the festival's top prize) and its home island's gradual decline as a popular tourist destination, yet it hasn't waned in popularity. Famous actors from all over the world, including popular Hollywood stars, continue to come to the festival each year, bringing extra verve to the peaceful beaches of eastern Lido. At this time of the year, members of the film industry, along with the journalists, fans, and paparazzi they attract, fill 1000-seat auditoriums for showings of both popular and smaller-market films.

i Contact information above is for La Biennale di Venezia offices, which operate the administration of the Venice Film Festival. ☒ Early Sept.

shopping

With innumerable designer stores, clothing boutiques, Murano glass shops, Burano lace vendors, Carnival mask workshops, and other stores operated by local artisans, Venice is a shopper's paradise. Every neighborhood has something to offer, but the best places can be found along the main streets of San Marco, Cannaregio, and San Polo as well as the areas adjacent to the Rialto Bridge. Though there are a fair number of shops with generic, overpriced merchandise who prey on tourists who haven't done sufficient comparison shopping, there are also a lot of great stores with incredible deals, especially for the shrewd negotiator. While the amount of English that shop owners speak is usually inversely proportional to how hard you press for a discount, prices can often be talked down. Failing that, tax refunds are often offered by stores that specialize in high-priced goods. If you're spending more than a few euros, it's worth asking about every possible discount, including those affiliated with *Let's Go* and **Rolling Venice** (if you have the card) as well as those that come from paying in cash. Some owners will deduct as much as 10% if any of these apply.

VENETIAN ARTISAN GOODS

Of the top three artisan goods made in Venice—glass, masks, and lace—only the masks are typically produced in the city itself. Glass is produced in the northern lagoon island of **Murano,** which has been a world capital for high-quality artisan glass goods since Venice's glass furnaces were banished from the city center in 1291, while lace is generally produced in **Burano,** a quiet island to the north of Murano whose economy is based primarily on fishing and the production of handmade lace. Though the islands offer numerous stores and the most extensive selection of glass and lace, there's no need to make a trip to the northern lagoon just to go shopping, as Venice itself has a solid number of reputable stores.

👍 CA' MACANA 🛍♿ DORSODURO

Dorsoduro 3172 ☎041 27 76 142 💻www.camacana.com

Venice is overrun with mask shops, but Ca' Macana is one of the few places that focuses exclusively on Carnival masks and regards its work as a serious art form. Though the shop has an unmatched selection of masks, it's Ca' Macana's workshops, where you can see masks being made by hand, that truly set it apart.

🪧 From Campo San Barnaba go south; the store is ahead on the left. The showroom and mask-making courses are in 2 different storefronts just north of Campo San Barnaba. $ Masks €15-60. ⏰ Open daily 10am-7pm.

MA.RE 🛍♿ SAN MARCO

V. XXII Marco 2088 ☎041 52 31 191 💻www.mareglass.com

MA.RE is stylish and cutting-edge without being jarringly avant-garde and offers pieces that are practical and functional rather than just glass for glass's sake. Unlike other stores specializing in kitsch and easily mass-produced artifacts, MA.RE makes sensible yet innovatively designed products. This is particularly evident in the beautiful wine, cocktail, and drinking glasses that manifest the talent of their Murano artists.

🪧 Exit the southwest corner of P. San Marco, continue west across a bridge, and keep walking for less than 2min.; the store is ahead on the right. $ Prices vary depending on quality of glass and product. ⏰ Open daily 10:30am-7pm.

DUE ZETA 🛍 SAN MARCO

Calle Larga San Marco 368-371 ☎041 63 17 79 💻www.duezeta.net

A lot of the glass sellers around San Marco greet tourists with a smile and a 50% markup, but the manager of Due Zeta is much more likely to introduce himself with a sneer and offers of steep discounts. The expansive store—which fills its three storefronts with an incredible selection—offers everything from inexpensive glass jewelry and souvenirs to gorgeous high-end glass artwork that is worth taking some time to admire, even if you're not in the market for a €2500 chandelier.

🪧 From P. San Marco, 2nd street to the north. $ Earrings and other jewelry as little as €3. Chandeliers up to €2500. ⏰ Open daily 9am-11pm.

P. SCARPA 🛍♿ SAN POLO

Campo Frari 3007 ☎041 52 38 681

One of the few lace shops outside of Burano that sells high-quality handmade products from the island, P. Scarpa captures the atmosphere of Burano perhaps better than any other store in Venice proper.

🪧 Along the southern edge of the square opposite the church. $ Prices vary. A lot. ⏰ Open daily 10:30am-7pm.

DESIGNER STORES

Most major Italian design houses and internationally recognized brands have outposts in Venice, the vast majority of which are along **Calle Larga XXII Marzo** just west of **Piazza San Marco.** Shopping for designer clothing and accessories is entirely different from shopping for most other local goods, since haggling over prices won't be well-received, and discounts are unlikely to apply. Purchases will be prohibitively expensive for a lot of budget travelers, but the shopping experience itself should be enjoyable. If you do purchase anything pricey, be sure to inquire about the possibility of a **Value Added Tax refund.**

👍 SALVATORE FERRAGAMO — 🛍♿ SAN MARCO

Calle Larga XXII Marzo 2098 — ☎041 27 78 509 💻www.ferragamo.com

Ferragamo, a design group originally based in Florence that now owns hundreds of stores all over the world, has earned a reputation over the years for making exceptionally high-quality products that never go out of style. Though perhaps most famous for their shoes and leather goods, Ferragamo's clothing, fragrances, and accessories have all garnered high praise from the fashion world. If you only bother to visit one designer store in Venice, make it this one, where you can experience Ferragamo's world-class customer service and see products by the design group that aren't available in North America.

🧭 Exit the southwest corner of P. San Marco and continue west for 2-3min.; the store is ahead on the left. ⏰ Open daily 10am-7:30pm.

ERMENEGILDO ZEGNA — 🛍♿ SAN MARCO

Bocca di P. San Marco 1242 — ☎041 52 21 204 💻www.zegna.com

Though top-quality men's suits continue to be Zegna's hallmark, the internationally acclaimed fashion house is by no means limited to men's formalwear. With perhaps more square footage than any other designer store in Venice, Zegna offers an incredible selection of men's and women's fashion and is the place to go for everything from swimwear to Venetian high society garb.

🧭 Exit the southwest corner of P. San Marco and turn right; the store is shortly ahead. ⏰ Open M-Sa 10am-7:30pm, Su 10am-7pm.

MARKETS

Though Venice has relatively few open spaces and streets, it is the setting for a number of respectable outdoor markets selling fresh fruit, vegetables, and seafood. Though the markets can be a bit intimidating to the timid traveler—you might be surprised by the vendors' brusque manners—if you're assertive, you'll find excellent values on the freshest and most delicious produce in the city. Prices are typically posted, so you don't have to worry about getting overcharged. Do make sure you're paying for produce that isn't blemished or bruised, though, since some vendors try to pass the damaged wares off on tourists, who are less likely to complain.

👍 RIALTO MARKET — 🍎♿ SAN POLO

San Polo

Once the biggest market in the Mediterranean, the Rialto Market still does business largely the way it has for nearly the past millennium. With wholesalers, retailers, restaurateurs, local shoppers, and tourists, things can get kind of crazy, but the spectacle of the market is part of what makes it great.

🧭 On the San Polo side of the Rialto Bridge, walk toward the Grand Canal and continue west. $ Prices are variable but cheap. ⏰ Open M-Sa 8am-noon. Fish available Tu-Sa 8am-noon.

TRADITIONAL BOAT MARKET — 🍎♿ DORSODURO

Campo San Barnaba

A relic from Venice's past without a fixed name or address, the 📖**boat** market docked near Campo San Barnaba is the best remaining example of Venice's answer to the supermarket. If you want to actually buy things, go to one of the markets listed earlier. If you want a cool experience, come here. In theory, it's a market run out of a boat, but it's actually so popular that it also occupies a storefront opposite the boat's moorings.

 # Exit Campo San Margherita in the southwest corner and continue west until you reach the bridge; the market is on the water. $ Prices are variable but quite cheap. ⏰ Open M-Sa 8am-6pm. Hours may vary, especially during winter.

essentials [i]

PRACTICALITIES

- **TOURIST OFFICES: APT Tourist Office** provides information, maps, tours, the Rolling Venice Card, and theater and concert tickets. Outposts are located throughout the city. *(Main Office: P. Rom ☎041 24 11 499 🖥www.turismovenezia.it i Additional offices near P. San Marco (San Marco 71) and on Lido (Gran Viale 6/A). ⏰ Open daily 9:30am-1pm and 1:30-4:30pm.)*
- **LUGGAGE STORAGE: Stazione Santa Lucia.** *(☎041 78 55 31 🖥www.grandistazioni.it # At the train station. i Cash only. $ First 5hr. €4, €0.60 per hr. up to 12, €0.20 per hr. thereafter. ⏰ Open daily 6am-midnight.)*
- **DISABILITY SERVICES: Informahandicap** provides information to physically disabled travelers in Venice, which, given the city's crazy design, is very useful. *(San Marco 4136 ☎041 27 48 144 🖥www.comune.venezia.it # Nearest vaporetto stop is Rialto. On Riva del Carbon, 2-3min. southwest of Rialto Bridge. ⏰ Open Th 9am-1pm.)*
- **POST OFFICES: Poste Venezia Centrale.** *(Main office at San Marco 5554, with branches all over the city ☎041 24 04 158 🖥www.poste.it # Nearest vaporetto stop Rialto. The post office is off of Campo San Bartolomeo, directly in front of the Rialto Bridge. ⏰ Open M-Sa 8am-7pm.)*

EMERGENCY!

- **POLICE:** There are police stations all over the city, but the main one is the **Carabinieri** office. *(Campo San Zaccaria, Castello 4693/A ☎041 27 411 # Walk straight and follow the signs from vaporetto San Zaccaria.)*
- **HOSPITALS/MEDICAL SERVICES: Ospedale Civile.** *(Campo Giovanni e Paolo Santissimi, Castello 6777 ☎041 52 94 111 🖥www.ulss12.ve.it # Walk east from vaporetto Fondamenta Nuove and turn right after 1st bridge. i Be forewarned: the hospital has limited hours and is likely to redirect you elsewhere for further treatment.)*

GETTING THERE ✈

By Plane

As many tourists are crestfallen to discover, though **Aeroporto Marco Polo** *(VCE ☎041 26 09 260 🖥www.veniceairport.it)* is billed as Venice's airport, once you've made it there, the journey to Venice's historic center has only just begun. You could opt to take a water taxi to reach the *centro*, which would cost about €100, but there are several more economical ways to make it to Venice from the airport. **Alilaguna** *(☎041 24 01 701 🖥www.alilaguna.it)* offers transport directly from VCE to the city center at €12 per passenger, but the service isn't necessarily the most expedient option. The ultimate budget solution is to take any one of a number of bus lines to **Piazzale Roma,** located near the Calatrava Bridge just minutes away from **Stazione Santa Lucia.** The buses, which offer convenient transportation throughout the region, are operated by **ACTV**

(☎041 24 24 💻www.hellovenezia.it) and cost as little as €2.50. This is comparable to the **ATVO Shuttle** bus, which also stops at Piazzale Roma and costs €3 for a one-way trip. Regardless of how you plan to get from Aeroporto Marco Polo to the city, be sure to get your ticket before leaving the airport—tickets for transportation services are most easily purchased at the windows there.

By Train

Most travelers who are already in Italy will either reach Venice by bus or by train. The extra-urban line operated by ACTV runs several buses per hour between Venice and the two nearest major cities, Padua and Treviso. However, each trip takes about an hour, and the consensus is that train travel is more economical and convenient, particularly for those traveling with luggage. Several train lines run through **Stazione Santa Lucia** *(☎041 26 09 260 💻www.veneziasantalucia.it)*, in the east of the city, bringing people from **Bologna** *($ €8.90. ⏰ 2hr., 30 per day.)*, **Florence** *($ €22.50. ⏰ 2-3hr., 20 per day.)*, **Milan** *($ €14.55. ⏰ 2½-3½hr.)*, **Padua** *($ €2.90. ⏰ 26-50min., 80 per day.)*, **Rome** *($ €42.50. ⏰ 3½-6hr., 20 per day.)*, and numerous local destinations.

GETTING AROUND

On Foot

Though Venice is a wonderful city with many great things to offer visitors, convenience of transportation isn't one of them. Within the city's six *sestiere*, there are absolutely no cars, buses, or trains, and the occasional skateboard or pushcart is about the only thing you'll see with wheels. While poets, musicians, and various members of the literati have waxed nostalgic about the beauty of Venice's romantic, tangled streets, those same winding walkways are likely to provoke less lyrical outbursts from those unfamiliar with the city. Even experienced travelers will likely find themselves frustrated when navigating the city, since maps struggle to provide adequate detailing of the city's smaller thoroughfares. Additionally, streets are often nameless or change names unexpectedly, and street numbers organized by neighborhood give only a general indication of where particular addresses are to be found. Your best bet is to memorize a few major landmarks, know the vaporetto stop nearest your hotel, know at least one *campo* near your hotel or hostel, and keep the cardinal directions in mind.

By Boat

In some cases, particularly when bridges are scarce, travelers will find it more convenient to get to their destination by boat. Before you spend a lot of money on an expensive vaporetto ticket, consider whether a 🗺**traghetto** might get you to your destination more quickly. There are several major stops in the city where you can catch these small ferries, essentially gondolas without the kitsch, that will take you across the Grand Canal for only €0.50. Signs toward *traghetti* stops tend to be clearly indicated, and odds are, wherever you are, there will be one nearby. *Traghetti* hours vary and are limited during the winter, but in general, they remain an excellent means of transport around Venice. The vaporetti offer more extensive service throughout the city and operate 24hr. per day but are also more expensive. A single vaporetto ride costs €6.50 and longer-term passes which offer unlimited service are also available *(⏰ 12hr. pass €16; 24hr. €18; 3-day €21; 4-day €28; 7-day €50)*, but the best option for students visiting in the short-term may be to purchase a three-day pass *(€22)* that includes unlimited transport via vaporetti and mainland-connecting buses as well as the benefits of the **Rolling Venice Card.**

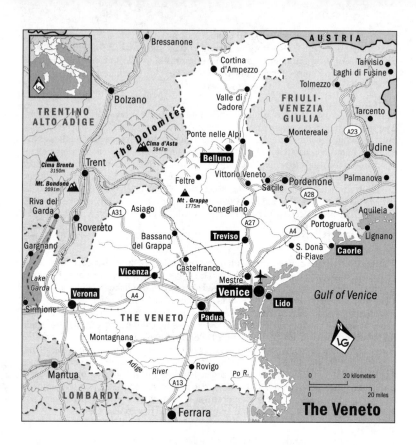

The Veneto

venice

PADUA, VERONA, AND BOLOGNA

While places like Milan and Venice tend to get most of the press, there's a lot more to northern Italy than the cities even Ron Burgundy could find on a world map.

You'll be pleasantly surprised to discover that less-known cities like Padua, Verona, and Bologna burst with vibrant intellectual life, incredible cuisine, and fascinating history. Padua and Bologna are home to two of Italy's most famous universities, with the **Università di Bologna** claiming the title of the oldest in the Western world. Cultured Verona, meanwhile, hosts Europe's premier opera series. Each city also lays claim to a culinary niche, Bologna having garnered worldwide fame for its invention of **tortellini** and **lasagna,** Padua creatively reinterpretating Venetian cuisine, and Verona marking itself as the capital of one of Italy's finest winemaking regions.

These three cities differ noticeably from one another, and attempting to draw excessive comparison between the them is really not worth the time; it's better that you see for yourself the wealth of rich experiences they have to offer. Sigh to the strains of a Puccini aria in Verona's Roman arena, burn your tongue on piping-hot *lasagne Bolognese* in Piazza Maggiore, and scrutinize Giotto's epic fresco cycle in Padua's Cappella degli Scrovegni. You'll quickly learn to love these Italian cities—and getting to know them won't hurt your chances at the next geography bee, either.

greatest hits

- **LA GRASSA.** Name a variety of pasta, and there's a good chance it originated in Bologna. That Bolognese sauce you've been eating on spaghetti for years started somewhere, you know (p. 243).

- **ROME OF THE NORTH.** Verona has carefully protected its ancient relics, and today you can watch an opera in the city's remarkable amphitheater (p. 230).

- **ALMA MATER.** Bologna has the world's oldest university, while Padua's is the second oldest in Italy. See where students have been studying, and taking week-long breaks from studying, since the 11th century (p. 218).

These are three great cities, but one is the clear champion when it comes to student life. Bologna *invented* students. And today it has 100,000 of them. Forget Cambridge, MA or Berkeley, CA: this is the granddaddy of student towns. Visit during the summer and you might never know; like any student town its character changes almost overnight once exams end. But during the year this is one of the highest concentrations of young people you could ever wish to meet. For a straightforward and ridiculously obvious place to start, try College Bar, which is basically everything its name makes it out to be.

Honestly, Padua doesn't deserve to be overshadowed by Bologna like this. The city actually has Italy's second-oldest university, but as Buzz Aldrin will tell you, one small step for a man means a whole lot of irrelevance for the guy right behind him. Don't let that deter you, however, since nightlife here is great, but again visit during the school year to get a real taste of it. As for Verona, student life is a little more muted. There are lots of 15-year-olds running around falling in love, though. Just watch out for family feuds, draughts of living death, and dodgy apothecaries. We don't want stories of woe after sunset in Verona's disco.

padua *padova* ☎049

Padua, one of the oldest cities in northern Italy, usually serves as a quick daytrip from Venice for most travelers. However, a visit of at least two days is necessary if you hope to scratch the surface of its illustrious history or its current identity as a rapidly developing metropolis. Even if you're not a student at the city's **Università di Padova** or on a Petruchian quest to wive it wealthily in Padua, take the time to explore its intriguing blend of old and new. With a population of 220,000, Padua is very much a modern city. It's got the high rise buildings, congested urban streets, and industrial production to prove it. But for all that, this economic center of Italy's Veneto region has retained many of its medieval qualities including breathtaking churches, spectacular *piazze*, and the vibrant intellectual life associated with a premier national university—one that counts **Copernicus** as an alumnus and **Galileo Galilei** as a former faculty member, no less. While a brief stay in Padua can leave you with the impression that the city's unique historical character has been worn away by the forces of modernity, those who can muster some persistance will be rewarded with a more realistic understanding of this diverse and extremely relevant place.

ORIENTATION

The train station, where most visitors will arrive in Padua, is at the northern end of the city. The area around the station tends to be largely commercial and will be of no interest to most visitors, who will spend the vast majority of their time exploring the sights in the city's historic center, which is concentrated around **Via Roma-Via Cavour-Corso Garibaldi.**

ACCOMMODATIONS

Padua is a fairly large city, but most accommodations are to the south, east, or southeast of the *centro*. Booking a room in these locations means you'll be farther from the city center and will likely have to contend with some highways while walking to most attractions. Aside from this inconvenience, you should be happy with your digs: Padua may not be as pretty as Venice, but it's also not as pricey.

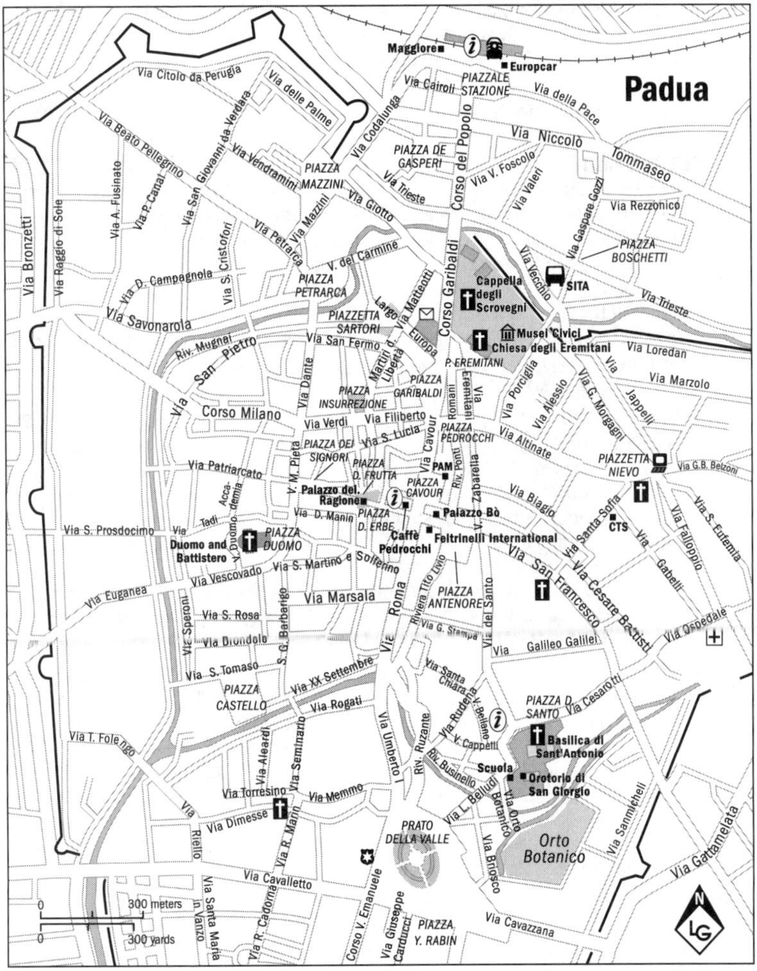

👍 BELLUDI 37 HOTEL [5]

V. Luca Belludi 37 ☎049 66 56 33 💻www.belludi37.it

Staying at Belludi 37 will cost a bit more than staying at another hotel in Padua, but even with the high rates, it's the best deal in town. Amenities include free bike rentals, excellent breakfast, free Wi-Fi, LCD TVs with DVD players, orthopedic beds, and some of the most comfortable, well-decorated rooms you'll find anywhere—even in this price range.

⇟ Exit Prato della Valle to the northeast on V. Luca Belludi and continue for 2-3min.; the hotel is ahead on the right. ℹ Breakfast included. Bikes available at front desk free of charge. Parking €10. Free Wi-Fi. $ Singles €80; doubles €120-150; junior suite €180. Additional bed €40.

OSTELLO CITTÀ DI PADOVA HOSTEL [1]

V. Aleardo Aleardi 30 ☎049 87 52 219 💻www.ostellopadova.it

If you're traveling in a larger group—and can share a room for four to six people—this hostel's the place for you. While you might not enjoy the elaborate decor or privacy you would find in most hotels (this is, after all, an *ostello*), the rates here are as low as you can hope for.

✈ Bus #3 to V. Umberto 1 or bus #12 or 18 to V. Cavalletto. From Prato della Valle (the large, elliptical square), take V. Cavalletto, turn right onto V. Marin, and after the Torresino church turn left. **i** *Breakfast included. Laundry service. Baggage storage.* $ *Dorms €19.* ⏰ *Max. 5-night stay.*

ALBERGO VERDI 💳♿📶❄ HOTEL [3]

V. Dondi dall'Orologio 7 ☎049 83 64 163 💻www.albergoverdipadova.it

A small hotel exceptionally close to most of Padua's major sights, Albergo Verdi only has 16 guest rooms, so if you're planning to stay here, reserve in advance. The rooms are both beautiful and functional, and if you book at the right time, you can get a sweet deal. Serious bonus points to Albergo Verdi for their 24hr. bar, one of the few places open all night in Padua.

✈ From Palazzo della Ragione, head west on V. Daniele Manin, turn right onto V. Monte di Pieta, turn left and walk through P. Capitaniato, and turn right onto V. Accademia; the hotel is immediately ahead. **i** *Breakfast included.* $ *Singles €40-100; doubles €40-150; suites €60-200.*

HOTEL AL FAGIANO 💳🚭📶❄ HOTEL [4]

V. Locatelli 45 ☎049 87 50 073 💻www.alfagiano.com

Surprisingly upscale for the price, Hotel Al Fagiano contains beautiful rooms decorated according to color themes meant to evoke different emotions. In addition to some of the most singular rooms you'll find in the city, the hotel presents a competent and well-informed staff and an enviable central location from which the entire city is accessible.

✈ From the northwest corner of Prato della Valle, turn onto V. Belludi and continue for about 2min. V. Locatelli intersects with V. Belludi; the hotel is near the intersection. **i** *Breakfast included.* $ *Singles €50-70; doubles €70-100; quads €90-110.*

HOTEL EDEN 💳🚭📶 HOTEL [3]

V. Cesare Battisti 255 ☎049 65 04 84 💻www.hoteledenpadova.it

Refreshingly, Hotel Eden tends to keep things simple. Its prime locale and surprisingly reasonable rates make it a standout. The look here is minimalist, favoring simple tile floors and solid colors over gaudy excess while emphasizing customer service and the quality of what they've got to offer.

✈ From the northeast corner of the Palazzo della Ragione, continue east along V. Cesare Battisti for 2-3min.; the hotel is ahead on the left. **i** *Breakfast included. Wi-Fi €2 per hr.* $ *Singles €45; doubles €65, used as triple €80, used as quad €95.*

HOTEL GIOTTO 💳♿📶 HOTEL [4]

Piazzale Pontecorvo 33 ☎049 87 61 845 💻www.hotelgiotto.com

Conveniently near **Basilica di Sant'Antonio da Padova** and the historic *centro*, Giotto caters to an English-speaking clientele. Thoroughly acceptable rooms are complemented by a front desk that's more than willing to help tourists plan excursions and responds to patron requests promptly.

✈ From Palazzo della Ragione, walk southwest for 5-7min.; the hotel is ahead shortly after the bridge. **i** *Breakfast included.* $ *Singles €59-80; doubles €79-120; triples €100-130.*

HOTEL MIGNON 💳🚭 HOTEL [4]

V. Luca Belludi 22 ☎049 66 17 22 💻www.hotelmignonpadova.it

A strong choice for groups of any size, Hotel Mignon might prove an irresistible value for parties of four or five who can enjoy the privacy and luxury of Mignon's high quality rooms at hostel-like prices. It is also well located and has nicely furnished rooms.

✈ From the northwest corner of Prato della Valle, turn onto V. Belludi and continue for about 1min. **i** *Breakfast included.* $ *Singles €54; doubles €71; triples €86; quads €108.*

SIGHTS

Seriously consider investing in a **Padova Card,** which will get you into most of the city's sights either for free or at a considerable discount. As an added bonus, the card is accompanied by a booklet jam-packed with up-to-date information about the city's attractions. With or without the card, though, Padua should prove a fascinating city to most visitors. Its dozens of historical sights are within walking distance of one another and constantly bring the city's fascinating history into the everyday life of its residents. Don't miss Prato della Valle, the mother of all Italian *piazze* (though, at 90,000 sq. m, it's kind of hard to overlook).

BASILICA DI SANT'ANTONIO DA PADOVA — ♿ CHURCH

V. Orto Botanico 11 — ☎049 87 89 722 💻www.basilicadelsanto.org

Basilica di Sant'Antonio is arguably Padua's single most impressive sight. The assemblage of Byzantine-influenced towers and domes on the church's exterior creates an arresting profile, and the interior is no less striking; a visitor could easily spend hours admiring the wide spectrum of artistic styles incorporated into the building's design over its 13 centuries of development. Highlights include the **Tomba di Sant'Antonio,** the ornate sepulcher of the church's namesake, the **Capella di San Giacomo,** and the **Oratorio di San Giorgio**—but after you've taken in these main events, spend some time exploring the dozens of smaller altars, tombs, capellas, and rooms throughout the rest of the cathedral, all with their own histories and styles.

🚏 Bus #3, 12, 18, A M, T. Or tram to Fermata Santo. $ Free. ⏰ Open daily 9am-1pm and 2-6pm.

CAPPELLA DEGLI SCROVEGNI — ♿ CHURCH

P. Eremitani — ☎049 20 10 020 💻www.cappelladegliscrovegni.it

Padua's premier tourist attraction, Cappella degli Scrovegni houses one of the most important works of the Italian Renaissance: Giotto's fresco cycle depicting the life of Mary, the mother of Jesus, and her role in human salvation. **Enrico Scrovegni,** a wealthy usurer who wanted to atone for the sins of his family, commissioned the chapel as penance. The chapel was completed between 1305 and 1306, but apparently didn't represent sufficient contrition for Dante, who placed Reginald Scrovegni, Enrico's father, in the seventh circle of hell in the *Inferno.* Regardless of Scrovegni's contrition or lack thereof, the chapel remains a masterpiece of Renaissance artwork, with 38 panels representing a level of realism that set the standard for many later Italian artists. The chapel's brick facade has endured damage due to those three great enemies of preservation—time, neglect, and war—but the interior retains its stunning imagery and color, thanks in part to careful restoration efforts and precise climate controls that limit the number of visitors allowed in the chapel at a given time. Some might complain that due to strict protective regulations the chapel is only marginally more accessible to the public than it was when Scrovegni constructed it as a private oratory for his family, but the authorities insist these limitations are necessary to preserve the city's greatest work of art. Budget at least 30min. for a visit since visitors are required to wait for 15min. in a climate-controlled room.

🚏 Bus #3, 10, 12, 18, A, M, T, AT. Or tram to Fermata Eremitani. ℹ Visitors admitted every 15min. $ €12, with Padova Card free. €1 reservation fee. ⏰ Open daily 9am-7pm. Open selected evenings 7-10pm.

MUSEI CIVICI EREMITANI — ♿ MUSEUM

P. Eremitani — ☎049 82 04 551 💻www.turismopadova.it

The Civic Museum of Padua is one of the top museums in the region, befitting a city with Padua's kind of history. The museum has an extensive archaeological collection, with pieces from all the different cultures and catastrophes that shaped the city and the broader Veneto. From artifacts of ancient Padua to artwork from the late Renaissance, the museum covers a comprehensive timeline in a series of collections that is surprisingly engaging. Though many visitors initally regard the Civic Museum as a way to spend a couple of minutes while waiting to enter the Scrovegni Chapel, most quickly realize that it's more than a mere stopover—it's a fantastic introduction to the city.

Bus #3, 10, 12, 18, A, M, T, AT. Or tram to Fermata Eremitani. $ €10, with Padova Card free. Open Tu-Su 9am-7pm.

PALAZZO DELLA RAGIONE — PALAZZO

P. delle Erbe - V. VIII Febbraio ☎049 82 05 006 www.turismopadova.it

The imposing arches of the Palazzo della Ragione constitute what, with the possible exception of the exterior of **Basilica di Sant'Antonio da Padova,** is the most impressive facade of any building in the city. The Palazzo has stood for almost 800 years as the seat of the town government and remains at the heart of the city, casting an impressive shadow over nearby restaurants, shops, markets, and cafes. Given its formidable exterior, you might expect an interior that would rival that of the Palazzo Ducale in Venice, but don't get your hopes up: the Great Hall is universally acclaimed due to its sheer size (2200 sq. m) and the breathtaking beauty of its frescoes, because...well, because that's all there is. Unless there's a temporary exhibition going on, the Great Hall is all you'll see, leading to a visit that may be frustratingly brief.

Bus #3, 12, 18, A, M, T, AT. Or tram to Fermata Ponti Romani. $ €4, with Padova Card free. During temporary exhibitions €2 for Padova Card holders. Open Feb-Oct Tu-Su 9am-7pm; Nov-Jan Tu-Su 9am-6pm.

MUSEO DEL PRE CINEMA — ♿ MUSEUM

Palazzo Angeli - Prado della Valle 1/A ☎049 87 63 838 www.minicizotti.it

Padua's Museum of Pre-Cinema is one of those small, quirky places where you can learn tons about a topic that, before you had entered, you didn't even know existed. With a staff and management who are clearly passionate about the topic, the small museum displays a fascinating collection of items relating to the development of film and illusion from the years before motion pictures involved, well, motion. The highlight here might be the 20min. film detailing early illusions that developed out of discoveries in the field of optics and how this technology fundamentally affected mass entertainment. The museum also features an excellent array of antiques, mainly from the late 19th and early 20th centuries, and interactive exhibits that allow visitors to explore the ingenious pre-cinema methods of illusion. **Tip:** if you plan your visit for mid-afternoon when the museum empties out, one of the museum's employees might volunteer to give you a brief private tour of the museum at no extra charge.

Bus #3, 12, 18, A, M, T. Or tram to Fermata Prato della Valle. $ €3, students, under 18 and over 65 and with Padova Card €2. Open M 10am-4pm, W-Su 10am-4pm.

ORTO BOTANICO — BOTANICAL GARDEN

V. dell'Orto Botanico ☎049 82 72 119 www.ortobotanico.unipd.it

A **UNESCO World Heritage Site,** the Botanical Garden of Padua was founded in the 16th century under the direction of the government of the Venetian Republic as a horticultural homework project for students of the city's university. The garden was meant to be a repository of important medicinal plants, a home to various forms of exotic vegetation brought to the Veneto by explorers, and a center for scientific inquiry into these various plants and their properties. Today, the garden remains affiliated with the university and continues to house an incredible array of foreign and domestic plants, but modern greenhouse technology has rendered this low-tech garden more significant historically than scientifically. Nevertheless, it's immaculately maintained and remains one of Padua's most beautiful tourist attractions, even if only the botanists will have a response more intelligent than, "ooh pretty flower!"

🚏 Bus #3, 12, 18, A, M, T, AT. Or tram to Fermata Santo. $ Free. ⏰ Open daily Apr-Oct 9am-1pm and 3-7pm; Nov-Mar 9am-1pm.

CHIESA DEGLI EREMITANI — ♿ CHURCH

P. Eremitani — ☎049 87 56 410 💻www.turismopadova.it

Built on the site of a former Roman arena, Chiesa degli Eremitani has historically been one of Padua's most important churches. Over its 700-year past, the building has endured more than its share of turmoil. During WWII, bombing destroyed a series of frescoes that had been held in regard comparable to that given to the ones featured in the nearby Cappella degli Scrovegni. Despite these travails, the church still stands today as one of the most esteemed in the Veneto.

🚏 Bus #3, 10, 12, 18, A, M, T, AT. Or tram to Fermata Eremitani. $ Free. ⏰ Open in summer M-F 8:15am-6:45pm, Sa-Su 10am-1pm and 4-7pm; in fall, winter, and spring M-F 8:15am-6:15pm, Sa-Su 10am-1pm and 4:15-7pm.

BATTISTERO DELLA CATTEDRALE — ♿ BAPTISTERY

P. Duomo — ☎049 65 69 14 💻www.padovacard.it

Attached to the Cathedral of Padua, the Battistero della Cattedrale is its most elaborate, interesting, and overlooked section. A small adjunct to the cathedral, it doesn't take long to see but features a series of frescoes by **Menabuoi** that are second in Padua only to Giotto's cycle in the Scrovegni Chapel. The remarkable detail of the frescoes, which cover the battistero's walls and ceilings, gives the place a much more dynamic appearance than you'll find in any of the city's larger churches.

🚏 Bus #10. Or tram to Fermata Ponti Romani. $ Free. ⏰ Open daily 10am-6pm

CHIESA DI SAN NICOLÒ — 🚫 CHURCH

V. San Nicolò — ☎049 87 62 318 💻www.sannicolo.padova.it

Padua's oldest church, San Nicolò was operational in the 11th century but houses artwork from centuries prior. The unassuming brick Roman-Byzantine facade conceals a fascinating interior, the highlights of which include a triptych from the fourth century, a sixth-century baptismal fountain, and a series of later works that rival anything featured in the Eremitani. Significantly smaller and less conspicuous than the other Paduan churches listed, San Nicolò escapes overcrowding.

🚏 Bus #3, 12, 18, A, M, T, AT. Or tram to Fermata Ponti Romani. $ Free. Written guide available for €0.50. ⏰ Open M-F 8am-6:30pm. Sa Mass 8am and 6:30pm. Su Mass 8:30, 10, 11am, and 7pm.

PALAZZO ZUCKERMANN — 🎫♿ MUSEUM

C. Garibaldi 33 — ☎049 82 05 664 💻www.turismopadova.it

A great complement to the works on display at the **Musei Civici Eremitani,** Palazzo Zuckermann houses Padua's collection of "applied decorative arts"—meaning glassware, silver, ceramics, and furniture that are of exceptional artistic merit. Appropriately located in one of Padua's premier *palazzi*, the collection also augments the historic narrative introduced in the Civic Museum through its display of these works with particular regard to their role in the history of Padua. Awaken your inner proletariat and appreciate some ass-kicking artwork that doesn't need namby-pamby climate control to make it through a few centuries.

🚏 Bus #3, 10, 12, 18, A, M, T, AT. Or tram to Fermata Eremitani. $ €10, with Padova Card free. ⏰ Open Tu-Su 10am-7pm.

PONTE SAN LORENZO — 🚫 BRIDGE, ANCIENT ROME

Ponte San Lorenzo at V. San Francesco and Riviera dei Ponti Romani

Built over 2000 years ago and now entirely subterranean, the Ponte San Lorenzo was the greatest triumph of Roman architecture in Padua. The bridge, the arches of which can still be viewed during limited hours, was built according to a precise geometry intended to provide adequate support while minimizing the width of the piers. This maximized the bridge's longevity and represented an architectural achievement unsurpassed by bridges in the region for a millennium after its completion. If you happen to be nearby during the limited viewing hours, definitely set aside some time to view these ancient arches.

🧭 Bus #3, 12, 18, A, M, T, AT or tram to Fermata Ponti Romani. $ Free. 🕐 Open Tu-W 10am-noon and 4-6pm, Th-F 10am-noon, Sa 10am-noon and 4-6pm, Su 10am-noon.

FOOD

Whereas in cities like Venice, most eateries near the famous locales are touristy rip-offs, in Padua, you'll actually want to head toward the *centro* and the big destinations for the best restaurants. It has avoided the proliferation of watered-down trattorias with English-language menus that plagues other cities. Plus, since the city center remains the most pleasant, walkable, and orderly section of town, it makes a fine place to eat a true Venetan feast. Definitely make time to drink a cappuccino at **Caffè Pedrocchi** *(V. VIII Febbraio ☎049 87 81 231 💻www.caffepedrocchi.it)* and contemplate your next literary masterpiece. Designed by Giuseppe Jappelli, the cafe was a favorite haunt of Lord Byron and Stendhal.

👍 DONNA IRENE — 💳♿🍸❄☀ RISTORANTE [4]

Vicolo Pontecorvo 1 — ☎049 65 68 52 💻www.donnariene.com

A can't-miss restaurant just south of Padua's major sights, Donna Irene specializes in the traditional cuisine of the Veneto region complemented by a few standard Italian classics, including an incredible Caprese salad that might be the best on the Italian mainland. The quality of the food is matched only by the restaurant's ambience. The place is easily reached from the *centro*, but set back in a quiet enclave, so it'll feel like you're eating in the gorgeous countryside of the Veneto rather than in the tumult of the city.

🧭 From Palazzo della Ragione, walk southwest for 5-7min.; immediately after the bridge, the restaurant is ahead on the left. Look for signs indicating the restaurant since it's set back from the road about 20m. $ Entrees €12-22. 🕐 Open Tu-Su noon-2:30pm and 7-11:30pm.

CLAFÉ — 🍽♿🍸❄ CAFE [2]

V. Cesarotti 63

Just a few minutes from the Basilica, Clafé is owned and operated by one of Padua's most enthusiastic and enterprising *restaurateurs* who's perpetually innovating new dishes and coming up with unique ideas to stay a few steps ahead of the competition. The small cafe is simultaneously chic and minimalist yet cozy and inviting and a lovely place to stop in for a drink while sightseeing or to enjoy a light lunch while people-watching on one of Padua's main pedestrian thoroughfares.

🧭 From the Basilica di Sant'Antonio, head north to V. Cesarotti, turn right, and continue for 2-3min.; the cafe is ahead on the left. $ Entrees €7-8. Wine €2-3.50. 🕐 Open Tu-F 7am-9pm, Sa 7am-7pm, Su 7am-3pm.

ZAIRO — 💳♿🍸☀ RISTORANTE [2]

Prato della Valle 51 — ☎049 66 38 03 💻www.zairo.net

From the outside, Zairo looks like a pretty conventional restaurant in a tourist-heavy area, but if you step inside, you'll find a surpisingly classy establishment with some of the best hearty Italian food around. The portions are sizable yet affordable, and while the menu offers myriad excellent entrees, Zairo's pizzas are their most popular selection.

🧭 East/southeastern corner of Prato della Valle. $ Entrees €6-15. 🕐 Open Tu-Su 11:30am-3:30pm and 6:30-8:30pm.

ENOTECA IL TORCHIO 💳♿🍸⛅ RISTORANTE, ENOTECA ❸

V. San Martino e Solferino 29 ☎349 55 62 390 💻www.iltorchio.eu

If you're looking for a light meal and a few drinks before a night out, Il Torchio and its nice selection of reasonably sized salads, pizzas, and pastas are perfect for you. Whatever you do order, be sure that you give the wine list adequate consideration—you'll find few places in Padua that complement the cuisine with such a diverse selection of drinks.

🪧 From the south side of Palazzo della Ragione, head west, make a left onto V. delle Piazze, and take the 1st right; the restaurant is immediately ahead. $ Entrees €12-19. ⏰ Open Tu-Su 11am-midnight.

AL RICORDO 💳♿🍸❄⛅ RISTORANTE ❸

V. San Francesco 175 ☎049 66 07 33

Centrally located Al Ricordo prepares traditional Veneto entrees but doesn't stop there, also serving an excellent menu of appetizers, an extensive dessert menu, and a nice selection of wines and beers. The grilled chicken makes a nice entree, but if you are planning to dine with at least a couple other people, we recommend going for a tapas-style meal and ordering a bunch of the intriguing appetizers.

🪧 From Palazzo della Ragione, walk southwest for 3-4min. $ Entrees €7.50-18. ⏰ Open daily 11am-3pm and 7-11pm.

NIGHTLIFE

The nighttime scene in Padua won't please the ravers, which is fairly typical for the Veneto region. Predictably, the city's a lot livelier during the school year, but in the summer, pretty much everything is shut down by 2am.

VIA ROMA 💳♿📶🍸❄⛅ BAR

V. Roma 96 ☎049 87 52 712

One of Padua's main hotspots, Via Roma is packed most evenings with a young, energetic, and eclectic clientele drawn in by top-notch cocktails, an impressive wine list, and the bar's welcoming vibe. Via Roma proudly displays its owners' creativity with trendy playlists and an interior featuring a unique blend of contemporary and antique decor.

🪧 From Prato della Valle, turn onto V. Umberto and continue straight for about 5-7min.; the bar is on the left. $ Drinks €2.50-7. ⏰ Open daily 7:30am-2am.

OTIVM 💳♿🍸⛅ BAR

V. Roma 69 ☎049 65 83 28 💻www.otivm.it

Otivm bills itself as a "lunch cafe" and touts its coffee, but the patrons who pack the bar well into the night clearly missed the memo. One of the most popular nighttime spots in Padua, Otivm is almost always packed with students and travelers in their mid-20s enjoying the strong and delicious drinks (descriptions that apply both to their coffee and their cocktails). With its flatscreen TVs, Otivm is an ideal place to watch major sporting events. Fortunately, it's easy to find on V. Roma. Otherwise its unpronounceable name would make it difficult to ask for directions.

🪧 From Prato della Valle, turn onto V. Umberto and continue straight for 6-8min.; the bar is on the right. $ Drinks €3-5.50. ⏰ Open daily 7am-2am.

MILANO CAFÉ 💳♿🍸❄⛅ CAFE

V. Santa Lucia 33 ☎347 73 30 828

With less of a student vibe and more of a sophisticated modern ambience, the Milano Cafe is a small lounge where you can go out and enjoy a few drinks and stimulating conversation without being drowned out by blaring music or drunk backpackers. Don't let the more refined atmosphere deter you, though, since the bar serves top-notch drinks and is popular with some of Padua's most discerning residents.

 # From Chiesa degli Eremitani, turn left onto C. Garibaldi, continue onto Riviera dei Ponti Romani, and turn right onto V. Santa Lucia; the bar is shortly ahead. $ Drinks €2.50-7. ⏰ Open M-Sa 8am-2am.

LES TULIPES CAFE BAR

V. San Martino e Solferino 19 ☎049 876 69 71

In its gorgeous interior, Les Tulipes Cafe plays up a flower motif without letting it become overbearing. The awesome color and lighting scheme gives the bar a congenial air even when it's not too crowded. The place is popular with students from the university and therefore tends to be less crowded during the summer, but it's always worth a visit.

 # From Palazzo della Ragione, head west, turn left onto V. delle Piazze, and make the 1st right; the bar is immediately ahead. $ Drinks €2.50-5.50. ⏰ Open Tu-Su 9am-midnight.

ARTS AND CULTURE

Padua's entertainment scene tends to be sporadic, featuring many festivals, university-affiliated events, and periodic concerts but few consistent theaters or cinemas. Many of the city's churches host occasional choirs or orchestral music, but these performances aren't on a consistent or fixed schedule. Maximize your chances of finding great artistic and cultural exhibitions by inquiring at a tourist office or in your hotel. There aren't any websites in English that offer completely up-to-date information, but if you're inclined to sort through the information in Italian, 💻**padovacultura.padovanet.it** is a great resource.

TEATRO VERDI DI PADOVA THEATER

V. dei Livello 32 ☎049 87 77 92 13 💻www.teatrostabileveneto.it

Teatro Verdi draws an incredible array of brilliant and thought-provoking shows, ranging from Shakespearean dramas to more contemporary works. The theater announces its scheduled performances months in advances of opening night, so check out their website to see what might be of interest, even if you have some difficulty navigating the Italian site.

 # From Palazzo della Ragione, head west on V. Daniele Manin and turn right onto V. Monte di Pieta; turn left and walk through P. Capitaniato, then turn right onto V. Accademia; the theater is shortly ahead. ⏰ Hours vary seasonally and depending on show. Call ahead or check their website.

SHOPPING

Though Padua is a relatively small city, there is some great shopping to be found. Daily markets near **Prato della Valle** usually offer fresh produce and other groceries but sometimes branch out into other sundry goods. If you want to see them at their best, you should try to arrive before noon on weekdays or anytime on Saturday. The best clothes shopping tends to be in the north end of the historic center, just north of the Palazzo della Ragione and to the southeast of the Scrovegni Chapel. Here you'll find many great designer stores and boutiques that range in price from astronomically expensive to fairly reasonable.

FUSODORO BOUTIQUE

V. Marsilio da Padova 21/25

A Paduan boutique so chic it feels the need to (unironically) advertise that pedestrian passersby can enter the store free of charge, Fusodoro offers an awesome selection of the top seasonal designs from several Italian designers, including a few smaller design houses you're not likely to come across elsewhere. While the prices are high, the clothes are colorful and casual while maintaining a cool and classic vibe. Fusodoro is unabashedly upscale, but the style is much more daring and innovative than the stolid ones you'll find in most comparable American or British boutiques.

 # From the northwest corner of Palazzo della Ragione, walk west until you reach a T intersection,

then turn right; the store is about 1min. ahead on the right. ⏰ Open M 4-7:45pm, Tu-F 9:30am-12:30pm and 4-7:45pm, Sa 9:30am-1pm and 4-8pm.

ESSENTIALS

Practicalities

- **TOURIST OFFICES:** There are several **Turismo Padova** offices throughout the city. *(Main office in the train station. ☎049 87 52 077 🖥www.turismopadova.it 🚏 Lines #3, 7, 10, 12, 41, 43, A, M, T. ⏰ Open M-Sa 9am-7pm, Su 9am-noon.)*
- **POST OFFICES: Poste Italiane.** *(C. Garibaldi 25 ☎049 87 72 111 🖥www.poste.it 🚏 Accessible by numerous lines including #3, 5, 9, 10, 11, 12, 13, 15, 16, 18, 22. Just across the street from the P. Eremitani. ⏰ Open M-Sa 8:30am-6:30pm.)*

Emergency!

- **POLICE:** There are several stations in the city, but Prato della Valle 41 is the main one. *(Non-emergency: ☎049 82 34 533 🚏 Bus #MDP, 12, 18, 22, or 24 to Prato della Valle, in the southern section of the city near the Orto Botanico. In the southwest corner of the square.)*
- **HOSPITALS/MEDICAL SERVICES: Ospedale Civile** provides emergency and non-emergency medical care. *(V. Giustiniani 2 ☎049 82 11 111 🖥www.sanita.padova.it 🚏 Bus #5, 6, 24, 41, or 43. From Basilica di Sant'Antonio, turn right onto V. Cesarotti and continue for about 5min.; the hospital is ahead on the right. ⏰ Non-emergency care M-F 7:30am-7pm. Emergency care 24hr.)*

Getting There

By Plane

Visitors seeking to go directly to Padua upon arrival in Italy are equally well-served by airports in Venice, Verona, and Bologna, which are all comparable in terms of convenience and offer relatively easy access to Padua by train. For more information, see the **Getting There** sections for those cities. If you're traveling within Italy, though, you'll be better-served by ground transportation.

By Train

Most travelers coming to Padua are coming from Venice or Milan, and in either case the easiest way to get to the city is definitely by train. The train station at **Piazzale Stazione** is in the north end of the city and a decent distance from where you're likely to be staying. Plan for a €5-10 taxi ride or 15-35min. walk to your hotel. Trains run to Padua from numerous destinations: **Bologna** *($ €7.75. ⏰ 1hr., 1-2 per hr.);* **Milan** *($ €12.35. ⏰ 2-3hr., 1-2 per hr.);* **Venice** *($ €2.90. ⏰ 18-41min., 3-6 per hr.);* **Verona.** *($ €4.95. ⏰ 40-80min., 2-3 per hr.)* Train tickets are available at the station, and trains are infrequently sold out.

By Bus

The bus station at **Piazza Boschetti** is near the train station and thus similarly inconveniently located. **Venice** *($ €3.10. ⏰ 45min., 1-2 buses per hr.)* is accessible by bus, but it's cheaper, quicker, and generally more enjoyable to take the train.

Getting Around

Padua has an excellent **bus** and **tram** system that runs throughout the city and to neighboring suburban areas, but it seems to be used primarily for longer distance transit. Most visitors sticking to the city's historic center will probably be fine getting around by foot or bicycle. You can walk from the Scrovegni Chapel to the Botanical Gardens in less than 20min. If you want to expedite things, this is a great biking city with bicycle lanes up the wazoo and motorists who tend to defer to cyclists, so check with your hotel to see if they rent **bikes** (many do) or see if there is a rental shop nearby. You can also get one as soon as you arrive at the shop in the train station.

(☎348 70 16 373 🖳www.turismopadova.it 🕐 Open 24hr.) If you're planning to go out to the countryside or are making a longer trip within the city, the buses or trams are a great option and are free to all holders of the Padova Card. If you need a **cab**, RadioTaxi (☎049 65 13 33) is a reliable option.

verona   ☎045

Fair Verona, best known to most English-speakers as the site of Shakespeare's *Romeo and Juliet*, has come a long way since the days when the Houses of Montague and Capulet fought in its streets. (OK, maybe the Bard embellished the history a bit, but a real-life Capello family did live here long ago.) Currently home to a thriving population of over 260,000 people, Verona is one of the liveliest and most economi-

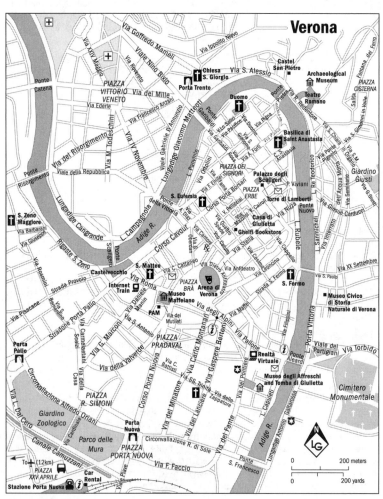

cally important cities in the Veneto region. Its ability to reconcile this modernity with its storied history through the preservation of numerous historic buildings and architecturally significant works from the Middle Ages has earned it a designation as a **UNESCO World Heritage Site.** Though its outskirts are filled with the types of buildings you might find in any mid-size European city, the *centro* holds a remarkable number of Roman buildings still in use today. In a setting like this, it's easy to drift into the romance of Shakespeare's famous tragedy. Equipped with a decent map and a good sense of adventure, any traveler can navigate this somewhat diffuse city and, in the process, quickly come to understand why Verona is regarded as one of the most historically significant locales in all of Europe and how it might have inspired one of the world's most famous love stories.

ORIENTATION

Verona is a sprawling city with over 700,000 people in its greater metropolitan area, but the good news for visitors is that it's actually fairly manageable. Getting around requires a fair amount of biking or walking, but pretty much everything of interest is within a 15-20min. walk of the **Arena.** Given the incredible number of well-preserved historic sights and buildings, the journey can be even more interesting than the ultimate destination. If you keep your eyes open, you're sure to discover more tucked-away churches, interesting bridges, and Roman walls than we could ever begin to list here. Keep in mind that the river marks the city's northern boundary—if you get caught on the wrong side of it, you might end up walking much more than you had originally intended.

ACCOMMODATIONS

Verona is one of the most difficult places in Italy to find budget accommodations. Often the city's visitors are older opera aficionados, so most hotels cater to a wealthier clientele. All the hotels listed here are within comfortable walking distance (less than 15min.) of the **Arena** and are among the city's most convenient. If you're tempted to book a room at a bed and breakfast, be forewarned: many of the B and Bs in Verona are less service-oriented than hotels. Don't be surprised if you show up and have to wait around a couple of hours for someone to answer the door, even if you've come at the scheduled arrival time.

HOTEL SAN LUCA

Vicolo Volto San Luca 8   ☎045 59 13 33 ▪www.sanlucahotel.com

    ✈♿(ᴙ)❄ HOTEL ❺

Hotel San Luca might be beyond the price range of many budget travelers, but anyone willing to shell out for a top-quality hotel should seriously consider this one since you get what you pay for and then some. Amenities here go above and beyond the standard for an Italian hotel in this price range, including exceptionally comfortable rooms and a breakfast buffet that is one of the best *Let's Go* has found.

✈ *From the southwest corner of P. Bra, continue south on C. Porta Nuova and turn right onto Volto San Luca; the hotel is immediately ahead.* ⓘ *Breakfast included.* ⑤ *Singles €78-181; doubles €116-208; triples €146-258.*

B AND B ALLE ERBE

Corte Sgarzarie 5   ☎39 29 15 50 00 ▪www.alleerbe.it

    ✈⊗ B AND B ❸

By far our favorite bed and breakfast in Verona, B and B Alle Erbe sits in a picturesque courtyard no more than 10min. from any of the city's major sights. The staff is extremely amiable and puts considerable time and energy into making sure that the rooms meet all of their guests' needs. Alle Erbe's beautiful setting and wonderful ownership more than make up for any inconveniences that come from rooming in a smaller establishment.

✈ *From P. Bra, go northwest on V. Fratta, turn right onto C. Cavour, and continue straight for about 5min.; the courtyard with the B and B is located on the left shortly before P. Erbe.* ⓘ *Breakfast included.* ⑤ *Singles €45-60; doubles €60-180.*

verona . accommodations

HOTEL SIENA
HOTEL [4]

V. Marconi 41 ☎045 80 03 074 🖥www.hotelsiena-verona.it

Complementing its lovely enclosed garden and excellent-value rooms with unparalleled service, Hotel Siena is small but nonetheless very accommodating of international travelers. It's a bit further from Verona's main sights than other places listed here, but travelers who want a tranquil hotel will find this to be one of the best options in the city.

From P. Bra, exit west onto V. Roma, turn left onto V. Daniele Manin, and continue straight for 3-5min.; the hotel is shortly before the intersection with V. Scalzi and V. della Valverde. *i* *Breakfast included.* [$] *Singles €50-90; doubles €65-135.*

HOTEL ARENA
HOTEL [3]

Strada Porta Palio 2 ☎045 80 32 440 🖥www.albergoarena.it

A great value hotel, Hotel Arena has some of the cheapest rooms on offer, particularly for travelers booking singles or doubles. Its quiet location not only offers convenient proximity to the Arena and Castelvecchio, but also (and perhaps more importantly) to Verona's best eateries.

From Castelvecchio, continue south along Strada Porta Palio for about 2min.; the hotel is on the right. *i* *Breakfast included.* [$] *Singles €35-75; doubles €60-115.*

HOTEL SANMICHELI
HOTEL [4]

V. Valverde 2 ☎045 80 03 749 🖥www.sanmicheli.com

Hotel Sanmicheli eschews spacious rooms and elaborate decor in favor of great rates and reliable service. Its distance from Verona's attractions is a minor inconvenience for the budget traveler trying to save a few euros.

From the southwest corner of P. Bra, exit south onto C. Porta Nuovo and stay right as it splits into P. Pradaval; the hotel is ahead after 2-3min. *i* *Breakfast included. Wi-Fi €2 per hr.* [$] *Singles €50-75; doubles €80-106. Extra bed €25.*

SIGHTS

Verona is full of Roman and Romanesque buildings that are among the most beautiful, historic, and architecturally significant in northern Italy. Most are concentrated around the historic *centro* and are within comfortable walking distance of one another. If you invest in a **Verona Card** *(1-day pass €10; 3-day €15),* you'll get free access to 12 sights, plus four more at a reduced charge. The card is available at most major sights and local *tabbaccherie.* If you're tempted by the many Romeo-and-Juliet attractions, do bear in mind that they tend to be overcrowded and of relatively little historic signficance.

ARENA DI VERONA
ANCIENT ROME

P. Bra ☎045 80 03 204 🖥www.arena.it

The Verona Arena, one of the best preserved and maintained Roman ampitheaters in the world, is both the city's most prominent Roman edifice and its top venue for theatrical and musical performances. Built nearly two millennia ago, the theater fell into disrepair in the centuries following the decline of the Roman empire, but, like many other buildings here, was partially reconstructed during the Renaissance. By the 18th century, it was again hosting sporadic performances. Used in antiquity for less refined (i.e., brutal) spectacles, the arena was lauded in modernity for its remarkable history as well as its excellent acoustics. As a result, over the past 150 years the theater has come to be regarded as one of the premier musical venues in all of Europe, hosting acts ranging from **Maria Callas** to KISS to Elton John. It's now most famous for its summer opera series, which draws musicians and opera aficionados from all over the world and has, to a large degree, shaped the contemporary cultural and economic identity of the city (see **Arts and Culture**).

From Stazione FS, bus #11, 12, 13, or 72 on M-Sa or #90, 92, 93, 96, or 97 on Su. [$] *€3,* *free with Verona Card. ⏰ Open M 1:30-7:30pm, Tu-Su 8:30am-7:30pm. Last entry 45min. before close. Hours subject to change in summer.*

MUSEO DI CASTELVECCHIO
💳🚭❄ CASTLE, MUSEUM

C. Castelvecchio 2 ☎045 80 62 611 💻www.comune.verona.it

The castle of Castelvecchio itself is as much of an attraction for many visitors as the museum to which it's home. Built by the **Scaliger dynasty** of Verona in the 14th century on the site of a defunct Roman fortress, the castle is the city's most notable medieval building for both architectural and historical reasons. Designed with the practical considerations of defensibility in mind, the castle has a foreboding grace—its brick rampart and towering walls stand as both aesthetic and military marvels. The castle has survived centuries of disputes between the powerful families of northern Italy, the Napoleonic invasions, and the Austrian occupation of Verona, and despite all this carnage its exterior remains virtually identical to the way it did when first constructed. The interior, however, has been completely renovated to accommodate an extensive collection of medieval and Renaissance artwork from the region. The collection, which features many frescoes and paintings similar to others you'll inevitably see during your time in Italy, benefits greatly from its setting. Legendary artist and architect **Carlo Scarpa** incorporated the collection into the ancient castle in such a way that the art on display and the exhibition space iself interact in at-times delightful ways.

🚏 From Stazione FS, take bus #21, 22, 23, 24, or 41 on M-Sa or #91, 93, 94, or 95 on Su. 💲 €6, students and over 60 €4.50, ages 8-14 €1, free with Verona Card. ⏰ Open M 1:30-7:30pm, Tu-Su 8:30am-7:30pm.

TORRE DEI LAMBERTI
🚶🚭 TOWER

V. dalla Costa 1 ☎045 92 73 027

The most prominent landmark in P. Erbe, the Torre dei Lamberti was originally built in the late 1100s but remained a work in progress for the better part of six centuries as it was rebuilt, added to, and reconstructed at various points throughout its history. Looking at the tower today, you'll recognize two clearly distinct layers of brick. Some visitors mistake this for a conscious design choice, but the difference in hues actually represents a gap in the construction of the tower. Now standing as the highest point in the city, the tower is among the city's most monumental secular buildings. It was built with the primary intent of protecting the city, while its famous bells—**Marangona** and **Rengo**—served to inform the citizens of important news. The smaller, Marangona, was used to signal the time of day and alert citizens of fires, while the larger's ringing convened city council meetings and warned citizens of impending military attacks. Today, thousands of visitors each year climb or take the elevator to the top of the tower to enjoy the best views of the city.

🚏 Bus #72 or 73. 💲 €2, free with Verona Card. Elevator access €1. ⏰ Open daily 8:30am-7:30pm.

COMPLESSO DEL DUOMO
💳♿ CHURCH

P. Duomo ☎045 59 28 13 💻www.chieseverona.it

An architecturally fascinating cathedral, the Complesso del Duomo was originally consecrated in the fourth century as a small and relatively simple church and was rebuilt several times over the next few centuries due to natural disasters. The cathedral's structure suffered during the 1177 earthquake that sparked Verona's Romanesque movement, a period which profoundly shaped the development of the modern cathedral. After being rebuilt in the new "in" style, the cathedral was renovated and developed further over the years, resulting in its eclectic mix of several architectural styles. Be sure to spend time admiring the detail of the building's exterior and its distinctive statuary. Also note that the cathedral is part of a complex that includes the square, a cloister, and library.

🚌 *Bus line #72.* 💲 *€2.50, free with Verona Card.* ⏰ *Open Mar-Oct M-Sa 10am-5:30pm, Su 1:30-5:30pm; Nov-Feb Tu-Sa 10am-4pm, Su 1:30-5pm.*

PIAZZA DELLE ERBE   ♿ PIAZZA

At the heart of Verona's historic center is P. delle Erbe, a site that has been the hub of Verona's political and cultural life for well over 1000 years. Under Roman rule, the *piazza* was where the forum could be found. Today, it's the site of daily events ranging from markets to civic administration to social gatherings. In addition to being one of the most heavily trafficked spots in the city, the *piazza* is home to several buildings that evince the rich cultural and architectural history of the city. The square's famous fountain, the **Palazzo Maffei,** and the **Torre dei Lamberti** complete a distinguished and aged skyline. If you're at a loss as to what to do in Verona, begin at P. delle Erbe. The square's tumult begins at dawn and continues well into the night, and numerous popular attractions can be found nearby.

🚌 *Bus #72 or 73.*

TEATRO ROMANO E MUSEO ARCHEOLOGICO   ◉⊗ MUSEUM, ANCIENT ROME

Regaste Redentore 2   ☎045 80 00 360 🖥www.estateteatraleveronese.it

Two sights in one, the Teatro Romano is a musical and theatrical venue second only to the Arena, and the attached Museo Archeologico is the city's most extensive collection of Roman-era artifacts. One of the major theaters in Roman Verona, The Teatro Romano, unlike the Arena, fell into significant disrepair after the fall of the Roman Empire and was all but forgotten for centuries. In the 19th century, it was excavated and rehabilitated to its present condition. It now frequently hosts contemporary musical acts, opera events, dramas, and even ballet performances. It differs significantly in appearance from the Arena, and visitors are often pleasantly surprised to find the stage is its only conspicuously contemporary feature: seating remains in much the same form that it took when it was excavated. For more information on performances, see **Arts and Culture.** The Museo Archeologico, similarly to the *teatro*, presents Roman artifacts without the typical contrived display you'll find in most museums, opting to arrange them in a series of buildings and walkways along the hillside overlooking the theater. This method of display is highly unconventional, but the museum makes it work. If you have the stamina to make it to the very top of the hill, you'll be rewarded with the best views of Verona this side of the Torre dei Lamberti.

🚌 *Bus #73 across the Adige river.* 💲 *€4.50, students and ages 14-30 and over 60 €3, free with Verona Card.* ⏰ *Open M 1:30-7:30pm, Tu-Su 8:30am-7:30pm. Last entry 45min. before close.*

CHIESA DI SANTA ANASTASIA   ◉♿ CHURCH

P. Sant'Anastasia   ☎045 59 28 13 🖥www.chieseverona.it

Chiesa di Santa Anastasia is Verona's largest church and one of the most impressive displays of Italian Gothic architecture in northern Italy. The church was built over the course of four centuries, with construction continuing off and on from the late 13th until the early 16th under the direction of the Dominican religious order. With a half-dozen altars and smaller chapels that would be worth visiting for their own artistic merit, the church is a veritable museum of Renaissance painting and sculpture. Be sure to look for *Saint George and the Princess of Trebizond*, Pisanello's signature work, on display in the church's **Pellegrini Chapel.**

🚌 *Bus #73.* 💲 *€2.50.* ⏰ *Open Mar-Oct M-Sa 9am-6pm, Su 1-6pm; Nov-Feb Tu-Sa 10am-4pm, Su 1-5pm.*

CASA DI GIULIETTA   ◉♿ PALAZZO, MUSEUM

V. Cappello 23   ☎045 80 34 303 🖥www.comune.verona.it

For the most part, Verona earns its reputation as a quiet town thanks to its historic buildings, managing to accommodate visitors from all over the world without becoming excessively touristy. This building—purported to be the home of Juliet Capulet—is the most notable exception to this rule. The house is of dubious historical significance at best, given that it has yet to be proven that the Juliet featured in Shakespeare's work was even a real person, but that doesn't deter hundreds of thousands of visitors from flocking to the house each year. Inside, several floors with displays of historic objects show what the building would have been like as a functional household during the time when Juliet might have lived, but again, the sentimental value here trumps the historical significance for many visitors. Though many purists and historians might be inclined to scorn the house, the cultural spectacle here is something else: throngs of visitors from all over the world scramble and shove to write love letters on the alleyway walls leading to the house while others jockey to take photographs from Juliet's famous balcony. Witnessing this kind of silly madness is worth a quick stop—even if you don't feel like dropping the €4 required for entry.

🚆 Bus #72 or 73. ⑤ €4. 🕐 Open M 1:30-7:30pm, Tu-Su 8:30am-7:30pm. Last entry 45min. before close.

ARCO DEI GAVI
C. Cavour 46

♿ ANCIENT ROME
🖳 www.comune.verona.it

Arco dei Gavi is one of Verona's most striking Roman relics. The arch, which after enduring numerous displacements and reappropriations over its 2000-year lifespan, now stands near its original location next to Castelvecchio and is a testament to the Romans' architectural prowess. Built to honor the prominent Gavi family, it still bears an original inscription with their name. Constructed of elegant white limestone from local quarries, the arch has been used in various practical and symbolic capacities, serving as both a decoration and a gate to the city several times throughout Verona's history. Though the arch was completely disassembled during the Napoleonic occupation, it was later reassembled using the original materials and now stands essentially as it was originally built.

🚆 From Stazione FS take bus #21, 22, 23, 24, or 41 on M-Sa or #91, 93, 94, or 95 on Su.

FOOD

Verona is one of the Veneto's top culinary cities and is famous above all else for its excellent wines. While visitors to Verona expect great *vino*, many are also surprised by the number of fantastic cafes and restaurants. There are a few touristy and overpriced options near the Arena, but plenty of smaller, family-owned restaurants prepare great traditional Veronese cuisine at reasonable prices.

🔲 TIGELLA BELLA
V. Sottoriva 24

📱♿🍴❄ RISTORANTE ❷
☎045 80 13 098 🖳www.tigellabella.it

Tigella Bella is an unconventional restaurant featuring small plates rather than full entrees, but it serves up delicious fried dumplings and *tigella* bread, a unique regional delight. A local favorite for the originality and creativity of its cuisine, Tigella Bella also offers an incredible wine list. Come with a larger group so you can sample a variety of the restaurant's specialities.

🚆 From the southeast corner of P. Bra, exit onto V. Pallone; take the last left before the bridge onto V. Marcello and continue for about 10min. until the street ends; turn left then immediately right, and the restaurant is immediately ahead. ⑤ Entrees €9. 🕐 Open Tu-Su noon-2:30pm and 7pm-12:30am.

CANGRANDE OSTERIA AND ENOTECA
V. Dietro Listone 19/D

📱♿🍴❄🍽 RISTORANTE ❸
☎045 59 50 22 🖳www.enotecacangrande.it

An exceptionally popular restaurant among locals and discerning visitors alike, Cangrande has garnered resoundingly positive reviews for its Veronese specialities, which range from exceptional meat and cheese plates to more unique regional delicacies. With excellent food and a wine list befitting the restaurant's extensive menu, Cangrande is a great place to sit outside well into a summer night to enjoy the music from the opera, which is audible from the restaurant's patio.

➜ From the southwest corner of P. Bra, exit west onto V. Roma and take the 1st right onto V. Listone; the restaurant is shortly ahead on the left. $ Entrees €7-21. ⏰ Open M-Sa 10am-1pm and 5pm-1am.

OSTERIA SGARZARIE 💳♿🍸❄ RISTORANTE [3]

Corte Sgarzarie 14/A ☎045 80 00 312

Located in one of Verona's most picturesque squares, Osteria Sgarzarie is as difficult to resist as its name is to pronounce. This restaurant specializes in authentic Veronese cuisine—if you've always wanted to try **horse** stew, you're in the right place—but tamer options like an incredibly delicious apple pie are available for those with more conventional tastes.

➜ From P. Bra, head northwest on V. Fratta, turn right onto C. Cavour and continue straight for about 5min.; the restaurant is ahead on the left. $ Entrees €8-17. ⏰ Open daily 12:30-2:30pm and 7:30-10:30pm.

LA TAVERNA DI VIA STELLA 💳♿🍸❄ RISTORANTE [3]

V. Stella 5/C ☎045 80 08 008 💻www.trovaristorantiverona.com

La Taverna di Via Stella is a true tavern, featuring a cozy, welcoming ambience and excellent, hearty portions of local specialties. You'll find several innovative preparations of duck, some of the best polenta you'll ever eat, and numerous vegetable side dishes that complement any meal on their well-rounded menu.

➜ From the Arena, exit northeast onto V. Anfiteatro and continue for 3-5min.; the restaurant is shortly ahead after V. Anfiteatro becomes V. Stella. $ Entrees €7.80-19.50. ⏰ Open daily 12:15-2pm and 7:15-11pm.

CREPERIA CUOVE AND AVANZI 💳♿🍸❄ CREPERIE [1]

V. Marconi 58 ☎32 91 69 98 34

After a long night out, crepes may be one of the few foods that rival kebabs on the list of crave-worthy foods available in Italy. We at *Let's Go* will take any one of these frou-frou pancakes that comes our way. But even our jaded palate took a delighted double take when we tried a flat one at Creperia Cuove and Avanzi—this place really takes it to the next level. Vaccari, the shop's talented, friendly owner and head chef, has prepared an astonishing menu of sweet and savory crepes that cost next to nothing. There is no better way to end a night of Verona bar-hopping than with one of these crepes.

➜ From the southwest corner of P. Bra, exit west onto V. Roma, make the 1st left onto V. Daniele Manin, and continue for 6-8min.; the creperie is on the right. $ Crepes €2.60-3.60. ⏰ Open Tu-Th noon-2:30pm and 6pm-1am, F noon-2:30pm and 6pm-3am, Sa 5pm-3am, Su 5pm-midnight.

TRATTORIA AL SOLITO POSTO 💳♿🍸❄ RISTORANTE [2]

V. Santa Maria in Chiavica 5 ☎045 80 14 220 💻www.alsolitoposto.verona.it

A restaurant that is among the city's best according to locals, Trattoria al Solito Posto tends to keep it simple with top-quality Veronese cuisine prepared with fresh, local ingredients. The polenta and risotto are among the restaurant's most popular items, but the menu is diverse enough to cater to pretty much all tastes.

➜ From the Arena, exit northeast onto V. Anfiteatro, continue for 4-6min., turn left onto V. al Cristo, and make the 3rd right onto V. Santa Maria in Chiavica; the restaurant is just ahead. $ Entrees €7.50-14. ⏰ Open M and W-Th noon-2:30pm, F-Su noon-2:30pm and 7:30-10pm.

NIGHTLIFE

Verona acquits itself surprisingly well for a quiet town mainly famous for an Elizabethan tragedy—several bars and clubs stay packed well into the night, even on weekdays. The nightlife tends to be pretty limited geographically, so you're going to want to stick to the historic *centro*.

PASION ESPAÑOLA
BAR

V. Marconi 4 ☎045 59 60 38

The best late-night bar in the city, Pasion Española is the place to go for drinks, music, and a great atmosphere after 1am. It doesn't open until 10pm, but it has an awesome environment the whole time and truly begins to shine after the city's other bars have already shut down. You might feel like a bit of a *traditore* for ordering Spanish wine when you're in the heart of Italy's wine country, but the selections are good enough that you'll feel less like Julius Caesar's dear Brutus and more like the legendary Caligula.

From the southwest corner of P. Bra, exit west onto V. Roma and make the 1st left onto V. Daniele Manin; the bar is on the right shortly after the 1st major cross street. $ Drinks €2-6. ⏰ Open M-Th 10pm-3am, F-Sa 10pm-4am, Su 10pm-3am.

BLOOM CAFE
CAFE

P. Erbe 24 ☎045 20 68 160

Bloom Cafe is distinguished by its excellent patio, attentive service, selection of high-end liquors, and great lounge music. The bar is a great place to go on a summer night if you want to sit on the patio and enjoy a few drinks, and if you're staying inside, you'll find that the bartenders are unusually friendly and chatty with English-speaking tourists.

Northwest corner of P. Erbe. $ Drinks €3.20-6.70. ⏰ Open daily 9:30am-2am.

CASA MAZZANTI CAFFÉ
CAFE

P. Erbe 32 ☎045 80 03 217 www.casamazzanticaffe.it

An ultra-hip bar with a huge TV displaying recent runway shows and one of the best live DJs in Verona, Casa Mazzanti Caffé might be the most sophisticated bar in the city, but it avoids taking itself too seriously. Sit on the patio to relax and make small talk. The bar is for alcohol connoisseurs and stimulating intellectual conversation, so size yourself up before you try that out.

Northwest corner of P. Erbe. $ Drinks €3-8. ⏰ Open daily 8am-2am.

ANSELMI
BAR

P. delle Erbe 22 ☎045 59 15 12

A bar that stands out among the many that surround P. Erbe, Anselmi manages to keep a lively crowd throughout the night without getting overly packed or chaotic. TVs and comfortable seating inside the bar, plus a light mist that cools patrons hanging out on the patio during hot summer nights, certainly help maintain the atmosphere. Anselmi has pulled out all the stops to create a chill and comfortable place for its patrons to enjoy their famously strong but tasty cocktails.

Northwest corner of P. Erbe. $ Drinks €2.75-7. ⏰ Open M-Tu 8am-2am, Th-Su 8am-2am.

ARTS AND CULTURE

Verona is famous for its performance arts scene, with phenomenal drama, dance, and, most of all, opera. The best acts take place primarily in the city's two main venues, the **Arena di Verona** and **Teatro Romano.** Within any given week, a visitor might have the opportunity to see five or even six different shows at these two venues alone. Sorting through what's playing can be somewhat daunting, so visit a local tourism office upon arrival to get help planning your high-culture experience.

ARENA DI VERONA
OPERA

P. Bra ☎045 80 03 204 www.arena.it

The summer shows at the Arena di Verona are one of the biggest reasons visitors come to Verona. If you weren't planning on seeing a show here, try to free up a few euros and revise your plans as soon as possible. The Arena di Verona hosts its world-famous summer opera series annually, so June, July, and August are prime opportunities to view some of the world's great theater in one of the world's most historic settings. Though you can pay serious money for tickets, they're also available for just over €20 if you manage to book a couple weeks in advance and avoid sold-out productions.

➔ From Stazione FS, take bus #11, 12, 13, or 72 on M-Sa or #90, 92, 93, 96, or 97 on Su. $ Opera tickets €23-198. ⏰ Most performances at 9pm.

TEATRO ROMANO ⊛♿ THEATER

Regaste Redentore 2 ☎045 80 00 360 💻www.estateteatraleveronese.it

A truly exceptional venue that has been transformed over the course of 2000 years from an opulent Roman ampitheater into a remarkably functional and comfortable ruin, Teatro Romano hosts diverse performances ranging from pop music to Shakespearean drama to contemporary dance. As famous as the Verona Arena is, there are actually quite a few connoisseurs who have expressed their preference for the Teatro Romano, which is lauded both for its authentic historical ambience and its incredible acoustics. Even if you're not a theater buff, you should see what's playing—the theater hosts such an impressive variety of acts that there is something for almost anyone.

➔ Bus #73 across the Adige river. $ Events vary significantly, and prices tend to fluctuate accordingly. Expect to pay slightly less than you might at the Arena di Verona for similar performances. ⏰ Box office at the theater opens 30min. before shows. Tickets can also be bought at Palazzo Barbieri (P. Bra 1) M-F 10:30am-1pm and 4-7pm.

SHOPPING 🛍

Verona has some interesting smaller stores in unexpected and inconspicuous locations, but **Via Mazzini** is clearly the most important shopping spot. This street is populated by a diverse array of stores including international brands, local stores, designer labels, and discount shops.

👍 **ENOTECA DAL ZOVO** ⊛♿🍸 ENOTECA [3]

Vicolo S. Marco in Foro 7 ☎045 80 34 369 💻www.enotecadalzovo.it

Verona is famous for the red wines produced nearby, and there's no better way to celebrate your stay in wine country than with a bottle or two from Enoteca dal Zovo. A small shop packed with hundreds of different fine wines and liquors, this is one of the best *enoteche* you'll find in northern Italy. With a great selection of local wines as well as an impressive variety of imports complemented by the encyclopedic knowledge of the shopowner, you should be able to find a few bottles to enjoy.

➔ From Castelvecchio, continue northwest along C. Cavour for 8-10min. and turn right onto the street immediately before P. Erbe; the enoteca is on the right. $ Wine €8-250. ⏰ Open daily 8:30am-1:30pm and 2:30-10pm.

ATHLETE'S WORLD 🏷♿❄ CLOTHING

V. Mazzini 19 ☎045 80 34 526 💻www.athletesworld.it

Athlete's World offers more than just athletic shoes, gym bags, and basketball shorts—it also stocks hip and stylish T-shirts, old-school Chuck Taylors with original patterns and prints, and sleek travel bags. If you're looking for any basic necessities, this a great place to start. Even if you're not going to buy anything, you still might want to step in to check out some of their creative and witty tees that somehow riff on American pop culture and style much more effectively than anything you'll find in an American or internet "comical T-shirt" store.

➔ From the north side of the Arena, continue on V. Mazzini for about 5-6min.; the shop is on the right. ⏰ Open daily 10am-7:30pm.

ESSENTIALS

Practicalities

- **TOURIST OFFICES:** The central tourist office is at V. degli Alpini 9. *(☎045 80 68 680 ➔ Accessible by bus #13, 51, 61, 62 70, 71, or 73. Walk south from Arena di Verona into P. Brà. ⏰ Open M-Sa 9am-7pm, Su 9am-3pm.)*
- **LUGGAGE STORAGE:** Can be found at **Stazione Porta Nuova.** *(Piazzale Porta Nuova ☎045 80 23 827 🖥www.grandistazioni.it ⏰ Open daily 7am-11pm.)*
- **POST OFFICES: Poste Italiane.** *(V. Carlo Cattaneo 23 ☎045 80 59 911 🖥www.poste.it ➔ From the Arena di Verona, turn onto V. Guglielmo Oberdan and make an immediate left onto V. Carlo Cattaneo; the post office is shortly ahead. ⏰ Open M-F 8am-6pm, Sa 8am-12:30pm.)*

Emergency!

- **POLICE:** *(V. Salvo D'Acquisto 6 ☎045 80 561 ➔ Bus #72. From city center, continue along C. Porta Nuova and turn right onto V. Antonio Locatelli.)*
- **HOSPITALS/MEDICAL SERVICES: Ospedale Civile Maggiore** provides emergency and non-emergency medical care. *(Piazzale Aristide Stefani 1 ☎045 81 21 111 🖥www.ospedaleuniverona.it ➔ Bus #41, 62, 7, or 71. On foot, cross the Ponti Garibaldi, continue along the Vle. Nino Bixio, and make a slight left at the 5-way intersection; the hospital is shortly ahead. ⏰ 24hr. emergency care. Departmental hours vary.)*

Getting There

By Plane

Verona has a small international airport, **Aeroporto Valerio Catullo (VRN)** *(Valerio Catullo ☎045 80 95 666 🖥www.aeroportoverona.it).* If you're coming straight here from within Europe, it makes a good option, particularly with **budget airlines** like Ryanair. A shuttle from the airport to the train station runs every 20min. *($ €4.50. ⏰ Departs airport 6:35am-11:35pm, departs train station 5:40am-11:10pm.)* and is the most convenient way to access the city from the airport.

By Train

If you're traveling to Verona from within Italy, you will almost certainly travel by train. **Verona Porta Nuova** station *(☎045 89 20 21 🖥www.grandistazioni.it ℹ Make sure you get off at Verona Porta Nuova, not Verona Vescovo.)* is where most travelers arrive. It offers service to and from: **Bologna** *($ €7.20. ⏰ 50-90min., 1-2 trains per hr.);* **Milan** *($ €9. ⏰ 1hr. 20min.-2hr., 2-3 per hr.);* **Rome** *($ €45-85. ⏰ 3hr., about 1 per hr.);* **Padua** *($ €5. ⏰ 40-80min., 3 per hr.);* **Venice.** *($ €6.15. ⏰ 1-2 hr., 2-4 per hr.)* A bus station is affiliated with Porta Nuova, but the service to Verona is very limited—trains will almost always be more convenient. The train station is south of the city center. From there, if you walk north toward the towers on the horizon, you should reach the city center in less than 20min.

Getting Around

Though Verona is a large city with a dispersed population, visitors will find little of interest outside the city center, and it's possible to see all of the city's major sights without renting a car or using public transportation. Most hotels are within easy walking distance (less than 15min.) of the *centro*, and those staying farther afield can take advantage of **buses** #13, 51, 61, 62 70, 71, and 73 to reach central Verona. **Bikes** are also a popular option, but they're of limited use in the compact city center where drivers tend to interpret speed limits as suggestions rather than legal maximums. A map is, of course, helpful, but once you know how to get to the city center from your hotel, you're unlikely to get lost. Familiarize yourself with a couple of main streets and the basic directions from your hotel to the city center before you begin your adventure. If you want to take a **taxi,** RadioTaxi can be called at any time of day (☎045 53 26 66 💬*www.radiotaxiverona.it*).

bologna ☎051

Bologna la grassa, la dotta, la rossa. It's a common refrain among locals trying to describe their city's greatest attributes. Fat, learned, and red—in these terms, the city sounds kind of like an obese commie professor, but, really, they sum up the place quite nicely. First, *la grassa.* The people of Bologna love their food, and they're famous for it. Stuffed pastas like tortellini are among the local creations, and *lasagne alla Bolognese* has of course gathered popularity far from Emilia-Romagna's dark, fertile soil. The town's other primary exports are caps and gowns—*la dotta.*

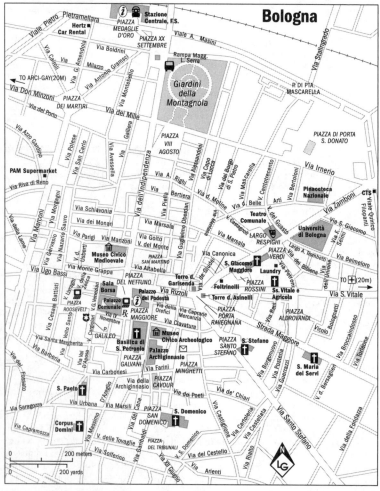

Bologna is home to the Western hemisphere's oldest university, the very first "Alma Mater" (its Italian name), whose 100,000 students the city while classes are in session and leave it feeling decidedly roomy come summertime. With youthful exuberance (and livers), these students lend the city hopping nightlife and plenty of inexpensive booze. What Bologna hasn't been so successful at spreading around Italy these days are the works of the national **Communist Party,** *la rossa,* which is headquartered in the city and has the sympathies of a number of its citizens.

Fat, learned, and red, Bologna boasts a culture that's as rich as its food. Numerous free museums house collections of Italian art and historical artifacts, and though the facade of its massive basilica has never been finished, the city also boasts a number of notable architectural specimens. It's got its oddities—two central towers, one of them leaning at a precarious angle straight out of Pisa—and its tattooed beauties: worshippers across Bologna are separated from the sky by the intricately frescoed ceilings of the city's many churches. Finally (and appropriately), the Bologna opera company remains a particular point of pride for residents—there couldn't be any place more perfect to hear *that* lady sing than this fat and juicy city.

ORIENTATION

Welcome to Bologna, a pedestrian's town. Almost everything happens inside the *centro* walls, and a walk straight across takes less than 40min., meaning anywhere worth going is easily reached on foot. Most travelers arrive at **Stazione Centrale,** in the north of the city. Just left of the station exit, **Via dell'Indipendenza,** which runs south to the *centro* at **Piazza Nettuno,** begins. The larger **Piazza Maggiore,** Bologna's medieval center, connects to P. Nettuno. From here, streets branch off and lead to the city's many museums. **Via Rizzoli** runs east from P. Nettuno to the **Two Towers of Bologna,** one leaning, and to **Via Zamboni,** hub of the city's university and a major student gathering spot. **Via Ugo Bassi** runs west from the *piazze* to **Via del Pratello's** numerous bars. **Via Archiginnasio** heads south alongside the basilica to Bologna's classiest quarter, where the entrances to designer shops gleam beneath elaborately patterned portico ceilings.

ACCOMMODATIONS

For a place with so many students, Bologna is woefully lacking in hostels—there's just one, and it's several kilometers from the *centro.* Other accommodations can be pricey and fill up quickly, especially at the beginning and end of the school year in September and May. Though no other hotels are too far apart, the most affordable properties can be found near **Via Marconi** and **Via Ugo Bassi.** For stays measured in months rather than nights, check out the rental listings taped unceremoniously to green trash barrels in the university area on **Via Zamboni.**

ALBERGO ATLANTIC — HOTEL [4]

V. Galleria 46 — ☎051 24 84 88 www.albergoatlantic.net

This new, immaculate hotel near Stazione Centrale can, in places, resemble a surrealist maze of stairs, but its rooms and public areas are flooded with light—many bedrooms have more than one window. Wood beams and exposed stone arches add a touch of traditional elegance, while TV, an internet connection, and hair dryers in the room provide many comforts.

From the train station, head straight down V. Galleria. ***i*** *Breakfast included. Free internet connection in room; no Wi-Fi.* $ *Singles €50-130; doubles €80-190; triples €100-250.* ⏰ *Reception 24hr.*

ALBERGO GARISENDA — HOTEL [3]

V. Rizzoli 9/Galleria Leone 1 — ☎051 22 43 69 www.albergogarisenda.com

The beds and bathrooms may be modern, but that's about it—and at Albergo Garisenda, that's a good thing. The owners have decorated the halls and guestrooms of this third-floor hotel with an electic collection of antiques ranging from carved armoires and a piano to turn-of-the-century sewing machines.

Take V. Rizzoli and turn right up the steps into Galleria Leone, where the door is on the left. i Breakfast included. Free Wi-Fi. $ Singles without bath €45-55; doubles €60-85, with bath €75-110.

ALBERGO CENTRALE HOTEL ❹

V. Della Zecca 2, 3rd fl. ☎051 22 51 14 www.albergocentralebologna.it

With two separate sitting rooms in which to relax and sweeping views of Bologna's rooftops (ask for a room on the hotel's upper floor), Albergo Centrale has some features more befitting of a luxury hotel than one with two stars. The kind staff will make sure travelers feel at home, which is saying something since the place sits on the third floor of an office building. You'll mingle with a lot of suits in the elevator up to your room, but no cubicle for you.

Just off V. Ugo Bassi. i Breakfast included. Smokers' rooms available. Ring bell after hours. $ Singles €65-80; doubles €85-120; triples €105-150.

ALBERGO PANORAMA HOTEL ❸

V. Livraghi 1, 4th fl. ☎051 22 18 02 www.hotelpanoramabologna.it

The flowers welcoming guests outside the elevator, *and* at the front desk, *and* in the hall may be fake, but the benefits of staying in this great location sure aren't. In addition to its proximity to most of Bologna's sights, the very well-appointed singles, each with armchair and large desk, make this hotel an excellent choice for solo travelers.

Just off V. Ugo Bassi. i Breakfast included. Only accepts Visa. $ Singles €40; doubles €60, with bath €80; triples €80-90; quads €90-100. Reception 7am-10pm.

OSTELLO DUE TORRE SAN SISTO (HI) HOSTEL ❶

V. Viadagola 5 ☎051 50 18 10 www.ostellodibologna.com

Amenities at this hostel include a basketball court, plentiful outdoor seating, and fields where the agriculturally minded can grow their own dinner. Actually, the latter isn't true. This quiet spot *is*, however, 4km outside Bologna's center and surrounded by farmland. Though the large dorm rooms are bunk-bed-free and the comfortable common room is full of student travelers, the hostel's remote location is a major drawback, and its pastoral setting invites numerous free-riding insects to share the bedrooms and bathrooms with legitimate, paying guests.

Take bus #93 from V. Mille at P. dei Martiri to San Sisto. For late-night service, take bus #21B from the train station. i Breakfast included. Wi-Fi €2.50 per 12hr. $ Dorms €17; singles €23, with bath €25; doubles €38. HI member discount €3. Lockout 10am-2pm. Reception closed during lockout.

SIGHTS

Bologna's academic heritage has given it dozens of **free** museums. The **University Museums,** too many to count on one hand (or two hands and two feet, for that matter), cover every imaginable discipline and are clustered at the far end of V. Zamboni *(hours vary; ask the tourist office or visit www.unibo.it)*, while the **Civic Museums** are more spread out.

PIAZZA MAGGIORE PIAZZA

P. Maggiore

P. Maggiore is the medieval heart of Bologna, with a unique mix of buildings in Romanesque styles and the bare brick of the Middle Ages. Aristotle Fiorvanti, who designed Moscow's Kremlin, was responsible for the redesign of one building on the square, the **Palazzo del Podesta.** This 15th-century building is a remarkable feat of engineering: its entire weight is supported by columns visible at street level. Another structure, the **Basilica di San Petronio,** presents a self-contained design contrast: its facade sits unfinished, with ornate stonework giving way to simple brick about halfway up. The people of Bologna, led by architect Arduino degli Arriguzzi, plotted in 1514 to make their basilica larger than Rome's St. Peter's, but the Pope would have none of it and funds were directed elsewhere. (As it stands, the church is currently the fifth-largest in the world.) Later, the building became famous for hosting the last portions of the long-running Council of Trent (though it started in 1545, Bologna hosted the ninth through 11th sessions in 1547) as well as being the site where Pope Clement VII gave Italy to German control in 1530. Today, the church—which, despite its size, is not Bologna's cathedral—is home to the **world's largest zodiac sundial,** a roped-off marble-and-gold strip running across the church floor at an odd angle. On its left side, the basilica also has a tiny museum with gleaming chalices and models that reveal more of the structure's architecture and history.

Take V. dell'Indipendenza south from Stazione Centrale. $ Free. Basilica open daily 7:45am-12:30pm and 3-6pm. Museum open Tu-F 9:30am-1:30pm and 3-5:30pm, Sa 9:30am-1:30pm and 3-4:30pm, Su 3-5:30pm.

BASILICA MADONNA DI SAN LUCA — CHURCH, PANORAMIC VIEW

34 V. San Luca — ☎051 61 42 339 www.sanlucabo.org

On a hilltop high above Bologna, this basilica holds a mysterious and prized icon of the Virgin Mary. The current church (not the first on the site) was constructed in 1723 by **Giovanni Giacomo,** using plans prepared by his father, Carlo Francesco. In the chapels that line the church's sides reside works by numerous noted artists, including Donato Creti's **Coronation of the Madonna** and frescoes by **Vittorio Bigari** that cover the walls surrounding the altar. Outside, views over the rolling countryside of Emilia-Romagna testify to the fertility of this region's land, though there are no stunning vistas of the city from here. The path to the basilica is historic in itself: the line of porticoes connecting the church to town—built to protect the Madonna icon as it was paraded up the hill—is the world's longest, at over 3.5km. The symbolism of the 666 arches from start to finish is unclear, but useful numbered tiles allow walkers to gauge how far they are from the summit.

Bus #20 from V. dell'Indipendenza to Villa Strada. Then take tourist bus or a 40min. hike to the church. $ Free. Open Mar-Oct M-Sa 6:30am-7pm, Su 7am-7pm; Nov-Feb M-F 6:30am-5pm, Su 7am-5pm.

PALAZZO ARCHIGINNASIO — ♿ PALAZZO

P. Galvani 1 — ☎051 27 68 11 www.archiginnasio.it

Built in 1563, the first permanent seat of Bologna's famous university has a lot of grafitti to show for its age, though maybe not the kind you have in mind. The coats of arms of over 5000 instructors and students cover the walls and ceilings of the palace's courtyard and hallways. Painted by students of law and the art from the 16th century to 1802, they were intended to be indelible markers of those who studied, but many (no one can put a precise number on it) have been painted over by later vandals. Today, the building houses the 800,000-volume **Biblioteca dell'Archginnasio,** arguably Italy's most important public library. Upstairs is the **Teatro Anatomico,** a theater in which dissections were once conducted for audiences of medical students and the general public. (Artists attended to improve the anatomic realism of their works.) Despite extensive WWII damage, this room has been restored to its former, wood-paneled glory, complete with a marble dissecting table at the center.

Walk down V. Archiginnasio alongside the basilica from P. Maggiore. $ Free. Open M-F 9am-6:45pm, Sa 9am-1:45pm. Closed 1st 2 weeks of Aug.

PINACOTECA NAZIONALE — ♿ MUSEUM

V. delle Belle Arti 56 — ☎051 42 09 411 www.pinacotecabologna.it

The focus on religious artwork at this *pinacoteca* (art gallery) can be staid, but the brushwork is astounding. God seems to pop right out of the frame in many of these pieces, especially the more Realist ones, which are the youngest works in this collection spanning from Ancient Rome to the 18th century. The entry staircase begins a series of epically sized canvases with Gaetano Gandolfi's *Nozze di Cana.* Other noted artists and works include **Raphael** in Gallery 15, plus *Sampson Victorious* by Guido Reni (of Bologna) and another mammoth work, Vasari's **Christ in Casa di Morta.**

✦ *From the 2 towers, take V. Zamboni. Turn left at the opera house and then right onto V. delle Belle Arti.* Ⓢ *€4, students and seniors €2.* Ⓙ *Open Tu-Su 9am-7pm.*

PIAZZA DEL NETTUNO
♿ PIAZZA

P. del Nettuno

Centered around Giambologna's surprisingly sexual 16th-century stone and bronze fountain **Neptune and Attendants,** this *piazza* next to P. Maggiore connects that larger square to the city's central streets. While you may find the buxom, water-spraying sirens surrounding Neptune a bit distracting, legend has it that the water god himself was once the subject of controversy. The story goes that Pope Pius IV disapproved of the large size of Neptune's original manhood and ordered that it be reduced. Of course, Giambologna complied, but creatively so: from the steps of the Sala Borsa, Neptune's member still appears as it did in the original package of which Pius so disapproved. When you're not ogling Neptune, take a closer look at the building upon whose steps you're standing, the **Sala Borsa.** It's a large public library and municipal center. Within the *piazza* you'll also find a pictorial memorial to Italians killed in battle while defending the republic. To the left, a small Plexiglas monument commemorates those who died in train bombings in 1974, 1980, and 1984.

✦ *Take V. dell'Indipendenza south from Stazione Centrale.* Ⓢ *Free.*

PALAZZO COMMUNALE
♿ MUSEUM

P. Maggiore 6   Collezioni Communali ☎051 21 93 526 🖥www.comune.bologna.it/culture
Museo Morandi ☎051 21 93 332 🖥www.museomorandi.it

Two museums for the price of one—and that price is zero! The **Collezioni Communali d'Arte** showcases art of the area around Bologna dating from the 13th through 20th centuries. In its Rusconi wing, you can check out reconstructed rooms complete with elaborately carved furniture and colored wallpapers from some of the city's homes. A tour through the museum includes a stop in the private chapel of the cardinals—the building once served as their home—which is frescoed by **Legato.** Take a look at the astonishing model of Bologna during the Renaissance, when wealthy families raced to build the tallest and most elaborate tower. In the diorama, these structures dot the skyline everywhere, but only a few of them remain today. On the other side of the second floor, the **Museo Morandi** pays tribute to Bologna's own master, Giorgio Morandi. Though acclaimed by critics, Morandi may be less appreciated by artistic neophytes encountering the numerous beige still-lifes covering these walls. If you can't get enough taupe in your life, Morandi's home, **Casa Morandi,** has recently been opened to the public (*V. Fondazza 36* Ⓢ *Free.* Ⓙ *Open in summer Sa-Su noon-7pm; in winter Th 11am-4pm, Sa-Su 11am-4pm).*

✦ *On the west side of P. Maggiore.* Ⓢ *Free.* Ⓙ *Open Tu-F 9am-6:30pm, Sa-Su 10am-6:30pm.*

MUSEO CIVICO MEDIOEVALE
♿ MUSEUM

V. Manzoni 4   ☎051 21 93 930 🖥www.comune.bologna.it/iperbole/museicivici

A medieval city has to store all its history somewhere. For Bologna, that place is here. From images and busts of the city's patron saints to wax seals and weaponry of local nobility, this museum offers an insight into the city's past. Upstairs, an impressive collection of arms from around Europe includes a German sword-gun combination. In the basement, sculpted funerary slabs honor the university's noted past professors.

✦ *Off V. dell'Indipendenza.* Ⓢ *Free. Audio tour €4.* Ⓙ *Open M-F 9am-3pm, Sa-Su 10am-6:30pm.*

MUSEO CIVICO ARCHAEOLOGICO

     ♿ MUSEUM

V. dell'Archiginnasio 2   ☎051 275 7211 ■www.comune.bologna.it/museoarchaeologico

Etruscan pottery from the Emilia-Romagna region is only one part of what's held in this museum. Enter through a courtyard with stone carvings from Roman-era buildings. Upstairs, a vast collection of well-maintained Roman pots displays magnificent scenes of gladiators, farmers, and senators in black and terra-cotta hues. Though there aren't any English labels on the dated, typewritten signs, all visitors will notice the contrast between the elaborate designs of Roman pottery and the simple, pressed patterns of the Etruscan pots on display.

⎯ *Walk from P. Maggiore to the left of the basilica.* Ⓢ *Free.* ⏱ *Open Tu-F 9am-3pm, Sa-Su 10am-6:30pm.*

THE TWO TOWERS

     ⓈⓈ TOWER

P. di Porta Ravegnana

The slanty *torre* in Pisa may be more famous, but you can still experience the thrill of seeing a building that's just slightly off its rocker by checking out Bologna's. After **Torre degli Garisenda** was left tilted by seismic activity, another family saw an oppurtunity to get ahead in the race to be the tallest. Indeed, the **Torre degli Asinelli** outdoes its predecessor by nearly 50m. Tourists hoping to glimpse Bologna from above (and maybe spot one of the 20 or so other towers remaining around the city) can climb 468 narrow wooden steps to the top of the newer (and less slanty) tower.

⎯ *At the end of V. Rizzoli. Entrance is on the Strada Maggiore side.* Ⓢ *€3.* ⏱ *Open daily 9am-6pm. Last entry 20min. before close.*

FOOD

   ⌨

Whatever locals list as Bologna's claims to fame (admittedly, quite a lot), this city is known internationally for one thing: its food. Heard of *lasagne alla bolognese?* How about tortellini? Stuffed pastas are among the dishes that were invented in this city, though Bologna has also been known for its hams and salamis, none of which bear much resemblance to American bologna. (Watch your pronunciation: that's "baloney" this time, and this time only.) In the *centro*, restaurants galore pack the side streets. Near P. Maggiore, **Via Pescherie Vecchie**, the former medieval market, sells everything from produce to meat freshly sliced off a carcass hooked to the ceiling. **Via Petroni** caters almost exclusively to the three student food groups of pizzas, panini, and kebabs, with prices that appeal to that clientele. Essentials can be bought at **PAM** supermarket. *(V. Marconi 28/A i Credit cards accepted.* ⏱ *Open M-Sa 7:45am-8pm, Su 9am-8pm.)*

▪ OSTERIA DELL'ORSA

  ⌨Ⓢ⚜✂ RISTORANTE ➊

V. Mentana 1/F   ☎051 23 15 76 ■www.osteriadellorsa.com

It's a new day, and that means a new pasta at Osteria dell'Orso, which specializes in Bolognese cuisine at tremendously affordable prices. Sit down with friends or strike up a conversation with the next group at the long benches of the several communal tables that constitute three quarters of the restaurant's indoor seating. The pasta menu changes daily, but a wide variety of panini *(€4-5)* and *crostini (€4)* are always available. Though *"Orsa"* means ■**bear**—as the osteria's logo will show—we're feeling bullish that this place will satisfy any eater.

⎯ *From P. Nettuno, take V. dell'Indipendenza, then turn right onto V. Marsala and left onto V. Metana.* Ⓢ *Entrees €6-10.* ⏱ *Open daily noon-1am.*

▪ SPACCA NAPOLI

  ⌨Ⓢ⚜❄✂ PIZZERIA ➊

V. San Vitale 45/A   ☎051 199 80 262

Diners at this sit-down pizza joint relax surrounded by kitschy fake bricks, but fear not: they're soon living the dream in a separate world of crisp, doughy crust and melty mozzarella (plus whatever toppings they've added on). The pies here can be big enough for two and are irregularly shaped, the true sign of a quality homemade pizza. Thinking outside the (pizza) box, try one for dessert, like the pizza with Nutella and Grand Marnier *(€6)*.

➔ Head down V. San Vitale from the 2 towers. $ Pizza €3-7.50. Primi and secondi €7-10. Special lunch menu of pizza, cover, and soda €6. ⏰ Open M-F noon-2:30pm and 7pm-midnight, Sa-Su 7pm-midnight.

tales of the tagliatelle

We vaguely remember hearing somewhere that art finds inspiration where it least expects it. For the culinary genius that invented tagliatelle, that couldn't have been more true. Legend has it that these long, flat ribbons of pasta native to Bologna were born when a talented court chef encountered the memorable hairdo of Lucrezia d'Este. Lucrezia was cast as something of a *femme fatale,* in part, perhaps, because of her long, blonde, and apparently pasta-like hair that fell well past her knees. Of course, it takes more than just chunky chains of hair to get a reputation like the one Lucrezia built up. Her passionate affair with her bisexual brother-in-law helped do that. Much later, when the famous poet and philanderer Lord Byron visited the site of Lucrezia's burial, he was purportedly quite taken with the love letters she and one of her many lovers had exchanged, and he claimed to have stolen a lock of her hair. We wonder why he bothered; a simple plate of tagliatelle would've had the same effect.

TRATTORIA ANNA MARIA 💳🚭🍸❄☁ RISTORANTE [3]

V. Belle Arti 17/A ☎051 26 68 94 💻www.trattoriaannamaria.com

Anna Maria has been instructing her chefs to use the freshest ingredients to make traditional Bolognese dishes for 20 years. No one's complaining about taking her orders, because clearly it's working. The restaurant's walls are covered in letters from satisfied diners as well as articles about the cuisine. There's even the occasional signed celebrity headshot from some low-level star who loved one of the four types of tortellini or the roast meats that are at the heart of the menu.

➔ From the 2 towers, take V. Zamboni, turning left onto V. Castagnoli at the opera house. Then make a right onto V. Belle Arti. $ Cover €3. Primi €13-14; secondi €11-14. ⏰ Open Tu-Su noon-3pm and 7-11:30pm.

GELATERIA GIANNI 💳🚭☁ GELATERIA [1]

V. Montegrappa 11 ☎051 23 30 08 💻www.gelateriagianni.com

Robin Hood trades blows with a Samurai on the Titanic as an Inferno explodes below. But this isn't the latest ill-conceived Hollywood summer blockbuster—it's the freezer of this well-loved local gelato chain. It rotates through 99 flavors, the names and tastes of which could only have been conceived by a true out-of-the-box ice-cream thinker. Here's a brief key to the sketch above: Robin Hood is pistachio and ricotta. Samurai? Mascarpone, ricotta, and powdered cocoa. Inferno combines white chocolate with black cherry, amarena, and wafer. White chocolate with almond and coconut shavings equals the Titanic. That last one sounds so good we could sink our teeth right in—that's actually true of all of them, but the Titanic is the only one for which the pun works.

➔ From P. de Nettuno, take V. dell'Indipendenza 1 block, then turn left onto V. Montegrappa and walk 4 short blocks. ℹ 2nd location, with fewer flavors, at V. San Vitale 12 next to the 2 towers. $ Small cup or cone €1.50-2, medium €3. ⏰ Open M-Tu noon-midnight, Th-Su noon-midnight.

PIZZERIA TRATTORIA BELFIORE 💳🚭🍸❄☁ PIZZERIA [1]

V. Marsala 11/A ☎051 22 66 41

Pizza's bargain basement—at street level, and with outdoor seating! The pizza is great and a great deal at this small, wood-paneled sit-down joint. Though the menu features a number of pastas, the pizzas are the focus here due to their dirt-cheap prices—the most expensive pies cost what the least expensive one at a number of places in the city might, and there's a large selection of pizzas under €3.50.

Just off V. Indipendenza on V. Marsala. $ Cover €2. Pizza €2.60-6. Primi €6.50-7.50; secondi €7-9. Open M and W-Su 12:30-2:30pm and 7:30pm-12:30am.

OSTERIA DEL SOLE RISTORANTE [1]

Vicolo Ramocchi 1/D ☎347 968 0171 www.osteriadelsole.it

Imagine this scenario: a wayward travel writer includes a place in the food section that doesn't serve food at all. Idiot, right? Well, here goes nothing. Bologna's oldest osteria, this spot has been serving two items—beer and wine—to locals for centuries. Students and old timers bring their bag lunches or purchase something from the myriad places next door, then sit at Osteria del Sole's worn wooden tables for good company and a cool glass of *vino bianco*.

Near P. Maggiore. Take V. Pescherie Vecchie and make the 1st left. $ Wine from €2. Beer from €3. Open M-Sa 10am-10pm.

NIGHTLIFE

One hundred thousand students require a lot of booze. Bologna provides generously, with a vast selection of bars, pubs, and nightclubs. **Via Zamboni** is student central and home to a mass of nightspots, while across town, **Via del Pratello** hosts a slightly older and more subdued crowd at its own multitude of watering holes. In summer, nightclubs close, and the partying moves to a number of outdoor discos, particularly in **Parco Margherita,** south of the city. In August, even the summer exchange students have departed and the city has moved to the beach, so don't expect a lot of action—anywhere.

COLLEGE BAR BAR

Largo Respighi 6/D ☎051 34 90 03 73 66

Cheap drinks and outdoor seating draw students to this small but packed watering hole. Books above the bar attempt a scholarly air, but it is fair to say that studying is on few people's minds here. Special deals appeal to many—six shots for €5 is sure to get the night off to a fast start. Couples make increasing use of the couches in the dark back room as the night gets older.

Take V. Zamboni and turn left before the opera house. The bar is on the left. $ Beer €3-5. Cocktails €4. Open M-F noon-3am, Sa-Su 6pm-3am.

CLURICAUNE IRISH PUB

V. Zamboni 18/B ☎051 26 34 19

The best Irish pub in Bologna—just ask an Irishman. (And there are only—only!—six of them. Pubs that is, not Irishmen.) Students and groups of expats gather to watch every soccer game and converse over their choice of one of the eight beers *(€4.50; Guinness €5)* on tap. While Irish beer coasters litter the bar, detritus like old street signs and bicycles hang from the ceiling on the pub's three levels.

Take V. Zamboni from the 2 towers. $ Cocktails €5.50. Open June-Aug M-Th noon-2am, F-Sa noon-2:30am; Sept-May daily 4pm-2am.

ALTO TASSO ENOTECA

P. San Franceso 6/D ☎051 40 88 06 79 www.altotasso.com

The owner of this popular establishment says his job is a higher calling than simply providing for thirsty students—though his bar carries out this task quite well. More important, he says, is showcasing the art on his walls. It's a bright display that rotates among young, local artists every two weeks. All lofty cultural benefits aside, though, it's the eight beers on tap and inexpensive but refreshing house wine (served from vats near the ceiling) that keep the patio overflowing nightly.

*Take V. Ugo Bassi and make a slight left onto V. Pratello, then the first left to V. San Francesco. **i** Occasional DJ sets follow no schedule but are often every 3-4 days when school is in* *session. $ Wine €2-5. Beer €2.50-5. Cocktails €5. ⏰ Open M-Th 4:30pm-2:30am, F-Sa 4:30pm-3am, Su 4:30pm-2:30am. Aperitivo 6-9:30pm.*

LA SCUDERIA
BAR, CLUB

P. Verdi 2 ☎051 65 69 619 🖥www.lascuderia.bo.it

The amount of outdoor seating at this incredibly popular student hangout must rival the number of seats in the Colosseum—the Roman games, though, didn't have table service. Here, on warm nights during the school year, the whole *piazza* is filled with clubgoers. In winter, disco lights replace moonlight as the party moves indoors for a more club-like atmosphere with dozens of black leather couches.

*Take V. Zamboni to P. Verdi, where the club's seating fills the piazza to the right. **i** Occasional outdoor live music in summer. $ Beer €2-4. Cocktails €6. ⏰ Open M-F 2pm-3am, Sa 5pm-3am.*

SIESTA CAFE
BAR

V. de'Castagnoli 14/C

The later it gets, the more conformist students water down the alternative crowd at this hole-in-the-wall bar. The drinks, fortunately, are anything but watery. Even better, they're cheap. A typical Bolognese *spritz* (a fruit drink similar to sangria) comes in two forms—the first is essentially alcohol with some red coloring *(€1)*. A more expensive version *(€3)* is closer to the real thing, with pieces of fruit floating around the rim.

Take V. Zamboni and turn left before the opera house. The bar is on the left. $ Cocktails €2. Beer €3. ⏰ Open daily 4pm-5am.

CASSERO
CLUB

V. Don Minzoni 18 ☎051 649 4416 🖥www.cassero.it

A cavernous dance floor and thumping beat inside plus a vast, sunken *piazza* for dancing, carousing, and occasional live music outside add up to plenty of space for the locals and students who frequent this popular party spot, Bologna's best-known gay and lesbian club. Despite being run by a GLBT organization, the club draws a variety of people from throughout the city's open-minded populace. Wednesday features pop music, on Friday nights the theme changes based on the week's special guest, and Saturday is the night for techno.

Take V. Marconi to P. dei Martiri and turn left onto V. Don Minzoni. $ Cover M-Tu €10, W €3, Th-Su €10. Beer €3. Cocktails €7. €15 ARCI-GAY card required for entrance; membership lasts 1 year and is good at any participating club in Italy. ⏰ Open daily in summer 7pm-6am; in fall, winter, and spring 9pm-6am. Aperitivo 7-9pm.

ARTS AND CULTURE

The **Bologna Festival** *(🖥www.bolognafestival.it)*, a classical music extravanganza that stretches from March to November, celebrated its 10th anniversary in 2010.

TEATRO COMUNALE
OPERA

Largo Respighi 1 ☎051 52 99 58 🖥www.tcbo.it

No matter the production that's in-house, there's always drama going on at Teatro Comunale, Bologna's oldest and best-known theater. That's because a fight over public funding for the arts during a fiscal pinch has sent the theater's protectors into a frenzy. "A people without theater is dead," screams a banner that dwarfs the posters of even the theater's top billing productions. Small-scale protests surround the building on a regular basis. Inside, the actual productions are notably more subdued and slightly better choreographed. Built after the original theater burned down in 1745, the theater was notable for its 19th-century productions of works by Rossini and Verdi as well as the Italian premieres of several Wagner works, which put him on the map in the world's most important opera nation.

Down V. Zamboni, on the left across from P. Verdi. $ Tickets €30-90. ⏰ Box office open Tu-F noon-6pm, Sa 10:30am-4pm, and 2hr. before performances. Season lasts Mar-Nov.

ESSENTIALS

Practicalities

- **TOURIST OFFICES: IAT** provides information on sights and the city. Walking and bus tours start here. *(P. Maggiore 1/E ☎051 23 96 60 🪧 In Palazzo di Podesta. ⏰ Open daily 9am-7pm.)* **Bolognaincoming** books hotels, but not hostels. *(P. Maggiore 1/E ☎800 85 60 65 🖥www.bolognaincoming.it 🪧 Located inside the tourist office. ⏰ Open daily 9am-7pm.)*
- **LUGGAGE STORAGE:** In Stazione Centrale. *(🪧 In Piazzale Ovest, to the left when entering the station. $ 1st 5hr. €4, 6-12hr. €0.60 per hr., €0.20 per hr. thereafter. ⏰ Open daily 6am-10pm.)*
- **GLBT RESOURCES: ARCI-GAY Cassero** has a library and counseling center, plus Cassero nightclub downstairs. *(V. Don Minzoni 18 ☎051 649 4416 🖥www.cassero.it 🪧 Take V. Marconi to P. del Martiri and turn right onto V. Don Minzoni. ⏰ Open daily 9am-7pm.)*
- **LAUNDROMAT: Lavarapido.** *(V. Petroni 38/B 🪧 Near V. Zamboni, off P. Verdi, on the right. ⏰ Open M-Sa 9am-9pm.)*
- **POST OFFICE:** *(P. Minghetti 4 ☎051 20 31 84 🪧 Southeast of P. Maggiore. ⏰ Open M-F 8am-6:30pm, Sa 8am-12:30pm.)*
- **INTERNET: Sportello Iperbole** provides free Wi-Fi, limited rather generously to 3hr. per day, and internet access limited a little less generously to 2hr. per week on non-personal computers. *(P. Maggiore 6 ☎051 20 31 84 🪧 In Palazzo Comunale. ℹ Reserve ahead for Wi-Fi. ⏰ Open M-F 8:30am-7pm, Sa 8:30am-2pm and 3-7pm.)*

Emergency!

- **POLICE:** *(P. Galileo 7 ☎051 16 40 11 11).*
- **LATE-NIGHT PHARMACY: Farmacia Communali.** *(P. Maggiore 6 ☎051 23 85 09 🪧 In Palazzo Communale. ⏰ Open 24hr.)*
- **HOSPITALS/MEDICAL SERVICES: Policlinco San Orsala Malpighi.** *(V. Pietro Albertoni 15 ☎051 63 61 111 🖥www.aosp.bo.it 🪧 Follow V. San Vitale to V. Massereti and turn left.)*

Getting There

By Plane

Aeroporto Guglielmo Marconi (BLQ) *(☎051 647 9615 🖥www.bologna-airport.it)* is northwest of the city center. ATC operates the **Aerobus** *(☎051 29 02 90)*, which runs from the airport to the train station's track D, with several stops in the *centro* along V. Ugo Bassi. *($ €5. ⏰ Every 15min. 6am-12:15am.)*

By Train

Stazione Centrale, in the north of the *centro*, is the main point of arrival. *(Ticket office open daily 5:30am-11:30pm. Info office ☎199 89 20 21 open daily 7am-midnight. West platform disability assistance ☎199 30 30 60 open daily 7am-9pm.)* Trains arrive from **Milan** *($ From €19. ⏰ 2-3hr., 2 per hr. 5:15am-11am.)*, **Florence** *($ €24. ⏰ 90min., 2 per hr. 7:15am-10:30pm.)*, **Rome** *($ From €36. ⏰ 3hr., 2 per hr. 7:15am-10:30pm.)*, **Venice** *($ €15. ⏰ 2hr., every 30min.-1hr. 5:57am-11:11pm.)*, **Padua** *($ €10. ⏰ 90min., every 30min.-1hr. 5:35am-12:45am.)*, and **Verona.** *($ €10. ⏰ 90min., every hr. 5:15am-11:35pm.)*

Getting Around

ATC *(☎051 29 02 90)* operates a comprehensive **bus** *($ 70min. €1, 24hr. €3)* system throughout the city, though most people walk in the *centro*. Purchase at newstands, *tabaccherie*. **Cabs** can be found in many *piazze*. *(☎051 37 27 27 or ☎051 53 41 41).*

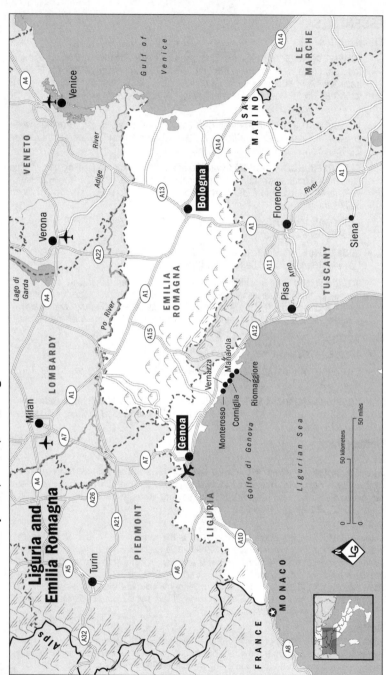

Liguria and Emilia Romagna

CINQUE TERRE

Once an undiscovered paradise, the Cinque Terre now offers a break to backpackers tired of city-hopping through Europe. Frequent train service makes the five charming cliffside villages that dot this stretch of the Italian Riviera easily accessible, yet the region's unique landscape, characterized by terraces built up over thousands of years of grape and citrus farming, prevents this Italian Shangri-La from becoming a tourism-fueled playground-by-the-sea. Yes, out-of-town visitors are a large majority of the summertime population, and English at times feels like the area's first language. But visitors willing to trek along the trails that connect the region's five towns find that a number of unrivaled vistas and secluded beaches remain. The tourist office says the walk, which winds through vineyards, along cliffs, and into forests, takes 5hr., but experienced hikers claim it can be done in less than four.

Part of the pleasure of exploring the area on foot comes from getting to know each of the five villages' distinct personalities. **Monterosso,** blessed with a welcoming expanse of sand, is the modern beach town, **Vernazza** the quieter but more beautiful sister by the sea. Hilltop **Corniglia** is tiny but offers the most stunning vistas of all five towns. **Manarola** has the best (and wackiest) swim spot, and **Riomaggiore** sees backpackers trying, successfully or not, to find last-minute rooms.

It would be a lie and a cliché to say that in the Cinque Terre there's not a car in sight. They're here, along with scooters and motorboats too. But in the face of all the beachfront hustle and tourist bustle, it's still possible to slip away into the vineyards, look down on the towns, and witness the beauty and majesty that make the Cinque Terre seem too perfect to be real.

greatest hits

- **I LIKE HIKE.** Leave your train ticket behind and hit the hiking trails to get between the five picturesque villages. Check out our map for a guide to the best places to admire the scenery (p. 260).

- **TAKE A BREATHER.** Backpacking can be hard, we know that. So take it easy and lie on Monterosso's beach (p. 252) for a few minutes. Or a week.

- **JAM BY THE MED.** La Cantina da Zio Bramante in Manarola is one of the best destinations for nightlife and surprising ensemble musical performances you'll find in all of Italy (p. 268).

student life

Cinque Terre may not have any actual universities, but that certainly doesn't mean it's short on students. The villages, particularly Monterosso, are packed with young people throughout the spring and summer. Many are American tourists here for everything from spring break partying to...summer partying. Check out the bars on P. Garibaldi for a good time once the sun has gone down. During the day, students can be found on the villages' beaches, the hikes between them, or maybe just still in bed, sleeping off their hangovers.

monterosso ☎0187

The biggest and most bustling of the towns on Cinque Terre's verdant stretch of coast, Monterosso feels the least like Italy and the most like the Bahamas, or Delaware, or, well...any other coastal places to which English-speakers flock in the summertime. It's a resort town through and through, with the added bonus of some quaint cobblestoned streets and colorful old buildings. The sheer number of restaurants, hotels, and shockingly bright umbrellas (yours for just a small fee!) that line the long beachfront sets this town apart from the rest.

ORIENTATION

Divided in two by a steep hill, Monterosso can nonetheless be walked from end to end in less than 10min. From the train station, turn left onto **Lungomare di Fegina,** where the sea view is obstructed (how rude!) by the umbrellas of beachside cafes. Free and private beaches are interspersed below this boardwalk-like avenue. Pass through the tunnel or take the slightly longer scenic route climbing to the right and enter **Piazza Garibaldi,** from which the tiny **Via Vittorio Emanuele,** inaccessible to cars, splits off to the left. Just further right is **Via Roma,** Monterosso's "Main Street" beneath which runs its 🛇**underground river.** Home to numerous restaurants, shops, and accommodations, V. Roma runs up the hill to parking and one of the roads that leads out of town.

ACCOMMODATIONS

Monterosso contains most of the Cinque Terre's hotels—probably as many as fill all the other villages combined—but even its side streets and oceanfront walkways are filled with rooms to rent. Prices do tend to be more expensive in this more touristy town.

HOTEL SOUVENIR ⊛⊗ HOTEL ❷
V. Gioberti 24 ☎0187 81 75 95

Though the owners urge their guests to party on the beach, the groups of backpack-lugging students who stay at Souvenir seem content to hang out in the in the hotel's large and comfortable rooms, many with bunk beds to accommodate bigger groups. The colorul outdoor chairs under a canopied patio are another popular hangout for eating, chatting, or just relaxing under the impressive array of tropical foliage.

⚑ *Head up V. Roma from the waterfront; turn right onto V. Gioberti, and walk to the end.* Ⓢ *Dorms €25-35; singles €45.*

HOTEL AMICI ➦⊗⟨ᵗ⟩❄ HOTEL ❹
V. Buranco 36 ☎0187 81 75 44 🖳www.hotelamici.it

Far, far away from the touristed world of Monterosso, there is a secret garden of terraces, citrus trees, and bright flowers. That garden just happens to be this

cinque terre

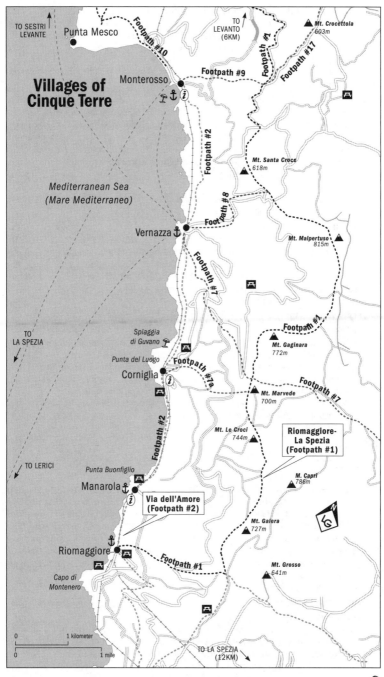

Villages of Cinque Terre

TO SESTRI
LEVANTE

Punta Mesco

TO
LEVANTO
(6KM)

Mt. Crocettola
603m

Footpath #10

Footpath #1

Footpath #17

Footpath #9

Monterosso

Footpath #2

Mediterranean Sea
(Mare Mediterraneo)

Mt. Santa Croce
618m

Footpath #8

Mt. Malpertuso
815m

Vernazza

Footpath #7

Footpath #1

TO
LA SPEZIA

Spiaggia
di Guvano

Mt. Gaginara
772m

Punta del Luogo

Footpath #7a

Footpath #7

Corniglia

Mt. Marvede
700m

Footpath #2

Mt. Le Croci
744m

**Riomaggiore-
La Spezia
(Footpath #1)**

TO LERICI

M. Capri
786m

Punta Buonfiglio

Manarola

**Via dell'Amore
(Footpath #2)**

Mt. Galera
727m

Riomaggiore

Footpath #1

Mt. Grosso
641m

Capo di
Montenero

N

0   1 kilometer

0   1 mile

TO LA SPEZIA
(12KM)

monterosso · accommodations

hotel's roof. After going up five floors in the elevator, guests can keep going up and up through the foliage if the lounge chairs and patio tables aren't good enough. The hotel also has spacious rooms with large bathrooms to match.

➜ From the waterfront, take V. Emanuele to P. Matteotti, turning left onto V. Buranco. Hotel has a large sign on the right. ℹ Breakfast included; board plans including lunch (available year-round) and dinner (June-Aug) available. Wi-Fi €2.50 per hr., €3.50 per 2hr. $ Bed in double or triple €50-70; singles €60-80. €5 surcharge per night for stays under 3 nights.

APPARTAMENTINI CINQUE TERRE — AFFITTACAMERE [4]

V. Molinelli 85/6 — ☎366 50 85 150 🖥www.appartamentini.it

Once guests manage to ascend the three-dimensional labyrinth of staircases snaking up the side of the building (the chaos you're envisioning is probably about right), they will find these three new apartments absolutely gleaming with modern cabinetry, flatscreen TVs, and ensuite kitchens with stove and fridge. An outdoor grass patio with table and chairs makes for a perfect romantic hangout.

➜ Turn right from the train station and then right onto V. Molinelli opposite the parking lot. The apartments are in the tall pink buildings to the left up the hill. $ Doubles €80.

ALBERGO AL CARUGIO — HOTEL [4]

V. Roma 100 — ☎0187 81 74 53 or 0187 81 77 05

These nine quiet rooms are farther from the bustle at the lower part of V. Roma but on top of another source of distraction—an auto repair garage. Still, the surroundings cannot distract at the back of the hotel, where the rooms have large patios with table and chairs in flowering gardens.

➜ Near the top of the hill on V. Roma. $ Doubles €60-80.

ALLE 5 TERRE AND CINQUE TERRE GUESTHOUSE — AFFITTACAMERE [2]

V. Molinelli 87 — ☎0187 81 78 28 🖥www.alle5terre.com

V. Gioberti 25 — ☎0187 81 78 28 🖥www.guesthousecinqueterre.com

The one-stop shopping isn't limited to wine and sauces, as the owners of **Cantina di Sciacchetrà** also rent rooms in two different properties. These guesthouse chambers are modern and sleek, with eye-popping zebra bedspreads, while some of the homier rooms at Alle 5 Terre feature leather furniture.

➜ To Alle 5 Terre, turn right from the station and then right onto V. Molinelli. The rooms are in a larger apartment building on the left. Cinque Terre Guesthouse is located on V. Gioberti, to the right off V. Roma. $ €25-35 per person. Apartment from €75.

SIGHTS

IL GIGANTE — MONUMENT, BEACH

V. Mollina, near V. Fegina

He's the best-looking lifeguard on the beach. Too bad he's so hard to get into bed. That's because he's a stone giant carved from a cliff, watching over one of Monterosso's **free beaches.** Beyond the giant's gaze, you'll be able to view more of the town's public shores, the most of any of the Cinque Terre towns. The uncontrolled stretches tend to be mixed in with roped-off private areas for hotel guests and paying customers. Look for the *ingresso libero* signs by the stairs or beach access to be sure that no cabana boys will come chasing you down with a bill.

➜ Turn right out of the train station onto Lungomare Fegina. $ Free.

CHIESA DEI CAPPUCINI — CHURCH, PANORAMIC VIEW

Above Monterosso

Climb to a point high above Monterosso—a Monterosso on the hill that most beachgoers never see, covered in foliage and cut off from the sounds of the world. From the Jesus statue halfway up, the full panorama of Cinque Terre is visible—all five towns and a swathe of ocean. Higher up, though, the view begins to be obscured by leaves, and a hiker gets different angles of Monterosso itself, fit snuggly into a valley that rises much higher than its peach-colored buildings. Finally, at the summit, the 17th-century church contains a magnificent golden cross by the Dutch artist, **Van Dyck,** who spent his most productive years in the Cinque Terre.

➤ Turn left from the train station and then left again onto V. Bastoni at the yellow sign for "Chiesa." Then climb up many flights of uneven steps to reach the church. $ Free.

FOOD

Monterosso's food offerings are as broad and varied as can be found in the Cinque Terre. This means nothing exotic, but a selection of Italian-style restaurants from several pizzerias and Ligurian seafood shops as well as focaccerias and *gelaterie* lining the waterfront streets. To make a picnic, visit **SuperConad Margherita.** *(P. Matteotti 9 ⏰ Open June-Sept M-Sa 8am-1pm and 4:30-8pm, Su 8am-1pm.)*

CANTINA DI SCIACCHETRÀ — 💳🚭🍸 ENOTECA [1]

V. Roma 7 — ☎0187 81 78 28

The one stop on V. Roma required for wine connoisseurs and thirsty students alike, this bottle-filled shop offers regional wines including its namesake, the world-renowned sweet wine, at dirt-cheap prices. Plus, samples are available at the lowest price of all: free. The enthusiastic and kind English-speaking staff are always eager to pour something but will also help customers navigate the selection of marmalades and sauces *(€5-10)*. For many backpackers, this place's outdoor seating is the beach (just ask the staff to open the bottle before you leave).

➤ On the left before the first underpass over V. Roma. $ Cinque Terre wine €5-20. Sciacchetrà €27. ⏰ Open daily 9am-11pm.

RISTORANTE L'ALTAMAREA — 💳🚭🍸🥡 SEAFOOD [3]

V. Roma 54 — ☎0187 81 71 70

Fresh fish and even fresher homemade pasta are the hallmarks of this well-loved restaurant's traditional Ligurian menu. Most locals already know the chef and his scrumptious creations, but tourists just discovering them for the first time come away equally satisfied. Fish ravioli is among the unique dishes recommended by diners and the staff alike.

➤ On the right after the 1st underpass on V. Roma. $ Primi €10; secondi €14-18. ⏰ Open M-Tu noon-3pm and 6-10pm, Th-Su noon-3pm and 6-10pm.

PIZZERIA LA SMORFIA — 🚫💳🚭🍸🥡 PIZZERIA [2]

V. Vittorio Emanuele 73 — ☎0187 81 83 95

A huge selection of 50 different pizzas (and 16 white pizzas, plus 10 calzones) draws locals, including workers from other nearby restaurants, to this crowded joint. Three employees frantically wait tables, cut pizzas, and make change to keep up with the rush and calls for beer that flow from the groups of young people under the awnings. The large pizzas will feed an army. The calzones shaped like bloated croissants are filled with deliciously melty cheese and sauces.

➤ Take the 1st left on the piazza after the tunnel onto V. Vittorio Emanuelle. The pizzeria is up on the left. $ Pizzas €4.50-7, large €9-14. Calzones €8. ⏰ Open daily 10:30am-3pm and 6-11pm.

PASTICCERIA LAURA — 🚫💳🚭🍸 CAFE [1]

V. Vittorio Emanuele 59

Quick and easy, Pasticceria Laura serves up some of the sweetest pastries around to locals who eat them at the bar and outdoor tables while reading the newspaper pink pages (sports section). Paired with a warm cappuccino, not much can beat a sugary cannoli. Here, that isn't cold cream in a crusty casing, but rather an airy, cream-filled puff of dough.

🍴 Pass through the tunnel, then take V. Vittorio Emanuele to the left from the piazza. Ⓢ Pastries €1. Espresso €1-2. 🕐 Open M 7:30am-10pm, W-Su 7:30am-10pm.

FOCACCERIA IL FRANTOLO

V. Gioberti 1

●Ⓧ BAKERY ❶

☎0187 81 83 33

The bread here comes piping hot out of the oven and straight into your hands, where the wonderful grease will stain the napkin and possibly your hands with that indelible mark of *focaccian* (is that a word? It should be) goodness. Il Frantolo serves an excellent brand of this special bread stuffed with olives, peppers, cheese, and more.

🍴 V. Gioberti to the right from V. Roma. Ⓢ Focaccia €1-3. 🕐 Open M-W 9am-2pm and 3:30-8pm, F-Su 9am-2pm and 3:30-8pm.

NIGHTLIFE

It seems difficult to call a collection of three bars a nightlife "hub," but, in Monterosso, that's what **Piazza Garibaldi** is. A few other bars, including one filled with raucous travelers, can be found on **Via Roma.** Many of the restaurants near the train station or past P. Garibaldi on the shoreline offer quieter spots where you can drink *sciacchetrà* while the sea breeze ruffles your hair.

📰 FAST BAR

V. Roma 13

●●Ⓧ♈♨ BAR

☎0187 81 71 64

It's fast times at Cinque Terre in this all-American bar, where it is the rare customer who speaks Italian rather than English. Visiting students chat at tables and mingle by the bar over draft beers and colorful cocktails sipped from long neon straws (apparently they weren't flashy enough already). The walls are papered with US dollar bills on which the poetic collegiate patrons scribble their profound messages to the universe ("Go Crimson!"). When the time difference allows, the owners show American sports on TV. Can anyone say "touchdown!"?

🍴 After exiting the tunnel, pass under the railroad bridge and head left onto V. Roma. The bar will be on the left. Ⓢ Shots €3. Beer €4-4.50. Cocktails €5-6. 🕐 Open daily 10am-2am. Aperitivo 6:30-8pm. Closed 2 weeks in Dec and all of Jan.

CA DI SCIENSA

P. Garibaldi 17

●●Ⓧ♈♨ BAR

☎0187 81 82 33

Don't worry about missing any of the action of the sporting world at Ca di Sciensa. TVs are everywhere you go and every way they come—outside, upstairs, flatscreen, big-screen, and even vintage versions with knobs. Join your friends in the extensive but frequently full outdoor seating for once-a-week live music.

🍴 From the tunnel, walk along the opposite side of the railroad bridge to P. Garibaldi. Ⓢ Beer €2-4. Cocktails €5. Sandwiches €5. 🕐 Open May-Sept daily 10:30am-2am; Oct-Apr M 10:30am-2am, W-Su 10:30am-2am. Aperitivo 7-8:30pm.

SCIUSCETTÚA CAFE

P. Garibaldi 22

●●ᶜ♈♨ BAR

☎0187 81 84 57

The restaurant is stone, arched, and cavelike, but that doesn't mean it's cold. The friendly staff, including three brothers who own the place, keep nights lively and bar patrons feeling welcome, but they guard their top-shelf liquors with care. You'll have to pay the premium to sip that sweet stuff.

🍴 From the tunnel, walk along the opposite side of the railroad bridge to P. Garibaldi. Ⓢ Cocktails €5-7.50. Appetizers €2.50-4.50. 🕐 Open daily Apr-Oct noon-2am. Aperitivo buffet 5:30-8:30pm.

CANTINA DI MIKY

Lungomare Fegina 104

●Ⓧ♈♨ BAR

☎0187 81 76 08 🖥www.ristorantemiky.it

No matter how small (or occasionally big) their audience, the bartenders here love to show off their behind-the-bar martini-shaking skills with some acrobatic flair. Hopefully, the groups seated at the large tables nearby won't be too dis-

cinque terre

tracted by the colorful changing lights to give them the attention they deserve.

⚑ To the right from the train station on the waterfront. Ⓢ Beer €4-5. Cocktails €6. ⏰ Open daily noon-midnight.

HIKING

The hike from Monterosso to Vernazza *(90min.)* is the most challenging of the four town-linking hikes, but without question, the pain is worth the gain: breathtaking vistas of the towns and spectacular panoramas of the sea crown the uphill journey. The start on the far-left side of Monterosso lulls hikers into a false sense of security with gradual ramps, before throwing them—BAM!—straight into a wall of steep, uneven, and seemingly unending steps. At higher elevation, the climb gives way to a relatively flat track notable for its wildflowers, butterflies, and gorgeous views over terraced vineyards back to Monterosso. Eventually, you'll begin to see the town of Vernazza. Watch the whitewashed ferryboats zipping by and pity them. Only the landlubbers have the privilege of this vista. The descent into Vernazza mirrors the ascent from Monterosso, struggling over rocky and uneven steps. This last stretch leads directly onto a tiny alley off a street in Vernazza's upper section.

cinque terre card

Cinque Terre Cards can be bought in the train stations and Cinque Terre National Park offices in each of the five towns. If you have any intention of hiking while in the area, you will need to purchase one, as they are required for access to the paths. They also grant reduced entry fees to various attractions in the towns and access to the bus routes within each town. A one-day pass costs €5, two-day is €8, three-day is €10, and seven-day is €20. You also have the option of buying an obviously-titled "with train" pass that includes unlimited access to the trains connecting the villages. This pass costs €8.50/€14.70/€19.50/€36.50, and is not worth the extra money since a) a train ride costs €1.40, so you'd have to ride it three times in one day to make it worth your money, and b) you're buying what is essentially a hiking pass, so who needs trains?

ESSENTIALS

Practicalities

- **TOURIST OFFICE: Cinque Terre National Park Office** provides information on trails and sells **Cinque Terre Cards,** which are necessary for hiking. *(P. Garibaldi 20 ☎0187 81 70 59 or 0187 80 20 53 🖳www.parconazionale5terre.it ℹ Also in the train station. ⏰ Open daily 8am-8pm.)* **Pro Loco** offers information on hiking and accommodations as well as **currency exchange.** *(V. Fegina 38 ☎0187 81 75 06 🖳www.prolocomonterosso.it ⚑ In front of the train station. ⏰ Open daily 9am-7pm.)*

- **ATMS: Banca Carispe.** *(V. Roma 49 and V. Roma 69 ⏰ Open daily 8:05am-1:15pm and 2:30-3:45pm.)* **Bancomat** has an ATM in the train station, on the ground floor.

- **INTERNET: The Net** has computers and Wi-Fi. *(V. Vittorio Emanuele 55 ☎0187 81 72 88 🖳www.monterossonet.com Ⓢ €1.50 1st 10min., €0.10 per min. thereafter, or €10 per 2hr. ⏰ Open daily 9:30am-9pm.)*

- **POST OFFICE:** *(V. Roma 73 ⏰ Open M-F 8am-1:30pm, Sa 8am-12:30pm.)*

monterosso • essentials

Emergency!

- **POLICE: Carabinieri** *(☎0187 81 75 24).* Also **Polizia Locale** in the Municipal Building *(P. Garibaldi ☎335 62 09 462).*
- **LATE-NIGHT PHARMACIES:** The pharmacy at **Via Fegina 44** posts after-hours rotations outside. *(☎0187 18 18 394 ⇞ Outside the train station. ℹ Cash only. ⏰ Open M-Sa 8:30am-12:30pm and 4-7:30pm, Su 9am-12:30pm and 4-7:30pm.)*
- **HOSPITALS/MEDICAL SERVICES:** There is a **doctor's office** in the municipal building *(P. Garibaldi).* Check the bulletin board for numbers of doctors on call. In a serious emergency call an **ambulance** *(☎118).*

Getting There

By Train

The station is on the waterfront on V. Fegina. *(☎0187 81 83 23 ⏰ Ticket office open daily 6:30am-7:25pm.)* The town lies on the Genoa-La Spezia line, and, as is not the case for some of the Cinque Terre villages, most trains stop here. Trains arrive directly from **Genoa.** *($ €5. ⏰ 90min., about every hr., departing Genoa 5am-10:20pm.)* A few trains come from **Turin** *($ €18. ⏰ 4hr.; 5:20am, 1:20pm, 5:20pm.)*, **Milan,** and **Florence,** but most arrivals from these cities transfer in one of the two points above. Local trains run between **Levanto** and **La Spezia,** with stops at each of the five villages. *($ M-F €1.40, Sa-Su €1.50. ⏰ 2-19min., every 30min. or less 4:51am-11:39pm.)* Train schedules to the towns are available at tourist offices.

By Ferry

From **La Spezia** *($ €12. ⏰ 2hr., 4 per day).* Ferries by **Navigazione Golfo dei Poeti** *(☎0187 81 84 40 or 0187 73 29 87)* connect the five towns. Departures from the dock to the right after exiting the tunnel run to **Riomaggiore** or **Manarola,** *($ Round-trip €11.50.)* or to **Vernazza** *($ Round-trip €6).*

Getting Around

Walking is the best way to do it.

Boat Rental

For where most mortals can't walk. Try **Samba.** *(☎0187 33 96 81 22 65 ⇞ Across from the train station, on the beach. ℹ Cash only. $ 2-person kayaks €25 per 3hr. ⏰ Open daily 9am-6pm.)*

By Bus

National Park Buses, a.k.a. green vans, run through town regularly, connecting it to points in the hills. *($ Free with Cinque Terre Card.)* Bus #1 connects the *centro sportivo* on the waterfront to Pietrafiore. *(⏰ About every 45min., 8:10am-6:35pm.)* Bus #2 goes from *centro sportivo* to Bivio and the church at Soviore, on top of the mountains. *(⏰ Every 30min.-1hr. 10:35am-6:30pm.)*

vernazza ☎0187

Judging by a quick walk down its primary street, Vernazza is a small haven for seafood restaurauteurs, colorful umbrellas, and tourists who like to be in bed by 10pm. Revolving around the central streets of **Via Roma** and **Via Visconti,** the town is mostly door after door of apartments occupied by welcoming Italians ready to take in the lonely wayfarer and his or her all-too-heavy luggage. The *piazza* by the beach is surrounded by restaurants serving up anchovies—a local specialty—in salads, soups, and pastas. When that's all been washed down with a cool wine from one of Vernazza's gourmet stores, only a dip in the fresh blue waters of the town's petite but oh-so-fine beach will do. Squished on three sides by pastel-colored buildings and on the other by a field of bobbing fishing boats, the sand here may nonetheless blanket Cinque Terre's most renowned swimming spot. Though there are tourists here, a trip to Vernazza during the day can still feel like an escape from the over-hyped beach resort aura.

ORIENTATION

One street, three names, and 100 million postcards. That's Vernazza in a nutshell, with the help of some hyperbole. The town's main street, **Via Roma,** runs from the train station and becomes **Via Visconti** about halfway to the water. Above the train station, it's called **Via Gavino** and is where you'll find many of the village's essential services. At the bottom of V. Visconti, restaurant-lined, umbrella-shaded **Piazza Marconi** overlooks Vernazza's tiny, picturesque harbor. From V. Roma/V. Visconti, many smaller "streets"—really staircases—and the trails to Monterosso and Cornigliarise connect with the homes and *affittacamere* (room rentals) above.

ACCOMMODATIONS

With a few exceptions, Vernazza's accommodations are almost all rental rooms owned by private citizens. Look for signs advertising *camere* in front of stores, restaurants, and doorways all over town.

ALBERGO BARBARA — HOTEL [4]

P. Marconi 30, top fl. ☎0187 81 23 98 www.albergobarbara.it

Ahoy there! Lifting that giant suitcase up a spiral staircase with only a rope to cling to may not be fun (though it really makes the nautical theme work), but it's worth it to get to the rooms above. Many have sea views and wooden rafters, and even those that look out the back are bright and airy. The maple chairs of the communal seating area on the second floor provide a spot for a relaxing drink or conversation with fellow guests.

To the right when coming from V. Roma. ℹ No elevator. Several flights up. $ Doubles €50, with bath €60-65, with sea view €100. ⏰ Closed Dec-Feb. Check-in until 5pm; if later, call ahead.

PENSIONE SORRISO — PENSIONE [4]

V. Gavino 4 ☎0187 81 22 24 www.pensionesorriso.com

While the toddler who runs the place is busy checking people in, his mother plays with blocks—wait, something's wrong there. This hotel's youngest resident is just one indication of the homey feel at Pensione Sorriso, where rooms are tucked away from the bustle of P. Marconi. Breakfast served in a communal dining room, free Wi-Fi access, and comfortable, brightly painted rooms make this humble *pensione* one of the best values in the village. The downstairs cafe is a lively gathering spot for young visitors as well.

Head uphill from the train station; the hotel will be on the right after the playground. ℹ Breakfast included. Free Wi-Fi. $ Singles €60, with bath and A/C €70; doubles €85, with bath €110, with bath and A/C €125.

HOTEL GIANNI FRANZI — HOTEL [4]

P. Marconi 5 ☎0187 82 10 03 www.giannifranzi.it

With rooms all over town, Gianni Franzi might be Vernazza's biggest real-estate mogul—and few would complain about that. The restaurant keeps 23 impeccable rooms decorated in antique furniture and bright bedspreads. They range from small singles with no view to expansive doubles with balconies overlooking the sea. A quiet, grassy seaside terrace helps travelers feel at home on the ocean no matter what room they've chosen.

Walk down V. Roma/V. Visconti and look left. $ Singles €45, with bath €70; doubles €65/€80, with bath and view €100. ⏰ Check in before 4pm. On W, when restaurant is closed, call upon arrival.

CAMERE DA MARTINA — AFFITTACAMERE [4]

P. Marconi 26 ☎0187 81 23 65 or 329 43 55 344 www.roomartina.com

The one and only Martina herself shows patrons to whichever of the four rooms they have chosen, each located in one apartment building next to the harbor on Vernazza's main square. What they may lack in thought-out and up-to-date design—one poster of the New York City skyline still has the Twin Towers on it—they make up for in comfort and practicality. Each room has a fridge, great for storing that vintage bottle from the shop downstairs.

⚡ *On the right side of P. Marconi when facing the water.* ⑨ *2- and 4-person rooms from €30-35 per person.* ⚏ *No reception; call ahead.*

SIGHTS

CASTELLO DORIA
⊛⊗ CASTLE

V. G. Guidoni

The Cinque Terre and its seas were a playground for the powerful families of Vernazza early in the last millenium, and from this castle, they observed and manipulated their domain—with the help of a strategic location and some artillery. (And thank goodness someone was protecting this harbor: at one point in the 13th and 14th centuries it was the primary port exporting the region's wine.) Today, though, the power is gone, and the thought of Vernazza controlling the sea—influencing anything, really—seems marvelously quaint. But the view, the commanding and description-defying view, remains for all to see. From the grassy deck of the castle roof, climb the foot-wide spiral staircase to the top of the tower, where a low stone wall is the only thing keeping viewers from tumbling to the rocks and sea below. (In America, this would have been shut down long ago with the help of a roomful of lawyers. Fortunately, we're in Italy.) The wall, well out of sight, is also the only thing between camera-toting travelers and the surrounding region's natural and historic beauty, all topped off with the colorful sprinkles of five cute little towns.

⚡ *Turn left onto V. G. Guidoni and walk up many steps, following the signs for "Castello."* ⑨ *€1.50. All proceeds benefit local charity.* ⚏ *Open daily 10am-7pm.*

VERNAZZA PORT
⅃ BEACH

P. Marconi

Once upon a time, this minuscule inlet was home to much of the wine shipping on the Italian Riviera. Now it sees a lot of toddlers in swim diapers taking their first dip with mom and dad. The small strip of sand located right in the heart of Vernazza has no services or lifeguard, but its small size and protected water mean it remains very family friendly. The harbor waters are fine for wading, but venture too far out and you may find yourself lost in the grid of buoys and fishing boats that make all those pictures so wonderfully Mediterranean.

⚡ *At the end of P. Marconi.* ⑨ *Free.* ⚏ *Open daily sunrise-sunset.*

FOOD

Vernazza is the perfect place for budget travelers to pack a picnic. Its gourmet shops, from delis to *pescherie* (fish shops), offer significant discounts over its many restaurants, which are concentrated around the waterfront in **Piazza Marconi. Salumi e Formaggi** (V. Visconti 19 ☎0187 82 12 40 *i* Cash only. ⚏ Open M-Sa 8am-2pm and 5:20-7:30pm, Su 8am-1:30pm.) sells produce and other staples, while just up the street, the small **Coop** (V. Roma 25 ⚏ Open M 8am-1pm and 5-8:15pm, Tu 8am-noon, W-Su 8am-1pm and 5-8:15pm.) stocks groceries of all kinds.

BAIA SARACENA
⊛⊗⅄⅂ PIZZERIA ❶

P. Marconi 16 ☎0187 81 21 13 ◼www.baiasaracena.com

The location—in an arcade next to Vernazza's quaint fishing port—is special, and so is the pesto pizza. For just €5 (margherita €4.50), patrons can get a large and amazingly filling slice as well as a soda. Even when it's raining, dozens of visitors gather with their slices to eat on the rocky sea wall as waves crash at their back.

For table service (when it's sunny), sit on the patio and savor the majestic view from a table.

➡ Far down on the left side of the piazza, right before the seawall. $ Whole pizzas €6.50-8.50. Bruschetta €5-6. Salads €5-8. ⏰ Open M-Th 10:30am-10:30pm, Sa-Su 10:30am-10:30pm.

BLUE MARLIN BAR
CAFE [1]

V. Roma 43 ☎0187 82 11 49 💻bluemarlin2@lycos.it

Here's something many travelers haven't seen in a while: eggs and bacon. And what a relief it can be to find those two staples on one's breakfast plate, as is possible here in the heart of Vernazza. And if eggs *(€4)* keep Americans happy, adding sausage or bacon *(€2)* should really put them in hog heaven. Despite a cuisine that seems particularly suited to Uncle Sam, this bar fills with patrons of all nationalities by mid-morning and tends not to empty out until just before closing, when the day's first meal is a distant memory.

➡ Down the hill from the train station; on the right. $ Pastries €1. Bruschetta €3-4. Pizza €5-7. Espresso drinks €1-2. ⏰ Open daily 7am-6:30pm. Hot breakfast served 8:40-11:30am.

TRATTORIA GIANNI FRANZI
RISTORANTE [2]

P. Marconi 5 ☎0187 82 10 03 💻www.giannifranzi.it

Serving as a coffee bar, hotel lobby, and lounge for local hangers-on, Gianni Franzi's front room seems to be bustling with activity at all hours of the day. In its stone-walled back room, however, the dining area is a quiet escape into a world of savory pastas and meats. The chefs are known locally for their pesto-making prowess.

➡ Walk down V. Roma/V. Visconti to the piazza and look to the left. $ Primi €8-15; secondi €10-20. ⏰ Open Mar 11-Jan 9 M-Tu 8am-11pm, Th-Su 8am-11pm.

PANIFICO DA GINO
BAKERY [1]

V. Vinsconti 3 ☎0187 81 22 95

Sometimes you just need it quick and easy. Lunch, we mean. That's what this bakery serves in its warm focaccia sandwiches, wrapped up and easy to eat during a stroll towards the waterfront. The store also carries a variety of loaves and rolls useful for backpackers who made a perfect picnic before setting out but forgot that all-important sandwich ingredient: bread.

➡ Down V. Roma on the right. $ Breads and rolls €1-3. Sandwiches €3, on focaccia €4. ⏰ Open M-Tu 7am-1pm and 5-7pm, Th-Su 7am-1pm and 5-7pm.

liguarian ambrosia

Wine bars and shops line the tiny capillaries of the Cinque Terre's streets, advertising the *produtti tipici* of the Liguria region—the famous Cinque Terre *bianco.* This wine is cultivated from grapes grown in the hillsides by the hiking trails through which tourists regularly meander. Those very trails began as crucial arteries for transporting grapes and other staples (and here, wine is a staple) to the central port at Vernazza. The scent of lemon and thyme perfuming the route reveals that the region's vineyards and farms are still very much committed to a traditional way of life. After a tough day of hiking or an even tougher one of reclining in the sun, try a cool glass of *sciacchetrà,* a sweet, thick, amber vintage that is the region's most famous product. At this point, you may never want to return to the modern (or sober) world.

hiking the cinque terre

The five villages on this stretch of the Ligurian coastline offer the perfect potential for enjoyable, and not particularly difficult hikes. For our descriptions of each hike, see the hiking section of each town. Here, we pick out our absolute favorite moments of the paths stretching from Monterosso to Riomaggiore. We hope you appreciate the beauty of this area as much as we did.

1. MONTEROSSO ASCENT WATERFALL. One more step. One more step. And then a few more. And then, before you get to the breathtaking views over the whole region, you get beauty on a miniature scale. As you cross over a small slate footbridge, a waterfall flows to the left and under the bridge. As most hikers pass right on by, take a short detour down below the bridge, where the noise of falling water drowns the din of footsteps from above. For the slow or step-climbingly-challenged, the rocks and roots here make a perfect spot for the first sit-down water or snack break (you're less than 20min. outside of Monterosso). For those who feel that, nah, we can keep going, stop and savor nature for a moment anyhow.

2. PUNTA LINA OVERLOOK. Come on, Vernazza, stop playing hard to get. From here, more than three-quarters of the way to the second town, hikers finally get their first glimpse of that fruit basket of buildings peeking out from behind its protective hill. Since the overlook is in a clearing at a bend in the trail, it's a spot where a number of people take a break—and photos—by taking a few steps down to gaze between the brush. A closed trail leads downhill here, but it is impassible, and plus, though it brings you closer to Vernazza on the map it also heads downhill, meaning the perspective is lost and photos get worse, not better.

3. LAST CHANCE BEFORE VERNAZZA. Ladies and gentlemen, the captain has indicated that the town is in sight and we've been cleared to make our final descent. We remind you that those wishing to avoid the chatty tourist throngs in the *centro* should consider stopping at this one little bench, after the guard shack and before the street begins. It does provide a close-up view of the bobbing boats and stone-cold castle, without all that hastle. Meal service will be provided by picnic basket.

4. MARKER 15 OVERLOOK. No need to mince words: this view is simply the best on the trail. Emerge from behind the brush and whoa—the gasps are audible (this is almost true, we swear.) Across the valley, floating high above the azure sea on a pillow of green foliage is Corniglia, with its beautiful sister Manarola just a few kilometers beyond.

5. GUVANO BEACH. Both clothing and decency seem to be optional at this beach, a steep 20min. climb down to the cove from the main trail. Lovers have been known to do more than simply suntan in the buff on the sands of Guvano. Geographically, it is known to locals as one of the most pristine and secluded spots around due to its fine sand beaches and turquoise water undisturbed by swim-diapered toddlers. The seclusion, however, may be better explained by its accurate but somehow untrustworthy rickety white sign from the trail that belies its not-quite-official status with park authorities.

6. PUNTA BUONFIGLIO. Just around the corner from Manarola is a quiet overlook that should be teeming with people. But it isn't, as the luxuries of town lure from so close. Above a rock wall, Punta Buonfiglio is the best-maintained stopping point on the trail, with grassy lawns perfect for croquet (you did bring your set, didn't you?) or picnics and a view over Manarola and the sea. A small playground keeps the little ones occupied, while amateur meteorologists amuse themselves analyzing one of the more quirky features, a windsock. But everyone, big and small, benefits from the first free public bathroom on the trail (donations accepted).

7. TUNNEL OF LOVE. The trail's final portion is famous as the "Via della'Amore." No spot on the walk says why better than the tunnel of love, where couples pause to leave a small mark on the concrete walls and a big smooch on each others' lips. Covered in painted, scratched, and drawn outlines of hearts and padlocks (the unbreakable bond, ya know?), in a big city the tunnel's mercilessly graffitied concrete might indicate a part of town you'd rather not be in, but on the Lover's Trail, after miles of magnificent scenery, this somehow seems a touching way to be re-acclimated from the paradise of the trail to something a little more familiar to city dwellers.

HIKING

The trail from Vernazza to Corniglia *(75min.)*, while still difficult due to a significant number of steps throughout, is more open than the previous walk. It begins along a wide trail with continuous views of the ocean over a brush-covered hill. With less shade comes more cacti (in Italy, who knew?). The hike's most impressive point is near **Marker 15**, over 200m up, where the trail overlooks Corniglia—itself a city on a hill—with Manarola's orange and pink hues standing out against the many azure inlets in the distance. After winding along above the turquoise water that sparkles like glittery sidewalks, you'll be about 15min. outside of Corniglia. Here, the terrain changes, and walkers wander through a working agricultural landscape, the air scented with thyme and lemon that grows on the surrounding trees. The trail spills onto a road outside of town. Turn right to head toward Corniglia's *centro.*

ESSENTIALS

Practicalities

- **ATMS: Banca Carispe** has a stand-alone machine at V. Roma 37. Also **Banca Carige** *(V. Gavino 18 ⏰ Open M-F 8:05am-1:20pm and 2:30-3:45pm.)*

- **LAUNDROMATS: Lavandara il Cargetto.** *(V. Carugetto 15 ☎333 78 99 499 ⚑ Turn right at V. Ettore Vernazza across from the pharmacy, then take the first left. Ⓢ Wash €5, dry €6. ⏰ Open daily 8am-10pm.)*

- **INTERNET: Phone Home Internet Point** has computers and Wi-Fi. *(V. Roma 38 Ⓢ €0.15 per min. 1st 30min., €0.10 per min. thereafter. Wi-Fi €3 per 30min. ⏰ Open daily May-Oct 9:30am-10pm; Nov-Apr 9:30am-8pm.)*

- **POST OFFICES:** Also includes a currency exchange. *(V. Gavino 30 ⏰ Open M-F 8am-1:30pm, Sa 8am-12:30pm.)*

Emergency!

- **POLICE: Municipal** *(P. dei Caduti 34 ☎0187 82 11 47 ⚑ Just uphill from the train station.)*

- **LATE-NIGHT PHARMACIES: Dott. Elena Niccolo** posts after-hours emergency numbers. *(V. Roma 2 ☎0187 81 23 96 ⚑ Down the hill from the station; on the left. ⏰ Open M-W 9:30am-1pm and 4-7:30pm, Th 9:30am-1pm, F-Sa 9:30am-1pm and 4-7:30pm.)*

- **HOSPITALS/MEDICAL SERVICES: Ambulatorio Medico di Vernazza** *(V. Gavino 5 ☎335 65 56 845 ⓘ Call 6-9pm for appointments. ⏰ Open M 11am-noon, Tu 5-7pm, W 4:30-5:30pm, Th 10:30am-noon, F 5-6pm.)*

Getting There

By Train

Vernazza is located on the line between Genoa and La Spezia. Trains arrive directly from **Genoa** *(Ⓢ €5. ⏰ 90min., approx. every hr., departing Genoa 5am-10:20pm.)* and **La Spezia** *(Ⓢ €1.40. ⏰ 20min., every 30min. or more, departing 4:30am-12:50am.),* just four stops away. A few trains come from **Turin** *(Ⓢ €18. ⏰ 4hr.; 5:20am, 1:20, and 5:20pm.),* **Milan,** and **Florence,** but most arrivals from these cities transfer in one of the two points above. Local trains run between **Levanto** and **La Spezia** with stops at the five villages. *(Ⓢ M-F €1.40, Sa-Su €1.50. ⏰ 2-19min., every 30 min. or less, 4:51am-11:39pm.)*

By Ferry

Boats run by **Navigazione Golfo dei Poeti** *(☎0187 81 84 40 or ☎0187 73 29 87)* connect Vernazza to **Monterosso.** *(Ⓢ €6 round-trip. ⏰ 15min., 8 per day departing Monterosso 10:30am-5:50pm.)* From Monterosso, ferries also connect to Manarola and Riomaggiore.

cinque terre

Getting Around

Cars are not allowed within the village, which only has one road wide enough to fit them. While this rule (and hundreds of steps) work to thwart delivery people, it's great for pedestrians. **National Park Buses** run to San Bernardino-Muro church high above the town. *(🕐 9:45am, noon, 3pm, and 6pm.)*

corniglia ☎0187

There's no beach in Corniglia, and to a significant extent, that—and the nearly 400 steps up from train to town—keeps the tourists away. As a result, this village at the center of the Cinque Terre provides a stunningly beautiful and refreshingly quiet respite from its neighbors down the coast.

ORIENTATION

From the train station, walk to the left along the tracks to the back-and-forth steps that lead to the town center. At the top of the climb, travelers find themselves on the very appropriately named **Via alla Stazione,** which leads into the town's **centro storico,** to the left. From the *centro*, follow **Via Fieschi** to many *affittacamere* and panoramic views on the left as well as a few restaurants to the right. The main trail to Vernazza and Manarola also crosses through this central intersection.

ACCOMMODATIONS

Although Corniglia is best as a daytrip because of its small size and inconvenient hilltop location, there are a number of *affittacamere* that tend to be more affordable than those in other towns.

OSTELLO CORNIGLIA HOSTEL [2]

V. alla Stazione 3 ☎0187 81 25 59 www.ostellocorniglia.com

Among a sea of signs advertising rooms, the bright yellow ostello stands out, and for good reason. This two-year-old, 24-bed hostel offers the most affordable accommodations in town. With brightly colored bunk beds and a flatscreen TV in the common room, Ostella offers backpackers comfort for a night. They'll have plenty of space to store all their gear in the palatial 7 ft. lockers.

In the yellow building to the right before the centro storico. i Breakfast €3. $ Single-sex 8-person dorms €24; doubles €55. Extra bed €20.

B AND B DA BEPPE B AND B [4]

V. Serra 2 ☎0187 82 11 63 or 338 49 52 022

Located on a small but well-lit street, the doubles and one apartment of this simple bed and breakfast don't offer sea views but bright rooms with table and chairs that invite relaxation away from much of Cinque Terre's bustle. The helpful elderly couple who own and run the B and B go back and forth offering advice, though sadly, non-Italian speakers will miss much of the banter's nuance.

To the right and then up the steps from the centro storico. $ Doubles €90.

SIGHTS

Corniglia's precarious position on a steep hill means that nearly every corner offers a beautiful vista or other enchanting discovery.

PANORAMIC VIEWS PANORAMIC VIEW

V. Solferino and V. Fieschi

Rapunzel's hair is not required to climb to the top of the **Torre** (tower), though some stamina might be needed to conquer even *more* stairs. Those who take on this low-tech Stairmaster will be rewarded with the highest view in town, which looks over Manarola to the left and down upon the turquoise waves. The busy sea lanes to La Spezia are also visible, with mammoth ships appearing like water-walking ants on the horizon. On clear days, even the hulking mound of Corsica is visible. Just down the road (and more steps—get used to it), **Terrazzo Panoramico Santa Maria** one-ups the tower from a lower vantage point, though the waves still crash far below. More than 180 degrees are visible in a panorama that includes Monterosso. Camera-shy Vernazza and Riomaggiore, however, hide behind their hills.

➔ To reach the tower from V. Fieschi, turn left at Largo Turagio and head up 2 flights of stairs, then up a 3rd flight to the right. The Santa Maria viewpoint is at the very end of V. Fieschi.

MARINA ⊗ BEACH

Below V. Marina

No sunbathing here, unless any prospective tanner is okay with being fried by the sun and pummeled by the waves that crash on the steaming rocks. This beach, located far below Corniglia, still draws a few adventurous fishermen (wearing unfortunately tiny swimsuits) and tourists willing to climb down—you guessed it—more steep and zig-zagging stone steps, these not as well maintained as those leading to town. For a place to picnic with the waves' white noise as the only break to the peace, however, there are few better locations. Park it on one of the several benches along the steps to the water.

➔ From V. Fieschi, turn right onto V. Marina and follow it down to steps that lead to the water's edge below.

FOOD

As a waypoint for backpackers, Corniglia offers a number of simple but satisfying dining options as well as several sit-down restaurants catering to those staying in town. **A Butiega** sells a variety of fresh fruits and vegetables, meats, and cheeses, plus essentials like soap, batteries, and beer. *(V. Fieschi 142 ☎0187 81 22 92 ⏰ Open daily in summer 8am-7pm.)*

TERRA ROSSA ENOTECA ⊗🍸 ENOTECA ❷

V. Fieschi 58 ☎0187 81 20 92

At the bottom of a terraced vineyard, under a nearly opaque awning of vines, seven tables sit hidden and waiting for weary patrons. With a postcard-like view of the town, valley, and sea below, Terra Rossa draws hikers, tourists, and locals seeking rest and a sip of Corniglia's *Polenza*, a dry white wine, or another Cinque Terre vintage *(€4-5)*. As if further enticement could possibly be needed, the restaurant also offers sweet delights at all hours of the day, from homemade breakfast cookies *(€3)* to *scriocco*, a selection of cheeses with honey and chutney *(€10)*.

➔ To the right from centro storico, overlooking the valley. $ "Finger food" €7-10. Wine €4-5. ⏰ Open M-Tu 8am-8pm, Th-Su 8am-8pm.

LA GATA FLORA ⊗ PIZZERIA ❶

V. Fieschi 109 ☎0187 82 12 18

Once the trail-fatigued backpacker realizes it's not vertigo that's making her see pots and pans hanging from the ceiling—they've been recycled as lights—she must deal with another sight quite uncommon in these parts: a rectangular pizza. Yes, with corners. The thick crust makes a filling meal, while the focaccia, also square, with toppings including tomato and olives, can hold you over as a tasty snack.

➔ From centro storico, turn right onto V. Fieschi; the pizzeria will be on the left. $ Whole pizzas €4.50-7, slices €2.50-3.50. Focaccia €1.80-3. ⏰ Open M 10am-3pm and 6-8pm, W-Su 10am-3pm and 6-8pm.

CANTINA DI MANANAN ⊗🍸❄ RISTORANTE ❸

V. Fieschi 117 ☎0187 82 11 66

Whether it's a desire to create exclusivity or a European dislike of working that keeps this restaurant open for just over 4hr. per day doesn't really matter: make time to visit the small stone-walled restaurant during its operating hours. The front entrance is covered in chalkboards scrawled with the dishes of the day, including the popular stuffed pastas.

From centro storico, turn right onto V. Fieschi; the restaurant will be on the left. $ Cover €1.80. Primi €10-12; secondi €12-18. ⏰ Open M 12:45-2:30pm and 7:45-9:15pm, W-Su 12:45-2:30pm and 7:45-9:15pm.

HIKING

Talk about an inauspicious start to this trail *(40min.)*. Even after climbing down 382 steps from Corniglia (a good reason to do the trail in this direction), the scenery scarcely improves, as the entry to this portion of the trail is past the train station, through a bunker-like concrete gully, and past a number of abandoned warehouses. A rope bridge marks the exit from these unfortunate surroundings, but don't get too excited. Compared to the first two sections of trail, the scenery here is only decent. The trail is much flatter and paved with gravel in many places, making it easier for hikers of all abilities. Near Manarola a few rocks at water's edge are perfect for sunbathing, as many have discovered—that's if you don't mind taking what the park calls a "dangerous descent," to reach them. Picnic areas are also plentiful at this end of the trail, which soon swoops around a rocky point and reveals a gradual ramp into the heart of Cinque Terre's fourth town.

ESSENTIALS

Practicalities

Corniglia's services are limited, so you better hope your lodging has things like laundry or you'll be lugging along a bag of dirty clothes to the larger towns.

- **TOURIST OFFICES: National Park Tourist Office** has information on trails and trains. *(☎0187 81 25 23 In the train station. ⏰ Open daily 7am-7pm.)*
- **ATM: Banca Carispe** *(V. alla Stazione 35).*
- **POST OFFICE:** *(V. alla Stazione 5 In the yellow municipal building. ⏰ Open M-F 8am-1:30pm, Sa 8am-12:30pm.)*

Emergency!

- **POLICE: Municipal** *(☎0187 82 11 47).*
- **HOSPITALS/MEDICAL SERVICES: Guardia Medica** *(☎338 376 0007).*

Getting There

By Train

Stazione Corniglia, a 15min. uphill walk from the village itself, is along the Genoa-La Spezia line, though a number of the trains that stop at other points bypass this small town. Trains arrive directly from **Genoa** *($ €5. ⏰ 90min., approx. every hr., departing Genoa 5am-10:20pm.)* and nearby **La Spezia.** *($ €1.40. ⏰ 15min., 30 per day, 4:30am-12:50am.)* A few trains come from **Turin** *($ €18. ⏰ 4hr.; 5:20am, 1:20pm, and 5:20pm.)*, **Milan,** and **Florence,** but most arrivals from these cities transfer in one of the two points above. Local trains run regularly to connect the five towns of the Cinque Terre.

By Bus

Green National Park shuttle buses run from the train station to town. *(☎0187 81 25 33 $ €1.50, round-trip €2.50. Free for holders of Cinque Terre Cards. ⏰ Every 30min.-1hr., 7:35am-8pm.)*

By Stairs

Three hundred and eighty-two of them, each one closer to the top than the last, guaranteed. Walk along the promenade by the rail tracks—not the bus road—to reach them.

Getting Around 🚌

Cars are not permitted within the village, so 🚶**walking** is basically the only option. Be warned that due to the town's geography, steep climbs are part of navigating Corniglia. Even bikes take up too much room for the narrow streets—and unless the rider is a "that's totally sweet dude" BMXer, your favorite two-wheeler wouldn't handle the steps all that well, anyway.

manarola ☎0187

One of the smallest of the five towns, Manarola concentrates the Cinque Terre's back-in-time Italian feel within just a few short blocks. With a rocky cove as the centerpiece for both local fishermen and out-of-town swimmers, Manarola offers a large dose of maritime charm. Though its main street may not seem to present a wide variety in the way of restaurants or nightlife, the town keeps its cards close to its chest. You'll need to give this village a more thourough examination to find the jewels, hidden in its basements and hills, that make the place unique.

ORIENTATION ✷

Manarola has one primary street that's known as **Via Birolli** toward the water and **Via Discovolo** on the other side of the train tracks. A tunnel leads from the train station to the central *piazza*, where stairs and a ramp lift pedestrians over the buried rail lines. To the right, V. Discovolo winds up past a number of *affittacamere* to the church, hostel, and some restaurants. To the left, over the hulking *piazza*, V. Birolli shoots straight down to the water past a number of restaurants.

ACCOMMODATIONS 🏠

Manarola is home to one of the few hostels in Cinque Terre, but numerous *affittacamere* provide most of the lodging for budget travelers.

👍 OSTELLO CINQUE TERRE 💳♿📶 HOSTEL ❷

V. Riccobaldi 21 ☎0187 92 02 15 🖥www.hostel5terre.com

It may have a summer camp atmosphere, but this is no wood-board bunkhouse. All rooms look out over Manarola and the sea beyond, and an airy restaurant with terrace serves as a gathering spot. What's more, an extensive board game collection and snorkel equipment for rent keep patrons entertained.

➔ From the train station tunnel, turn right and walk 300m uphill to the church, where the hostel will be to the left. ℹ Wi-Fi €1 per 15min. $ 6-bed dorms €23; doubles €65; quads €100. ⏰ Reception 7am-1pm and 4pm-1am. Lockout 10am-5pm. Closed Nov-Feb.

CAPELLINI AFFITACAMERE 🚫💳🚫♿ AFFITTACAMERE ❹

V. Birolli 88 ☎0187 92 04 10

Although she doesn't own a computer, the kind, motherly keeper of these simple but comfortable rooms literally goes out of her way to make guests feel at home, as she has to descend from the fourth floor for every request. The rooms, on Manarola's main street, each have a few pieces of antique furniture like leather armchairs, plus a table, chairs, and fridge: perfect for a quiet night in.

➔ Turn left from the tunnel, over the piazza; the property is on the right. $ Doubles €60; triples €75.

DAVIDE ROOMS 🚫💳🚫♿ AFFITTACAMERE ❹

V. Chiuso Marina 17 ☎0187 92 04 07

Pack as many people as you can into Davide's grandiose though spare doubles and triples (the prices stay the same) holding a bed, futon-couch, and little else besides Cinque Terre posters and maps on the walls. Really, Davide would probably prefer that travelers not attempt to fill their room with more guests than the number of beds, but negotiate and do what you must.

➤ *Turn left from the tunnel, cross the piazza, and take the 1st right up the steps to V. Chiuso Marina.* $ *Doubles €60-65; triples €60-90.*

LA TORRETTA
♿ 📶 ❄ B AND B [5]

Vico Volto 20 ☎0187 92 03 27 💻www.torrettas.com

The digits before that decimal point may scare some (the entire villa can be rented for a mere €2000 a night), but they come with some serious luxury. Free nightly tastings of wine and local specialties are held on the breezy terrace, which has one should-be-more-common amenity: a telescope for stargazing. Check out those celebrities sunbathing on their yachts out at sea—or the heavens, if you want. Inside, canopied beds and large rooms are attended by a professional staff befitting such a hip boutique bed and breakfast.

➤ *Turn right from the tunnel and then right at the church piazza at the top of the hill. Entrance to the B and B is by the overlook fence.* $ *Singles €100; doubles €120; quads €190.*

SIGHTS

👍 ROCKY BEACH
♿ BEACH

At the end of V. Birolli

A **boat** putters by, a swimmer uses it to screen the defender, and—he scores! Yes indeed, water polo is one of the primary pastimes—after fishing from small, enthusiastically colored boats, of course—practiced in Manarola's compact cove. The rock face leading down from the town doesn't dissuade swimmers from nearby homes or from two continents away, and neither does the occasional marine traffic. Sunbathers populate the hard surfaces, both slanted and flat, along the boat ramp, while more adventuresome types jump 15 ft. from the central outcropping. And it's not just crazy teenagers: dads do belly flops into the salty water too. No matter what, take a dip in the refreshing, clean sea at probably the best place to swim in Cinque Terre. Ironically, the quieter area to sunbathe is nearer to the *piazza*, where a small concrete pier next to the rocks allows for flatter bronzing (what a luxury) and easy entry to the water.

➤ *Turn left from the tunnel and head down to the water on V. Birolli.* $ *Free.*

MUSEO DI SCIACCHETRÀ
♿ MUSEUM

V. Discovolo 203

Cheers! And then drink, with scarcely a second thought. That's how it normally goes, but to discover where that glass of intensely sweet, peach-colored dessert wine came from, visit this small one-room museum. It showcases the history of the region, a story very intertwined with wine. The now-famous trail linking the towns was once a trade route through which grapes, lemons, and thyme were brought to the wider world. Also, see the tools used to harvest the tens of kilos of delicate grapes needed to produce just one liter of *sciacchetrà*. A 15min. video on the process *(available in English)* is played on request.

➤ *Turn right from the tunnel; the museum is up the hill on the right.* $ *Free with Cinque Terre Card, which is required for admisison.* ⏰ *Open daily 9:30am-1pm and 1:30-7pm.*

FOOD

👍 TRATTORIA DAL BILLY
♿ ❄ RISTORANTE [2]

V. Rollandi 122 ☎0187 92 06 28

Maybe it's the locals' choice of restaurant because of the view. It certainly could be because of the food. Or perhaps it's just because residents are the only ones who want to make the hike up the steep road in order to dine at Trattoria dal

Billy. If it's the latter—**lightbulb!**—visitors should take the hint: the walk is worth it. Locals love the fresh seafood (caught by a fisherman whose gleaming mug adorns the walls) and homemade Ligurian pastas. Many are so large, even with whole lobsters in the dish, that they are best consumed by two, but the staff can prepare dishes for lonely parties of one.

✦ *Turn right from the tunnel, then follow the road uphill 300m to the church piazza. Then turn right up the steps at the far side of the piazza and follow the small street to the trattoria.* ⑤ *Cover €2. Primi €6-10; secondi €9-17.* 🕐 *Open M-F noon-2:30 and 6-10:30pm, Th 6-10:30pm, F-Su noon-2:30pm and 6-10:30pm.*

LA CAMBUSA
V. Birolli 110

✦⊗♨ PIZZERIA ❶
☎0187 92 10 29

The display case is always full. Maybe that's because there are so many choices that no customer can bear to pick just one dish. Beneath the hand-painted sign and fake ivy of this seatless establishment (not counting a few benches outside) every bread product and delicacy known to humanity awaits, from cannoli *(€1)* and pastries to focaccia with tons of different toppings. Plus, distinctly un-Italian deep-dish pizza slices.

✦ *Turn left from the tunnel and cross the piazza. The pizzeria is on the right.* ⑤ *Focaccia €1.80-2.50. Panini €3. Pizza slices €2.* 🕐 *Open daily 8am-8pm.*

MARINA PICCOLA
V. lo Scalo 16

✦⊗♈❋♨ RISTORANTE ❸
☎0187 92 09 23

A patio with white tablecloths overlooks a rocky grotto—the location is simply perfect, and everyone notices. Tourists throng to this place for seafood pastas like shrimp linguine and shrimp risotto with shellfish seemingly pulled from the harbor moments before reaching the plate.

✦ *Turn left out of the tunnel and walk to the waterfront, where Marina Piccola is to the right.* ⑤ *Primi €8-16; secondi €9-16.* 🕐 *Open M noon-2:30pm and 7pm-midnight, W-Su noon-2:30pm and 7pm-midnight.*

IL PORTICCOLO
V. Birolli 92

✦⊗♈❋♨ RISTORANTE ❷
☎0187 92 00 83 ▪www.ilporticcolo5terre.com

One of Manarola's most prominent restaurants, Il Porticcolo isn't shy, putting itself out there with a large, protruding patio that extends some ways into the street. While the prices catch many a visitor's eye, divine dishes like the *gnocchi al pesto* keep some locals coming back as well.

✦ *Turn left from the tunnel; the restaurant will be on the right past the piazza.* ⑤ *Primi €5-9; secondi €7-16.* 🕐 *Open M-Tu 11am-11:30pm, Th-Sa 11am-11:30pm.*

NIGHTLIFE

The Cinque Terre's undiscovered hotspot is here in Manarola, but it's close to the only game in town.

◪ LA CANTINA DA ZIO BRAMANTE
V. Birolli 110

✦⊗♈♨ BAR
☎0187 76 20 61

How much more fun would elementary school music class have been with a few bottles of wine? Ignore the flagrant illegality of that proposal for a moment, then look to this cantina for the answers. The owner and friends jam on the guitar (or didgeridoo) nightly at the front of the room cluttered with microphones, amps, and songbooks. Patrons join in on the bongos, tambourines, and the tables. Music starts at 9:30pm, and the crowd—locals young and old and tourists who become regulars over the course of their vacation—arrives soon after, but it has to stop by midnight. The owner says his mom sleeps above the family-run business.

✦ *Turn left from the tunnel and cross the piazza; it is on the right.* ⑤ *Wine €2.50-4.50. Cocktails €5-6.* 🕐 *Open M-W 9:30am-1am, F-Su 9:30am-1am.*

HIKING

All's fair in love and walking, as the final stretch of Cinque Terre's famous "Trail #2" (the blue line on the tourist-office map) demonstrates. Known as **Via dell'Amore,** or the "Lover's Trail," this 20min. walk can be completed by anyone, and with elevators at both ends, it is nearly wheelchair accessible except for a few steps in the middle. *(Visitors with disabilities should call the park in advance at ☎0187 76 00 91 for lift information.)* Smooth and paved, this hike provides more than just a mild introduction to the sea views further along. Its uniqueness comes from the so-called "tunnel of love" graffitied with sappy hearts and Cupid's arrows by countless paramours over the years, though some have painted elaborate murals. A cheesy but nonetheless popular trail tradition is to affix a lock to the park fences with your one and only and throw away the key as a symbol of everlasting affection.

ESSENTIALS

Practicalities

- **ATM: Banca Carispe.** *(275 V. Discovolo ✥ Just outside the tunnel.)*
- **POST OFFICES:** *(216 V. Discovolo ✥ To the right outside the tunnel. ⏰ Open M-F 8am-1:15pm, Sa 8am-12:30pm.)*

Emergency!

- **PHARMACIES:** *(238 V. Discovolo ☎0187 92 01 60 ⏰ Open M 9am-1pm and 4-7:30pm, Tu-Th 9am-1pm, F-Sa 9am-1pm and 4-7:30pm.)*
- **HOSPITALS/MEDICAL SERVICES: Croce Bianco Riomaggiore** *(☎0187 92 07 77).*

Getting There

By Train

Trains arrive directly from **Genoa** *($ €5. ⏰ 90min., approx. every hr., departing Genoa 5am-10:20pm.)* and nearby **La Spezia.** *($ €1.40. ⏰ 15min., 30 per day, 4:30am-12:50am.)* A few trains come from **Turin** *($ €18. ⏰ 4hr.; 5:20am, 1:20pm, and 5:20pm.),* **Milan,** and **Florence,** but most arrivals from these cities transfer in one of the two points above. Local trains run regularly to connect the five towns of the Cinque Terre.

By Ferry

Ferries operated by **Navigazione Golfo dei Poeti** *(☎0187 81 84 40 or ☎0187 73 29 87)* connect the town to **Monterosso** and **Riomaggiore.** *($ Round trip €6. ⏰ 15min., 8 per day, departing Monterosso 10:30am-5:50pm.)* From Monterosso, ferries also connect to Vernazza.

Getting Around

National Park **buses** connect the center of town to **Volastra** in the hills above. *(⏰ About every hr. 7am-11:30pm. Check the schedule in the tourist office for specific times, which change frequently.)* Other than this, your feet are all you'll need.

riomaggiore ☎0187

Riomaggiore, the touristy town at the other end of the Cinque Terre from Monterosso, lacks a beach but is intimately connected with the sea. The water's not even visible from the village's main drag—but don't tell the fishermen rinsing their **boat** hulls or the nearby boat rental companies trawling for customers. Those visitors who set up camp in Riomaggiore and prefer not to tan on rocks and swim in the wake of passing boats take the train to the sandy beaches of Monterosso each morning. As the sun sets (and with it the opportunity for soaking up the rays) they return in droves to descend upon the town's numerous seafood restaurants and affordable bars, adding to this town's vibrant culture.

ORIENTATION

From the train station, a tunnel leads to the center of town at **Piazza del Vignaiolo.** The town's central street, **Via Colombo,** heads steeply upward past numerous bars, restaurants, and hotels, eventually becoming **Via de Santaurio** and reaching the intersection with **Via de Gasperi,** which circles the valley and boasts marvelous views of the buildings below. Between V. Colombo and V. de Gasperi and accessible by a number of staircases lies the town's main church, accompanied by its **Castello,** from which visitors can marvel at spectacular views of the sea. At the lower end of V. Colombo across from the tunnel exit, a staircase leads down to the marina, which is invisible from the main square and home to colorful, bobbing skiffs, a number of seafood restaurants, and the ferry terminal.

ACCOMMODATIONS

At the extreme end of Cinque Terre, Riomaggiore has more than its fair share of room rentals and *locanda* (inns), meaning that this is the best place to look for last-minute lodging (though that doesn't guarantee anything will be available if you arrive in mid- to late summer). Most hotels and room rentals are on **Via Colombo,** but looking on a few back streets and above the town center can yield rewards.

👍 MAR-MAR — 👥🚭 AFFITTACAMERE [2]

V. Malborghetto 4 — ☎0187 92 09 32 💻www.5terre-marmar.com

Talk about assorted flavors—from student dorms to vast apartments, this room rental company seems to have it all. Each room includes an ensuite bath, but beyond that, little is shared by the 30 different properties. Some have TV, others balconies, and prices vary accordingly. Those who choose to spend less can still benefit from the community terrace, a space for all renters that overlooks the water.

➜ After the tunnel, turn left up V. Colombo. Mar-Mar is ahead on the left. $ Dorms €15-20; doubles and apartments €60-120. ⏰ Office open daily 9am-1pm and 2-5pm.

EDI — 💳🚭 AFFITTACAMERE [4]

V. Colombo 111 — ☎0187 92 03 25

With many boasting full kitchens and terraces, Edi's apartments are dressed to impress and priced to please. (One-bedroom apartments with living room and bathtub for €60?! It's a real possibility.) The best deals, however, are on the couple of rooms reserved for young people, which include many of the same amenities—minus the sea view, but you can find that at the beach—for even lower rates.

➜ From the tunnel, head about halfway up V. Colombo, where Edi is on the right. $ Student rooms for 2-3 people €50-75; doubles €60-100; apartments €60-180.

LOCANDA DALLA COMPAGNIA — 💳🚭📶❄ B AND B [4]

V. del Santaurio 32 — ☎0187 76 00 50 💻www.dallacompagnia.it

The most popular accessory at this cheery bed and breakfast should probably be a skateboard for guests to zoom down the steep hill of V. Colombo. Though perched at the top of the road, this *locanda* is still only minutes (perhaps seconds for those on wheels) from the water and restaurants in the lower end of the town. It features five brightly colored rooms and an open breakfast area as well as a few "mini-apartments" farther from the main building but with similar amenities.

*➜ At the top of V. Colombo, in the small piazza on the right. **i** Breakfast included in most rates. $ Doubles outside the hotel €30-50, in main building €60-100. Small discount for payment in cash. ⏰ Check-in noon-6pm.*

HOTEL CA DEI DUXI — 💳🚭📶❄ HOTEL [5]

V. Colombo 36 — ☎0187 92 00 36 or 0187 76 05 63 💻www.duxi.it

Ca dei Duxi's six rooms have a rustic feel. If it weren't for the sea breeze on the terrace (available in several rooms), the wood beams, beds, and arched stone breakfast area could have travelers believing they were in Tuscany, not Cinque Terre. But hotel guests keep coming back, not just for the water and sunshine but for the young, friendly staff and rooms with A/C and fridge. The owners also rent rooms and apartments with fewer amenities at lower prices.

*# Up V. Colombo at the steps on the left. **i** Breakfast included. Wi-Fi available in lobby. $ Hotel doubles €70-120; triples €90-130. Rooms outside hotel €50-60, with private bath €60-75. Apartments outside hotel €60-80. ⏰ Lobby area open 11am-9pm.*

SIGHTS

ARTWORK OF SILVIO BENEDETTO — ♿ PUBLIC ART

In P. Rio Finale, the tunnel, and all over town — 🖥www.silviobenedetto.it

Buenos Aires native Silvio Benedetto has made it his mission to beautify Riomaggiore through monumental works of art, and all visitors to the town are beneficiaries of his project. From the moment one exits the station, a striking mural catches the eye. Benedetto's *Storia di Uomini e de Pietre* (*History of Man and Stone*) immortalizes the region's hardworking farmers in dramatic poses and eye-catching colors, showing how they created the unique terraced landscape over thousands of years by stacking eight million cubic meters of sandstone. Benedetto's installation in the train tunnel also focuses on the landscape, representing the changes in the Cinque Terre over time and through the seasons in a mosaic that begins with small natural elements and ends with more durable, modern terra cotta. The starfish marks the tunnels exact center. Exploring the rest of town, visitors will unexpectedly find Benedetto's influence in many places, including Riomaggiore's municipal building, lending a little bit of whimsy to this less secluded sea town.

 # First admire the mural outside the train station. Then proceed through the tunnel to town, focusing on the mosaic to the right, and don't miss the tile installation outside the tunnel's end. Above town, the municipal building on V. T. Signori also has a mural. $ Free.

CASTELLO — CASTLE

Above V. T. Signori and P. della Chiesa

Mother nature has a kind reward for those hearty travelers who, having made the hike from Manarola or even Monterosso, are willing to climb a few more steps to Riomaggiore's ancient *castello*. After the bustle of V. dell'Amore, this is a quiet retreat with an even more magnificent sea view, the same one that allowed sentries defending the city hundreds of years ago to see for miles. Look down on the trail below, Riomaggiore's pink and yellow buildings, and the village's protected, rocky harbor.

*# From V. Colombo, follow the signs for "Castello" up the steps to P. della Chiesa. Outside the front doors of the church, take the steps up to the right, which lead to the castle. **i** For those less inclined to walk (see the hiking pun?) a lift rises 38m from the station to a promenade just below the Castello. $ Castle free. Lift €0.50 per person or €1 per family. ⏰ Open daily 8am-8pm. Lift closes at 7:45pm.*

FOOD

The lower one goes, the more restaurants one finds in Riomaggiore. They line the bottom of **Via Colombo** and the marina, but a few worthwhile places are also high above town. Those looking for a picnic or an inexpensive bite should stop at one of the many *alimentari* (grocery stores) that occupy lower V. Colombo.

TE LA DO IO LA MERENDA — PIZZERIA, TAKEOUT [1]

V. Colombo 161 — ☎0187 92 01 48

Can the menu at this tiny hole-in-the-wall takeout joint get any bigger? Sure it can: the staff hangs handwritten pages of new dishes and specials all over the outside and from the clotheslines inside. Serving more than typical pizza and pasta, this quick and scrumptious spot draws patrons all day with local specialities including crispy *farinata* and vegetarian Ligurian pastas, even without giving their hungry guests a single place to sit down.

At the bend in V. Colombo, on the right. $ Medium pizzas €5-7, slices €2-3. Ligurian dishes to go €5-8. ⏰ Open daily 8am-8pm.

DAU CILA SEAFOOD ❸

V. San Giacomo 65 ☎0187 76 00 32

Some townspeople say that this is not only their favorite restaurant in town, but it is also the only restaurant that serves fresh fish brought into Riomaggiore harbor. While our survey says that's probably not true, there is fresh fish to be had. One of the scaly critters stares back at diners from an outdoor cooler as they peruse the menu, its forlorn-looking fish face seeming to say, "You really want to eat me?" Sorry bud, it's already too late for you. See ya later...on my plate.

From the tunnel, take the steps down toward "Marina." Once outside, Dau Cila is on the left. $ Salads and primi €9-12; secondi €12-18. ⏰ Open daily noon-3pm and 6-11pm.

RIPA DEL SOLE RISTORANTE ❸

V. de Gasperi 282 ☎0187 92 01 43 💻www.ripadelsole.it

Removed from the conglomeration of touristy spots in the valley below, this place has a fancier feel without fancier prices. That means good eats, good views, and better company. (Please, no Hawaiian shirts or cameras around the neck.) The restaurant's menu focuses on seafood-based pastas, plus the occasional special addition from the chef, such as the popular truffles.

Walk all the way up V. Colombo and V. del Santuario and turn left. Or, take the new public elevator from P. Chiesa to V. de Gasperi. $ Primi €10-11; secondi €10-20. ⏰ Open Tu-Su noon-2pm and 6:30-10pm.

GELATERIA CENTRALE 2 GELATERIA ❶

V. S. Giacomo 105 ☎0187 76 00 66

It's not often that *Let's Go* recommends the number two of anything. But in this case, being the second twin doesn't make this seafront ice cream shop second-best. An unbeatable view of the harbor helps this shop dethrone its sister *(on V. Colombo)*, which serves the same treats, all made in-house.

From the tunnel, take the steps down toward "Marina." Once outside, take the ramp on the left upward . $ Gelato €1.50-3.50. ⏰ Open daily 10am-10pm.

TRATTORIA VIA DELL'AMORE RISTORANTE ❸

P. Rio Finale 8 ☎0187 92 08 60

The name and the location are a bit misleading: despite being beneath the steps to the trail after which it's named, this is not the tourist haven one might expect. While visitors proceed to the town center on the other side of the tunnel, locals travel just steps away from the railway station to escape and unwind over pastas, fish, and meats. The trattoria offers a *prix-fixe* menu *(€22)* that includes a *primo*, *secondo*, dessert, the cover charge, and water.

From the train station, turn left. Restaurant is at the foot of the steps to V. dell'Amore. $ Cover €2. Primi €9-11; secondi €10-14. ⏰ Open M-Tu noon-3:30pm and 5:45-11pm, Th-Su noon-3:30pm and 5:45-11pm.

NIGHTLIFE

Not to be confused with that other Rio (look a few thousand miles west), this Cinque Terre town certainly lacks a hard-partying club scene. Still, compared to its neighbors, Riomaggiore boasts a number of bars where you can relax with a drink or two and find some friends.

BAR CENTRALE

🍸⊗♿ BAR

V. Colombo 144

☎0187 92 02 08

The central gathering point for Riomaggiore's visiting international crowd isn't much to see on its own (except for caffeine-junkies itching to see its high-tech espresso machine). When the people start flowing in and the backpacker crowd begins to swap travel tales, however, it becomes easy to see why visitors return night after night. The bar's owner rocks V. Colombo annually with a raucous Fourth of July party that includes a DJ and live band playing for all the Yanks.

✦ *Up V. Colombo on the left.* Ⓢ *Beer €3.50-5. Cocktails €5.50-7.* ⌚ *Open daily 7am-1am.*

A PIE DE MA, BAR AND VINI

🍸⊗♿ BAR

V. dell'Amore

☎0187 92 10 37

Who knows how many lovers have taken a break from smooching on the path above for a cocktail overlooking the sea—a pretty romantic location in itself? Who knows how many lovers on the path at night have heard the band below and stopped by for some after-dusk dancing? One thing is for sure: here, love is just as much in the air as the guitair strains. And there are plenty of tables for two. The A Pie de Ma drinks can't hurt the relationship either.

✦ *From the train station, take the steps up to V. dell'Amore. Turn right at the sign just before the ticket booth.* 𝒊 *Live music most F-Sa at 9pm or 9:30pm.* Ⓢ *Wine €2-6. Beer €2.50-4.50. Cocktails €5-6.* ⌚ *Open daily 10am-midnight.*

ESSENTIALS

Practicalities

- **TOURIST OFFICES: National Park** is next to the train station. Sells **Cinque Terre Cards** and has **Wi-Fi** as well as 6 computer stations on upper level. *(☎0187 76 07 15* Ⓢ *Internet access €0.80 per 10min.* ⌚ *Open daily 8am-7:30pm.)*

- **ATM: Banca Carige** offers currency exchange. *(V. Colombo 215* ⌚ *Open M-F 8:20am-1:20pm and 2:30-4pm.)*

- **LAUNDROMATS: Wash and Dry Lavarapido.** *(V. Colombo 109* 𝒊 *Cash only.* Ⓢ *Wash and dry both €3.50 per 30min. Detergent €1.* ⌚ *Open daily 8:30am-7:30pm.)*

- **POST OFFICES:** *(V. Pecunia 7* ☎0187 80 31 60 ✦ *Up the stairs from V. Colombo and to the left.* ⌚ *Open M-F 8am-1pm, Sa 8am-noon.)*

Emergency!

- **POLICE: Municipal.** *(V. Santaurino 123c* ☎0187 92 09 75 ✦ *Above V. Colombo on the right.)*

- **LATE-NIGHT PHARMACIES: Farmacia del Mare** posts late-night pharmacy information outside. *(V. Colombo 182* ☎0187 92 01 60 ⌚ *Open M-Sa 9am-1pm and 4-8pm, Su 9am-1pm.)*

- **HOSPITALS/MEDICAL SERVICES: Croce Bianca** *(V. Colombo 68* ☎92 07 77*).*

Getting There

By Train

Riomaggiore is a stop for almost all regional trains. Trains arrive directly from **Genoa** *(*Ⓢ *€5.* ⌚ *90min., about every hr., departing Genoa 5am-10:20pm.)* and nearby **La Spezia.** *(*Ⓢ *€1.40.* ⌚ *15min., 30 per day, 4:30am-12:50am.)* A few trains come from **Turin** *(*Ⓢ *€18.* ⌚ *4hr.; departing Turin at 5:20am, 1:20pm, and 5:20pm.),* **Milan,** and **Florence,** but most of the time, travelers from these cities must change trains. Frequent local trains connect the five villages of Cinque Terre.

By Ferry

From **La Spezia** *($ €12. ⏰ 2hr., 4 per day.)* Ferries operated by **Navigazione Golfo dei Poeti** *(☎0187 81 84 40 or ☎0187 73 29 87)* connect the five towns. Departures are from the marina. Take the steps down from the station tunnel, then keep left and walk back up on V. San Giacomo, where the ticket office is located. Ferries run to **Monterosso** or **Manarola** *($ Round-trip €11.50.)*, and to **Vernazza.** *($ Round-trip €6.)*

Getting Around

By Bus

National Park Buses run from the town center on V. Colombo to the hilltop parking lot, *castello*, and cemetery. Some travel to Biassa, several kilometers away in the mountains. *($ Free for Cinque Terre Card holders. ⏰ Every 30min.-1hr., 7am-10:30pm.)*

On Water

Il Corsaro Rosso, "the red pirate," rents kayaks and snorkel equipment and recommends the best spots to visit. *(Riomaggiore Marina ☎328 17 86 457 or ☎328 69 35 355 ⇄ Down the stairs toward "marina" and to the right by the boats. $ Single-person kayaks €5 per hr., €25 per day; 2-person €10/€45; 3-person €15 per hr. ⏰ Open daily May-Sept 9am-6pm.)*

Under Water

Diving Cinque Terre offers daily snorkeling and scuba excursions. *(V. San Giacomo ☎0187 92 00 11 ⇄ Down the stairs in the corridor toward the marina. $ Snorkeling excursions €18. ⏰ Open daily Easter-Sept 9am-6pm. Scuba and snorkel boat trips depart M-F 2:30pm, Sa-Su 10am and 2pm.)*

FLORENCE

With Michelangelos crammed into every corner and Botticellis stacked clear to the sky, Florence isn't quite a real city—it's more like a storage facility for the Renaissance. Race through the Tuscan capital in three to five days, consuming masterpieces like a fresco-eating Pac-Man, and you're bound to remember Florence as a beautiful—if blurry—delight. Look too closely, though, and the seams begin to show. A large portion of the city's seemingly 16th-century buildings and frescoes are actually 19th-century reproductions, sometimes making it feel as if you're in a chase scene out a cheap cartoon where the same handful of background cells have been reused over and over again. Add in the overwhelming tourist crush and the lack of any local industry aside from the manufacture of plaster *Davids*, and it can all start to seem a bit like Disney World.

So don't stretch out your stay. With little green space, performance art, or nightlife, Florence is the place for concentrated sightseeing at its best. In the end, you'll find it's better to give the city just a few days of intense museum- and church-going and leave feeling as though you've seen only the tip of a remarkable iceberg than overstay and never want to visit another gloriously frescoed cathedral again. Because really, they truly are glorious.

greatest hits

- **LINES BE DAMNED.** There's a reason people wait in 4hr. lines to get into the Uffizi. See possibly the world's greatest collection of Renaissance art, and follow our guide to understanding the art and avoiding the lines (p. 289).

- **BOBOLI TOP.** The luscious Boboli Gardens south of the Arno River offer views and rare greenery (p. 297).

- **GELATO GIANTS.** Where is it better, Rome or Florence? Head to Grom (p. 300) or Gelateria dei Neri (p. 305) to find out where you stand in the eternal ice cream debate.

- **THE JOYS OF ACCADEMIA.** Michelangelo's *David* is the centerpiece of this museum in San Marco. There are numerous replicas all over the city (Florentines like to remind you of why they're great), but this is the real thing (p. 295).

student life

To find people studying things other than the sublime carving of the *David*, head to Santa Croce. Here you'll find every student's favorite things: cheap food and cheap beer. **Eby's Bar** is probably the single-best place in the city to get cheap Mexican food, no matter what time of day. And in a city somewhat devoid of quality nightlife, the *piazze* **Sant'Ambrogio** and **Ghiberti** are your best bets for finding students on a weekend night.

orientation

Our coverage of Florence is divided into neighborhoods that roughly correspond to the major church districts. These distinctions are mostly for convenience's sake, to divide the city into more manageable chunks. In a short visit, you are unlikely to notice any significant variation from one area to the next, but here are some rules of thumb. Near the Uffizi things are expensive. The eastern third of the city is student-oriented and contains some bright patches of nightlife. The train station has the cheaper eats, sleeps, and shopping. The other side of the river is home to more locals and **trees.** Everything is very quiet near the city walls. All roads lead to the Duomo.

call me!

The phone code for Florence is ☎055.

THE DUOMO

In a city where the streets were lain with 15th-century logic and everything looks pretty much the same, you'll find the Duomo an invaluable navigational aid. No matter how lost you get, you'll probably be able to find your way back here, so learn to get to your hostel from the Duomo and you're all set. Likewise, it makes a handy meeting point when you're trying to coordinate plans without a cell phone.

PIAZZA DELLA SIGNORIA

Near the **Uffizi** and river, this *piazza* is where the well-heeled and the honeymooning spend their time and money. With cheaper food and lodging options to the immediate east and north, you'll come here mostly to hang out in the spacious *piazze* and see some of the city's most famous sights.

SANTA MARIA NOVELLA

Santa Maria Novella train station will likely be your first introduction to Florence, and whether you first venture east or south will color your earliest impressions of the city. To the east of the train station you'll find the cheap accommodations and casual food joints you'd expect of a neighborhood that serves as a transport hub. To the south await the church that gives the station its name, a pastoral *piazza*, and streets filled with folks hanging out late into the evening. Don't bother venturing north or west, as you'll be leaving Florence's historic center before you've even set foot in the heart of the city.

SAN LORENZO

Slightly east of the train station is this land of budget accommodations and 99 cent stores. San Lorenzo's vendors and the fresh food market of **Mercato Centrale** make this part of Florence an excellent base, even if staying here means you'll be a bit removed from the city's nightlife.

SAN MARCO

By "San Marco," we mean pretty much everything from **Piazza San Marco** itself north up to the edge of the old city. The defining characteristic of this area is the sheer number of museums and bus stops per sq. ft. Stick to the south edge late at night, though—north of the *piazza* is one of the quietest areas of the old city, and once the buses stop running, it can be unsafe. Travel with a friend if you're passing through this part of San Marco late at night.

SANTA CROCE

Wander eastward from the Duomo and you'll likely find yourself in Santa Croce. The neighborhood runs east along the Arno away from central Florence. With few big-name tourist attractions and a lot of university students, this part of town is where you'll primarily find cheap lunches and evening entertainment—or perhaps just a lot of English-speaking students clutching copies of this book and asking where the party's at. Florentine nightlife is more about hanging around outside and drinking with friends than pumping bass and exclusive clubs. It'd be a pretty cool trick if we turned some *piazza* into nightlife central just by sending you all there, but really, why mess up a good thing?

WEST OLTRARNO

This is the cool part of the Oltrarnos—the area on the south side of the Arno. It feels more authentic and lived-in than the other side of the river but still has a high density of hostels and museums. All-in-all a nice scene, and worthy of a visit if you're in town for more than a day or two.

EAST OLTRARNO

Aside from the **Piazzale Michelangelo,** there probably isn't much to bring you here. We've set the Oltrarnos' east-west dividing line at the **Ponte Vecchio,** but you'll find a large residential stretch between the immediate Ponte Vecchio area and the nightlife of **Ponte San Niccolo.** Head uphill for views.

accommodations

Travel in a small group to get your money's worth in Florence, particularly during the low season. Two to four people can score gorgeous rooms in three-star hotels for a lower per-person rate than you'll find at a hostel. Although most hotel rooms are doubles, it is not difficult to find triples, quads, and even family suites. For the solo traveler, options are a little more limited. Florence is home to only a few good hostels, and most otherwise affordable accommodations charge a pretty penny for singles. However, if you're only in town for a few days, there are plenty of acceptable options in central locations. If you're sticking around a little longer, consider commuting from a hostel outside the city, where you'll find better deals, cleaner air, and more adventurous travelers. Whatever your situation, keep in mind that low season is called "low" for a reason: nightly room rates can drop by €10-20 when the city is less flooded with out-of-towners seeking beds. In our listings, we've stuck to high-season rates, so those of you traveling to Florence in February can silently gloat every time you read a price estimate and think about how much lower your rate will be.

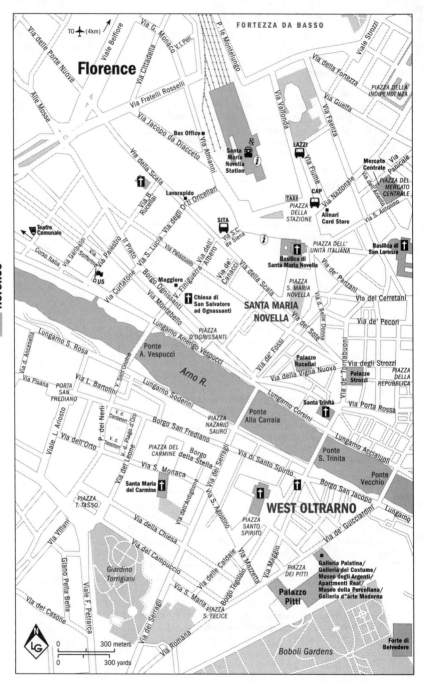

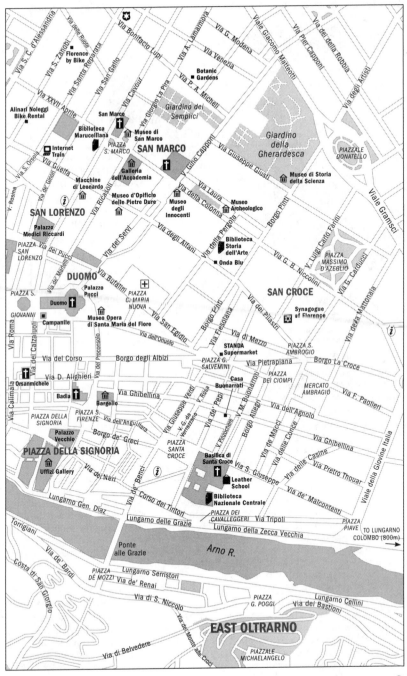

Hotel Abaco

1 Via dei Banchi
Santa Maria Novella
50123 Florence, Italy
Tel: +39 055.2381919
Fax: +39 055.282289

2010 LET'S GO recommends

STAY WITH US IN A 16TH CENTURY PALACE!

The Hotel Abaco is situated on the 2nd floor of a 16th century palace, in the heart of Florence. Steps from Santa Maria Novella railway station and the Cathedral. Near the most important monuments, museums and art galleries.

Furnished in Barocco Style, the Hotel Abaco is very comfortable with a warm friendly atmosphere. Perfect for those looking for a relaxing holiday.

www.hotelabaco.it email: abacohotel@tin.it

THE DUOMO

There are a lot of options in the most central part of the city, though none are super cheap. The Academy is your best bet, particularly if you can book in advance. To go up a notch, check out the many nice small hotels, mostly found to the east and north of the Duomo. While Florence *is* tiny, it's still nice to be at its center.

👍 ACADEMY HOSTEL — 🌐♿📶❄ HOSTEL [2]

V. Ricasoli 9 ☎055 23 98 665 🖥www.academyhostels.com

This is the poshest hostel in Florence, and if you're planning ahead, it is the place to stay. For a few euro more than **Archi Rossi** and **Hostel Plus**—the other good hostel options in town—you get free pasta and wine every evening at 6:30pm as well as towels, privacy screens, bedside tables, and no bunk beds. Academy is also far smaller than the other options, sleeping only 30 people at a time. For better or for worse, the price keeps away the hordes of drunk teenagers and the more adventurous backpackers, so the Academy mostly attracts middle-ground types who book in advance. The uncommonly helpful day staff learn names and, like the ritziest of concierges, know the city inside and out. Lockout may seem inconvenient, but it keeps the place spotless.

🧭 Less than a block north of the Duomo, on the left. ℹ Breakfast and dinner included. Credit card min. €150. Free Wi-Fi. $ Dorms €29-34. 🕐 Reception 24hr. Lockout 11am-2pm.

HOTEL LOCANDA ORCHIDEA — 💳♿📶 HOTEL [3]

V. Borgo Degli Albizi ☎055 24 80 346 🖥www.hotelorchideaflorence.it/history.html

A lovely, homey little place, with tile floors, leather couches, and a narrow terrace that's overgrown in a romantic sort of way. It's charmingly cluttered and den-like in most of the common space, but the shared bathrooms are large and clean.

🧭 V. Borgo Degli Albizi leads from the southeast of the Duomo piazza. ℹ Tea and coffee all

day. Good ceiling fans. $ Singles €30-55; doubles €50-75; quads €80-120. ⏰ Reception 8am-10pm.

HOTEL CASCI — HOTEL [4]

V. Cavour, 13 — ☎055 21 16 86 💻www.hotelcasci.com

Twenty-four rooms of varying sizes each have wood shutters, cable on actually new-ish TVs, and big ol' bathtubs. A very large breakfast room hosts a very large, American-style breakfast buffet (gluten-free upon request). Flexible triples and larger family rooms make this a good option for a small group traveling together.

➜ North of the Duomo, on the right. ℹ Breakfast included. Free Wi-Fi. $ Doubles €80-150; quads €150-230. 10% discount for paying cash. ⏰ Reception 24hr.

PIAZZA DELLA SIGNORIA

This is the area where your parents would stay, so the budget options are limited and usually shady. However, among all the posh hotels are a few that would make excellent splurges.

HOTEL BRETAGNA — HOTEL [4]

Lungarno Corsini 6 — ☎055 28 96 18 💻www.hotelbretagna.net

Beautiful historic suites with frescoed ceilings merit a price tag that's twice as high, and even this hotel's standard rooms are lovely. A tiny balcony off the lobby looks out on the Arno—at sunset, it's a fine place for a coffee or smoke. Breakfast is served in a hall lined with antique porcelain adjacent to a banquet hall that would not be out of place in one of the city's major *palazzi*.

➜ Facing the river, it's 2 blocks right of Ponte Vecchio. ℹ Breakfast included. $ Doubles €90-110; historic rooms €110-140. Several larger suites available. ⏰ Reception 24hr.

HOSTEL VERONIQUE / ALEKIN HOSTEL — HOSTEL [2]

V. Porta Rossa 6, 2nd and 4th fl. — ☎055 26 08 332

These are two barebones hostels on two floors of the same building, run by mother and son. Rooms are all private and sleep two to four. The bathroom on the hall is shared. The place could use a better paint job, but otherwise it's clean and serviceable.

➜ Just north of Mercato Nuovo. ℹ Free Wi-Fi. Cash preferred. $ Beds around €25. ⏰ Alekin (he of the title) will sleep in the hostel if there are any late arrivals expected.

RELAIS CAVALCANTI — HOTEL [4]

V. Pellicceria 2 — ☎055 21 09 62 💻www.relaiscavalcanti.com

Antique photographs line the pastel hall off of which you'll find airy rooms named after artists. Painted armoires and, in some cases, bathtubs are room highlights. Complimentary coffee and pastries all day.

➜ V. Pellicceria is off of P. della Signoria. ℹ Free Wi-Fi. $ High-season standard rooms €90; doubles €110. ⏰ Reception 9am-1pm, and they're around in the afternoon if there are check-ins coming. Will give a key to guests.

SANTA MARIA NOVELLA

As in almost any city, there are plenty of budget hotels located right next to the train station. If you roll into town late and are just looking for somewhere to crash, head straight to **Via Fiume,** which is lined with hotels. The area between the station and river offers some posher options. Whatever you're looking for, make sure to ignore the monstrous Majestic Hotel that is very visible from the train station—despite the building's valuable real estate, it is empty and abandoned.

PENSIONE LA SCALA — PENSIONE [4]

V. della Scala 21 — ☎055 21 26 29

Don't be scared off by the name of the building in which Pensione La Scala is situated—Residence Bellevue. This place may be a bit mental, but it's no institution. Rather, it's a comfy, personal bed and breakfast with a stuffed crocodile, frescoed ceilings, a nifty vintage radio that sometimes works, and a dining room table full of books and papers. It will be cleared for breakfast only if you're able to get on avuncular proprietor Gabriel's good side. Gabriel lives on premises and describes himself as Santa Claus—especially to those who are quick to flash a smile, show up on an under-booked night, or pay cash.

Down from the train station, on the left. i Cash preferred. $ Doubles €80-90; triples €120-135; quads €160-180. ⏰ Reception 24hr., but Gabriel would rather not be woken up at odd hours.

HOTEL CONSIGLI

HOTEL [3]

Lungarno Amerigo Vespucci 50 ☎055 21 41 72 www.hotelconsigli.com

If you are traveling in a small group, this gorgeous hotel on the Arno is a no-brainer. The grand staircase of the 16th-century building leads to airy rooms with original frescoes on the ceilings: the family-size suites are an especially impressive option for a well-behaved group of four. Brave a narrow spiral staircase to have a glass of wine on the enormous terrace overlooking the river. And with the American consulate right next door, you're sure to be first in line for the airlift if Florence is invaded by zombies.

Follow the river west, up past the consulate. i Breakfast included. Remodeling project underway in 2010, prices (and quality) may rise thereafter. $ Doubles €90; triples €120; family suite €130.

DESIREE HOTEL

HOTEL [3]

V. Fiume 20 ☎055 23 82 382 www.desireehotel.com

All the hotels in this old, palatial building have attractive stained glass—but Desiree gets the lion's share, with stained glass plentiful in both the lobby and in some of the 18 unique rooms. Other rooms have little balconies, chandeliers, or big antique armoires, and even the plainer rooms have flowers painted on the bathroom tiling. Sip your coffee on the sunny, small balcony off the breakfast room when the weather's nice.

V. Fiume is parallel to the train station. $ Singles €75; doubles €100; quads €140. ⏰ Reception 24hr.

SAN LORENZO

Most of the budget accommodations in San Lorenzo are clustered around **Via Nazionale** and **Via Faenza,** with good proximity to the train station and the cheap food of **Mercato Centrale.** There's a fine Roman-style drinking fountain at the corner of Nazionale and Faenza as well, so fill your bottles.

OSTELLO ARCHI ROSSI

HOSTEL [2]

V. Faenza 94r ☎055 29 08 04 www.hostelarchirossi.com

The large garden courtyard might be the only green space you'll see in Florence outside of church cloisters. The quirky garden is charming enough that you will forget you are in a massive 100+ bed hostel, and the walls packed with notes, drawings, and signatures from previous guests will give you something new to look at every time you walk up the stairs. Pay a little extra for an ensuite room, because the communal bathrooms are shared by too many. On the plus side, this hostel has more computers than most American public schools. Despite some trade-offs, this is the best hostel in Florence. Good luck trying to find somewhere to scrawl your own name—look for *Let's Go* across from the water cooler.

From the train station, take V. Nazionale and then a left onto V. Faenza. i Beer on sale at desk. $ Dorms €21-27. ⏰ Reception 6:30am-2am.

HOSTEL PLUS

HOSTEL [2]

V. Santa Caterina D'Alessandria 15 ☎055 46 28 934 www.plushostels.com

It's a chain hostel, sure, but it's the nicest darn chain hostel our *Let's Go* researchers have ever seen. With so many rooms, it can feel a little empty when

HOTEL ANNABELLA***
via Fiume 5 - 50123 Florence, Italy
at only 100 mt. from the Central Train Station of Firenze SMN

www.hotelannabella.it
e-mail: info@hotelannabella.it
SKYPE: annabella6914
phone #: +39-055-281877
fax #: +39-055-2396814
* * * * * * * * * * * * *
A NEW charming hotel located in the ancient city center, very close to all points of attraction and interest like Uffizi, Accademia, Palazzo Vecchio, Duomo, Ponte Vecchio, Exhibition Center, Conference Center, etc. All rooms are equipped with private bath, shower, toilet, A/C, direct phone, satellite TV; some rooms have balcony too. Roof terrace, WIFI on request. Baggage storage: FREE OF CHARGE. Open 24 hours a day - Concierge service, NO CURFEW!

HOTEL BIJOUB&B**
via Fiume 5 - 50123 Florence, Italy
at only 100 mt. from the Central Train Station of Firenze SMN

www.hotel-bijou.it
e-mail: info@hotel-bijou.it
SKYPE: annabella6914
phone #: +39-055-214156
fax #: +39-055-280515
* * * * * * * * * * * * *
Located in the city center, nearby all points of attraction. Rooms equipped with bath, A/C, direct phone, Satellite TV; WIFI Internet on request. Some rooms have balcony too.
CHEAP ROOMS FOR STUDENTS!
Panoramic terrace on the roof. Baggage storage: FREE OF CHARGE. Open 24 hours a day - Night concierge service, NO CURFEW!

For both hotels, CHEAP RATES, DISCOUNTS & SPECIAL OFFERS FOR LET'S GO READERS & STUDENTS!

there aren't nine million tourists around, but that just means more space for you on the spacious terrace bar. Climb up another level to the flat roof, which sports some folding chairs, a guard rail, and, the best panoramic **view** of Florence you'll find outside Giotto's tower. Down in the basement is a restaurant *(€10 for breakfast, pasta dinner, or a bottle of wine)*, another full bar, a disco complete with ball, a sauna, a Turkish bath, and a heavily chlorinated swimming pool flooded with colored lights. Rooms themselves are standard dorms—avoid the nauseating Pepto-pink walls of the all-female floor—but otherwise it's chain-hostel standard. Security is a little iffy—this researcher just waltzed right in and hung out on the roof for an hour.

➔ Follow V. Nazionale way up until it changes names. ℹ Breakfast €10. $ Dorms €20-25. ⏰ Reception 24hr.

👍 SOGGIORNO ANNAMARIA / KATTI HOUSE — B AND B [3]

V. Faenza 21 — ☎055 21 34 10 💻www.kattihouse.com

If you are traveling with a small group and don't mind sharing queen-size beds, stay here. This lovely B and B feels more like a flat that you're borrowing from some posh aunt. Wood-beamed ceilings, grandfather clocks, and comfortable living rooms characterize these suites of rooms. On the second floor, four bedrooms share a big, sunny living room with a built-in bar. Each bedroom sports a TV and a tea kettle (as we said, posh aunt).

➔ On V. Faenza, look for the doorway with all the Let's Go stickers. ℹ Breakfast included. $ Singles €70; doubles €85; quads €130.

HOTEL ESTER — HOTEL [3]

V. Largo Alinari 15 — ☎055 23 02 185 💻www.roominflorence.com

Down the block from the train station, the two levels of Hotel Ester boast an array of private rooms with flatscreen TVs, mini-fridges, and overhead fans. The longer the hike, the better the view—the third story rooms boast a lovely prospect, while the larger rooms across the street at sister hotel Luna Rossa are a good deal for groups *(quad €120).*

🪧 From train station, turn left at the McDonald's; Hotel Ester is about 1 block down on the right. Luna Rossa and Maison de Charme are across the street and adjacent, respectively, but share Hotel Ester's reception. $ Mar-Oct doubles €75, with bath €90; Nov-Feb €55/60.

HOLIDAY ROOMS 💳🚭📶❄ HOTEL ❸

V. Nazionale 22 ☎055 28 50 84

Good luck navigating the byzantine V. Nazionale numbering system to find this simple hotel, but once you arrive, you'll agree that its convenient location makes it a gem. Attractive, small rooms adorned with art prints and shuttered windows are complemented by flatscreen TVs, wooden armoires, and computers ensuite. The colorful communal kitchen sports a full set of appliances and a shelf of books that provides ample entertainment alternatives to watching the water boil.

🪧 From the train station, walk down V. Nazionale for about 5min.; no point watching the building numbers, just look for the name on the right. You'll hit it after you pass V. Chiara. $ Doubles €60-70.

SAN MARCO

This is not a great neighborhood for accommodations: the cheaper options can't compete with the ones you'll find in neighboring San Lorenzo. If you plan to go out late at night on weekends, don't stay here. It's a little too deserted after midnight for comfort.

DAVID INN 🍳🚭📶 HOSTEL ❷

V. Ricasoli 31 ☎055 21 37 07 💻http://hostelfirenze.splinder.com

One of the few small hostels in Florence, David Inn sits on the top floor of an otherwise residential building, and is the sort of place that provides you with somewhere to sleep—and not much else. No common space except for a couple squashy couches against an orange wall. The dorms are your basic bunk-bed situation, and the kitchen is tiny. But the small hostel scene in town is fairly dire, so if Academy is full or too posh for your hosteling tastes, then try here.

🪧 About a 5min. walk north of the Duomo, on the right. ℹ Luggage storage. $ Dorms €24-26. ⏰ Reception 24hr.

OSTELLO GALLO D'ORO 💳🚭📶 HOSTEL ❷

V. Cavour 104 ☎055 55 22 964 💻www.ostellogallodoro.com

San Marco's other small proper hostel option calls a quieter location on the other side of the neighborhood its home. The building's big shared entryway is a little confusing, but you want the stairs on the right. The place has a college dorm feel, with rooms that line a single hallway. It's small, friendly, and clean, and has its own tiny balcony for a coffee or a smoke.

🪧 5min. up V. Cavour from San Marco, on right. ℹ Breakfast included. $ Beds €28-30. ⏰ Reception 24hr.

HOTEL GIOIA 💳♿📶❄ HOTEL ❸

V. Cavour 25 ☎055 28 28 04 💻www.hotelgioia.it

The 28 rooms here are reminiscent of an American chain hotel—they must've ordered the bedspreads from Holiday Inn's supplier—but if you're skeeved out by all these hotels with no proper entrance of their own, then this hotel's video-monitored, dedicated entry from the street will provide a pleasant surprise. Inside, four couches are arranged in a square around a television, which makes for a somewhat greater socializing potential than what's to be found at other hotels.

🪧 Easy to find–has its own door! ℹ Breakfast included. $ Doubles €65-90. ⏰ Reception 24hr.

HOTEL SAN MARCO
⊛⊗📶❄ HOTEL [3]

V. Cavour 50 ☎055 28 18 51 💻www.hotelsanmarcofirenze.it

The white walls of this little hotel are far cleaner than their scuffed counterparts in the entryway. The guest kitchen is fully equipped and the breakfast tables are small and relatively private, although the TV is frequently blasting Italian soap operas.

➔ Just past the Gran Caffe from the piazza. $ Singles €40-50; doubles €70. ⏰ Reception 24hr.

HOTEL BENEVUTI
💳♿❄ HOTEL [3]

V. Cavour 112 ☎055 57 21 41 💻www.benvenutihotel.it

The wood paneling on the walls lends a sort of Brady Bunch aesthetic, but the 20 rooms are clean, simple, and recently renovated. Ask for a room with A/C or one that faces the courtyard for a quiet evening.

➔ North of San Marco on V. Cavour, about 5min. ℹ Breakfast included. Elevator possibly too small for many wheelchairs. $ Doubles €60-75; triples €70-90. ⏰ Reception 2pm-midnight.

SANTA CROCE

Looking to minimize the stumble home after a night out? Unfortunately, you are probably out of luck, because affordable accommodations in Santa Croce are difficult to come by. Check out places in the adjacent Duomo area, or perhaps try shacking up with a student at the university.

HOTEL ARIZONA
💳♿📶 HOTEL [5]

V. Luigi Carlo Farini 2 ☎055 24 53 21 💻www.arizonahotel.it

If you're studying at the university and your parents come to visit, this might be a good place to put them; otherwise, you'll do better in another neighborhood. The small reception area has squishy armchairs, an upright piano, and a generous stack of magazines (mostly Italian fashion and, oddly, *Smithsonian*). The oodate rooms are a bit cramped, but some compensate with little balconies looking on to the street. All the rooms are more or less the same.

➔ To the right of the synagogue. ℹ Minibar ensuite. Wi-Fi €4 per hr. $ High-season singles €130; quads €179. ⏰ Reception 24hr.

HOTEL ARISTON
💳⊗📶 HOTEL [3]

V. Fiesolana 40 ☎055 247 6980 💻www.hotelaristonfirenze.it

Sad gray hallways lead to characterless but spacious rooms with big closets and ceiling fans. The lobby has a small bar, an array of breakfast tables, and a plaster *David*. Windows face either the street or an air shaft.

➔ You can see the neon hotel sign from the intersection at Pietrapiana. ℹ Breakfast included. Free Wi-Fi. $ High-season doubles €65-70. ⏰ Reception 24hr.

WEST OLTRARNO

This side of the river has a decent concentration of good hostels, but they aren't significantly cheaper than the more centrally located places. You have to really want to be in West Oltrarno to stay here.

👍 OSPITALE DELLE RIFIORENZE
⊛♿📶 HOSTEL [1]

P. Piattellina 1 ☎055 21 67 98 💻www.firenzeospitale.it

Carved out of an old monastery, this socially aware hostel still feels like a religious escape. Live like a monk in a little pre-fab cell for two or three and hang out in the cavernous common space, featuring an ornate but decaying 15th-century ceiling that looks like something off the Titanic. All kinds of classes are run here including yoga, capoeira, and ceramics. Some of them are free, others are free for your first session. The folks at this nonprofit, co-operative hostel are a special sort—take one of their booklets providing walking tours of the people's Florence, which shift the historical perspective from the Medici to the Medici's handmaids.

☞ From P. Santo Spirito, the "ostello" signs direct you to this one. ⅈ Free Wi-Fi. Ⓢ 3- to 4-bed dorms €15; doubles €40; triples €45. ⊠ Reception 7am-noon and 3pm-2am. Curfew 2am.

HOSTEL SANTA MONACA
☝⊗⁽ᵗ⁾ HOSTEL ❶

V. Santa Monaca 6 ☎055 26 83 38 ▣www.ostello.it

This former monastery has all the charm of a local community center, despite the occasional cast-iron gate or vaulted ceiling. Rooms are simple, bathrooms are shared, and everything is kept clean during a strict 10am-2pm lockout. A nice large mess hall lined with picnic tables and a digital projector for sporting events are the few perks. A small grocery store is next door, but the "kitchen" is poorly equipped and overcrowded at meal times. You'll reap the benefits of Santa Monaca's proximity to the P. di Santo Spirito after-dinner scene—as long as you're back for the 2am curfew.

☞ From P. Santo Spirito, take a right onto V. Sant'Agostino and then a left onto V. Santa Monaca. ⅈ Free Wi-Fi. Ⓢ Dorms €17.50-20.50. ⊠ Reception 7am-2am. Curfew 2am. Lockout 10am-2pm.

SOGGIORNO PITTI
☝⊗⁽ᵗ⁾ HOTEL, HOSTEL ❷

P. Pitti 8 ☎329 06 40 765 ▣www.soggiornopitti.com

This is a sort of a hotel-hostel combo—the feel is hostel, with a big comfy common space, but most of the rooms are private, with double beds and twins. The bathrooms are clean but not terribly plentiful. That being said, it is a serviceable hostel and benefits from the best location of the three in West Oltrarno. But if you look elsewhere in Florence you'll find nicer options than this.

☞ Across the street from Palazzo Pitti. Ⓢ Dorms €20; doubles with bath €70; quads €92. ⊠ Reception 8am-11pm.

EAST OLTRARNO

Unless you have a reason to stay here, you might as well book a room at a nice bed and breakfast another few kilometers away in Bagno a Ripoli. Either way, you'll still have to take a bus to reach the sights.

PLUS CAMPING MICHELANGELO
☝⊗⁽ᵗ⁾ CAMPING ❶

Vle. Michelangelo 80 ☎055 68 11 977 ▣www.camping.it

▶Camping sure sounds nice, doesn't it? A bit of the ▶great outdoors, some greenery, roughing it a little? Don't be fooled. Whether you're packing a tent or renting a bungalow, this campsite has all the appeal of the neighboring Piazzale Michelangelo—which is to say, of a parking lot. The bungalows sleep two or three in bunk beds. You have to share a key, and there's no locker in the tent, so we don't recommend going halvsies on one with a stranger. Bathrooms are in a facility at the top of the hill akin to the locker room at a large gym. Wi-Fi is expensive and limited. The cafe is your only option for food that doesn't require a good walk, though at least the view is nice from its seating area.

☞ To the left of Piazzale Michelangelo, or take the #12 bus to the Camping stop. Ⓢ 2-bed tents €29; 3-bed €36. ⊠ Reception 24hr.

HOTEL DAVID
☝♿❄ HOTEL ❺

Vle. Michelangelo 1 ☎055 68 11 695 ▣www.davidhotel.com

A large, standard sort of hotel right over the Ponte San Niccolo—the bridge that marks the very eastern edge of the city center. If you have a reason to be this far east, then it's a good—if expensive—option.

☞ On the south end of Ponte San Niccolo. ⅈ Buffet breakfast included. Ⓢ Doubles €150. ⊠ Reception 24hr.

sights

Hope you like the Renaissance! Seriously, that's the big game in town here. If you search really hard you can find museums or attractions that don't have their roots in the 16th century, but there aren't many. If you do like the Renaissance, this is literally the best place in the world for you. Options abound, so it's best to take your time and appreciate things rather than letting them become a devalued mush of crucifixes and portraits of semi-attractive women.

THE DUOMO

Your Duomo-related sights are pretty much the main event for this neighborhood—the church itself, and the other bits and pieces of the Duomo complex.

DUOMO
               ♿ CHURCH
P. del Duomo 1   ☏055 23 02 885 🖥www.operaduomo.firenze.it

Honestly, it's better on the outside. The Duomo complex is enormous and distinctive, looming over every other Florentine building. All roads seem to lead to the Duomo and its shockingly colorful facade, capped with that giant red gelato-cone of a dome. It's famous, it's old, and it's free: clearly it must be the greatest tourist attraction known to humanity.

Well, it's all right. There are a lot of really great churches in Florence, and the Duomo just happens to be the biggest. It truly is enormous, but once you've stood in line behind half a dozen cruise-ship excursion groups to file your way inside the mighty cathedral, you might find yourself wondering—"is that all there is?"

Fortunately, it's not. Unfortunately, all the good parts have been divvied up, so you can only sample a bit at a time. All the statues, paintings, and other adornments have been moved into the Museo across the street, and you have to pay separately to climb the dome or the tower. For free, you get a rather empty, cavernous church.

There are certainly highlights. The inside of the vast dome is ornately frescoed and extremely impressive, even from ground level. On the opposite side of the nave a 24hr. clock by **Paolo Uccello** oxymoronically runs counter-clockwise. If you take the stairs in the middle of the church's floor down to the basement, you can pay €3 to see the archaeological remnants of the Duomo's previous incarnations, which is cool if you like that sort of thing.

And in a bit of irony, that notable green-white-and-pink marble facade that's so impressive from the outside—well, it's a fake. Or rather, it's not contemporary to the cathedral itself. The Duomo's facade was left unfinished in the 16th century and was eventually removed completely, leaving the great cathedral buck naked. Only in the late 19th century—last Thursday by Florentine standards—did the Duomo receive its famous decoration. Like much of Florence, it's not actually from the Renaissance—it's the Victorian equivalent of a Renaissance Faire.

Still really pretty, though.

♯ *Come on, you can't miss it.* **i** *Audio tour available in English.* Ⓟ *Free. Archaeological site €3. Audio tour €5, students and under 18 €3.50.* ⏲ *Open M-F 10am-5pm, Sa 10am-4:45pm, Su 1:30-3:30pm. 1st Sa each month only open 10am-3:30pm.*

CAMPANILE AND DOME
             ➚⦿ CHURCH
P. del Duomo   ☏055 23 02 885 🖥www.operaduomo.firenze.it

Normal travel not tiring enough for you? Try climbing 400+ stone steps! These two sights are combined into one review here because, well, there's no reason to split them up. Both involve climbing a heck of a lot of stairs to see an extremely rewarding view. The major distinction is which you would rather see up close: the inside or the outside of Brunelleschi's dome.

If you would rather see the inside, then climb his architectural miracle. You'll ascend a lot of twisty, narrow stairs for a long time. Halfway to the top, you can step out on a platform at the base of the cupola for a closer look at the Duomo's vast fresco through murky anti-suicide Plexiglas. Then it's back to the stairwell for the last couple hundred stairs before emerging to a truly worthwhile view of Florence and the surrounding hills.

The Campanile is much the same, but when you reach the summit, you get a perfect next-door view of the dome. Relatedly, if you're going to do that corny thing from the movies and meet your lover on top of the Duomo, make sure you settle on whether to meet at the dome or the tower. Otherwise, you might be staging your reunion via shouting and semaphore flags.

*‡ Enter the dome from the north side of the rounded part of the Duomo. Enter the Campanile at the base of the big tower thing. **i** Not for the out-of-shape. $ Dome €8. Campanile €6. Tour of the dome and the cathedral's terraces €15. ⏰ Dome open M-F 8:30am-7pm, Sa 8:30am-5:40pm. Campanile open daily 8:30am-7:30pm.*

a man with a plan

After 100 years of construction, the Duomo still had a gaping hole. The architects found themselves stumped—during construction, they had not realized that the dome the design called for would have to be larger than anything previously built or even considered possible. After several decades of leaving the church open to the elements, the commission for the construction was awarded to an unlikely candidate: **Filippo Brunelleschi,** who had been trained as a goldsmith, not an architect. How did Brunelleschi end up gaining the commission for the largest dome of his age? Legend states that he proposed a competition: whichever architect could make an egg stand up on a slab of marble would take over the dome's construction. When everyone else attempted and failed, Brunelleschi cracked the egg at the bottom and placed the newly flat edge on the marble. Fortunately, he was as talented at architecture as he was at rule-bending, and his ingenuity led to the spectacular dome that is still the most stunning sight on Florence's skyline.

MUSEO OPERA DI SANTA MARIA DEL FIORE — ♿ MUSEUM

P. Duomo 9 — ☎055 22 02 885 💻www.operaduomo.firenze.it

If the Duomo seems a little empty compared to the other big name churches, that's because all the good stuff got moved here. Preservation concerns over the years led the cathedral to be stripped of its statues, paintings, and other shiny objects. They remain on display, if not in their proper context, in this winding little museum where you can escape the Duomo complex's crowds and get up-close and personal with the goods. There's a *pieta* that Michelangelo originally intended for his own tomb, some nifty trios of statues in the courtyard, and the incredibly creepy 👁**Mary of the Glass Eyes** (you'll know it when you see it).

On the second floor, models and sketches of the Duomo detail the long genesis of its 19th-century facade. And if you like the mechanics of this sort of thing more than the pretty pictures, there's a great display of the fixed pulleys and hoists used to construct Brunelleschi's dome.

*‡ Behind the Cupola. **i** Most texts in Italian, but the more important ones are also in English. $ €6. Audio tour €3.50. ⏰ Open M-Sa 9am-7:30pm, Su 9am-1:40pm.*

BAPTISTERY OF SAN GIOVANNI — ♿ MUSEUM

P. Duomo — ☎055 22 02 885 💻www.operaduomo.firenze.it

The octagonal building beside the Duomo is the Baptistery, and nearly all Florentines until the 19th century were baptized here, including big names like **Dante.** It features an incredible mosaic ceiling and some highly intricate ornamentation—but if you're feeling cheap and churched out, you can pretty much get the idea from looking in through the exit. In fact, the outer doors of the Baptistery are as much a big deal as the inside. Ghiberti's splendid golden eastern doors (facing the cathedral steps) were dubbed the **"Gates of Paradise"** by Michelangelo, and if we trust anyone to prescribe aesthetic judgment on a work of art, it's him.

✈ The octagonal building next to the Duomo. $ €4. ⏰ Open in summer M-W 12:15-6:30pm, Th-Sa 12:15-10:30pm, Su 8:30am-1:30pm; in winter M-Sa 12:15-6:30pm, Su 8:30am-1:30pm. In both seasons open 1st Sa of the month 8:30am-1:30pm.

PIAZZA DELLA SIGNORIA

✓ UFFIZI GALLERY — ♿ ❄ MUSEUM

Piazzale degli Uffizi 6 — ☎055 238 8651 🖥www.firenzemusei.it

Welcome to the Uffizi. The first thing you should know about this museum is that the *David* is not here—he's on the other side of town, in the Accademia. Also, the *Mona Lisa* is in France, and de Nile ain't just a river in Egypt.

If you're looking for an art history lesson, don't expect to find one in this listing. You won't find one in the galleries' texts either: although the explanatory panels are in both Italian and English, they are not hugely informative. Your best bet is to take an audio tour *(€5.50)* or to stick with *Let's Go.* We'll do our best to point out some of the main things you might not notice on your own.

The Uffizi's rooms are numbered. Look to the lintel of the doorway to figure out what room you're in. Our instructions will assume that you are going through the galleries sequentially.

Start the Uffizi from the top. Don't crumple up your ticket at the bottom of your bag (or paste it directly into your notebook like we did) because, after climbing two flights of the Uffizi's grand staircase, you'll be asked to flash your ticket once more. At this point, you're standing in an enormous hallway lined with statues and frescoed to within an inch of its life.

The first room you'll actually enter is **Room 2,** which begins the long parade of Jesuses that you'll be visiting today. **Rooms 3-4** are particularly gilded. In Martini's *Annunciation,* Gabriel literally spits some Latin at Mary, who responds with the mother of all icy stares. In **Room 6,** take some time with Beato Angelico's fun *Scenes From the Lives of Hermits.*

The next few rooms are all well and good, but **Rooms 10-14** are the main event. Where there be crowds and benches, there be the postcard works. Not that you need us to tell you this, but Botticelli's *Birth of Venus* is on the left—that's right, behind all those people. Push your way to the front to enjoy all the little details that don't come across in the coffee mug and mousepad reproductions, like the gold trim on the trees, the detail of the fabrics, and Venus's rather poor haircut. It's like she tried to get the Rachel but left on an extra 4ft.

Room 15 features works by a fellow named Leonardo da Vinci. If you're able to tell which are by him without reading the plaques, give yourself a pat on the back for being a good art historian.

If you're getting sick of Catholicism, skedaddle to **Room 20** to view a couple rare portraits of Martin Luther. Ninety-five theses, three chins. **Room 22** has a Mantegna triptych on the right with a curved center panel that makes it seem almost 3D. **Room 25** varies the Jesus-ness with some scenes from Joseph's story in Exodus on the right. There's a seriously ginormous baby in **Room 29's** Parmigianino painting, which is called *Madonna of the Long Neck* for reasons that will be obvious.

A really interestingly composed painting of a woman bathing hangs on the near-right wall of **Room 31.** What do you look at first? Don't be shy, we know you're eyeing her luscious breasts. And then you probably look at her legs and thighs, and perhaps the rest of her. And then, if you haven't yet turned away, maybe you will notice King David in the top left corner. The woman is Bathsheba, and Brusasorci's painting is remarkable for making you, the viewer, mimic the intensity of David's ogling gaze.

On the left in **Room 35** is a *Massacre of the Innocents* by Daniele Ricciarelli. Though feminists might be excited about the painter's vaguely female name, sadly, Daniele was a dude like every other artist in the Uffizi. Despite the pile of dead babies in this painting, *Let's Go* does not condone the making of **dead baby jokes.**

Finally you'll reach the **Room of Niobe,** an impressive palatial space full of statues posed as if frozen while cowering in horror, not unlike the poses of the ash corpses in Pompeii. These statues were discovered in the Villa Medici gardens and are supposed to be the unfortunate children of Niobe about to be slain by the gods as revenge for their mother's pride in her progeny.

The last couple of rooms have some 18th-century stuff. But you don't care about that. You waited in line for 3hr. and then proceeded through an endless line of rooms filled with Renaissance art, so maybe it's time to just go home. **Congratulations** on finishing the Uffizi; now you can go act like a Botticelli expert among all your friends, even if the only thing you remember is Venus's terrible haircut.

It's the long narrow part of P. della Signoria. Enter (or stand in line) on the left, reserve tickets on the right. To avoid the lines without paying for a reservation, try arriving late in the day, when your time in the museum will be limited by closing. i 2-3hr. wait in line is average. $ €10, EU citizens ages 18-25 €5, EU citizens under 18 and over 65 and the disabled free. €4 reservation fee. Audio tour €5.50. ⏰ Open Tu-Su 8:50am-6:50pm.

friends in high places

If you know you want to hit a lot of the museums in Florence, consider becoming their friend first. You'll receive a single entrance to all the state museums, including the Uffizi, the Accademia, the Boboli Gardens, the Museo di San Marco, and the Bargello, among others (though not the various churches and church-related sights). It costs €60, or €40 for those under 26, but paying the entrance for all the above museums will cost you a lot more. Become a member at 🖥www.amicidegliuffizi.it or visit the Welcome Desk in Sala delle Reali Poste, inside the Uffizi museum complex. *(☎055 52 13 560 ⏰ Open Tu-Sa 10am-5pm.)*

THE BARGELLO — MUSEUM

V. del Proconsolo 4 ☎055 23 88 606 🖥www.firenzemusei.it

For a change of pace, the Bargello offers a nice dose of 19th-century eclecticism: it's a bit like London's Victoria and Albert Museum, with objects organized by function and material. The building was once a brutal prison, but fortunately for visitors, there's no trace of this original purpose left in the architecture. The courtyard, once the site of public executions, is now adorned with terra-cotta coats of arms and family crests. Several statues remain from what must have been an extremely suggestive fountain. Look for the water spigots located in such charming locations as between a lady's legs. There's also an enormous cast cannon bearing the head of St. Paul, a devoted disciple of the prince of peace who probably wouldn't be too happy about having his face emblazoned on heavy artillery. Pass the pair of great stone lions wearing iron crowns—very *Narnia*—to find a hall full of pagan (not so *Narnia*) sculptures such as Adonis, Bacchus, and a 1565 work celebrating Florence's victory over Pisa.

The courtyard stairs bring you to some stone fowl and a series of numbered galleries. Minutely carved ivories, from tiny portraits to hair combs to a giant chess board are in **room 4.** The variety of objects that people have thought to carve from elephant tusk is astounding.

Room 6 holds a huge collection of Maiolica, an earthenware pottery that is decorated before being glazed. **Room 8** will introduce you to the Ninja Turtle you know least well. This *Salone Di Donatello* was designed for his 500th birthday in 1887, and has remained unchanged since.

Room 9 contains probably the only Arabic script you'll see in Tuscany. This chamber is devoted to Islamic art and has some very interesting ceramics and fabrics.

Room 10 is a true Victorian *wunderkammer* (or wonder-cabinet). There's the case of pipes, the case of bottles, and the collection of keys and locks. There are even table settings, scientific instruments, metalwork, jewelry, and that 17th-century spork you've been missing.

On the third floor, check out the fantastic tiny bronzes in **Room 15. Room 13's** glazed terra cotta in blues, greens, and yellows creates a color scheme that will make you feel as if you've been sucked into a game of old-school Oregon Trail.

⇟ Behind the Palazzo Vecchio. $ €4, EU citizens ages 18-25 €2, EU citizens under 18 and over 65 free. ⏰ Open daily 8:15am-5pm. Closed 1st, 3rd, and 5th Su each month, and 2nd and 4th M.

PIAZZA DELLA SIGNORIA

♿ PIAZZA

P. della Signoria

Don't be fooled by the *David* in front of the **Palazzo Vecchio**—the real deal is in the **Accademia.** The reproduction in the *piazza* fills David's original location and stands just as proud as his original did when he (allegedly) was installed facing Pisa to celebrate Florence's dominance over the Tuscan region. To the left of the statue is a giant fountain which Michelangelo despised so much that he called it a waste of perfectly good marble. To the big guy's right you'll find the **Loggia,** a portico full of statues that's as legit as any room in the Uffizi. Hang out amid the art students sketching, listen to the street musicians, and enjoy the free outdoor art. Don't miss Giambologna's spiraling *Rape of the Sabines.*

⇟ This is the main piazza around the Uffizi. $ Free.

PONTE VECCHIO

♿ BRIDGE

Ponte Vecchio

This is Florence's famous shop-covered bridge. It has been called the "old" bridge for, oh, 400 years or so, ever since the Florentines first built a second bridge over the Arno and had to find a way to distinguish this one from their new *ponte.* When the Nazis evacuated Florence, Ponte Vecchio was the only bridge they didn't destroy. Now it is full of gold and jewelry shops—more like kiosks, in many cases—as well as shadier street vendors and buskers. Come on a weekend afternoon, and you are guaranteed to be in the wedding photos of at least half a dozen bridal parties. Come at night for a romantic view of the river—and of other couples seeking the same.

⇟ From the Uffizi, walk to the river. It's the one with the shops on it. $ Free.

PALAZZO VECCHIO

❀♿ MUSEUM

In P. della Signoria ☎055 276 8465

The real draw here is that it's the only museum you can visit post-*aperitivo.* In addition, the place has got some pretty impressive architecture and views. The vast and ornate **Room of the 500's** gilded ceiling is divided into panels that frame truly massive paintings. On the second floor, the **Salon of Leo X,** a terrace with an incredible view of the city and the surrounding hills, provides a great photo op. There's a lot of repetition in this *palazzo*, though, and it can all begin to look the same. That's until you reach the **Sala dei Gigli,** which boasts a pretty rocking view of the Duomo as well as a fantastic map room that's worth all the chintz before it.

‡ The huge one in P. della Signoria. $ €6, ages 18-25 and over 65 €4.50. Tours free if requested at time of ticket purchase. ⏰ Open M-W 9am-midnight, Th 9am-2pm, F-Su 9am-midnight. Activities and tours with costumed reenactors, skits, etc. available; call for times.

CASA DI DANTE ♿ MUSEUM

V. Santa Margherita 4 ☎055 21 94 16 🖥www.museocasadidante.it

Don't go here. Normally we only list sights that we do recommend, but we wouldn't want you to think our omission an oversight. We really do think you should skip the Casa di Dante. It isn't really Dante's house. It isn't even really a reproduction. It's just a building sadly lacking in artifacts. Whether you're an expert Dantista or you don't know your *Paradiso* from your *Purgatorio*, there's nothing for you here.

‡ On the corner of V. Dante Alighieri and V. Santa Margherita; it's very well sign-posted. $ €4. ⏰ Open Apr-Sept daily 10am-6pm; Oct-Mar Tu-Su 10am-5pm.

SANTA MARIA NOVELLA

For an additional off-beat option, check out the **Farmaceutica di Santa Maria Novella.**

MUSEO DI FERRAGAMO ♿ MUSEUM

P. Santa Trinita 5r ☎055 33 60 456 🖥www.museoferragamo.it

That's right, the shoe guy. This small but excellently designed museum celebrates the work of the great cobbler to the stars, whose eloquent and anecdotal memoirs are liberally quoted in the museum's display text. Exhibits rotate every two years; a new installation arrived in late 2010, focusing on footwear in the second half of the 20th century. We know you may have a skeptical look on your face right now, but you don't have to be Carrie Bradshaw to appreciate a fashion and culture exhibit as thoughtfully assembled as this one. The gift shop is surprisingly tiny, but check out the real Ferragamo store upstairs to ogle shoes you can't possibly afford.

‡ Enter at P. Santa Trinita, the side of the building facing away from the river. i Ticket proceeds fund scholarships for young shoe designers. $ €5, under 10 and over 65 free. ⏰ Open M 10am-6pm, W-Su 10am-6pm.

PALAZZO STROZZI ♿ MUSEUM, PALAZZO

P. degli Strozzi ☎055 27 76 461 🖥www.palazzostrozzi.org

While this may seem like yet another old palace, impressive like all the others, it isn't the seen-one-seen-'em-all Renaissance decor that makes Palazzo Strozzi worth visiting. The Center for Contemporary Culture Strozzina, which produces shows of recent and contemporary art in the palace's exhibit halls, is the main draw here. Recent shows have included an exhibit of De Chirico, Ernst, and Magritte as well as a series of interactive installations tracing the effect of media on modern living. The programming changes regularly, so check the website or stop by if you want to shake a little 21st century into Florence's 15th-century aesthetic.

‡ West of P. della Repubblica. $ Prices and hours vary; check website for details.

BASILICA DI SANTA MARIA NOVELLA ♿ CHURCH

P. di Santa Maria Novella ☎055 21 59 18 🖥www.chiesasantamarianovella.it

If you're only going to bother with one of the non-Duomo churches, consider making it this one. The cavernous church features some glorious stained glass which, due to the church's north-south orientation, reflects beautifully on to the floors in the morning and late afternoon. The Filippino Lippi-designed chapel to the right of the altar is almost cartoonish in the drama and action of its panels. Cappella Strozzi on the left has a sadly faded fresco of Purgatory, inspired by Dante. Try to make out the goblins, centaurs, and less familiar mythological figures like the man-dove. The basilica also features an impossibly handsome gift shop in a room dominated by a gold-trimmed reliquary cabinet and a red and blue ceiling so bright it must have been restored yesterday.

Just south of the train station; can't miss it. ℹ *Audio tour stations in the middle of the sanctuary for €1; some travelers wait around for others to pay up the euro and get bored, then finish their turn.* $ *€3.50, over 65, travelers with disabilities, and priests free.* ⏰ *Open M-Th 9-5:30pm, F 11am-5:30pm, Sa 9am-5pm, Su 1-5pm.*

SAN LORENZO

Two of the best experiences in San Lorenzo are its open-air markets, one eponymous and the other named **Mercato Centrale.** For information on those, see **Markets.**

keeping up with the medici

It's impossible to tour Florence without hearing about the Medici, the family that ran the show here between the 15th and 18th centuries. While the Medici are best known for their banking skills, political prowess, and patronage to the arts and sciences, no family is without its eccentricities. Here's a crib sheet that'll help you keep the multi-faceted Medici men straight:

1) The first Medici to make it big was **Cosimo the Elder.** He was incredibly wealthy due to his father (Giovanni di Bicci) having founded the Medici Bank. He established his family's de facto rule in Florence by appealing to the working class, buying favors, and raising taxes on the wealthy. The players may change, but politics stays the same.

2) Cosimo had a son who was nicknamed **Piero the Gouty** because of the infection in his foot. He found it difficult to rule Florence with a swollen big toe, so he didn't last very long.

3) Despite their power, the Medici weren't always the coolest kids in the cafeteria. Rival families and a priest conspired to "sacrifice" Piero's son **Lorenzo** during a church service. After a brief period of expulsion (it's a long story), the Medici made a comeback in the early 1500s, helping to patronize artists like Leonardo da Vinci and Raphael.

4) Cosimo I de Medici is famous for establishing the Uffizi and Pitti Palace, ruling Florence, and patronizing the arts. He also deserves props, though, for embodying the "work hard, play harder" motto. In his free time he managed to father 15 children with four different women.

5) Cosimo II established the Medici family as patrons of science and technology. Cosimo *numero due* was Galileo's sugar daddy, supporting his research, giving him a place to stay, and offering him the chance to schmooze with the upper classes. In return, Galileo dedicated his books to the Medici, named some stars after them, and allowed the family first dibs on his new inventions, like the telescope.

PALAZZO MEDICI RICARDI ♿ MUSEUM

V. Camillo Cavour 1 ☎055 27 60 340 🖥www.palazzo-medici.it

After innumerable treks through the detritus of Medici public life, you may be wondering what they were like at home. Answer: more of the same. The Medici palace sports another lovely garden, another fine chapel, and yet another pile of fantastic art. Just try to keep up with *these* Joneses.

Start with the tiny chapel. The frescoes are so cluttered with faces of generations of Medici attending the Adoration of the Magi that you'll find just as much to look at as you would in a grander commission. Then head downstairs to the interactive explanatory exhibit. Motion sensor technology lets you point at a projection of the chapel's frescoes and, without touching anything, cue explanations in Italian, French, or English. It's a neat way to learn more, but if you're excessively tall or short, be prepared to flail unsuccessfully until the guard adjusts the camera.

The palace also plays a working role in provincial government today. The **Quattro Stagioni** hall hosts the provincial council, and the gold-on-white stucco panels of the **Sala Luca Giordana,** flanked by painted mirrors and frolicking cherubim, are incongruously complemented by a projection screen, a conference table, and rows of plexiglass chairs. If nothing else, be happy for the members of the provincial council who get to gaze at fleshy angels when they zone out during dull meetings.

From San Lorenzo you can see the back of the huge brown palace. Enter from the reverse side, on V. Cavour. $ €7, groups of 15 or more and ages 6-12 €4. ⏰ Open M-Tu 9am-7pm, Th-Su 9am-7pm.

florence

MEDICI CHAPELS

♿ MUSEUM

P. Madonna degli Aldobrandini 6 ☎055 23 88 602 www.firenzemusei.it

Ah, the Medici. If you thought they were opulent alive, wait until you see them dead! The **Cappella Principe,** an octagonal chapel that's the final home of a handful of Medici, is the grander of the two on display in this museum, despite being unfinished. Some of the Medici were smart enough to commission their own statues, and they're doing swell. Others went with the popular trend of having sons commission honorary statues after their fathers' death. This, of course, led to lots of empty statue slots. There are other late additions as well—the frescoes may look the part, but they were painted in the 1870s. As some tour guide quipped while we were eavesdropping, while the French were inventing Impressionism, the Florentines were still in the Renaissance. The **New Sacristy** is smaller and less colorful, but given its design by Michelangelo, it's nothing to sniff at.

The roundish building to the right of San Lorenzo. ℹ Likely visit length: half hour tops. $ €6, EU citizens 18-25 €3, EU citizens under 18 and over 65 free. ⏰ Open fairly daily 8:15am-4:50pm. Closed 1st, 3rd, 5th M and 2nd and 4th Su each month.

BASILICA DI SAN LORENZO

♿ CHURCH

P. San Lorenzo ☎055 26 45 184 www.sanlorenzo.firenze.it

The Basilica di San Lorenzo was consecrated in 393 CE: this is why Europeans scoff at Americans who think of 19th-century churches as old. The austere basilica is grey and white, but the cupola by the altar is a bit more glam. In the old sacristy is a small cupola painted with gold constellations on a midnight blue background that represent the sky over Florence on July 4th, 1442. Cool if you care about that sort of thing, but otherwise, spend your €3.50 on a big gelato and take it to the cloister on the left side of the basilica. The cloister is free and peaceful and has some of those rare Florentine trees. The domes and towers of nearby attractions peek out over the walls of the courtyard, making for a nice panorama.

In P. San Lorenzo, which is just a little north of the Duomo. $ €3.50. ⏰ Open M-Sa 10am-5pm, Su 1:30-5pm.

SAN MARCO

There is a very high museum density around this square, second only to the Uffizi area. You could easily lose days visiting all the museums, so choose wisely.

GALLERIA DELL'ACCADEMIA ♿ MUSEUM

V. Ricasoli 60 ☎055 23 88 612 www.firenzemusei.it/accademia

Sometimes tourist attractions gain their reputation for a reason. The *David* is pretty legit. Do you see those veins on his hand? The guy's a beast.

Four other statues by Michelangelo share *David*'s hall. They're unfinished, with figures that appear to be trapped in the remaining block of marble, like Han Solo encased in carbonite. You may understand on an intellectual level that the master's statues are carved from a single piece of marble, but seeing these unfinished works drives it home. One big damn rock. One man. A bunch of chisels. It's kind of miraculous, really.

Beyond its main event, the Accademia is a small museum, albeit a good one. The musical instruments gallery, to the right when you enter, is surprisingly informational. The collection itself contains the typical array of ancient instruments such as **serpents** and trumpet marines, but there are some excellent interactive elements, like models that help you understand the mechanical difference between a harpsichord and a piano. On one of a half-dozen computers provided, you can also hear samples of the collection's instruments in action—believe it or not, this is not standard for major musical instrument galleries, so take advantage of the opportunity to hear a **hurdy-gurdy.** Yes, that's a real thing. Skip trying the water spring bowl, though, unless you want to be stuck with seriously grimy hands until you find a bathroom.

Past the *David* gallery on the left is a 19th-century workroom overflowing with sculpted heads and busts. Notice the little black dots freckling the pieces? They hark back to the Accademia's days as an actual academy. These are plaster casts were created for teaching, and the black dots are nails that students used as reference points as they made copies for practice. Gorgeous crucifixes and Russian Orthodox stuff make a quick spin through the upstairs worthwhile.

Note: At your most contemplative pace, the Accademia won't take more than an hour. Bear that in mind when weighing the choice between paying extra for a reservation or waiting in a line that lasts far longer than you'll spend in the actual museum.

Line for entrance is on Ricasoli, off of San Marco proper. ***i*** *Make reservations at the Museo Archeologico, the Museo di San Marco, or the Museo del'Oficio. The non-reservation line is shortest at the beginning of the day. Try to avoid the midday cruise ship excursion groups.* $ *€6.50, EU citizens ages 18-25 €3.25, EU citizens under 18 and over 65, and art students free. €4 reservation fee applies to all.* ⏰ *Open Tu-Su 8:15am-6:50pm. Last entrance 30min. before close. .*

MUSEO DI SAN MARCO ♿ MUSEUM

P. San Marco 3 ☎055 23 88 608 www.firenzemusei.it

The first floor of this museum is divided into small cubbies the size of West Village studios. These are the cells of old monks, and each one has a different painting on the wall. Pop inside and imagine spending four decades copying manuscripts by hand in here. Then imagine what it would be like if an angel arrived to announce that you were about to experience an unplanned pregnancy—twice—by looking at Fra Angelico's two **Annunciation** frescoes. The most famous, which you'll probably recognize from postcards, is at the top of the staircase, while a less popular incarnation is on the wall of one of the cells.

The more traditional gallery space has a nice collection of illuminated manuscripts and Gregorian chants. If the graduals inspire you to do some singing yourself, we recommend finding an empty cell, shutting the door behind you, and having at it. The resonance is lovely. If you don't know any chants, don't worry. Try singing The Beatles' "Yesterday" slowly. It should do the trick.

🍴 *The north side of the piazza.* ℹ️ *Approximate visit time: 30min.* Ⓢ *€4, EU citizens ages 16-25 €2.* 🕐 *Open M-F 8:15am-1:50pm, Sa 8:15am-6:50pm, Su 8:15am-7pm.*

BOTANIC GARDENS
🚶♿ GARDENS

V. Micheli 3 ☎055 23 46 70 ✉️msn.unifi.it

Listen. There are way more impressive botanical gardens in the world. Don't come here to learn about horticulture or to feel transported to a Chinese bamboo forest, but just to sit somewhere green and relax. It is probably the best smelling place in historic Florence outside the **Boboli Gardens,** especially so after the rain. Grab a bench to rest both your feet and your nostrils. The Botanic Gardens are also a fine place to sneak a siesta, if you don't mind getting poked on the shoulder when a guard reluctantly decides to enforce the anti-vagrancy rules.

🍴 *Continue past San Marco; gardens are on the right and kind of obvious.* ℹ️ *Info text also in Braille.* Ⓢ *€6.* 🕐 *Open Apr-Oct M-Tu 10am-7pm, Th-Su 10am-7pm; Oct-Mar M 10am-5pm, Sa-Su 10am-5pm.*

MUSEO D'OPIFICIO DELLE PIETRE DURE
🚶♿ MUSEUM

V. Degli Alfani 78 ☎055 26 51 11 ✉️www.opificiodellepietredure.it

That name is a mouthful, but it boils down to a whole lot of mosaics. And when you've been staring at paintings for days, it is fun to mix it up with some truly excellent examples of a surprisingly different medium that's distinct from other visual arts.

🍴 *From San Marco, 1 block down Ricasoli then left on Alfani.* Ⓢ *€4, EU citizens age 18-25 €2, EU citizens under 18 and over 65, and art students free.* 🕐 *Open M-Sa 8:15am-2pm.*

SANTA CROCE

Although plaques marking the water line of the 1966 Arno flood can be found all over Florence, the Santa Croce area was the hardest hit. Be on the lookout for the watermarks—some of which will be well over your head—and imagine the incredible efforts it took to save and restore Santa Croce's art from the floodwaters.

🕍 SYNAGOGUE OF FLORENCE
🚶♿ SYNAGOGUE, MUSEUM

V. Luigi Carlo Farini 4 ☎055 21 07 63 ✉️www.firenzehebraica.net

It may not be Renaissance vintage, but this is one Florentine house of worship that is well worth a visit. Florence is mum when it comes to the history of its working class, minority, or otherwise non-Medici population, and the synagogue is one of the only sites where average citizens get the spotlight. The story of the Jewish community and Italy's role in WWII is every bit as vital to your understanding of the city of Florence as a stack of Botticellis. Prior to WWII, there were 40,000 Jews in Italy, 2400 living in Florence. The synagogue contains a memorial to the Florentines killed in the camps; although the list is relatively short, the number of shared surnames indicates that a handful of large families were wiped out completely. That this building is still standing is miraculous—when the Nazis evacuated the temple was rigged to explode, but amazingly all but one of the bombs failed to detonate, saving it from total destruction—and a visit to it offers an incredibly moving and different experience from anywhere else in Florence.

🍴 *From the Basilica di Santa Croce, head north on V. dei Pepi for 7 blocks. Take a right onto Pilastri and an immediate left onto V. Luigi Carlo Farini.* ℹ️ *Yarmulkes required and provided. Check bags and cameras at lockers before entering.* Ⓢ *€5, students €3.* 🕐 *Open Apr-Sept M-Th 10am-6pm, F 10am-2pm; Oct-Mar M-Th 10am-3pm, F 10am-2pm. Closed Jewish holidays. The 1st fl. of the museum is open during the 2nd half of every hr.*

BASILICA DI SANTA CROCE
🚶♿ CHURCH

P. Santa Croce ☎055 24 66 105

This basilica is an enormous complex worthy of costing more than the other big churches in town, though really it's the dead celebrities buried here that jack up the price of admission. Fork over the dough and pay your respects to Florence's greats. Rossini's tomb is subtly decorated with treble clefs and violin bridges. Galileo gets a globe and an etching of the solar system (*his* solar system) to mark his grave. Machiavelli is just sort of chilling. Dante's tomb is probably cool, but it was blocked with scaffolding when we visited. Michelangelo, all things considered, really should have a grander place of burial, but since he didn't design it, we take what we can get. Even Marconi is here—that's right, the guy who invented the radio.

 # Take Borgo de' Greci east from P. della Signoria. [$] €5, ages 11-17 €3, disabled free. Combined with Casa Michelangelo €8. Audio tour €5. ⏰ Open M-F 9:30am-3:30pm, Sa-Su 1-5:30pm.

CASA BUONARROTI ⊗♿ MUSEUM

V. Ghibellina 70 ☎055 24 17 52 💻www.casabuonarroti.it

When Michelangelo hit it big, he did what any new celebrity would do—he bought a bunch of houses and then never lived in them. Unlike the completely fabricated Casa di Dante, Casa Buonarroti is not a reproduction. It was, in fact, home to several generations of the big guy's descendents, making it a good destination for Miche-*fan*-gelos.

 # From Santa Croce, walk a block to the left to find V. Ghibellina. [$] €6.50, students and seniors €4.50. ⏰ Open M 9:30am-2pm, W-Su 9:30am-2pm.

WEST OLTRARNO

Palazzo Pitti

The major sights of West Oltrarno are all helpfully condensed into the enormous Palazzo Pitti. It's not hard to find the complex: just cross the Ponte Vecchio and continue along the same street until you reach the very obvious *palazzo*. The Palazzo Pitti museums are batched under two ticket combos: **Ticket One** gets you into Galleria Palatina, Galleria d'Arte Moderna, and Apartamenti Reali. **Ticket Two** is for the Boboli Gardens, Museo degli Argenti, Galleria del Costume, and Museo della Porcellana. Overall, if you're choosing one ticket combo over the other, we recommend ★**Ticket Two.**

★ **BOBOLI GARDENS** 🎫⊗ GARDENS

Palazzo Pitti Complex

The Boboli Gardens feels a little like a cross between Central Park and Versailles, which means it's really wonderful. Imagine you're a 17th-century Medici strolling through your gardens—but don't imagine your way into a corset, ladies, because the gardens are raked at a surprising incline. They're also easily large enough for you to lose yourself here for an entire afternoon. For the best vantage point climb farther up and in. Head uphill from the palace, past several large and attractive fountains. When you feel as if you've climbed the Campanile and reached the top level, you aren't done yet. Follow the path to the right behind a wall, and you'll emerge onto the peak of the hill. This is the very edge of Florence. Immediately below, a verdant green valley rolls into the distance and the packed red buildings of the city give way to sprawling monasteries and thickset trees. It's a stunning view. Don't forget to turn around; the view of Florence behind you ain't too shabby either. As with any gardens, Boboli is most fragrant and lovely right after the rain, but make sure the downpour is really finished or you'll be spending a lot longer in the porcelain museum than any person ever should.

i Ticket 2. [$] €10, EU citizens ages 18-25 €5, EU citizens under 18 and over 65 free. ⏰ Open daily June-Aug 8:15am-7:30pm; Sept 8:15am-6:30pm; Oct 8:15am-5:30pm; Nov-Feb 8:15am-4:30pm; Mar-May 8:15am-6:30pm. Closed 1st and last M of each month.

GALLERIA PALATINA 🎫♿ MUSEUM

Palazzo Pitti Complex

This enormous gallery would be more of a draw in a city that didn't also include the Uffizi. The two museums sometimes offer joint exhibits, despite being on opposite sides of town—at the time of writing, the Uffizi's mysteriously Caravaggio-less Caravaggio show only made sense upon a visit to the Palatina's Caravaggio-filled version of the same show. The permanent collection is housed in rooms named not for the art, but for the ceilings. We are still in a *palazzo*, remember, so the organizational logic is still that of a rich royal wanting to clutter his brocaded walls with all the big-ticket masterpieces he could commission. The quirkiest object in the collection sits alone in a small chamber between the Education of Jupiter and Ulysses rooms. It is Napoleon's 🛁**bathtub.** That's right: *The* Napoleon. *His* bathtub. Your entire vacation was just made worthwhile, wasn't it?

i Ticket 1. Ⓢ €12, EU citizens age 18-25 €6, EU citizens under 18 and over 65 free. 🕐 Open Tu-Su 8:15am-6:50pm.

GALLERIA DEL COSTUME
🕊️♿ MUSEUM
Palazzo Pitti Complex

If you like the costume gallery at the Met, you'll love Palazzo Pitti's Galleria del Costume. The galleria's fashion collection isn't just Medici-era vintage—it stretches all the way into the modern day. A true Italian knows that clothes are every bit as sacred as paintings of angels, so the couture is presented engagingly and thematically. Pieces from the collection rotate, but the current exhibit categorizes styles not by chronology, but by gimmick—one display includes classically-inspired sheath dresses from 1890, 1923, 1971, and 1993. It's fascinating to see the same basic ideas get reinterpreted every other generation and fun to play the "guess the decade" game before reading the title cards—you'll be surprised how easy it is to confuse the 1920s for the 1980s. The one permanent display is for the true Medici completist. Here, the actual burial clothes of several dead Medici, torn from their rotting corpses for your viewing pleasure, have been preserved. You're welcome.

i Ticket 2. Ⓢ €10, EU citizens ages 18-25 €5, EU citizens under 18 and over 65 free. 🕐 Open daily June-Aug 8:15am-7:30pm; Sept 8:15am-6:30pm; Oct 8:15am-5:30pm; Nov-Feb 8:15am-4:30pm; Mar-May 8:15am-6:30pm. Closed 1st and last M of each month.

MUSEO DEGLI ARGENTI
🕊️♿ MUSEUM
Palazzo Pitti Complex

In this treasure museum, you will be overwhelmed with the abundance of riches, quite literally. If the museum were a 10th of its size, it might be the greatest thing ever. As it is, it's just a little too much sensory overload. The collection includes incredible minute ivories, precious jewels with portraits engraved on the surface, dazzling crowns, Chinese porcelain, jade mosaics, sterling silver bedpans, and a wide array of chalices from the palaces. And don't forget to look around—the collection is housed in some of the most impressively and elaborately frescoed rooms of any palace in Florence.

i Ticket 2. Ⓢ €10, EU citizens ages 18-25 €5, EU citizens under 18 and over 65 free. 🕐 Open daily June-Aug 8:15am-7:30pm; Sept 8:15am-6:30pm; Oct 8:15am-5:30pm; Nov-Feb 8:15am-4:30pm; Mar-May 8:15am-6:30pm. Closed 1st and last M each month.

APARTAMENTI REALI
🕊️♿ MUSEUM
Palazzo Pitti Complex

The back end of the Galleria Palatina gets it right by doing away with the pesky art and sticking to the rich people's bedrooms. Take a quick stroll through the apartments of the great and pick out tapestries, tassels, and toilettes for your own palace.

i Ticket 1. Ⓢ €12, EU citizens ages 18-25 €6, EU citizens under 18 and over 65 free. 🕐 Open Tu-Su 8:15am-6:50pm.

MUSEO DELLA PORCELLANA ✏[X] MUSEUM

Palazzo Pitti Complex

The top of that hill in the gardens is home to a porcelain museum. Sounds dull, right? Turns out, whoever spent the centuries amassing this collection of dishware really knew what he or she was doing. Play the Imaginary Wedding Registry game and plan future dinner parties in your Tuscan villa.

⌖ At the highest point of the Boboli Gardens. Just keep walking up. ℹ Ticket 2. $ €10, EU citizens ages 18-25 €5, EU citizens under 18 and over 65 free. ⏰ Open daily June-Aug 8:15am-7:30pm; Sept 8:15am-6:30pm; Oct 8:15am-5:30pm; Nov-Feb 8:15am-4:30pm; Mar-May 8:15am-6:30pm. Closed 1st and last M of each month.

GALLERIA D'ARTE MODERNA ✏♿ MUSEUM

Palazzo Pitti Complex ☎055 23 88 616

Only in Florence could people define "modern art" as stuff that predates the French Revolution. This gallery contains works from the 1780s onwards, but it is mostly mired in 19th-century Naturalism. The good parts of 19th-century art are pretty much left out or squashed into a single room on "Pointillism, Symbolism, and Social Themes." In an entire city devoted to the Renaissance, "social themes" gets one wall. The best part is the exit. That's not meant to be (entirely) derogatory—the staircase is actually really beautiful.

ℹ Ticket 1. $ €12, EU citizens ages 18-25 €6, EU citizens under 18 and over 65 free. ⏰ Open Tu-Su 8:15am-6:50pm.

EAST OLTRARNO

There's not much here except the Piazzale Michelangelo and, uphill, a bit more green space than you'll find in the rest of the city center.

PIAZZALE MICHELANGELO ♿ PANORAMIC VIEWS

Piazzale Michelangelo

It's a parking lot. Still, it's the most scenic damn parking lot you'll ever see. Cross the river and bear east until you reach the base of the steps. It's about a 10min. walk uphill to the *piazzale*—a walk both cheaper and more pleasant than the one up the Campanile, but still requiring decent shoes. You can take the #12 or 13 bus if you're lazy, but the short **hike** is rather pleasant itself. At the summit, you'll be rewarded with a broad cement *piazza* upon which an oxidized reproduction of the *David* and a whole lot of parked cars enjoy a killer view. Ignore everything behind you and watch the sun set over the city.

⌖ From pretty much any bridge, walk left along the river until P. Guiseppe Poggi, where you will find the base of the steps. It's up from there. ℹ Wheelchair-accessible only by bus. $ Free. ⏰ Open 24hr.

food

While Florence isn't a culinarily distinct city, it remains a great place to find good food. There are trattorias everywhere, and almost every one of them is tasty. The only major variance between them all will be in cover charge and distance from a major *piazza*. If they begin to feel a bit too similar to one another, head to smaller places: the markets, the hole-in-the-walls, the local favorites. Whatever you do, you can't go wrong.

THE DUOMO

The places along the **Piazza del Duomo** all seem to have been cast from the same mold. They cost about the same, they offer similar fare, and they all have a rockin' view of the Duomo. For slightly more variety, venture a couple blocks from the main *piazza*.

GROM
☆ 🍴♿ GELATERIA ❶

V. del Campanile ☎055 21 61 58 🖥www.grom.it

Grom is a high-end *gelateria,* which means it has a posh location right off the Duomo, branches in New York City, and a slightly higher starting price than the city's other top-notch *gelaterie.* Nevertheless, it's the best of the sweet stuff in the Duomo area. Sure, you'll find it mentioned in every guidebook and, if you catch it at the wrong time of day, you'll be waiting in line for 15min. Just come back later. The gelato will still be delicious.

⌖ Just south of the Duomo. $ Starting at €2. ⏰ Open daily Apr-Sept 10:30am-midnight; Oct-Mar 10:30am-11pm.

VESTRI CIOCCOLATO D' ANTOIE
GELATERIA ❶

Borgo degli Albizi 11r ☎055 23 40 374 🖥www.vestri.it

Another brilliant gelato place, this one featuring the best pistachio in town, according to our very scientific research that consisted of eating too much pistachio gelato. The prices are a little higher than others, but it's gelato, so we're talking a difference of a few euro cents. Plus, top-notch combo flavors like the *cioccolata fondente* with mint make it worth the pennies. There's a bit of a boutique feel to the place, the only seating is a bench right outside, and sometimes the line is long, but no matter. This is the best gelato within a half-mile radius.

⌖ Coming from the Duomo, it's on the right after Borgo degli Albizi opens up into a piazza. $ Starting at €1.80. ⏰ Open daily 10:30am-8pm.

florence

CAFFE DUOMO
🍴♿🍸 RISTORANTE ❷

P. del Duomo 29-30r ☎055 21 13 48

There are a number of nice trattorias all in a row here, staring up at the Duomo. They're all roughly equivalent and offer specials, so browse them all and decide which you like best. We prefer this one for its lighter lunch specials, particularly the cheese and cold cut platter with a glass of Chianti *(€12 for 2 people).* The young staff have also been known to dance to Justin Bieber when business is slow.

⌖ In the shadow of the Duomo. $ Entree and a glass of wine for €9. ⏰ Open daily noon-11pm.

TRATTORIA LA MADIA
🍴♿🍸 RISTORANTE ❷

V. del Giglio 14 ☎055 21 85 63

If you are tired of unsalted Tuscan bread, come here for a welcome dose of sodium. The bruschetta is especially good, as are the seafood specialties, and all are pleasantly salty compared to the same dishes in every other identical trattoria.

⌖ Off V. dei Banchi, toward Santa Maria Novella. $ Primi €10; secondi €10-18. ⏰ Open Tu-Su 1-10pm.

PIAZZA DELLA SIGNORIA

Considering that this area teems with tourists of the well-heeled variety, there are still a surprising number of budget-friendly eateries. Good rule of thumb—the farther north or east you are of the Uffizi, the better off you are.

DA VINATTIERI
☆ 🍴♿ SANDWICHES ❶

V. Santa Margherita 4r ☎055 29 47 03

This is a literal hole-in-the-wall that's well worth tracking down. Unlike most of the panini in town, these are actually made to order. As in, the guy picks up the leg of ham and cuts off a slice for your sandwich. You can step into the tiny shop or just order a quick *lampredotto (€3.50)* from the alley through the counter window. Choose from the long menu of sandwich suggestions or invent your own—they all cost the same anyway. The stools in the alley make for a fine perch while polishing off your lunch. The proprietor sometimes pops out for a smoke or a chat, but give it a minute. He'll be back.

⌖ Across the alley from Casa di Dante, so just follow the signs for that attraction. Shares a corner with Lush, which you can smell from 2 blocks away. $ Panini €3-3.50. ⏰ Open daily 10am-8pm.

👍 FESTIVAL DEL GELATO 💳♿ GELATERIA [1]

V. Del Corso 75r ☎055 29 43 86

We had dismissed this tacky, neon-flooded *gelateria* as a certain tourist trap, but when a local recommended it, we caved and gave the disco gelato a try. At our first bite of *cioccolata fondente*, the garish fluorescence melted into warm candlelight and fireflies and a violinist in white tie began to...OK, no, the place still looked ridiculous, but hot damn, that's good gelato.

🪧 Look for the neon. You seriously can't miss it. $ Gelato from €1.80. ⏰ Open daily noon-midnight.

OSTERIA DELL PORCELLINO 💳♿🍸⛅ RISTORANTE [3]

V. Val di Lamona 7r ☎055 26 41 48 💻www.osteriadelporcellino.com

This beautiful osteria has an alleyway to itself which it fills with wrought-iron tables and colored lights. Don't come for lunch, when the adjacent Mercato Nuovo is bustling. Instead, wait until the evenings when the *piazza* clears out and the space is well worth the €2 cover.

*🪧 Right off Mercato Nuovo. **i** Vegetarian menu. $ Cover €2. Primi €7-10; secondi €14-22. ⏰ Open daily noon-3pm and 5-11pm.*

CORONAS CAFE 💳♿🍸⛅ CAFE [1]

V. Calzaiuoli 72r ☎055 239 6139

Cheap sandwiches and pastries *(€1-3.50)* as well as an open layout on the corner make this cafe a good spot for eating alone and people-watching. The excellent gelato is available in enormous American-appetite-sized cones if you want to be *that* guy.

🪧 Just north of P. della Signoria, on the corner. $ Pastries €1-3.50. Panini €3.50. ⏰ Open daily 10am-1am.

CANTINETTA DEI VERRAZANO 💳♿ CAFE [1]

V. Dei Tavolini 18/20r ☎055 26 85 90

The pizzas *(from €1.80)* here are cheaper and better than what you'll find at similar places. They're also tiny, but what do you expect at this price? Offers a wide variety of biscotti and cakes as well.

🪧 Off V. Calzaluioli, north of P. della Signoria. $ Pizzas from €1.80. ⏰ Open daily 8am-9pm.

OSTERIA GANINO 💳♿⛅ RISTORANTE [2]

P. de' Cimatori 4r ☎055 21 41 25

Hide from the sun under big umbrellas and a hedge of leafy green plants at this pleasant *osteria* in a low-traffic *piazza*. Sample the wide variety of desserts *(€4-5)* or one of the many vegetarian options.

🪧 Across from the American Express office. $ Primi €7-11. ⏰ Open M-Sa noon-11pm.

GUSTO LEO 💳♿🍸⛅ PIZZERIA [2]

V. del Proconsolo 8-10r ☎055 28 52 17 💻www.gustoleo.com

Come to this friendly, brick restaurant near the major sights for its enormous calzones and pizzas. Wide selection of large salads and a cute little lion cartoon as a logo.

🪧 Coming from P. Della Signoria, it's on the right. $ Pizzas €5.40-8.90. Calzones €7.60. ⏰ Open daily 8am-1am.

SANTA MARIA NOVELLA

Pizzerias, cafes, and kebab shops abound near the train station and church. This is a good neighborhood to find a generic, cheap, quick eat but not a destination if you're looking for a sit-down meal.

CAFFE GIACOSA 💳♿🍸⛅ CAFE [1]

Inside Palazzo Strozzi ☎055 42 65 04 86

Backpacking is murder on your lower lumbar, and the curved wooden wall at

Caffe Giacosa fits just right in the small of your back. Lean back with a cappuccino (€1.30), and it's as good as ibuprofen. The prices triple for table seating, but who cares? The nice wooden wall in the self-serve area is the point of the visit. The pots of tea (€2) are made of fancy bagged stuff—a lot better than nothing for tea-drinkers stranded in coffee country.

✈ Inside Palazzo Strozzi, which is west of P. della Repubblica. Has a 2nd location down the street at V. della Spada 10. ⓢ Cappuccino €1.30. Pot of tea €2. ☼ Open daily 10am-10pm.

OPERA ET GUSTO
≈♿⚲❄ RISTORANTE, CONCERT VENUE ❸

V. Della Scala 17r
☎055 28 81 90 🖳www.operaetgusto.com

This sleek joint is a little-black-dress sort of place, with black-and-red decor and limited lighting. The draw is the live performances most nights, which tend towards jazz combos and light world music but sometimes encompass diverse theatrical art forms. Considering the entertainment, the cover (€2) is a steal.

✈ Coming from Santa Maria Novella, on the left. ⓘ Show 9-10:30pm. ⓢ Cover €2. Primi €10-12; secondi €11-22. ☼ Open daily 8:30pm-2am.

OSTERIA E PIZZERIA CENTROPOVERI
≈♿⚲❄ PIZZERIA, RISTORANTE ❷

V. Palazzuolo 31r
☎055 21 88 46 🖳www.icentopoveri.it

Two adjacent restaurants with the same name but different menus. The long dining rooms with curved ceilings will make you feel like you're eating in a tunnel, but the light at the end is the excellent pizza (€4-9) on the pizzeria side, and the Tuscan specialties in the osteria, with a *prix-fixe* menu (€35) featuring *bistecca alla fiorentina*.

✈ Corner of Porcellana. ⓢ Cover €2 in osteria. Pizza €4-9. Primi €7-10; secondi €9-19. ☼ Open daily noon-3pm and 7pm-midnight.

50 ROSSO
≈♿⚲♨ CAFE ❶

V. Panzani 50r
☎055 28 35 85

A lovely open-walled cafe with a takeaway happy hour and no surcharge for sitting. Open during basically all reasonable eating hours. The Nutella crepes are divine.

✈ From P. Santa Maria Novella, you'll find the start of V. Panzani in the northeast corner of the piazza, nearer the train station. ⓢ Panini €2.50. Cappuccino €1.20. ☼ Open daily 6:30am-12:30am.

TRATTORIA IL CONTADINO
≈♿⚲ RISTORANTE ❷

V. Palazzuolo 69/71r
☎055 23 82 673

This weekday-only trattoria has wine racks on the wall and lazy ceiling fans—the good deal is a lovely *prix-fixe* menu of *primo*, *secondo*, veggie, and wine (lunch €11, dinner €13).

✈ From P. Santa Maria Novella, take a right onto V. Palazzuolo. ⓢ Prix-fixe menu €11-13. ☼ Open M-F noon-9:40pm.

LA GROTTA DI LEO
≈♿⚲ RISTORANTE ❶

V. Della Scala 41/43r
☎055 21 92 65

This brick-walled trattoria is bigger than it looks, with two grotto-esque dining rooms and a couple outdoor tables. Try the house specialty, tiramisu (€4).

✈ Coming from P. Santa Maria Novella, take a right onto V. della Scala. ⓢ Pizza €5-8. Primi €5-8. ☼ Open daily 11am-1am.

SAN LORENZO

Honestly, if you're around here during the day, you should be getting your food at Mercato Centrale (See **Markets**). But Trattoria Mario is the choice if you get to Mercato after the stalls close up. Other food options vary widely in this crowded, lively area.

TRATTORIA MARIO

RISTORANTE 2

V. Rosina 2r ☎055 21 85 50 www.trattoriamario.com

If you're starting to wonder where all the Italians are hiding, show up late for lunch at Trattoria Mario. Diners are packed into tables with strangers, and regulars will flag the waitress if they want a newcomer to be seated at their table. And then perhaps they will buy you wine. Lots and lots of wine. The food is pretty good too, with the day's offerings written on brown paper by the kitchen.

Just off Mercato Centrale, on the right. $ Daily specials €6-9. Open M-Sa noon-3:30pm.

NEGRONE

RISTORANTE 1

P. del Mercato Centrale ☎055 21 99 49

Mercato Centrale isn't just for groceries. The edges are lined with cafes, cafeterias, and panini stands that cater to workers and wise visitors. Negrone stands out as both the oldest, dating back to 1872, and the best. Crowd around the counter to order whatever happens to be on offer, take your tray, and squeeze in somewhere at the picnic tables along the wall. The food is fantastic and dirt-cheap, plus the atmosphere is far livelier than any cookie-cutter trattoria. Don't forget to bus your tray when you're done!

Along the wall of the Mercato. $ Primi and secondi €4-7. Cup of house wine €1. Open M-Sa 7am-2pm.

ANTICA GELATERIA FIORENTINA

GELATERIA 1

V. Faenza 2a ☎388 05 80 399 www.gelateriafiorentina.com

Off-beat flavors like rosewater, cheesecake, and green tea will add some variety to your gelato diet, and although the peanut butter chocolate was probably concocted to please Americans starved of their lunchbox staple, it at least succeeds in its goal. Antica is super cheap too, with cones starting at a single flavor for €1. If you want to go whole-hog American, there's a ginormo cone *(€15)* in which you can try every flavor on tap. Don't mix the cheesecake and green tea. Also, don't look too closely at the **Torture Museum** across the street.

Toward the far end of V. Faenza, on the left. $ Cones from €1. Open daily noon-midnight.

TRATTORIA ZAZA

RISTORANTE 2

P. del Mercato Centrale 26r ☎055 21 54 11 www.trattoriazaza.it

The tented alfresco seating is typical for a *piazza ristorante*, but the quirky logo on the menu—a naked child being stung on the buttocks by a bee—should give you a clue to the offbeat glamour of the inside dining rooms. Lurid frescoes coat the vaulted ceilings, while staid dead white men watch you devour fresh pasta from gilded portraits. For those not inclined to the bloody *bistecca alla fiorentina*, there are abundant creative salad options—try Zaza's, with chicory lettuce, walnuts, brie, and Roquefort dressing.

Behind Mercato Centrale. $ Cover €2.50. Primi €7-11. Open daily 11am-11pm.

BAR CABRAS

CAFE 1

V. dei Panzani 12r ☎055 21 20 32

Italy takes its regional specialties seriously, so you're hard pressed to find a decent cannoli outside its southern home turf. But for the best cannoli between Sicily and Boston's North End, go no further than this tiny cafe by the train station. Not looking for regionally misplaced pastries? It's also a full bar. We were going to add a cheesy Godfather pun here too, but the pastry is looking so tempting that we're gonna leave the pun and take the cannoli.

Just down the street from the train station. $ Cannoli €2.50. Open daily 8am-8pm.

RISTORANTE LE FONTICINE

RISTORANTE 2

V. Nazionale 79r ☎055 28 21 06 www.lefonticine.com

While it appears deceptively small from the front dining room, a walk deeper inside this restaurant past the open kitchen reveals a beautiful lantern-lit dining room cluttered with framed paintings. Poke your head into the adjacent wine cellar and select a bottle to accompany the *prix-fixe menu dello chef (€25).*

⇆ To the right of the V. Nazionale fountain, hence the name. $ Primi €6-13; secondi €8-16. ⏰ Open daily noon-2:30pm and 7-10:30pm.

OSTERIA ALL'ANTICO MERCATO 🎟♿🍸☀ RISTORANTE ❷

V. Nazionale 78r ☎055 28 41 82 💻www.anticomercatofirenze.it

The €10 combo meals are the draw here—try the *bruschetta e spaghetti bolognese.* Those sick of carbs will be happy to find that "Big Salads" get their own section of the menu, and gluten-free lasagna and pasta are also prominently offered. You get the same view whether you're dining inside or out—the dining room features a mural of the street outside sans noisy cars and mopeds.

⇆ Toward San Lorenzo. $ Combo meals €10. ⏰ Open daily noon-11pm.

IL PIRATA 🎟♿🍸 RISTORANTE ❶

V. de' Ginori 56r ☎055 21 86 25

How could we not review the pirate cafe? Unfortunately, the place is sort of phoning in the pirate theme, but it's nevertheless refreshing to see a cafe mural that trades in knock-off Botticelli for knock-off Captain Hook. The dinner buffet *(all you can eat and a bottle of wine; €10)* is better and more varied than the other buffets in the area, with dozens of dishes available for the hungry landlubber.

⇆ From P. San Lorenzo, walk north up V. de' Ginori for a few minutes. i Takeout available. $ Lunch specials €5.50-7.50. Buffet €7.50, with wine €10. ⏰ Open daily 11am-11pm.

SAN MARCO

This is a poorly defined neighborhood, so it is hard to generalize. Odds are, you're looking for somewhere to eat after hitting up one of the many museums. Get something from Gran Caffe to go and enjoy it in the botanical garden. V. San Gallo, which runs parallel to the garden, is a bit livelier in the evening.

GRAN CAFFE SAN MARCO 🎟♿📶🍸❄☀ CAFE ❶

P. San Marco 11r ☎055 21 58 33 💻www.grancaffesanmarco.it

This place just keeps getting bigger. Enter from the main *piazza*, and it's a *gelateria*. Enter from the side street, and it's a pizzeria. Walk further in, and it's a cafeteria, coffee bar, and garden cafe. Make your way to the tented garden for a bit of quiet. It's a bit chintzy but cheap. The enormous gooey bowls of lasagna *(€4.50)* are reheated, but since when has a bit of reheating hurt lasagna?

⇆ The south end of the piazza. $ Huge variety of options, but meal-type food will run you from €3 panini to €7 secondi. ⏰ Open daily 8am-10pm.

RISTORANTE PIZZERIA DA ZEUS 🎟♿🍸❄ PIZZERIA ❶

V. Santa Reparata 17r ☎328 86 44 704

Dodge a bank-account lightning bolt with Zeus's student special—pizza and a soft drink. The large rear dining hall is air-conditioned, and the *prix-fixe* menu *(drink, a salad or pizza or primi dish, a dessert, and coffee; €6.50)* is one of the cheapest in town.

⇆ Off V. XXVII Aprile. $ Pizza and soft drink €5, prix-fixe menu €6.50. ⏰ Open daily noon-11 pm.

VIN OLIO 🎟♿🍸 RISTORANTE ❷

V. San Zanobi 126r ☎055 48 99 57 💻www.vinolio.com

Vin Olio is a quiet, grown-up sort of joint, with subdued art and fans slowly whirring under the high, beamed ceilings. The front room has a small bar, featuring cocktails *(€3)* and grappa *(€1.80)*. Try the penne with duck meat.

⇆ From P. dell'Indipendenza, take V. XXVII Aprile to V. San Zanobi. $ Antipasti €5-9; primi €8-9. Grappa €1.80. Cocktails €3. ⏰ Open daily 11am-midnight.

DIONISO 🎟♿🍸 GREEK ❷

V. San Gallo 16r ☎055 21 78 82

Sick of typical Tuscan cuisine? Have a little baklava! It's your predictable Greek joint, in that predictable shade of blue that seems to be international code for "here be filo dough." The menu's in Italian and Greek only, but we are confident you can recognize the Greek for "souvlaki."

⚑ *Just to the west of San Marco.* Ⓢ *Baklava €3.50. Souvlaki and gyro plates €11. Ouzo €3.* ⌚ *Open M-Sa noon-3pm and 7:30pm-midnight, Su 7:30pm-midnight.*

SANTA CROCE

Where there are students, there's cheap food. We've picked out some highlights for you, but student whimsy shifts quickly. Visiting the university area during lunchtime on a weekday and seeing where the crowds are may be a better strategy for discovering tasty places than relying upon our listings. You can count on finding an abundance of kebab joints, automats, and other sources of cheap drunkfood to fuel the student population.

EBY'S BAR

●⛊♂♿ MEXICAN ❶

V. dell'Oriuolo 5r and Borgo Pinti 2r   ☎055 90 62 116

Heck yes, burrito joint! America has the leg up on Europe in a certain area—Mexican food just ain't a thing on the continent. Kebabs aren't super big stateside, though, so we guess it's sort of a fair trade. Nonetheless, not even the best kebab in Italy can quite fill a craving for a bean-and-cheese-stuffed tortilla doused in hot sauce. Imagine our joy, then, when we found a top-notch burrito joint right on the edge of Santa Croce's nightlife scene. Eby's is even good! Not quite SoCal good, but definitely New York good. This is a place that knows its purpose: a boasting sign on the door proudly announces the availability of "LATE NIGHT CHICKEN QUESADILLA." Order your €4 burrito on the corner of Borgo Pinti and Dell Oriuolo, then cross to Eby's colorful bar and upstairs dining room. Or chill with a €12 pitcher of sangria at the tables in the covered Volta di San Pietro alleyway—shared by none other than a kebab shop! So many options to satisfy a case of the drunkies! Drunktions, one might say. Oh dear, we're on a lollercoaster! No, seriously, the food is so good that you can come here sober, too.

⚑ *Head away from Santa Croce, west from P. de Salvamini.* Ⓢ *Nachos €3. Burrito €4. Sangria pitcher €12.* ⌚ *Open daily 10am-3am.*

GELATERIA DEI NERI

●⛊ GELATERIA ❶

V. Dei Neri 20/22r   ☎055 21 00 34

Our job description compels us to have our thrice-daily dose of gelato at a different *gelateria* each time to sample Florence's wide range of offerings. So why can't we stop eating at this one? It might have something to do with the mousse-like *semifreddo*—try the tiramisu—or the insanely spicy Mexican chocolate, which we found too intense to even finish. The €0.50 mini-cones are perfect for trying each of the 30+ flavors on tap. We wish there was nice seating close enough to reach before having eaten all of one's gelato—but we'll happily take it as all the more reason to go back for more.

⚑ *On the right when heading to city center.* Ⓢ *Cups and cones from €1.50.* ⌚ *Open daily 9am-midnight.*

LA GHIOTTA

●⛊❄ CAFE ❶

V. Pietrapiana 7r   ☎055 24 12 37

Take a number at this student-y rotisserie with student-y prices—the line is out the door during lunchtime. Pick your meal from platters behind the counter or order one of 20 varieties of pizza *(€5.50)* and cram into the seats in the back. You'll eat even cheaper if you take it to go—get half a rotisserie chicken for a couple euros, go for a giant slab of eggplant parmigiana, or try whatever else they happen to have when you visit.

⚑ *From Borgo Alegri, take a right.* Ⓢ *Primi €5-6; secondi €5-7. Liter of wine €6.* ⌚ *Open daily noon-5pm and 7-10pm.*

ALL' ANTICO VINAIO 🚭♿🍸 CAFE [1]

V. De' Neri 65r ☎055 23 82 723

Self-service wine! What an idea! Walk up to the counter on the street, plop down €2, pour yourself a small-ish glass of wine, and enjoy. It's actually not as good a deal as it seems, given how dirt-cheap wine by the bottle is in this town. But still, self-service wine! If you bother going inside the tiny storefront, there's a student special of sandwich and a drink for €4.

 # 2 blocks behind Uffizi. ⏰ Open daily 8am-9pm.

IL GIOVA 💳🚭⛱ RISTORANTE [2]

Borgo la Croce 73r ☎055 24 80 639 💻www.ilgiova.com

Settle down with a giant slice of watermelon on the mismatched chairs of this busy little lunch joint. At night, the outside tables fill the otherwise deserted intersection with couples and young people sipping wine. Menu changes daily.

 # At the corner of V. della Mattonaia. $ Primi €5; secondi €7. ⏰ Open M-F noon-5pm and 7:30-11pm, Sa 12:30-4:30pm and 7:30-11pm.

CIBREO CAFFE 💳♿🍸❄⛱ CAFE [2]

V. Andrea del Verrocchio 5r ☎055 23 45 853

If you want to experience the classiness of the Cibreo theater scene minus the wallet drain, try visiting this cafe for a not-quite-budget lunch or, if you're really cheap, a coffee. The dark wood of the inside seating will make you feel like you are crashing a university's faculty club, sipping old-fashioned cocktails (like the Sidecar and, well, the Old Fashioned) with patch-elbowed professor types.

 # Facing the main Cibreo theater, it's behind you on your left. $ Primi €8; secondi €15. ⏰ Open Tu-Sa 8am-1am.

RUTH'S KOSHER VEGETARIAN FOOD 💳🚭❄ KOSHER [2]

V. L.C. Farini 2/A ☎055 24 80 888 💻www.kosheruth.com

There are probably some visitors to Florence who are stuck eating every meal here, and that must get old. For the carnivorous Christian getting sick of all that *bistecca alla fiorentina* or the nostalgic New Yorker who misses the Lower East Side, however, Ruth's provides some nice variety. Have a falafel while surrounded by Israelite kitsch like Hebrew calendars, maps of Israel, and photos of bearded old Jews. If you look Jewish, the locals may stop by your table to say hi.

*# To the right of synagogue. **i** Kosher. $ Falafel platter €9. Entrees €9-12. ⏰ Open M-Th 12:30-2:30pm and 7:30-10pm, F 12:30-2:30pm, Sa 7:30-10pm, Su 12:30-2:30pm and 7:30-10pm.*

KOCCO 💳♿🍸⛱ RISTORANTE [2]

V. Farini 1/2 ☎055 23 44 020

This is the neighborhood for a rare dose of religious diversity—across the street is the **Synagogue** and inside Kocco there is a giant gold Buddha. The table service is expensive, but the unshaded outdoor seating is unpleasant at midday anyway. Go for the light lunch special: *primo*, bottled water, and coffee for €7 or the same with a *secondo* for €8. Come back at 6:30pm for the €4 *aperitivo* buffet.

 # At the corner of Pilastri, across from the Synagogue. $ Lunch specials €7-8. ⏰ Open daily noon-11pm.

LA SEMOLINA 💳♿🍸⛱ RISTORANTE [2]

P. Ghiberti 87r ☎055 23 47 584

Semolina's exterior is a bit run down, but come in the evening to sit under the umbrellas and enjoy large portions of pasta and some excellent risotto. During the day, regulars hang out on the patio and chat with passersby. It's priced a little higher than equivalent options and may refuse to serve tap water, but the food is good.

➤ *On the far corner of P. Ghiberti; it's the one with the plants and tents.* $ *Cover €2. Pizzas €5-7. Pasta €6-11.* ⏰ *Open daily noon-midnight.*

S. CROCE
💳♿🍸❄☀ RISTORANTE ❷

P. Santa Croce 11r ☎055 24 79 896

S. Croce is slightly pricier than it should be but good for being on a major *piazza*. The menu offers a nice range of salads in addition to the usual options, and even the side salad is surprisingly substantial *(€4.50)*.

➤ *To the left of the Basilica di Santa Croce.* $ *Cover €1.50, but when they're not busy a sign will announce that there's no cover. Pizza €5.50-8. Pasta €8.50. Salads €8.50.* ⏰ *Open daily 11am-11pm.*

WEST OLTRARNO

A lot of West Oltrarno's restaurants are quirkier than their counterparts on the other side of the river. Unfortunately, they're also a little bit more expensive and more likely to have a cover. Still, the locals who frequent these joints must know something we don't.

DANTE
💳♿🍸 RISTORANTE ❷

P. Nazario Sauro 12r ☎055 21 92 19 💻www.trattoria-dante.net

An excellent choice for students—with any meal, students get a free bottle of wine. No joke. The pizza is the same as anywhere, but dude, **free wine.** Also hosts lots of images of Dante on the wall, as you'd expect. Free wine!

➤ *A block south of Ponte alla Carraia, on the right.* $ *Cover €2.50. Pizzas €6-9. Pastas €8-10.* ⏰ *Open daily noon-11pm.*

OSTERIA SANTO SPIRITO
💳♿🍸☀ RISTORANTE ❷

P. Santo Spirito, 16r ☎055 23 82 383

Delightful wooden tables behind bamboo screens line the street in front of this osteria, while inside large round tables are suffused with a flickering red light. Linger after your pasta for the *crème brulée (€6)* and other posh desserts.

➤ *Far end of the piazza from the church, on the right.* $ *Pizza €6-9. Primi €7-12. Wine by the bottle from €12.* ⏰ *Open daily noon-11:30pm.*

GELATERIA LA CARRAIA
💳♿ GELATERIA ❶

P. Nazario Sauro 25r ☎055 28 06 95 💻www.lacarraiagroup.eu

An excellent gelato option right across the river, with cones starting at €1. Try the After Eight. Not much ambience in the shop itself, but go stand by the river—it's right outside.

➤ *Right over the Ponte alla Carraia.* $ *Gelato from €1.* ⏰ *Open daily 11am-11pm.*

PIZZERIA IL TIRATOIO
💳♿🍸❄☀ PIZZERIA ❷

P. de Nerli 1r ☎055 28 96 13

This pizzeria offers simple outdoor seating on a *piazza* that's mostly a parking lot, but it's got a small knot of locals hanging out at any hour of the day, nabbing the specials scrawled on a white erase board in the street.

➤ *From Borgo San Frediano, turn right.* $ *Cover €1.50. Pizza €5-7. Primi €7.50-10. Bottled beer €5. Bottle of wine €8.* ⏰ *Open M-Tu 5pm-1am, Th-F 5pm-1am. Open for lunch on weekends; call ahead for specific times.*

EAST OLTRARNO

The actually eastern part of East Oltrarno is rather far from most attractions, but if you venture out here, you'll find dinner joints frequented by locals and a whole lot less English on the menus. Our choices are right off the Ponte Vecchio, which is the area most likely to be frequented by our readers.

BIBO
💳♿🍸❄☀ RISTORANTE ❷

P. di Santa Felicita 6r ☎055 23 98 554

A quiet restaurant right past the Ponte Vecchio, Bibo is kinda on the tacky side of niceness, with electric candles on pink tablecloths, but it works.

➜ Bear left after crossing Ponte Vecchio. $ Pastas €9-10. ⏰ Open daily noon-11pm.

RISTORANTE CELESTINO
💳♿🍸❄☀ RISTORANTE [2]

P. di Santa Felicita 4r ☎055 23 96 574 💻www.ristorantecelestino.it

Slightly nicer than its neighboring trattoria, Celestino has a grotto feel, with climbing vines winding about the outdoor seating. The site was once a monastery, but now, it is full of mostly Tuscan wines. The €15 *prix-fixe* menu of chef's specials is a good deal.

➜ Turn left after Ponte Vecchio. $ Soups €6-8. Pastas €8-10. ⏰ Open daily noon-3pm and 7-11pm.

SNACK LE DELIZIE
💳♿🍸☀ CAFE [1]

P. di Santa Felicita 2/3 ☎055 29 53 33

This is a simpler option in a *piazza* crowded with restaurants. Five euros here can get you a pizza margherita with olives.

➜ Turn left after Ponte Vecchio. $ Pizzas €5-7. ⏰ Open 24hr.

nightlife

People don't come to Florence to party. They come to Florence to stare at pretty things. During peak season, major sporting events, and other cultural happenings, the streets will fill with young people clutching wine bottles. At other times, you will be better off simply hanging out with the people in your hostel. For more hopping after-hours entertainment, head to Santa Croce or deal with one of the bazillion American or Irish pubs that litter the city.

THE DUOMO

This isn't exactly a traditional nightlife area. You'll find a couple of bars right by the Duomo, but mostly, you're going to be pushing into the edges of other neighborhoods. When the weather is beautiful and the town is particularly crowded, people hang out on the Duomo steps all evening.

SHOT CAFE
💳♿📶🍸 BAR

V. dei Pucci 5 ☎055 28 20 93

At least it looks different from the other American bars? This aggressively quirky little bar is covered in inner tubes and stuffed fish because, well, why not? The music is American "oldies," if you define oldies as anything recorded between 1920 and 2005. The TV is usually tuned to MTV—now that's retro.

➜ A block north of the Duomo. ℹ Happy hour 1st drink €3.50, 2nd €3, 3rd €2.50. Free Wi-Fi. $ Shots €2.50. Pitchers €9. ⏰ Open daily 5pm-3am. Happy hour until 9pm.

ASTOR CAFE
💳♿🍸 BAR

P. Duomo 20r ☎055 23 99 318

A contemporary cafe for all times of the day. Lunch specials draw people during the day, with *antipasti*, *primi*, water, and beer or wine for just €10. Sleek black furniture shifts the focus to nightlife, when the big projection screen is lit with sporting events. On non-sporty weekend nights, live music livens up the scene. Outdoor seating looks up at the Duomo.

➜ NE side of the piazza. $. Bottled beer €5. 1L of what's on tap €10. ⏰ Open daily 8am-3am.

PIAZZA DELLA SIGNORIA

The nightlife scene here is mostly of a DIY variety. The **Loggia, Piazza Della Repubblica,** and **Ponte Vecchio** are all excellent places to hang out with a **beer,** so get one to go from Old Stove or a watering hole in a pubbier part of town. It should also be noted that the Ponte Vecchio is a fine place for a snog and that *Let's Go* does not condone drunk-riding the P. della Repubblica carousel.

top 5 smooch spots

Florence is undeniably romantic, with movie-set side streets and constant streams of wine. If you're inspired to indulge in a Florentine romance, here are some options preferable to hostel bunk beds.

- **PONTE VECCHIO.** It's as cliché as the Eiffel Tower and not remotely private, but no one bats an eye at some smooching along the most famous bridge in town. Hope the constant stream of wedding parties isn't a turn-off, though.
- **PONTE SANTA TRINITA.** Keeping along the Arno, score a little more isolation and an even better view on one of the broad stone triangles over the edge of this less trafficked bridge. Come early (or very late) to find one unoccupied, though—this is prime canoodling real estate.
- **THE DUOMO.** Want to tick blasphemous make-out session off your "Never Have I Ever" list? The steps in front of Florence's most recognizable church are scenic and quiet after midnight, but more daring couples could try climbing the dome or tower. Right before closing, the 300+ steps of winding stairwells will be mostly deserted, and your hearts will already be racing from the climb. If you make it to the top, the view ain't too shabby either.
- **PIAZZALE MICHELANGELO.** It might seem like an obvious choice, but it's a bit too parking lot to really set the mood. Try a corner along the hike up to the more secluded piazzale or keep going up the hill to find a small park that's far darker, deserted, and every bit as scenic.
- **LEAVE THE CITY.** Take your romance out under the Tuscan sun and head to the hills. Hostels in adjacent towns let you escape the crowds and perhaps snag a private room while staying within a backpacker's budget.

NOIR

💳♿🍸❄ BAR

Lungarno Corsini 12/14r ☎055 21 07 51

This super-classy watering hole spills over to the other side of the street, where patrons balancing cocktails and munchies lean against the wall of the Arno. Inside is dark, trendy, and loud, with low, cushioned benches lining the walls. Fill your plate from the extensive *aperitivo* buffet and go watch the sunset over the river.

➜ Facing Ponte Vecchio, it's on your right. $ Bottled beer €5. Cocktails €6-7. ⏰ Open daily noon-3am.

OLD STOVE

💳♿🍸👤 IRISH PUB

P. della Signoria 30r ☎055 29 52 32 🖥www.theoldstovepub.com

Hey look, it's another Irish pub! Which, of course, actually means American because Irish people know better than to go to Florence for drinking. The dive-bar inside pales in comparison to the social and open outdoor seating. Wednesdays are Dollar Days—pay in US$ all day long. Other branches by the Duomo and *Il Porcellino.*

➜ Walk to the side of P. della Repubblica that doesn't have the carousel, and look down the street to the left. There it is. ℹ Happy hour pints €4. $ Pints €6. Cocktails €7. ⏰ Open M-Th noon-2am, F-Sa noon-3am, Su noon-2am. Happy hour M-Th 5-9pm.

TWICE

💳♿🍸 CLUB

V. Giuseppe Verdi 57r ☎055 24 76 356

Twice is the sort of place for clubbing when you don't feel like making a big production out of it. No cover means a bit of a mixed bag crowd in terms of both age and attire, but, as is the case for many places in the Florentine nightlife scene, Italian men and American women dominate the clientele. The weird mix of music should have you giggling every time some forgotten hit from 8th grade starts to play. Epileptics take heed: Twice loves the strobe light.

⇆ From Duomo, head east on V. Oriuolo, then right onto V. Giuseppe Verdi. $ Beer €6. Cocktails €8. ⏰ Open daily 9pm-4am.

SANTA MARIA NOVELLA

There are a number of options in this area, but they are spread out, making bar-hopping difficult. If you are on the river side of the area, it's best to cross over to West Oltrano. If you are near the train station, well, you're screwed.

SPACE CLUB ELECTRONIC
💳♿🍸 CLUB

V. Palazzuolo 37 ☎055 29 30 82 💻www.spaceelectronic.net

Do you wish you could go clubbing in Epcot? Then this utterly ridiculous club is the place for you. Descend into the depths of its space-age neon dance hall for a taste of the European clubbing scene, or as close as you'll get to that in central Florence. If the bouncer waves you in, don't be fooled into thinking you got a free entrance—you pay the steep cover *(€16)* when you leave. And hold tight to your drink ticket when crowding around the aquarium bar, because the fine for losing it is sky high. Special events like guest bands and foam parties are extensively advertised on posters around town, so keep an eye out. The club's location means it's one of the few in the area from which you'll likely be able to return home without hailing a cab.

⇆ From river, take V. Melegnano to V. Palazzuolo, then turn right. $ Cover €16 and it only goes up from there. ⏰ Open daily 10pm-4am.

JOSHUA TREE
💳♿🍸❄ BAR

V. della Scala 37r 💻www.thejoshuatreepub.com

The dark, bold colors of this Irish-style pub may remind you of the nicer of your college haunts. It is smaller than similar places in town which means it doesn't feel deserted in the early hours of the evening. Good place to start your adventures, or to just hang out on a weeknight.

⇆ At corner of V. Benedetta. $ Pints €5. ⏰ Open daily 4pm-2am. Happy hour 4-9:30pm.

PUBLIC HOUSE 27
💳🚫🍸 BAR

V. Palazzuolo 27/r ☎339 30 22 330 💻www.publichouse27.com

Public House 27 has a slightly more punk feel than the other bars in the area. It gets busy early, and with a €3 pint, the price is right.

⇆ At the corner of Porcellana. $ Pints €3. ⏰ Open M-Sa 5pm-2am, Su 2:30pm-2am.

CENTRAL PARK
💳♿🍸❄⛅ CLUB

V. del Fosso Macinate 2 ☎055 35 99 42 💻www.centralfirenze.it

If you have money to burn and are willing to take a cab home, try trekking out to this enormous club in the middle of Parco delle Cascine. You'll be greeted by four outdoor dance floors with four different musical themes—hip hop, house, mainstream, and '70s/'80s. Be sure to pregame because the drinks are all €10. And hope that Daddy's paying for your trip—the cover is an absurd €20.

⇆ From the river, go to Ponte della Vittoria, the westernmost bridge of the city center. Follow Vle. Rosselli north (careful, it's busy), then turn left onto V. Fosso Macinante. $ Cover €20. All drinks €10. ⏰ Open daily 10pm-4am.

SAN LORENZO

The headquarters of drunk backpackers from North America and down under.

MOSTODOLCE
💳♿🍸❄ BAR

V. Nazionale 114r ☎055 23 02 928 💻www.mostodolce.it

The one pub in the area likely to have one or two Italians present. Large and comfortable, with big crowds for sporting events and artisanal beers brewed in Prato. If you're around for a while (or drink fast), get the "10th beer free" punch-card.

On the corner of V. Guelfa. $ Pints from €6. ⏰ Open daily 5pm-2am.

DUBLIN PUB BAR

V. Faenza 27r ☎055 27 41 571 www.dublinpub.it

Dartboards, beer ads, drunk Americans—the works. There are a few tables outside, but beware the splash of zamboni-like street-cleaners after midnight. Across the street is a fine *gelateria* for when you want to wash down the beer with something sweet.

The far end of V. Faenza. $ Pint of cider €4.40. Pint of Guinness €6. Pizza €5. ⏰ Open daily 5pm-2am.

KITSCH THE PUB BAR

V. San Gallo 22r ☎328 90 39 289 www.kitsch-pub.com

What do you expect from a place that has "kitsch" as its name? Tarot readers, that's what. Also red velvet, stained glass, and a surprisingly late happy hour with cocktails *(€5)* and beer from 11pm to 1am.

Off V. Cavour. $ Shots €3.50-4.50. Cocktails €5-6. ⏰ Open daily 5pm-3am. Aperitivo 6-9:30pm.

THE FISH PUB BAR

P. del Mercato Cenrale 44r ☎055 26 82 90 www.thefishpub.com

The "free crazy party!" announced on the promoter's fliers doesn't usually materialize, but at least the flier gets you a free shot. It's mostly orange juice but, hey, refreshing! And you can get five more of them for €5. On the plus side, come any time before midnight with your friends and you can totally take over the joint.

Right off Mercato Centrale. $ 5 shots for €5. Cocktails €7. ⏰ Open daily 3pm until "late night." Happy hour 3-9pm.

SAN MARCO

The intersection directly to the west of San Marco is pretty lively, but other than that, you'll want to avoid this area if you're looking for proper nightlife. The area north of San Marco is particularly deserted, especially after the buses stop running.

THE CLUBHOUSE BAR

V. de' Ginori 6r ☎333.26 95 434 www.theclubhouse.it

An American sports bar that, with its white tiles and blue-tinged lighting, might be best suited for watching swimming. Plasma TVs and martinis are at your disposal all day, and at night, the pints are €5.50. Excellent weekday lunch specials *(pizza, water, and espresso €5; with primo or secondo instead of pizza €6-7).*

Off V. dei Pucci. $ Shots €3. Beer €5.50. ⏰ Open daily noon-2am. Kitchen open until 11pm.

FINNEGAN IRISH PUB IRISH PUB

V. San Gallo 123r ☎055 49 07 94 www.finneganpub.com

Another **Irish pub!** This one has outdoor seating, dedicated screenings of football and rugby games, dart boards, those usual pub booths, and rugby paraphernalia on the walls. You know the drill. Good place for casually watching the game, whatever the game may be, and hanging with the regulars.

North of San Marco. $ Beer €5. ⏰ Open M-Th 1pm-12:30am, F-Sa 1pm-1am, Su 1pm-12:30am.

WINE BAR NABUCCO BAR

V. 27 Aprile 28r ☎055 47 50 87 www.nabuccowine.com

This sunny, citrus-colored bar has you covered from dawn to dusk. Start your day with the international breakfast menu *(€1-4.20)*, then take advantage of the free Wi-Fi and coffee bar *(coffee €1, latte €1.10)* until lunch is served. Then it's just a few hours until you can enjoy the *aperitivo* buffet as a pregame for when Wine Bar Nabucco begins living up to its name. Try the frozen Bailey's.

Corner of V. Santa Reparata. i Free Wi-Fi. $ Breakfast items €1-4.20. Nutella coffee €2. Frozen Bailey's €4. ⏰ Open daily 8am-midnight. Aperitivo bar 6:30-9:30pm.

SANTA CROCE

This is the place to go for Florentine nightlife. On nice evenings, **Piazza Sant'Ambrogio** and **Piazza Ghiberti** are swarmed with young people carrying drinks from the few area bars. Venture too far from the main drag, however, and Santa Croce is as dead as the rest of the city.

glbt nightlife

A number of bars and clubs in this area cater to a **GLBT** clientele—however, they would prefer not to be listed in guidebooks. Many of these establishments are unmarked or tucked down alleys. If you can get yourself in the correct general vicinity, the staff at neighboring bars can usually direct you the rest of the way. For a list of gay-friendly nightlife options, contact the organization Arcigay (*www.arcigay.it*).

florence

LAS PALMAS — BAR

Largo Annigoni ☎347 27 60 033 www.laspalmasfirenze.it

Hundreds of locals pack this stretch of blacktop, transforming what may or may not qualify as a *piazza* by day into a rowdy block party by night. There's a lovely neighborhood feel here, with groups of students, families, and older folk crammed into the scores of tables covered by piles of food from the generous *aperitivo* buffet and children entertaining themselves at the foosball and table tennis games off to the side. A big stage bordering the space features performances and movies all summer as well as live screenings of sporting events.

Off of P. Ghiberti, in front of the La Nazione building. i Check website for full-season performance and screening schedule. $ Beer €5. Pizza €5-8. Primi €7-10. ⏰ Open daily May-Sept, hours vary.

SANT'AMBROGIO — BAR

P. Sant'Ambrogio 7r ☎055 24 10 35

This bar seems to single-handedly service the entire P. Sant'Ambrogio scene. And since this *piazza* is responsible for about 40% of Florentine nightlife overall, that's saying something. The plentiful outdoor seating located across the *piazza* from the bar itself spills over onto the steps of the church, creating a pleasant evening bustle. By nightfall, the whole area is full of young people sipping drinks from Sant'Ambrogio.

The piazza is at the end of V. Pietrapiana. $ Wine €4-7. Hard liquors €6-7. ⏰ Open M-Sa 8:30am-2am. Aperitivo happy hour 6-9pm.

PLAZ — CAFE, BAR

V. Pietrapiana 36r ☎055 24 20 81

Sit under a tent on this busy little *piazza* and do some quality web surfing (courtesy of free Wi-Fi) while attacking an enormous salad (*€8*) or sweet crepe (*€5*). At night the scene shifts, and you'll begin to see drunk university students stumble past as you sip an aromatic (*€9-10*).

On P. die Ciompli. $ Cover €1.50. Aperitivo buffet from €8. ⏰ Open daily 8am-3am.

KITSCH BAR

✱⅋ﾟ BAR, CONCERT VENUE

Vle. Gramsci 1r

☎055 23 43 890

If a summer evening's booze-fueled wanderings take you straying to the edge of the historic city center, a small outdoor stage featuring local musicians will probably attract you to Kitsch. On evenings that don't feature live music, you can still find a bar that, bedecked with a giant Buddha, knock-off Klimt, and patio with glowing floors, certainly lives up to the place's name.

⚑ *The traffic circle on the far right edge of your map, just above the river.* Ⓢ *Aperitivo buffet €8. Happy hour beer and cocktails €5.* Ⓣ *Open daily 6:30pm-2am. Aperitivo buffet 6:30-10:30pm. Happy hour 10pm-1am.*

I VISACCI

✱⅋ﾟ BAR

V. Borgo degli Albizi 80/82r

☎055 26 39 443

Five shots for €5 is a deal offered at a few places in town, but it's good to know which they are. This is an excellent joint for a pre-game—if you ever make it out the door after the €5 cocktails and three beers for €10.

⚑ *Coming from Duomo, take a left off Proconsolo.* Ⓢ *5 shots for €5. 3 beers for €10. Cocktails €5.* Ⓣ *Open daily 10am "till late."*

WEST OLTRARNO

▧ VOLUME

✱⅋ﾟ BAR

P. di Santo Spirito 5r

☎055 23 81 460

There's a great quirky atmosphere in this *"museo libreria caffe."* Cluttered and busy, Volume sports mismatched chairs low to the ground and stacks of books, a juke box (*€0.50 per song*) and a giant old printing press for good measure. The place is just as much about gelato and sweets as it is about cocktails, but the gelato is fancy, starting at €2.50. Don't drunkenly nibble on the cones in the display case—they're coated with something icky to keep the flies away.

⚑ *Right of the church, sandwiched between 2 larger establishments.* Ⓢ *Cocktails €7. Crepes €4-7.* Ⓣ *Open daily 11am-3am.*

POP CAFE

✱⅋ﾟ BAR

P. di Santo Spirito 18a

☎055 21 38 52 ▣www.popcafe.it

This simple setup on a lively *piazza* is enlivened by a DJ and cheap drinks. Beer, shots, and *prosecco* are all €3 at the bar, €4 at the outside tables. Non-carnivores take heed—the *aperitivo* buffet is vegetarian, as is the weekday lunch menu. Stumble back in the morning, because they proudly offer bagel sandwiches.

⚑ *To the left of the church.* Ⓢ *Beer, shots, and prosecco €3-4. Bagel sandwiches €5.* Ⓣ *Open daily 11:30am-2am.*

CABIRIA

✱⅋ﾟ BAR

P. di Santo Spirito 4

☎055 66 26 18

If you penny-pinch by always ordering the menu's cheapest item, you're in luck—all the *primi*, salads, and pizzas here are €6. Options! The *aperitivo* buffet is also a good choice. At night, the DJ blasts legit oldies, and if it gets a bit intense, the outdoor seating is plentiful but crowded.

⚑ *To the right of the church.* Ⓢ *0.5L of wine €6. Primi, salads, and pizza €6.* Ⓣ *Open daily noon-3pm and 7pm-3am. Aperitivo 7-9pm. Kitchen closes 10pm.*

EAST OLTRARNO

Far east of any part of the city you're likely to visit, East Oltrarno is where the locals go to party. Since they're real people with real jobs, things are only happening here on weekends. Investigate **Piazza Poggi**, at the base of Piazzale Michelangelo, and the area just over the **Ponte San Niccolo** to get your game on. In late summer, bars along the southern banks of the Arno enliven the entire scene.

JAMES JOYCE PUB
🚬♿🍸☁ BAR

Lungarno b. Cellini 1r ☎055 65 80 856

This enormous, popular bar is lively with students, particularly on nice weekend evenings. You don't even have to step inside to order another round of drinks—a window in the bar opens onto the patio. There's foosball and literary kitsch on the walls, and a generally local, fun vibe.

‡ On the right, following the perilous traffic circle after the Ponte San Niccolo. $ Shots €3-4. Wine from €4.50. Bottled beer €5. ⏰ Open daily until 3am.

NEGRONI
🚬♿🍸☁ BAR

V. de' Renai 17r ☎055 24 36 47 💻www.negronibar.com

This is the principal bar of the lovely P. Poggi, where patrons spill out of the official outdoor seating to populate the small green square and the banks of the Arno. The petite interior is hopping when the DJ's there or the weather's bad.

‡ On P. Poggi. $ Grappa €4. Beer €5.50. Aperitivo €7-11. ⏰ Open M-Sa 8am-2am, Su 6:30pm-2am. Aperitivo 7-11pm.

FLO
🚬🚫🍸☁ BAR

Piazzale Michelangelo 84 ☎055 65 07 91 💻www.flofirenze.com

If the climb to the Piazzale at night leaves you needing a drink to recover, check out Flo. The scene is noisy and crowded, but the view is divine. If you're staying at the camping hostel next door, then the music from Flo is likely to keep you up. Might as well join the party.

‡ To the left of the Piazzale, or take the #12 or 13 bus. $ Beer €6. Cocktails €8. ⏰ Open daily 7pm-3am.

arts and culture

You may have heard there was this Renaissance thing here once. As you might guess, this is very much a visual arts town. To read about Florence's prodigious collection of art, see **Sights.** If you're hoping to encounter art other than paintings and sculptures, head to Lucca.

CHIESA DI SANTA MARIA DE' RICCI
♿ CLASSICAL MUSIC

V. del Corso ☎055 21 50 44

An unassuming little church with a loud voice, this *chiesa* boasts a pretty spectacular pipe organ. Fortunately for the music-starved traveler, it likes to show it off. Organ vespers are played every evening at 7pm, followed by a recital of organ music from 8-10 pm. The programs are crowd pleasers—of the vast literature for organ you probably only know Bach's *Toccata and Fugue*, and the odds of hearing it here are in your favor. The performances are not exactly masterful, but they're free and very, very loud.

‡ From the Duomo, take V. dei Calzaioli south and turn left onto del V. del Corso. $ Free. ⏰ Daily vespers 7pm, recital 8pm.

STADIO ARTEMIO FRANCHI
🚬♿ SPECTATOR SPORTS

Vle. Manfredo Fanti 4/6 ☎055 58 78 58 💻www.fiorentina.it

As is true for most Italian cities, Florence has a soccer team, and that soccer team is one of the primary obsessions of the city's residents. Purple-clad Fiorentina waver on the brink of success but never quite seem to achieve it, making them a great team to support if you're more into roller-coaster rides than easy victories. Catch a game here on Sundays throughout most of the year. The stadium is mostly uncovered, though, so pick a day when it's not raining.

‡ Take bus #7, 17, or 20 or train from Santa Maria Novella to Firenze Campo Marte. The bus takes you directly to the stadium; it's a short walk from the train. i Call ahead for wheelchair-accessible

seats. ⏰ Ticket office open M-F 9:30am-12:30pm and 2:30-6:30pm. Most matches Su afternoons Sept-May.

TEATRO VERDI ♿ THEATER

V. Ghibbellina 99r ☎055 21 23 20 🖥www.teatroverdionline.it

This grand concert hall lined with box seats is home to orchestra concerts and other live music events.

*From P. Santa Croce, walk up V. Giovanni da Verazzano. **i** Credit card required for phone or online reservations. ⏰ Box office open daily 4-7pm during the theater season. Alternative box office at V. Alammani 39 (near the train station) open M-F 9:30am-7pm, Sa 9:30am-2pm.*

CALCIO STORICO ♿ SPECTATOR SPORTS

P. Santa Croce

Europeans love really rough sports. As if the English with their rugby weren't enough, the Florentines play this bizarre game with Renaissance origins. Legal moves include head-butting and choking. To figure out what on earth is going on here, head to P. Santa Croce for the three annual matches held in the third week of June. If you think you've walked into a riot, you're in the right place.

*In P. Santa Croce. **i** Check with newspapers of a tourist office for exact times. ⏰ 3rd week in June.*

shopping

Florentines cook up some of the snazziest window displays you'll ever see—you'll be tempted to stop in nearly every store you pass. If you're going to be in the city for a while, wait for the sales. The best months for shopping are January and July. As retailers prepare for the August slump, when the locals desert the city for the seashore, they chop prices drastically. Mid-July is also the season of scorching temperatures, so you'll have more than one reason to stay inside the air-conditioned stores.

OPEN-AIR MARKETS

MERCATO CENTRALE ♿ SAN LORENZO

P. Mercato Centrale

It's best to come here to eat, but you can come to sightsee too. Watch real Florentines (and clever tourists) peer at tomatoes and squeeze melons in the vast produce market. On the main floor, stalls hawk dried fruit, fresh fish, divine *mozzarella di bufala*, logs of salami, and all the other raw materials of Italian food. You don't have to just buy groceries—along the edges, counter cafes and cafeterias sell panini and lunch dishes. **Negrone** is the best bet.

*It's the huge green-and-red building in the middle of all those sidewalk vendors. **i** Some stalls accept credit cards, others don't. $ Market rate. ⏰ Open M-F 7am-2:30pm, Sa 7am-5pm.*

SAN LORENZO ♿ SAN LORENZO

San Lorenzo

Unless you're very serious about going off the beaten path, this is where you'll come for souvenir and knockoff shopping. You'll find leather bags, jackets, belts, journals, and gloves, as well as stationery, hats, tapestries, pashminas, doodads, and tourist schlock.

*The area around San Lorenzo and Mercato Centrale **i** Some are cash only, some take credit cards. ⏰ Open daily 9am-7pm.*

MERCATO NUOVO (MERCATO DEL PORCELLINO) ♿ PIAZZA DELLA SIGNORIA

P. di Mercato Nuovo

A similar selection to the San Lorenzo market can be found here, but the posher location means higher prices in this ancient marketplace. Then again, there are instances of the real deal mixed in with the knock-offs, so this is a good spot if you know enough to judge the quality of what you're looking at. Also check out the bronze boar *(il Porcellino)* and pop a coin in his drooling fountain mouth for good luck.

→ From Ponte Vecchio, take V. Santa Maria north. ℹ Most, but not all, take credit cards. ⏰ Open daily 9am-7pm.

CLOTHING

Many department stores dot the area around P. della Signoria and Santa Maria Novella. Here are some good picks for filling out a travel wardrobe with more European styles.

PROMOD — 💳♿ SAN LORENZO

V. dei Cerretani 46-48r — ☎055 21 78 44 💻www.promod.eu

Akin to H and M or Forever 21, Promod sells bargain-priced, relatively disposable current fashions. Stocks mostly women's clothing

→ Take V. Cerretani west from the Duomo. ⏰ Open daily 10am-8pm.

GOLDENPOINT — 💳♿ SAN LORENZO

V. dei Cerretani 40r — ☎055 28 42 19 💻www.goldenpointonline.com

Goldenpoint deals in women's swimsuits and lingerie. It offers no bargains, but there's a bigger selection of swimsuit sizes and styles than elsewhere. Curvy women take note: Italian swimsuits offer far better support than American styles. Other locations at V. Panzani 33 *(☎055 21 42 96)* and V. dei Calzaioli 6 *(☎055 27 76 224).*

→ Take V. Cerretani west from the Duomo. ⏰ Open daily 10am-7pm.

MASKS

The *commedia dell'arte* tradition is alive and well in Italian mask-making, and though you'll find masks to be more of a big deal in Venice, this shop is worth a visit. Chintzier options are easy to find in San Lorenzo and standard souvenir stores.

👍 ALICE'S MASKS ART STUDIO — 💳⊘ SAN LORENZO

V. Faenza 72r — ☎055 28 73 70 💻www.alicemasks.com

Even if you have no interest in buying a mask, stop by this tiny cluttered shop to ooh and ahh at the gorgeous, handmade masks for theater, panto, and Carnival. Professor Agostino Dessi and his daughter Alice have been supplying masks to major exhibitions, films, and performances since the '70s. Mask-making workshops take place the last week of every month. Email agostinodessi@tiscalinet.it for rates.

→ Between the railway station and the Medici Chapel. $ Masks from €50. 5-lesson course €500. ⏰ Open daily 9am-1pm and 3:30-7:30pm.

GOLD

You should probably do some research on how to judge the quality of gold before doing any major jewelry shopping, whether in Florence or anywhere in the world. If you think you know what you're looking at, then the Ponte Vecchio, lined with numerous goldsmiths and jewelers as well as shady street sellers, is the place for you (see **Sights**). There are also a smattering of stores around the city, including the following.

THE GOLD CORNER — 💳♿ SANTA CROCE

P. Santa Croce 15r — ☎055 24 19 71 💻www.goldcorner.it

The Gold Corner's helpful, English-speaking staff await to talk you into frivolous purchases. Many designer brands are available at this fairly busy store where you can actually get a chance to browse for a minute before being attacked by a salesperson. Only a minute, though.

→ Facing the basilica, it's on your right. ⏰ Open daily 10am-7pm.

LEATHER

Florence is famous for its soft, quality leather, but as with any luxury good, you need some amount of background knowledge before making any big purchase. If you really want to learn about leatherworking, try visiting the **Scuola del Cuoio** within the basilica of Santa Croce. Founded by the Franciscan friars in the 1930s, this leather school continues to offer courses lasting from one day to six months to anyone interested in learning the craft of leatherworking. They don't come cheap, though. Visit 💻www.scuoladelcucio.com for information, or enter their storefront in the basilica via the apse entrance at V. San Giuseppe 5r.

TORNABUONI 💳♿ DUOMO

P. Duomo 21/22r ☎055 28 01 98 💻www.tornabuonionline.com

This large leather-goods shop stocks a huge selection of purses. Prices start at several hundred euros, but they start offering discounts as soon as you walk in the door. Ask if you're contemplating a purchase.

⇞ North side of P. Duomo. $ Handbags starting around €200. ⏰ Open daily 10am-7pm.

ARTISAN GOODS

If you want the fancy handmade goods, you're going to have to pay through the nose.

✎ **FARMACEUTICA DI SANTA MARIA NOVELLA** 💳♿ SANTA MARIA NOVELLA

V. Della Scala 16 ☎055 21 62 76 💻www.smnovella.com

You can smell the talcum and perfume before setting foot in this time capsule of a perfumery. The Santa Maria Novella monks have been bottling medicines since the 13th century, but this "modern" pharmacy is straight from the Victorian age. Elixirs, perfumes, juleps, salts, spirits, waters, and protective oils are all available here, displayed on shelving and sold in packaging that has been updated little over the course of the past century. The current *farmaceutica* is still run by descendents of the 19th-century owners.

⇞ At the corner of V. della Porcellana. Coming from P. Santa Maria Novella, take a right onto V. della Scala. $ Free to browse. ⏰ Open daily 10:30am-7:30pm. In Aug, closes Sa at 1pm.

essentials [i]

PRACTICALITIES

- **TOURIST OFFICES:** Tourist Information Offices, or **Uffici Informazione Turistica,** are staffed by qualified, multilingual personnel who can provide general information about visiting Florence and city services. There are numerous locations around the city, but one of the most useful is at **Piazza Stazione 4** *(☎055 21 22 45 ⏰ Open M-Sa 8:30am-7pm, Su 8:30am-2pm.)*
- **CONSULATES: UK** *(Lungarno Corsini 2 ☎055 28 41 33).* **USA.** *(Lungarno Vespucci 38 ☎055 26 69 51).*
- **LUGGAGE STORAGE:** At Stazione di Santa Maria Novella, by platform 16. *(i Cash only. $ 1st 4hr. €4, 6th-12th hr. €0.60 per hr., then €0.20 per hr. thereafter. ⏰ Open 6am-11:50pm.)*
- **POST OFFICES:** *(V. Pellicceria 3 ☎055 27 36 481 ⇞ South of P. della Repubblica. ⏰ Open M-F 8:15am-7pm, Sa 8:15am-12:30pm.)*
- **POSTAL CODE:** 50100.

EMERGENCY!

- **POLICE: Polizia Municipale** *(☎055 32 85).* 24hr. non-emergency helpline *(☎055 32 83 333).* Help is also available for tourists at the mobile police units parked at V. de' Calzaioli near P. della Signoria and Borgo S. Jacopo in the Oltrarno near the Ponte Vecchio.
- **LATE-NIGHT PHARMACIES: Farmacia Comunale** is in Stazione Santa Maria Novella and is open 24hr. *(☎055 21 67 61).* Other 24hr. pharmacies include **Farmacia Molteni** *(V. Calzaioli 7r ☎055 21 54 72 ➔ Just north of P. della Signoria.)* and **Farmacia All'Insegna del Moro.** *(P. San Giovanni 20r ☎055 21 13 43 ➔ A little east of the Duomo.)*
- **HOSPITALS/MEDICAL SERVICES: Ospedale Santa Maria Nuova** near the Duomo has a 24hr. emergency room *(P. Santa Maria Nuova 1 ☎055 27 581).* Tourist medical services can be found at V. Lorenzo Il Magnifico 59. *(☎055 47 54 11 ➔ In the north of the city, near P. Liberta.)*

GETTING THERE ✈

By Plane

Aeroporto Amerigo Vespucci. *(V. del Termine 11 ☎055 30 615 main line; 055 30 61 700 for 24hr. automated service 🖥www.aeroporto.firenze.it ℹ For lost baggage, call ☎055 3061302.)* From the airport, the city can be reached via the **VolainBus shuttle.** Pick up the shuttle from the Departures side—exit the airport and look to the right. Drop off is at Santa Maria Novella station. *($ €5. ⏰ 25min., every 30min. 5:30am-11:30pm.)*

By Train

Stazione Santa Maria Novella will likely be both your entry point to and exit point from the city. The ticket station is open daily 6am-9pm. Self-service kiosks are available 24hr. The Information Ofice is next to track 5. *(⏰ Open daily 7am-9pm.)* Luggage storage is by platform 16 (see **Practicalities**). Trains run to and from **Bologna** *($ €42. ⏰ 37min., 2 per hr. 7am-10:35pm.),* **Milan** *($ €52. ⏰ 1¾hr., 1 per hr. 7am-9pm.),* **Rome** *($ €44. ⏰ 95min., 2 per hr. 7am-10:45pm.),* **Siena** *($ €6.20. ⏰ 90min., 6 per hr. 8:10am-8:10pm.),* **Venice** *($ €42. ⏰ 2hr., 2 per hr. 8:30am-8:30pm.),* and numerous local destinations.

By Bus

Three major intercity bus companies run out of Florence. **SITA** *(V. Santa Caterina da Siena 17 ☎800 37 37 60 🖥www.sita-on-line.it)* runs buses from **Siena, San Gimignano,** and other Tuscan destinations. **LAZZI** *(P. Stazione 4/6r ☎055 215155; for timetable info ☎055 35 10 61 🖥www.lazzi.it)* buses depart from P. Adua, just east of the train station. Routes connect to **Lucca, Pisa,** and many other local towns. **CAP-COPIT** *(Largo Fratelli Alinari 10 ☎055 21 46 37 🖥www.capautolinee.it)* runs to local towns. Timetables for all three companies change regularly, so call ahead or check online before traveling.

GETTING AROUND

By Bus

Since buses are the only public transportation in Florence, they are surprisingly clean, reliable, and easy to manage. Not to mention adorably orange and tiny! They are operated by **ATAF** and **LHNEA.** Buy a ticket before boarding from most newsstands and tabacconists, from a ticket vending machine, or from the ATAF kiosk in P. Stazione *(☎800 42 45 00 $ 90min. ticket €1.20, €2 if purchased on board; 24hr. €5; 3-day €12.)* Time-stamp your ticket when you board the bus—there are sporadic ticket checks, and if you forget, are caught without a stamped ticket, or can't successfully play the "confused foreigner" card, it's a €50 fine. You're unlikely to need to use the buses unless you're leaving the city center. The network is extensive, with several night-owl buses taking over for the regular routes in the late evenings, so if you are venturing out of town, pick up a schematic bus map from the ATAF kiosk or use the trip planner at ◼www.ataf.net.

Unlike most city bus systems, Florence's is organized well enough that you can travel on the fly. Every bus stop is named, as in a Metro system, and the name is posted clearly on top of the bus stop, making it possible to identify your stop even if you don't know what it looks like. At each bus stop, the entire schedule for every line that stops there is posted on the pole. The top of the schedule tells you what direction the bus is going when it stops there (San Marco to La Fonte is outbound, La Fonte to San Marco is inbound). Then there is a list of every stop, in order, so you can identify whether this particular bus is going where you need to be. A simple 24hr. diagram tells you at what minutes in each hour the bus will stop. Most buses originate at either P. Stazione or P. San Marco. #12 and #13 run to the Piazzale Michelangelo. #7 runs to Fiesole.

By Taxi

To call a cab, try calling ☎055 4390, 055 4499, 055 4242, or 055 4798. Tell the operator your location and when you want the cab, and the nearest available car will be sent to you. Designated cab stands can be found at P. Stazione, Fortezza da Basso, and P. della Repubblica. Cabs between fares can also often be found at Santa Maria Novella.

By Bike

It takes some confidence to bike in the crowded parts of central Florence, but cycling is a great way to check out a longer stretch of the Arno's banks or to cover a lot of territory in a fast-paced day. **Mille E Una Bici** (☎055 65 05 295) rents out 200 bikes in four locations, and they can be picked up and returned at any of four locations: P. Stazione, P. Santa Croce, P. Ghiberti, and Stazione F.S. Campo Di Marte. **Florence By Bike** (V. San Zanobi 91r and 120-122r ☎055 48 89 92 ◼www.florencebybike.it) is another good resource. Staff will help renters plan routes, whether for an afternoon or for a multi-day trip outside of town.

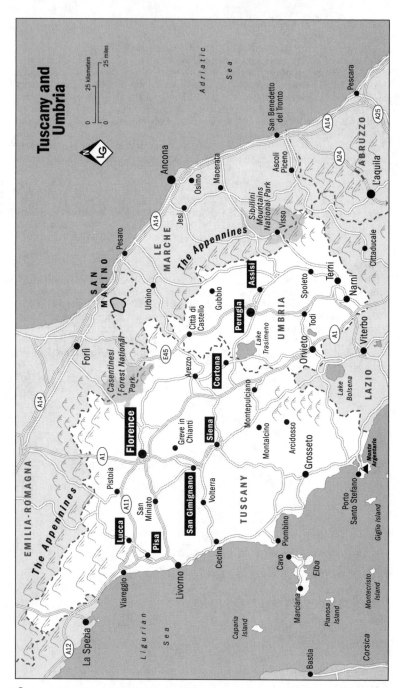

Tuscany and
Umbria

0   25 kilometers
0   25 miles

Adriatic
Sea

Pescara

San Benedetto
del Tronto

A25

ABRUZZO

A24

L'Aquila

Ascoli
Piceno

Cittaducale

Ancona

Macerata

Narni

A14

Osimo

Visso

Sibillini
Mountains
National Park

Terni

Jesi

The Appennines

Spoleto

Viterbo

A1

Pesaro

LE
MARCHE

Assisi

Todi

SAN
MARINO

Urbino

Perugia

Orvieto

Gubbio

UMBRIA

LAZIO

Città di
Castello

Lake
Trasimeno

Lake
Bolsena

Forlì

Casentinesi
Forest National
Park

E45

Arezzo

Cortona

A14

Montepulciano

Monte
Argentario

Florence

Greve in
Chianti

Siena

Montalcino

Arcidosso

Porto
Santo Stefano

Giglio Island

EMILIA-ROMAGNA

A1

Pistoia

San
Gimignano

Volterra

Grosseto

A11

San
Miniato

TUSCANY

Lucca

Pisa

Cecina

Piombino

Cavo

Elba

The Appennines

Viareggio

Livorno

Marciana

Pianosa
Island

Montecristo
Island

La Spezia

A12

Caparia
Island

Ligurian
Sea

Corsica

Bastia

TUSCANY AND UMBRIA

Central Italy is considered one of the most romantic destinations in the world. Maybe it's all the wine, or the rolling green hills, the narrow medieval streets, the incredible panoramic views in every direction...It's all a bit swoon-inducing. Don't worry though: Tuscany and Umbria are more than just a region-sized honeymoon suite. Full of incredible architecture and intense local pride, the towns and cities that dot the area boast a unique and often gory history. (For many centuries, the towns were locked in battle to the death.) Some features are shared by all—the soaring Duomo, the occasional Etruscan ruin, a unifying resentment of Florence—but these cities are not interchangable.

There's **Siena** and its centuries of neighborhood rivalries that explode in the biannual Palio. Famous **Pisa** has a lot more to its name than a certain tilty tower. **Lucca** is green and slow paced, with the sound of Puccini spilling nightly onto its incredible walls. The streets of **Cortona** are so steep that some of its buildings' basements boast panoramic views, and the similarly vertical streets of **San Gimignano** catch the heels of ritzy tourists by the zillions. **Assisi** is a sun-drenched, ancient city of devotion, while neighboring **Perugia** delivers a zippy blend of nightlife, jazz, and chocolate. There's no need to squash every central Italian city into a single trip, and an attempt to hit six in a week will make them all seem a standardized, scenic blur. Take your time. After all, these hills and stones have been here for millennia—they're not going anywhere.

greatest hits

- **AS LUCCA WOULD HAVE IT.** The whole city of Lucca gets the *Let's Go* thumbs up. Within its city walls lies the perfect Tuscan town (p. 342).

- **LEAN ON ME.** It might be the most famous sight in Italy, but that doesn't mean you won't gasp the first time you lay eyes on Pisa's greatest structural failure (p. 334).

- **A LITTLE BIT CAMPO.** Siena's central square (p. 325) offers it all: beautiful buildings, nice restaurants, sociable nightlife, and crazy wild horse races based on ancient and bitter rivalries. Who could ask for more?

student life

Unsurprisingly, the seven cities in this chapter differ markedly in their student life. San Gimignano, Lucca, and Assisi? Kind of quiet. Pisa and Perugia? Rocking. Siena and Cortona? Somewhere in between. So, if you're more interested in hanging out with students than in medieval monasteries or Renaissance towers, choose your destination carefully. And if you do so, the possibilities are great. Pisa is the obvious highlight. With three universities placed into a medium-sized city, the youth culture is extremely prominent. Try P. delle Vettogaglie for great nightlife. Cortona is another, surprisingly lively, student town. In this rather random home of the University of Georgia's satellite campus, the population of American study abroad students goes through the roof come summer. From Cortona, stumble (or take the train) to Perugia, the Umbrian capital and owner of the largest student population between Bologna and Rome. Come during the school year if you want to experience its great nightlife scene. If you find yourself here in the summer, expand your artistic appreciation by taking in the Perugia jazz festival. It may not be a classic student attraction, but now's the time to broaden your horizons. Or, see how long you can convince a stranger you're actually a performer taking a break, then engage them in conversation on bass solos. If they see through your charade, who cares, you've got six other cities to head to and million more gullible Italians to fool.

siena ☎0577

Thanks to the biannual Palio, Siena shares a reputation with Spain's Pamplona for being a city that's completely crazy two days of the year and asleep the other 363. That's really not a fair rep though, because the Sienese provide plenty to see even when they aren't racing bareback around Il Campo. Take the steep pedestrian-only streets of Siena's *centro*, for one. The completely befuddling medieval layout is Tuscany taken to its illogical—and seriously charming—extreme. Amid the trapped-in-time Gothic architecture, you'll find that Siena is also a respectable university town with a campus indistinguishable from the city around it—you'll only realize you're at the university when you poke into a church and discover it's actually a Linguistics department. Offering pleasant Campo-centric nightlife, relative freedom from overwhelming Florentine tourist crowds, and a twisty jumble of streets hiding secrets that will take a semester to unlock, Siena is perhaps the best study-abroad city in Tuscany—and one of the best to visit as well.

ORIENTATION

First of all, you should know that the train station is far away from the town center. Exit the station and follow the signs to the bottom of the parking garage, where you can catch a bus to the *centro*—look at the digital display board to see which bus is on its way and whether it's going where you need it to. That being said, you should try to arrive in Siena by bus instead of rail. Almost all intercity buses arrive in **Piazza Matteotti**, in the northwest of the *centro*. The upper part of this *piazza* opens up onto a park-like area and then the **Fortezza Medicea,** an old fortress. Walk in the direction your bus was going in order to head deeper into the *centro*, where you will soon see many direction signs for **Il Campo,** the Duomo, and a variety of hotels. You will depend on these signs heavily during your time in Siena. The printed maps available around town often try to iron things out a little bit for legibility purposes, but take a look at

Siena on an online map to get a frightening sense of the curling dead-ends and streets that wander uphill and lead nowhere. Good luck. Just remember that Il Campo is in the center and then try to remember how you got there—that way, you should be able to find your way home again afterward.

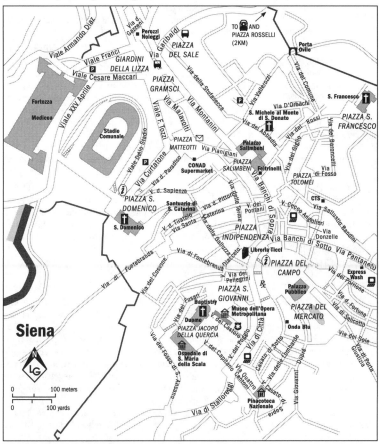

ACCOMMODATIONS

We are sad to report that there are exactly eight dormitory beds in the entirety of Siena. Solo travelers had better nab one of those eight in advance or daytrip from elsewhere. If you have a friend with whom to share a bed-and-breakfast double, however, there are quite a few good options. No matter what you're looking for, you need to plan ahead when trying to visit in early July or early August—at these times, every room in the city is booked (and has been months in advance) for the Palio. The period in late August between the two races is pretty quiet though, and rooms will rent at mid-season rates.

CASA DI ANTONELLA

B AND B ❸

V. delle Terme 72

☎339 30 04 883 ✉anto.landi@libero.it

You'll feel like you've scored your own flat at this hands-off B and B where check-in consists of wandering inside to find the room marked by a Post-it with your name on it. Although the owner, Antonella, only comes round to prepare breakfast, you won't be lacking for anything in the six airy, comfortable double rooms with lovely ceiling frescoes, oscillating fans, and shared bath. Plus, there's no one to stop you from using the kitchen.

➜ *From P. Matteotti, take V. dei Termini and then turn right onto the parallel V. delle Terme.* ***i*** *Breakfast included.* Ⓢ *Doubles €50-60.*

SIENA IN CENTRO
💳♿📶 B AND B [3]

V. di Stalloreggi 14-16 ☎0577 43 041 💻www.bbsienaincentro.com

Three B and B properties are bundled together as Siena in Centro. All boast similar decoration and amenities. Casa del Giglio, with ornate headboards and fancy curtains, is the nicest, but Casa del Conte and B and B dei Rossi are lovely as well. Each of the properties' breakfast nooks feel cozy, but there is little other common space. The reception for all three, which are a short distance from one another, can be found at V. di Stalloreggi.

➜ *For reception, follow signs from the Duomo to the Pinacoteca but bear right onto V. di Stalloreggi.* ***i*** *Breakfast included. Bike rental and laundry service available. Internet access only at reception.* Ⓢ *Singles €40-80; doubles €60-120; triples €90-150.*

PICCOLO HOTEL ETRUSIA
💳♿❄ HOTEL [3]

V. delle Donzelle 3 ☎0577 28 80 88 💻www.hoteletruria.com

Look for an ivy-covered entryway to find this pleasant little hotel with a comfortable sitting area. The hotel keeps a 1am curfew, but a few of the rather straightforward rooms have a separate entrance from the street. Request these at booking if you would like to avoid an early bedtime.

➜ *North of V. Banchi di Sotto. In the area north of Il Campo, there are signs directing you here.* ***i*** *Breakfast €6.* Ⓢ *Singles €40-50, with bath €45-55; doubles as singles €60-70, doubles with bath €80-110; triples €90-138. Extra bed €10-28.* ⏰ *Reception 7am-1am.*

YHA OSTELLO DI SIENA
🚭♿📶 HOSTEL [1]

V. Fiorentina 89 ☎0577 52 212 💻www.ostellosiena.com

Sadly, Siena's one hostel barely counts as a hostel, and it's barely in Siena. Offering mostly double rooms and a single eight-bed dormitory, the place is a 15min. bus ride from the *centro*. What it lacks in location it also lacks in character—it's a standard-issue hostel, with bathrooms that are clean-ish and rooms that are nice-ish, but if you're shlepping outside the *centro*, you'd like to be getting a little more than this. Pity it's the only game in town. Attention aspiring entrepreneurs: head to Siena and open a hostel. You'd make a fortune.

➜ *From train station, take bus #77 or 4. From the centro take #10, 15, or 77. Ask the driver to let you off at the ostello.* ***i*** *Breakfast included. Limited Wi-Fi.* Ⓢ *Dorms €20; doubles €40.* ⏰ *Reception 24hr.*

CAMPING SIENA COLLEVERDE
💳♿ CAMPING [2]

Strada Shiacciapensieri 47 ☎0577 33 40 80 💻www.sienacamping.com

It's neither near the *centro* nor is it rustic, but if you're here for a while and really pinching pennies, this campsite may do the trick. The mobile home accommodations are all private, which is good because you're in rather close quarters. On the bright side, the grounds are spacious, with a big swimming pool, a bar, and a market, and the RVs have private baths—to really take it up a notch, get one with a kitchenette too. Be warned that you are not within walking distance of the *centro*, and the last bus runs before midnight. This lodging option is best if you have your own transportation or no interest in hitting the town after hours.

➜ *If on foot, do not follow the Camping signs from the train station. These signs are for cars and will take you the long way. Walk to the nearby bridge over the train tracks and cross it. There's a big intersection—take the right-hand fork, Strada di Malizia, where you will be walking against the traffic. The street twists around in the beginning, but otherwise it is a straight km to the campsite.* $ *2- to 5-person RV €45, with kitchenette €65-115; tents €5.70-6.70; campers €12.50-13.80.* ⏰ *Reception 24hr.*

SIGHTS

You'll find a wealth of things to see in Siena, but the biggest attractions are **Il Campo** and the area around the **Duomo.** The six sights of the Duomo complex—Duomo, Baptistery, Crypt, Museo dell'Opera, Santa Maria della Scala, and Museo Diocesano—can be visited with a single cumulative ticket, available at the ticket booth to the right of the cathedral up until 30min. before the sights close. The ticket is valid for 48hr. from first use, so you don't even have to cram all the sights into one day, and with the exception of the Museo Diocesano, they are all helpfully clustered in the same *piazza.* At €12 regular and €5 for students, this is one of the best cumulative-ticket deals in the region. The cathedral, crypt, and Santa Maria della Scala are particularly worth visiting. Call ahead for specific accessibility information for the different venues.

IL CAMPO — ♿ PIAZZA

P. del Campo

Originally conceived as a space for large civic events, Il Campo continues to be the heart of the *centro.* During the twice-annual **Palio,** this shell-shaped *piazza* is crammed with as many bodies as can be packed into its boundaries when the famous horse race tears around the square's outer edge. Even without the Palio, the *piazza* hums with the life of the town. By day, Il Campo is a restaurant-lined expanse of gently slanted, sun-warmed brick—a surprisingly nice place for a snooze, considering you're essentially napping in the middle of the street. For fun, watch the tourists meandering through the *piazza,* which has no obvious walking routes and could likely generate some interesting randomized-traffic data. You know, if you think randomized-traffic data is interesting. In the evenings, Il Campo is transformed into a communal patio, as the students of Siena plop themselves on the brick in small clusters to drink and hang out until the early hours.

Follow the ubiquitous signs pointing you to Il Campo.

DUOMO — ♿ CHURCH

P. Duomo 8 — ☎0577 28 30 48 💻www.operaduomo.siena.it

Of the many impressive cathedrals in Tuscany, Siena's Duomo might be the

in-siena-ty

Pretty much everwhere in the world thinks it has the best sports fans. People worship their own sports god. They follow your team "religiously," and consider themselves part of the be-jerseyed devout. They think they're better than the people on the other side of the stadium. Well, they're all wrong, because they aren't from Siena.

Twice a year, Siena plays host to the *Palio di Siena,* a horse race so epic that it blurs the line between enthusiasm and clinical insanity in every one of the town's residents. In these events, reason is suspended in favor of uncensored fanatic fervor, with each neighborhood racing its own horse through an incredibly dangerous course in Il Campo, where the horse that finishes first, with or without a jockey, is declared the victor. And though these races attract tourists from around the world, don't doubt that the Palio remains a largely local affair. Indeed, over the centuries, rivalries between neighborhoods have only become stronger, and the fans only more devout. How many towns, we ask you, baptize their children in fountains that represent their equine loyalties? In Siena they do, and if you want to see real fanatical fandom, this is the place to be in late July or early August.

best. The first thing you notice is the floor—or rather, the abundant metal posts cordoning off chunks of the floor to stop distracted tourists from trampling over the large marble cartoons underfoot. The earlier examples from the 14th century use a technique called *graffito*—thin grooves were chiseled out of slabs of white marble and then filled in with black *stucco*, creating an image worthy of a coloring book. The later examples also use marble inlay to create richly colored designs that almost look as if they had been painted. Overhead, carved busts of centuries of popes look down on visitors. Imagine what *they* talk about at night. Turn around to check out the beautiful stained-glass representation of the Last Supper. Off the left aisle, the small, richly adorned **Piccolomini Library** displays an excellent collection of graduals and illuminated manuscripts. And don't skip the gift shop, which has a rather nice selection of stationery modeled on the library's illuminated manuscript collection. Sadly, no one has yet been clever enough to turn those *graffito* designs into a proper coloring book.

⚜ *Follow the ever-present signs. Ticket booth is on the right of the cathedral.* Ⓢ *€3. Combined ticket with other Duomo sights €12, students €5.* Ⓩ *Open June-Aug M-Sa 10:30am-8pm, Su 1:30-6pm; Sept-Nov M-Sa 10:30am-7:30pm, Su 1:30-5:30pm; Nov-Feb M-Sa 10:30am-6:30pm, Su 1:30-5:30pm; Mar-May M-Sa 10:30am-7:30pm, Su 1:30-5:30pm.*

SANTA MARIA DELLA SCALA
⚑♿ MUSEUM

P. Duomo 1 ☎0577 53 45 11 🖳www.santamariadellascala.com

Actively tending to pilgrims, the poor, and the orphaned for over a millennium, the Santa Maria della Scala complex is one of the oldest hospitals in Europe. It was also a mighty and wealthy institution, the city's third-biggest site for artistic installations after the Duomo and **Palazzo Pubblico.** Today, the building is no longer in use as a hospital—instead, it is currently under renovation to become the new home of the city's Pinacoteca in 2013. Sadly, you'll find little on display relating to the building's fascinating history. One brilliantly frescoed ward displays a photograph of the same ward in the early part of the century, when a row of cots stood under the same frescoes. For even more reductiveness, check out the second-to-last fresco on the right, which illustrates a scene in this very ward from many centuries before. Another notable section of the complex is the church of **Santissima Annunziata**—an enormous 1730 painting of a scene from the Gospel of John fills the church's entire apse. Unlike much 18th-century work in the region, this one actually looks like it's from 1730. The complex's many other galleries are filled with the permanent collection from the hospital's history as well as rotating exhibits from the Pinacoteca and elsewhere. If you want to learn more about the Palio, check out the small exhibit of contrada flags and other ephemera related to the famous race in the lower level.

⚜ *Across from the entrance to the Duomo.* ℹ *Individual tickets available at the museum, combined tickets at the general Duomo ticket booth.* Ⓢ *€5.50, students €3. Combined ticket with other Duomo sights €12, students €5.* Ⓩ *Open daily 10:30am-6:30pm.*

CRYPT
⚑♿ CHURCH

P. Duomo ☎0577 28 30 48 🖳www.operaduomo.siena.it

The crypt is not actually a crypt, but you can see why they thought it was when they discovered the space during a 1999 excavation. Imagine digging along the outer edge of a cathedral to lay some new pipes and suddenly breaking into an underground cavern lined with 13th-century frescoes, still brightly colored thanks to centuries of being sealed off. That's a tale to tell at your next dinner party. Visiting the discovery today, you walk through the crypt on a false floor several feet above the real one, with windows underfoot allowing you to see the brickwork and floor of the cavern as it was found. It's quite a nifty space.

⚜ *Just past the ticket booth, on the left.* Ⓢ *€6. Combined ticket with other Duomo sights €12,* *students €5. ☑ Open daily June-Aug 9am-8pm; Sept-Oct 9:30am-7pm; Nov-Feb 10am-5pm; Mar-May 9:30am-7pm.*

MUSEO DELL'OPERA
♥�§ MUSEUM

P. Duomo ☎0577 28 30 48 ▣www.operaduomo.siena.it

The Duomo's museum houses Sienese masterpieces that were once displayed in the cathedral, including an excellent collection of statues of prophets by Pisano. On the upper floors, check out a beautiful silver rosebush and a jumble of reliquaries that hold bits of saints. Follow the signs to the **Facciatone,** at the end of the Hall of Vestments. A staircase inside the wall leads to what would have been the top of the facade of the New Cathedral had construction not been halted by the Black Death in 1348. From here, enjoy a splendid view of the city and the surrounding mountains. It's also enjoyable to look down on Il Campo and watch all the little tourists scurrying about.

🌗 *Opposite the Duomo, on the left. ⑤ €6. Combined ticket with other Duomo sights €12, students €5. ☑ Open daily June-Aug 9am-8pm; Sept-Oct 9:30am-7pm; Nov-Feb 10am-5pm; Mar-May 9:30am-7pm.*

BAPTISTERY
♥⊗ CHURCH

P. San Giovanni ☎0577 28 30 48 ▣www.operaduomo.siena.it

This building where, for centuries, Sienese children were baptized is small but sumptuously decorated, with a ceiling fresco illustrating the Apostles' Creed and a 15th-century marble, bronze, and enamel baptismal font. The polychrome marble exterior is quite grand and a worthwhile pairing with the Duomo.

🌗 *From the ticket booth, ahead and downstairs. ⑤ €3. Combined ticket with other Duomo sights €12, students €5. ☑ Open daily June-Aug 9am-8pm; Sept-Oct 9:30am-7pm; Nov-Feb 10am-5pm; Mar-May 9:30am-7pm.*

PALAZZO PUBBLICO AND TORRE DEL MANGIA
♥⊗ MUSEUM, PALAZZO

P. Il Campo 1 ☎0577 29 26 14 ▣www.comune.siena.it/main.asp?id=885

This grandiose town hall, whose construction began in 1297, forms the lower wall of Il Campo. Built to show up hotshot Florence, the tower here is slightly taller than that of its rival's. (Proving that size doesn't matter, Siena was decimated by the Black Death shortly after the tower's completion, while Florence went on to become the birthplace of the Renaissance.) Insecure in more ways than one, the civic government then passed ordinances preventing citizens from building anything that would rival the *palazzo* in size, so the tower still looms mightily over the surrounding area, which you can observe from the view inside the tower itself. The *palazzo* is also home to the **Museo Civico,** which showcases the building's elaborate frescoes and architecture, including a chapel with a fantastic wood-carved choir and a series of paintings illustrating the unification of Italy. Upstairs, a broad loggia overlooks the southern quarter of the city. The Palazzo Pubblico continues to function as a legislative house, so you may find this gallery populated with politicans in suits having a smoke. The chambers themselves are not open to tourists, but if the doors off the loggia happen to be open, poke your head in to catch a glimpse of Sienese government at work.

🌗 *It's the big thing at the bottom of Il Campo. ⑤ Museum €7.50, students €4. Tower €8. Both €13. ☑ Museum open Mar 16-Oct 10am-7pm; Nov-Mar 15 10am-6pm. Tower open Mar-Oct 15 10am-7pm; Oct 16-Feb 10am-4pm. Last entry 45min. before close.*

FONTEBRANDA
⊗ FOUNTAIN

V. di Fontebranda

The creation of this ancient fountain in medieval Siena fundamentally re-centered the city's social life and managed to score a mention in Dante's *Inferno.* First constructed in 1081 and then rebuilt in 1246, the covered fountain was originally divided into three basins. The spillover from each filled the next, with the first for drinking water, the second for watering animals, and the third for mills and other industrial uses. Although the water in the fountain today is non-potable, it is still fresh—on a hot summer day, the area around the water's surface radiates coolness.

Follow signs to Santuario di Santa Caterina, then continue downhill on the sanctuary's left. The fountain will be on your right, down a few stairs. $ Free.

FORTEZZA MEDICEA ♿ FORTRESS

P. della Liberta

No Tuscan town is complete without a fortress, and Siena delivers this well-maintained example. A grassy path around the top is one of the only good jogging locations in town (not to mention some of the only grass), and the views of the sunset and the rest of the city are fantastic. In the summer, the amphitheater seating in the courtyard is host to movie screenings.

From P. Matteotti, take Vle. Tozzi and Vle. Maccari north around the stadium. You'll see the fortress. $ Free.

FOOD

Thanks to Siena's slightly higher population of homegrown residents than those of similar Tuscan cities, the town has a large number of groceries and delis—great news for cheapskates. Avoid the restaurants that border Il Campo unless you want to pay €9 for a bowl of pasta.

LA PIZZERIA DI NONNO MEDE ♿ 🍸 PIZZERIA 2

V. Camporeggio 21 ☎0577 24 79 66

It takes a little bit of effort to find this pizzeria, but that's because it's hiding itself for the locals. There's a bunch of patio seating overlooking the town skyline, and on clear summer evenings, every inch of that seating will be packed: make a reservation or expect to wait for a table. The pizza menu is the big draw. This is the place to try an adventurous topping situation—the apple-gorgonzola white pizza is particularly impressive.

There are stairs behind Fontebranda that lead uphill and to the right—they'll take you directly to the pizzeria. Or from Casa di Santa Caterina, if you're facing it, take the street that's on the right and follow it until it opens out onto the piazza. $ Cover €1.60. Pizza €5-7.50. Primi €6-7.50. 🕐 Open daily noon-3:30pm and 7pm-1am.

LA FONTANA DELLA FRUTTA ♿ 🍸 GROCERY 1

V. delle Terme 65-67 ☎0577 40 422

For a budget lunch, you can't beat the takeout counter at this corner grocer. The packaged goods and produce are reasonably priced and lovely, but head to the counter for excellent cold pastas, stuffed tomatoes, sauces, and vegetable dishes sold by the kilogram. Split several quarter-kilos of different cold pastas, grab a couple of table-wine juiceboxes, ask for some plastic utensils, and have a lovely picnic on Il Campo while laughing at the fools burning money in the real restaurants.

At the corner of V. Santa Caterina. $ Most of the cold pastas run around €11 per kg. 🕐 Open daily 8am-8pm.

SALE E PEPE ♿ 🍸 RISTORANTE 1

V. Garibaldi 23 ☎0577 60 00 89 www.ristorantesalepepe.it

This extremely affordable dinner option is making a funny in its name—it's just off Piazza del Sale, you see, and Sale e Pepe means salt and pepper. Not laughing? A better reason to eat here are the dozen pastas that come with 0.5L of water and a coffee *(€5.50)*. They have a nice bread list as well and are probably the only restaurant in Italy that charges supermarket price for bottled water.

Off P. del Sale. $ Pasta, secondo, water, and coffee €10. Breads €3.50. 1L of wine €4.50. 🕐 Open daily 11am-11pm.

SAVINI 🍴♿ BAKERY ❶

V. dei Montanini 9 ☎055 91 21 61 🖥www.dolcezzesavini.com

Since 1959, this bakery has been producing delicious Sienese specialties like *panforte*, a sort of trail mix from the Crusades now sold by the paper-wrapped block, and *ricciarelli*, sugary almond cookies. Savini now has locations in half a dozen Tuscan cities. Plenty of cookies, cakes, and other pastries are available as well. There's no seating, but the clothing shop across the street has a beanbag out front.

From P. Gramsci take V. Cavallerizzo, then turn right onto Montanini. $ Most pastries €1-2.50; also sold by the kg. ⏰ Open M-Sa 7:30am-7:30pm, Su 8am-1pm.

LA COMPAGNIA DEI VINATTIERI ENOTECA ❷

V. Delle Terme 79 ☎0577 23 65 68 🖥www.vinattieri.net

This *enoteca* is quite literally a wine cellar. Walk down a flight of stairs to reach the stone-walled dining room lined with their selection of 100 wines from around the world. The layout is welcoming, with large tables for joining strangers and a piano. During dinner hours you can get pastas and other dishes, and when the kitchen is closed, cheese and meat assortments are available to complement your wine tastings. Occasionally jazz combos and other music groups perform, so check the website.

At the corner of V. dei Pittori. $ Pastas €9-10. Wine from €3. ⏰ Open daily noon-midnight.

NIGHTLIFE

There are plenty of nice bars in Siena, but the cheerful efforts of the student population have brought about a true BYOB scene. Pick up a couple of bottles and head to Il Campo for the nightly block party. The tourist-trappy restaurants surrounding the *piazza* become tourist-trappy bars at night, so load up elsewhere to avoid €8 pints.

SAN PAOLO PUB 🍴 PUB

Vicolo San Paolo 2 ☎0577 22 66 22 🖥www.sanpaolopub.com

For reasonably priced drinks and food that's *almost* on Il Campo—if you sit outside and crane your neck a bit, it's like you're there—this alleyway pub is your best bet. It's small enough to seem crowded all day, and the alley allows for spillover when the place is legitimately crowded at night. The extensive sandwich menu is a big draw, with 40 excellent sandwiches costing only €3.50.

In a little covered alley, just off Il Campo—it's one of the streets directly opposite the Palazzo. $ Beer €4.20. Cocktails €5. Hot and cold sandwiches €3.50. ⏰ Open daily noon-2am. Aperitivo buffet 6-8pm.

ENOTECA ITALIANA ♿ ENOTECA

P. Libertà 1 ☎0577 22 88 11 🖥www.enoteca-italiana.it

Unique to Italy, the Enoteca Italiana is a public institution founded in 1960 to educate the people about Italian wine and wineries. The collection includes over 1600 different wines—1607 at last count, according to one waiter—which are presented on a rotating tasting menu each week. At €11, they're fairly reasonable, considering you're getting educated and tipsy at the same time. For further enlightenment, check out the small wine museum where you can discover the origins of the vintages currently on offer, sign up for one of their wine-tasting classes, or, if you're really classy, speak with one of their consultants about additions to your personal cellar.

Inside Fortezza Medicea, on the left. $ Tasting menu of 2 glasses of wine €11. ⏰ Open M-Sa noon-1am.

CAFFE DEL CORSO 🍴♿ BAR

V. Banchi di Sopra 25 ☎0577 22 66 56 🖥www.caffedelcorsosiena.it

If you've been mystified by Italian distinctions between different types of mixed drinks, then Caffe del Corso is here to help! One wall of this corner pub is covered with the drink list, helpfully divided into categories like *aperitivi* (Bloody Mary, martini, cosmo), after-dinners (margarita, Sidecar, whiskey sour), and long drinks (Screwdriver, Gin Fizz, mojito). The drinks may have lots of distinctions, but they have one thing in common—they all cost €5. Play the "what category is a Long Island Iced Tea?" game (long drink) from the sidewalk seating, where you can see that drink list and order from it through a large window looking into the bar. There is more seating upstairs, where you might consider grabbing a pizza off the dinner menu.

➜ 2 blocks up from Il Campo, on the right. $ Cocktails €5. Pizza €5-7. ⏰ Open Tu-Su 8:30am-3am. Kitchen closes at midnight.

DUBLIN POST 🎵♿📶🍸☀ IRISH PUB

P. Gramsci 20/21 ☎0577 28 90 89 💻www.dublinpost.it

Yet another Irish pub in Italy. You know the drill. This one has a lot of outdoor seating. It's outdoor seating on the bus-stop *piazza*, to be sure, but at least you can watch people leaving town—perhaps they're en route to the real Dublin, where the Guinness isn't a ridiculous €6.

➜ Directly across from the end of the line for all buses. ℹ Frequent live music. Free W-Fi. $ Beer pints €5. ⏰ Open M-Sa noon-1am, Su 3pm-1am. Happy hour 6-9pm.

ESSENTIALS

Practicalities

- **TOURIST OFFICES: APT Siena** provides maps for a small fee. Also has pamphlets, brochures, and a bookstore. *(P. del Campo 56 ☎0577 28 05 51 💻www.terresiena.it ➜ Right in Il Campo; look for the"i.")*
- **LAUNDROMATS: OndaBlu** is a self-service wash and dry and also has a Wi-Fi point. *(V. del Casato di Sotto 17 ☎516 25 68 98 💻www.ondablu.com ➜ Just off Il Campo.)*
- **POST OFFICES: Poste Italiane.** *(P. Matteotti 37 ☎0577 21 42 95 ➜ Just past the main bus stops. ⏰ Open M-F 8:15am-7pm, Sa 8:15am-1:30pm.)*

Emergency!

- **POLICE:** *(V. del Castoro 1 ➜ Near the Duomo.)*
- **LATE-NIGHT PHARMACIES:** Several pharmacies in the *centro* share a late-night rotation–visit any one of them to check the rotation board outside and get the number of the pharmacy on duty. The easiest to find is **Farmacia del Campo.** *(V. di Cittá 15 ☎0577 28 02 34 ➜ 1 block off Il Campo, far side of the Palazzo.)*
- **HOSPITALS/MEDICAL SERVICES: Santa Maria alle Scotte.** *(Vicolo delle Scotte 14 ☎0577 58 51 11 ➜ Take bus #3 or 77 from P. Gramsci. ⏰ Open 24hr.)*

Getting There

Siena is surprisingly difficult to reach. Coming from Florence is easy, but if you're arriving from elsewhere, you're almost certainly going to have to transfer trains or buses at least once.

By Bus

Siena is one of the few Italian towns that possesses a train station but might actually be better reached by bus. From Florence at least. **TRA-IN/SITA** *(☎0577 42 46 💻www.trainspa.it)* buses drop off in P. Antonio Gramsci, about 5min. north of P. del Campo. (Some also drop off at the train station, see below.) The ticket office is in the underground terminal. *(⏰ Open 7am-7pm.)* From **Florence.** *($ €6.80. ⏰ 90min., at least 1 per hr.)*

By Train

The train station is in **Piazza Rosselli,** 15min. outside town by bus #3, 4, 7, 8, 10, 17, or 77. *(Ticket office open daily 6:30am-1:10pm and 1:40-8:10pm.)* Trains arrive from **Florence** *($ €6.30. ⏰ 90min., every hr. 8am-8pm.)* and Poggibonsi. *($ €2.40. ⏰ 30min., 2 per hr.)*

Getting Around

Although Siena has an extensive **bus** system, it will be almost entirely unnecessarily for a short-term visitor unless you are staying outside the *centro.* Nearly all buses finish their route at P. Matteotti in the northwest of the *centro*—if you need to get somewhere that's farther afield, someone at the underground station in the *piazza* can help you out. Otherwise, this is a walking city. Although cycling is permitted, you won't see many bicycles around—the hills and crowds make a set of wheels a nuisance more than a convenience. If you want to take a **taxi,** try calling RadioTaxi *(☎0577 49 222)* or head to the cab stands in P. Matteotti and P. Independenza.

pisa ☎050

This is what Pisa has to offer: one tower, leaning. One airport, budget airline hub. Three universities.

That may not sound like much, but the tower is actually really cool, the airport is remarkably easy to get to, and the universities, well, you can thank them for the city's many student-friendly bars. If Florentine nightlife left you doubting the Tuscan party scene, come to Pisa, where the density of pubs will leave you leaning at a 3.99° angle too.

Unless you're visiting someone at one of the universities or flying out of the airport, however, there's little reason to stay overnight in Pisa. The tower doesn't take long to see, and the theoretically picturesque alleys along the Arno would be far more charming if they didn't smell like urine. *Let's Go* recommends staying a night or two in nearby **Lucca,** and making Pisa a half-day trip from there.

But if you're studying abroad in Pisa, then lucky you! This is a university town full of young people and bars, where the beer is cheap and the beach is 20min. away. Have a great semester, and don't forget to go to class.

ORIENTATION

Whether arriving in Pisa by train or by plane, you will enter the *centro* via the **train station.** The city knows why people visit it, so street signs bearing the image of a leaning tower and an arrow are abundant. When you leave the station, you will be south of the Arno—the **Piazza dei Miracoli** is on the other side of the river, in the northwest of the *centro.* Follow either the "Torre" or "Centro" signs to get there. Otherwise, walk straight—leaving the *stazione* you will be on **Corso Italia**—to reach the river.

ACCOMMODATIONS

Those staying overnight in Pisa are likely in transit—therefore, our picks weigh access to the train station and airport over proximity to the tower.

WALKING STREET HOSTEL HOSTEL ❷

C. Italia 58 ☎393 06 48 737 www.walkingstreethostel.com

This hostel is nice enough to make you wish you had a reason to stay in Pisa longer. The dorm rooms that face C. Italia have an entire wall of 300-year-old stained glass—that's floor-to-ceiling stained glass, in your dorm room—and common space is plentiful and comfortable, with a pool table and dart board in two Chinese-themed red lounges. Guests may use the kitchen, and the small terrace is good for smoking or drying laundry. Moreover, two buzzes are required to access the building, making this hostel more secure than most.

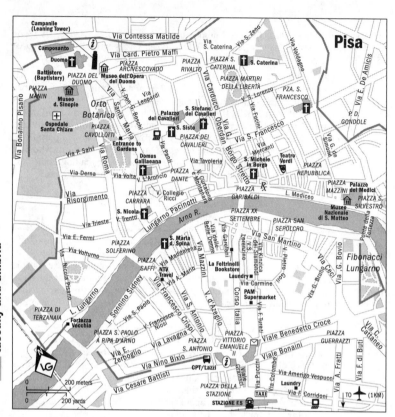

Pisa map

⚑ On C. Italia, equidistant between the train station and the river. *i* Complimentary coffee and tea. Security 24hr. Ⓢ Dorms €22. ⌚ Reception until 3am.

HOSTEL PISA

⊛Ⓧ(╰) HOSTEL ❶

V. Sainati 8

☎349 68 88 446

If you get the sense that some dude just decided to turn his house into a hostel and called it Hotel Pisa, then you are absolutely correct. Carlo is a backpacker himself, but the sort who cares more about community than security. If you're the same, you'll love it here. The bathrooms are knees-touching-the-wall tiny, the Ikea-furnished dorms are rather warm, and no one bats an eye at the door that is left open pretty much all the time. Nevertheless, the neighborhood is quiet, and the hostel's side yard contains a little bar and television around which you can usually find Carlo and his new friends. His digs are a bit far from the *centro*, but that's why he lends out well-maintained bicycles to his guests. You won't need to borrow one when it's time to skip town, though: the proximity to the train station couldn't be better.

⚑ Leave the train station at track 14, take a right onto V. Quarantola, then, after 5min., make a left onto V. Sainati. *i* Complimentary coffee and tea. Free Wi-Fi. Ⓢ Dorms €20. ⌚ Carlo is usually present and awake until the early morning, but if he isn't, the door's open.

HOTEL HELVETIA

⊛ఉ(╰) HOTEL ❸

V. Don Gaetano Boschi 31

☎050 55 30 84

Our pick for slanty-building-proximity is this lovely bargain hotel with a beautiful, well-kept garden that proudly features a cactus to rival the city's famous tower—the plant is 10m high and the tallest of its kind in Pisa, according to the owner. Not that competitors are plentiful. (There's also a huge trampoline, but don't get excited: it's for his kids.) Four floors of private rooms have brick trim, ceiling fans, wood shutters, and iron bedstands. The breakfast room's bright mural takes its cue from the Keith Haring one downtown, and the front hall makes sure you know where you're going with a painted map of Pisa and two huge posters of the entire Pisa Centrale train schedule.

🧭 V. Don Gaetano Boschi begins in the southeast corner of P. dei Miracoli. ℹ Coffee machine available for a nominal fee. Free Wi-Fi. Only 1 wheelchair-accessible room, which is a suite. $ Singles €35; doubles €45, with bath €62; quad suite €100. Extra bed €20. ⏰ Reception 24hr. Leave keys at desk when going out.

CAMPING VILLAGE TORRE PENDENTE 👍♿📶 CAMPING [1]

V. Delle Cascine ☎050 56 17 04 💻www.campingtorrependente.it

If you're lingering for more than a couple nights in the city or want to be near Stazione Pisa San Rossore, consider this camping hostel, which is pretty nice as such places go. The standalone cabins are proper shingled things with kitchenettes and even lawn furniture on their shaded decks. Shared bungalows are a bit more RV-style, but come equipped with a sink and a range on their patios. Tents, however, are completely rudimentary Boy-Scouts-style affairs. Some crammed-together, semi-shaded RV lots and a bathhouse round out the campsite's main landmarks. An internet point and small market on the grounds add to its convenience, but the real perk here is the large, clean swimming pool. If you're not bikini-ready, of course, you can always head to the nearby bocce pitch. We don't recommend walking back to the site from the *centro* after dark, though, as you'd have to pass through a mildly sketchy underpass.

🧭 Follow the "Camping" signs from the west side of P. dei Miracoli. When you reach the underpass, walk through it. ℹ Breakfast €3. Linens €4. Credit card min. €100. $ From €58 for a double within a shared caravan to €132 for a 2-bedroom, 2-bath maxi-caravan for up to 5 people. Same options €45-98 in low season. Dorm caravan €24 per person. Many other tent/RV/bus/etc permutations available. ⏰ Security 24hr.

ROYAL VICTORIA HOTEL 👍♿📶 HOTEL [4]

Lungarno Pacinott 12 ☎050 94 01 11 💻www.royalvictoria.it

This three-star hotel screams class. Half the rooms face the Arno, some with a little balcony to boot. As a quieter option, the other half face an ivy-covered tower. All feature gorgeous carved wooden furniture and glass-fronted armoires. There's a salon on each floor, but take an *aperitivo* from the elegant formal lobby and carry it up to the incredible fourth-floor terrace to watch the sunset over the river.

🧭 On the north side of the river, toward the center. ℹ Breakfast included. Parking available for €20. Wi-Fi available for a fee. $ High-season singles €70; doubles €100-130; suite €190. Up to 40% less in low season. ⏰ Reception 24hr.

RELAIS UNDER THE TOWER 👍🚫♿📶 HOTEL, HOSTEL [2]

V. Santa Maria 165 ☎050 520 0231 💻www.hotelpisacentro.it

Twins and bunk beds share rooms in this semi-hostel where rooms are private or dorm depending on demand. Though it can't make up its mind about what kind of rooming house it is, Relais Under The Tower's name is pretty literal—you won't find another hostel-like place closer to the monuments. Guests may use the kitchen and tiny breakfast nook.

🧭 Just south of the tower. ℹ Toast and coffee included. Free Wi-Fi. $ Dorms €20-25; doubles €45-50, with bath €65-100. ⏰ Reception's around until the last person checks in. Hostel guests receive a key to the front door.

SIGHTS

All of Pisa's grime and crass tourism instantly melt away when you walk among the glistening white monuments of **Piazza Duomo.** The writer Gabriele D'Annunzio called this medieval square the *Piazza Dei Miracoli*, or Piazza of Miracles, and the name is both apt and widely used. (That D'Annunzio was also a fascist is beside the point—he had a good sense for a catchy name, and that's all that matters for our discussion of Pisa.) This is a side of the Middle Ages that we tend to forget given the period's pervasive "Dark Ages" misnomer—these monuments are graceful, classical, snowy white, and all built before the 14th century. The well-maintained, thick green grass and the unobstructed sunshine make for a *piazza* of clean lines, bright colors, and stark contrasts. Entrance to the *piazza* itself is free, and possibly the best part of Pisa is just hanging out in the shadow of the tower and watching tourists try to direct one another in how to take *that* photo. ("OK, now move your hand to the left. The other left. My left.") This *piazza* is definitely sights-central in Pisa: there isn't all that much else to see in this city. If you want to expand your visit beyond the big shiny buildings, the last two listings in this section offer some options. As always in Italy, there are plenty of churches into which you can wander.

LEANING TOWER — TOWER

P. Duomo ☎050 83 50 11 www.opapisa.it

Jaded travelers that we are, we expected Pisa's famous tower to be something of a tourist trap, on par with a leaning Big Block of Cheese. We were very wrong. Turns out the postcards, placemats, and neckties simply cannot do justice to the ridiculous slant of this seriously tipsy structure. It really is awesome, shocking as that may be. And if you're getting sick of the sense o' wonder inspired by most great European monuments (we told you we were jaded), get stoked for the tower. Your first reaction will be less OMG and more LOL. LMAO, even. It really is hilariously tilted. Oh man, Tower, you crack us up.

After 800 years of work, the construction, reconstruction, and restoration of the tower were finally finished in 2010, so you, lucky visitor of 2011 or later, have the good fortune to see the complete tower in all its un-scaffolded silly glory. Your best approach is from the east. Try not to catch a glimpse of the monuments before reaching the east gate, where you'll get a truly knockout view of the tower at its most absurd.

Climbing the tower is not really necessary considering the price and the wait. If you've climbed another major belltower in Tuscany, you basically have the idea: lots of steps, a steep climb, and a great view at the top. The one major difference, of course, is that it's slanted all over the place and very slippery, so try not to fall.

Follow the abundant signs toward "Tower." i Wheelchair-accessible only by arrangement, call ahead. Make reservations in the Museo del Duomo, online, or next to the tourist info office. Visitors under 18 must be accompanied by an adult. No bags permitted (cameras okay). Your ticket is for a specific time; be prompt. The climb is 300+ stairs, narrow, twisty, and very slippery; consider your health and tendency to vertigo before attempting. $ €15. Open daily June-Sept 8am-11pm; Oct 9am-7pm; Nov-Dec 24 10am-5pm; Dec 25-Jan 6 9am-6pm; Jan 7-Feb 10am-5pm; Mar 9am-6pm; Apr-May 8am-8pm. Last entry 30min. before close. Visit lasts 30min. and is guided.

BATTISTERO — ♿ CHURCH

P. Duomo ☎050 83 50 11 www.opapisa.it

The Battistero is the great round thing in front of the cathedral, designed by **Diotisalvi** in 1152. The anonymous designer of the belltower echoed its roundness shortly after to give the *piazza* symmetry—a symmetry that was soon thwarted by that tricky shifting soil. The Battistero is round, high-ceilinged, and entirely marble. Physics time! What does all that mean for sound wave propagation?

fantastic failures

It's oddly comforting to know that horrible failures can bring with them the best kind of fame. Because, unless the original contractor charged with the task of building the Tower of Pisa was banking on off-vertical angles being the next hot thing in bell tower construction, that's exactly what the *Torre Pendente* is. A pretty miserable failure that's become a wildly popular tourist sight: every year, we flock by the thousands to see this vertical mass of white marble leaning foolishly 3.99° away from where it should be.

Perhaps even more interesting than our mystifying fascination with the Leaning Tower of Pisa is the centuries-long effort the town has made to preserve, in whatever way they can, a building that was from the onset foundationally unstable and structurally unsound. The first three floors of the tower were completed in 1178, after a period of the brand of military success and economic prosperity that apparently makes one say, "Hey! Let's celebrate by building a modestly sized monument out of unassuming white marble!" Set on just a 3m-deep foundation, the tower immediately began to sink. In all likeliness, the whole thing would have crumbled had construction continued, but as luck would have it, Pisa was distracted from any architectural endeavors for the next century. Something about a war against those pesky folks from Genoa, Lucca, and Florence, over, we imagine, access to a severely limited supply of competent builders.

During this period, the soil under the tower settled enough to encourage one Giovanni di Simone to resume construction in 1272, despite the rather conspicuous tilt already affecting the tower's appearance. In an effort to compensate for the imbalance, di Simone had the idea to build the upper floors unevenly, with one side taller than the other; because of his admirable creativity (if less than admirable execution) the tower is actually curved, as well as leaning. Everyone took a break from the construction of the tower in 1284, when they realized it was decidedly less futile to fight with other provinces than with the laws of gravity. Not until 1319 would the tower be finished. Presumably they had a party with a smattering of applause and some half-hearted toasts with medium-quality champagne. It had, after all, been quite a tiring affair.

Of course, the tower's restoration is anything but finished. Despite repeated applications of lead weights, shifting of earth, and more cowbell, it wasn't until 2008 that a massive preservation effort finally stopped the incessant shifting of the tower. Perhaps, however, it was a mistake to fix the problem. In 2010 the Guinness Book of World Records certified the Capital Gate building in Abu Dhabi—which had been deliberately engineered at an 18° slant—as the "World's Furthest Leaning Man-Made Tower." So congratulations, United Arab Emirates. This distinct honor is now yours. As is, we think, the next millennium or so of perpetual restoration.

pisa · sights

That's right: interesting acoustic properties!

If you share our enthusiasm for the science of sound, then the rest of this paragraph is for you. The Battistero is so resonant that a choir singing inside can supposedly be heard from 2km away. Don't get too excited, though—for some reason, this remarkable space isn't used for performances. Instead, the guards do an "acoustical demonstration" every half hour, in which a staff member sings a couple notes so visitors can hear the resonance. Unfortunately, the chosen interval is the totally dull sol-mi, repeated several times. Someone bring these people one of the graduals in the **Museo,** quick! Even worse, the demonstrator's timbre isn't clear enough to bring out the overtones which, if a proper singer was letting loose, would be incredible. Most regrettable of all, the Battistero is always crowded and always guarded. As a result, conducting your *own* "acoustical demonstration" is frowned upon. Sigh.

✂ *In P. Duomo.* ℹ *Wheelchair-accessible only by arrangement; call ahead.* Ⓢ *Joint admission with the other non-leaning monuments: 1 monument €5, 2 monuments €6, all 5 €10. Handicapped persons and 1 guest free. Buy tickets at the biglietteria north of the tower or at the Museo delle Sinopie.* ☼ *Open daily Apr-Sept 8am-8pm; Oct 9am-7pm; Nov-Dec 24 10am-5pm; Dec 25-Jan 6 9am-6pm; Jan 7-Feb 10am-5pm; Mar 9am-6pm. Last entry 30min. before close.*

CAMPOSANTO
♿⛪ CEMETERY

P. Duomo ☎050 83 50 11 ▪www.opapisa.it

For a major tourist attraction, the Camposanto, sitting within an enormous, austere, white courtyard, is surprisingly peaceful. Walk over well-worn marble tombs to examine the resting places of the luckier folk whose tombs rest against the wall rather than underfoot. Fragments of frescoes remain on display, remnants of the building's appearance before it was heavily damaged by the Nazis.

✂ *In P. Duomo.* ℹ *Wheelchair-accessible only by arrangement; call ahead.* Ⓢ *Joint admission with the other non-leaning monuments: 1 monument €5, 2 monuments €6, all 5 €10. Handicapped persons plus 1 guest free. Buy tickets at the biglietteria north of the tower or at the Museo delle Sinopie.* ☼ *Open daily June-Sept 8am-11pm; Oct 9am-7pm; Nov-Dec 24 10am-5pm; Dec 25-Jan 6 9am-6pm; Jan 7-Feb 10am-5pm; Mar 9am-6pm; Apr-May 8am-8pm. Last entry 30min. before close.*

DUOMO
♿⛪ CHURCH

P. Duomo ☎050 83 50 11 ▪www.opapisa.it

This impressive cathedral would not be at all out of place in Florence. The vast, ornate interior is watched over by an enormous mosaic Jesus. Check out the gloriously ornate ceiling. Even the pews are stylish, with open curlicued backs that let you see right through two dozen rows of seats. Sadly, the church's art lacks explanatory texts in any language—a bummer for those cheapskates among us unwilling to shell out €1 for the coin-operated audio tours. Here's a little background for you skinflints: the church of Pisa has sat here since before Constantine's peace pact, the **Edict of Milan,** was signed in 313 CE. The building may seem sort of randomly off-center in terms of the city's geography now, but a river once flowed right past the *piazza*. Pisa's central port was approximately where the San Rossore train station now stands, making this site the former entrance to the city. Today's "temple of snow-white marble," as it is called in the funeral inscription of its architect, **Buschetto,** was founded in 1064 and constructed throughout the Middle Ages. A 1595 fire, however, destroyed much of the church's interior, which explains why it now looks pretty much like all the other Renaissance stuff in Florence. Be happy to know that you're not crazy—there actually is a difference between the Middle Ages and Renaissance.

✂ *In P. Duomo.* ℹ *Wheelchair-accessible only by arrangement; call ahead.* Ⓢ *€2. Free during Mass. Joint admission with 4 other non-leaning sights €10.* ☼ *Open daily Apr-Sept 8am-8pm; Oct 9am-7pm; Nov-Dec 24 10am-5pm; Dec 25-Jan 6 9am-6pm; Jan 7-Feb 10am-5pm; Mar 9am-6pm. Last entry 30min. before close. Mass Su 8am-1pm.*

MUSEO SINOPIE
♿⛪ MUSEUM

P. Duomo ☎050 83 50 11 ▪www.opapisa.it

The nearby Camposanto was severely damaged by Nazi shelling, and restoration work did not even begin until 1979. When preservationists finally began reconstructing the edifice's shredded frescoes, they discovered enormous preparatory drawings underneath. In response, Museo delle Sinopie was created so that visitors could see these sketches, with catwalks providing multiple vantage points from which to view the drawings. Once a hospital for the poor and orphaned, the museum building retains its original walls and ceiling.

A 3D multimedia station provides more information on the square's monuments, explaining in detail the stabilization efforts for the tower. If you are stuck in the mercilessly unshaded *piazza* on a hot summer day, it may be good to note that the museum is ❄**air-conditioned.**

✠ *In P. Duomo.* ⓘ *Wheelchair-accessible only by arrangement; call ahead.* Ⓢ *Joint admission with the other non-leaning monuments: 1 monument €5, 2 monuments €6, all 5 €10. Handicapped persons and 1 guest free. Buy tickets at the biglietteria north of the tower or at the Museo delle Sinopie.* ⓩ *Open daily June-Sept 8am-11pm; Oct 9am-7pm; Nov-Dec 24 10am-5pm; Dec 25-Jan 6 9am-6pm; Jan 7-Feb 10am-5pm; Mar 9am-6pm; Apr-May 8am-8pm. Last entry 30min. before close.*

MUSEO DELL'OPERA DEL DUOMO

❤♿ MUSEUM

P. Duomo   ☎050 83 50 11 🖳www.opapisa.it

The Duomo's museum contains yet more information on the construction, reconstruction, and preservation of the cathedral and its surrounding buildings. If you ever happen to travel back in time to Pisa in 1064, you'll be able to tell them exactly how they can keep their buildings from getting all tilty. Maybe you should tell them to start construction elsewhere. The museum also has a fair amount of Roman, Etruscan, and Egyptian art and artifacts.

✠ *In P. Duomo.* ⓘ *Wheelchair-accessible only by arrangement; call ahead.* Ⓢ *Joint admission with the other non-leaning monuments: 1 monument €5, 2 monuments €6, all 5 €10. Handicapped persons and 1 guest free. No other discounts. Buy tickets at the biglietteria north of the tower or at the Museo delle Sinopie.* ⓩ *Open daily Apr-Sept 8am-8pm; Oct 9am-7pm; Nov-Dec 24 10am-5pm; Dec 25-Jan 6 9am-6pm; Jan 7-Feb 10am-5pm; Mar 9am-6pm. Last entry 30min. before close.*

GIARDINO SCOTTO

♿ PARK

Lungarno Leonardo Fibonacci   ☎050 83 50 21

For a small park, Giardino Scotto sure brings the goods. Its main draws are the ruins and Roman walls, upon which you can go clambering around if you'd like. There's also a permanent outdoor movie theater in the park where first- and second-run films are screened every night of the summer. The playground is straight out of a high-end playspace supply catalogue, with an in-ground trampoline and a spinning gazebo-go-round. Along the park's edges, rows of desk-like benches are crowded with university students using the park as an outdoor library on sunny weekends .

✠ *The park is just south of the river, east of the centro, in the bend where it turns.* Ⓢ *Free.* ⓩ *Open daily July-Aug 9am-8:30pm; Sept 9am-8pm; Oct 9am-6pm; Nov-Jan 9:30am-4:30pm; Feb-Mar 9am-6pm; Apr 9am-7pm; May-June 9am-8pm.*

CHIESA DI SANTA MARIA DELLA SPINA

❤♿ CHURCH

South bank of the Arno

If you turned to your copy of *Let's Go* to find out what the deal was with that little church half-floating in the Arno, then you've come to the right listing. It's really what it seems to be: an itsy bitsy Gothic church smack on the south bank, and...that's pretty much it, though sometimes the *chiesa* hosts art exhibits. You can go inside, but mostly it's just a cute little thing across the river, the only building on the banks.

✠ *Look at the river from the north shore. You'll see the church on the west side of the south shore.* Ⓢ *€2.* ⓩ *Open Tu-F 11am-1:45pm and 3-5:45pm, Sa-Su 11am-1:45pm and 3-6:45pm.*

FOOD

This port city is blessed with lots of seafood, plus restaurants that double as bars offering lovely *aperitivo* buffets and late hours. Just south of the monuments on **Via Santa Maria,** you will find about a half dozen pizzerias. They have similar menus, hours, and prices, and all have some form of outdoor seating on the busy street. Choose whichever looks nicest to you. Pizzas go for €4-8, and as is impossible in Florence, you can get pies with actual toppings in the €4-5 range.

👍 ARGINI MARGINI
💳♿🍸☀ SEAFOOD [2]

Lungarno Galilei ☎329 88 81 972 💻www.arginiemargini.com

The Arno smells far sweeter when you're sipping wine on a dock along its sandy shore. In the summer months at the edge of the south shore, head to Argini Margini's small floating dock for fresh seafood and live jazz and classical music. *Aperitivo* and cocktails are also served along the pier. Best of all, due to the magic of Pisan prices, this beautiful location won't cost you an arm and a leg—charges are about average for the city. Sweet deal.

➡ Look over the edge of the river, and you'll see it. $ Cover €1. Seafood priced at market rate, by the kg. Aperitivi and cocktails €3.50-5. ⏰ Open in summer M-Th 6-11pm, F-Sa 6pm-midnight, Su 6-11pm.

LA BOTTEGA DEL GELATO
💳♿ GELATERIA [1]

P. Garibaldi 11 ☎050 575467 💻www.labottegadelgelato.it

Big scoops of good-by-all-but-Florentine-standards gelato, right on Pisa's main bridge. Take your cone and stroll along the Arno.

➡ On P. Garibaldi. $ Gelato from €1.50. ⏰ Open daily in summer 11am-1am; in fall, winter, and spring 11am-10pm.

DOLCE PISA
💳♿🍸☀ CAFE [1]

V. Santa Maria 83 ☎050 56 31 81

At this pleasant cafe a bit farther down the otherwise busy street off the monuments, entire swaths of the menu are €5, including the lunch menu (lasagna, gnocchi, etc.), a large selection of salads, and a long list of smoothies—try the spinach-less Popeye (kiwi, tomato, tabasco, salt, pepper) or one of their lovely pastries. You can eat whatever you order in the cute little tea salon or at the outdoor tables for no surcharge.

➡ From the monuments, it's about a 5min. walk down V. Santa Maria; it's on the right. $ Pastries €0.90. Most entrees €5. Cappuccino €1.20. ⏰ Open M-Tu 7:30am-11pm, Th-Su 7:30am-11pm.

OSTERIA I SANTI
💳♿🍸❄☀ RISTORANTE [2]

V. Santa Maria 71/73 ☎050 28 081 💻www.osteria-isanti.com

With a real canopy, tall green plants, and twinkling Christmas lights, Osteria i Santi offers nicer outdoor seating than most of the options in this area. Dishes cost €6.50-9, with lasagna and spaghetti on the low end and seafood risotto and baby octopus on the high. Sure, there are slightly garish, enormous portraits of saints watching you eat, but St. Sebastian is pretty cute if you like arrows.

➡ From the monuments, walk down V. Santa Maria; it's on the right. $ Cover €1.50. Dishes €6.50-9. ⏰ Open daily noon-3pm and 7-10:30pm.

IL BARONETTO
💳♿🍸❄ RISTORANTE [1]

V. Domenica Cavalca 62 ☎340 25 91 646 💻www.ilbaronetto.com

Il Baronetto's quiet side street is far less foul-smelling than other Pisan side streets, so it's a good place for a nice lunch. The pizza menu is extremely diverse—pies come in a phenomenal 45 varieties, many of them under €6.

➡ Off V. Curatone. From river, turn right. $ Cover €1.50. Pizza €4-8. Primi €7-10. ⏰ Open M-Sa 8:30am-3:30pm and 5:30-9:30pm.

Good news, everybody! Pisa was once a major port city, and ports mean ocean, and ocean means—beach! Viareggio is the resort town for posh beach trips, but to escape smelly old Pisa and get some sand and surf on the cheap, head to Marina di Pisa.

Quick disclaimer before you get too excited: you can take the beach out of Pisa, but you can't take Pisa out of the beach. Don't expcet the postcard beaches and Windex-blue waters of southern Italy. Here the Mediterranean looks about as dull as, well, the Atlantic. But a beach is a beach, right? It's also west-facing, so you'll get lovely sunsets—and the eye-level sunshine right until then, so wear sunblock, kids.

The success of your trip to Marina di Pisa may well be determined by how you handle the bus ride there. The bus to Marina di Pisa runs from the Lazzi station in P. Vittorio Emanuele. A one-way ticket is €1.80. The bus is not numbered, but it leaves every 20min. from 6:45am to 9:30pm (but check on that time for the last bus; don't get stranded by schedule changes or strikes). If you're not sure where to go, just look for people in swimsuits and follow them. After about 20min. the bus will reach Marina di Pisa—you'll know because you'll see the ocean. It's around now that you have to start making key decisions. The first few stops are by the free public beach, which is a rock beach. Take a look from the bus window and see if it looks good to you—you have a couple of stops to make up your mind. If you are not a fan of rock beaches (is anyone?), hang tight on the bus. For the next 10min. the bus will pass along a stretch of private beaches and beach clubs. If you've got a pair, get off the bus now and waltz right in, looking like you own the place. As long as you don't sit down on one of their fancy lounge chairs, you should be fine—though *Let's Go* doesn't recommend trespassing, especially if you can't even sit down once you're in. If you do want a seat, then you'll want a public beach. You can tell these by the fact that they do not have fancy lounge chairs or umbrellas. But they do have sand. And an ocean. You can wait on the bus until you see one, or get off and wander down the shore for a bit. There are also a few beaches attached to a bar or restaurant—we recommend ⚑**Sunset Cafe** if you happen across it. In these spots you'll be good to go, though you might be asked to buy a beer or something. A hardship, we know.

If you chose to sit on the bus reading this instead of getting off, however, you've probably missed all the action by now. But you still have a chance of some beach rays. At the end of the line is another free rock beach. It ain't luxury, but hey, it's the Mediterranean; you don't have much to complain about.

pisa · nightlife

NIGHTLIFE

You really don't need our help with this one. Pisa is jam-packed with bars and pubs, many of them quite cheap. Basically, if you are paying more than €2.50 for a bottle of beer, then you'd better really like the place. Florentine *piazza*-based nightlife is less popular here, if only because the *piazze* aren't as pretty and the pubs are more plentiful. The main gathering spot, **Piazza delle Vettogaglie**, is a near-hidden square lined with small pubs, picnic tables, and cheap late-night food options. Beer here is consistently around €2-3. If the first bar you try is more expensive, try next door. Use our listings to get started, then have fun finding more watering holes from there.

SUNSET CAFE (MARINA DI PISA) — BAR

V. Litoranea 40 ☎345 08 73 007 🖥www.sunset-cafe.it

Spend your entire beach day at this bar—you won't regret it. With its own cove along Marina di Pisa's long string of private beaches, Sunset Cafe has the whole seaside ambience thing down. During the day, the beach is full of lounge chairs. At night, Sunset replaces them with wicker mats, enormous cushions, and big candles. Up near the bar, sitting areas for large groups or cozy couples are shaded by thatched umbrellas and bamboo screens. Around 7pm the *aperitivo* buffet comes out, an extravagant affair with enough options to easily serve as dinner. And that sunset? It really is marvelous.

➡ Take the bus to Marina di Pisa and get off at New Camping Internazionale. The entrance for Sunset Cafe is directly opposite. 💲 Bottled beer €4.50. Cocktails €6. ⏰ Open daily noon-2am, but hours vary depending on business.

BAZEEL — BAR

Lungarno Pacinotti 1 ☎340 28 81 113 🖥www.bazeel.it

A big corner bar on a major *piazza*, Bazeel dominates the scene around the Ponte di Mezzo, the most central of the *centro* bridges. When it's hot, there are frozen cocktails. When it's cold, hang out on the catwalk above the cavernous indoor seating.

➡ Just over the north side of the bridge. 💲 Beer €3-4.50. Frozen cocktails €6.50. ⏰ Open daily 2pm-2am.

AMALTEA — BAR

Lungarno Mediceo 49 ☎050 58 11 29

Munch from a generous *aperitivo* buffet while watching the sun set over the river from this other *piazza* dominator with a *gelateria* conveniently located next door. Amaltea gets a mixed crowd of students and grown-uppier types, making the atmosphere lively but pleasant.

➡ In P. Cairoli, on the river. 💲 Bottled beer €3.50-4.50. Cocktails €4.50-6. ⏰ Open daily 5pm-2am.

ESSENTIALS

Practicalities

- **TOURIST OFFICES:** The office at **Piazza Vittorio Emanuele II** provides maps, an events calendar, and other assistance. *(P. Vittorio Emanuele II 13 ☎050 42 291 🖥www.pisaunicaterra.it ⏰ Open daily 9:30am-7:30pm.)* Another office is at **Piazza Duomo.** *(☎050 56 04 64 and 334 64 19 408 🖥www.pisaunicaterra.it ➡ In Museo dell'Opera. ⏰ Open daily in summer 9:30am-7:30pm; in fall, winter, and spring 10am-5pm.)* **Airport office.** *(☎050 50 25 18 🖥www.pisaunicaterra.it ⏰ Open daily 11am-11pm.)*
- **ATMS: Deutsche Bank.** *(On the corner of V. Giosue Carducci and V. San Lorenzo ➡ Between P. Cavalieri and P. Martiri della Liberta. ⏰ Open 24hr.)*
- **LUGGAGE STORAGE:** Can be found at the left end of Binario 1 in the train station. *(ℹ Self-service lockers were broken at time of printing and are unlikely to be repaired in the near future. 💲 €3 per 12hr., €5 per 24hr., €9 per 48hr. ⏰ Open daily 6am-9pm.)*
- **LAUNDROMATS: Lavenderia** provides washers, dryers, and detergent. *(V. Carmine 20 💲 Wash €4, dry €4. ⏰ Open daily 7am-11pm.)*
- **INTERNET: Internet Surf** has computers and Wi-Fi. *(V. Giosue Carducci 5 ➡ Off V. San Lorenzo. 💲 €2.50 per hr., students €2 per hr. ⏰ Open daily 9am-10pm.)*
- **POST OFFICES:** *(P. Vittorio Emanuele II 8 ☎050 55 30 84 ➡ On the right of the piazza. ⏰ Open M-F 8:15am-7pm, Sa 8:15am-1:30pm.)*

Emergency!

- **POLICE: Polizia Locale** for non-emergencies (☎*050 58 35 11).* **Polizia Municipale** (*V. Cesare Battisti 71/72* ☎*050 91 08 11).*

- **LATE-NIGHT PHARMACIES: Lugarno Mediceo 51.** (☎*050 54 40 02* ✚ *North shore of river, in the east.* ✿ *Open 24hr.)*

- **HOSPITALS/MEDICAL SERVICES: Santa Chiara** provides emergency assistance. (*V. Bonanno* ☎*050 99 21 11* ✚ *Near P. del Duomo.)*

Getting There

By Plane

Galileo Galilei Airport (☎*050 84 93 00* ▢*www.pisa-airport.com)* is so close to the city you could walk, but assuming you don't want to do that, the train shuttle (*€1.10)* is only 5min. The shuttle arrives at platform 14 **Pisa Centrale.** The airport is a major ▢**budget airline** hub, often acting as the arrival point for travelers visiting the whole of Tuscany, including Florence. No intercontinental flights service Galileo Galilei, but you can fly direct to Pisa from most big European cities.

By Train

Pisa Centrale will be your main port of entry from other Italian destinations. (*P. della Stazione* ☎*050 41 385* ✚ *South of P. Vittorio Emanuele II.* ✿ *Biglietteria open 6am-9pm, but there is always a long line; check out the 24hr. self-service machines.)* Trains run to **Florence** (Ⓢ €5.70. ✿ *60-80min., on the 32s and 54s 4:15am-1:12am.)*, **Rome** (Ⓢ *€17.85.* ✿ *4hr., approx. every hr., 5:45am-7:56pm.)*, and **Lucca.** (Ⓢ *€5.10.* ✿ *27min., approx. 2 per hr., 6:20am-9:50pm.)* If leaving from **San Rossore,** Pisa's secondary station in the northwest of town, buy tickets from *tabaccherie.*

By Bus

Lazzi (☎*058 35 84 876* ▢*www.lazzi.it)* and **CPT** (☎*050 50 55 11* ▢*www.cpt.pisa)* run buses that leave from and arrive in P. Sant'Antonio. (*Ticket office open daily 7am-8:15pm.)* To **Florence** (Ⓢ *€6.10.* ✿ *2hr., 1 per hr.)*, **Lucca** (Ⓢ *€2.* ✿ *40min., 1 per hr.)*, and **Marina di Pisa.** (Ⓢ *€1.80.* ✿ *25min., every 20 min.)*

Getting Around

On Foot

Pisa is easily walkable. From the train station to P. dei Miracoli—the longest diameter of the city and also the route you're most likely to take—it's about a 20-25min. walk, depending on the route.

By Bus

LAM ROSSA runs a loop between the airport, train station, tower, and several other points in Pisa every 20min. (*€1.10).*

By Taxi

RadioTaxi (☎*050 54 16 00)*

By Bike

Pisa is somewhat less bike-friendly than other Tuscan cities, with lanes that tend to disappear right when you actually need them. Rental available at **Eco Voyager.** (*V. Uguccione della Faggiola 41* ☎*050 56 18 39* ▢*www.ecovoyager.it* Ⓢ *€4 per hr., €12 per day, €50 per week.* ✿ *Open M-F 9am-midnight.)*

Ask a native of Lucca to compare Florence to his beloved hometown, and he is likely to mutter dismissively about canine excrement. The fiercely proud Lucchesi have every reason to be protective of their little fortified Brigadoon, as it is everything Florence is not: musical, uncrowded, green, and slow-paced. You can throw away your map here and just get lost—the walls will keep you safe as you wander amid labyrinthine alleys, distinctive *piazze*, and bicycling Lucchesi balancing cappuccinos. The amazingly intact 16th-century walls that hug the city not only provide a gorgeous 4km stroll, but also keep out most cars, generic trattorias, and two-days-per-country Round-the-Worlders. As the birthplace of **Puccini**, Lucca is also an extremely musical city, with at least one concert every day of the year—your first stop might be at one

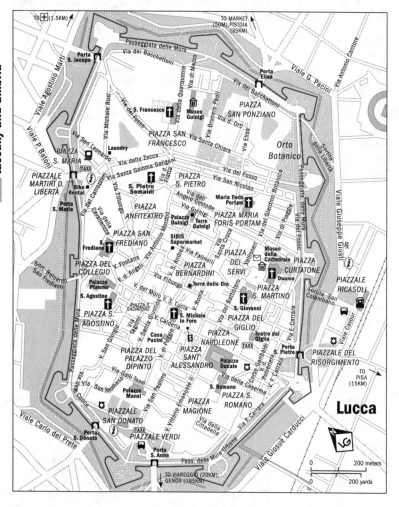

of the ubiquitous poster kiosks to find out which university choir is touring through town that day.

Let's Go recommends staying at least a night or two in Lucca and using it as a base to visit Pisa rather than the other way around. You don't want to miss the walls at sunset.

ORIENTATION

Your first step is to put down this book. But wait! Finish reading this section before you toss us to the wayside. Lucca is not a place for checklist tourism. Whether you are here for an afternoon or a week, the best thing to do is get lost. Put a map in your pocket in case of emergency, resist the temptation to follow the stops of the carefully signposted Tourist Route, and have at it. You'll find that despite the secret passages, hidden *piazze*, and winding alleys, these medieval streets are so distinctive that in a day you'll know your way around.

When you do look at a map, you'll see a big square inside the ellipse of Lucca's walls. That marks the original Roman city boundaries, and within it, the streets form a surprisingly reliable grid. If you sense that two streets might run parallel, within the Roman section, you can assume they do.

If you must know, **Piazza Napoleone** is in the south, a little west of the cathedral, around which you'll first enter the walls (if coming from the train station—there are about a dozen points of entry around the city). **Via Fillungo,** lined with posh shops and department stores, runs roughly north-south. **Piazza San Michele** is in the center of the Roman section and left of center of the modern city. The other major gateway to the town is **Piazzale Verdi** in the west. If the streets seem like they are begining to spiral in on themselves, you are probably nearing the elliptical **Piazza dell'Anfiteatro** in the north. East of the canal on **Via Del Fosso** you'll find the city's "new" section—a 16th-century extension that does feel rather different from the original city's grid. It's also a bit more lived-in and every bit as lovely. The walls, of course, are all around you.

ACCOMMODATIONS

There's just one hostel in town, but it's big enough to accommodate everyone. You can also get a room at a great B and B for what you would've spent on a hostel in Florence.

LA GEMMA DI ELENA

▶⊗⦿ B AND B ❷

V. Della Zecca 33   ☎0583 49 66 65 ▣www.virtualica.it/gemma

Most B and Bs feel like they were decorated by a chintzy aunt. This one feels like it was decorated by that awesome guy from college who lived in Tibet and now edits an antiquing blog. It's spacious yet cluttered in an utterly lived-in way, with colorful sarongs on the wall and a wind chime hanging from the chandelier. None of the linoleum matches, and each room is different. It's a pity you can't use the wonderful kitchen, but you can look at it and daydream about getting your own flat in Lucca some day. The friendly proprietor Jon is from the Netherlands, so his English (and, presumably, Dutch) is excellent.

✈ *Off of V. Del Fosso.* ℹ *Breakfast included. Parking available. Free Wi-Fi.* ⑤ *Singles €35; doubles €55, with bath €65. In low season €5-10 less.* ◲ *Reception open until the last guest arrives. Guests receive a key to the front door.*

OSTELLO DELLA GIOVENTU (HI)

▶⊗ HOSTEL ❶

V. della Cavallerizza 12   ☎0583 46 99 57 ▣www.ostellionline.org

Goodness knows why someone thought Lucca needed an enormous HI hostel, but that means all the more space for you! This former library has impossibly high ceilings and cavernous common spaces. If only there were more people to fill them. There's also a huge breakfast room with seating for about nine billion and a courtyard facing the historic wall. The semi-private bathrooms aren't attached to the dorm rooms, but each room has a designated bathroom of its own on the same hall. Bummer about the lack of breakfast and internet and the sheer size of the place, which makes it a bit impersonal. Otherwise, though, it's a lovely option.

 # Just past V. San Frediano. It's the only hostel in town, so you can safely follow the "ostello" signs. i Security 24hr. $ Dorms €18-22. ⏰ Reception until midnight.

B AND B LA TORRE B AND B 3

V. del Carmine 11 ☎0583 95 70 44 🖥www.roomslatorre.com

This small hotel's hallway is lined with fantastic photographs of the most classic Italian grandmother ever—specifically, the proprietor's grandma, who was the subject of a *New York Times* photo essay a while back—as well as the obligatory framed shot of Italy's favorite crooner...Elvis. Small but tidy rooms feature brass beds and wicker furniture, but the real deal here is the apartment for two to four people that's rented as part of the hotel. This one-bedroom apartment with a full modern kitchen is on P. Anfiteatro and is an absolute steal *(€80)*. In other news, lovelorn travelers, fear not! *Let's Go* is here to help. No, we're not about to set you up with the proprietor—he's taken. However, he met his girlfriend when she stayed at La Torre...on *Let's Go*'s recommendation. (Send *your LG*-enabled love stories to us at feedback@letsgo.com.)

 # Across from the Mercato. i Parking available. Free Wi-Fi. $ Singles €35, with bath €50; doubles €50/80; quads €120. €20 per additional person. ⏰ Reception 8am-8pm.

GUESTHOUSE SAN FREDIANO B AND B 3

V. Degli Angeli 19 ☎0583 46 96 30 🖥www.sanfrediano.com

There's nothing generic in this very personal B and B decorated with letters from former guests, photos of the owner's family, and a mannequin wearing the military uniform of the guesthouse chef's grandfather. The nine rooms have an Alpine lodge feel, with pointed wood-beam ceilings and the occasional skylight. The bathrooms are orange and have bathtubs, while the windows overlook a quiet street.

 # Off V. Cesare Battisti. i Breakfast kits included in room; restocked daily with "little Italian breakfasts." Cash preferred. Wi-Fi €4 per hr. $ Singles €40-50, with bath €60-70; doubles €50-70/70-95. Extra bed €20-25. ⏰ Reception 8:30am-12:30pm and 3-6pm. Guests receive key to front door.

RELAIS SAN LORENZO B AND B 4

V. Cesare Battista 15 ☎0583 19 90 191 🖥www.sanlorenzorelais.it

The rooms in this floral-scented B and B are named after Puccini operas, but you won't find Mimi's garret here. If you can bear to leave your gorgeous carved wooden bed in your high-ceilinged room, have a sherry or a chess game in the parlor by the fireplace. If you want to go all out, the suite is an absolute stunner—ask for dinner served by a waiter on your huge private veranda.

 # Off V. San Giorgio. i Breakfast included. Free Wi-Fi. $ Singles €55-80; doubles €75-95; suite €130-140. ⏰ Reception open until last guest arrives.

ALBERGO LA LUNA HOTEL 5

Corte Compagni 12 ☎0583 49 36 34 🖥www.hotellaluna.com

The 30 rooms in this hotel are spread over two kitty-corner buildings, but in both locations, you'll find doubles (some with queens, some with two twins) featuring exposed wood beams, armchairs, and desks. In the building with reception, there's also the occasional 16th-century ceiling and a couple huge suites with chandeliers and hot tubs. The second building is always locked, but the staff will buzz you in at reception. The included breakfast buffet, Wi-Fi, and a stand full of umbrellas for borrowing can all be found in the lobby.

 # Off V. Fillungo. i Breakfast included. Wi-Fi in lobby. $ Singles €90; doubles €109-125; 4- to 6-person suites €180. Extra person €20. ⏰ Reception 24hr.

PICCOLO HOTEL PUCCINI HOTEL [5]

V. Di Poggio 9 ☎0583 55 421 www.hotelpuccini.com

Sleep across the street from where Puccini slept! All right, guess that's not the biggest draw for most people, but others will drool at the chance to see the birthplace of the great maestro whenever they gaze out their window. For the rest of us, there are also rooms that face a quiet wall. Three of the 14 rooms are singles with full-size beds. In the small but comfortable lobby, you'll find a nifty and functioning 1946 cabinet radio—if only it could still broadcast live performances of Toscanini conducting *Turandot* at the Met—and, of course, a big portrait of Puccini.

Off P. Cittadella. i Italian breakfast €3. Wi-Fi available for a fee. $ Singles €70; doubles €95. Reception 24hr.

SAINTE JUSTINE B AND B [3]

V. Santa Giustina 30 ☎0583 587 964 www.saintejustine.it

Sainte Justine is a small and brightly colored B and B with just five rooms on two floors. The baths are off the hallway, but still private.

Off V. del Loreto. i Breakfast included. All rooms are doubles. $ Doubles €50, with bath €60. Reception open until last guest arrives.

SIGHTS

This is not a city for tick-box tourism: the main sight is the town itself. Just go have a wander. We're here if you want to read about the things you see.

THE WALLS ♿ WALLS

All around the city

Some cities have a park. This park has a city. Lucca's walls were built as fortification in the second half of the 16th century, an expansion of previous Roman and medieval walls. Despite all their ramparts, sally ports, and cavaliers, however, they never had to face an enemy worse than an 1812 flood. By the 19th century, the walls' defensive purpose had given way to more civic and metaphorical significance. Today, the 4.2km of walls are mossy and tree-covered, with benches and playgrounds, and the old army quarters now serve as public facilities, cafeterias, and study centers. At any time of the day or evening, the town's residents can be found strolling or hanging out on their beautiful walls. Metaphorically, the walls continue to be a defense—they protect this Tuscan Atlantis from the outside world, keeping this ancient, tiny city's rhythm from being disrupted by the frantic tick-tock of tourism and modernity. "Once it was a place for military protection," says the city's official guide of the walls, "and now it protects memories."

Walk away from the town center and you're certain to hit them. i For more information, visit the Opera Delle Mura at Castello Porta San Donato Nuova, ☎0583 58 23 20 www.operadellemura.it, or just pick up the guide to the walls from the tourist office. $ Free.

PIAZZA ANFITEATRO ♿ PIAZZA

In the north of the city

If Lucca's streets begin to seem like they're curving in on themselves, you are probably nearing P. Anfiteatro. Once the site of a Roman amphitheater—hence the name—this is now simply an elliptical *piazza*. Which, when you think about it for a moment, is probably not something you've seen before. The faces of all the buildings line up to create a smooth curved wall around the *piazza*, while their varying heights keep the overall image jagged and asymmetrical. There's nothing here except for a handful of nice trattorias and a Puccini gift shop, but the "square's" artful shape alone makes it entirely worth seeking out. It's a fine place to hang out in the wee hours of the morning, when the chairs and tables left out overnight by the trattorias are deserted.

🪧 *Follow V. Fillungo to its northernmost point, where it curves east. You'll then be at P. degli Scalpellini, where there is an entrance to the P. Anfiteatro.* 💲 *Free.*

👍 TORRE DELL'ORE AND TORRE GUINIGI — TOWERS

V. Fillungo 24 (Dell'Ore) and V. Sant'Andrea 41 (Guinigi) ☎0583 31 68 46 (Guinigi only)

The city of Lucca began renting Torre Dell'Ore to clock-runners in 1390, and it has told Lucca's time ever since. The steep climb to the top takes you through the innards of a working timepiece, with all its mechanisms and bits on display. At the top, you'll have an incredible view of this teeny walled city and the surrounding Tuscan hills.

Tower Guinigi isn't a clock, but it does have a rooftop garden. Hang out in a lovely shaded *giardino* full of oak trees at the highest point of the city—and if you lose track of the time, well hey, there's that clocktower right at eye level!

🪧 *Torre Dell'Ore is roughly in the center of the city. Guinigi is a bit to the east, off V. Guinigi.* **i** *As Tuscan tower climbs go, these aren't as difficult as some.* 💲 *1 tower €3, both €5; students and over 65 €2/4.* ⏰ *Torre Dell'Ore open daily June-Sept 9:30am-7:30pm; Oct-May 9:30am-6:30pm. Torre Guinigi open daily May-Sept 9am-midnight; Oct-Feb 9am-5pm; Mar-Apr 9am-7:30pm.*

PUCCINI OPERA — ♿ MUSEUM

V. Santa Giustina 16 ☎0583 95 58 24 🖥www.pucciniopera.it

Whether you're a Puccini diehard or haven't even seen *RENT*, this small and free exhibit should be mandatory viewing during a visit to Lucca. It's only a couple rooms, but the texts go a long way towards explaining why Puccini is important to opera and his hometown. Artifacts include vintage poster art, costume design sketches, and souvenir schlock from the original runs of his masterpieces *Turandot*, *La Bohème*, *Madame Butterfy*, and *Tosca*. Display cases in the center contain letters to and from the great maestro himself, although most go untranslated. For more Puccini pilgrimage, grab one of the ubiquitous red postcards that bears his signature bowler hat and mustache. On the back of the card, a map directs you to his childhood house a few blocks away. Sadly, the residence is not open to the public, but you can take a picture with the statue of the composer in the *piazza* out front, and even eat a snack in one of several opera-named restaurants nearby. The postcards also indicate the birthplace of **Boccherini,** but apparently no one cares about him. His cello stuff is good, though, so give him a chance!

🪧 *Off P. San Salvatore.* 💲 *Free.* ⏰ *Open M 10am-7pm, W-Su 10am-7pm.*

PALAZZO PFANNER — ♿ MUSEUM

V. Degli Asili 33 ☎0583 95 40 29 🖥www.palazzopfanner.it

This is a small sight but a pretty neat one if you are into classical gardens, antique medical instruments, or beer. Clearly that covers pretty much everyone. Originally the *palazzo* was the home of eccentric 18th-century Saxon scholar **Georg Martini,** but in the 19th century it was bought by a *nouveau-riche* brewer named **Felix Pfanner**—hard not to like a guy who made his fortune through beer. You might even say we're pfans. The five rooms of the palace open for public viewing have been set up as they were in the Pfanners' time, and in the kitchen, you can see the vintage tools of micro-brewery. Felix's son, **Preto,** was a great surgeon and war hero, so the main parlor also features a cool selection of medical tools, circa WWI. There's an uncomfortably large collection of catheters and gynecological tools, but if that makes you twitchy, check out the induction apparels for the then-popular alternate current therapy. Outside, the garden, also visible from the city walls, is lined with gravel, old statues, and roses. A bamboo thicket and a wall of mums offer a bit of surprise, and the dozens of lemon trees give the air a lovely scent.

🪧 *Near the San Frediano gate in the walls.* 💲 *Palazzo or garden €3.50, both €5.50, students €4.50. In Apr and Oct €0.50 less.* ⏰ *Open daily Apr-Oct 10am-6pm.*

ORTO BOTANICO

◉ ♿ GARDEN

V. del Giardino Botanica 14   ☎0583 44 21 61 ▣www.comune.lucca.it

The Tuscans love their botanical gardens, even in cities that are already so green and beautiful that it's almost besides the point. This one is superbly maintained, with a winding path up a little hill and a pond full of extremely vocal frogs. Friday evenings in the summer are the best times to visit, as it is on these nights that you can stroll the candlelit gardens to the drifting strings of free performances in the courtyard.

⚑ *In the southeast corner of the city.* Ⓢ *€3, under 14 and over 65 €2, disabled persons and 1 guest free.* ⌚ *Open daily July-Sept 14 10am-7pm; Sept 15-Oct 10am-5pm; Mar 20-Apr 10am-5pm; May-Jun 10am-6pm. Nov-Feb only available by reservation.*

PIAZZA NAPOLEONE

♿ PIAZZA

P. Napoleone

If you need further evidence that Lucca is the best small town ever, look no further than its bustling town square. On one side of the L-shaped *piazza*, an enormous inflatable screen shows major sporting events and tinkly music spills out of a nice carousel *(€1 per ride)*. Around the turn in front of Teatro Verdi, candles in brown paper bags occasionally cordon off a section of pavement for community tango sessions. A number of campus-y poster kiosks full of signs advertising the town's many upcoming concerts and performances populate the square, and next to the theater, a box office sells tickets for events going on throughout town.

⚑ *Just above the southern center walls.* Ⓢ *Free.*

DUOMO DI SAN MARTINO

◉ ♿ CHURCH

P. San Martino   ☎0583 49 05 30 ▣www.museocattedralelucca.it

Lucca's churches all have a similar, distinctive style: a long, rectangular sanctuary (no cruciform layouts here) divided into three aisles by arches. The Duomo di San Martino is an excellent example of this structure. On the facade, carvings for each month of the year provide a public-access farmers' almanac, reminding you that September is the time to crush grapes with your feet and so forth. Inside, on the right, you can visit the **Tomb of Ilyaria** *(€2)*, an important piece of marble carving that is the oldest surviving work of Renaissance artist **Jacopo della Quercia.** On the left, inside a gilded, cage-like structure, is Il Volto Santo, or the Holy Face, which according to tradition was carved by Nicodemus. Next door in P. Antelminelli, the **Museo della Cattedrale** offers a nifty collection of graduals and other sparkly things from the Middle Ages to the 15th century.

⚑ *From P. Napoleone, take V. Duomo directly to the duomo.* Ⓢ *Duomo free. Tomb of Ilyaria €2. Baptistery €2.50. Museo €4. All 3 €6.* ⌚ *Open M-F 9:30am-5:45pm, Sa 9:30am-6:45pm, Su 9:30-10:45am and noon-6pm. In winter may close earlier. No tourist visits to the cathedral during Mass.*

BASILICA DI SAN FREDIANO

♿ CHURCH

P. di San Frediano

Look up as you enter the *piazza* in front of San Frediano—you'll want to take in the splendid dynamism of the Byzantine mosaic Jesus on the church's facade as it catches the sunlight. Enter to see that sparkling light referenced in the small bursts of bright stained glass adorning the church's plain stone altar. To the left, the dessicated corpse of Saint Zita is on display in a glass casket. Like Snow White, but more gruesome.

⚑ *Off the north end of V. Filllungo, across from the P. Anfiteatro.* Ⓢ *Free.* ⌚ *Open daily in summer 9am-noon and 3-5pm; in winter 9am-noon and 3-6pm.*

LUCCA

◉ ♿ MUSEUM

V. Della Fratta 36   ☎0583 57 17 12 ▣www.luccamuseum.com

This brand-new contemporary art center is a versatile space that bills itself as a "living museum," bringing a rare dose of modernity into Lucca's visual palette. Their first four shows have tended toward the block-of-color-on-white-wall type of contemporary art, but their shows of **Man Ray** and **Kandinsky** hint that there's hope yet for this living museum to grow.

➹ At the intersection of V. Santa Gemma Galgani, V. della Zecca, and V. dei Fossi. $ Prices vary, but exhibits run from free to €10, sometimes with student discounts. ⏰ Open Tu-Su 10am-7pm. Last entry 1hr. before close.

CHIESA DI SAN MICHELE ♿ CHURCH, PIAZZA

P. di San Michele

This church and the *piazza* in the center of the city are crowded at any time of day with locals and tourists hanging out and having coffees, some sitting on the church steps. The *chiesa* has stood in this location since the eighth century, but it was continually rebuilt and remodeled through the 17th. Note the unique carvings, designs, and zebra stripes of the columns on the facade.

➹ A little left of the centro—ignore the town's 16th-century extension and the church is at the old Roman city center. $ Free. ⏰ Church open daily in summer 9am-noon and 3-6pm; in winter 9am-noon and 3-5pm. Piazza open 24hr.

FOOD

Many of Lucca's loveliest dining spots are tucked into alleyways and hidden courtyards, but at night they are easy to find. Just follow the candles or paper lanterns lining the sidewalk: they likely lead to a quiet and charming dinner spot. Closing for siesta is not uncommon here, so if you want to eat after 2pm or 3pm, look for somewhere that's *sempre aperto*—always open. Fresh produce, meat, and fish are available at the **Mercato** in P. del Mercato. *(⏰ Open M-Sa 8am-1:30pm.)*

SAN COLOMBANO 💳♿🍸☀ RISTORANTE, CAFETERIA [2]

Baluardo di San Colombano ☎0583 46 46 41 🖥www.caffetteriasancolombano.it

The conversion of the walls' old *baluardi* (bulwarks) into public spaces brought about the creation of this, the walls' only restaurant, which was carved out of an enormous battlement. There's a pretty seamless transition between indoor and outdoor seating in San Colombano's E-shaped space. The inside restaurant lies on the left "tine," the outdoor tables sit in the center, and a more casual cafeteria is on the right. Multiple large projection screens are great for showing simultaneous sporting events, and lit, plastic lounge seats look like melting ice cubes. Dinner patrons are hit with a €2 cover, but staff refills the bread basket frequently. The Lucchese specialties are excellent—try the macaroni with gorgonzola and pear sauce. Bottles of wine will run you anywhere from €12 to €200, but there are several nice local wines at the bottom end.

➹ Along the wall, in the southeast. $ Cover €2. Crepes €3-4. Primi €7-9. Cocktails €6. ⏰ Open Tu-F 8am-1am, Sa 8am-2am.

LUCCA IN TAVOLA 💳♿🍸☀ CAFE [1]

V. San Paolino 130/132 ☎347 81 55 631 🖥www.luccaintavola.it

Diners are encouraged to draw on the plain brown placemats at this sidewalk cafe, and the walls are adorned with past visitors' drawings of Lucca and love letters to the bruschetta *(€4.50)*. Although the four-language menu and the location right off Piazzale Verdi would imply that Lucca in Tavola caters to tourists, the food is nonetheless excellent and cheap.

➹ Just off Piazzale Verdi. $ Crepes €4.50-5.50. Bruschettas €4.50. Pizza €5-6.50. ⏰ Open daily 10am-11pm.

BASION CONTRARIO 💳♿🍸☀ RISTORANTE [2]

V. San Paolino 69 ☎0583 53 403

Truffles are the specialty here, with an entire second menu of truffle *antipasti*, truffle *primi*, and truffle *secondi*, all running in the €17-19 range. For a somewhat less pricey but no less gourmet meal, stick to the truffle-free menu, where *primi* are a more reasonable €6-13. The extensive dessert menu—featuring, you guessed it, more truffles, and not of the chocolate variety—is likely to leave you drooling.

🧭 At the intersection of V. Galli Tossi. $ Desserts €4-5. ⏰ Open daily noon-3pm and 7pm-midnight.

ANTICO SIGILLO 💳♿🍸❄⛅ RISTORANTE [2]

V. degli Angeli 13 ☎0583 91 042 🖥www.anticosigillo.it

Candles in white paper bags invite passersby on busy V. Fillungo to peer down a passageway and into a romantic courtyard. The restaurant proper is across the street, but the seating is nestled under the arches of this courtyard lit only by candles. Typical Lucchese dishes are the specialty, with a changing list of chef's specials and some rather excellent bread.

🧭 Courtyard entrance off V. Fillungo. $ Cover €1.50. Primi €7-12. Chef's specials €8-15. ⏰ Open daily 2-11pm.

FUORI DI PIAZZA 💳♿🍸❄⛅ PIZZERIA [2]

P. Napoleone 16 ☎0583 49 13 22

With beer available by the liter, this place would be listed under nightlife if only it were open later. No matter. For a €1 cover, you can sit right on P. Napoleone with your own personal tap and a giant pizza. It's not posh, but it's lively and friendly.

🧭 Right on P. Napoleone. $ Cover €1. Pizza €4.50-6.50. Liter of beer or wine €8. ⏰ Open daily 10:30am-9:30pm.

GINO'S BAR 💳🚭🍸⛅ RISTORANTE [2]

P. XX Septembre 4 ☎335 70 15 311

You don't have to leave P. Napoleone to escape the street noise—this small restaurant dominates a sort of feeder *piazza* up a few steps and under a large leafy tree. The inside is nothing much, but sitting on the raised deck while having a simple *primi* or a cocktail and watching everyone else hurrying around on the main *piazza* is a thing of beauty.

🧭 Just off P. Napoleone. $ Primi €6-8. Cakes €3. Shots €3-5. Cocktails €5. 0.5L wine €6. ⏰ Open Tu-Su 11am-11pm.

OSTERIA SAN GIORGIO 💳♿🍸⛅ RISTORANTE [2]

V. San Giorgio 26 ☎0583 95 32 33

The exposed wood ceiling and slightly rounded walls of this trattoria may make you feel like you're inside a wine barrel, but that's certainly a good thing. The lovely courtyard is particularly romantic at night, with wicker seats under an enormous suspended umbrella and soft candlelight. The menus are lovingly bound in extremely soft leather, and inside them you'll find a solid *prix-fixe (primo, secondo, and vegetable; €18).*

🧭 By P. Sant'Agostino. $ Soups €7. Primi €7-12. Cocktails €6. ⏰ Open daily noon-3pm and 7-11pm.

NIGHTLIFE

Smatterings of nice bars and *enoteche* dot the old city, but areas of particular concentration include the intersection of V. Vittorio Veneto and C. Garibaldi, **Piazza San Michele,** and **Piazza San Frediano.**

👍 **ENTE ENTO** 💳♿🍸❄⛅ ENOTECA

V. della Polveriera 8 ☎0583 14 52 21

There are a half dozen bars, pubs, and *enoteche* around the intersection of V. Veneto and C. Garibaldo, but the super-mod Ente Ento is our favorite. This *enoteca* fancies itself an old movie. The chic interior is entirely black and white, with glossy photos of Bogie and James Dean on the wall—a splash of red on Marilyn's lips provides the space's only dash of color. The *aperitivo* buffet is one of the nicer in town, and you can take it outside to nibble while facing Lucca's lovely walls.

🛵 Across from Baluardo Santa Maria. Ⓢ Bottled beer €4. Cocktails €5. 🕐 Open M-Tu 7am-1am, Th-F 7am-1am, Sa 7am-2am, Su 7am-1am.

PULT

♥&⫯⛱ ENOTECA, RISTORANTE

V. Fillungo ☎0583 49 56 32 🖵www.pult.it

You will pass PULT many times—its location in the center of V. Fillungo makes it hard to miss. This lively restaurant and wine bar dominates the P. dei Mercanti with clusters of cushioned wicker couches and tables bearing curiously balanced apples on candlesticks. During mealtimes, it's packed with people eating. During drinking times, it's packed with people drinking—come for one of the frequent chef tastings and wine tastings. This is definitely a place to hang out conspicuously. If you know anyone in Lucca, you'll probably see him or her while you're sitting here with a glass of wine, and *you'll* certainly be seen by whoever walks by.

🛵 In the middle of V. Fillungo, more or less. Ⓢ Liqueurs €4. Bottled beer €5. Wine bottles €25. Primi €10-18. 🕐 Open Tu-Su noon-3:30pm and 7:30-1am. Kitchen closes 11pm.

GELATERIA VENETA

♥&⛱ GELATERIA

V. Vittorio Veneto 74 ☎0583 16 70 37 🖵www.gelateriaveneta.net

While it may seem odd to list a *gelateria* as a nighttime destination, visit adorable Veneta in the evening and you'll understand. The locals have made it an after-dinner hotspot in the manner of a 1950s ice cream parlor full of bobby-soxers and drugstore Romeos. In the early evening, it's full of teenagers smooching over sundaes. In the later evening, the long benches outside fill with groups making a gelato pitstop on their way from one bar to the next. Compared to Florentine gelato, this stuff, which you can get in several locations around Lucca and from the occasional bicycle vendor on the walls, is good but not great. No matter: sample a cone from Gelateria Veneta, a *Lucchese* staple since 1927, for the experience. In classic soda fountain fashion, Veneta's flagship location also serves sundaes, crepes, and other treats.

🛵 At the intersection with C. Garibaldi. ℹ Other locations at V. Beccheria 10 (☎0583 49 68 56) and Chiasso Barletti (☎0583 49 37 27). Ⓢ Cover €1. Cones from €2. Sundaes €4.50-7. Crepes €3.50-5.50. 🕐 Open daily 10:30am-1am.

BETTY BLU CAFE

♥&⫯⛱ BAR

V. del Gonfalone 16-18 ☎0583 49 21 66 🖵www.betty-blue.eu

Internet cafe by day, bar by night. In the afternoon, Betty Blu is full of folks using the several computers and Wi-Fi or drinking coffee. Sometimes a couple of dodgier fellows pull at the two slot machines. At night, the stools on the *piazza* fill up with a more standard crowd of young locals who have come to enjoy mega-guacamole.

🛵 Between V. della Zecca and Porte dei Borghi. Ⓢ Bottled beer €5. Cocktails €8. Internet and Wi-Fi €2 per 15min., €4.50 per 1hr. 🕐 Open daily 11am-1am.

ARTS AND CULTURE

Lucca is an extremely musical town. The **Puccini Festival** ensures at least one performance every single day of the year, and summertime sees an explosion of concerts and musical events. Additionally, it's a very popular destination for university choirs and orchestras on tour, so stop by the box office at Teatro Verdi, visit 🖵www.comune.lucca.it, or take a look at one of the many poster kiosks to see what's happening during your visit.

PUCCINI E LA SUA LUCCA — OPERA

Chiesa di San Giovanni ☎340 81 06 042 www.puccinielasualucca.com

Hometown hero **Giacomo Puccini** is celebrated every single night of the year in Lucca with recitals of his arias and art songs often paired with vocal music by Mozart and Verdi. That makes this the only permanent **festival** in the world and suggests that these folks don't really understand the concept behind festivals. We certainly aren't complaining, though, even if the church in which performances are held is a bit too resonant to be an ideal recital hall, and texts and translations are not provided. The performers' talent level is extremely high, and the program is different every single night—no daily march through the greatest hits here. All performances are at 7pm at the Chiesa di San Giovanni. Programs available in advance online. In the fall, a Puccini opera is produced in full, and the Christmas and Easter seasons bring a handful of extra concerts and gala events.

Off V. Duomo; coming from P. Napoleone, it's the church on the left that's before the Duomo. $ Nightly concerts €17, students €12. Galas and staged opera performances €15-40. Discount on following night's recital with ticket stub from previous night. ⏰ Tickets on sale at Chiesa di San Giovanni daily 10am-7:15pm. Advance sales online or at authorized festival sales points.

MUSIC OF THE TREES — CLASSICAL MUSIC

Giardino Botanico www.comune.lucca.it

If you are lucky enough to be in Lucca on a Friday night in June, July, or August, then you should be here. The city's botanical garden hosts chamber music concerts on summer Fridays at 9pm, free and open to the public. Better still, the whole garden is open and illuminated with candles along the pathway. If you thought the botanical gardens were nice during the day, wait until you explore them in the flickering light while Italian arias drift out of the courtyard.

In the botanical garden in the southeast corner of the city. $ Free. ⏰ Performances F in summer at 9pm.

SUMMER FESTIVAL — FESTIVAL

P. Anfiteatro ☎0584 46 477 www.summer-festival.com

In July, Lucca returns P. Anfiteatro to its original amphitheater purpose with a concert series that demonstrates the town can do non-classical music just as well as it does Puccini. Previous line-ups have included ZZ Top and Crosby, Stills and Nash.

Gates and seating vary per concert, but all are based out of P. Anfiteatro. $ Prices vary, but generally €30-50, with a couple free concerts each year. Free to disabled persons. ⏰ Concerts every few days in July.

ESSENTIALS

Practicalities

- **TOURIST OFFICES: Ufficio Regionale** includes an internet point, currency exchange, booking assistance, and a tourist bus checkpoint. *(P. Santa Maria 35 ☎0583 91 99 31 www.luccaturismo.it Look for "i" sign, on the right. ⏰ Open in summer 9am-8pm; in fall, winter, and spring 9am-1pm and 3-6pm.)* **Ufficio Provinciale** provides general tourist assistance. *(Corile Carrara ☎0583 58 31 50 Beside P. Napoleone. ⏰ Open daily 10am-1pm and 2-6pm.)* **Centro Accoglienza Turistica,** the main branch of Lucca's primary tourist office, schedules guided tours and provides audio tours, information about events, and an internet point. *(Piazzale Verdi ☎0583 58 31 50 www.luccaitinera.it Look for "i" sign, on the left. ⏰ Open daily 9am-7pm.)* A **second branch** may be closed in 2011. *(P. Curatone ☎0583 49 57 30 On Vle. Guisti, outside city walls near train station. ⏰ Open daily 10am-1:30pm and 2:30-5:30pm.)*
- **CURRENCY EXCHANGE:** Is available at **Ufficio Regionale** tourist office.

- **ATMS:** **UniCredit Banca.** *(Corner of V. San Paolino 🧭 50m from bank, off Piazzele Verdi. ⏰ Open 24hr.)* **Deutschebank.** *(Corner of V. Fillungo and V. Mordini 🧭 Beside bank. ⏰ Open 24hr.)*
- **LAUNDROMATS:** **Levanderia Niagara.** *(V. Michele Rosi 26 ☎349 16 45 084 🧭 Off P. San Michele. $ 7kg wash and dry €4. ⏰ Open daily 7am-11pm.)*
- **INTERNET:** **Tourist Offices** all provide computers with internet. The office at P. Verdi has **Wi-Fi** (when it's working). Betty Blu internet cafe has both computers and Wi-Fi and keeps the longest hours. *(V. del Gonfalone 16-18 ☎0583 49 21 66 💻www.betty-blue.eu 🧭 Between V. della Zecca and Porte dei Borghi. $ €2 per 15min., €4.50 per 1hr. ⏰ Open daily 11am-1am.)* Wi-Fi is also available at the train station in Piazzale Ricasoli. *($ €1.50 per 20min.)*

Emergency!

- **POLICE:** **Polizia Municipale.** *(Vle. Camillo Benso Conte di Cavour 1 ☎0583 45 51 🧭 Outside the walls to the south.)* **Carabinieri.** *(Cortile degli Svizzeri ☎0583 47 821 🧭 In the southwest of the centro.)*
- **LATE-NIGHT PHARMACIES:** **Farmacia Comunale.** *(P. Curatone 🧭 Outside the city walls, opposite Baluardo San Colombano. ⏰ Open 24hr.)*
- **HOSPITALS/MEDICAL SERVICES:** **Campodi Marte** provides emergency medical attention. *(V. dell' Ospedale ☎0583 95 57 91 🧭 Outside the city walls, in the northeast corner. ⏰ Open for emergencies 24hr.)*

Getting There

By Train

The **train station** is in Piazzale Ricasoli, just south of the city walls. *(⏰ Ticket office open daily 6:30am-8:10pm. Station open M-F 4:30am-12:30am, Sa-Su 5:30am-12:30am.)* To **Florence** *($ €5.10. ⏰ 80min., on 32s and 39s 5:05am-10:32pm.)*, **Pisa** *($ €2.40. ⏰ 30min., on 42s and 12s 7am-9:42pm.)*, and numerous local destinations. Change in Pisa or Florence for **Rome, Venice,** and other far-flung destinations.

By Bus

Lazzi *(☎0583 58 78 97 💻www.valibus.it)* in Piazzale Verdi. To **Florence** *($ €5.10. ⏰ 70min., 1-2 per hr.)*, and **Pisa.** *($ €2.40. ⏰ 50min., 1-2 per hr.)*

Getting Around

By Taxi

RadioTaxi *(☎0583 33 34 34)*. Taxi stands (marked with code identifying the pick-up point for when you call) at train station, P. Napoleone, P. Santa Maria, and Piazzale Verdi.

By Bike

You will find the same rates and hours at each of the major rental places around town. *($ Street bikes €2.50 per hr., €12.50 per day; mountain bikes €3.50/17.50; tandem bikes €5.50 per hr. ⏰ Open daily 9am-7:30pm.)* Here are some options: **Chrono** *(C. Garibaldi 93 ☎0583 490 591)*, **Cicli Bizzarri** *(P. Santa Maria 32 ☎0583 49 66 82)*, **Cicli Rai** *(V. San Nicolao 66 ☎348 89 37 119)*, **Poll Antonio Biciclette** *(P. Santa Maria 42 ☎0583 49 37 87)*, **Promo Tourist** *(Porta San Pietro ☎348 38 00 126)*, and **tourist office** *(Piazzale Verdi ☎0583 58 31 50 💻www.luccaitinera.it)*.

san gimignano ☎0577

Both picturesque and formidable, the 14 towers of San Gimignano loom over the city's small *piazze* and wandering walls. The towers date back to a period when prosperous families used the town square as their personal battlefield. During sieges, they were a handy vantage point from which to dump boiling oil on neighbors. Now, however, there's very little need for scalding fluids, as San Gimignano's impressive skyline and the region's dry, white Vernaccia wine draw nothing more dangerous to the town than tourists by the bus-load—30 bus-loads a day from Poggibonsi, to be precise.

You will never again see so many older folk gamely chugging their way up steep hills as you will in this town. V. San Giovanni is congested with tourists and tour-

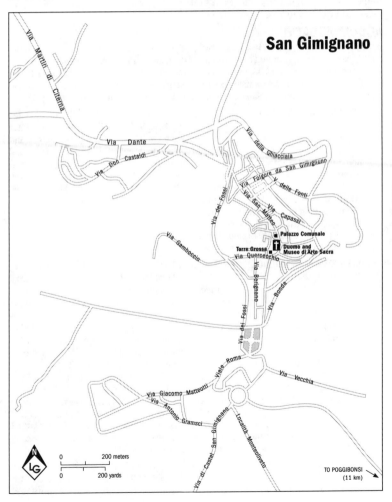

San Gimignano

Via Martiri di Citerna
Via Dante
Via Don Castaldi
Via della Ghiacciaia
Via Folgore da San Gimigliano
V. delle Fonti
Via dei Fossi
Via San Matteo
Via Capassi
Via Gamboccia
Palazzo Comunale
Torre Grossa
Duomo and Museo di Arte Sacra
Via Quercecchio
Via Berignano
Via Bonda
Via dei Fossi
Viale Roma
Via Vecchia
Via Giacomo Matteotti
Via Antonio Gramsci
Via di Castel San Gimignano
Località Momealdveto

N LG

0 — 200 meters
0 — 200 yards

TO POGGIBONSI
(11 km)

ist schlock, and you can hardly move for fearing of stepping into a photograph or onto a Pinocchio doll. Luckily, San Gimignano's infernal verticality means that the crowds rarely wander off the *very* beaten path—you need only walk a few meters down (more likely up) a side street to be completely alone. Strap your feet into some legit walking shoes and explore the towers of San Gimignano from the outside in.

ORIENTATION

The bus from Poggibonsi will let you off right outside the city walls. When you enter the gate, you will be on **Via San Giovanni**—the main tourist drag. Follow that uphill to reach **Piazza Duomo** and the adjacent **Piazza della Cisterna,** which you can identify via the big well *(cisterna)* in the center. This is the path on which you will find most things, and most tourists. Past P. Duomo is **Via San Matteo,** which leads you through to the other side of the city and **Porta San Matteo.** There are signs pointing the way to most sights and many restaurants as well.

ACCOMMODATIONS

San Gimignano is small. It's beautiful, and it's a nice place to be after dark when all the daytrippers have gone home. There are a lot of daytrippers for a reason, however: you can easily see the town in a day. As a result, accommodations are mostly geared toward well-off older visitors. Ask at the tourist office for a list of all the hotels, bed and breakfasts, and *affittacamere* in the greater San Gimignano area if you're really intent on staying.

OSTELLO IN CHIANTI (HI)

💳♿📶 HOSTEL [1]

V. Roma 137 ☎055 80 50 265 💻www.ostellodelchianti.it

So, this hostel is actually nowhere near San Gimignano, but by kilometers and travel minutes, it *is* the nearest option that qualifies as a proper hostel—and quite a nice one at that. The town of Tavarnelle Val di Pesa is tiny but charming, overlooking vast vineyards. With frequent buses to San Gimignano (via Poggibonsi) and Florence, it's an excellent base for exploring the Chianti region. Moreover, the hostel itself is quite nice and comfy, with large, sparsely populated dorms and an uncommonly helpful staff.

🧭 To get from the hostel to San Gimignano, take the bus toward Siena and change at Poggibonsi for the shuttle. ℹ Breakfast €1.80. Parking available. $ Dorms €15; private rooms with bath €17-22.50 per person. ⏰ Reception 8:30am-11:30pm.

FORESTERIA MONASTERO DI SAN GIROLAMO

🚫💳🚫♿ CONVENT [2]

V. Folgore 30/32 ☎0577 94 05 73 💻www.monasterosangirolamo.it

There are no hostels or hostel-priced beds in all of San Gimignano, so if you're on a budget and absolutely must spend the night in town, we hope you don't have sphiscophobia (that's the fear of nuns). You might have to ring a few times and knock at several doors to find a sister to check you in, but you'll be led to a small, simple room with weirdly tall bunk beds and tasteful images on the wall. Guests are confined to a couple hallways of this very large, fully operational convent. A visitor willing to risk the wrath of the nuns would find a stone courtyard, a beautiful cloister, and some spectacular views of the towers of San Gimignano—but *Let's Go* does not recommend such escapades.

🧭 Exit the city walls at any point and walk around to Porta S. Jacopo, in the northeast. The convent, though largely unmarked, is most of the buildings on the left. Or, from Porta San Matteo, walk 2 blocks uphill, then turn left onto V. XX Septembre, which becomes V. Folgore. ℹ Breakfast €3. Parking €2. Male and female guests welcome. Reserve ahead by emailing monasterosangimignano@gmail.com. $ Dorms €27. ⏰ Reception 11am-1pm and 4-6pm.

L'ANTICO POZZO

💳♿📶❄ HOTEL [5]

V. San Matteo 87 ☎0577 94 20 14 💻www.anticopozzo.com

Even if you aren't staying here, you should pretend you're thinking about it so that you can go check out their underground cavern. Right off the lobby, just after the nifty grotto bar and the old well that gives the hotel its name, steps lead down into an excavated cellar. In the 17th century, when the hotel was a rather palatial house, these caverns would be pumped full of imported ice or stoked with huge fires—they were a centralized heating and cooling system. Now, the modern rooms have cooling systems of the more mundane variety, but there are still big bathrooms (some with tubs) and a lovely terrace where you can take breakfast under big white umbrellas.

 # Halfway between P. Duomo and San Matteo, on the left. i Breakfast included. Wi-Fi available for a fee. Call ahead for wheelchair accessibility. $ Singles €80-90; doubles €110-130; triples €150. ⏰ Reception 7am-1am, with a porter overnight.

LOCANDO IL PINO B AND B [3]

V. Cellolese 6 ☎0577 94 04 15 💻www.ristoranteilpino.it

This small, homey bed and breakfast is run by the same guy who manages an adjacent restaurant. His English is minimal, so be prepared to pantomime that you want a bed rather than a table or you might end up with very uncomfortable and board-like sleeping quarters. Inside the five rooms, you'll find wood-beamed ceilings, big wood armoires, and lacy, gently wafting curtains.

 # Turn left just after entering the walls at Porta San Matteo. i Breakfast €5. $ Doubles used as singles €45; doubles €55; triples €70.

SIGHTS

There's not much to see in San Gimignano other than the beautiful city itself. This makes it a very doable daytrip.

PALAZZO COMUNALE AND TORRE GROSSA MUSEUM

P. del Duomo ☎0577 99 03 12

This "common palace," or town hall, was built in the late 13th century, and the famous "Sala di Dante" on the first floor supposedly hosted a visit from the great bard himself. Although the texts are in Italian in this small-ish (as far as such things go) palace, you don't need any explanation to enjoy Lippo Mommi's fresco cycle **Virgin Enthroned in Majesty.** Wander through a few richly decorated rooms, then head up the stairs to the tower. It's a slippery climb to the top of the tallest of San Gimignano's seven remaining towers, but after scaling the last ladder and ducking underneath the bells, you'll find a remarkable view.

 # Facing the Duomo, the entrance is on your left. $ €5, students and under 18 and over 65 €4. Entry to all civic museums €7.50/€5.50. ⏰ Open daily Mar-Oct 9:30am-7pm; Nov-Feb 10am-5:30pm.

DUOMO AND MUSEO DI ARTE SACRA ♿ CHURCH, MUSEUM

P. del Duomo and V. Costarella 1 ☎0577 94 22 26

Lacking the frames, chapels, and side altars that break up the frescoes of most big cathedrals in this region, the San Gimignano Duomo is simply a huge expanse of color. The floor-to-ceiling, brightly colored frescoes create one continuous panel of fluid decoration depicting the stories of the New Testament. The perspective in some of them is a little wack, but hey, this ain't Florence, so don't expect perfection. Note the incredible rear wall featuring a row of apostles under an abstract, swirly rainbow window. Across the street, the **Museo di Arte Sacra** houses spillover from the church's collection in small rooms punctuated by iron gates, wood beams, and rounded stone walls.

 # Enter the Duomo on the left side. The museo is the opposite side of the courtyard from there. i Duomo is wheelchair-accessible; museum is not. $ Duomo €3.50, students and under 18 €1.50. Museo €3/€1.50. Combined entry €5.50/€2.50. ⏰ Duomo open Apr-Oct M-F 10am-7pm, Sa 10am-5:30pm, Su 12:30-5:30pm; Nov-Mar M-Sa 10am-5pm, Su 12:30-5pm.

ROCCA DI MONTESTAFFOLI AND MUSEO DEL VINO

☺☒ FORTRESS

Villa della Rocca

☎0577 94 12 67

Besides some stone walls and a well overgrown with ivy, there's nothing particularly citadel-like left at this ruined fort. Still, it makes for an attractive little park with some spectacular views. Buskers and peddling artists are frequently found within the crumbling walls, and in summer, outdoor movies are shown on a small screen. The adjacent **Museo di Vino** is unimpressive, but their wine tastings are affordable.

⌗ *Follow the signs from P. Duomo.* ⓢ *Rocca and museum free. Taste 4 wines for €6.* ☼ *Rocca open dawn to dusk. Museum open daily Mar-Oct 11:30am-6:30pm.*

museums are torture

Ask the staff at any of San Gimignano's three (that's right, three) torture museums which one was first, and they'll all have the same answer: "We were." Sadly, *Let's Go* has failed to determine the lineage of these storefront exhibits, or why someone thought little San Gimignano would draw the torture-hungry hoards. But if you are psyched at the idea of seeing plastic mannequins in spiked collars and iron maidens (you sick freak), then these are the "museums" for you. You can find the Museo Pena di Morte at V. San Giovanni 16, the Museo della Tortura at Porta San Giovanni 123, and the other Museo della Tortura at V. del Castello 1/3.

FOOD

⟳

Bargains are rare in a town as highly touristed as this one. Likewise, since it seems no one makes San Gimignano his or her actual *home*, you'll be hard-pressed to find a real grocery store. In this respect, it's fortunate that you probably aren't here for long. Bring a sandwich for lunch and splurge on a nice restaurant for dinner. Market days are Thursdays until 1pm in the main *piazze*.

▨ GELATERIA DI PIAZZA

☺& GELATERIA ❶

P. della Cisterna 4

☎0577 94 22 44 ▣www.gelateriadipiazza.com

It's easy to tell which *gelateria* in San Gimignano is considered the best—the door to this centrally located artisanal shop is plastered with awards and recommendation stickers. All those critics were likely won over by Gelateria di Piazza's rich chocolates and unique sorbets, with flavors like gorgonzola cheese and walnuts—that's right, savory gelato—and a Vernaccia flavor based on San Gimignano's specialty wine. A fancy-schmancy digital display will help you pick your *gusto* by reminding you what's on the menu for the day.

⌗ *In the north side of the piazza.* ⓢ *Small cone €1.80. Chocolate-dipped cone with 3 flavors €2.80.* ☼ *Open daily 9am-11pm.*

RISTORANTE IL CASTELLO

➥&⟨ɯ⟩ɣ⌂ RISTORANTE ❷

V. del Castello 20

☎0577 94 08 78 ▣www.enotecailcastello.it

This *ristorante* is named after a 12th-century Gonfiatini palace, and a suit of armor still stands watch over the entrance to prove the point. There's a glass-enclosed courtyard with palm trees, a balcony with a view of the valley, a dining room with colorful hanging lamps and picnic benches, and a wine bar excavated out of the limestone of the hill. The food is classic Tuscan, with *ribollita*, wild boar *tagliatelle*, and the like on the menu.

⌗ *Take a right off P. della Cisterna.* ⓢ *Soups and pastas €7-13. Pizza €6.50-7.50. Secondi €11-13.* ☼ *Open daily Apr-Oct M-Th noon-2:45pm and 7-9:45pm; Nov-Mar noon-2pm and 7-9pm.*

CAFFE DELLE ERBE 💳♿🍸⛅ CAFE [2]

V. Diacceto 1 ☎0577 90 70 83

This nice cafe on a somewhat less busy *piazza* offers fancy panini, cold plates like *Caprese* and *bresaola* (dried and salted beef, beets, arugula, parmesan, tomato, oil), and your standard sort of *primi.*

⇆ On P. delle Erbe. $ Panini €4.50-6.50. Primi €7. Cold plates €6.50-9. ⏰ Open M-W 8:30am-11pm, F-Su 8:30am-11pm.

TRATTORIA CHIRIBIRI 💳🚭🍸 RISTORANTE [2]

P. della Madonna 1 ☎0577 94 19 48

The dining room may be underground here, but they've painted windows and shutters on to the wall to open things up a bit while you enjoy scrumptious wild boar lasagna and roasted rabbit.

⇆ Off V. San Giovanni, on the right. Enter up the alley on the left. $ Cover €1.55. Primi €5.50-7.50; secondi €7-15. ⏰ Open daily 11am-11pm.

NIGHTLIFE 🍷

Nothing stays hopping too late in San Gimignano, but you can always make it a "do it yourself" night in P. della Cisterna by picking up a bottle of crisp local Vernaccia *(€4.50)* from **La Buca** *(V. San Giovanni 16 ☎0577 94 04 07).*

CAFFE COMBATTENTI 💳♿🍸⛅ CAFE

V. San Giovanni 124/127 ☎0577 94 03 91 💻www.sangimignano.com/aco008e.htm

This cafe right at the main gate to San Gimignano looks like a general store, with candy shelves, hanging meat, and pastries on display. Across the street, their wine shop ships bottles of *vino* and olive oil all over the world. Take a seat next to the gate before the last bus to Poggibonsi and sip your cocktail while watching the city empty out.

⇆ Right past the main entrance into the city. $ Wine from €3. Cocktails €4. Bottles of beer €4.50-5. Crepes €4-5.50. ⏰ Open daily 9:30am-11:30pm.

BAR PIAZZETTA 💳♿🍸⛅ BAR

Piazzetta Buonaccorsi 5 ☎0577 94 03 21

This spacious neighborhood bar, somewhat off the main tourist path, has been providing adult beverages to locals and wanderers since 1927. Plenty of seating, but all prices are a euro or two more for table service.

⇆ Just before Porta San Matteo. $ Wine from €2, bottles from €12. Bottled beer €2.50-3.50. Cocktails from €4. ⏰ Open in summer daily 6am-midnight; in fall, winter, and spring M-Tu 6am-11pm, Th-Su 6am-11pm.

ESSENTIALS ℹ

Practicalities

- **TOURIST OFFICES: Ufficio Informazioni Turistiche** provides free maps, *affitta-camere* listings, bus tickets, lists of internet points, etc. It also runs various walking tours, daily. *(P. Duomo 1 ☎0577 94 00 08 💻www.sangimignano.com ⇆ Right in P. Duomo, look for the "i" sign. ℹ 2hr. winery tours with tastings; reserve at office. $ 2hr. winery tour €20. ⏰ Open daily in summer 9am-1pm and 3-7pm; in fall, winter, and spring 9am-1pm and 2-6pm.)*
- **LAUNDROMATS: Wash and Dry.** *(V. del Pozzuolo 8 ⇆ Left of V. San Giovanni. $ Wash and dry for up to 5kg €11. ⏰ Open M-Sa 9am-1pm and 3-7pm.)*
- **CURRENCY EXCHANGE: Protur** provides a 24hr. number for emergency money exchange. *(P. della Cisterna 6 ☎0577 94 06 61 ⏰ Open daily 10am-1pm and 3-6pm.)*
- **INTERNET: Libreria La Francigena** provides public internet access. *(V. Mainardi 12*

☎0577 94 01 44 ⚔ *Enter at Porta San Matteo and make the 2nd right. ☾ Open M-Sa 11am-7:30pm.)*

- **POST OFFICE:** *(P. delle Erbe 8 ⚔ Behind the Duomo. ☾ Open M-F 8:15am-1:30pm, Sa 8:15am-12:30pm.)*
- **POSTAL CODE:** 53037

Emergency!

- **POLICE: Carabinieri** state police. *(Piazzale Montemaggio ☎0577 94 13 12 ⚔ Outside Porta San Giovanni, the main gate of the old city.)* **Polizia Municipale,** town police station. *(V. Santo Stefano ☎0577 94 03 46 ⚔ From P. della Cisterna, take V. de Castello and then a left on V. Santo Stefano.)*

- **LATE-NIGHT PHARMACIES: Farmacia** has a 24hr. phone number. *(P. della Cisterna 8 ☎348 002 1710 ⚔ Next to the gelateria. ☾ Open daily 9am-1pm and 4:30-8pm.)*

- **HOSPITALS/MEDICAL SERVICES: Ospedale Valdelsa** provides emergency room and hospital care. It's in Poggibonsi, so try not to get sick. If you do, call an ambulance. *(Campostaggia—Poggibonsi ☎0577 99 41 ⚔ Call ☎118 for ambulance: they'll know the way to the hospital. Or take shuttle down to Poggibonsi. ☾ Open 24hr.)*

Getting There

Other than driving or biking a really long way, taking the shuttle bus from Poggibonsi is the sole option for getting to San Gimignano. Poggibonsi is an active train station, easily reached from Siena, Florence, or Empoli by hourly trains. Exit the station and look at the big departures board outside to see when the next shuttle to San Gimignano arrives. The shuttle leaves from Area 2 (up a little bit, on the right), takes about 20min., runs every 15-30min., and costs €1.80.

Getting Around

Although San Gimignano is tiny and pretty much walkable, its hills are a bit of a nuisance. Two **bus** lines run a loop through the city for €0.50 *(daily ticket €1),* mostly providing transport between the parking lots, the Coop, and the Duomo. Cars are not an option within the city walls. If you're interested in alternative transportation options, **Bellini Bruno** may be worth investigating. It provides bike, scooter, motorcycle, and car rental. *(V. Roma 41 ☎0577 94 02 01 ▣www.bellinibruno.com ⚔ Downhill and to the right from Porta San Giovanni. ⓘ Provides delivery and pickup of vehicles at your accommodations.)*

cortona ☎0575

It is hard to imagine that this tiny, impossibly hilly town once rivaled mighty *Firenze* for Tuscan dominance. But in the summer, Cortona sure rivals it for tourists per square inch. Nearly empty in the winter—the tourist office reports the summer population as 3000 and the winter population as "much, much less"—the town's three *piazze* and one main drag swell on breezy summer evenings with students from the University of Georgia's satellite campus and grown-up types from one of the many professional conferences held in town. Folks come here for the twisty, steep medieval streets and the breathtaking scenery, and because most streets end with a steep drop over the gorgeous green valley, panoramic views are a dime a dozen. Make sure to bring good shoes, though: you can't walk more than 50m on a flat surface in the entirety of Cortona.

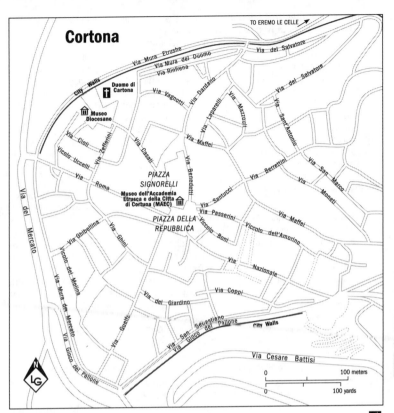

ORIENTATION

To get a proper sense of Cortona's topography, take a map, pinch it somewhere in the middle, and pull up. There you go.

You will arrive in town via the Camucia-Cortona train station, which is at the very bottom of the steep and sizable hill. A bus runs from outside the tiny station to Cortona's **Piazza Garibaldi** every 20-30min. or so, but don't plan to arrive or leave on a Sunday, when the bus runs its loop just twice the entire day. This same bus is also the only public transportation in Cortona unless you count the outdoor escalator leading up to P. Garibaldi. From that *piazza*, walk uphill for the hostel. Walk left along **Via Nazionale**—Cortona's one bustling street—to reach **Piazza Della Repubblica.** Just to the right of that square is **Piazza Signorelli.** Most other streets of interest extend downhill or uphill from these *piazze.*

ACCOMMODATIONS

For some reason, Cortona is a place where people like to hold conferences. If the first hotel you try is completely booked, don't panic—it might just be the annual meeting of Stair Climbers of America Society, and everything else is empty.

CASA BETANIA
V. Gino Severini 70

⤷⊗((•)) HOTEL ❸
☎320 70 98 101

Despite the presence of a proper hostel in town, this hotel is actually the best budget option, whether you're alone or in a group. The rooms are small but lovely, with filmy, colored curtains. The ensuite baths are also tiny, the kind in which you'll stand next to the toilet while you shower. Come for the common spaces. The salon, with a black chandelier and a shiny, silver bar paired with antique wooden furniture, looks like it was decorated in a compromise between a mother and an angsty teenage daughter. There's also a pentagonal conference room and a chapel because, well, it is Italy after all. Bypass it though and go downstairs to reach the terrace. Of all the wonderful panoramic views in Cortona, this is one of the best, on a large tree-shaded patio with nice lounge chairs and a vegetable garden. Who needs a big bedroom when you have this?

⇟ Walk downhill from P. Garibaldi. Cross Vle. Battisti (the 1st major cross street), take a right through the gate, and walk down the drive. When returning, continue walking downhill on Battisti until you reach the escalator up to P. Garibaldi. ℹ Breakfast €4. Wi-Fi available for a fee. $ Singles €32, with bath €42; doubles €44/€48; triples €60/€66; quads €86; quints €106. ⏰ Reception 8:30am-12:30pm and 2:30-7:30pm.

OSTELLO SAN MARCO (HI) 🍴🚭 HOSTEL ❶

V. Maffei 57 ☎0575 60 13 92 💻www.cortonahostel.com

This HI hostel is heartbreaking—it could be one of the best hostels in Italy but can't quite manage the task. The medieval lobby is like something out of Hogwarts, and you won't find a more impressive view from your bunk bed anywhere else. Unfortunately, that lobby is locked most of the day, and there is no other common space in the cavernous, frequently empty hostel. Internet access is nonexistent, although the girl at the desk can tell you where to mooch Wi-Fi in town. That being said, the basic facility is excellent. It's too bad that, without much competition in town, there's no pressure to offer the amenities that would make this hostel great.

⇟ From V. Garibaldi, walk 5min. uphill on V. Santa Margherita. It's right down the 1st left. ℹ Breakfast included. Only group reservations in winter. $ Dorms €16. ⏰ Reception 4-8pm. Call if arriving at another time. Check-out strictly at 9:30am.

INSTITUTO SANTA MARGHERITA 💳♿📶❄ HOTEL ❸

Vle. Cesare Battisti 17 ☎0575 63 03 36 💻www.comunitacortona@smr.it

The "institute" part is a bit apt for the feel of this nun-run hotel, but the rooms themselves have nicely painted wood furniture, ensuite baths, and a preponderance of twin beds that are occasionally pushed together but usually arranged in the chaste *I Love Lucy* fashion. The breakfast room has an altar, but otherwise the big common spaces, huge patio, and terrace are largely unfurnished and tidy. The larger family rooms, with their long row of twin beds, have a dormitory feel, but you'll like them better when you calculate their per-person rate.

⇟ Walk downhill from P. Garibaldi. When you hit Vle. Battisti (the 1st major cross street), the hotel is on the corner on the left. When returning, continue walking downhill until you reach the escalator up to P. Garibaldi ℹ Breakfast €5. Only 2 rooms with A/C. Only 2 rooms are wheelchair-accessible. $ Singles €40; doubles €54; triples €70; quads €80; quints €95. A little less in winter. ⏰ Always buzz to get the desk's attention.

DOLCE MARIA 💳🚭📶 B AND B ❸

V. Ghini 12 ☎0575 63 03 97 💻www.cortonastorica.com

The six ornately decorated rooms in this bed and breakfast are of the lace doily variety, but unique features like huge antique fireplaces give the rooms charm. The building is the historic residence of the Burboni family, whomever they may be, and retains a very house-like layout. The breakfast room is quite beautiful. Consider taking advantage of the adjacent restaurant run by the same owner.

⇟ From P. Signorelli, take V. Ghibellina downhill and turn left onto V. Ghini. ℹ Breakfast included. $ Doubles €85-100; quads €130. ⏰ Reception 3-8pm. Owner lives on premises, so call ahead if arriving at a different time.

HOTEL SAN LUCA
HOTEL [4]

P. Garibaldi 1 ☎0575 63 04 60 www.sanlucacortona.com

With a navy-and-yellow color scheme torn straight from the Ralph Lauren catalog, Hotel San Luca has a lobby full of Don Draper accoutrements like shoe-buffers, newspaper racks, and brandy snifters. For the Clark Kents, there's an indoor telephone booth. For the Stephen Colberts, a portrait of a bald eagle. And for everyone else, the enormous panoramic terrace on the bottom floor has several large jacuzzis as well as a gym and spa. For the same price here you can get a room on the noisy *piazza* or with a small balcony over the valley, so plan ahead to call dibs.

It's the only thing in the piazza aside from the bus stop. ***i*** *Breakfast buffet included, served on the terrace in summer. Non-guests are welcome to come and pay to use their Wi-Fi.* $ *Singles €75-90; doubles €95-120; triples €140-160; 4- to 5-person suite €150-170.* *Reception 24hr.*

SIGHTS

EREMO LE CELLE
MONASTERY, HIKE

40min. north of the city ☎0575 60 33 62 www.fraticappuccini.it

Getting here is a **hike,** but it's worth it. Photos do not do justice to this 13th-century monastery built into the face of the mountain—think Mesa Verde, but not ruins. At one time, 200 monks lived in the Franciscan cells—they earned the name Franciscan, by the way, since St. Francis actually hung out here while writing his memoirs—but now there are only half a dozen brothers maintaining the site and providing ministry to the nearby towns. Churched-out tourists may find the rough, sparse chapels more impressive and moving than a dozen Duomos. The grounds are almost entirely open to visitors—if there's somewhere you're not supposed to go, it will be signposted—so take the time to explore this astonishing, ancient complex. If the walk to get here wasn't too taxing, leave the structure to the left to find a proper hiking trail, along paths maintained by the feet of meditating monks. (It doesn't loop or lead to any particular destination, so be aware that you'll have to turn back eventually.)

From P. Mazzini, outside Porta Colonia on the north side of town, 2 roads head downhill to the right. 1 goes steeply downhill to Santa Maria Nuova, which you can see from the piazza. You want to take the other road. The walk is about 3km along a paved, low-traffic road that moves mostly downhill—the view as you curve around the valley is spectacular. The path to the monastery is signposted, but only infrequently. At one point the road splits, and it is ambiguous where the sign is pointing—you want the left fork, going downhill. Eventually you will start seeing signs that you are reaching something—a dumpster, a small park, a place on the left that might be a summer camp. The road ends in a parking lot. Turn around, and you'll see the gate of the monastery. Remember that the return trip will be uphill—some backpackers report that kind locals are willing to offer a lift, but Let's Go does not recommend hitchhiking. $ *Free.* *Visitors most welcome during daytime, for obvious reasons.*

MUSEO DELL'ACCADEMIA ETRUSCA E DELLA CITTA DI CORTONA (MAEC)
MUSEUM

P. Signorelli 9 ☎0575 63 72 35 www.cortonamaec.org

This surprisingly enormous museum is about Cortona: not just modern Cortona, but political Cortona, artistic Cortona, ancient Cortona, and cultural Cortona too. If it's relevant to the land you are standing on, it's in this museum. Cortona is Etruscan territory, so you would be forgiven for thinking MAEC was primarily an archaeological museum. The first 14 rooms do concentrate on the pottery shards and arrowheads you would expect, but the recommended path that starts four levels underground creates a neat echo of the layers of an archaeological site. Just when it seems like the Etruscans are running out of steam, MAEC jumps ahead a few millennia to **Gino Severini,** Cortona's hometown 20th-century

Futurist painter. It's all very confusing until you accept the jumble of historical periods you will be experiencing in the next several dozen rooms. A large series of display cases house Renaissance funerary urns alongside Etruscan bronzes. Medieval sacred art shares a room with a detailed sculpture of the Bay of Malta. Some important person's personal apartment is preserved, complete with an ivory chess-and-checkers set, a wall of rapiers, and an iron chest with lockwork so intricate that it could hold Mad-Eye Moody. In case you thought you'd left them behind in Florence, a giant Medici coat of arms welcomes you into the Sala Medicea, likely lined with folding chairs because it is still used for official occasions. Your reward for making it to the end? One more reminder of the place that inspired it all: an incredible view of the valley from the museum's terrace.

🧭 In P. Signorelli, it's the building that looks like a museum. $ €8, with Museo Diocesano €10. 🕐 Open Apr-Oct daily 10am-7pm; Nov-Mar Tu-Su 10am-5pm.

DUOMO AND MUSEO DIOCESANO CHURCH, MUSEUM

P. Duomo 1 ☎0575 62 830

Of Tuscany's *duomi*, this ain't the most impressive. It's mostly gray, with a richly decorated altar. On the right is an interesting *Pietà* in which Mary looks like a child until you get up close and see the age in her face. It's by an unknown 13th-century artist. You can find the greater selection of art in the Museo Diocesano across the *piazza*. That museum includes a substantial collection of brightly colored Signorellis—the emotional *Pietà* is the most affecting. A series by Cortona's Futurist homeboy, **Severini,** depicts the stations of the cross and also lines the stairwell.

🧭 From P. Signorelli, walk downhill between MAEC and the teatro. $ Duomo free. Museum €5, with MAEC €10. 🕐 Duomo open daily in summer 7:30am-1pm and 3-6:30pm; in fall, winter, and spring 8am-12:30pm and 3-5:30pm.

BASILICA DI SANTA MARGHERITA AND FORTEZZA MEDICEA CHURCH

V. Santa Margherita ☎0575 60 31 16 💻www.santamargheritadacortona.org

As if the views all over Cortona weren't enough, you can climb to ever greater heights and further enjoy the prospect. The trek up to the basilica is lined with small roadside shrines. Inside the church, you can pay your respects to the corpse of **Saint Margherita** herself. For the fortress, head yet farther uphill, where you will be rewarded with mosaics, temporary art installations, and a wholly unobstructed 360° view.

🧭 From P. Garibaldi, take V. Santa Margherita uphill and follow the road as it curves its way up the hill until you reach the church. For the fortress, take a right out of the church and follow a path farther uphill. $ Basilica free. Fortress €3. 🕐 Basilica open daily in summer 8am-noon and 3-7pm; in fall, winter, and spring 9am-noon and 3-6pm.

CHIESA DI SAN FRANCESCO CHURCH

V. Berrettini 4 ☎0575 60 32 05

This one is mostly important for those interested in pilgrimages. This unassuming church houses a relic of the Holy Cross. St. Francis's robes are also here, and they may be the ones he wore when he left Asissi for Cortona. The church itself dates from the 13th century and was designed by **Friar Elias.** It became the prototype of all Franciscan churches, with a single gothic nave and a trussed roof.

🧭 Take V. Maffei from P. Signorelli and you'll hit the church. $ Free. 🕐 Open daily 9am-6:45pm

CHIESA DI SANTA MARIA NUOVA CHURCH

Localita Santa Maria Nuova ☎0575 60 32 56

Look over the edge of Cortona's north wall, and you'll see a church nestled in the slope of the hill a bit below you. It's rarely open, but the walk down the hill is lovely anyway. If you're really curious to see the inside of the 16th-century church, you can look for the caretaker Paola. She'll let you in. On Saturdays from April to September at 7pm they perform mass in eight languages.

✠ North and downhill of the city. Exit the city at P. Mazzini and look down. ⑤ Free. ⚙ Unless attending mass, the inside is only open by appointment.

FOOD

The sit-down restaurants in town keep limited hours, closing between lunch and dinner, but there are plenty of other options. The small **◆Despar** in P. della Repubblica stocks basic groceries, and the deli counter makes incredible sandwiches for €3-4 (*P. della Repubblica 22/23* ☎0575 62 544 ⚙ *Open M-Sa 7am-1:30pm and 4-8pm, Su 9am-1pm.*) On Saturdays from 8am until around 1:30pm, **Piazza Signorelli** hosts a flea market that includes a fair number of stands selling fresh produce, meat, and cheese.

just a few more minutes

Restaurants in Cortona don't really believe in fixed opening, or especially closing, hours. Show up during a mealtime and they'll probably be open. If there's enough business they'll stay open later, and then a little later, and pretty much just until everyone feels like going home. We've tried to indicate roughly when each establishment is open, but if you have your heart set on somewhere, it's best to check ahead with the restaurant to see if they'll be open.

cortona . food

◆ FUFLUNS
V. Ghibellina 3

🍴⊗✝ RISTORANTE ❷
☎0575 60 41 40 🖥www.fuflunscnc.it

The cheap and varied pizza selection might seem tempting—and the neverending stream of takeout boxes proves that the *Cortonese* have been thoroughly tempted—but Fufluns is special for another reason. *Let's Go* knows that penny-pinchers tend to be faced with the choice of the same three pasta dishes at the bottom of any restaurant's price range, but at Fufluns you'll find awesome homemade pastas made with eccentric ingredients—blueberry!—plus actual meat *secondi* in the €6-8 range. That blueberry pasta may look like a bowl of raw flesh, but it is actually delicious. Basically, the food is so good at Fufluns that we don't have to resort to padding our word-count with jokes about their adorable name.

✠ Downhill from P. della Repubblica, on the left. ⑤ Cover €1.50. Pizzas €4-6.50. Blueberry pasta €7. L of beer €7-8. ⚙ Open M 12:15-2:30pm and 7:15-10:30pm, W-Su 12:15-2:30pm and 7:15-10:30pm.

◆ GELATERIA SNOOPY
P. Signorelli 29

⊛ⓖ GELATERIA ❶
☎0575 63 0 197

Good grief, that's good gelato! We doubt this is an authorized use of the Snoopy name, but one taste of the incredibly dark *cioccolato fondente* and you'll be doing the happy dance too. Other draws include this creamery's abnormally generous portions—the smallest size is three scoops (€1.50)—and its proximity to the popular Lion's Well pub. Customers sign the walls over images from the great beagle's life—look for the *Let's Go* thumbpick on the nose of the WWI Flying Ace.

✠ Across from MAEC. ⑤ 3 scoops €1.50. ⚙ Open daily 11am-late.

TAVERNA PANE E VINO
P. Signorelli 27

🍴ⓖ✝🅰 RISTORANTE, ENOTECA ❷
☎347 34 93 583 🖥www.pane-vino.it

This barrel-shaped tavern does indeed focus on bread and wine—with a dozen different bruschettas (€3.50) and over 900 different wines rotating through a weekly tasting menu. The rest of the menu focuses on *Cortonese* and Tuscan

www.letsgo.com **𝓟 363**

specialties, including—and we are quoting them on this—"Cortona's fake 'tuna' with white beans (not for vegetarians!!!!)."

☀ *Opposite the teatro.* Ⓢ *Primi €6-9. Wine mostly €3. Half bottles from €6-19, excluding the fancy stuff.* ⓩ *Open Tu-Su 12:30-2:45pm and 7:30-11pm.*

LA BUCACCIA
V. Ghibellina 17

☀⊗⊘ ♀♨ RISTORANTE ❷
☎0575 60 60 39 ▦www.labucaccia.it

A little chef's hat is the menu's symbol for typical Cortona dishes, and predictably, it can be found next to nearly every entry at this homey trattoria. La Bucaccia is located on a particularly steep bit of hill, but that doesn't stop the restaurant from providing outdoor seating—instead, each table is on a little platform of its own, creating a stairway of tables down the alley. Inside is more level, with the stone interior familiar to Cortona restaurants, plus a giant Archimedes Screw in the center. Try the fondue-like *caccoteca* dishes, which are made of local tangy cheese.

☀ *Uphill from Porta Bifora or downhill from P. della Repubblica.* Ⓢ *Primi €8-9. Caccoteca €8-10.* ⓩ *Open daily for lunch and dinner.*

TONINO'S
P. Garibaldi 1

☀♿ ♀♨ RISTORANTE ❷
☎0575 63 05 00 ▦www.ristorantetonino.com

Take advantage of Hotel San Luca's excellent panoramic perch (p. 361) without having to stay there by eating at their attached restaurant. The menu is the usual run of trattoria options, but you have a more interesting selection in terms of where to sit. There's the patio on busy, breezy P. Garibaldi, which affords the chance for fine people-watching but is marred by an annoying outdoor TV. Or keep your view more pristine and go around to the incredible glass-enclosed terrace, which seems to almost hover over the valley.

☀ *Attached to Hotel San Luca, the only other thing on the piazza.* 𝒊 *Discount for UGA students.* Ⓢ *Primi €7-8. Glass of wine €3.* ⓩ *Open daily 1pm-1am.*

BAR 500
V. Nazionale 44/46

☀♿ ♀♨ CAFE ❶
☎0575 60 44 50

It's just a cafe, but Bar 500 has these amazing pizza-panini things. Picture two pizzas smooshed face to face. To top it off, these concoctions are sprinkled on top with olives and mushrooms. The owner has a fantastic ugly-adorable English bulldog who sometimes visits.

☀ *Halfway between P. Garibaldi and P. della Repubblica.* Ⓢ *Cover €1. Pizza-paninis €5.* ⓩ *Open daily in summer 11am-11pm; in fall, winter, and spring 11am-7pm.*

LA SALETTA
V. Nazionale 26-28

☀♿♨ CAFE ❶
☎0575 60 33 66 ▦www.caffelasaletta.it

If you're tiring of the typical unsalted Tuscan breads, check out this cafe's wide selection of alternatives. While they offer excellent variations on the traditional bread, the La Saletta gets its name—which translates to, roughly, The Saltery—from its menu of flat, salty breads, many baked with interesting things thrown in, like wild boar or goat cheese.

☀ *From P. Garibaldi, on the right.* Ⓢ *Breads €3-7.* ⓩ *Open daily noon-midnight.*

NIGHTLIFE

For such a small place, in the summer, at least, Cortona has a surprisingly hopping evening scene. This is in large part thanks to the UGA students who turn the town into a borough of Athens, GA. The action still consists mostly of people walking around with drinks purchased at one of the two busy bars or sitting with bottles on the steps of one of the two *piazze*. In the winter, though, they roll up the sidewalks.

THE LION'S WELL
P. Signorelli 28

☀♿ ♀♨ BAR
☎0575 60 49 18

The Lion's Well sits on the busiest *piazza* and has a lot of outdoor seating.

There's also a flatscreen TV outside: this is a recipe for pub success. The Lion's Well is always crowded with a group of American undergrads and locals rubbing elbows. The bar itself is nothing special but seems to be where it's at.

The pub is in P. Signorelli, next to Snoopy's. $ Wine €3. Shots €3-4. Beer €3.50-4. Open daily 11am-3am or 4am or when business dries up for the day.

ROUTE 66 BAR

V. Nazionale 78 ☎0575 627 27 www.route66cortona.it

Route 66 must lose an awful lot of wine glasses to the gaping maw of the valley. The bar benefits from a location at the corner of V. Nazionale and P. Garibaldi, although the patio's mandatory waiter service *(with €2 cover)* and TV blaring away are less than appealing. There's also a dance floor downstairs, but in nice weather, you'll likely only go inside to order a drink from their long cocktail list before heading back out to enjoy it at the edges of the *piazza*. The stone ledge separating the square from the drop into the valley becomes a de facto bar littered with abandoned glasses at the end of the evening, so head outside and make a toast to *Toscana*.

The corner of P. Garibaldi and V. Nazionale. $ Wine €3-4. Beer €4. Cocktails €6. Open daily 11am-4am or whenever people go home.

ARTS AND CULTURE

TEATRO SIGNORELLI THEATER

P. Signorelli ☎0575 60 18 82 www.teatrosignorelli.com

This classic La Scala-style house plays host to various concerts, festivals, and conferences throughout the year. It's a great old theater with plush, red-velvet seats and boxes all the way to the ceiling—relics of a time when going to the theater was about seeing and being seen. On the ceiling directly above the pit, there's a large clock, presumably for bored musicians.

In P. Signorelli, the building that looks like a theater. $ Prices vary, but standard ticket €10-40. Concerts start at 9:15pm.

TUSCAN SUN FESTIVAL FESTIVAL

Terretrusche Ticketing, at Vicolo Alfieri 3 ☎0575 60 68 87 www.tuscansunfestival.com

Annual festival in early August, featuring a wide array of activities over eight days, including cooking and handicraft workshops, tours, movies, dance lessons, wine tastings, and lectures. In the evenings at Teatro Signorelli, there are performances by major musicians like Renee Fleming and Joshua Bell.

Multiple locations around Cortona. $ Prices vary. Early August.

FESTIVAL DI MUSICA SACRA FESTIVAL

V. Zefferini 16 www.cortonacristiana.it

This annual sacred music festival and conference takes place in July. You can find performances, several of them free, at venues all over Cortona. There are also lectures and classes, including a five-day course in singing Gregorian chant.

Various locations around Cortona. $ Many events free, other prices vary. July.

ESSENTIALS

Practicalities

- **TOURIST OFFICES: Ufficio Turismo** provides maps, bus schedules, taxi-calling, and bus and train tickets—it's the only place to buy train tickets for Camucia. *(V. Nazionale 42 ☎0575 63 03 52 www.apt.arezzo.it On the left, coming from P. Garibaldi. Open in summer M-Sa 9am-1pm and 3-8pm, Su 9am-1pm; in fall, winter, and spring M-F 9am-1pm and 3-6pm, Sa 9am-1pm.)*
- **CURRENCY EXCHANGE: Banca Etruria** provides 24hr. ATM. *(V. Santa Margherita 5 Just off P. Garibaldi.)*

- **INTERNET: Hotel San Luca** provides what seems to be the town's only Wi-Fi. Non-guests are welcome to pay to use it in the lobby. (*P. Garibaldi 1* ☎*0575 63 04 60* ✝ *On P. Garibaldi, can't miss it.* ✆ *Open 24hr.*)

- **POST OFFICES:** (*V. Benedetti 2* ☎*0575 60 25 22* ✝ *Uphill from P. della Repubblica.* ✆ *Open M-F 8:15am-1:30pm, Sa 8:15am-12:30pm, Su 8:15am-1:30pm.*)

- **POSTAL CODE:** 52044.

Emergency!

- **POLICE: Polizia Municipale.** (*P. Repubblica 13* ☎*0575 63 72 25* ✝ *On the right coming from P. Garibaldi.* ✆ *Open M 9:30am-12:30pm, Tu 9:30am-12:30pm and 3-5:30pm, W 9:30am-12:30pm, Th 9:30am-12:30pm and 3-5:30pm, F-Sa 9:30am-12:30pm.*)

- **LATE-NIGHT PHARMACIES: Farmacia Centrale** is in a 24hr. rotation with other pharmacies in Camucia (*V. Nazionale 38* ☎*0575 60 32 06*).

- **HOSPITALS/MEDICAL SERVICES: Ospedale Santa Margherita di Cortona** provides hospital care in Fratta, about 4 mi. northwest of Cortona (*Localita Fratta 15* ☎*0575 63 91*).

Getting There

There is no train station in Cortona. You'll want to use the **Camucia-Cortona** station, in the downhill satellite town of Camucia. Even this is a small station—there is no *biglietteria*, so buy tickets at the automated machine or from the tourist office in Cortona. Outside the station, the **LFI bus** (☎*0575 30 07 38* ▣*www.lfi.it* Ⓢ *€1.*) will take you the 15min. up to P. Garibaldi every 20min. or so. Be warned that the bus runs only twice on Sundays. From Camucia, trains arrive from **Florence** (Ⓢ *€7.30.* ✆ *90min., 1 per hr. 4:14am-9:25pm.*), and **Rome** (Ⓢ *€9.40.* ✆ *2½hr., from every 2hr. 8am-10:34pm.*) To get here from **Perugia** (Ⓢ *€3.40.* ✆ *50min.*) or **Asissi** (Ⓢ *€4.30.* ✆ *1hr. 10min.*), change in Foligno. (✆ *6 per day 9:34am-9:34pm.*)

Getting Around

On Foot

There is no public transportation within Cortona, unless you count the outdoor escalator up to P. Garibaldi. The LFI **bus** will take you to Camucia, Terontola, or Arezzo. Take note that navigating Cortona in a wheelchair is nearly impossible.

By Cab

There is no centralized taxi service. The tourist office can provide a list of names and phone numbers of individual drivers. You might want to have her call for you to get a rate quote.

perugia ☎075

In Perugia, there's plenty to do but not a whole lot to see. The city has an excellent art gallery and lovely Duomo, plus the usual round of incredible panoramic views from ancient city walls, but odds are, if you're looking for that sort of thing, you'll end up in Siena first. As pretty as the Tuscan towns but without the big name, Perugia wisely compensated by finding itself two claims to fame wholly unrelated to the Renaissance—**chocolate** and **jazz.** During the Eurochocolate festival in October and Umbria Jazz Festival in July, Perugia's population swells beyond capacity as pilgrims from around Europe descend on the city and completely max out its tourism infrastructure. Even when the festivals aren't in session, the Perugina factory is ready to satisfy sweet-tooths, and a lively year-round jazz scene should appease improvisation aficionados. The wealth of excellent pubs may exist largely to support the summer's jazz babies, but fear not! During the winter, Perugia's many university students are up to the task of keeping the bars full.

ORIENTATION

If you've been making your way through tiny Tuscan towns for the past few weeks, getting to the Umbrian capital will be a shock. Perugia is actually enormous, an unattractive urban sprawl full of actual people living lives unrelated to the tourism industry. Nonetheless, there is, in fact, the usual *centro storico* for all your tourism consolidation needs—it just exists on a different plane, literally. You will likely arrive from the **train station** or the bus station across the street. If you're facing the train station, turn left and walk across that parking lot to the mini-Metro. Tiny red light-rail trams will spirit you up the mountain to the *centro* (the stop is **Pinchetto,** the end of the line). Escalators will bring you the rest of the way up inside the old walls.

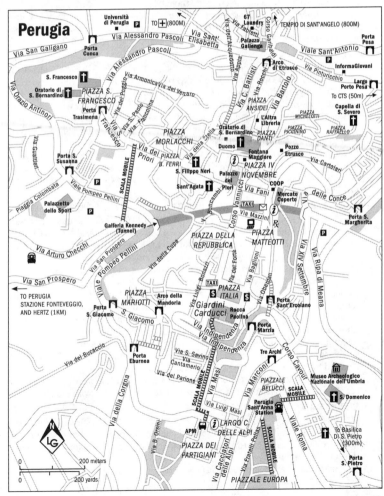

ACCOMMODATIONS

Book in advance for the Umbria Jazz and Eurochocolate Festivals. The rest of the time, you're likely to have the town to yourself.

OSTELLO PERUGIA
💳♿ HOSTEL [1]

V. Bontempi 13 ☎075 57 22 880 💻www.ostello.perugia.it

This hostel's main perk is its location right in the *centro*. Dorms are plain and divided by gender between two floors, but the common spaces are indeed spacious. The kitchen has eight ranges to accommodate many cooks in the kitchen and a row of picnic tables for when the meal's ready. The view from the small terrace can't be beat. A large library (large enough to merit use of the Dewey Decimal System) contains mostly academic texts in Italian and German, but hey, it's a library in a hostel. The midday lockout is lame, so plan ahead. And really plan ahead to book your bed for the Umbria Jazz Festival, when you definitely don't want to be stuck staying outside the city.

➜ From P. IV Novembre, facing the Duomo, take the street that's behind you to the right, V. Bontempi, and bear right until the hostel. ℹ Linens €2. [$] Dorms €15. ⏰ Reception 7:30-10am and 4pm-midnight. Curfew 3:30am. Strict lockout 11am-3:30pm. Closed Dec 15-Jan 15.

HOTEL PRIORI
💳♿📶❄ HOTEL [3]

V. Vermiglioli 3 ☎075 57 23 378 💻www.hotelpriori.it

This hotel is a bit of a maze—there are so many rooms scattered through so many hallways behind so many unnecessary doors that you might suspect it was originally one of those "riot-proof" college dormitories. In reality, it was just a 15th-century house. When you get lost, there are a lot of signs pointing you to the lobby or the breakfast room, the latter being the better destination. Breakfast is served on a glass-enclosed (and, mercifully, climate-controlled) patio on the panoramic terrace. Appropriate to a town with a chocolate factory, there's also a great glass elevator—take it to the top floor to really feel like you'll head up and out.

➜ On the corner of V. dei Priori. ℹ Breakfast included. [$] Singles €45-70; doubles €65-95. Extra €20 for ensuite A/C. ⏰ Reception 24hr.

PERUGIA FARMHOUSE BACKPACKER HOSTEL
⊛🚭📶 HOSTEL [1]

Strada Torre Poggio 4 (San Sisto) ☎339 56 20 005 💻www.perugia-farmhouse.it

The swimming pool is absolutely gorgeous, and the farmhouse bit ain't no lie: chickens, a donkey, two mean geese, an affectionate turkey, and a horse roam these grounds. Importantly, despite what you might read on the internet, no night transportation from the city connects to the hostel. The last bus leaves Perugia at 9:15pm. Given the city's expensive taxis, this is a very poor base for any car-less individual hoping to live it up after 10pm. You'll have plenty of fun at the farmhouse itself, though, with the chickens providing breakfast, the other farm animals providing company, a communal kitchen, and a DIY party atmosphere—Thursday night talent shows around the pool are highly recommended. For the location, beds should be a few euros cheaper, and management seriously needs to invest in a few fans—the east-facing dorms are ovens at dawn. All the same, it's hard to quibble when the pool is so darn nice.

➜ From the train station, take the C or D bus toward Pila. Get off in front of Bar Olympia and walk back 20m for Strada Torre Poggio. ℹ Breakfast included. Free Wi-Fi. [$] Dorms €18-23.

ALBERGO ANNA
⊛🚭 HOTEL [3]

V. dei Priori 48 ☎075 57 36 304 💻www.albergoanna.it

Stuffed lounges full of framed photos and chintzy armchairs, combined with random details like colorful terra-cotta fireplaces in otherwise plain rooms, make this small hotel memorable.

➜ Downhill from C. Vannucci, the street that splits Palazzo dei Priori. [$] Singles €30-40, with bath €40-50; doubles €60-90.

LA ROSETTA

🍴♿📶❄ HOTEL 5

P. Italia 19 ☎075 57 20 841 💻www.perugiaonline.com/larosetta

This hotel has a posh-circa-1922 look, and despite the beautiful Renaissance ceiling frescoes in a couple of the suites, the decoration scheme is very early-to-mid-20th century. There's even a card room with green felt covered tables off the lobby. The rooms chichi it up a bit with golden upholstery and gilded art prints, but the undercurrent of late Deco can't be erased.

🚶 The hotel is 1 side of P. Italia, but enter through the restaurant courtyard on the right. $ Singles €81-100; doubles €120-210.

SIGHTS

👁

The **Perugia City Museum Card** is a fantastic deal, particularly for students. The "A" Card for €10 grants unlimited entry to one adult and one person under 18 to five museums and is valid for 48hr. The "U" Card for university students is only €6, and grants admission to five museums for one month from first use. All card holders may pick up a free video guide from the Galleria Nazionale as well. Participating sights include the Galleria Nazionale, Museo Archeologico, Pozzo Etrusco, and nine other smaller sights. The card is available at the ticket office of all participating museums. For information, contact the Consorzio Perugia Citta Museo. *(V. Podiani 11 ☎075 57 72 805 💻www.perugiacittamuseo.it)*

★ PERUGINA MUSEO STORICO

🍴♿ MUSEUM

6km southwest of the city ☎075 52 76 796 💻www.perugina.it

This is a chocolate factory. Do you really need to know more than that?

All right, fine—here's a taste of what's to come: lots and lots of free chocolate. As if to reward you for schlepping outside town to find the factory, you are greeted in the lobby by a table overflowing with free samples of the freshest chocolate imaginable. Feel free to stuff your face—it's not like they can wrap this stuff up at the end of the day and sell it. Pull an Augustus Gloop and go to town. The museum itself is pretty interesting, too, particularly if you're into media history and social anthropology. The collection is mostly a jumble of wrappers, advertisements, packaging, and other ephemera from a century of Perugina chocolates—amazingly, the logo of the company's signature Baci chocolate has barely changed in 80 years. There's also a replica of a one ton Bacio (that's the singular of Baci) that was created for the annual chocolate-carving competition in Perugia a few years back. In less than 3hr., one ton of solid chocolate was consumed by the hordes in attendance. The museum also screens a pretty awesome reel of Baci television ads from the last 80 years. The montage moves through soldiers presenting Baci to girls who have waited on the home front to screaming teenagers lobbing Baci at The Beatles to a series of viral videos from recent years. Don't miss the historic photos of folks like **Joe DiMaggio** holding boxes of Baci or the display explaining just how chocolate is made—bet you didn't know that **[?] cocoa beans are actually the size of your head.** If you're feeling hungry again, double back to the lobby for more chocolate. Finally, you may get to go on an actual tour of an actual chocolate factory. It was under renovation when we were here, but it's scheduled to reopen before we go to print. Let us know how it is, you lucky gits.

🚶 From the train station, take the A bus out of town to San Sisto. It passes right by the Perugina factory, which is enormous and cannot be missed. ℹ Reservations required for guided tours and the factory tour. $ Free. ⏰ Open M-F 9am-1pm and 2-5:30pm.

PIAZZA IV NOVEMBRE

♿ PIAZZA

P. IV Novembre

Competitive though central Italian cities may be, this *piazza* does not commemorate the destructive flooding of Florence on November 4th, 1966, but rather the

Italians' version of Armistice Day on November 4th, 1918, when Austria-Hungary surrendered to Italy. The *piazza* itself is truncated by the steps of the **Duomo,** which shades the always crowded square. The fountain in the center of the *piazza* was decorated by the Pisanos and is a good local landmark. Always the epicenter of Perugia's BYOB nightlife, during the Umbria Jazz Festival the *piazza* is completely overwhelmed. That crunching sound underfoot as you push through the crush of bodies at 4am comes from a weekend's worth of plastic cups blanketing the ground.

⌖ Bordered by the Duomo and the National Gallery.

GALLERIA NAZIONALE DELL' UMBRIA — ⊛♿❄ MUSEUM

C. Vannucci — ☎0755 72 10 09 💻www.sistemamuseo.it

If you're starting to get the feeling that Tuscan and Umbrian art museums aren't so much curated exhibits as they are a jumble of stuff thrown into a room a few centuries ago, then you'll be pleased by Perugia's major gallery. Shockingly enough, the art is well-lit and decently spaced out. There are even artificial walls in the middle of galleries so that important pieces can be displayed alone. This offers possibly the region's best opportunity to appreciate—rather than just see—Renaissance art.

⌖ In P. IV Novembre, opposite the Duomo. ℹ Frequent special exhibits, ask at the desk. $ €6.50, students €3.25, under 18 and over 65 free. ⏰ Open Tu-Su 8:30am-7:30pm. Last entry 1hr. before close.

MINIMETRÒ AND ROCCO PAOLINA — ✎♿ TRANSPORT

Around the *centro* — ☎075 50 58 753 💻www.minimetrospa.it

OK, so maybe it's a little absurd to list a tram as a sight, but when you were a kid, didn't you consider the Monorail an integral part of Disney World? Perugia's Minimetrò is basically adorable. Teeny little red cars go buzzing up and down 3km of track between seven stations, and that's it. They come so frequently (about one per minute) that you can easily score a car to yourself if you feel like having a silly tram-car photo shoot. The cars are silent and fast, and when they turn around at the end of the track, it's pretty much the cutest thing ever. Truly, though, these things aren't just significant for being the most *awww*-inducing public transit vehicles around: excellent design and engineering allowed the creation of this fast and cheap rail system into the *centro* that doesn't impact the historic skyline. Similarly impressive is the series of **public escalators** inside the walls of the city, particularly inside the former **Rocca Paolina,** connecting P. Italia to the bus station and arena at P. dei Partigiani.

⌖ Escalator off of P. Italia. There are many signs for the Minimetrò stops. $ Minimetrò €1. Escalators free. ⏰ Minimetrò operates M-Sa 7am-9:20pm, Su 8:30am-8:30pm. Escalator operates daily 6:30am-1:45am.

POZZO ETRUSCO — ⊛⊘ WELL

P. Danti 18 — ☎075 57 33 669

It's a big hole in the ground, but it's a really important one. This well was dug by the Etruscans in the third century BCE and watered the city for millennia. Perugians were forced to use the well again during WWII, when bombs destroyed water lines to the city. Now, you can descend a series of dark, wet, slimy steps into the well itself and stand over the water on a small footbridge. The damp walls continue to leak fresh water from the deep underground springs that the well has tapped since ancient times.

⌖ Look for the entrance off P. Danti next to Dempsey's Bar and follow the covered alley down to the well's entrance. $ €3. ⏰ Open daily 10am-1:30pm and 2:30-6:30pm.

FOOD

👍 IL PORCHETTO
⊗♿🍸 STREET FOOD ❶

P. Matteotti

Somewhere between a hole-in-the-wall and a food cart, this distinctly pre-war, semi-permanent green kiosk appended to the front of the post office is a simple affair. They have a pig; you want a pig sandwich. They slice a chunk off whatever part of the pig happens to be up next for slicing and stick it on a roll. You give them €2.50. Done and done. A Porchetto sandwich carved straight from the pig is a Perugian standby, and you'll see them available at festivals and markets elsewhere in town. This particular kiosk, however, has been servin' 'em up since 1921. Get a bottle of beer (in a plastic cup, per local regulation) along with your hearty sandwich, and you have a swell takeout dinner.

 # In front of the post office. [S] Porchetto €2.50. Bottle of beer €2-3. ⏰ Open 7pm-late, depending on business.

TRATTORIA DAL MI' COCCO
💳♿🍸 RISTORANTE ❷

V. Garibaldi 12 ☎075 57 32 511

In the outskirts of the *centro* toward the university, this extremely popular small restaurant offers only a *prix-fixe* menu. That means, what they're offering is the only thing they're cooking today—you'll never order wrong here. Count on a meal that includes an *antipasto*, a *primo*, a *secondo*, bread, a dessert, and a liqueur. Reservations recommended, particularly when school's in session.

 # Leave the city walls at Arco Etrusco, and continue north on V. Garibaldi. It's on the left, a bit easy to miss. [S] Prix-fixe menu €13. ⏰ Open Tu-Su 11am-2pm and 8:15-10pm.

LA LANTERNA
💳♿🍸⛱ RISTORANTE ❸

V. Rocchi 6 ☎075 57 26 397

Three large, wildly different dining spaces fill this popular restaurant. The main indoor dining room is brick-lined, with high, vaulted ceilings and copper pans on the wall. Sit on the outdoor seating in P. Danti if you want to sacrifice character for excellent people-watching. Around the corner, an Oriental garden is lined with colored sheets to create a watery light.

 # Behind the Duomo, off P. Danti. Garden is a bit downhill and around the corner. [S] Cover €2. Primi €6-10; secondi €7-13. ⏰ Open in summer daily 12:30-2:30pm and 7:30-10:30pm; in fall, winter, and spring W-Su 12:30-2:30pm and 7:30-10:30pm.

LA TANA DELL'ORSO
💳♿📶🍸⛱ RISTORANTE ❷

V. Ulissa Rocchi 32 ☎075 57 29 536 💻www.latanadellorso.com

This restaurant is a favorite of the study-abroad crowd—some students report getting special rates for being regulars. The menu is not extensive, but the kitchen is open late. Plus, there's free Wi-Fi. Avoid the overpriced hamburgers—no matter how homesick you are, a meat patty is not worth €11.

 # From P. Danti, take V. Rocchi; it's on the left. [S] Entrees €6-11. ⏰ Open daily 11:30am-3am.

NIGHTLIFE

There are tons of lovely bars in this student town, many tucked away down small alleys or under covered streets. The heart of the nightlife is **Piazza IV Novembre**—Italians just can't resist boozing it up on the steps of their Duomo. No glass bottles are permitted here, but local establishments pour out drinks into clear plastic cups. No one seems to mind, though all those cups make a nice crunch-crunch underfoot at the end of the night.

👍 IL BIRRAIO
💳♿🍸⛱ BAR

V. delle Prome 18 ☎075 57 23 920 💻www.ilbirraio.net

This partially underground bar has an *Arabian Nights*, hookah-lounge feel, while offering microbrews and artisan beers. At the entrance, you ascend past giant copper brewing things to enter the airy, pastel upper level with dozens of painted wooden stools along a friendly blue bar. Downstairs is dominated by floor cushions and low tables. Il Birraio is enormous and will probably be deserted in the summer when there are good outdoor bar options—its small outdoor provides a nice view but lacks the interior's atmosphere—but come early to snag a pile of pillows when the weather drives the nightlife indoors.

🧭 Follow signs to Porta Sole. $ Beer €3-5. 1L Sangria €10. ⏰ Open Tu-Sa 11am-2am, Su 11:30am-2am.

👍 LA TERRAZZA — BAR

Mercato Coperto

Under the covered archway off of P. Matteotti and past the flea-market stalls is a large, bustling outdoor pub with an incredible 270° panoramic view of Perugia. Try a *rum e pere* shot—that's rum and a chaser of pear juice. Recommended drinking method is to swish the pear juice around and coat your mouth before shooting the rum.

🧭 V. del Mercato, accessed from P. Matteotti. $ Rum e Pere €3. ⏰ Open M-F 11am-2am, Sa 11am-2:30am, Su 11am-2am.

👍 ELFO'S PUB — IRISH PUB, JAZZ BAR

V. Sant'Agata 20 ☎347 078 5981

Crowded in a pleasant way, Elfo's Pub is the only establishment on a small, steep side street which becomes an extension of the bar itself in the later hours. This is a pretty good version of the whole Irish pub thing. Elfo's is known for hosting jam sessions throughout the year, and it's an unofficial satellite of the Umbria Jazz Festival. During the festival, late-night shows start every evening shortly after the finish of whomever was playing the Arena. Being an Elfo's barfly is one of the best ways to take in some serious free jazz and hang with musicians instead of partiers.

🧭 From C. Vannucci take V. Priori, which splits the Palazzo dei Priori, downhill. 2nd left, more downhill. $ Shots €3-4. Beer pints €5-6. ⏰ Open M-Sa 8pm-2:30am. Closed in late Aug.

CAFFE MORLACCHI — BAR

P. Morlacchi 8 ☎075 57 21 760

Comfortable and spacious, this cafe across the street from Teatro Morlacchi gets a before- and after-theater crowd—to drive it home, out front they have, not a bench, but a row of wooden theater seats. Inside is quirky and friendly, with anthropomorphized decorations like terra-cotta flowerpots with scary, scary troll eyes.

🧭 Downhill from P. IV Novembre, past P. Cavalliotti. $ Espresso €0.80. Bottled beer €4-5. ⏰ Open M-Sa 8am-1am.

FESTIVALS

👍 UMBRIA JAZZ FESTIVAL — SUMMER

☎075 50 18 228 💻www.umbriajazz.com

The time of the Umbria Jazz Festival is the time to head to Perugia. If you're a jazz fan, then you probably already know about this festival and can judge your interest for yourself. If you're one of those people who's more likely to hear about the festival and say, "jazz is cool, I guess," don't think twice: come. The whole thing is 10 days of constant free music. The stage at the snack bar in Giardini Carducci has free acts every day of the festival. The stage in P. IV Novembre has two or three free sets each night. 👍**Elfo's Pub** and several other pubs host jam sessions in the late evening, with no cover. Ristorante La Taverna and several other restaurants host jazz buffets, jazz dinners, and jazz *aperitivi* if you're willing to pay the cost of food for your music. And if you really want to cough up some cash for the big-name acts, general admission seats at the

Arena Santa Giuliana are as cheap as €13. You can even listen from right outside the arena. Basically, you don't have to spend any money at all to be completely sated with jazz, and you get to experience Perugia at its most happening. Each evening, C. Vannucci and P. IV Novembre become a giant party (on weekends perhaps too giant) with thousands of young people milling about, drinking, dancing, and generally showing Perugia how to have a good time. If you're in central Italy in early July, this is simply the place to be. Umbria Jazz 11 will run July 8-17, 2011.

$ Free-€56, depending on the event, venue, and seat. Mostly free.

EUROCHOCOLATE FALL

☎075 50 25 880 🖥www.eurochocolate.com

For nine days in mid-October, Perugia opens its doors to Lindt, Cadbury, and other great chocolatiers of the world. The city is transformed into a sweet-tooth's paradise as all the major *piazze* are filled with chocolate stands, chocolate statues, chocolate spas, and chocolate art. Free samples are abundant—hover near one of the artists sculpting huge blocks of chocolate and grab the shavings. Best of all, the experience is completely free—unless you want to bring home your very own giant chocolate *Pieta*.

➜ P. Italia, P. IV Novembre, and the other piazze of Perugia centro. $ Free. ⏰ Mid-Oct.

ESSENTIALS

Practicalities

- **TOURIST OFFICES: Infopoint "Loggia dei Lanari"** provides brochures, accommodation listings, and lovely shiny guides with tourist itineraries and self-guided walking tours. *(P. Matteotti 18 ☎075 57 36 458 🖥www.turismo.comune.perugia.it ➜ At the entrance to the Loggia. ⏰ Open M-F 9am-1pm and 2:30-6:30pm, Sa 9am-1pm.)*
- **POST OFFICES:** *(P. Matteotti 1 ➜ Across from the tourist office. ⏰ Open M-Sa 8am-6:30pm.)*
- **ATMS:** There are a handful of 24hr. ATMs along C. Vannucci and in P. Italia.

Emergency!

- **POLICE: Polizia Locale.** *(V. Cortonese 157 ☎075 57 22 335)*
- **LATE-NIGHT PHARMACIES: Farmacia San Martino** posts rotation for 24hr. service. *(P. Matteotti 26 ☎075 57 22 335 ➜ Across from the post office.)*
- **HOSPITALS/MEDICAL SERVICES: Ospedale Silvestrini** provides emergency service *(☎075 57 86 400)*.

Getting There

By Plane

Perugia's very small airport, **International Airport of Umbria (PEG)** *(☎075 59 21 41 🖥www.airport.umbria.it ➜ 16km east of the city.)*, receives a few flights each day from a select group of cities like Milan, London (Stansted), Barcelona, Tirana, and Bucharest. Yep, that's a pretty random list. That's because this is a pretty random airport. There is a shuttle bus linking PEG with the city itself, and there are few enough flights arriving that the bus schedule can intersect with each of them. The shuttle will drop you off at P. Italia or at the train station. *($ €3.50.)*

By Train

Trains to Perugia arrive in **Stazione Fontivegge** in P. Vittorio Veneto. *(⏰ Ticket office open daily 6:30am-12:50pm and 1:20-8:10pm. Automated machines 24hr.)* Get here from **Assisi** *($ €2.40. ⏰ 30min., 14 per day 8am-8pm.)*, **Florence** *($ €10.10. ⏰ 2hr., every 2hr. 7am-9pm.)*, or **Rome.** *($ €20. ⏰ 2½hr., 5 per day 7:45am-8pm.)* From Rome, it's also possible to change trains in Foligno to where there is more frequent service. To get to Perugia from Cortona, also change in Foligno.

By Bus

SULGA *(☎075 50 09 64 🖥www.sulga.it)* runs a service to **Florence,** stopping in **Siena.** *($ €10.50. ⏰ 2½hr.; M-F 1 per day, from Florence 6pm, from Perugia 9:30am.)* The same company links Perugia with cities as far away as **Milan** *(⏰ 6½hr., 1 bus per day on M-Tu and F-Sa, from Milan 4:45pm, from Perugia 4:40am.)* and **Naples.** *(⏰ 4½hr.; 1 per day, from Naples 8:15am, from Perugia 2:30pm.)* Check their website for information on the infrequent service. **APM** *(☎075 57 31 707 🖥www.apmperugia.com)* buses run between Perugia and **Assisi.** *($ €3. ⏰ 50min., 9 per day.)*

Getting Around

By Bus

APM *(☎075 50 67 81 🖥www.apmperugia.it)* connects the main train and bus station with the outer edges of the city for €1.50 per ride.

By Minimetrò

This light rail connects Stazione Fontivegge and Pincetto (the *centro*). *(☎075 50 58 753 🖥www.minimetrospa.it $ €1. ⏰ Operates M-Sa 7am-9:20pm, Su 8:30am-8:30pm. Extended hours during Umbria Jazz Festival.)*

By Taxi

Radio Taxi provides taxis. *(☎075 50 04 888 🖥www.radiotaxiperugia.it ⏰ 24hr.)* Find cab stands at P. Italia, P. Partigiani, Ospedale Silvestrini, the airport, and the train station. ⚠**Warning:** prices will rise steeply and arbitrarily during the Umbria Jazz Festival.

assisi ☎075

It's easy to see how Assisi could have inspired St. Francis's rejection of worldly goods for a life of poverty and prayer—this hillside town glows with a simple, profound, and moving beauty. As the birthplace of the saint, it has been attracting pilgrims for nearly a millennium and is thus well-adjusted to its role as a tourist destination. Fortunately, Francis's spirit has kept the souvenir schlock and wax museums away from his hometown, letting serene Assisi remain filled with a lot of long, pretty streets and a heck of a lot of churches. It's a relatively small town that can be seen in a daytrip, but it is also unhurried and elegant. If possible, take your time and spend a night here so that you can stroll the ancient streets while the sunset dances on the stone. Listen carefully, and you might hear the whispers of the olive trees, grape vines, and oaks below—who says communing with nature is just a saintly thing?

ORIENTATION

The closest train station is in the town of Santa Maria degli Angeli at the base of the hill upon which Assisi sits. From the station, you'll take APM Line C to ascend the mountain. There's also a beautiful walking path that provides a much grander introduction to Assisi, but it's a long unshaded drag only suitable for a time when you are without bags and have good weather. Take the bus to the end of the line at **Piazza Matteotti,** in the east of Assisi. The city is on the south face of the hill, so north is up in both maps and topography. The **Basilica di San Francesco** marks the western terminus of the city—the several long avenues that traverse the town all end up there. **Piazza del Comune,** in the *centro*, provides another orientation point with the tourist office and a concentration of hotels and restaurants.

ACCOMMODATIONS

In Assisi, the standard lodging option is a family-owned hotel-restaurant combo. Every rooming house seems to have an eatery attached, and every restaurant has rooms to let. You can usually swing a discount at your hotel's associated trattoria.

OSTELLO DELLA PACE

HOSTEL [1]

V. di Valecchie 177 ☎075 81 67 67 🖥www.assisihostel.com

You will never want to leave this hostel. That's because it will take you so darn long to find it, and once you have, you'll be facing an uphill hike to get anywhere else. To be fair, it's also very nice. Unfortunately, however, due to the strict and excessively long 9:30am-4pm lockout, you'll be wracked with separation anxiety each morning. When you are actually allowed inside, you'll find comfortable lounge areas with a piano and guitar, plus a beautiful garden to escape Assisi's relentless sunshine. The hostel looks a bit like a derelict building from the side when you finally reach it, tucked in the middle of an olive grove somewhere in the fields on the lower slopes of Assisi, but no, that's it, and it looks more like a real hostel from the front.

⇟ From the train station, take the local bus C up to Porta San Pietro (on the bus map, the stop is marked for the Ostello). Then walk back downhill the way you came. At the split, bear right, and you'll see a sign for the hostel, pointing you toward a dirt road. Follow the road downhill for a while through the fields until you see a farmhouse; that's your new home. i Breakfast included. $ Dorms €19. 🕐 Reception 4pm-midnight. Lockout 9:30am-4pm.

PALLOTTA

HOTEL [3]

V. S. Rufino ☎075 81 26 49 🖥www.pallottaassisi.it

This tiny eight-room hotel seriously cares about details. First of all, there's tea. Not just the beverage but a proper tea time, with pastries, served every afternoon in the lobby. In Italy, this is practically unheard of. The small building's third floor is really the windowed garret of a tower and could easily have been turned into a suite, but instead, it's a common room with a 360° view. Even Pallota's brochure is amazing—someone must have had a talented nephew or something, because the thing is a beautifully illustrated picture book featuring the Big Red Clifford of cats perched on the Assisi skyline. This is a fairly simple hotel to receive such treatment, but these kinds of details make it stand out from the rest.

⇟ Just past the Duomo, on your left, up a flight of stone stairs on the outside of the building. i Breakfast and tea included. Laundry available. Train station pickup available. 10% discount at the restaurant. Parking €5. Free Wi-Fi. $ Singles €35-45; doubles €58-75; triples €70-90.

VEDUTA SANTA CHIARA

HOTEL [3]

Vicolo Sant'Antonio 1 ☎075 81 52 20

This small, simple hotel makes interesting use of its architecture. Like many places in Assisi, it's somewhat perched on top of 13th-century walls, and rather than work with the old structure, the hotel just surrounds it. One room has an ancient stone wall right in the middle—a TV is balanced on top of it. Random chunks of antiquity dot the walls and floor of other chambers. If nothing else, this sort of space is certainly an authentic experience of Italians' casual relationship with the super-old. Another small hotel and good budget option, Grotta Antica *(V. dei Macelli Vecchi 3 ☎075 81 36 20 🖥www.grottaantica.com)*, a restaurant, and a bar are all owned and operated by the incredibly sweet Annemarie, her mother, and her husband, who can all frequently be found running between their various businesses.

⇟ From P. del Vescovado, take a right onto V. Sant'Agnese, then a left onto Viccolo Sant'Antonio. i Cheap breakfast available at the family bar. $ Singles €35; doubles €50.

SIGHTS

The city itself is officially a sight—in 2000 Assisi was declared a **World Heritage Site** by UNESCO. There's no real need to point out any one street or *piazza* when they're all enchantingly beautiful, but we do anyway.

BASILICA DI SAN FRANCESCO

♿ CHURCH, CRYPT

V. San Francesco ☎075 81 90 01 💻www.sanfrancescoassisi.org

St. Francis is the main event in Assisi, and remarkably, this has been the case for a millennium. The St. Francis show began quite early on, when the pope laid down the cornerstone for the town's basilica just two years after the saint's death in 1228. Construction moved very quickly for the time, with both churches that comprise the structure completed and consecrated in just 30 years.

For a man whose mission statement was a vow of poverty, St. Francis sure scored a grand basilica in his name. Appropriately, however, its splendor is in the architecture, not baser riches. The unique basilica is divided into two churches built one on top of the other. Enter through the upper church, the **Basilica Superiore,** a remarkable, if not particularly surprising, vaulted affair with beautifully carved seats on the altar and murals of scenes from the saint's life. Exit to the right of the altar to find a lovely, peaceful courtyard and stairs descending to the **Basilica Inferiore.** This church is more unusual, with low, richly tiled ceilings. The entrance to the **crypt** of St. Francis himself is down a flight of narrow stairs in a space far more in keeping with the Franciscan aesthetic, though the rough-hewn stone and plain wood benches are shockingly modern additions. When St. Francis was first entombed at the basilica in 1230, Brother Elias, the then-vicar of the Franciscan order, had the crypt sealed off for fear that the saint's body would be vandalized, as many churches wished to have a Francis relic for themselves. Brother Elias's plan was so successful that the tomb was not rediscovered until 1818. The current bare-stone, neo-Romanesque crypt dates only from the 1920s.

Outside the basilica, you can pick up a free audio tour to learn about more adventures in basilica-building politics. When reconstruction on the sections of the building that were damaged in the 1997 earthquake is going on, visitors are sometimes allowed to put on hardhats and check out the work. It's also worth noting that the Franciscans, despite their sackcloth, are more fashion-conscious than their counterparts in the region: inappropriately clad visitors are given not the usual Kimono of Shame, but a far more tasteful Pashmina of Shame.

⇞ Most roads in town lead here. Head west. $ Free. ⏰ Basilica Superiore open daily in summer 8:30am-6:45pm; in fall, winter, and spring 8:30am-6pm. Basilica Inferiore open daily in summer 6am-6:45pm; in fall, winter, and spring 6am-6pm.

ROCCA MAGGIORE

FORT

At the top of V. della Rocca ☎075 81 55 234

Best *rocca* in central Italy! Come with a group of friends, and you will have a funny **photo-op** field day. Trek uphill past a weird shrine to abandoned chewing gum and reach the entrance—it's worth the hike even on a hot day, because the fort's thick stone walls provide the best sort of A/C. This old garrison is on the whole a bit "museified," but in the most haphazard of ways. Oh hey, giant crossbow in the middle of a room. What up, stack of parade banners in the corner. Hold up, scary faceless mannequins! Seriously, it's like the place is begging you to amass a year's worth of Facebook profile pictures. If you need more props, the fortress gift shop sells toy crossbows and rifles alongside the rosaries. Be sure to venture down the long, dark, low-ceilinged passage inside the wall to reach the incredible lookout point. You could probably pace through the whole thing in 1hr., but it's far more fun to bring a picnic, a camera, and perhaps some chainmail and make it an afternoon.

⚓ There are signs from P. San Rufino and from P. Matteotti, but in general, from those areas, head uphill. You can see it: it's the big castle thing. ⑤ €5, students and over 65 and under 17 €3.50. ⌚ Open daily June-Aug 9am-8pm; Sept-Oct 9am-7pm; Nov-Feb 10am-4:30pm; Mar 10am-5:30pm; Apr-May 9am-7pm. Closed in bad weather.

CATTEDRALE DI SAN RUFINO (DUOMO)
P. di San Rufino

 ⛪ CHURCH
☎075 81 22 83

Though the big-name church in town, St. Francis's Basilica isn't actually Assisi's Duomo. A church dedicated to **San Rufino** has stood in Assisi since 1028 and became its cathedral in 1305. The Duomo's current Neoclassical appearance is the result of a 1571 refurbishment which gave it a beautifully sculptured facade. All the same, it's a relatively modest cathedral as far as these things go.

⚓ From P. del Comune, V. San Rufino heading northeast will lead you to the church. ⑤ Free. ⌚ Open in summer M-F 7am-12:30pm and 2:30-7pm, Sa-Su 7am-7pm; in fall, winter, and spring daily 7am-12:30pm and 2:30-6pm.

ABAZIA DI SAN PIETRO
P. San Pietro

 ⛪ CHURCH
☎075 81 23 11

An unadorned but soaring stone space, Abazia di San Pietro is austere thanks to a radical reconstruction in 1954 that removed some offending Baroque altars. The elaborate creche and diorama to the left of the altar is of interest—it's like one of those miniature holiday train displays but with less trains and more cattle.

⚓ Just off Porta San Pietro, in the southwest of the city. ⑤ Free. ⌚ Open daily 7:30am-7pm.

FOOD

RISTORANTE DA CECCO
P. San Pietro 8

 🍴♿️🍸❄️🐕 RISTORANTE ❷
☎075 81 24 37 🖥www.hotelberti.it

A crowded, country-kitchen sort of restaurant with checkered tableclothes and stone walls, da Cecco has made fresh pasta its specialty—try the *strangozzi* with sausage, cream, and mushrooms (€8). Menu in four languages.

⚓ Just off the piazza on V. Borgo San Pietro. ⑤ Cover €2. Primi €7.50-9. ⌚ Open daily noon-2:30pm and 7:10-9:30pm.

IL DUOMO PIZZERIA
V. Porta Perlici 11

 🍴🚫🍸 PIZZERIA ❷
☎075 81 63 26 🖥www.assisiduomo.com

This dining room makes use of its 13th-century building's natural architecture— the worn-smooth stone and rounded walls will make you feel like you're in a pizza oven. Don't worry, though: it's not that warm. It *is* yummy, however, with 30 inexpensive varieties of pizza awaiting—try the ricotta and spinach. The first dining room of this secretly huge place opens onto a courtyard space with two more levels of seating.

⚓ From the Duomo, take a right. ⑤ Pizza €4.50-7.80. Primi €6.30-8.40. ⌚ Open noon-3pm and 7-10pm.

LA ROCCA
V. Porta Perlici 27

 🍴♿️🍸❄️🐕 RISTORANTE ❷
☎075 81 22 84 🖥www.hotelarocca.it

The elegant blue dining room and scenic terrace seem a bit too classy for the excellent prices on the menu of this hotel-restaurant. The "Menu Franciscan" in particular—*primo, contorno,* fruit, and cover (€9.50)—seems a deal cheap enough for the poverty-lovin' saint himself.

⚓ Where V. Porta Perlici turns through the porta itself. ⑤ Cover €1.30. Salads €2.50-4.50. Primi €6-7.50. ⌚ Open M-Tu 12:15-1:45pm and 7-9pm, Th-Su 12:15-1:45pm and 7-9pm.

assisi · food

ESSENTIALS

Practicalities

- **TOURIST OFFICES: Ufficio Turismo** provides excellent self-guided walking tours of Assisi and the region as well as themed itineraries. Most generally useful and best-titled is the *"guida...verso lo stupore."* For those whose Italian is a bit rusty, that translates to the "guide...toward astonishment." *(Palazzo San Nicolo ☎075 81 38 680 🖥www.assisi.regioneumbria.eu and www.comune.assisi.pg.it ⇆ In P. del Comune.* ⏰ Open in summer M-Sa 8am-2pm and 3-6pm, Su 10am-1pm and 2-5pm; in fall, winter, and spring M-Sa 8am-2pm and 3-6pm, Su 9am-1pm.)
- **LUGGAGE STORAGE:** At the train station. *(☎075 80 40 286 $ €2.60 per item for 12hr. ℹ No overnight storage. ⏰ Open daily 6:30am-7:30pm.)*
- **LAUNDROMATS: Service Acqua Azzurra.** *(V. San Bernardino da Siena 6 ☎075 80 40 927 ⇆ In Santa Maria Degli Angeli, by the train station. ⏰ Open daily 8am-10pm.)*
- **INTERNET: Bar Caffe Duomo** has Wi-Fi. *(P. San Rufino 5 ⇆ Across from the Duomo.)* **Bar Bibiano** has computers with internet. *(Vle. Marconi ☎075 81 26 39).*
- **POST OFFICES:** *(P. San Pietro ☎075 81 51 78 ⏰ Open M-F 8am-1:30pm, Sa 8am-12:30pm.)*

Emergency!

- **POLICE: Polizia Locale** *(P. Santa Chiara ☎113 ☎075819091).* **Carabinieri** *(P. Matteotti ☎075 81 908).*
- **HOSPITALS/MEDICAL SERVICES: Ospedale di Assisi** *(V. Valentin Muller 1 ☎075 80 43 616).*

Getting There

By Train

Stazione Ferroviaria is near Basilica di Santa Maria degli Angeli. *(P. Dante Alighieri ☎075 80 40 272 ℹ Tickets available at the ticket office, station bar, automated machines, and in Assisi at Agenzia Viaggi Stoppini at C. Mazzini 31. ⏰ Ticket office open 1-7:35pm.)* Trains arrive from: **Camucia-Cortona** *($ €4.30. ⏰ 1½hr., 6 per day 8am-9:30pm.);* **Florence** *($ €11. ⏰ 2½hr., 7 per day 5:50am-9:30pm.);* **Perugia** *($ €2.40. ⏰ 30min., 14 per day 8am-8pm.);* **Rome.** *($ €17. ⏰ 2hr., 4 per day 7:45am-8pm.)*

By Bus

APM buses arrive in P. Matteotti. They're a cheap option for trips between Assisi and **Perugia.** They leave Perugia from P. Partigiani. *($ €3. ⏰ 1¼hr., 9 per day.)*

Getting Around

By Bus

APM *(☎800 51 21 41 🖥www.apmperugia.it)* services Assisi with three shuttle lines. Lines A and B do loops around major sights and monuments every 40min. Line C runs from the train station to P. Matteotti every 30min. Buy tickets at *tabaccherie* and the train station bar for €1.50.

By Taxi

Radio Taxi provides 24hr. taxi service *(V. Arco dei Priori 1 ☎075 81 31 00 🖥www.radiotaxiassisi.it).* A cab stand is in front of the train station.

BAY OF NAPLES

If there's one thing unifying the smorgasbord of cities that fills the Bay of Naples, it might just be the traffic—buses whipping around Amalfi's winding cliffs recall the omnipresent scooters that zoom through Naples's equally twisting streets. With no traffic lights in either case, only honks and vrooms let you know if something is coming round the bend. Watch out.

Equally hard to anticipate are the immense contrasts in scenery and character you'll find throughout the region. Indeed, you may be wondering how such a diverse assortment of locales can all be packed in the same chapter—it's hard to equate Naples's piles of trash with Capri's piles of sand. You'll find that in many ways, this diversity's a good thing, for the plastic-looking streets and colorful trinkets of Amalfi beach towns don't possess quite as much staying power as *Napoli*'s century-old churches and catacombs. Head to the dirty and practical big city for cultural riches and treat the rest of the Amalfi Coast like a dollhouse—pretty, popular, but not all too habitable. Somewhere between the grime and glitz sit Pompeii and Herculaneum, cities which unexpectedly combine the best of their southern and northern neighbors: as the footprints of once bustling cities, their remains contain both the quaint streets of the bay's beach towns and the artistic masterpieces of a metropolis like Naples.

In short, the Bay of Naples could be its own Italy—it has enough scenic variety and sights to keep any itinerary fresh for well over a week. And when we said transit unifies the place, we weren't just talking about the ready-to-run-you-over kind: frequent buses and trains make the whole region easily navigable, even during short stays.

greatest hits

- **PIZZA PIONEERS.** Naples invented pizza, and by now they've definitely figured out how to make a good pie. Pretty much anywhere in Spaccanapoli will prove stunningly delicious (p. 394).

- **RUINED FOR LIFE.** Pompeii might be more famous, but Herculaneum (p. 407) is our pick of the cities that got on the wrong side of Mt. Vesuvius.

- **COASTING.** The postcard cities of the Amalfi Coast are all spectacular, but move a little away from the beach to reach Ravello, a hilltop town with a phenomenal music festival (p. 429).

For student life around the bay, it's best to stick to the big cities. Sorrento is a remarkably friendly city for young people. Though it attracts its fair share of seriously wealthy Western tourists, it's also home to great bars and the famed *limoncello*. C. Italia is lined with great options. Amalfi and Positano are great towns to visit during the day, hang out on the beaches and enjoy yourself, but you'll quickly notice these aren't really places where people study. Similarly, Capri is just a little too beautiful for anything as real as a university to take hold there. So your best bet might be the enigma that is Naples. Avoid the area around the train station, but a little farther west in the *centro storico* you'll find plenty of young people at the bars along V. Enrico de Marinis. This area is right next door to the University of Naples Federico II, the world's oldest state university which still boasts a huge student body. And, of course, while in Naples remember to enjoy some of every student's favorite: pizza. Next time you're back at college and ordering a late-night pie, you'll remember your visit to the home of this greatest of inventions, and probably wish that you were back there. So eat up now, and make your friends jealous with all the stories later.

naples *napoli* ☎081

Naples is a bustling, hectic city—revel in it if you like, revile it if you must, just don't be scared by it. Travelers who know where they're going (or just look like they do) will fare best. Traffic zooms through the streets in lanes half the width of the painted lines. Red lights are mere suggestions. Crossing the street is a battle of wills—one of which has a V8 engine on its side. Yet Neapolitans take it all in stride. Cheerful chaos is a lifestyle they have eagerly adopted, though they now take out the trash, and much of the crime and grime has gone with it. Laughing together in one hearty chuckle, locals seem to spend every waking hour on the town, drinking, smoking, carousing, and eating.

Especially eating. This city invented **pizza,** and it sure knows how to make a good slice. The challenge is less finding the best than finding something else to eat: with pies so savory and inexpensive, it's hard to try something a little different. Still, the seafood that has defined the Mediterranean diet for centuries overflows the fishermen's holds in the picturesque bay.

It's a shame tourists often treat this city as a mere stopover while exploring nearby attractions. All they see is the train station—unruly and unclean, the worst of stereotypical Naples, but many areas have the beauty of a resort town. Scrub off the grime and graffitti, and there's much to be found in the city's architecturally masterful *centro*. Don't trust us? Trust UNESCO, which recently deemed Naples' historical center a **World Heritage Site.** For millennia, the city has been an outpost for the world's greatest civilizations, so forgive Naples its untidiness and petty crime: the continent and, really, the world as they stand in the modern era owe a lot to this scrappy city.

ORIENTATION

The *centro* and the most interesting areas of Naples are arranged roughly in an "L" shape along the coast. To the northeast, in an unappealing and unsafe neighborhood, is Stazione Centrale on **Piazza Garibaldi.** From the corner of the *piazza* opposite the station, **Corso Umberto I** runs through the university district to **Via Depretis** and the

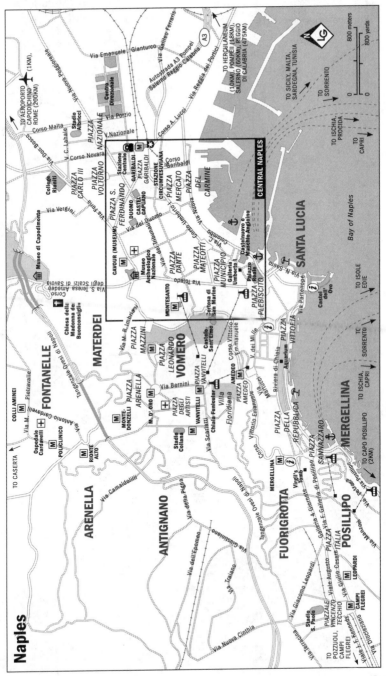

Naples

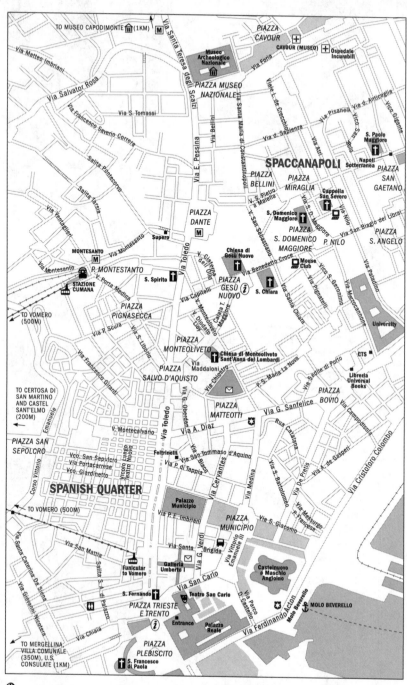

bay of naples

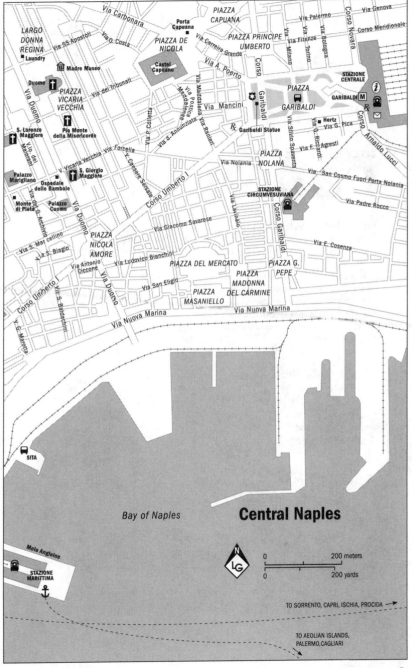

Central Naples

Bay of Naples

TO SORRENTO, CAPRI, ISCHIA, PROCIDA →

TO AEOLIAN ISLANDS,
PALERMO, CAGLIARI

200 meters

200 yards

hostelofthesun
napoli**naples**italy

PRIVATE ROOM
€ 25 per person
DORM BEDS from € 16

accomodation in
naples italy

Hostel of the Sun is perfectly located in the center of Naples. It is in a safe area of the city and is a comfortable, clean and very welcoming base for your stay in Naples. Just across the street from the bus stop to Pompeii, Amalfi coast and the ferry port to the islands of Capri and Ischia, HOTS is conveniently located for day trips as well as visits to some of the main sights in the city itself, and of course to try the famous Napoletan pizza!

Free at Hostel of the Sun
· **WiFi in every rooms**
· **Air conditioning in all rooms**
· **Breakfast**
· **Guest Kitchen**

other facilities:
24hr reception - lockers - luggage storage - lounge room - maps and trip advice - satellite tv dvd room - laundry service
No Lockout, No Curfew.

Hostel of the Sun
via Melisurgo 15 - 80133 Napoli - Italy
phone and fax: (+39) 081 4206393
info@hostelnapoli.copm
www.hostelnapoli.com
skype: hostelofthesun

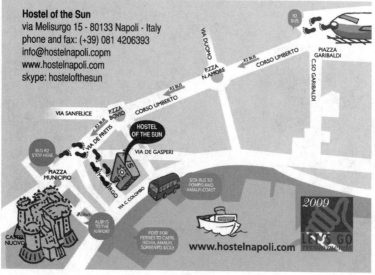

www.hostelnapoli.com

port. **Via Duomo** and **Via Mezzocannone** lead up from there toward the **Centro Storico** (also known as Spaccanapoli.) **Via Toledo** connects the western edge of that area and the **Museo Nazionale** to the historical sights, including **Piazza del Plebiscito,** located to the south. The fashionable, shop-lined **Via Chiaia** leads from these sights to the Riviera-like waterfront hidden from many tourists, along which run **Via Caracciolo** and **Riviera di Chiaia.** These streets extend all the way to the picturesque and calm **Mergellina** district. All of this unfolds around the soaring hill at the city's center, on which sits the **Vomero** and where you'll find stunning panoramic views. Accessible primarily by funicular, this hilltop neighborhood is a shopping district centered on the perpendicular **Via Scarlatti** and **Via Bernini.**

Centro Storico

The Centro Storico, also known as Spaccanapoli, is Naples's oldest neighborhood, filled with tiny alleys and beautiful architecture. Located west of the station and east of P. del Plebiscito, the area is much more pleasant than the chaos by Stazione Centrale. It is also paradise for pizza lovers.

Stazione Centrale

Naples's transit hub, Stazione Centrale opens onto the vast, chaotic **Piazza Garibaldi,** full of vendors and traffic that stops for no man or woman. Hotels surround the *piazza* and fill its nearby streets. The neighborhood is seedy, and many streets are, in fact, lined with trash. From the far left corner of the *piazza*, **Corso Umberto I,** one of the city's main boulevards, leads away from the bustle toward the university area and, eventually, the port. From the same corner, **Corso Garibaldi** runs south to the sea, passing **Stazione Circumvesuviana** on the way. From the far right corner, V. Alessandro Poerio follows the line of the **Metro** in the direction of the Museo Nazionale.

Piazza del Plebiscito and Spanish Quarter

Piazza del Plebiscito was once one of the most important locations in Naples, home to the Palazzo Reale and a stunning church. Today, it has declined in vitality but remains central to the city. **Via Toledo** runs north through **Piazza Trieste e Trento,** home of Teatro San Carlo, to P. Dante and Spaccanapoli. The Spanish Quarter is west of this main road and features a number of small but bustling streets heading up the hill and lined with hanging laundry.

Chiaia, Vomero, and Outskirts

Numerous neighborhoods less known to tourists but more beautiful than much of Naples lie to the west of the *centro storico*. **Vomero,** on a high hill above the city, is connected to its lower areas by three funicular railways. The one most often used, Centrale, departs V. Toledo for **Piazza Fuga.** Back near sea level, the fashionable **Chiaia** district borders the seafront, as does quiet **Mergellina** farther to the west. **Via Francesco Caracciolo** and **Riviera di Chiaia** run parallel to the water and surround **Villa Communale,** one of the city's finest parks, palm trees and all. Nearest to the *centro* along the water is Castel dell'Ovo, one of the city's famous monuments. Away from the water, **Via Chiaia** and **Via dei Mille** are sleek and clean shopping streets that bustle all day long.

ACCOMMODATIONS

The first thing most travelers see upon arriving in Naples is a neon junkyard of hotels in the hectic and unpleasant area near **Stazione Centrale.** Don't trust anyone who approaches you in the station—people working on commission are happy to lead naive tourists to unlicensed and overpriced hotels seedier than those you could find on your own. There are several comfortable and inexpensive options in this area; just be careful when returning at night. **Centro Storico** and **Piazza del Plebiscito** have much better-located options, though at noticeably higher prices. Progressing further west, **Vomero, Chiaia,** and **Mergellina** boast numerous hospitable bed and breakfasts in quiet areas that provide excellent views of the city or the sea.

Centro Storico

Accommodations in Naples's historical heart are more convenient and thus pricier, but they'll put travelers just a dough's throw away from the ancient streets that are the pizza capital of the world.

6 SMALL ROOMS
➥⊗(�) ❄ HOSTEL ❶

V. Diodato Lioy 18 ☎081 79 01 378 ▓www.6smallrooms.com

Modesty may be a virtue, but the Australian owners of this beautiful hostel seem to be taking it a bit far with the name of this place. Most of the "small" rooms are huge, with high ceilings and fun, elaborate murals of the city and ancient Roman gods. A tremendous communal kitchen doubles as a breakfast room where guests gather to chat—when they're not in the spacious common room with flatscreen TV, DVD and music collection, and even guitars on which to strum the night away.

✦ Ⓜ1: Dante. Walk down V. Toledo, turn left onto V. Tommaso Senise, and make the 1st right onto V. Diodato Lioy. *i* Breakfast included. Free lockers. Some rooms with A/C. No bunk beds. Free Wi-Fi. Resident cats and dogs. ⑤ Dorms €20; singles or small doubles with bath and A/C €25-45; doubles €50-55, with bath €55-65; triples €60-75; quads €80-95. 10% Let's Go discount. ⌚ Reception 8am-midnight. Keys provided after hours.

NAPLES PIZZA HOSTEL
➥♿(ᵻᵻ) HOSTEL ❶

V. San Paulo ai Tribunali ☎081 19 32 35 62 ▓www.naplespizzahostel.com

When guests open the door to their room, it's clear this hostel is a step above the rest. Most chambers have loft beds up a set of steps above the other bunks, creating a secret, secluded single within a dorm. One guest apparently enjoyed her stay so much that she painted a mural of—what else?—happy students eating Neopolitan pizza on the orange walls of the common room.

✦ Taking V. Tribunali from the station, turn right onto V. San Paulo ai Tribunali. *i* Breakfast included. Laundry €5. All-female dorms available. Communal kitchen. Free Wi-Fi. ⑤ 5-bed dorms €15-18; singles €25-35, with bath €35-40; doubles €35-45/€45-55; triples €49-65/65-70, quads €65-70/71-79. ⌚ Reception 24hr.

HOTEL NEAPOLIS
➥⊗(ᵻᵻ)❄ HOTEL ❸

V. Francesco del Giudice 13, 3rd fl. ☎081 44 20 815 ▓www.hotelneapolis.com

It's easy to stay connected at this luxurious budget hotel, which not only takes reservations via Skype but also has computers with free internet in every room, from the smallest single to the superior doubles. Even with a large computer desk, the 24 rooms are spacious and have fine draperies and bedding.

✦ Ⓜ1: Dante. From P. Dante, head through Porta Alba down V. dei Tribunali and turn left onto V. Francesco del Giudice. Enter the courtyard and take the elevator. *i* Breakfast included. Skype name: Hotel Neapolis Ricivimento. ⑤ Singles €35-50; doubles €60-90.

ALLOGIO MIRAGLIA
➥⊗ PENSIONE ❷

P. Luigi Miraglia 386 ☎081 45 53 82 ▓www.bedandbreakfastmiraglianapoli.it

This bed and breakfast takes travelers on a quick trip to paradise—if the palm-lined desert-island bedspread counts. There's no real sandy beach, but a few comfortable rooms and a breakfast served in bed or the small dining room help whisk away lingering memories of the hectic Naples below.

✦ Take V. dei Tribunali to P. Miraglia. *i* 1 double has toilet inside, all others outside; all showers outside rooms. ⑤ Singles €25; doubles €40; triples €60; quads €75.

Stazione Centrale

The area around P. Garibaldi is littered with cheap hotels, their bright signs glaring enough to fill a Las Vegas junkyard, so you're virtually assured that rooms will be available. Just exercise caution when returning after dark.

HOTEL GINEVRA
➥⊗(ᵻᵻ)❄ HOTEL ❷

V. Genova 116 ☎081 28 32 10 ▓www.hotelginevra.it

Exiting Naples's train station is always an adventure, but few expect a full-blown safari. Get ready for it as you walk into this hotel and encounter the jovial staff behind the desk—or is that a tiki bar? This is no joke (well, maybe it is a *little* tongue-in-cheek kitschy): the "ethnic" rooms come with elephant carvings on the door, bamboo on the walls, and vines on the ceiling—not to mention a flatscreen TV. Superior rooms have more amenities, including minibars and A/C. Some have murals of the Amalfi Coast.

➤ Take the 1st right out of the station onto C. Novara, then the next right onto V. Genova. $ Singles €25-35, with bath €35-45; doubles €35-50, "ethnic doubles" €40-65, superior €45-70; triples €45-65, with bath €50-75. 10% Let's Go discount.

HOSTEL PENSIONE MANCINI
🚭📶❄ HOSTEL, PENSIONE [1]

V. P.S. Mancini 33 ☎081 55 36 731 💻www.hostelpensionemancini.com

The helpful owners make this hostel, located in a distinctly average building, stand out. Bedrooms are comfortable, some with balconies. But the overwhelming hospitality of an owner who organizes outings for and shares extensive knowledge of the city with his guests makes it stand out.

➤ Directly across the piazza from the station. $ Dorms €13-16; singles €25-30, with bath €40-45; doubles €35-45/40-50; triples €54-66/60-70; quads €60-68/70-80. 10% Let's Go discount.

HOTEL ZARA
💳🚭📶❄ HOTEL [2]

V. Firenze 81 ☎081 28 71 25 💻www.hotelzara.it

Comfy common areas with deep couches, large TV, and a fish tank make socializing easy, while the simple rooms make for a good night's sleep.

➤ Walk down the right side of P. Garibaldi from the station and turn onto V. Milano, then right onto V. Firenze. $ Singles €25-35; doubles €30, with bath €35; triples €50/60.

Piazza del Plebiscito and Spanish Quarter

Find hostel central in the clean area near the port just a few minutes walk from P. del Plebiscito. Other accommodations, from luxury hotels to petite B and Bs, await discovery on the surrounding steep streets.

★ HOSTEL OF THE SUN
💳🚭📶❄ HOSTEL [1]

V. Melisurgo 15, 7th fl. ☎081 42 06 393 💻www.hostelnapoli.com

This hostel is quite simply the most fun place you can stay in Naples. The exuberant—somehow even that strong word seems too weak—staff begins everyone's stay with an in-depth and amusing introduction to the city and a collection of free maps to stuff in pockets. They keep it going by hosting several outings weekly, occasionally cooking for guests, and relaxing with them in the colorful and comfortable common room which features a flatscreen TV, DVDs, computers, and Nintendo Wii. (The owner has been known to challenge guests; those who beat him get a free stay, though he claims an undefeated record.)

➤ Take the R2 bus from C. Umberto I near the station, get off at the 2nd stop on V. Depretis. i Breakfast included. Private rooms with ensuite A/C. Free lockers. Free internet and Wi-Fi. $ 5- to 7-bed dorms €16-20; doubles €55-60, with bath €60-70; triples €75-80/€70-90; quads €80-90/€85-100. 10% Let's Go discount. ⏰ Reception 24hr.

★ HOTEL AND HOSTEL BELLA CAPRI
💳♿📶❄ HOSTEL [1]

V. Meilsurgo 4, 6th fl. ☎081 55 29 494 💻www.bellacapri.it

The ground-floor hotel for people over 30 here is kept well-hidden from the groups of students who occupy the upper floor. Every night is a social occasion, with guests cooking in the communal kitchen, chatting, and gathering for near-nightly outings to bars in the *centro*. Satellite TV and three computers beckon to keep them in, but the excitement of Naples outside of the port area usually succeeds in drawing students from their rooms and to the streets.

➤ R2 bus from C. Umberto I near the station to the 2nd stop on V. Depretis. After hours, ring bell. i Lockers with €5 deposit. All-female dorms available. Free internet and Wi-Fi. $ Dorms €15-21; singles €40-50, with bath €50-70; doubles €50-60/€60-80; triples €70-80/€80-100;

quads €80-90/€90-110. 10% Let's Go discount. Wash and dry €7. ⏰ Reception 24hr.

I FIORI DI NAPOLI
💳🚫♿📶❄ B AND B [3]

V. Francesco Girardi 92, 3rd fl. ☎081 19 57 70 83 💻www.ifioridinapoli.it

This inn is a mighty fine place for travelers who don't mind being surrounded by vines. Flower murals decorate the walls, and the real things grow in the hallways and on the sunny rooftop terrace. The seven rooms are named after various species of flora and appointed brightly to match. Two dining-and-sitting rooms, a communal kitchen, plus the local knowledge of a kind owner makes this B and B a great value.

🧭 From V. Toledo, take V. Montecavalo and turn right onto V. Francesco Girardi. The B and B is on the left, with no sign. Ring bell and take stair A to 3rd fl. ℹ Some rooms with ensuite A/C. Internet available on 1 computer in breakfast room. Ⓢ Doubles used as singles €35, with bath €40; doubles €60/€70.

HOTEL TOLEDO
💳🚫♿📶❄ HOTEL [4]

V. Montecalvario 15 ☎081 40 68 00 💻www.hoteltoledo.com

The peaceful rooftop terrace is just one highlight of this Spanish Quarter property's common areas. They also include a large bar with throne-like dining chairs and couches that guests sink into while enjoying a nightcap.

🧭 From P. Dante, walk down V. Toledo and turn right onto V. Montecalvario. Ⓢ Singles €50-65; doubles €70-100; suites €100-120.

Chiaia, Vomero, and Outskirts

Farther from the city center, the neighborhoods get nicer and the rooms pricier. Seek out smaller B and Bs for the best rates and most personal service.

👍 CAPPELLA VECCHIA 11
💳🚫♿📶❄ B AND B [4]

Vicolo Santa Maria a Cappella Vecchia 11, 1st fl. ☎081 24 05 117 💻www.cappellavecchia11.it

Meeting other travelers has never been easier than at the communal breakfast table of this well kept B and B. The common room has comfortable couches and a public computer, while bedrooms with comfortable beds and large bathrooms come in a pleasantly shocking purple-and-green color combo.

🧭 From V. Santa Caterina just before P. dei Martiri, turn onto the small alleyway of Vicolo Santa Maria a Cappella Vecchia. Take the stairs to the right. ℹ Breakfast included. Free Wi-Fi. Ⓢ Singles €50-70; doubles €80-110.

OSTELLO MERGELLINA (HI)
🚫💳🚫♿📶 HOSTEL [1]

V. Salita della Grotta 23 ☎081 76 12 346 💻www.ostellonapoli.com

Far from the bustle that makes Naples what it is, this hostel is a little out of the way. Nonetheless, the sun shines brightly and the turquoise water beckons just steps away in the quiet Mergellina neighborhood, where the hostel provides small bedrooms and a comfortable but spare lobby with flatscreen TV.

🧭 ⓂMergellina. Make 2 sharp rights onto V. Piedigrotta, then a right onto V. Salita della Grotta. Turn right onto driveway after overpass. ℹ Breakfast included. Wi-Fi in lobby. Ⓢ Dorms from €15; singles from €25; doubles from €40. ⏰ Reception 24hr.

HOTEL CIMAROSA
💳🚫♿📶❄ HOTEL [4]

V. Cimarosa 29 ☎081 55 67 044 💻www.hotelcimarosa.it

Up the steps of this hotel, ascend into the Space Age. There's a wavy, blue ceiling light that casts the entire hall in an eerily hip light, not to mention the illuminated sculptures that fill wall nooks. Who doesn't need that extra artsy touch? Inside, 19 spacious rooms feature floor-to-ceiling windows—eight of which have views of the bay—plasma TVs, and large showers.

🧭 From the funicular in P. Fuga, turn right onto V. Cimarosa. Ⓢ Singles €60-70; doubles €90-110.

HostelsofNaples
naples italy napoli

www.hostelsofnaples.com

Hostel & Hotel BellaCapri
Via Melisurgo, 4 (scala B 6° piano)
80133 - Napoli
Tel. +39.081.5529494
Fax. +39.5529265
info@bellacapri.it
www.bellacapri.it
bella.capri

Naples - Italy - Napoli

Via P.S. Mancini, 33
80139 Napoli (NA)
Tel: 081 553 6731
info@hostelpensionemancini.com
www.hostelpensionemancini.com
hostel.pensione.mancini

hostel
pensione
Mancini

Naples Pizza Hostel
Via San Paolo ai Tribunali 44
80135 Naples - Napoli Italy
Ph. CC39 C81119323562
www.naplespizzahostel.com
info@naplespizzahostel.com
naples.pizza.hostel

Hotel Bellini
Via San Paolo ai Tribunali 44
80138 Naples - Napoli Italy
Ph. 0039 0819323562
www.hotelbellini.net
info@hotelbellini.net

HB

RING
Via Gaetano Morgera,72,
Forio, Island of Ischia,
Gulf of Naples, Italy
Phone: 0039 081 987 546
Phone: 0039 081 997 136
Mobile Phone: 0039 333 698 5665
Skype Phone: ringhostel
Fax: 0039 081 987 942
Email: info@ringhostel.com
Web: www.ringhostel.com

VILLAEVA
Via Grotta Azzurra
Trav.la Fabbrica, n.8-16
80071 Anacapri (Na) Italy
Tel. +39 0818371549 Fax/Tel +39 0818372040
villa.eva@capri.it - www.villaeva.com

Le Sirene
Via degli Aranci, 160 - 80065
Sorrento [NA] - Italy
Tel. 081 807 2925 - Fax 081 877 1371
info@hostellesirene.com - www.hostellesirene.com

If you're thinking about visiting Naples and sourrondings, you'll find us right here to welcome and astonish you: it has always been a habit for us to make our guests feel at home.

SHOW THIS PAGE AT ANY OF OUR PARTNERS HOSTELS AND YOU WILL GET 10% DISCOUNT.
FOR INDIVIDUALS AND 15% DISCOUNT FOR GROUPS OF AT LEAST 10 PEOPLE.
SPECIAL DISCOUNT'S FOR STUDENT'S AND SCHOOL GROUPS DURING LOW SEASON.

* For school groups contact us via e-mail with your request.
* Mentioned discount NOT applicable with other offers.

www.hostelsofnaples.com
info@hostelsofnaples.com

DISCOUNT PAGE!!

SIGHTS 👁

Been there, done that. So the Greeks, Romans, and Spanish have each said about the city of Naples, and each of their conquests has left a unique mark on this remarkably historical metropolis. Home to a world-renowned antiquarian museum and an ancient underground system that remains a remarkable feat of engineering, Naples has got the really-old thing covered. Meanwhile, the **Palazzo Reale** gives an uncensored glimpse into the life of an 18th-century royal and a reminder of the steps the city has taken into the modern age.

Centro Storico

Part wide boulevards with ornate achitecture, part Roman alleys, Naples's Centro Storico has a history that is palpable. Churches hold exquisite art, while museums offer a glimpse into the city's Roman and Greek past. Many churches with free admission provide small historical tidbits as well. Note that modest dress is required for all churches.

👍 NAPOLI SOTTERANEA (UNDERGROUND NAPLES) ⊛⊗ ANCIENT ROME

P. San Gaetano 68 ☎081 29 69 44 🖥www.napolisotterranea.org

Get down and dirty 35m below the city exploring ancient Greek aqueducts, World War II bomb shelters, and more. Before moving underground, the fascinating guided tours begin with a visit to an ancient Roman theater now built into apartment houses. **Emperor Nero,** noted psycho but not a recognized virtuoso, twice performed here, insisting to an audience that the earthquake they felt as he sung was merely applause of the gods. Beneath the historical center, Mussolini-era graffiti remain as signs of the 3000 Neopolitans who made the tunnels their home for three years during the Allied bombardment of the city. Visitors wander through passageways, grottoes, and catacombs, and while most of the tunnels are cavernous and well lit, the last part of the tour has patrons shimmying through a tiny tunnel in the rock with only candles illuminating the way.

→ Take V. Tribunali and the entrance is to the left of San Paolo Maggiore church. ℹ Tours offered in English. $ €9.30, students €8. 10% Campania Artecard discount. ⏰ 90min. tours depart every 2hr. M-F noon-4pm, Sa-Su 10am-6pm.

👍 MUSEO ARCHEOLOGICO NAZIONALE ⊛♿ MUSEUM, ANCIENT ROME

P. Museo Nazionale 19 ☎081 29 28 23

🖥museoarcheologiconazionale.campaniabeniculturali.it

Even if the prospect of more archaeological specimens has no appeal for you, you've got to be intrigued by the more salacious stuff on display at this museum. It's home to the ever-popular **Gabinetto Segreto** ("Secret Cabinet"), a trove of sexual artifacts recovered from the ash-entombed archaeological site at Pompeii. Of course, the entire museum is not pornographic—heck, some of it's even good for kids—as it contains the most significant collection of artifacts from the nearby towns that were destroyed by Vesuvius's famed eruption. One of Europe's oldest and best-regarded museums, the Museo Nazionale is expansive, and an audio tour or guidebook is worth the price. Check out the **Farnese Bull,** one of the largest surviving statues from antiquity. It's sculpted from a single slab of marble that was reworked by Michelangelo. The mezzanine level contains exquisite mosaics from Pompeii, notably the **Alexander Mosaic,** with a young and fearless Alex the Great routing the Persian army.

→ [M]Cavour. Turn right from the station and walk 2 blocks. $ €10, EU citizens ages 18-24 €5, under 18 and over 65 free. ⏰ Open M 9am-7:30pm, W-Su 9am-7:30pm.

CAPPELLA SAN SEVERO ⊛⊗ CHURCH, MUSEUM

V. de Sanctis 19 ☎081 55 18 470 🖥www.museosansevero.it

Here's one fewer church in a city full of them—this 1590 chapel has been converted into a private museum. Several remarkable 18th-century statues, of which

Giuseppe Sanmartino's 🖼**Veiled Christ** is by far the best known, fill the corridors.

⚶ *To the right when walking away from P. San Domenico Maggiore* Ⓢ *€6, ages 10-25 €4, with Artecard €5.* Ⓞ *Open M 10am-5:40pm, W-Sa 10am-5:40pm, Su 10am-1:10pm.*

COMPLESSO MONUMENTALE DI SAN LORENZO MAGGIORE 🌐🅧 ANCIENT ROME

V. dei Tribunali 316   ☎081 37 23 720 💻www.sanlorenzomaggiorenapoli.it

Now why would those silly Romans put a market underground? In short, they didn't, but the built-up city around their old stomping ground has left an ancient bazaar—with shops, a bakery, and tavern—beneath Naples's streets. It's on display here, along with the delicately frescoed cloister and relatively barren nave of the church under which the market was found.

⚶ *As you come from P. Dante on V. Tribunali, the entrance is on the right across from Napoli Sotteranea.* Ⓢ *€9, students €7.* Ⓞ *Open M-Sa 9:30am-5:30pm, Su 9:30am-1:30pm.*

Stazione Centrale

The hubbub that engulfs Stazione Centrale is a sight in itself. Beyond that, you'll have to head toward the *centro storico* for more to see.

PIO MONTE DELLA MISERICORDIA 🌐🅧 MUSEUM

V. Tribunali 253   ☎081 44 69 44 💻www.piomontedellamisericordia.it

Life on the run was good to Caravaggio, or so it appears. After killing a man in a 1606 duel, the master became a fugitive from justice and fled to Naples, where he was commissioned to paint one of his masterpieces, **The Seven Works of Mercy,** for this small chapel. One of the painting's most surprising elements is a young woman nursing an imprisoned man at her breast. Caravaggio envisioned this as a most basic merciful act but, like other creative men (John Steinbeck, we're looking at you), seems to have overlooked that this would be really, really awkward. His painting is the centerpiece of a round nave surrounded by works of art.

⚶ *On V. Tribunali, before V. Duomo when coming from the station.* Ⓢ *€5, students €4.* Ⓞ *Open M-Tu 9am-2pm, Th-Su 9am-2pm.*

PIAZZA GARIBALDI ♿ PIAZZA

P. Garibaldi

Don't worry about missing this *piazza*—it truly is a sight to behold, if not the prettiest picture to put on a postcard. P. Garibaldi is to Naples as Naples is to Italy: its most incomprehensibly chaotic outpost. Street vendors stake out their sidewalk claims like 1849 California miners, only here the Gold Rush comes from tourists' pockets in exchange for cheap sunglasses and knockoff bags. A spider web of roads and Neapolitan drivers who won't stop add to the disorder. Unlike the streets in much of Naples, the ones here really are lined with trash. At the end of the *piazza* farthest from the trains, **Garibaldi** himself watches over the scene.

⚶ *Outside Stazione Centrale and at the end of C. Umberto.*

DUOMO ♿ CHURCH

V. Duomo 149   ☎081 44 90 97

Hearing about hidden beauty gets old in Naples—why can't some of the good stuff be out in the open on the city's streets? Yet in the city's cathedral, here it is again: an ornate 13th-century interior behind a 19th-century facade. The church has been altered many times over the centuries, but the Baroque paintings and gold metal fittings of its **Cappella del Tesoro di San Gennaro** remain the main attraction. Two containers of congealed blood from the saint for whom the chapel is named (in English, St. Januarius, a former bishop of Naples) sit in the requilary. Keep your eyes on those vials: according to legend, if they do not liquefy on the day of the **Festa di San Gennaro,** it's time to start running, as disaster is about to strike the city. (Not scared? Go visit Pompeii.)

⚶ *From Stazione Centrale, take C. Umberto I to V. Duomo and turn right.* Ⓢ *Church free. Archaeological site €1.50. Museum €6, students €4.50.* Ⓞ *Church open M-F 8:30am-noon, Sa-Su*

8:30am-1pm and 5-7pm. Excavations open M-F 9am-12:30pm and 4:30-7pm, Sa-Su 9am-1pm. Last entry 30min. before close. Museum open M by group reservation, Tu-Su 9:30am-5pm.

Piazza del Plebiscito and Spanish Quarter

◼ PALAZZO REALE
P. del Plebiscito 1

◉⊗ MUSEUM
☎081 40 05 47

King in the castle! Err, *palazzo*, that is. Whatever the name, visitors can play royalty for a day wandering through the magnificent halls of this sprawling structure, once the seat of Bourbon kings and Spanish viceroys in Naples. Wander through artwork-filled rooms and see—but don't dare sit in—the velvet-draped golden throne of former kings, whose exploits are recounted in the aptly but not succinctly named fresco, *The Splendor of the House of Spain and Some Episodes in the Life of Ferrante of Aragon*, on the ceiling in a subsequent room. The palace is also an intellectual mecca, as it contains the 1,500,000 volume **Biblioteca Nazionale,** which holds carbonized scrolls from the Villa dei Papiri in Herculaneum. As if this *palazzo* wasn't packed with enough stuff already, the **Teatro di San Carlo,** Europe's oldest continuously active theater, calls the place home as well. Its acoustics are reputedly better than those of Milan's **La Scala.**

✦ *In P. del Plebiscito, across from the basilica.* ⑤ *€4, students €2. Audio tour €2.50, though we advise against it since, in all rooms, you'll find informative signs in English.* ⏲ *Open M-Tu 9am-8pm, Th-Su 9am-8pm. Last entry 1hr. before close.*

CASTELLO NUOVO O MASCHIO ANGIONO
V. Vittorio Emanuele II at P. Municio

◉㋖ MUSEUM
☎081 42 01 241

When **Charles of Anjou** needed a castle in 1279, beachfront property was cheap, so he took up a lot of it and had this large castle constructed. Today, it's still an integral part of the city's skyline. The castle once had seven towers, but **Alfonse of Aragon** (he called himself the Magnanimous—no big deal) did some remodeling, leaving the building with the five turrets it sports today. He also added the most impressive part of the structure, an intricately carved, arched entrance inspired by Roman architecture. Inside, the castle's exhibitions are limited, though you'll find a decent collection of medieval art and royal artifacts on the first floor. Don't miss the bronze doors that once guarded the castle. They survived destruction during a successful Genoese siege of the city but were scarred by a cannonball when the Genoese hauled them back home as booty. **Baron's Hall,** up steps to the left of the courtyard, is a former meeting place with a stunning dome, while the splendid **Cappella Palatina** provides a cool retreat from the sun-baked courtyard.

✦ *Take the R2 bus from P. Garibaldi or walk from V. Toledo or the centro storico.* ⑤ *€5.* ⏲ *Open M-Sa 9am-7pm.*

BASILICA DI SAN FRANCESCO DI PAOLO
P. del Plebiscito 10

⊗ CHURCH
☎081 76 45 133

Designed to mimic the Pantheon in Rome, this towering domed church is no copycat. It's interior is soaring—54m high and 34m in diameter—and bright like its Roman counterpart, but the basilica is not exactly like its pagan counterpart, as it features carved statues of saints surrounding the nave (though we could get into an interesting conversation about Catholicism's use of sainthood as a way to appeal to pagan polytheism here if we really wanted to get deep). The building dominates P. del Plebiscito.

✦ *The building with the large dome.* 𝒊 *Modest dress required.* ⑤ *Free.* ⏲ *Open M-Sa 8am-noon and 3:30-7pm, Su 8:30am-1pm and 4-7pm.*

bay of naples

Chiaia, Vomero, and Outskirts

CASTEL SANT'ELMO

CASTLE, MUSEUM

V. Tito Angelini 20 ☎081 22 94 401 💻www.polomusealenapoli.beniculturali.it

Stop, gulp in some air, and step up to the wall and gaze out. You'll need that oxygen, because this view—standing eye level with airplanes—truly takes the breath away. Sweeping from the hills, across the *centro storico* and port to Chiaia and Mergellina along the turquoise water, the vista is amazing. Then, in the distance, there are Vesuvius and Capri, ferries leaving foamy white streaks between them. Once a defensive outpost, the ramparts of P. d'Armi atop this castle are one of Naples's loveliest places. They're also now part of a creative art installation by **Giancarlo Neri** which uses lighting to artificially "compete" with the moon in certain parts of the city. **Napoli Novecento,** an extensive modern art museum featuring canvases and sculpture from the last century of Neopolitan modern art, can be found in the old fortress as well.

In Vomero. From the funicular at P. Fuga, turn right up the steps and follow the signs along V. Morghen to the castle. The ticket office is to the right in the gate. $ *€5, EU students ages 18-25 €2.50.* ⏰ *Open M 8:30am-7:30pm, W-Su 8:30am-7:30pm. Guided tours of the museum offered hourly 9am-6pm.*

MUSEO NAZIONALE DI CAPODIMONTE

MUSEUM

V. Miano 2 ☎081 74 99 111 💻www.museo-capodimonte.it

Here is a true rarity among museums, especially in Italy: a collection that features

"everywhere else"

This was how my itinerary was described when I took the job of researching in Italy for *Let's Go.* Others had research routes that focused on a single city (Rome, Venice, Florence) and its environs. I went to the "other" places, bouncing around the country's north before landing in very southern Naples. What has become abundantly clear to me over the past eight weeks is that "everywhere else" is, in fact, somewhere after all. Destination by destination, here's what I learned:

Milan is more than a financial capital. It's a sprawling metropolis with hopping nightlife, gourmet restaurants (some at less than gourmet prices), and collections of exquisite art.

Turin, a city I knew nothing about, has a modern history to rival Rome's ancient one. It's home to opulent Savoy palaces and domed basilicas perched on verdant green hills. It seems that nothing more than a river separates this cosmopolitan city from the rugged beauty of the Alpine foothills.

Cinque Terre is touristed, but even its tiny, jewel-like towns that sit perched on rocks contain more than turquoise water and beaches. Intimate restaurants set in the hills above town and rocky trails offering stunning vistas make these villages so much more than your average seaside resort.

Bologna is a student paradise–100,000 of them call the city home, eating high-quality, cheap grub, then partying until 4am in medieval *piazze* and waking up in time for class the next day.

And Naples is not really full of trash. Much of it is beautiful and better explored over the course of a few days before you run off to the islands and coastline nearby.

Of course, as soon as I finish my route I'll be off to spend some time in the "Big Three" Italian cities, taking the train up to Rome, Venice, and Florence. But that doesn't mean the best of Italy is yet to come. I'm pretty sure I've found that already.

–William White

classical works alongside contemporary art. Though it's famous for its **Farnese Collection,** once owned by a family of the same name, the museum has much more going for it than that. Formerly a royal palace, the *museo* boasts many rooms that are precious artifacts in themselves, though unlike 2D paintings, these works of art can hold visitors inside them. In the second floor's Neapolitan collection, works by **Caravaggio** and numerous 19th-century masters from the city are on display.

In the north of the city. [M]Cavour, then bus C63 or R4. $ €7.50, EU students ages 18-25 €3.75. ⏰ Open M-Tu 8:30am-7:30pm, Th-Su 8:30am-7:30pm.

CASTEL DELL'OVO (EGG CASTLE) ♿ CASTLE

Borgo Marinari ☎081 24 00 055

All that fuss over an egg? Yes indeed, throughout the city's history one measly egg has caused a string of panics. According to legend, the enchanted egg in question was placed in this castle's foundation by **Virgil.** If its fragile shell were to break, the city of Naples would crumble. After the yellow-brick castle sustained significant damage when one of its arches collapsed, none other than the queen herself had to reassure the public that the egg was safe. Originally a monastery, the castle was later converted to be used for defensive purposes but is now mostly used for its beautiful views, especially at sunset.

Walk down V. Santa Lucia from south of P. del Plebiscito. $ Free. ⏰ Open M-Sa 8:30am-7pm, Su 8:30am-2pm.

SPAGGIA ROTONDA DIAZ 🚭 BEACH

V. Francesco Caracciolo

Capri and Ischia, Sorrento and Amalfi—they're all so far away. Spaggia Rotonda is right here in the heart of Naples, and it's a Neapolitan **beach** at its finest. This is the perfect spot for working on the southern Italian tan you see on everyone around you.

Walk down V. Caracciolo along the waterfront from Mergellina or Chiaia. $ Free. ⏰ Open daily sunrise to sunset.

FOOD

When in Rome, do as the Romans do. When in Naples, eat **pizza.** If you ever doubted that Neapolitans invented the crusty, cheese-covered pie, the city's pizzerias will take that doubt, beat it into a ball, throw it in the air, spin it on their collective finger, punch it down, cover it with sauce and mozzarella, and serve it *alla margherita.* Centro Storico is full of excellent choices, especially along **Via Tribunali,** the pizza corridor of the world..

Centro Storico

GINO SORBILLO 🚭🍸❄ PIZZERIA [1]

V. dei Tribunali 35 ☎081 44 66 43 🖥www.sorbillo.eu

Making pizza and children since 1935, Gino Sorbillo has created a dynasty: a family of 21 pizza-making children, several of whom own their own shops nearby. His eponymous shop also gave birth to the *ripieno al forno* (literally "fried in the oven"), a.k.a. the calzone. Twenty-one scrumptious specialty pizzas bear the names of the family's numerous offspring.

Between V. Arti and Vico San Paolo. $ Pizza €3-8. Service 10%. ⏰ Open Sept-July M-Sa noon-3:30pm and 7-11:30pm.

PIZZERIA DI MATTEO 🚭🍸❄ PIZZERIA [1]

V. dei Tribunali 94 ☎081 45 52 62 🖥www.pizzeriadimatteo.it

This place has its priorities straight: while diners at Pizzeria Di Matteo have to take the stairs, the pizza rides to the dining room in an elevator. The Neapolitans that fill the tables aren't bothered by the unhurried service, and tourists who are shouldn't be. If they could just imagine the fluffy dough of Matteo's standout

marinara pie melting in their mouths, they'd be more than happy to wait for it.
On V. dei Tribunali near V. Duomo. The only door seems to lead into the kitchen, but this is indeed the entrance. $ Pizza €2.50-6. ⏰ Open M-Sa 9am-midnight.

ANTICA TRATTORIA DEL CARMINE — RISTORANTE, SEAFOOD 3

V. dei Tibunali 330 ☎081 29 43 83

Recommended by locals as a great date spot or stop for some quality fish or pasta, this trattoria with a multi-level dining room under brick arches retains the rustic, ancient charm of Naples's historic center. Try the linguine with seafood *(€13)* or go for a simpler pasta or fish from the extensive menu.

Directly across from Napoli Sotteranea. $ Primi €4-13; secondi €7-10. Fish €7.50-13. ⏰ Open Tu noon-4pm, W-Su noon-4pm and 7-11pm.

SORRISO INTEGRALE — VEGETARIAN 2

Vico S. Pietro a Maiella 6 ☎081 45 50 26 🖥www.sorriosointegrale.com

Naples making you feel like you're becoming round and sprouting tomato sauce and mozzarella? At some point, take a break from pizza and pasta to try this small, hidden organic and vegan restaurant with a constantly changing menu

Near P. Miraglia, on the small connecting street between Vico S. Pietro a Maiella and P. Bellini. Inside the gate on the right when heading to P. Bellini. $ Cover €2. Primi €4.50; secondi €5.50-7.50. ⏰ Open daily noon-4pm and 7-11pm.

FANTASIA GELATI — GELATERIA 1

V. Toledo 381 ☎081 55 11 212 🖥www.fantasiagelati.it

The podium for this proud gelato gold medalist is the place it's always been: the streets of Naples. There's no need for a flashier showcase, as Fantasia earns admirors enough among the locals and visitors who wander in off the street to sample fruit flavors made from real juices. There are also many creatively titled scoops like Cuore Nero ("Black Heart"), a deep, dark chocolate.

[M]Dante. On V. Toledo south of P. Dante. i Other locations at P. Vitelli 22, V. Gilea 80, Largo Lala 30, and V. Fragnito 39. $ Cones €1.50-5, gluten-free €2. ⏰ Open in summer daily 7am-1am; in fall, winter, and spring Tu-Su 7am-11pm.

LEOPOLDO — BAKERY 1

V. Toledo 8 ☎081 55 12 909 🖥www.leopoldo.it

This tiny shop fills little blue boxes with kilos of Neopolitans, all tied up with their signature yellow ribbon. The packaging is a nice touch, but it's hard to imagine the individual who doesn't promptly tear off that ribbon and devour the box's contents soon after arriving home. If you count yourself guilty of such self-indulgence, you're not to be blamed, for from Leopoldo's simple cannoli to its cartoonish frosted animal cakes, everything here is irresistibly sugary and oh-so-delicious.

[M]Dante. South of P. Dante. $ Pastries from €0.50. ⏰ Open daily 10am-7pm.

Stazione Centrale

As many takeout places and cafes line **Piazza Garibaldi** as do street vendors. Most food here is grab-and-go for travelers on the move, though there are a few sit-down spots for visitors with more time before the train arrives.

ANTICA PIZZA DA MICHELE — PIZZERIA 1

V. Cesare Sersale 1/3 ☎081 55 39 204 🖥www.damichele.net

All the people here must know something. They take numbers from the chef inside, then wait around in the hot midday sun, sometimes for 1hr. What they're waiting for has been called, by some, the best pizza in the world. The options may be limited to margherita and marinara *(€4.50)*, with the option of double cheese *(€5.50)*, but once a pie is in front of you, you know it's the real deal. Thin, crispy, and just right, the pizzas emerge from the oven at the back and, needless to say, their stays on the plates are short-lived.

Walk down C. Umberto I and turn right. i Takeout available. $ Sodas €1.50. ⏰ Open M-Sa 10am-11pm.

MIMI ALLA FERROVIA SEAFOOD ❸

V. Alfonso d'Aragona 19/21 ☎081 55 38 525 www.mimiallaferrovia.it

Many of the diners here may arrive by train, but the seafood comes by boat, fresh from the bay. Chefs waste no time cooking the salty harvest in delicious shellfish dishes and *secondi* plates to serve here at Mimi alla Ferrovia, one of the few full-service restaurants near Stazione Centrale. Served by black-tied waiters in an elegant dining room, the professionals and tourists who dine here must find it a refreshing retreat from the summer heat.

Across the piazza from the station, take V. Poerio and turn right onto V. Alfonso d'Aragona. $ Primi €7-10. Meat and fish dishes €8-13. Service 15%. ⏰ Open M-Sa noon-3pm and 7-10:30pm.

RISTORANTE BERGANTINO RISTORANTE ❷

V. Milano 16 ☎081 55 38 996

Pass through these doors and the inevitable end is coming—for the rather vulnerable-looking fish in this restaurant's big tank, that is. Though, truthfully, those sea creatures will likely see Bergantino's doorway once more when they're sitting in the stomach of one of the restaurant's satisfied patrons. Even those who don't speak Italian will find the friendly banter and laughter of the servers here entertaining, though the low din resonating throughout the dining room might remind you of your high school's cafeteria.

From the station, walk along the right side of the piazza and turn right. $ Cover €1.50 plus 12% for service. Pizza €3.50-12. Pastas €5-8. ⏰ Open M-Sa 11:30am-4pm and 6-10:30pm.

Piazza del Plebiscito and Spanish Quarter

The area has its share of touristy cafes, mostly on **Via Toledo.** Step into the Spanish Quarter's alleys for something more authentic—and for an alternative to pizza, too.

HOSTERIA TOLEDO RISTORANTE ❷

Vicolo Giardinetto 78/A ☎081 42 12 57 www.hosteriatoledo.it

If you doubt that this place has its fair share of happy customers, step inside Hosteria Toledo, which calls itself a landmark, and allay your suspicions. Postcards from admirers dangle from the ceiling and taped-up photographs of happy eaters line the walls. Specializing in pasta and seafood, this homey spot has axed pizza from its menu in a dramatic, anti-establishment move largely unheard of in the Neapolitan culinary scene. Those who are flustered by this shocking development can try the chef's surprise—it rarely disappoints, though the price will be a surprise as well.

Take Vicolo Giardinetto off V. Toledo. Restaurant is at the intersection with V. Sperzanella. $ Primi €6.50-8; secondi €7-14. Service 10%. ⏰ Open M 1-4pm and 7pm-midnight, Tu 1-4pm, Th-Su 1-4pm and 7pm-midnight.

TRATTORIA NENNELLA RISTORANTE ❷

Vicolo Lungo Teatro Nuovo 105 ☎081 41 43 38

From construction workers to bankers, Neopolitans gather here for long and leisurely lunches at unbelieveably low fixed prices from a menu consisting of a *primo*, *secondo*, *contorno*, fruit, and wine. In summertime, patrons sit outdoors in the street, where views of the unchoreographed neighborhood hubbub should be fascinating for the uninitiated.

Walk up Vicolo Teatro Nuovo and look for the signs near Vicolo Lungo Teatro Nuovo $ Prix-fixe menu €10. ⏰ Open M-Sa noon-3pm and 7-10:30pm. Closed in Aug.

LA SFOGLIATELLA MARY BAKERY ❶

Galleria Umberto I ☎081 40 22 18

The summer weather may be scorching (hey, it's the South) but somehow, a piping hot *sfogliatelle* still hits the spot. Naples's signature pastry is a flaky, triangular puff of dough filled with a variety of tasty pastes. Mary makes some of the city's best, though it has to be eaten on the run—there's not a single seat at this tiny stand.

🪧 Just inside the entrance of Galleria Umberto I off V. Toledo. [$] Pastries from €0.80. Sfogliatelle €1.50. Fruit tarts €2.50. ⏰ Open M-Sa 8am-8pm, Su 8am-3pm.

LA BOTTEGA DELLA PASTA 💳🚭 TAKEOUT [1]

Vico D'Afflitto 41 ☎081 41 00 06

If you don't want to do to a real restaurant, skip the supermarket and get some fresh, genuinely Neapolitan pasta at this local shop. Though they may not speak English, the helpful ladies behind the counter will help you pick the best type for what you're cooking, no matter what culinary creations are floating through your head.

🪧 Take Vico D'Afflitto from V. Toledo. The shop is about halfway up on the right. [$] Pasta €5-7 per kg. Lasagna €10-12 per kg. ⏰ Open Tu-F 9:30am-8pm, Sa 9:30am-2pm and 4:30-8pm, Su 9:30am-2pm.

7 SOLDI 💵🚭🍸❄ RISTORANTE [1]

Vico Tre Re a Toledo 6 ☎081 41 87 27

The name means "seven pence," but more than seven Neopolitans—and foreigners—are fans of this Spanish Quarter restaurant if the lunchtime crowd is any indicator. The chatty staff serve up massive salads *(€5-7)*, some with whole crustaceans piled on top, beady eyes begging not to be eaten and all, plus pizzas fresh from an oven near the entrance.

🪧 Turn onto Vico Tre Re from V. Toledo near P. Trieste e Trento. [$] Pizza €3-7. Secondi €5-8. ⏰ Open Tu-Su noon-4pm and 7pm-midnight.

Chiaia, Vomero, and Outskirts

👍 FRIGGITORIA VOMERO 💵🚭 BAKERY [1]

V. Domenico Cimarosa 44 ☎081 57 83 130

Super-quick, super-cheap, and about as Neapolitan as a place can be, this no-frills fast-food joint fills its flour-dusted display cases with fried dough creations. Sweet **arancino di riso** is a Neapolitan classic and local favorite, but the biggest crowd-pleaser has to be the dirt-cheap pricing: most items are under €1, so buy a whole bunch.

🪧 In Vomero. Head away from the funicular at P. Fuga and look across the square. ℹ No seating available. [$] Fried foods €0.20-2. Panini €2.50 ⏰ Open M-Sa 9:30am-2:30pm and 5:30-8:30pm.

PIZZERIA GORIZIA 💳🚭🍸❄☂ PIZZERIA [2]

V. Bernini 29-31 ☎081 57 82 248

From late lunch through late at night, this place is packed with local diners. They're rewarded with a delicious pizza *crudaiola (€8)*, a piping-hot and pie with *mozzarella di bufala*, tomato, prosciutto, oregano, and olive oil.

🪧 In Vomero. From the funicular at P. Fuga, take V. Cimarosa to the left and turn right onto V. Bernini. [$] Cover €1. Pizza €5-8. Primi €6-13; secondi €8-15. ⏰ Open Tu-Su 12:30-4pm and 6:30pm-midnight.

HAPPY MAX KEBAB 💵♿ KEBAB [1]

P. Giulio Rodino 35

Try what locals call the best kebab in Naples—just don't look for any seating or superfluities.

🪧 In Chiaia. Take V. Chiaia from V. Toledo and turn right onto the small piazza and V. Filangieri before P. dei Martiri. [$] Sandwiches €3.50. ⏰ Open daily 11:30am-midnight.

GRAN CAFFÈ CIMIRINO 💵🚭🍸❄☂ CAFE [1]

V. Gonzaga Filangieri 12/13 ☎081 41 83 03

Grab a cappuccino and croissant to-go or an espresso and brioche to savor at the

naples . food

outdoor tables. And savor you should, for the brew here is locally lauded as the best coffee in the city. Pay first at the register to the right, then step right up and experience the aroma you're enjoying in liquid form.

➡ In Chiaia. Take V. Chiaia from V. Toledo and turn right onto V. Filangieri before P. dei Martiri. $ Pastries €0.60-2.50. Coffee drinks €1-2. ⏰ Open M-Th 7am-10pm, F-Su 7am-1am.

NIGHTLIFE 🌙

The discos in Naples may be few and far between—literally—but the city is not without after-hours activity. Its *centro* and fashionable outer neighborhoods bustle with bars and, better yet, students in *piazze* drinking cheap beer from—where else?—local pizza joints. **Piazza Gesù Nuovo** and **Piazza Duomo** are filled with students, some of whom firmly believe in the healing power of certain botanicals, but the most popular *piazza*, known as **Kesté,** is also one of the more obscure to outsiders. *(➡ From C. Umberto I, walk up V. Mezzocannone and take the 1st left onto V. Enrico di Marinis.)* The environs of **Piazza del Martiri** contain tons of bars, though unlike those in the previous *piazze*, the ones here are less convenience store and more the Ritz. Some nightclubs call the place home as well, though they're virtually all closed in July and August. **Piazza Bellini** is relaxed and bookish, with computers and Wi-Fi replacing the DJ booth and bass. If a short funicular or longer Metro ride is in the cards, you could join the young and hip in Vomero's **Piazza Vanvitelli.** Avoid the area around **Stazione Centrale,** it is very sketchy at night.

Centro Storico

The *centro* offers a pleasing selection of bars scattered throughout the area. Students gather nightly at a *piazza* on **Via Enrico de Marinis,** just off V. Mezzocannone and conveniently only a few minutes walk from some of Naples's best hostels. At bars and pizza joints in this area, large beers start at €2 or less.

👍 TROPICANA 🚫⊗🍸❄ CLUB, LATIN

V. San Giuseppe dei Ruffi 14 ☎338 23 08 288

Whether they come from Buenos Aires or Bolivia, Brazil or Bogota, they're welcome here. Those who don't speak a Latin language are warmly welcomed too, but their nation's flag won't be on the wall at this salsa and Latin music club, one of Naples's most hopping hidden spots. A packed, small dance floor moves into a frenzy when the DJ starts spinning, and the sardine-smooshed patrons make the most of it by dancing with whomever's nearby.

➡ Just off V. Duomo. When walking uphill, turn left. $ 1st drink €5, €3.50 per drink thereafter. ⏰ Open daily midnight-6am.

LEMME LEMME BY INTERNET BAR 🚫⊗📶🍸❄⛅ BAR

P. Bellini 74 ☎081 29 52 37

Sway to the beat, check your email, grab a drink, or check the score—the free internet at this popular bar is great for everything except your social life. Stay away from the screen and mingle with the locals who gather on this pretty *piazza.* You can friend them all on Facebook later.

➡ Ⓜ Dante. Walk through Porta Alba and turn left onto V. Santa Maria di Constantinopoli; the piazza is immediately to the right. $ Beer €3-5.50. ⏰ Open M-Sa 9am-3am, Su 5pm-3am.

ARTS CAFE 💳⊗🍸❄ CLUB

V. San Giuseppe dei Nudi 9 ☎081 21 88 467, 081 56 41 206 💻www.artscafe.eu

An older crowd gathers for a nightly old-school spectacle at this club featuring everything from jazz quartets to Vaudeville-esque shows in its simple venue near the Museo Nazionale.

➡ From V. Santa Teresa degli Scalzi (V. Roma) across from the museum, take the zigzagging street upward to the cafe. $ Drinks €5, with dinner €20. ⏰ Open daily 6pm-1am.

Piazza del Plebiscito and Spanish Quarter

LES BELLES CHOSES
⊛⊗❄❖☂ IRISH PUB

V. Cesario Console 15/16 ☎081 24 51 166

Les Belles Choses is a little like a pug: not so beautiful, but oh-so-friendly. The interior is dark and covered in an intentional clutter of street signs and mismatched furniture, but the beers are cool and the staff and patrons are warm.

✚ *Just south of P. del Plebiscito.* Ⓢ *Beer €3-4. Cocktails €6.50.* ☼ *Open M-Tu 6:30pm-1:30am, W-Sa 6:30pm-4am, Su 6:30pm-1:30am. Sometimes open later depending on crowds.*

BARRITO
⊛⊗❄❖☂ BAR

V. Cesario Console 17/19 ☎392 15 65 636 ▣www.elbarrito.it

A fancy-looking interior draws slightly more elegant patrons than the Irish pub next door. Mainly older locals gather under the sidewalk umbrellas in front beneath the rosy glow of pink neon signs.

✚ *Just south of P. del Plebiscito.* Ⓢ *Beer €3-5. Cocktails €6.* ☼ *Open daily 10am-2pm.*

Chiaia, Vomero, and Outskirts

◧ GOODFELLAS
⬟⊗❄❖ BAR

V. Morghen 34 ☎340 92 25 475 ▣www.goodfellasclub.com

This is a good old sports bar—except there's hardly any sports on TV. Screens show MTV along with the occasional soccer match, while cover bands take to the stage three nights weekly at 11pm. Sports-wise, the Chicago Bulls jerseys and baseball posters on the wall could still get any red-blooded soul into the mood for a beer and some football (of whichever variety you prefer).

✚ *In Vomero. Up the stairs from the funicular in P. Fuga and to the left.* Ⓢ *0.5L wine €3.50. Beer €5. Cocktails €7.* ☼ *Open Tu-Su 8pm-2am.*

◧ S'MOVE
⬟⊗❄❖☂ BAR

Vico dei Sospiri 10/A ☎081 76 45 813 ▣www.smove-lab.net

This bar is the closest one can come to getting groovy in summertime Naples, as a DJ spins house, funk, or rap most nights to create the feeling of being at a disco, without most of the dancing. Young patrons cluster at the bar and around high outdoor tables with their mojitos and crushed drinks—the bartender's specialties.

✚ *In Chiaia. From P. dei Martiri, take V. Alabardieri, then make the 2nd left.* Ⓢ *Beer €5. Cocktails €7-8.* ☼ *Open daily 7pm-4am. Aperitivo 7-9pm.*

VINTAGE
⬟⊗❄❖☂ ENOTECA

V. Bernini 37/A ☎081 22 95 473 ▣www.vintageweb.it

Vomero's first wine bar makes quite an impression. On nights when a DJ plays inside, the sound bursts onto the street and draws in a line of young people who would otherwise stay at the tables outdoors. Then the dance floor gets hot and sweaty in an almost anti-*enoteca* way. (This is not your mother's wine bar.)

✚ *In Vomero. From the funicular at P. Fuga, take V. Bernini past P. Vanvitelli.* Ⓢ *Wine €5. Cocktails €7.* ☼ *Open M-Th 7pm-1am, F-Sa 7pm-3am. Happy hour 7-9:30pm. Closed 2 weeks in Aug.*

L'OCA NERA
⬟⊗❄❖ IRISH PUB

V. Bernini 17 ☎081 55 81 649

This place has the classic look of an Irish pub and the extensive beer selection to match. Satellite TVs in every room keep diners' minds off the table conversation. Play darts but *please* be accurate—in keeping with Neapolitan safety standards (or lack thereof), there is no backboard to stop errant needle-nosed objects from zooming past the target and hitting people sitting behind.

✚ *In Vomero. From the funicular at P. Fuga, turn left onto V. Cimarosa, then turn right onto V. Bernini.* Ⓢ *Beer €4-6; gourmet varieties up to €15. Cocktails €6.* ☼ *Open daily 7:30pm-1:30am.*

naples · nightlife

ARTS AND CULTURE

Naples is known more for carefree lifestyles and a disregard for rules than arts and refinement, yet the city presents a number of opportunities to experience something a bit more unique than a red-light-running scooter. On September 19 and the first Saturday in May, the city stops all its scooters to celebrate its patron saint in the **Festa di San Gennaro.** Join the crowd to watch the procession on V. Duomo in May and see San Gennaro's blood (normally kept in the city's Duomo) miraculously liquefy, keeping the former settlement safe for another year.

Opera, Theater, and Classical Music

TEATRO DI SAN CARLO PIAZZA DEL PLEBISCITO

V. San Carlo 98 ☎081 79 72 331 or 79 72 412 www.teatrosancarlo.it

La Scala's southern foil, Teatro di San Carlo puts on magnificent productions in Europe's oldest operating opera house—a theater that many say has better acoustics than the jewel of Milan. This is an argument in which you might not want to engage with a resident of that northern city, but stopping in here for a show will let you see if the claims are true. The symphony *(Oct-May)* and opera *(Dec-June)* seasons both offer great opportunities to put those ears to good use and hear sound on a grand scale.

In P. Trieste e Trento, near P. del Plebiscito. i All tickets go fast, buy in advance. $ Gallery tickets from €12. Box office open M-Sa 10am-7pm, Su 10am-3:30pm.

TEATRO STABILE DI NAPOLI PIAZZA DEL PLEBISCITO

P. Municipo ☎081 55 13 396 www.teatrostabilenapoli.it

Shakespeare is on the menu—in English, with subtitles—of Naples's most renowned theater company, which performs primarily at Teatro Mercadante in P. Municipo. Unlike American theater, Italian shows run for just a few weeks, so check the schedule and plan your stay according to what strikes your dramatic fancy.

From Stazione Centrale, take bus R2. $ From €15. Box office open M-Sa 10:30am-1pm and 5:30-7:30pm, Su 10:30am-1pm.

TEATRO NUOVO SPANISH QUARTER

V. Montecalvario 16 ☎081 49 76 267 www.nuovoteatronuovo.it

Try something a bit more modern at this theater, a showcase for new productions in the Spanish Quarter. Featuring occasional dramatic laboratories in which the public can participate, the theater has made a name for itself by differing from establishment venues like the two listed above.

[M]Dante. Walk down V. Toledo and turn right onto V. Montecalvario. $ Tickets from €10. Season runs Oct-Apr.

Festivals

AMALFI COAST MUSIC FESTIVAL SUMMER

Locations in Naples and Amalfi Coast towns ☎+1 301-587-6189 www.musicalstudies.com

Annually in June and July, Naples and the Amalfi coast open their theaters and music venues to a group of outsiders looking to learn about music from the best of the best. While they do so, these musicians stage nightly classical music concerts throughout the region, from solo piano to full orchestra performances. Mozart's ballets have been a highlight in past years, and of course, the surroundings delight no matter what the performance.

Most shows in Naples take place at the Complesso Monumentale di San Lorenzo Maggiore, V. dei Tribunali 316. $ Tickets free-€10. June-July. Concerts nightly at 9pm.

NEAPOLIS FESTIVAL SUMMER

Mostra d'Oltremare, P. Tecchio www.neapolis.it

Perfect for students, this festival attracts local and international pop and rap artists to show off their skills on outdoor stages near the soccer stadium. With thousands of people packed in, travelers can't help but party with some Neapolitans while swaying to the synthesized beats.

☝ Ⓜ*Mostra. On the piazza outside the station.* Ⓢ *€30.* ⏰ *Mid-July. Doors open daily at 4pm.*

Sports

STADIO SAN PAOLO

Piazzale Vincenzo Tecchio

✈♿ OUTSKIRTS
☎081 23 95 623 ▣www.sscnapoli.it

If it's game day, light blue is the color of choice in this bustling metropolis. The Neopolitan football club lacks the international following of many Italian teams, but what it loses there, it more than makes up for with rabid home crowds who still have a crush on their late-1980s hero, Argentinian **Diego Maradona**. For the semifinal of the 1990 World Cup (held in the stadium), Maradona went so far as to ask the Italian fans to cheer for Argentina (who were playing *against* Italy), which the Italians politely declined. Maradona answered with the game-winning penalty kick. Hardly fazed, today the city council has sought to rename the stadium after Maradona—with a minor snag being an Italian law forbidding the naming of buildings after anyone who hasn't been dead for at least 10 years. Whatever it's called, however, the stadium filled with 60,000 screaming Neapolitans is a snapshot of true city life that cannot be rivaled.

☝ Ⓜ*Mostra, in the Fuorigrotta area. Directly outside the station.* Ⓢ *Tickets from €15.* ⏰ *Season runs Sept-June; most games Su afternoons.*

SHOPPING

Very low prices can make Naples an enticing place to score that killer deal—as long as you remember that there's a reason the street vendor grabs his wares and runs when a police car turns the corner. His livelihood depends on his craftiness, and given the opportunity to outwit you, he will. If a transaction seems too good to be true, **it is.** On that note, ▣**never buy electronics from street vendors.** Many tourists, even those who checked the name-brand packaging, have ended up with the most expensive bag of salt they ever bought. What should you do? Haggle, bargain, and barter to your heart (and wallet's) content. Where haggling *won't* get you too far is at designer stores, which are surprisingly abundant in the city's nicer areas, including **Piazza Martiri, Via dei Mille,** and **Via Scarlatti.**

Designer Stores

Designer shops line the streets near **Piazza dei Martiri,** particulary **Via dei Mille.** Fashionable locals flock to Vomero's pedestrian-only **Via Scarlatti** for a much calmer, window-gazing stroll.

ASCIONE

Angiporto Galleria Umberto I 19

✈⊗ PIAZZA DEL PLEBISCITO
☎081 42 11 11 ▣www.ascione.it

This glittering jewelry store proves that, in Naples, "fruits of the sea" don't just end up on restaurant plates. Here, beautifully colored coral from the Mediterranean ends up in silver and gold settings. Made in nearby Torre San Greco, these coral baubles are ready to be worn as a conversation-starting necklace or a romantic ring.

☝ *In the galleria, off V. Toledo* Ⓢ *Jewelry from €200.* ⏰ *Open M-Sa 9:30am-1pm and 3-6pm.*

CANE ROSSO

V. Carlo Poerio 42

✈⊗ CHIAIA
☎081 24 05 207

From Naples to Milan, sneakers are a crucial element of the Italian outfit. They can be worn with jeans or with a suit, but if they don't catch the eye immediately, something must be wrong. This store sets out to solve that problem in an explosively colorful fashion, with brand-name sneakers in canary yellow, fuschia, and every point on the rainbow in between.

➜ From Riviera di Chiaia, turn onto Vle. Ravaschieri and then turn left onto V. Carlo Poerio. $ Sneakers €75-200. ⏰ Open M-Sa 10am-1:30pm and 4:30-8pm.

Bargain Stores

Via Chiaia has a concentration of stylish but inexpensive clothing outlets en route to the more expensive area near **Piazza dei Martiri.** Vomero offers other shops exploding with color, but prices jump in this well-off enclave.

👍 CERAMICHE DI VIETRI — VOMERO

V. Sergio Abate 14 ☎081 57 86 924 💻www.ceramichedivietri.com

The colors of Naples are here to take home and enjoy. The blue of the sea, yellow of the sun, purples, reds, and millions of coral colors. This small shop next to a bustling outdoor market keeps the Neapolitan artisan tradition alive by selling handpainted ceramics with cartoonish, bubbling fish and waving, delicate reefs. Step inside to take home a fragile but beautiful piece of this gorgeous coastline.

➜ [M]Medaglie d'Oro. Walk down V. Fiore and turn right. $ Small plates €6.50; extra-large €32. Bowls €12. ⏰ Open M-Sa 9:30am-1:45pm and 4:30-7:45pm.

IL CAMICIAIO — CHIAIA

V. Chiaia 180 ☎081 41 57 65

The shirt you get will probably be gray, but on the bright side, shopping here means saving more of those colorful euro bills. With a selection biased toward beige and that color's dull friends, this men's shop offers a selection that's sleek and fitted but certainly doesn't jump out of the window display.

➜ Take V. Chiaia from V. Toledo. $ Pants from €10. Shirts from €20. ⏰ Open M-Sa 9:30am-2:30pm and 4-6:30pm.

Markets

👍 ARTIGANO ♿ VOMERO

Between V. da Camaino and V. Fiore

If you're ready to haggle but maybe not to fight with the vendor as you attempt to buy that nice souvenir T-shirt, it's better to avoid P. Garibaldi and head to Vomero. Everything, even the markets, are a little cleaner up here, and the crowd is a little less rough. Many of the same wares at similar prices are available despite the significantly higher-class digs. After all, a street market is a street market is a street market.

➜ [M]Medaglie d'Oro. In the triangle just to the southwest of the piazza. $ Dresses from €3. Fresh fruits and vegetables from €1 per kg. ⏰ Open M-Sa 8:30am-2pm.

FIERA ANTIQUARIA NEAPOLITANA ♿ STAZIONE CENTRALE

Villa Communale, V. Caracciolo 💻www.fierantiquarianeapolitana.it

Filled with artisans and vendors selling ancient artifacts and more recent antiques, this *fiera* is a feast for the eyes, though the hefty pricetags discourage purchases of the exquisite items. Hundreds of would-be shoppers wander through aisle after aisle to browse rare stamps, books, coins and art.

➜ From V. Chiaia, walk through P. dei Martiri and onto V. Calabritto, which emerges at the eastern end of Villa Communale. $ Prices vary widely, but many rare antiques can be expensive. ⏰ Open 3rd Sa-Su each month 8am-2pm. Also open on the 4th Sa-Su except June-Aug.

ESSENTIALS

Practicalities

- **TOURIST OFFICES: EPT** offers booking services, free maps, and the indispensable guide **👍Qui Napoli,** which includes abundant hotel and restaurant listings. *(P. dei Martiri 58 ☎081 41 07 211 💻www.eptnapoli.info ⏰ Open M-F 9am-2pm.)* There is another, often crowded, branch in Stazione Centrale. *(☎081 26 87 79 ⏰ Open M-Sa 9am-7pm, Su 9am-1pm.)* Friendly **AASCT** provides info on accommodations, transportation, and things to do. *(V. San Carlo 9 ☎081 40 23 94 🖳www.inaples.it ⇆ Outside Galleria Umberto I, near P. Trieste e Trente. ⏰ Open daily 9am-7pm.)*

- **CONSULATES: Canada.** *(V. Carducci 29 ☎081 40 13 38 ⇆ In Chiaia, 2 blocks from V. dei Mille. ⏰ Open M-F 9am-1pm.)* **UK.** *(☎081 42 38 911; emergency ☎06 42 20 23 54 ⏰ Open M-F 9:30am-12:30pm and 2-4pm.)* **USA.** *(P. della Repubblica 2 ☎081 53 88 111; emergency 033 79 45 083 ⇆ At the far west end of Villa Communale, on the waterfront. ⏰ Open M-F 8am-1pm and 2-5pm.)*
- **INTERNET:** Internet points are clustered around V. Mezzocannone and P. Bellini. **Lemme Lemme by Internet Bar** offers computer terminals and free Wi-Fi. *(P. Bellini 74 ☎081 29 52 37 $ Computers €0.05 per min. ⏰ Open M-Sa 9am-3am, Su 5pm-3am.)*
- **POST OFFICES:** Head here for a window into true Neapolitan life. The defunct telecommunications hall next door has an oddly library-like atmosphere in which to relax in the shade. As may be obvious, you can also mail things from here. *(P. Matteoti ☎081 55 24 233 ⏰ Open M-F 8:15am-6pm, Sa 8:15am-noon.)*

Emergency!

- **POLICE: Polizia Municipale** *(☎081 75 13 177)*. **Polizia del Stato** can be found at V. Medina, near P. Matteoti, or at P. Garibaldi 22, directly across the *piazza* from the station.
- **HOSPITALS/MEDICAL SERVICES: Incurabili** is more helpful than its name might suggest. *(P. Cavour ☎081 25 49 422 ⇆ [M]Cavour (Museo). The emergency ward is directly up V. Maria Longo.)*

Getting There

By Plane

Aeroporto Capodichino (NAP) *(Vle. Ruffo Fulco di Calabria ☎081 84 88 87 73 or 081 75 15 471 🖳www.gesac.it ⏰ Open daily 5:30am-11:30pm.)* is located in the northeast of the city and is a great point of access to the whole Bay of Naples area. Twenty airlines operate from the airport, including Alitalia, British Airways, Lufthansa, and EasyJet. The red and white **Alibus** shuttle travels from the airport arrivals terminal to the seaport near P. Municio and to P. Garibaldi. *($ €3.10. ⏰ 15-20min.)* City bus **3S** *($ €1.10. ⏰ Every 30min.)* also runs from the arrivals terminal to P. Garibaldi but has many more stops and can be a target for pickpockets. **Taxis** to and from Stazione Centrale and most destinations in the *centro* should not have fares higher than €23—confirm with the driver before getting in.

By Train

Stazione Centrale is in the crazy part of Naples, by P. Garibaldi. **Trenitalia** *(☎199 30 30 60)* runs from **Rome.** *($ From €12. ⏰ 1-3hr., every 30min. 5:40am-10:10pm.)* **Eurostar** trains operated by Trenitalia arrive from **Milan** via **Bologna, Florence,** and **Rome.** *($ €98. ⏰ 5hr., every hr. 6:30am-5:15pm.)* **Circumvesuviana** *(☎081 77 22 111 🖳www.vesuviana.it)* trains are used primarily to access outlying tourist sights such as Pompeii. Trains originate in **Sorrento.** *($ €3.40. ⏰ 50min., every 30min.-1hr. 5am-10:25pm.)* Stazione Centrale is not the final stop: trains continue one more stop down C. Garibaldi to **Stazione Nolana.**

Getting Around

The **UnicoNapoliticket** *(☎081 55 13 109 🖳www.napolipass.it)* is valid for all modes of transportation in the city. Tickets come in three varieties: 90min. *(€1.10)*, full-day *(€3.10)*, and weekend *(€2.60)* and can be bought at newsstands and *tabaccherie.* All regional buses and trains are included in the **UnicoCampania** system *(🖳www.unicocampania.it)*. Prices depend on the zone of your destination. *($ €1.70-8.20; daily tickets €3.50-16.40.)* Schedules change frequently and are published in the daily newspaper *Il Mattino.*

By Bus

Public bus lines crisscross the city; most accommodations and tourist offices provide maps. Most buses run from 6:30am to just before midnight. **R1** runs from P. Bovio to Vomero, while **R2** connects the train station at P. Garibaldi to P. Municipio along C. Umberto I. Cleverly-named **3S** connects the three stations: the airport, train station, and the ferry port at Molo Beverello.

By Metro

Currently, the Metro (☎800 56 88 66 ▪www.metro.na.it) is useful for reaching far-away destinations (such as P. Cavour, Montesanto, P. Amedeo, or Mergellina) but not for exploring the *centro*, though it is being expanded. Trains run 6am-11pm. The lines extend west from P. Garibaldi to **Pozzuoli** from underground at Stazione Centrale. Line 1 stops at **Piazza Cavour** (Museo Nazionale), **Piazza Amedeo** (from which the funicular runs to Vomero), and **Mergeilina.** Transfer at P. Cavour for Line 2 to P. Dante and P. Medaglie d'Oro.

By Funicular

Three funicular lines connect the lower city to elevated Vomero: **Centrale** runs from V. Toledo to P. Fuga; **Montesanto** from P. Montesanto to V. Morghen; and **Chiaia** from V. del Parco Margherita to C. Cimarosa. Centrale and Cimarosa make intermittent stops at C. Vittorio Emanuele. (🕐 *Every 10min.; M-Tu 6:30am-10pm, W-Su 6:30am-12:30am.*)

By Taxi

A number of companies operate the city's white taxis (☎081 88 88; 081 570 70 70; 081 55 60 202; 081 55 15 151). Only take official, licensed taxis with meters and always ask about prices upfront; even recognized companies have been known to charge suspiciously high rates. Meters start at €3 Monday through Saturday 7am-8pm, €5.50 Sunday and nights. Each additional 65m costs €0.05. There may also be surcharges for luggage. Fees double for trips beyond city limits.

bay of naples

pompeii *pompei*

Sailing around the Bay of Naples, you'll see Mt. Vesuvius from nearly all vistas. It lurks formidably as though to say, "Don't forget about me." Well, given the crowds that stream to Pompeii annually, we hardly think the massive volcano is being forgotten (even if it *has* been dormant more than half a century.) On August 24, 79 CE, it earned its infamy, erupting and blanketing the nearby city of Pompeii in a cloud of ash. Tragic though the eruption was for the residents of this ancient metropolis, the preservation of its streets, artifacts, and even people is unparalleled, making this frozen snippet of life nearly two millennia ago a gold mine for archaeologists and a sort of morbid historical "playground" for tourists. Excavations of Pompeii, which started in 1748, have revealed an entire city, most of which is walkable in a day. Streets covered in large, stone blocks, fading frescoes, chipped mosaics, and a labyrinth of small rooms may get repetitive after a few hours—eerie how much it resembles a circa-2011 suburb in that way—but nonetheless spark some thoughts about what this ancient city must have been like. Chances are it was more interesting than its modern-day reincarnation: the small *centro* about 1km away doesn't offer too much to the traveler, except possibly a cheaper meal than what can be found by the ancient city. Head to the ruins in the morning and, if hunger calls, stroll down to the new city for a meal and to escape from the crowds.

ORIENTATION

The ruins cover 66 hectares of land extending east to west, though only 45 are accessible to the public. The area around the **Circumvesuviana**, the **Porta Marina** entrance, and **Piazza Esedra** is full of expensive restaurants and souvenir shops. A 20-25min. walk down V. Plinio and then V. Roma will lead you to the modern city's *centro*. There, the Trenitalia train station is down V. Sacra in P. XXVIII Marzo. Inside the ruins, many of the most important sights are located on the western side, closer to the Porta Marina entrace. These sights include the **Forum** and the **House of the Faun.** A little to the east is the old city's **brothel,** and in a rather peaceful spot at the far eastern corner, you'll find Pompeii's **amphitheater.** Working your way back from there toward the entrance, you'll pass the **Great Theater** on the southern edge of the ruins.

SIGHTS

For the price of one ticket at Pompeii, you'll have the run of an entire ancient city, but that doesn't mean touring the ruins is a simple undertaking. Pompeii was a true metropolis, complete with basilicas, bars, and brothels, and that kind of scope can be intimidating. Plenty of tour guides will try to coerce you into joining their group *(most €10-20).* Rather than shelling out the money to become one of the crowd, opt for an informative audio tour *(€6.50, 2 for €10).* While both options will teach you a lot, one of the most fun ways to experience Pompeii is to navigate its maze-like streets solo—you'll likely get lost even with a map. Before heading out, pick up a free map and guidebook at the info office by showing your ticket. *(€11, EU citizens ages 18-24 €5.50, EU citizens under 18 and over 65 free. Valid 1 day; no re-entry. If you plan on seeing more sites, a combined ticket allows entry to Herculaneum, Oplontis, Stabia, Boscoreale and Pompeii over the course of 3 days for €20, reduced €10.* ◪ *Ruins open daily Apr-Oct 8:30am-7:30pm; Nov-Mar 8:30am-5pm. Last entry 90min. before close.)* Of course, the pleasure of going it alone can be mitigated when the city is packed, and at times it's hard to walk down one of Pompeii's cobbled streets without running into another visitor. Come in the early summer or fall for slightly less crowded circumstances.

Near the Forum

Entering from Porta Marina, you first hit the **Basilica,** the remains of a building originally used for legal purposes and business matters. Now an open space occupied by columns that resemble tree stumps, it's a small taste of the many columned structures to come. Immediately beyond the Basilica is the **Temple of Venere** provides a great view of the surrounding landscape. To the left is the grassy **Forum,** the first-century city's political, religious, and economic center. Head to the **Granai del Foro** on the left for a startling peek at four body casts created by pouring plaster into air pockets in the ash that were formed by disintegrated bodies. You may not be able to tell that one of them is a dog, but the three human figures, one of whom is a pregnant woman, are contorted in heart-wrenching positions of fear. Passersby throw coins of prayer through the metal gates in memory of these individuals' awful ends. For a look at less disturbing human forms, head to the **Tempio di Apollo,** where copies of Apollo and Diana statues that once dominated the area stand. (The originals are in Naples's **Museo Archeologico Nazionale**) As this area is closest to the main entrance and the cafeteria, it is predictably the most crowded. Head elsewhere for a quieter walk.

Near the House of the Faun

The wide V. delle Terme and V. della Fortuna surround the area around the stunning **Casa del Fauno,** the biggest and perhaps best preserved residence in the ruins. Your attention will undoubtedly be drawn to the bronze faun statue at the house's center, but don't miss the mosaic-covered surrounding rooms—unfortunately, these mosaics can only partially make up for the absent Alexander mosaic now displayed at the Naples Museo Archeologico Nazionale. At the time of its discovery, that tiled decoration suggested some relation between the house's wealthy owner and Alexander the

Great. Head to the intimate **House of the Small Fountain** for a peek at a beautifully decorated fountain, complete with mosaics, frescoes, and petite sculptures. The smallish **House of the Vettii** is home to frescoes of Priapus and his biggish member—as the god of fertility, he can be forgiven for weighing his crowning "jewel" on a scale. If you can take your eyes off the amusing picture, admire the brighter-than-usual red walls which have immortalized the color "Pompeii red," a warm earthy hue.

Near the Brothel

While all of Pompeii's ruins are full of strolling tourists, none are as packed as the **Lupanare**, the ancient city's brothel. Looks like it's just as popular now as it was centuries ago. If you can squeak past the tourist groups, take notice of the explicit frescoes lining the walls, which show popular bedroom positions as a source of "inspiration" for the men who frequented the place. The small rooms, occupied only by stone beds which were luckily covered in comfier mats, leave more to the imagination. The upstairs rooms are not accessible but were used for more expensive transactions. Nearby, the large **Stabian Baths** feature a body cast and a wall of impressive mosaics.

Near the Amphitheater

That big green block on your map indicates the **amphitheater,** a massive structure that could hold 20,000 spectators and hosted Colosseum-like gladiator battles in its day. Much quieter now, the arena stands as another vivid reminder of what this city used to be. The adjacent **Great Palaestra** provides a nice break from the hard-to-navigate stone blocks scattered about the rest of the city and some shade under its trees. Less serene is the **Garden of the Fugitives,** where you'll find more plaster casts of the bodies of individuals who didn't flee the city in time. The **House of Octavius Quartio** and **House of Venus** are more peaceful. At these ancient abodes, gardens have been planted based on modern knowledge of ancient horticulture.

Near the Great Theater

Though less impressive in size than the amphitheater, the **Great Theater** has a bit more culture to it—both ancient and modern. Originally a stage hosting plays, it now serves as a performance space for summer music concerts, giving it some life apart from the tourist hordes. The nearby **Small Theater** was the site of ancient poetry readings. An acoustically designed rooftop surrounding the theater's rim amplified the voice of the reciting poet. Nearby, the **Botanical Garden** provides a nice punch of greenery, shade, and pleasant smells.

ESSENTIALS

Practicalities

- **TOURIST OFFICES:** Tourist Offices are located at V. Porta Marina Inf. 12 (☎081 85 07 255 ⚓ *At the Circumvesuviana station.)* and at V. Sacra 1. (☎081 536 32 93 ▣*www.pompeiturismo.it ⚓ Near the Trenitalia station.)* Both offer information on and maps of the modern city of Pompeii, sell tickets for sightseeing buses around Campania, and stock pamphlets about museums in the area. (Ⓓ *Both open daily 8:30am-6:30pm.)*

- **LUGGAGE STORAGE: Bag check** at the archaelogical site is free and mandatory for large bags.

- **POST OFFICES:** *(P. Esdera 1 ☎081 85 06 164 ⚓ Right near the V. Porta Marina Inferiore entrance. Ⓓ Open M-F 8am-1:30pm, Sa 8am-12:30pm.)*

Getting There

The best way to get to Pompeii's archaeological site is by the **Circumvesuviana train** from Naples's Stazione Centrale (Ⓢ *€2.40. Ⓓ 20-30min., every 15min.)* or from Sorrento. (Ⓢ *€1.90. Ⓓ 20-30min., every 20min.)* Get off at Pompei Scavi. From the train, the ruins' main entrance, **Porta Marina,** is to the right. If you proceed onward down V. Villa dei

Misteri, you can enter at the less crowded entrance at **Piazza Esedra.** Instead of the Circumvesuviana, you can take a **Trenitalia** train. *($ €2.40. ⏰ 20-40 min., every 30min. Ticket office open daily 6:40am-8:28pm, with 3 15min. midday closings.)* The train will drop you off in modern Pompeii's *centro.* From the station, walk up V. Sacra until you reach P. Bartolo Longo. Turn left down V. Colle San Bartolomeo. It's a 20-25min. walk to the archaeological site's main entrance, so it is better to enter at the less crowded **Piazza Anfiteatro,** a short way down V. Plinio.

herculaneum *ercolano*

Once you've gotten over Herculaneum's hard-to-pronounce name, there's very little to begrudge this delightful ancient Roman town. A smaller archaeological site than the more famous Pompeii, Herculaneum is much easier on the sightseer than its big sib—you can cover its grounds in an afternoon without fatigue or boredom ever setting in. Not only is it better preserved and less crowded than good old Pompy, but it's also situated in a beautiful natural enclave. Sparkling water less than 1 mi. away and lush green trees surrounding the ruins make Herculaneum worth a daytrip even if you're not an archaeology fanatic. Best of all, the modern city that cradles the ancient one has not become a tourist trap, meaning you'll find plenty of residential life, shops, and cheap restaurants if you want to spend the afternoon. Slow down and gear up for this undiscovered lost city.

ORIENTATION

From the train station, head down the hill onto **Via IV Novembre.** The ruins are a 5min. walk away.

SIGHTS

HERCULANEUM (ERCOLANO SCAVI)

ANCIENT ROME

At the intersection of C. Resina and V. IV Novembre ☎081 732 4338 www.pompeiisites.org

Herculaneum is a city upon a city. You'll know you've reached the ancient Ercolano when cotton-candy pink houses suddenly cede to dusty, copper-colored ones. Even before buying a ticket to enter the ruins, take a moment to look around. The public walkway leading to the information desk provides one of the best views of the city in its entirety. To the right is the 4.5 hectare region open to the public. (Another 16 or so hectares are not visible.) From this elevation, you get the best sense of how deeply the city was buried by the explosion and of how much was vertically preserved. About 16m of pyroclastic rock covered the region, making its second-story structures even better preserved than those of Pompeii.

The large archways directly below the elevated promenade provide a good introduction to the city's tragic fall—or, rather, what fell upon it. In these cavities lie the skeletons of over 300 victims, likely those who were waiting for boats to take them from the city before the volcano hit. Luckily for squeamish visitors, the skeletons are not available for viewing. Instead of skeletons, you get the pots, beds, and even baths the skeletons used back when they were covered in flesh. Descending into the ruins, you'll come across frescoes and mosaics that rival those of intact churches, baths where you could later retreat to clean off all that Roman soil, and roofs that could shelter you from the rain. Walking around Herculaneum is a bit like walking through a functional city. If you feel like an intruder or a diary-reader...well, you should.

Though this city (really more of a town) is smaller than Pompeii, you could easily spend hours exploring its nooks and crannies. Make sure not to miss the

Casa del Tramezzo di Legno, one of the site's largest and most detailed complexes: large frescoes, a marble table at its center, and wooden dividers give the room its name. The **Casa della Cervi** (House of the Deers) is a bit like a museum: still-life frescoes (now covered in Plexiglas) line the walkway, while the central courtyard was once home to life-size statues depicting dogs destroying deers. (No evidence that Herculaneum's citizens were alliteration authorities.) Just across the way, **Casa del Relievo di Telefo** contains a beautiful line of columns and an incredible relief of Telephus, Hercules's son. (Among his many accomplishments, Hercules was also a hotshot here, as he was the town's supposed founder.) Not only were they artistically inclined, but the people of Herculaneum knew how to live: the **Larga Taberna** contains a series of holes that were used for serving food and wine. They cleaned themselves in style too—the **Terme Suburbane** (Suburban Baths) is a three-room complex whose middle area contains an intricate black-and-white mosaic on its floor. If you're still upset about not seeing those skeletons, visit the **Casa dello Scheletro** (House of the Skeleton) and the adjoining rooms, which contain a stunning turquoise mosaic and meditative altarpiece.

Appreciate the age of this sight, but allow the modernity that rubs up against old Herculaneum to enrich your experience of the ancient town. Rooftops of modern dwellings peek out beyond the ruins' perimeter, and the sounds of city residents penetrate the otherwise silent streets of the remains. Like a remarkable mini-Rome, where rubble and modern brick live side by side, Herculaneum is maybe not as much a city upon a city, as it is two cities in one.

✣ *See* **Orientation.** *i Mandatory and free bag check by the ticket window. Free map and guide at the information point beyond the ticket window. Audio tours (available in English) can be obtained past the park entrance. Gift shop, bathrooms, and snack bar past park entrance. $ €11, EU citizens ages 18-24 €5.50, EU citizens under 18 or over 65 free. Access to 5 sites (valid 3 days) €20/10/free. Audio tour €6.50, 2 for €10. ⏰ Open daily Apr-Oct 8:30am-7pm; Nov-Mar 8:30am-5pm. Last entry 90min. before close. Information point open daily 8:30am-1:30pm and 2-5pm.*

FOOD

While most people make their way down to the archaeological site as though unable to resist gravity, we advise that you take a slower stroll through the neighborhood as a precursor to your visit. The streets are full of residents, cheap shops, and trattorias dishing up stellar food at uninflated prices. To tide yourself over for the tour ahead, stop by **Luna Caprese** for a delicious pizza made exactly to your liking. *(V. Quattro Novembre 68 ☎081 77 71 543 $ Pizza €3-4.50. ⏰ Open M-Sa noon-3:30pm and 6:30-10:30pm.)*

ESSENTIALS

Practicalities

- **TOURIST OFFICES:** At Herculaneum's tourist office you can pick up a small map of the modern city and ruins, though the excavation sight provides much more information. *(V. IV Novembre 82 ☎081 78 81 243 💻www.comune.ercolano.na.it ✣ 3min. down the hill from the train station. ⏰ Open M-Sa 8am-6pm. Occasionally closes in the afternoon.)*

Emergency!

- **POLICE: Carabinieri** *(V. Nicolo Marcello Venuti 30 ☎081 77 76 022).* **Local Police** *(☎081 78 81 400).* **State Police** *(☎081 78 87 111).*

Getting There

To get to Herculaneum, take the **Circumvesuviana train** from Naples's Stazione Centrale to Ercolano Scavi *($ €1.80. ⏰ 17min., every 15min.)* or head to the same destination from Sorrento. *($ €1.90. ⏰ 45min.)* From the station, head downhill 500m to the main gate. The ticket office is 200m farther to the left.

Taxis can be found near the train station in Piazzale della Stazione Circumvesuviana (☎081 73 93 666).

isle of capri ☎081

Capri certainly qualifies as an oasis. Before even landing at its dock, visitors have their cameras going, snapping postcard shots of the aquamarine water and pastel houses dotting the island's cliffs. Pebble beaches, stunning vistas, and rocky hikes add to this escape's at times unbelievable beauty. Yet walking around the narrow streets of the isle's residential area, you may feel as though you're in a Disneyland for the Bill Gateses of this world. Narrow streets split off the main thoroughfares and lead to dollhouse-like homes labeled not with street numbers, but rather with endearing names painted on ceramic tiles. It's hard to believe these residences are inhabited by real people and not characters out of a glossy Hollywood film. Find yourself in the people-ridden *centri* of Capri and Anacapri, where sparkling jewelry and equally shiny menus lure in tourists, however, and you'll discover that this "oasis" is only really that for the select few with the means to access it. Don't let us get you too down, though. Spend a day here swooning at gorgeous vistas and daydreaming about a life more glamorous than your own. Surrender to the fantasy of it all, and you'll leave Capri with the Cinderella feeling of having been princess for the night in your very own private oasis.

ORIENTATION

The Isle of Capri consists of two towns: **Capri,** closer to the port, and **Anacapri,** higher up and farther west.

Capri

Capri centers around **Piazza Umberto I.** Radiating from here, the main streets are **Via Roma** (mostly practical stores), **Via Vittorio Emanuele** (designer shops), **Via Botteghe,** and **Via Longano** (mostly restaurants). Off these thoroughfares, dozens of unmapped streets branch off, though most are residential lanes lacking merchants. Pay attention to the painted tile signs that indicate street names as well as commercial stores and restaurants when looking for unmapped places.

Anacapri

The prefix "ana" means "above," and Anacapri is indeed well up a hill from Capri. Once you've made the trek up (or taken the bus), you'll probably be in **Piazza Vittoria,** the upper town's center. Most of the action is down the long **Via Giuseppe Orlandi,** which is full of restaurants, merchants, and most of the interesting places to visit.

ACCOMMODATIONS

Rooms in both Capri and Anacapri are pricey year-round, thanks to the popularity of the lovely island they call home. The most conveniently located hotels also tend to be the most expensive, making any stay here at least a bit of a splurge for the budget traveler. Seek out harder-to-find bed and breakfasts and smaller side-street *pensioni* for somewhat reduced prices. Reserve in advance and arrange a check-in time with the owner, as, quite often, 24hr. reception does not apply.

Capri

HOTEL QUATTRO STAGIONI ⊛⊗⊛⊛ HOTEL ❸

V. Marina Piccola 1 ☎081 83 70 041 ▣www.hotel4stagionicapri.com

The humorous and hospitable staff make this one of the sunniest spots on the island, even if its look isn't as refined as other options. Simple furnishings, a

Isle of Capri

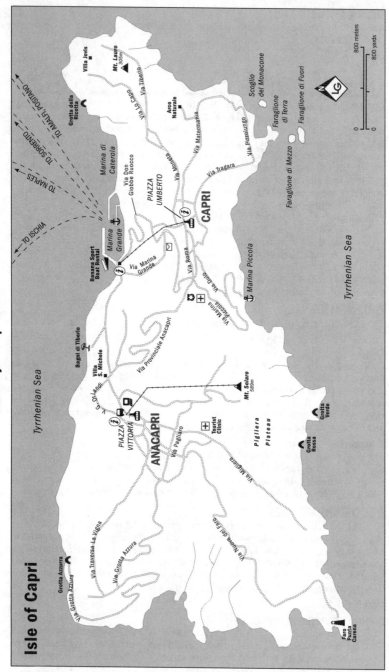

bay of naples

relatively unfrequented patio, and a removed location make Quattro Stagioni a break from the glitz of the *centro*. Rooms are sunny, clean, and quiet.

➤ Bus to V. Marina Piccola. ℹ Breakfast included. All rooms with bath ensuite. 10% Let's Go discount M-F. Free Wi-Fi. [S] Singles €40-70; doubles €70-130. Extra bed €20-30. ⏰ Reception 24hr.

👍 VILLA PALOMBA

💵🚭📶❄ B AND B [3]

V. Mulo 3 ☎081 83 77 322

Possibly the best deal on the island if you can manage the slight trek to get here. A vine-covered patio with great views gives you plenty of relaxing space, while the wicker furniture and flower-decorated sheets' old-fashioned feel matches the motherly attention paid to you by the hostess. Free Wi-Fi is a huge plus and will keep you connected to the world outside this secret garden.

➤ From V. Marina Piccola, walk down stairs on the right onto V. Mulo; walk through tunnel and slightly downhill, following signs. ℹ Breakfast included. All rooms with bath ensuite. A/C €10 per day. Free Wi-Fi. [S] Singles €45-65; doubles €80-130. ⏰ Door service until 8pm.

HOTEL IL PORTICO

💳🚭📶❄ HOTEL [4]

V. Truglio 1/C ☎338 18 28 700 💻www.ilporticocapri.com

Ideally located between the port and Capri's *centro*, this spot offers the reliability of a hotel and the feel of a bed and breakfast. Sparkling clean rooms (and since they're white, you can tell) smell like flowers and, if you step out onto the balcony, the sea.

➤ Off V. Marina Grande on the way to Capri's centro. [S] Doubles €80-160; triples €140-190

Anacapri

👍 VILLA MIMOSA BED AND BREAKFAST

💵🚭📶❄ B AND B [3]

V. Nuova del Faro 48/A ☎081 83 71 752 💻www.mimosacapri.com

Anacapri might already resemble a fairy-tale land, but if you had any doubts, Villa Mimosa's hanging bird cages and antique sculptures adorning the garden will do the trick. Save for the occasional food run, you won't want to leave this retreat: rooms are even equipped with private terraces. Lack of Wi-Fi is a bit inconvenient, but it just adds to the escape, right?

➤ 100m down the hill on the right from the last stop of the Marina Grande-Anacapri bus. ℹ Breakfast included. All rooms with bath ensuite. Public computer with free internet. [S] Doubles €70-100. ⏰ Call to arrange check-in time.

SENARIA HOTEL

💳🚭📶❄ HOTEL [5]

V. Follicara 6 ☎081 83 73 222 💻www.senaria.it

Senaria retains the perks of a hotel without becoming a generic rest stop. With only 12 rooms and a public terrace, it's small enough that you might get to know your temporary neighbors. Especially large rooms with tall ceilings and simple white curtains should put you at peace, and if you haven't gotten enough exercise from the island's hills, take advantage of the discount at the nearby gym.

➤ Take Marina Grande-Anacapri bus to V. Caprile. Follow signs downstairs, just off the piazza. ℹ Breakfast included. All rooms with bath ensuite. Free Wi-Fi. [S] Doubles €100-170. ⏰ Reception 24hr.

BAR DUE PINI RESIDENCE

💳🚭📶❄ APARTMENTS [4]

P. Vittoria 3 ☎081 83 71 404 💻www.2pini.com

You can easily pay these rates for a room half the size. Due Pini's six apartments located on the surrounding streets of P. Vittoria are thus steals, offering extra-spacious "doubles" and "triples," if you want to call them that. Make up the extra euro by cooking your own meals in the adjoining kitchenette. Access to a Jacuzzi and park are added perks that make these residences worth the cost.

➤ In P. Vittoria. ℹ Most apartments have fully equipped kitchen; all have private bath. Wi-Fi downstairs in bar for a fee. [S] Doubles €90-135; triples €170-180. ⏰ Reception 8am-6pm at bar downstairs.

SIGHTS 👁

Capri is hardly a cultural experience to rival Rome or even Cinque Terre. The best things to see here are the island's natural beauty and its posh buildings and shops. Walk down V. Le Botteghe and V. Vittorio Emanuele to see every designer store known to Milan lining streets half as wide as those of the big city. In addition, there are churches—this is Italy, after all. Most churches are small, free, and pastel-colored like the houses surrounding them. One worth visiting is the **Chiesa di San Michael,** a Baroque church with a stunning Majolica tile floor. The depiction of Adam and Eve in Earthly Paradise actually recalls the views from Anacapri, reminding you that you're in a paradise of your own. *(In P. San Nicola, off V. Giuseppe Orlandi. $ €2. ⏰ Open daily 9am-7pm.)*

VILLA SAN MICHELE ●⊗ VILLA, ANCIENT ROME

Vle. Axel Munthe 34 ☎081 83 71 401 🖥www.villasanmichele.eu

If free views aren't enough for you, then you can pay for one. The Villa San Michele does have something on the rest of the island though—actual history. Originally an ancient Roman villa, its remains were maintained by Axel Munthe, who used them as a home (and quite likely a retreat to nurture his literary and scientific inclinations) at the end of the 19th century. Here, he wrote the famous *The Story of San Michele*—see if you can trace the story's origin while walking through its birthplace's beautiful gardens and sculpture loggia.

 # A 5min. walk down V. Capodimonte out of P. Vittoria; the street becomes Vle. Axel Munthe. $ €6. ⏰ Open May-Sept 9am-6pm; Oct and Apr 9am-5pm; Nov-Feb 9am-3:30pm; Mar 9am-4:30pm.

THE GREAT OUTDOORS 🌴

Beyond Capri's rampant commercialism lies its stunning natural beauty—and that's the best reason to come. Most **🥾hikes** are hilly but not terribly rugged, making a pair of sneakers enough for hitting the paths. The **Arco Naturale,** a triumphant stone arch, can be reached by starting in P. Umberto I, heading down V. le Botteghe, and finally veering right onto V. Matermania. Head down a steep staircase, and you'll hit the spot. Turn back around and make your way left, passing the Grotta di Matermania and the **Villa Malaparte,** a rare work of modern architecture in a country filled with ancient and Renaissance-era buildings. When the road opens out onto V. Pizzolungo, the **Faraglione,** Capri's famous three rocks, is around the way. The walk is about 1½hr. Head to the tourist office for detailed maps of other suggested hikes.

GROTTA AZZURRA ●⊗ CAVE

On the island's northwest coast, below Anacapri ☎081 83 70 973

Despite being blue, this is Capri's golden star—and when we say blue, we mean swimming-pool aquamarine. The walls of this water-filled cave shimmer almost artificially when sunlight beams through from beneath the water's surface. Though you can appreciate the grotto without knowing a stitch of history, anyone bitter about paying the hefty entrance fee may be interested to know that Roman statues were discovered here (they now reside in the **Museo Archeologico Nazionale** in Naples). Legend has it that spirits reside in the caves—if the authorities don't catch you taking a prohibited swim, maybe the ghosts will.

 # A popular option for reaching the Grotta Azzurra is to take a cruise with the Grotta Azzurra company. Boats leave from Marina Grande every hr. 10am-1pm (€14). A cheaper option is the bus from Anacapri to Grotta Azzurra leaving from Vle. de Tommaso (15min., every 10-20min. 6:30am-10:30pm). You can also walk from Anacapri down V. Pagliara, V. Tuoro, V. Damecuta, and V. Grotta Azzurra for 50min. Once there, catch a Cooperativa Battellieri rowboat to the entrance. $ Coop. Battellieri boat €7.50. Entry €4. ⏰ Last boat at 5pm.

MONTE SOLARO 💳⊗ PANORAMIC VIEWS

V. Caposcuro 10 ☎081 83 71 428 💻www.capriseggiovia.it

It might be nearly as expensive as the ferry to Capri, but the ascent 589m above the island is worth it. For 13min., titillate or tremble as your chairlift climbs up to the summit. From the island's highest point, you can enjoy an unrivaled panorama of land and sea: Ischia, Naples, and the Appenines loom in the distance, though standing there you wouldn't wish yourself anywhere else.

➡ The chair lift leaves from V. Caposcuro 10, just off P. Vittoria in Anacapri. ℹ Cafe and terrace at the top. $ Round-trip €9. ⏰ Ticket office open 9:30am-5pm. Last ride to Monte Solaro at 5pm; last ride back to Anacapri at 5:30pm.

FOOD 🍴

The Isle of Capri is famous for the **Caprese salad**—rich mozzarella balls tossed with sweet red tomatoes and fresh basil. *Limoncello*, a lemon-flavored yellow liqueur, seems to epitomize the island's sweetness and bright feel. It's hard to find a budget meal here, but cafes often have decently priced panini to tide you over.

Capri

Pricey restaurants and cafes in the *centro* cater to tourist crowds. High-quality spots can be found on smaller streets, though that doesn't mean they're any cheaper. If you want a picnic for your day, head to well-stocked **Supermarket Deco** at V. Marina Grande 35/37, which has good prices and, by Italian standards, great hours. *(☎081 83 77 221 ⏰ Open M-Sa 8am-9pm, Su 8am-1pm.)*

👍 **TINELLO** 💳⊗ SEAFOOD ❷

V. L'Abate 3 ☎081 83 76 578

Finally, a restaurant without a photo-supplemented (dear Italy: we know what pasta carbonara is; we don't need a picture), touristic, or pages-long menu: this tiny spot feels like it could be in an old city center rather than ritzy Capri. The only thing reminding you of the water is the exquisite seafood menu, featuring fish of the day served grilled or baked in *"acqua pazza"* (crazy water). Eight small tables keep it classy without being flashy.

➡ From Chiesa Santo Stefano, walk up stairs to the covered V. L'Abate. $ Primi €7-15; secondi €10-15; dolci €5-7. ⏰ Open daily noon-2:30pm and 7:30-11pm.

VERGINIELLO 💳⊗🍸☀ RISTORANTE ❸

V. Lo Palazzo 25 ☎081 83 70 944

The whole package: terrace seating for a view, straw covering for some shade, and great value for some help re-padding that dented wallet. Despite its central location and amazing panorama, this large restaurant retains the feel of a family-run trattoria, with its light-hearted staff generous portions.

➡ Take V. Roma from P. Umberto I and walk down the stairs on the right past the post office. $ Cover €2. Primi €7-14; secondi €12-22. ⏰ Open daily noon-3pm and 7:30pm-midnight.

Anacapri

More budget-friendly, though less fancy, options make Anacapri a good spot when hunger calls. **Galardo** doubles as a supermarket and convenience store if you need basics. *(V. Giuseppe Orlandi 299 ⏰ Open daily 8am-1:30pm and 4:30-8:30pm.)*

👍 **PASTICCERIA GELATERIA SAN NICOLA** ⊗♿☀ BAKERY, GELATERIA ❶

V. San Nicola 7 ☎081 83 72 199

Size *does* matter. What this shop lacks in square footage, it makes up for in the size of its pastries. Unlike more glamorous spots, this closet-sized bakery makes treats that are actually fresh and well-priced. Try their massive *biscotto all'amerena*, a long cookie stuffed with a mix of nuts and amaretto flavoring and topped with crunchy meringue *(€1)*.

➜ Take V. Giuseppe Orlandi away from P. Vittoria and turn right onto V. San Nicola. $ Pastries €0.80-3. Cannoli €1.50. Gelato €2.50-3. ⏰ Open daily 7am-9pm.

👍 TRATTORIA IL SOLITARIO
💳🚭☀ PIZZERIA [2]

V. Giuseppe Orlandi 96 ☎081 83 71 382 🖥www.trattoriailsolitario.it

Tucked away behind a garden and sporting its *own* garden inside, this pizzeria feels miles away from the commerical flair of Anacapri. It has probably the best prices on the island for a sit-down pizza, yet it isn't lacking in flavor or creativity as a result: the *ammiraglia* is a white pie topped with an unusual combo of mussels, calamari, clams, shrimp, and mozzarella (just to remind you it's still pizza). Homemade bread makes the €1.50 cover charge actually worth it.

➜ A short walk down V. Giuseppe Orlandi from P. Vittoria; follow signs to the right. $ Cover €1.50. Pizza €3.50-8. Primi €5.50-15. Caprese salad €6. ⏰ Open in summer daily noon-3pm and 7:30-11:30pm; in fall, winter, and spring M noon-3pm and 7:30-11:30pm, W-Su noon-3pm and 7:30-11:30pm.

AGORÁ
💳🚭🍸☀ RISTORANTE, ENOTECA [3]

P. Caprile 1 ☎081 83 72 018 🖥www.agora-capri.com

Fine Mediterranean food meets live music and wine. Sounds like Italy to us. Along with "normal" pizzas (though when they're this good, normal seems like an understatement), more creative brick-oven specialties set this place apart from its neighbors. Vegetarians will cave for the *pane* pizza stuffed with veggies, provola, and *fior di latte* cheese *(€6)*. Anyone will cave for the wine selection which justifies Agorá's status as an *enoteca*. With tall ceilings and a white theme going, the place feels light even without being in the sun.

➜ On the left in P. Caprile. $ Pizza €5-7.50. Salads €5.50-7.50. Primi €8-14. ⏰ Open daily 6:30-11:30pm.

SNACK BAR ORLANDI
💳🚭🍸☀ CAFE [2]

V. Giuseppe Orlandi 83/83A ☎081 83 82 138

Just a step from P. Vittoria, this bright cafe has all the standards—pizza, salads, and liquid pick-me-ups—but combines them in a lunch menu that makes the value better than standard. At €10, their midday combo of salad, *primo*, drink, and service is a steal. They're not on the menu, but helpful hints from the friendly staff are part of the deal.

➜ A short walk down V. Giuseppe Orlandi from P. Vittoria; on the left. $ Primi €8-10; secondi €8-12. Pizza €6-7. Fixed lunch €10. ⏰ Open daily 9am-8pm.

NIGHTLIFE

With ferry and hotel costs what they are, the Isle of Capri is not the young traveler's party town that other beach locales sometimes are. People who can afford to stay here head to expensive lounges and discos. The economically minded might consider the ridiculously early 5:40am ferry back to Naples, which means you can "stay the night" partying in Capri instead of booking a hotel room. Given the cost of most spots however, sleeping in Naples or living it up in Capri will probably end up costing about the same.

Capri

BYE BYE BABY
💳🚭🍸❄☀ CLUB

V. Roma 6 ☎081 83 75 065 🖥www.byebyebabycapri.com

Funky furniture sits in the lounge areas of this downstairs disco, though you won't be doing much sitting as the night wears on. The nightly DJ spins mostly commercial beats under a giant disco ball and across from stunning views of the water. The hefty price of drinks draws a sophisticated crowd, so don't expect to get in donning beachwear and flip-flops.

➜ Take V. Roma from P. Umberto 1 and descend steps on right. $ Entry M-Th with purchase of drink. F-Sa and special events cover €20; Includes 1 drink. Cocktails €10. ⏰ Open Tu-Su 11pm-5am.

MEDJ PUB 🍸 PUB

V. Oratorio 9 ☎081 83 75 148

The cheapest spot to get a cocktail or beer, even by non-resort standards. Without the hip decor or nightly DJ of nearby clubs, it attracts a younger crowd looking for good conversation loosened up by a few too many drinks.

➔ From P. Umberto I, take V. P.S. Cimino and turn left onto V. Oratorio. $ Beer €2.50-4. Shots €4. Cocktails €5-6. ⏰ Open in summer daily 8pm-2am; in fall, winter, and spring Tu-Su 8pm-2am.

Anacapri

Quieter than its downstairs sister, Anacapri has little else than late-night cafes and pubs in the way of nightlife. The view from your terrace better be beautiful.

BOCCADILLOS ♿ 🍸 PUB

V. Giuseppe Orlandi 208 ☎081 83 73 783

The wooden interior of this pub and "game room" stays open during the day for customers at the adjacent cafe (owned by the same family). At night, customers move from outside tables to stools or head to the floor to play pool or foosball or watch soccer. Cheap food and cocktails attract an unpretentious crowd that can't stomach the clubs of Capri. There's not much in the way of music, so bring your bar voice.

➔ At the end of V. Giuseppe Orlandi, as it intersects with V. Pagliaro. $ Beer €3-4. Cocktails €5-6. Panini and pizza €3-5. ⏰ Open daily 7pm-1am.

BLOOM ♿ 🍸 BAR

V. Caprile 5/B ☎081 83 71 716

It's actually just as good to come here during the day for their cheap and filling panini (even a New York-style hot dog with mustard and sauerkraut), but with late hours and great cocktail deals to match, Bloom is an OK place to bring some friends and settle down at a wooden bench. Low-key music and a big interior make this a good hangout spot, but don't expect the action to get too hot.

➔ From the end of V. Giuseppe Orlandi veer left to the start of V. Caprile; Bloom is just past the post office. $ Beer €3-5. Cocktails €5-6. Panini €5-5.50. Pastas €7-10. ⏰ Open M 5:30pm-3am, Tu-Su noon-3am.

ESSENTIALS

Practicalities

- **TOURIST OFFICES: Info points** offer free maps, a list of accommodations and restaurants, and information on sights and tours. There are three locations: to the right of the dock at **Marina Grande** *(☎081 83 70 634)*, in **Piazza Umberto** in Capri *(☎081 83 70 686)*, and in Anacapri just off P. Vittoria at **Via Giuseppe Orlandi 59** *(☎081 83 71 524 🖥www.capritourism.com, www.infocapri.molti ⏰ All branches open M-Sa 8:30am-8:30pm, Su 9am-3pm.)*
- **CURRENCY EXCHANGE:** There's only one on the island. *(P. Vittoria 2, Anacapri ☎081 83 73 146 ⏰ Open M-Sa 8:30am-6pm.)*
- **LUGGAGE STORAGE:** In Capri. *(➔ Once you've taken the funicular into Capri, walk down the steps from P. Umberto I. $ Each bag €3 per day. ⏰ Open daily 8am-10pm.)* In Anacapri. *(P. Vittoria 5 $ Each bag €2 per day. ⏰ Open daily 9:30am-5pm.)*
- **INTERNET: Capri Graphic** offers internet and office supplies in Capri. *(V. Listrieri 17 ☎081 83 75 212 ➔ From P. Umberto I walk down V. Longano and make a right onto V. Listrieri. $ €2 per 10min., €6 per hr. ⏰ Open M-Sa 9am-1pm and 4-8pm.)* In Anacapri try **Hotel Due Pini.** *(P. Vittoria 3 ☎081 83 71 404 $ €1 per 10min., €5 per hr. ⏰ Open daily 8am-6pm.)*
- **POST OFFICES:** In Capri. *(V. Roma 50 ☎081 97 85 211 ➔ 3min. from P. Umberto*

I. ⏰ Open M-F 8am-6:30pm, Sa 8am-12:30pm.) In Anacapri. *(Vle. de Tommaso 8 ☎081 83 71 015 ⏰ Open M-F 8:30am-1:30pm, Sa 8:30am-noon.)*

Emergency!

- **POLICE: Carabinieri** has offices in Capri *(V. Provinciale Marina Grande 42 ☎081 83 70 000 ⇟ By the port. ⏰ Open until 8pm.)* and Anacapri *(V. Caprile ☎081 83 71 011).* There is also **City Police** in Capri *(V. Roma 70 ☎081 83 74 211).*
- **HOSPITALS/MEDICAL SERVICES: G. Capilupi** in Capri. *(V. Provinciale 2 ☎081 83 81 205 ⇟ At the 3-pronged fork at the end of V. Roma. ⏰ 24hr. service for emergencies.)*

Getting There

By Ferry

Capri is an island and has no airport; therefore, it's time for **ferries and hydrofoils.** Capri's main port is Marina Grande. Various companies run ferries to and from Naples and Sorrento. **Caremar** *(☎89 21 23 💻www.caremar.it)* is the cheapest option but not the most frequent, running both ferries and hydrofoils to and from **Naples** *($ Ferries €10, hydrofoils €14.50. ⏰ Ferries 80min., hydrofoils 50min.; depart Naples every 2-4hr. 5:40am-9:10pm, depart Capri every 2-4hr. 5:45am-10:20pm.)* and hydrofoils to **Sorrento.** *($ €9.80. ⏰ 25min.; depart Sorrento 7:45am, 9:25am, 2:30pm, 7pm; depart Capri 7am, 8:40am, 1:40pm, 6:15pm.)* **SNAV** *(☎081 42 85 555 💻www.snav.it)* runs the most frequent hydrofoils to and from **Naples** *($ €16. ⏰ 45min., every 30-80min. 6:50am-7:10pm.)* and **Sorrento** *($ €13.50. ⏰ Every 20-85min. 7:35am-6:30pm.)*

Once There

Once you've actually arrived on the island, the fastest way to get to Capri's *centro* from the port is by funicular. *(⏰ Every 15-30min. 5:25am-1:45am.)* For information on tickets, see **Getting Around.** If you want to walk, it'll take about 20min. up the winding streets. To get to Anacapri directly from the port, take the hourly bus leaving from outside the ticket office in Marina Grande. *(⏰ Every 30min. in the afternoon, otherwise every hr. 5:45am-9:05pm.)*

Getting Around

Once in Capri and Anacapri's town centers, navigating the narrow and steep streets is only practical on foot. To get between major points, take **buses** or the **funicular** *(€1.40 per ride).* You can buy a €1 rechargable card and fill it with €2.20 for 1hr. (includes one bus and one funicular ride) or €6.90 for the week. Rechargable cards are rarely worth it for daytrips but are practical if you're here for a while and planning to bus around the island a lot. The ticket office is to the right of the port. *(☎081 83 89 515 **i** Cash only. ⏰ Open daily 6:30am-11pm.)* From Capri *centro*, ATC buses run to **Anacapri.** *(⏰ Every 10min. during the day, 20min. early and late, 6am-2am.)* All buses depart from the start of V. Roma in Capri. From Anacapri *centro*, buses head to other island destinations like Grotta Azzurra and Faro. All buses stop in P. Vittoria in Anacapri. For a **taxi,** head to the hubs at the Marina Grande port, P. Umberto I in Capri *(☎081 83 70 543),* or P. Vittoria in Anacapri *(☎081 83 71 175).*

sorrento ☎081

Sorrento is the practical traveler's paradise. Located on a train, bus, and ferry route that connects it with the Amalfi Coast's other cities, Sorrento makes dazzling, high-cliffed Bay of Naples beauty easily accessible. While many travelers use Sorrento as a springboard for daytrips, its mix of paved streets and urban grit with shopping and beach bumming—the epitome of leisure—make it worth exploring in its own right.

Before hopping on that train to more serene destinations, kick back with a glass of *limoncello* (as common as water here) and a *cono* of mint gelato for some daytime relaxation. Don't forget your heels, though—staying out into the wee hours of the morning is as popular with Sorrento's young crowds.

ORIENTATION

With its flat layout and paved sidewalks, Sorrento is very easy to navigate. Circumvesuviana trains and SITA buses pull into **Piazza de Curtis.** From there, head up the steps to **Via degli Aranci,** which has plenty of cheap accommodations and stores along its sidewalks, or down the hill to **Corso Italia,** which leads into the *centro.* A short walk will take you to the palm-tree-filled **Piazza Tasso** and the parallel **Via San Cesareo,** which is cluttered with souvenir and *limoncello* shops. From the *piazza,* steep stairs lead to the waterfront, a small public beach, and the port.

ACCOMMODATIONS

Being a beach town, Sorrento has its fair share of hotels—sometimes it feels as though they make up a third of the buildings here. With so many cheap hostels and one-star hotels only a few minutes from the *centro,* Sorrento is a great base for hopping around the Amalfi coast. Though not as conveniently located, one train-stop away in Sant'Agnello, **Seven Hostel** is a great option. The clean and spacious dorms there are complemented by free Wi-Fi, breakfast, and fun common areas. *(V. Iommella Grande 99 ☎081 878 6758 🖥www.sevenhostel.com ℹ Credit cards accepted. $ Dorms €19-30.)* If you can't get enough of the beach and sky, you can stay at a campsite, **Nube D'Argento,** a 15min. walk from central Sorrento. *(V. Capo 21 ☎081 878 1344 🖥www.nubedargento.com $ €8-11 per person; €5-10 per tent. Bungalows €9-11.)* For more options, check the tourist office's extensive list.

👍 ULISSE DELUXE HOSTEL

HOSTEL [1]

V. del Mare 22 ☎081 87 74 753 🖥www.ulissedeluxe.com

With its air-conditioned rooms, marble foyer, and discounted access to its private fitness center, Ulisse Deluxe is not easily reconciled with conventional expectations about hostel living. Doubles are more like those of a hotel, with their spacious rooms (yes, multiple rooms) and sparkling-clean ensuite bathrooms. Dorms may be bunked but they're well-kept and have fashionable wooden armoires. It's close to the beach, though with the on-site pool, you might opt to stay sand-free.

➜ Walk down C. Italia nearly to its end and then head downstairs just before the hospital. Walk 3min. toward the right down V. del Mare. ℹ Breakfast €5. All rooms with ensuite bathroom. Free Wi-Fi. Public internet point €10 per day. $ Dorms €18-25; doubles €60-80; triples €90-120; quads €120-160. ⏰ Reception 24hr.

BED AND BED DIANA CITY

HOTEL [3]

C. Italia 5 ☎081 80 74 392 🖥www.dianacity.com

You don't have to veer out of central Sorrento or resort to dormitory living to find an affordable room: this newly opened spot is as convenient as it is cheery. Colorful rooms decorated with bright paintings and linens remind you of the beach, and the sand is only 10min. away.

➜ From P. Tasso, head 10min. down C. Italia, away from the train station. $ Doubles €59-79.

OSTELLO LE SIRENE

HOSTEL [1]

V. degli Aranci 160 ☎081 80 72 925 🖥www.hostellesirene.com

The bunk beds in the small rooms at this hostel don't allow for much wiggle room, but le Sirene's proximity to the beach and train is convenient. Rooms have ensuite baths, which would be a plus if the floors weren't wet and a bit dirty.

➜ From train station, follow signs down V. degli Aranci and walk 5min. $ 8-10 bed unisex dorms €16; 6- to 7-bed (co-ed) €18; 4-bed (co-ed) €19-20. Doubles €45-60.

SIGHTS

Beaches

Sorrento doesn't offer much in the way of religious and artistic must-sees, but its location on the coast makes it a great starting point for scenic hikes and leisurely days on the sand. Most visitors hit the **beach,** head up **Corso Italia** for shopping, or hop on a SITA bus to hit nearby cities on the Amalfi coast. Sorrento's main beach is the **Marina Grande,** easily accessible by walking down V. de Maio and climbing down 100 steps to the winding road. From there, the port is to the right and a sizeable stretch of private beach is to the left. The tiny public area, which will undoubtedly be crowded, is just beyond. Alternatively, walk down C. Italia in the direction of St. Agnello, the smaller neighbor of Sorrento. (You can also get there by taking the 5min. train ride from Sorrento). From P. Municipio by the Circumvesuviana station in St. Agnello, head left onto Vle. dei Pini and then veer left again onto C. Marion Crawford (yes, that is actually the name of the street, and no, she was not Italian) to reach **Marinella Beach.** Marinella Beach is considerably smaller than Marina Grande, though arguably more serene. The best and farthest beach is **Puolo Beach,** accessible by a 45min. walk from P. Tasso or by the A bus. To reach it on foot, follow V. del Capo for 30min., turn right onto V. Marina di Puolo, and head down the path to the shore. Unlike the nearby **Punta del Capo,** this beach is actually sandy.

Other Sights

If you don't just want to lie around in the sun (who are you?), you can check out the sight listed below or head to the tourist office (see **Practicalities**), which offers walking maps and booklets with sight-seeing itineraries.

👍 CAPO DI SORRENTO ♿ BEACH, RUINS

On the coast, 10-15min. northwest of V. del Capo.

For a break from the tourist crowds and crowded beaches near the *centro*, head down C. Italia to the Capo di Sorrento, a small protrusion of beach and cliff off the otherwise flat coast. Either walk 30min. up the paved V. Capo, passing mostly hotels and greenery, or take the EAVBUS A line. When you reach Calata di Punta del Capo, head right down the steep cobblestone road which eventually becomes soil and winds to the coast. Near the base, you'll pass a small sign marking the **Ruins of Villa di Pollio Felice.** They truly are ruins—without the post, you would barely know they existed. Continue on past the few crumbling arches and make the steep descent to an aquamarine pool of water which will most likely be occupied by swimmers, though far fewer than fill Sorrento's main beaches. A short walk further leads to flat rocks and more water, where a family-heavy crowd switches off between sunbathing and swimming.

🚶 Facing the water, take C. Italia left and continue as it winds into V. del Capo. ℹ The walk is easy and doesn't require sneakers.

FOOD 🍴

Eating good food and staying cool in Sorrento is easy—*gelaterie* and *limoncello* merchants seem to come in pairs. If you've never tasted the sweet yellow drink, pop into **Limonoro** for a free sample and a piece of *limoncello*-filled chocolate. *(V. San Cesareo 49/53 ☎081 807 2782 💻www.limonoro.it. ℹ Accepts credit cards. ⏰ Open daily 8am-9pm.)* Sit-down restaurants line the touristy C. d'Italia, and while they're not as expensive as those in most beach towns, better spots can definitely be found on peripheral streets. Likewise, fruit stands and *salumerie* are plentiful, but your best bet for stocking the picnic basket is either the **STANDA** supermarket *(C. d'Italia 225 ℹ Accepts credit cards. ⏰ Open M-Sa 8:30am-1:55pm and 5-8:55pm, Su 9:30am-1pm and 5-8:30pm.)* or the **SISA,** which has even better prices. *(V. degli Aranci 157. ℹ Cash only. ⏰ Open M-Sa 8:30am-1:30pm and 5-8:30pm.)*

👍 PRIMAVERA GELATERIA ❄♿ GELATERIA, PASTICCERIA ❶

C. Italia 142 ☎081 80 73 252 💻www.primaverasorrento.it

When the Pope and bikini-clad supermodels can agree on something, you know it's good: photos of each line the walls of this famed *gelateria*, where proud owner Antonio Cafiero dishes up over 70 flavors of gelato and sweets. Try his invention, the *caffe al nocciola*, a liquid concoction of hazelnut and coffee served in a chocolate-lined cone. Or do like countless movie stars have and devour a *delizia al limone*, a sponge cake smothered in lemon-flavored cream, though you probably won't end up with your photo on the wall unless you can manage a 3 ft. high stack of them. Believe it or not, some people have.

🚶 5min. down C. Italia from P. Tasso. $ Pastries €1.50-3. Cones €2.50-12. The €12 cone is unimaginably large. ⏰ Open daily summer 9am-1am; fall, winter, and spring 9am-midnight.

IL GIARDINIELLO 💳♿🍸❄⛅ RISTORANTE ❷

V. dell'Accademia 7/9 ☎081 87 84 616 💻www.giardiniellosorrento.com

Retreat from the sun and crowds to this leaf-covered restaurant while watching Nonna Luisa mix dough for her namesake *torta di nonna.* Classic *Sorrentina* dishes, like gnocchi with tomatoes and basil, are accompanied by a large selection of wine and are often served by the owners themselves.

🚶 From P. Tasso, head down V. de Maio, turn left onto V. Santa Maria Grazie, and continue as the street becomes V. Accademia. $ Cover €1. Pizza €4.50-7. Primi €4-7. Fish and meat €6-14.50. ⏰ Open in summer daily 10:30am-midnight; in winter M-W 10:30am-midnight, F-Su 10:30am-midnight.

SALTO 🍴♿🍸☀ PIZZERIA [1]

V. degli Aranci 147 ☎334 31 22 016

Portions and menu sizes are rarely this gigantic, even in Naples. Drop by Salto's minuscule shop before hitting the beach or the train for a pizza, made any way you like it.

From the train station, head down V. degli Aranci away from the centro. Across the street from hostel. $ Pizza €2.50-4, slices €0.80. Panini €3-3.50. Primi €3.50. ⏰ Open daily 9am-1am.

NIGHTLIFE

For such a small town, Sorrento is home to a surprising number of hopping evening spots. Head down **Corso Italia** for a lively array of bars and cafes teeming with gelato-lickers and cocktail-sippers. Though this town doesn't boast the beach discos of other coastal cities, you can still break it down at spots like **Daniele's Club,** which has a small dance area and caters to a distinctly tourist crowd. *(P. Tasso 10 and down the steps ☎081 877 3992 💻www.bagattelle.net ⏰ Open daily 9pm-4am.)*

ENGLISH INN 🍴🍸❄☀ CLUB, BAR, RISTORANTE

C. Italia 55 ☎081 807 4357 💻www.englishinn.it

English keeps the crowd hustling every night and well into the morning. Customers consistently pack its downstairs restaurant for English grub like fish and chips *(€10)*, but the real action happens upstairs in the vine-covered rooftop garden. A nightly DJ, plenty of TVs, and a cheap bar (with bartender's choice happy hours) give rowdy guests their choice between dancing, drinking, or watching it all unfold. The fun and laid-back staff are happy to take requests on anything from music to group drink discounts. When the wee hours start to set in, treat yourself to a hot breakfast in classic English fashion—nice and big.

5min. from P. Tasso. $ Shots €2. Beer €3-3.50. Cocktails €5. Pizza, pasta, and panini €5-9. ⏰ Open daily 8am-4am. Kitchen closes at 2am. Upstairs garden open 7:30pm onward. Happy hour 10pm.

INSOLITO 🍴📶🍸 BAR, CLUB

C. Italia 38/E ☎081 87 72 409 💻www.insolitosorrento.it

If you want to disguise your foreign status and slip in with a sleeker Italian crowd, Insolito's glass bar and modern mini-disco will fit the bill. Despite its "prettier-than-thou" look, the place stays down-to-earth thanks to its cheap happy hours. Just don't expect the raucous crowd that can be found at other touristy spots.

5min. down C. Italia from P. Tasso. $ Cocktails €5-8. ⏰ Open daily 8am-5am.

ESSENTIALS

Practicalities

- **TOURIST OFFICES: Info Points** are the most convenient sources of information and are scattered throughout the town. They provide free maps, a small guidebook on Sorrento, and bike rental. Locations at the **Marina Piccola** *(near the port)*, in **Piazza de Curtis** *(outside the train station)*, in **Piazza Tasso,** and in **Piazza Andrea Veniero** *(near the end of C. Italia). (⏰ All open daily at 10am; some close at 8pm, others at 9pm.)* The main **Tourist Office** provides free maps, train and bus schedules, and small guides about Sorrento. *(V. Luigi de Maio 35 ☎081 807 4033 💻www.sorrentotourism.com From P. Tasso, take Luigi De Maio to the end of P. Sant'Antonino and continue toward the water. ⏰ Open M-Sa 8:30am-4pm.)*
- **CURRENCY EXCHANGE:** The *centro* is full of exchange places, but **Golden Store** has better rates than most. *(V. del Corso 38C ☎081 878 1413 5min. from P. Tasso. ⏰ Open daily 8am-10pm.)*
- **INTERNET: Insolito.** *(C. Italia 38/E ☎081 877 2409 💻www.insolitosorrento.it $ Wi-Fi €4 per hr. ⏰ Open daily 8am-5am.)*

- **POST OFFICES:** *(C. Italia 210 ☎081 877 2429 ⏰ Open M-F 8am-6:30pm, Su 8am-1pm.)*

Emergency!

- **POLICE: Carabinieri** *(Vicolo III Rota ☎081 80 73 111).* **Police** *(Vicolo III Rota ☎081 80 75 311)* right off C. Italia heading toward St. Agnello.
- **HOSPITALS/MEDICAL SERVICES: Santa Maria della Misericordia** keeps miserable hours. *(C. Italia 129 ☎081 533 1112 ⏰ Open to public for appointments M-Sa 1-3pm and 7-8:30pm, Su 1-4pm and 7-8:30pm.)*

Getting There

By Train

Chances are you're traveling to Sorrento from Naples. That's the closest big city and, therefore, the closest airport. Circumvesuviana trains roll into the station in P. de Curtis 6. *(☎800 05 39 39 ⏰ Every 15-30min. 5:01am-11:26pm.)* The train runs to **Naples** *([$] €3.40. ⏰ 1hr.)* and makes stops along the way in **Pompeii** *([$] €1.90. ⏰ 20-30min.)* and **Herculaneum.** *([$] €1.90. ⏰ 45min.)*

By Ferry

If taking the Circumvesuviana scares you too much (sure, Mt. Vesuvius is dormant, but who knows when that might change?), you can take the ferry across the Bay of Naples. Ferries arrive at the port on the Bay. Take the B or C city bus to P. Marina d'Italia or walk from P. Tasso down the steps to the port. Ticket offices open and close in accordance with the first and last boats of the day. **Linee Marittime Partenopee** *(☎081 80 71 812 🖥www.consorziolmp.it)* runs hydrofoils from **Naples** *([$] €10. ⏰ Every 2hr. from Naples 9am-6:25pm, from Sorrento 7:20am-4:25pm.)* and **Capri.** *([$] €14. ⏰ Roughly every hr. from Capri 8am-7pm, from Sorrento 7:20am-6:20pm.)* **Metro del Mare** *(☎199 60 07 00 🖥www.metrodelmare.net)* runs ferries from **Positano** *([$] €9. ⏰ 4-5 per day from Positano 9am and 12:30-6:10pm, from Sorrento 9:30am-1:15pm and 6:05pm.)* and **Amalfi.** *([$] €11. ⏰ 1hr.; 4-5 per day from Amalfi 8:35am, noon, 1:50, 5, 5:40pm; from Sorrento 9:30am-1:15pm and 6:05pm.)*

By Bus

SITA buses *(☎089 405 145 🖥www.sitabus.it)* stop in P. de Curtis in front of the Circumvesuviana train station and are the best way to travel to Sorrento from the Amalfi Coast. Buy tickets from **Unicocampania** bus drivers or the kiosk in P. de Curtis. For prices and logistics see the box below. Buses run to **Positano** *(⏰ 45 min., every 30min. 6:30am-midnight.)* and **Amalfi.** *(⏰ 90min., every 30min. 6:30am-midnight.)*

> **bay of buses**
>
> To get around Sorrento and the Amalfi Coast, buses are your friends. Tickets work on a system where you buy them for a given amount of time, and then are entitled to unlimited rides within that timeframe. Tickets are also valid for EAVBUS service within Sorrento, and the Circumvesuviana trains. A 45min. ticket costs €2.40, 90min. €3.60, 24hr. €7.20, and a 3-day pass €18. For information on where to buy them, check the **Getting There** section for each town.

Getting Around

Though walking is easy, **EAVBUS** does run orange buses throughout the city *([$] One-way ticket €1).* Integrated SITA tickets (see box above) are also valid on EAVBUS lines. For information on finding your way around the city, see **Orientation.**

positano ☎089

Like the two-piece bathing suit that originated here (a.k.a. the bikini), Positano is a city in two parts. In one, you have the hot, crowded coast and, in the other, the cool cliffs which cushion it on either side. The divided layout matches the cultural clash that seems to define this small town: literati like **Jack Kerouac** and **Tennessee Williams** famously celebrated the beauty here, and now countless tourists simply bundle it into their rounds along the Amalfi Coast. Though Positano's unique geography makes it harder to navigate than surrounding cities, hiking, tanning, shopping, or hitting the town after dark are equally feasible options in its diverse landscape. Just don't expect to do any of those activities in the solitude Kerouac might have enjoyed—Positano's history and beauty have cemented its status as one of the coast's most popular destinations.

ORIENTATION

Though not huge, Positano is tricky to navigate. The *centro* sits nestled on the coast between two high cliffs but is not accessible by SITA buses—coming from other cities, you'll have to walk or take a local bus down. From the **Chiesa Nuova** stop, the winding **Viale Pasitea** and a few short-cut staircases lead to the **Spiaggia Grande,** the town's recreational and commercial heart. Alternatively, from the **Positano Sponda** stop, **Via Cristoforo Colombo** is a gentle slope which winds into **Via dei Mulini** and heads to **Piazza Flavio Gioia,** which is full of shops and close to the tourist office. A footpath from Spiaggia Grande leads along the coast to **Spiaggia del Fornillo,** a somewhat less crowded option. Be prepared for winding, pedestrian streets near the water and curving car-ridden roads farther up the cliffs. The area around Chiesa Nuova may not be the city center, but it has great restaurants, cheaper accommodations, and the best views.

ACCOMMODATIONS

Expect anything from expensive four-star hotels to charming and cheap bed and breakfasts. The most affordable spots are located on the hill descending from the **Chiesa Nuova** SITA bus stop. Closer to the coast and up the other side around **Positano Sponda,** bigger and costlier hotels are more common.

OSTELLO BRIKETTE — HOSTEL ❷

V. Guglielmo Marconi 358 ☎089 87 58 57 www.brikette.com

Positano's only hostel delivers with a laid-back staff, a social and panoramic terrace to rival those of nearby hotels, and bright, spacious dorms. Though you can't use the kitchen, cheap bar grub and beer and a communal refrigerator should save you from Positano's more expensive options. That's not to mention the bountiful breakfast options, including America's two favorite morning foods: pancakes and eggs *(€2-4).* The only thing you don't have is the beach lapping at your door, but the hostel's location near the bus actually makes it more convenient than central hotels.

*From Chiesa Nuova stop, walk 100m to the left of Bar Internazionale and climb steps. **i** Breakfast €2-4. Bag storage after checkout €2 per bag. Free Wi-Fi. $ 8-bed dorms €22-24; doubles €65, with bath €75; triples with bath €120. Reception 24hr.*

CASA COSENZA — PENSIONE ❹

V. Trara Genoino 18 ☎089 87 50 63 www.casacosenza.it

Tiled floors, arched ceilings, and stripped wooden doors set this lovely guesthouse apart from other accommodations this close to the coastal center. Casa Cosenza's only single is snug but great if you like simplicity and ocean views. Doubles are much more spacious and feature terraces or balconies with views that make them feel even bigger. Plants and a tiled walkway leading to the rooms might remind you of the countryside instead of the ocean. Though breakfast is expensive, the continental offerings could be satisfying enough to last you through lunch.

From the tourist office, exit onto V. Trara Genoino, heading up stairs in the direction of V. Pasitea. Look for signs on the right of the small street. i Breakfast €10. All rooms with ensuite bathroom. Free Wi-Fi. $ Singles €50-60; doubles €100-120. Extra bed €40.

B AND B VILLA PALUMBO B AND B [4]

Vle. Pasitea 334 ☎089 87 59 82 www.villapalumbo.it

If you're thinking about staying in one of Positano's hotels, consider the five bedrooms offered at this small bed and breakfast instead. Lace curtains lead to private terraces with unbelievable views of the coast and cliffs. Though rooms aren't huge, they are well cared-for, and the sunny vistas make them feel airy. The friendly owner serves homecooked breakfast on the public terrace and even leaves a bottle of wine and snack in each room upon arrival.

From Chiesa Nuova stop, walk downhill for 5min. and look for sign on the left. i Breakfast included. Rooms have private bath. $ Singles €50-70; doubles €60-80; triples €70-90. Reception 8am-9pm. Call ahead to arrange arrival time.

THE GREAT OUTDOORS

More than other cities along the Amalfi coast, Positano offers great outdoor opportunities ranging from lazing on the beach to sweating your way up the surrounding hills. After taking a stroll through the center's bustling boutiques, head to **Fornillo Beach,** Positano's most secluded and scenic. Tucked away past the Torre Trasita and the main docking area, it's a bit quieter than the rest. To reach it, take V. Positanese d'America, a footpath starting at the port's right side and winding down the coast. The more centrally located **Spiaggia Grande** has only a small public area near the docks, making for a less-than-clean swim. Nearby, **Blue Star** rents motorboats and rowboats if you want to drift down the water on your own. Or, consider taking a tour of the Blue and Emerald Grottoes in a more directed itinerary *(☎089 81 18 88 www.bluestarpositano.it).*

If you've had enough water, head inland for some **hiking.** A 45min. climb will take you up the side of **Montepertuso,** which is pierced by a huge hole. From its top, you can take the **Path of the Gods** *(about 4hr.).* Hit up the tourist office for maps and information on the excursions—but before setting out, get ready with water and good shoes. The trails are not for the light of heart *or* those wearing flip-flops.

FOOD

Positano's *centro* is full of elegant restaurants—or at least, restaurants disguising tourist-trappery with elegance. While it won't be hard to satisfy seafood cravings near the coast, head up the hill toward Chiesa Nuova for great views, fewer people, and slightly better prices. The **Mini Market A.D.** stocks basics and is close to Chiesa Nuova bus stop. *(V. Pasitea 352 ☎089 81 23 437 i Credit cards accepted. Open M-Sa 7:30am-1:45pm and 4:30-9pm, Su 8am-1pm.)*

C'ERA UNA VOLTA RISTORANTE [2]

V. Guglielmo Marconi 127 ☎089 81 19 30 www.ristoranteceraunavolta.info

When they're not scribbling down takeout orders from hungry backpackers and locals, the busy waiters will be running to your table, delivering piping-hot plates in record time. This place has excellent pizza that will fuel you up for a day of rushing or resting—though, when you see the views of the coast from C'era una Volta's rooftop terrace, you'll probably choose the latter. It may be an uphill trek from the beach, but, with lower prices and that fabulous view, it's all the better for its elevated locale. Luckily for hostelers, all they have to do to get here is roll out of bed.

Down the street from the Chiesa Nuova bus stop. $ Cover €1. Pizza €4-7. Primi €6-8.50; secondi €7-18. Open M-W noon-3pm and 7-11pm, Th 7-11pm, F-Su noon-3pm and 7-11pm.

positano . food

SARACENO D'ORO

🍴🚫🍷🛋 RISTORANTE ❸

V. Pasitea 254

☎089 81 20 50 ◾www.saracenodoro.it

Under soft red arches and twinkling lights, indulge in a meal that perfectly captures this part of Italy—everything from the coastal view to the homemade *scialatielli allo scoglio* (finely-cut pasta with seafood) shouts, "Amalfi!" Large doors open out onto small sidewalk tables, making the restaurant as airy as it is aromatic—you can be assured, that fish smell is drifting from the kitchen, not the ocean below. Though half the joy comes from lingering a while, margherita pizzas on the go (€5) can save you some time and money.

🍴 *Halfway up V. Pasitea between the Chiesa Nuova SITA stop and the tourist office; walk up the hill or take an orange city bus.* Ⓢ *Cover €2. Pizza €6-10, takeout €4-8. Pasta €10-15. Meat and fish €9-15.* Ⓞ *Open daily Mar-Dec noon-3pm and 6pm-midnight.*

TRATTORIA GROTTINO AZZURRO

🍴🚫🍷🛋 SEAFOOD ❷

V. Guglielmo Marconi 303-305

☎089 87 54 66

Seafood restaurants often have a somewhat stuffed-shirt attitude, perhaps thanks to their usually elevated prices. Fortunately, with its white walls and wooden tables, the simple interior of this laid-back trattoria looks more like a tugboat than a cruise ship. There's no need for aesthetic flair because, as the natives of Positano know, this spot has the best seafood around. No pizza means you'll have to content yourself with a proper spoon, fork, and plate. Don't worry: with food this good, it won't be hard.

🍴 *Outside the Chiesa Nuova SITA bus stop.* 𝒊 *No reservations.* Ⓢ *Primi €6-10; meat entrees €10-12, seafood entrees €12-24.* Ⓞ *Open M-Tu 11am-3pm and 7-10:30pm, Th-Su 11am-3pm and 7-10:30pm.*

ESSENTIALS

🔳

Practicalities

- **TOURIST OFFICES: Azienda Autonoma di Soggiorno e Turismo di Positano** provides free maps of the city as well as information on hotels, restaurants, and transportation options. *(V. del Saracino 4 ☎089 87 50 67 ◾www.aziendaturis-mopositano.it 🍴 Near the end of V. dei Mulini, in Positano's centro.* Ⓞ *Open M-Sa 8:30am-8pm, Su 8:30am-2:30pm.)*

- **CURRENCY EXCHANGE: Angela Collina** exchanges currency and has a **Western Union.** *(P. dei Mulini 6 ☎089 87 58 64 🍴At the start of V. dei Mulini.* Ⓞ *Open daily 9am-2pm and 4-9:30pm.)* The most **ATMs** and **banks** are clustered around V. dei Mulini.

- **LUGGAGE STORAGE: Blu Porter** has baggage pickup and deposit. *(In front of the pharmacy at Vle. Pasitea 22 ☎089 81 14 96 ◾www.positanobluporter.it* 𝒊 *Cash only.* Ⓢ *€5-10 per day, per bag.* Ⓞ *Open daily 7am-7pm.)*

- **POST OFFICES:** *(V. Guglielmo Marconi 320 ☎089 87 51 42 🍴 Near the Chiesa Nuova SITA stop.* Ⓞ *Open M-F 8am-1:30pm, Sa 8am-12:30pm.)*

Emergency!

- **POLICE: Police.** *(V. Guglielmo Marconi 111 ☎089 87 50 11 🍴 At the intersection with V. Pasitea.)* **Municipal police.** *(Località Mulini ☎089 87 52 77).*

- **HOSPITALS/MEDICAL SERVICES: Red Cross.** *(Vle. Pasitea 246 ☎089 81 19 12).*

bay of naples

Getting There

By Bus

Positano is best reached by blue **SITA** buses. There is no central bus station: Positano's many bus stops all sit on the elevated road above the coastal *centro*. From the stops, either walk 10-20min. down the steps or road, or take a small orange bus marked "Positano Interno" to the coast. *($ €1. ⏰ Every 10-15min.)* Arriving in Positano, either get off at **Chiesa Nuova** (in front of "Bar Internazionale") or **Positano Sponda** (near V. Cristoforo Colombo and closer to the *centro*). From any of Positano's stops, buses run to and from **Sorrento** *(⏰ 1hr., 31 per day 7:10am-12:40am.)* and **Amalfi.** *(45 min., 31 per day 6am-12:50am.)* Buy tickets at *tabaccherie*. The cost of the ticket depends on the length in time of your trip. *($ 45min. €2.40, 90min. €3.60, 24hr. €7.20, 3-day €18.)*

By Ferry

By water, ferries and hydrofoils arrive at the port on **Spiaggia Grande. Metro del Mare** *(☎089 19 96 00 700 🖥www.metrodelmare.net)* runs ferries between Positano and **Amalfi** *($ €9. ⏰ 6-7 per day, from Amalfi 8:35am and 11:45am-5:40pm, from Positano 10:15am-6:35pm.)*, **Naples Molo Beverello** *($ €14. ⏰ 4 per day, from Naples 8:25-9:20am and 3:10pm, from Positano 12:15-6:10pm.)*, and **Sorrento.** *($ €9. ⏰ 4-5 per day, from Sorrento 9:30am-1:15pm and 6:05pm, from Positano 9am and 12:30-6:10pm.)* **Alicost** *(☎089 81 19 86 🖥www.lauroweb.com/alicost.htm)* runs ferries and hydrofoils to **Capri.** *($ €14.50-16.50. ⏰ 30-60min.; from Capri 3:30pm, 4:25pm, 5pm, 5:30pm; from Positano 8:50am, 10am, 10:55am.)*

Getting Around

Walking is pretty much the only option for getting around Positano, which, given its small size, is not really a problem. There are many steps and uneven paths, though, so exercise caution or you could end up looking really stupid. For more information on getting around or how to get from the bus stops to the town center, see **Orientation** or **Getting There.**

amalfi ☎089

Amalfi is the cool kid on the block—universally known, the subject of wild rumors, the one everyone else wants to be. Not surprising, as it's the perfect marriage of waterfront and commercial *centro* yet somehow escapes becoming either fully urban or completely beach resort. More than any other coastal spot, Amalfi walks the line between artificial and natural beauty—the Escher-like Duomo and Disneyland-style houses sit beside sparkling blue waters, jagged cliffs and lush green trees. This unique combo makes this town highly sought-out (read: expensive and crowded). To escape, head to the neighboring Atrani, 10min. away on foot, which offers cheaper options and some originality of its own. No, it's not just the copycat kid fauning over the hotshot, even though it's name *is* awfully similar.

ORIENTATION

Amalfi is shaped like an upside-down T: its base lying on the waterfront and its thin center extending slightly uphill. It's all easily walkable in an hour. **Piazza Flavio Gioia** (the bus and boat hub) leads into **Piazza Duomo,** which funnels into the narrow **Via Lorenzo d'Amalfi** and **Via Pietro Capuano.** These two central thoroughfares are lined with merchants, small food shops, and cafes; while most of the nicer restaurants can be found up steps on either side; look for signs. **Corso delle Repubbliche Marinare** runs along the coast and becomes **Via Pantaleone Comite.** Follow this road to get to neighboring **Atrani,** a 10min. walk around the large cliff. Atrani's much quieter center is located down a circular ramp in **Piazza Umberto.**

ACCOMMODATIONS

Cheap accommodations in Amalfi are few and far between. For better prices, head to **Atrani.** If you do want to shell out your euro, you'll likely get good services and great views of the water, though you'll still have to pay to step on the sand.

HOTEL LA CONCHIGLIA
⊛ ⊘ 📶 HOTEL [4]

Piazzale dei Protontini ☎089 87 18 56 🖥www.amalfihotelconchiglia.it

The bright aquamarine shutters and decorative tiling of this hotel match Amalfi's beautiful water. This family-run place 10min. from the *centro* is secluded from crowds but still provides guests with beach proximity and plenty of relaxing space on the terraces and garden. Eleven clean rooms aren't fresh-and-crispy new, but they have charming white curtains and painted tile accents that give the place the feeling of an old-fashioned summer home. Owner Alfonso speaks little English but if you can muster up broken Italian, he'll be happy to tell you the secrets of Amalfi, his lifelong hometown.

⇄ Facing the water from the bus stop, walk right on the waterfront along Lungomare dei Cavalleri for 10min. Look for hotel sign when you reach Salita S. Caterina. ℹ Breakfast included. Rooms with ensuite bathroom and fan. Free Wi-Fi. $ Singles €55; doubles €80-90; triples €110-120. Beach access, 2 chairs, and umbrella €18. ⏰ Reception 8am-8pm; call ahead to arrange arrival time.

A SCALINATELLA HOSTEL
⊛ ⊘ 📶 HOSTEL [2]

P. Umberto I ☎089 87 14 92 🖥www.hostelscalinatella.com

Helpful staff and cheap prices are the only appealing thing about an otherwise bare-bones hostel. Its location in the more secluded Atrani is a plus, though you won't have anything near hotel-like amenities.

⇄ From Amalfi, walk 10min. along V. Pantaleone Comite overlooking the waterfront; after the tunnel, head down the circular ramp on the right into Atrani's centro. Reception in P. Umberto I until 10am. After that, head up V. dei Dogi and follow signs to the right up the steps. ℹ Breakfast included. Laundry €7. $ 4-bed dorms €25; doubles, triples, and quads €70-140. ⏰ Call about arrival time to make sure staff is around. Showers open 6-10am and 5-10pm.

HOTEL LIDOMARE
💳 ⊘ 📶 ❄ HOTEL [3]

V. Piccolomini 9 ☎089 87 13 32

The nearly silent surrounds of Hotel Lidomare will make you wonder if you're still in Amalfi. Get a room with a terrace, though, and you'll have no trouble remembering how close the ocean is—great views of the water await. Antique bookshelves, curious wall decorations, and beautiful mosaics distinguish Lidomare from more generic hotels. You can't use it, but ask to see the old-fashioned kitchen anyway for a peek at where your breakfast fixings are carefully prepared. Prices are surprisingly good for the area.

⇄ Head out of P. Duomo through the alleyway and up the steps to the left. ℹ Breakfast included. All rooms with ensuite bathroom. Wi-Fi €5 per 3hr. $ Singles €45-60; doubles €80-120. ⏰ Reception 24hr.

SIGHTS

DUOMO DI SANT'ANDREA, CLOISTER OF PARADISE AND CRYPT
⊘ CHURCH

P. Duomo ☎089 87 13 24

After you utter your first "wow" at seeing Amalfi's blue waters, your second one will come when you pass its Duomo, the proud star of the city's busiest *piazza.* Admire the peculiar black-and-white facade and its strong geometric patterning before climbing over 60 steps to the top. The interior might not be worth the wait if you arrive after the free "hours of prayer," but the quiet **Cloister of Paradise,** with its arcade of interlaced white columns, makes for a nice stroll. Get your money's worth by popping into the **crypt,** which holds the body of St. Andrew, and the small museum, which displays intricate jewelry and ornamentation from the church's treasury.

 # To enter basilica during prayer, go through main doors up the stairs; to enter midday, head up the stairs and left to the ticket desk. $ Basilica free during hours of prayer; €3 midday entry only with combined ticket to museum, crypt, and cloister. ⏰ Basilica open for prayer daily 7:30-10am and 5-8pm. Open with museum, crypt, and cloister 10am-5pm.

PAPER MUSEUM (MUSEO DELLA CARTA) — MUSEUM

V. delle Cartiere 23 ☎089 83 04 561 🖳www.museodellacarta.it

Compared to others in Italy, this museum is as lightweight as, well, a piece of paper. Nonetheless, the town takes pride in the place, which is housed in a 14th-century papermill that may become more notable once you know that Amalfi is famed for its artisan production of a certain kind of thick paper. The included tour adds a bit of amusement to the place and lets you watch this miraculous thing—paper—being made.

 # 10min. up V. delle Cartiere from the P. Duomo. i Admission includes tour (available in English). $ €4, students and groups €2.50. ⏰ Open daily 10am-6:30pm.

THE GREAT OUTDOORS

Beaches are the reason most people come to Amalfi. The town's main beach is the **Marina Grande,** which, though unremarkable, is well-loved and easily accessible (translation: crowded). Head around the Torre di Amalfi to neighboring **Atrani,** where a much quieter sandy stretch awaits. If lying in the sun and dipping into the calm waters isn't your idea of fun, try a rigorous **hike** through Amalfi's stunning countryside. One of the most popular hikes connects Amalfi to Ravello through Pontone. The 2hr. uphill climb starts at the **Museo della Carta.** From here, continue on the partially paved path, following signs for Ravello. Monuments you'll pass on the way include the churches of **San Giovanni Battista** and **Santa Maria del Carmine.** The shorter 1hr. hike from Atrani to Ravello consists mostly of steep stairs and provides a scenic route ending up beside the **Villa Cimbrone.** The tourist offices in both Ravello and Amalfi provide detailed hiking maps.

FOOD

Most higher-quality restaurants are located up side steps off the main streets. The local favorite dish is *scialatelli* (a coarsely cut pasta), often topped with excellent seafood. **La Grande Mela** supermarket offers a better and less expensive selection of basic foodstuffs than the specialty grocers which line V. Pietro Capuano *(V. dei Curiali 6 ☎089 87 11 60 # Turn right into the alley at the start of V. d'Amalfi. ⏰ Open M-Sa 8am-1:30pm and 5-8:30pm, Su 8am-1:30pm.)*

BAR BIRECTO — CAFE [1]

P. Umberto I ☎089 87 10 17 🖳www.ilbirecto.com

You've had pizza, gelato, and beer before—the first two are practically Italy's middle names—but finding them on the cheap, especially in Amalfi's touristy streets, is another story. Bar Birecto's happy hour combos *(all the above for €5)* is nothing less than spectacular. Combine the sweet food and drink deal with free Wi-Fi and chill service from longtime owner, Luigi, and you've got a winner. One liter pitchers of cocktails *(€7)* and mixed beer drinks like the cielo blue *(beer, rum, and Blue Caracao; €4)* will have you wondering if that's the blue Amalfi water or just a similarly colored cocktail before you. Either way, you'll want to dive in.

 # In Atrani. From Amalfi, walk 10min. along V. Pantaleone Comite overlooking the waterfront; after the tunnel, head down the circular ramp on the right into Atrani's centro. i Free Wi-Fi. $ Gelato

€2-3.50. Pizza €4-6. Primi €5-7. Beer €2.50-6. Cocktails €4-5. ⏰ Open daily 7am-2am. Happy hour 3-7pm.

TRATTORIA E PIZZERIA DA MEMÉ 💳🚭🍸⛱ RISTORANTE [3]

Salita Marino Sebaste 8 ☎089 83 04 549

This family restaurant is set back away from Amalfi's beach going crowds. Locals gather at small tables scattered on stone steps leading to the fresh interior. Though the brick-oven pizza is a real steal, their specialty is homemade pasta topped with fresh seafood.

➡ Walk up V. Lorenzo d'Amalfi from P. Duomo. As it becomes V. Pietro Capuano, look for signs on the left of the street and turn up the stairs. $ Cover €1.50. Primi €6.50-15; secondi €8-15. ⏰ Open in summer daily noon-3pm and 6:30pm-midnight; in fall, winter, and spring Tu-Su noon-3pm and 6:30pm-midnight.

PIZZA EXPRESS 🥡🚭 PIZZERIA [1]

V. Pietro Capuano 46

Pop into this tiny joint for the best prices and quickest service in town. Its hole-in-the-wall status, however, means you'll have to head elsewhere with your goods.

➡ From P. Duomo, walk up V. Lorenzo d'Amalfi and continue as it becomes V. Pietro Capuano. $ Pizza €2.50-5, slices €1-1.50. Calzones €4. ⏰ Open in summer daily 9am-10pm; in fall, winter, and spring M-Th 9am-10pm, Sa-Su 9am-10pm.

IL MULINO 💳♿🍸⛱ RISTORANTE [3]

V. delle Cartiere 36 ☎089 87 22 23 💻www.ristoranteilmulino.biz

Locals who have had enough of the beach and its tourists head here for excellent food in a plain setting. About as far away from the *centro* as you can get before reaching countryside, only Italian voices can be heard floating around in the background. If you can do without a table, their takeout menu lets you grab a pizza for a mere €3, one of the best deals in town.

➡ 3min. from the Paper Museum, past the end of V. Pietro Capuano. $ Pizza €5-8, takeout €3-6. Primi €6-12. Fish or meat €7-11. ⏰ Open daily noon-3pm and 7-11pm.

ESSENTIALS

Practicalities

- **TOURIST OFFICES:** The **Azienda Autonoma Soggiorno e Turismo di Amalfi** provides free maps of the city and surrounding area (including hiking maps), bus and ferry schedules, and hotel and food listings. *(C. delle Repubbliche Marinare 27, through the courtyard. ☎089 87 11 07 💻www.amalfitouristoffice.it ➡ 5min. from P. Flavio Gioia, in the direction of Atrani. ⏰ Open M-Sa 9am-1pm and 2-6pm, Su 9am-1pm.)*
- **POST OFFICES:** *(C. delle Repubbliche Marinare ☎089 83 04 831 ℹ Also has currency exchange. ⏰ Open M-F 8am-6:30pm, Sa 8am-12:30pm.)*
- **POSTAL CODE:** 84011.

Emergency!

- **POLICE: Carabinieri.** *(V. Casamare 19 ☎089 87 10 22 ➡ To the left of V. delle Cartiere's start, on the way to the Museo della Carta.)* **Police.** *(In P. Municipio ☎089 87 16 33 ➡ Around the corner from Tourist Office.)*
- **HOSPITALS/MEDICAL SERVICES: Guardia Medica** *(V. Casamare before the Carabinieri ☎089 87 14 49).*

Getting There

By Bus

Amalfi is best reached by blue **SITA** buses which run up and down the coast *(☎089 87 35 89 🖥www.sitabus.it).* Buses arrive in and depart from P. Flavio Gioia near the port. There is no central office, but tickets can be bought at nearby *tabaccherie* or at the **Touring Point** at Vico dei Pastai 9, just off the *piazza*. The cost of the ticket depends on the length in time of your trip. *($ €2.40 for 45min., €3.60 for 90min., €7.20 for 24hr., €18 for 3 days.)* Buses run between Amalfi and **Sorrento** *(⏰ 90min.; depart M-Sa every 30min., slightly reduced on Su, 6:30am-midnight.)*, **Ravello** *(⏰ 25min., every 15-30min, 6:30am-midnight.)*, and **Salerno.** *(⏰ 75min., depart every 15-45 min. 5:15am-12:45am.)* To get between Amalfi and **Positano** (45min. away), just hop on an Amalfi-Sorrento bus—they all stop in that other coastal town.

By Boat

Ferries and hydrofoils (docks beside the bus stop) are a more expensive option, but provide nice views and service some places buses don't reach. **Metro del Mare** *(☎199 60 07 00 🖥www.metrodelmare.net)* runs ferries to **Salerno** *($ €8.50. ⏰ Depart Salerno 8am, 11:30am, 5:15pm; depart Amalfi 10:40am, 4:45pm, 7pm.)*, **Positano** *($ €9. ⏰ 6-7 per day, from Positano 10:15am-6:35pm, from Amalfi 8:35am and 11:45am-5:40pm.)*, **Naples** *($ €14-15. ⏰ 2hr.; 6 per day; from Naples 8:25-9:20am, 3:10pm, and 5:20pm, from Positano 8:35am-5:40pm.)*, and **Sorrento.** *($ €11. ⏰ 1hr.; 4-5 per day; from Sorrento 9:30am-1:15pm and 6:05pm; from Amalfi 8:35am, noon, 1:50, 5, 5:40pm.)* **Alicost** *(☎089 87 33 01 🖥www.lauroweb.com/alicost.htm)* runs ferries and hydrofoils to and from **Capri.** *($ €15-17. ⏰ 50-80 min.; 5 per day; from Capri 9:30-9:40am and 3:30-5:30pm; from Amalfi 8:25am-11:35am.)*

Getting Around

The biggest transportation decision most travelers face in Amalfi is dive or belly-flop. Walking will get you around quite easily; for more information, see **Orientation** (p. 425). Atrani is a 10min. walk away, although if that's too far, you can get there in half the time (save five whole minutes!) by catching a Ravello- or Salerno-bound bus, which will drop you off in Altrani. For information on schedules, ticket purchase, and prices, see **Getting There.**

ravello ☎089

If the Amalfi Coast is a house, Ravello is the attic a lot of visitors don't see but actually stores much of the coolest stuff. This tiny town sits quite literally above all of Amalfi's coastal cities and offers phenomenal views down on them. It has beautiful gardens, elegant villas, and and a classical music festival that makes you think the place might be heaven itself (it certainly has enough altitude to make you wonder). Come here to get away from the bustle—everything from the music to the older crowds begs you to slow down.

ORIENTATION

Ravello is a small hilltop town, easily walkable in an hour. After getting off the bus at **Via G. Boccaccio,** walk through the tunnel into **Piazza Duomo.** From there, a few main streets, including **Via Roma** and **Via della Francesca** (headed for **Villa Cimbrone**), branch off, leading to stunning views and Ravello's outdoor sights.

SIGHTS 👁

Like the aforementioned attic, Ravello packs a lot of cool stuff into a small space. If you don't want to go the more cultural route, consider doing some hiking around the area (see **Amalfi Sights**). Routes are well marked and fairly easy to do; the tourist office provides detailed maps.

👍 VILLA RUFOLO
💳♿ GARDENS

P. Duomo ☎089 85 76 21 💻www.villarufolo.it

Ravello is most renowned for its yearly music festival (see **Festivals**), much of which is performed in the serene grounds of the 13th-century Villa Rufolo. There's a reason the festival is based here—these grounds are so stunning that they inspired **Richard Wagner:** it was in his honor that the town initiated the festival. The villa's lands, once the possession of Ravello's wealthiest family, feature a cloister and the **Torre Maggiore** (visible from outside the walls), but the natural beauty is its most obvious and pleasing element. A garden full of diverse and rare flora complements the blue seascape gleaming below.

➜ *Right off P. Duomo.* $ *€5, under 12 and over 65 €3.* ⏰ *Open daily 9am-9pm. Last entry 15min. before close.*

VILLA CIMBARONE
⊘⊗ GARDENS, PANORAMIC VIEW

V. Santa Chiara 26 ☎089 85 74 59 💻www.villacimbrone.com

Not that you need a break from anything (Ravello's streets are that calm), but if you want a bit more beauty, head to the Villa Cimbarone, a short walk from P. Duomo. The six-hectare expanse of land was once coveted for its relative fertility in comparison with the rockier expanses in most of Ravello, but was eventually abandoned. In the 20th century, **Ernest William Beckett** bought the neglected land and determined to turn it into a work of landscape art—his revitalization of the grounds is one of the most stunning manifestations of English design in Italy. Though he didn't sculpt the views of the coast with his own hands, they are just as beautiful as his more contrived design.

➜ *From P. Duomo, head down V. San Francesco and continue as the street becomes V. Santa Chiara. The villa is about 10min. away.* $ *€6, children €4.* ⏰ *Open daily 9am-8pm.*

FOOD 🍎

The restaurants in musical Ravello serve up some seriously delicious food that'll have you singing their praises, but you may end up singing the blues when the bill arrives—things here aren't cheap.

👍 CUMPÀ COSIMO
💳⊗🍸 RISTORANTE ❸

V. Roma 44/46 ☎089 85 71 56

After 81 years of business, this family-run trattoria has carved itself a spot in Ravello's cliffs and in the hearts of its residents. On top of top-notch service to locals, the friendly owners show their love for their coastal neighbors, printing business cards on handmade paper from Amalfi's **Paper Museum.** You're here for food, though, not history. Rich crepes with ham and cheese are a family specialty *(€11)*, but for those who can't make up their mind, the testing plate *(€15)* may be the better choice. The platter lets you sample some of Ravello's best pasta, all house-made. Between bites, chat with the longtime owners and learn more about Ravello lore.

➜ *Down V. Roma, just past the tourist office.* $ *Pastas €9-15; meat/fish €9-40; cheese €9-10.* ⏰ *Open Mar-Sept daily noon-3:30pm and 6:30-10:30pm; Oct-Feb Tu-Su noon-3:30pm and 6:30-10:30pm.*

RISTORANTE PIZZERIA VITTORIA

🍴⊗🍸☕ RISTORANTE ❷

V. dei Rufolo 3 ☎089 85 79 47 📧www.ristorantepizzeriavittoria.it

For a twist on the old pie, try the 0.5m pizza "plank," with your choice of three toppings (€18). The inner garden's small tables may barely accommodate the giant-sized entree, but with a friend, you'll have no trouble finishing it off.

🍴 *From P. Duomo, head out onto V. dei Rufolo for 2min.* Ⓢ *Cover €2. Pizza €5-9. Primi €9-12; secondi €15-18.* 🕐 *Open daily 12:15-3pm and 7:15-11pm.*

FESTIVALS

RAVELLO FESTIVAL
SUMMER

P. Duomo 7 ☎089 85 84 22 📧www.ravellofestival.com

Ravello really spoils us sometimes. As if the view weren't enough, the town goes and gives us one of the world's largest classical music festivals each summer. If classical music's your thing, you'll probably be in heaven. If it's not, you can just look at the view. After witnessing Ravello's stunning beauty during a visit here in 1880, German composer Richard Wagner based some of his **Parsifal** on the Villa Rufolo gardens. Cashing in on this (really rather minor) legacy, the town has for more than 50 years hosted an annual series of concerts that attracts renowned performers. The festival has expanded to encompass dance, art shows, and discussion groups as well. In a small town, having a festival so grand that it gets a new theme each year—2010's was "Madness"—is quite an achievement, and one of the two things (yes, the other is indeed the view) that sets Ravello apart from other Amalfi Coast destinations.

🍴 *Most performances take place in Villa Rufolo gardens, although the reach of the festival extends over the whole town.* ℹ *Check the website, ticket office at the above address, or the tourist office for a schedule of events.* Ⓢ *Concert tickets €20-70.* 🕐 *Festival runs July-Sept. Ticket office open daily May-Sept 10am-8pm.*

ESSENTIALS

Practicalities

- **TOURIST OFFICES: Azienda Autonoma Soggioro e Turismo di Ravello** provides free maps of the town and surrounding area (including hiking maps), information on the Ravello Festival, and hotel and restaurant listings. *(V. Roma 18 ☎089 85 70 96 📧www.ravellotime.it 🍴 A 2min. walk from P. Duomo.* 🕐 *Open daily 9:30am-1pm and 2-6pm.)*

- **INTERNET: Bar Calce** provides internet and Wi-Fi. *(V. Boccaccio 11 ☎089 85 71 30 🍴 Beside SITA bus stop.* ℹ *Cash only.* Ⓢ *€1.50 per 15min., €5 per hr. Discounts on internet if you buy food.* 🕐 *Open daily 8:30am-1:30pm and 3:30-10pm.)*

- **POST OFFICES:** *(V. Boccaccio 21 ☎089 85 86 61 🍴 Beside SITA bus stop.* 🕐 *Open M-F 8am-1:30pm, Sa 8am-12:30pm.)* Also has an **ATM,** though others are throughout the town.

Emergency!

- **POLICE: Carabinieri.** *(V. Rogadeo 1 ☎089 85 71 50 🍴 At the end of V. Roma, make a right.)* **Polizia Locale.** *(P. Fontana Moresca ☎089 85 74 98 🍴 At the end of Vle. Gioacchino D'Anna.)*

- **LATE-NIGHT PHARMACIES:** Unlike most Italian towns, Ravello does not have many pharmacies. Try **Farmacia Russo.** *(V. Boccaccio 15 ☎089 85 71 89 🍴 Right by the SITA bus stop.* 🕐 *Open daily 9am-1pm and 5-8:30pm.)*

Getting There

■

Ravello is a 25min. ride from **Amalfi** on a blue **SITA bus.** Buses arrive and leave from the end of V. Giovanni Boccaccio regularly. (🕑 *Every 10-30min. 5:45am-12:25am.*) You can also call a **taxi** (☎*089 85 80 00*) from the bus stop. Alternatively, ⛰**hike** 1hr. up fairly even stairs from **Atrani** (through Castiglione and Scala) or 2hr. from Amalfi (through Pontone). For more information, see **Amalfi Sights.**

Getting Around

⊏

Ravello is small and navigated almost exclusively by foot. For more information on how to navigate by foot, see **Orientation.**

ESSENTIALS

You don't have to be a rocket scientist to plan a good trip. (It might help, but it's not required.) You do, however, need to be well prepared, and that's where we come in. Essentials is the chapter that gives you all the nitty-gritty you need to know for your trip: the hard information gleaned from 50 years of collective wisdom (and that phone call to Bologna the other day that put us on hold for an hour). Planning your trip? Check. Staying safe and healthy? Check. The dirt on transportation? Check. We've also thrown in communications info, meteorological charts, and a ◨**phrasebook,** just for good measure. Plus, for overall trip-planning advice from what to pack (money and as little underwear as possible) to how to take a good passport photo (it's physically impossible; consider airbrushing), you can also check out the Essentials section of ◨www.letsgo.com.

We're not going to lie—this chapter is tough for us to write, and you might not find it as fun of a read as 101 or Discover. But please, for the love of all that is good, read it! It's super helpful, and, most importantly, it means we didn't compile all this technical info and put it in one place for you (yes YOU) for nothing.

greatest hits

- **PASSPORT: YES, VISA: NO.** Remember to take your passport! But if you're spending less than 90 days in Europe (note: Europe, not just Italy), no visa is required (p. 434).

- **RAIN, RAIN, GO AWAY.** See our climate table (p. 445) to get an idea of what the weather might be like during your trip. Yes, that word was "might."

- **DON'T PANIC!** We list information inside for all embassies of English-speaking countries in Italy. In an emergency, they'll be your first resort (p. 435).

- **ACCESSIBLE TRAVEL.** Navigating Italy's antiquated cities can be a little tricky in a wheelchair. Read inside to learn how it can be done, even through the canals and stairways of Venice (p. 439).

planning your trip

entrance requirements

- **PASSPORT:** Required of any citizens, of anywhere.
- **VISA:** Required of non-EU citizens staying longer than 90 days.
- **WORK PERMIT:** Required of all non-EU citizens planning to work in Italy.

DOCUMENTS AND FORMALITIES

You've got your visa and your work permit (if necessary), just like Let's Go told you to, and then you realize you've forgotten the most important thing: your passport. Well, we're not going to let that happen. **Don't forget your passport!**

Visas

Those lucky enough to be citizens of the European Union do not need a visa to travel to Italy. You citizens of Australia, Canada, New Zealand, the US, and other non-EU countries do not need a visa for short trips to Italy, but if your trip lasts more than 90 days, you will need one. Take note that this 90-day period begins when you enter the EU's **freedom of movement** zone (for more info, see **One Europe,** below), so ask yourself if you really want to spend 89 days in Slovakia and apportion your time wisely. If you really can't pull yourself away from the wonders of Bratislava, visas can be acquired at your neighborhood Italian consulate or embassy (see the next page for details). With this visa safely tucked away in your backpack, you'll be free to stay between 90 and 365 additional days in Italy.

one europe

The EU's policy of freedom of movement means that most border controls have been abolished and visa policies harmonized. Under this treaty, formally known as the Schengen Agreement, you're still required to carry a passport (or government-issued ID card for EU citizens) when crossing an internal border, but, once you've been admitted into one country, you're free to travel to other participating states. Most EU states are already members of Schengen (excluding Cyprus), as are Iceland and Norway. For more consequences of the EU for travelers, see **The Euro** feature later in this chapter.

Double-check entrance requirements at the nearest embassy or consulate of Italy (yep, they're still listed on the next page) for up-to-date information before departure. US citizens can also consult ▇travel.state.gov.

Entering Italy to study requires a special visa. For more information, see the **Beyond Tourism** chapter.

Work Permits

Admittance to Italy as a non-EU traveler does not include the right to work, which is authorized only by a work permit. For more information, see the **Beyond Tourism** chapter.

- **ITALIAN EMBASSY IN AUSTRALIA:** *(12 Grey St., Deakin, Canberra ACT 2600 ☎02 6273 3333 ▣www.ambcanberra.esteri.it ☼ Open M-F 9am-noon.)*

- **ITALIAN EMBASSY IN CANADA:** *(275 Slater St., 21st fl., Ottawa, ON K1P 5H9 ☎613-232-2401 ▣www.ambottawa.esteri.it ☼ Open M-Tu 9am-noon, W 9am-noon and 2-4pm, Th-F 9am-noon.)*

- **ITALIAN EMBASSY IN IRELAND:** *(63/65 Northumberland Rd., Dublin 4 ☎01 660 1744 ▣www.ambdublino.esteri.it ☼ Open M-W 10am-noon, Th 1:30-3:30pm, F 10am-noon.)*

- **ITALIAN EMBASSY IN NEW ZEALAND:** *(34-38 Grant Rd., PO Box 463, Thorndon, Wellington ☎04 473 5339 ▣www.ambwellington.esteri.it ☼ Open M-Tu 9am-1pm, W 9am-1pm and 3-4:45pm, Th-F 9am-1pm.)*

- **ITALIAN CONSULATE GENERAL IN UK:** *(38 Eaton Pl., London SW1X 8AN ☎020 7235 9371 ▣www.conslondra.esteri.it ☼ Open M-F 9am-noon.)*

- **ITALIAN EMBASSY IN US:** *(3000 Whitehaven St. NW, Washington, DC 20008 ☎202-612-4400 ▣www.ambwashingtondc.esteri.it ☼ Open M 10am-12:30pm, W 10am-12:30pm, F 10am-12:30pm.)*

- **AUSTRALIAN EMBASSY IN ITALY:** *(V. Antonio Bosio 5, Rome ☎06 85 27 21, emergency ☎800 87 77 90 ▣www.italy.embassy.gov.au ☼ Open M-F 9am-5pm.)*

- **CANADIAN EMBASSY IN ITALY:** *(V. Zara 30, Rome ☎06 85 444 ▣www. canadainternational.gc.ca/italy-italie ☼ Open M-Th 8:30-11:30am.)*

- **IRISH EMBASSY IN ITALY:** *(P. di Campitelli 3, Rome ☎06 69 79 121 ▣www. ambasciata-irlanda.it ☼ Open M-F 10am-12:30pm and 3-4:30pm.)*

- **NEW ZEALAND EMBASSY IN ITALY:** *(V. Clitunno 44, Rome ☎06 85 37 501 ▣www.nzembassy.com/italy ☼ Open M-F 8:30am-12:45pm and 1:45-5pm.)*

- **BRITISH EMBASSY IN ITALY:** *(V. XX Settembre 80a, Rome ☎06 42 20 00 01 ▣www.britain.it ☼ Open M-F 9:15am-1:30pm.)*

- **AMERICAN EMBASSY IN ITALY:** *(V. Vittorio Veneto 121, Rome ☎06 46 741 ▣rome.usembassy.gov ☼ Open M-F 8:30am-12:30pm.)*

planning your trip . time differences

TIME DIFFERENCES

Italy is 1hr. ahead of Greenwich Mean Time (GMT) and observes Daylight Saving Time. This means that it is 6hr. ahead of New York City, 9hr. ahead of Los Angeles, 1hr. ahead of the British Isles, 8hr. in Northern Hemisphere summer and 10hr. in Northern Hemisphere winter behind Sydney, and, in the same fashion, 10hr./12hr. behind New Zealand. Don't get confused and call your parents while it's actually 4am their time! Note that Italy changes to Daylight Saving Time on different dates from some other countries, so sometimes, though not often, the difference will be one hour different from what is stated here.

money

GETTING MONEY FROM HOME

Stuff happens. When stuff happens, you might need some money. When you need some money, the easiest and cheapest solution is to have someone back home make a deposit to your bank account. Otherwise, consider one of the following options.

the euro

Despite what many dollar-possessing Americans might want to hear, the official currency of 16 members of the European Union—Austria, Belgium, Cyprus, Finland, France, Germany, Greece, Ireland, Italy, Luxembourg, Malta, the Netherlands, Portugal, Slovakia, Slovenia, and Spain—is the euro.

Still, the currency has some important—and positive—consequences for travelers hitting more than one eurozone country. For one thing, money-changers across the eurozone are obliged to exchange money at the official, fixed rate and at no commission (though they may still charge a small service fee). Second, euro-denominated traveler's checks allow you to pay for goods and services across the eurozone, again at the official rate and commission-free. For more info, check a currency converter (such as www.xe.com) or www.europa.eu.int.

Wiring Money

Arranging a **bank money transfer** means asking a bank back home to wire money to a bank in Italy. This is the cheapest way to transfer cash, but it's also the slowest and most agonizing, usually taking several days or more. Note that some banks may only release your funds in local currency, potentially sticking you with a poor exchange rate; inquire about this in advance. Money transfer services like **Western Union** are faster and more convenient than bank transfers—but also much pricier. Western Union has many locations worldwide. To find one, visit ■www.westernunion.com or call the appropriate number: in Italy ☎800 788 935, in Australia ☎1800 173 833, in Canada ☎800-235-0000, in the US ☎800-325-6000, and in the UK ☎0800 731 1815. Money transfer services are also available to **American Express** cardholders and at selected **Thomas Cook** offices.

pins and atms

To use a debit or credit card to withdraw money from a cash machine (ATM) in Europe, you must have a four-digit Personal Identification Number (PIN). If your PIN is longer than four digits, ask your bank whether you can just use the first four or whether you'll need a new one. Credit cards don't usually come with PINs, so if you intend to hit up ATMs in Europe with a credit card to get cash advances, call your credit card company before leaving to request one.

Travelers with alphabetic rather than numeric PINs may also be thrown off by the absence of letters on European cash machines. Here are the corresponding numbers to use: 1 = QZ; 2 = ABC; 3 = DEF; 4 = GHI; 5 = JKL; 6 = MNO; 7 = PRS; 8 = TUV; 9 = WXY. Note that if you mistakenly punch the wrong code into the machine multiple (often three) times, it can swallow (gulp!) your card for good.

essentials

THE STUDENT TRAVEL GUIDE written **for** students **by** students

the latest **hotspots, the** best **deals**

work, study, volunteer, and
travel abroad

LET'S GO

Blogs, photos, videos,
and free content
online!

www.letsgo.com   facebook.com/letsgotravelguides

US State Department (US Citizens only)

In serious emergencies only, the US State Department will forward money within hours to the nearest consular office, which will then disburse it according to instructions for a US$30 fee. If you wish to use this service, you must contact the Overseas Citizens Services division of the US State Department (☎+1-202-501-4444, from US 888-407-4747).

TAXES

The **Value Added Tax** (**VAT;** *imposto sul valore aggiunta,* or IVA) is a sales tax levied in EU countries. Foreigners making any purchase over €155 are entitled to an additional 20% VAT refund. Some stores take off 20% on-site. Others require that you fill out forms at the customs desk upon leaving the EU and send receipts from home within six months. Not all storefront "Tax-Free" stickers imply an immediate, on-site refund, so ask before making a purchase.

TIPPING AND BARGAINING

In Italy, as in the rest of Europe, tips of 5-10% are customary, particularly in restaurants. Italian waiters won't cry if you don't leave a tip—just get ready to ignore the pangs of your conscience later on. Taxi drivers expect the same kind of tip, but lucky for you alcoholics, it is unusual to tip in bars. Bargaining is appropriate in markets and other more informal settings, though in regular shops it is inappropriate. Hotels will often offer lower prices to people who arrive looking for a room that night, so you will often be able to find a bed cheaper than what is officially quoted.

safety and health

GENERAL ADVICE

In any type of crisis, the most important thing to do is **stay calm.** Your country's embassy abroad is usually your best resource in an emergency; registering with that embassy upon arrival in the country is a good idea. The government offices listed in the **Travel Advisories** feature at the end of this section can provide information on the services they offer their citizens in case of emergencies abroad.

Local Laws and Police

In Italy, you will mainly encounter two types of boys in blue: the *polizia* (☎113) and the *carabinieri* (☎112). The *polizia* are a civil force under the command of the Ministry of the Interior, whereas the *carabinieri* fall under the auspices of the Ministry of Defense and are considered a military force. Both, however, generally serve the same purpose—to maintain security and order in the country. In the case of attack or robbery, both will respond to inquiries or desperate pleas for help.

Drugs and Alcohol

Needless to say, **illegal drugs** are best avoided altogether, particularly when traveling in a foreign country. In Italy, just like almost everywhere else in the world, drugs including marijuana, cocaine, and heroin are illegal, and possession or other drug-related offenses will be harshly punished.

If you carry **prescription drugs,** bring copies of the prescriptions as well as a note from your doctor, and have them accessible at international borders.

The legal drinking age in Italy is (drumroll please) 16. Remember to drink responsibly and to **never drink and drive.** Doing so is illegal and can result in a prison sentence, not to mention early death. The legal blood alcohol content (BAC) for driving in Italy is under 0.05%, significantly lower than the US limit of 0.08%.

essentials

The following government offices provide travel information and advisories by telephone, by fax, or via the web:

- **AUSTRALIA: Department of Foreign Affairs and Trade.** (☎+61 2 6261 1111 🖳www.dfat.gov.au)

- **CANADA: Department of Foreign Affairs and International Trade (DFAIT).** Call or visit the website for the free booklet *Bon Voyage...But*. (☎+1-800-267-8376 🖳www.dfait-maeci.gc.ca)

- **NEW ZEALAND: Ministry of Foreign Affairs.** (☎+64 4 439 8000 🖳www.mfat.govt.nz)

- **UK: Foreign and Commonwealth Office.** (☎+44 20 7008 1500 🖳www.fco.gov.uk)

- **US: Department of State.** (☎888-407-4747 from the US, +1-202-501-4444 elsewhere 🖳travel.state.gov)

SPECIFIC CONCERNS

Travelers with Disabilities

Those in wheelchairs should be aware that travel in Italy will sometimes be extremely difficult. Many cities predate the wheelchair—and sometimes it seems even the wheel—by several centuries and thus pose unique challenges to disabled travelers. Venice is particularly difficult to navigate in a wheelchair given its narrow streets and numerous bridges (many with steps). Be aware that while an establishment itself may be wheelchair-accessible, getting to the front door in a wheelchair might be virtually impossible. **Accessible Italy** (☎+378 941 111 🖳www.accessibleitaly.com) is an organization that offers advice to tourists of limited mobility heading to Italy, with tips offered on subjects ranging from finding accessible accommodations to organizing wheelchair rental.

Natural Disasters

Italy is liable to occasional earthquakes and volcanic eruptions (see **Pompeii,** or **Herculaneum**). If Vesuvius decides to become active during your trip (this could actually happen), your best resource will be your country's embassy.

PRE-DEPARTURE HEALTH

Matching a prescription to a foreign equivalent is not always easy, safe, or possible, so if you take **prescription drugs,** carry up-to-date prescriptions or a statement from your doctor stating the medications' trade names, manufacturers, chemical names, and dosages. During flights, be sure to keep all medication with you in your carry-on luggage.

All basic drugs can be bought at Italian pharmacies, and sometimes supermarkets. Pharmacies are incredibly wide-spread but generally quite small, so you often have to ask the pharmacists to receive what you're looking for. Most pharmacists tend to speak at least a little English, and will often be able to guide you towards the purchase you need.

Immunizations and Precautions

Travelers over two years old should make sure that the following vaccines are up to date: MMR (for measles, mumps, and rubella); DTaP or Td (for diphtheria, tetanus, and pertussis); IPV (for polio); Hib (for *Haemophilus influenzae* B); and HepB (for

Hepatitis B). For recommendations on immunizations and prophylaxis, check with a doctor and consult the Centers for **Disease Control and Prevention (CDC)** in the US or the equivalent in your home country. *(☎+1-800-CDC-INFO/232-4636 🖳www.cdc.gov/travel)*

getting around

For information on how to get to Italy and save a bundle while doing so, check out the Essentials section of **🖳www.letsgo.com.** (In case you can't tell, we think our website's the bomb.)

BY PLANE

Commercial Airlines

For small-scale travel on the continent, *Let's Go* suggests taking advantage of **🖳budget airlines,** but more traditional carriers have also made efforts to keep up with the low-price revolution. The **Star Alliance Europe Airpass** offers low economy-class fares for travel within Europe to 220 destinations in 45 countries. The pass is available to non-European passengers on Star Alliance carriers, including United, U.S. Airways,

budget airlines

The recent emergence of no-frills airlines has made hopscotching around Europe by air increasingly affordable. Though these flights often feature inconvenient hours or serve less popular regional airports, with ticket prices often dipping into single digits, it's never been faster or easier to jet across the continent. The following resources will be useful not only for crisscrossing Italy but also for those ever-popular weekend trips to nearby international destinations. Be warned—these airlines try to squeeze their profit margins any way they can, and calling some of the phone numbers listed below will cost as much as a euro per minute, so it may be best to use their websites.

- **BMIBABY:** Departures from East Midlands in the UK to Venice and Alghero. *(☎0871 224 0224 for the UK, +44 870 126 6726 elsewhere 🖳www.bmibaby.com)*
- **EASYJET:** Flies from multiple locations in Europe to most major Italian cities (but not Florence). *(☎+44 871 244 2366 🖳www.easyjet.com $ UK£50-150.)*
- **RYANAIR:** From numerous European airports to Italian cities both large and small. *(☎899 018 880 in Italy, 0871 246 0000 in the UK 🖳www.ryanair.com)*
- **STERLING:** Flies from Denmark to Rome, Venice, Florence, Naples, and Sicily. *(☎70 10 84 84 for Denmark, 0870 787 8038 for the UK 🖳www.sterling.dk)*
- **TRANSAVIA:** Flies from the Netherlands and Denmark to several Italian cities, including Rome and Venice. *(☎899 009 901 in Italy 🖳www.transavia.com $ From €49 one-way.)*
- **WIZZ AIR:** Flies from many Eastern European destinations to most major Italian cities. *(☎899 018 874 in Italy 🖳www.wizzair.com)*

BACKPACKING
by the numbers:

117   photos snapped

41   gelato flavors (3 lbs gained)

23   miles walked (in the *right* direction)

6   buses missed

4   benches napped on

2½   hostel romances

1   Let's Go Travel Guide

0   REGRETS.

LET'S GO

www.letsgo.com

we'd rather be traveling, too.

Continental, and Air Canada. (🖳*www.staralliance.com*) **EuropebyAir's** snazzy FlightPass also allows you to hop between hundreds of cities in Europe and North Africa. (☎*+1-888-321-4737* 🖳*www.europebyair.com* Ⓢ *Most flights US$99.*)

In addition, a number of European airlines offer discount coupon packets. Most are only available as tack-ons for transatlantic passengers, but some are standalone offers. Most must be purchased before departure, so research in advance. For example, **oneworld**, a coalition of 10 major international airlines, offers deals and cheap connections all over the world, including within Europe (🖳*www.oneworld.com*).

rail resources

- **WWW.RAILEUROPE.COM:** Info on rail travel and railpasses.

- **POINT-TO-POINT FARES AND SCHEDULES:** 🖳www.raileurope.com/us/rail/fares_schedules/index.htm allows you to calculate whether buying a railpass would save you money.

- **WWW.RAILSAVER.COM:** Uses your itinerary to calculate the best railpass for your trip.

- **WWW.RAILFANEUROPE.NET:** Links to rail servers throughout Europe.

- **WWW.LETSGO.COM:** Check out the Essentials section for more details.

BY TRAIN

Trains in Italy are generally comfortable, convenient, and reasonably swift. Make sure you are on the correct car, as trains sometimes split at crossroads. Towns listed in parentheses on European train schedules require a train switch at the town listed immediately before the parentheses.

You can either buy a **railpass,** which allows you unlimited travel within a particular region for a given period of time, or rely on buying individual **point-to-point** tickets as you go. Almost all countries give students or youths (under 26, usually) direct discounts on regular domestic rail tickets, and many also sell a student or youth card that provides 20-50% off all fares for up to a year.

BY BUS

Though European trains and railpasses are extremely popular, in some cases buses prove a better option. Certain smaller Italian destinations, including some Tuscan towns and the Amalfi Coast, have no train links and can only be reached by road. For long-range travel, buses are often cheaper than railpasses; **international bus passes** allow unlimited travel on a hop-on, hop-off basis between major European cities. **Busabout,** for instance, offers three interconnecting bus circuits covering 29 of Europe's best bus hubs. (☎*+44 8450 267 514* 🖳*www.busabout.com* Ⓢ *1 circuit in high season starts at US$579, students US$549.*) **Eurolines,** meanwhile, is the largest operator of Europe-wide coach services. We get misty-eyed just thinking about their unlimited 15- and 30-day passes to 41 major European cities. (☎*086 1199 1900* 🖳*www.eurolines.com* Ⓢ *High season 15-day pass €345, 30-day pass €455; under 26 €290/375. Mid-season €240/330; under 26 €205/270. Low season €205/310; under 26 €175/240.*)

keeping in touch

BY EMAIL AND INTERNET

Hello and welcome to the 21st century, where you can check your email in most major European cities, though sometimes you'll have to pay a few bucks or buy a drink for internet access. **Internet cafes** and the occasional free internet terminal at a public library or university are listed in the **Practicalities** sections of cities that we cover. For lists of additional cybercafes in Italy, check out ▇cafe.ecs.net.

Wireless hot spots make internet access possible in public and remote places. Unfortunately, they also pose security risks. Hot spots are public, open networks that use unencrypted, unsecured connections. They are susceptible to hacks and "packet sniffing"—the theft of passwords and other private information. To prevent problems, disable "ad hoc" mode, turn off file sharing and network discovery, encrypt your email, turn on your firewall, beware of phony networks, and watch for over-the-shoulder creeps.

BY TELEPHONE

Calling Home from Italy

Without a doubt, the cheapest, easiest, and downright coolest way to call home is ▇Skype (▇www.skype.com). You can even videochat if you have one of those new-fangled webcams. Calls to other Skype users are free; calls to landlines and mobiles worldwide start at US$0.021 per minute, depending on where you're calling. Skype's only drawback is that it requires an active internet connection.

For those who can't find Wi-Fi or prefer to pretend that it's still the 20th century, **prepaid phone cards** are a common and relatively inexpensive means of calling abroad. Each one comes with a Personal Identification Number (PIN) and a toll-free access number. You call the access number and then follow the directions for dialing your PIN. To purchase prepaid phone cards, check online for the best rates; ▇www.call-ingcards.com is a good place to start. Online providers generally send your access number and PIN via email, with no actual "card" involved. You can also call home with prepaid phone cards purchased in Italy.

Another option is a **calling card,** linked to a major national telecommunications

international calls

To call Italy from home or to call home from Italy, dial:

1. THE INTERNATIONAL DIALING PREFIX. To call from Australia, dial ☎0011; Canada or the US, ☎011; Ireland, New Zealand, the UK, or Italy ☎00.

2. THE COUNTRY CODE OF THE COUNTRY YOU WANT TO CALL. To call Australia, dial ☎61; Canada or the US, ☎1; Ireland, ☎353; New Zealand, ☎64; the UK, ☎44; Italy, ☎39.

3. THE CITY/AREA CODE. *Let's Go* lists the city/area codes for cities and towns in Italy opposite the city or town name or on the chapter opening page, next to a ☎, as well as in every phone number. If the first digit is a zero (e.g., ☎049 for Padua), omit the zero when calling from abroad (e.g., dial ☎49 from Canada to reach Padua).

4. THE LOCAL NUMBER.

service in your home country. Calls are billed collect or to your account. Cards generally come with instructions for dialing both domestically and internationally.

Placing a collect call through an international operator can be expensive but may be necessary in case of an emergency. You can frequently call collect without even possessing a company's calling card just by calling its access number and following the instructions.

Cellular Phones

Sadly, the world refuses to be a simple place, and cell phones bought abroad, particularly in the US, are unlikely to work in Italy. Fortunately, it is quite easy to purchase a reasonably-priced phone in Italy. Plus, you won't necessarily have to deal with cell phone plans and bills; prepaid minutes are widely available and phones can be purchased cheaply or even rented, avoiding the hassle of pay phones and phone cards.

The international standard for cell phones is **Global System for Mobile Communication (GSM)**. To make and receive calls in Italy, you will need a GSM-compatible phone and a **SIM (Subscriber Identity Module)** card, a country-specific, thumbnail-size chip that gives you a local phone number and plugs you into the local network. Many SIM cards are prepaid, and incoming calls are frequently free. You can buy additional cards or vouchers (usually available at convenience stores) to "top up" your phone. For more information on GSM phones, check out ▣www.telestial.com. Companies like **Cellular Abroad** (▣*www.cellularabroad.com*) and **OneSimCard** (▣*www.onesimcard.com*) rent cell phones and SIM cards that work in a variety of destinations around the world.

BY SNAIL MAIL

Sending Mail Home from Italy

Airmail is the best way to send mail home from Italy. **Aerogrammes,** printed sheets that fold into envelopes and travel via airmail, are available at post offices. Write "airmail," or *"per posta aerea,"* on the front. Most post offices will charge exorbitant fees or simply refuse to send aerogrammes with enclosures. Surface mail is by far the cheapest but also slowest way to send mail. It takes one to two months to cross the Atlantic—good for heavy items you won't need for a while, like souvenirs that you've acquired along the way, or gifts you're obligated to send home but don't actually care about people receiving promptly.

Sending Mail to Italy

Federal Express offers express mail services from most countries to Italy (☎+1-800-463-3339 ▣*www.fedex.com*). Postage within Italy is very reasonably priced and will rarely cost you more than a euro (except for weighty packages).

There are several ways to arrange pickup of letters sent to you while you are abroad. Mail can be sent via **Poste Restante** (General Delivery; **Fermo Posta** in Italian) to almost any city or town in Italy with a post office, and it is generally reliable (though in Italy it's not a surprise for things to be a little untimely). Address Poste Restante letters like so:

Leonardo DA VINCI
c/o Ufficio Postale Centrale
FERMO POSTA
48100 Ravenna
Italy

The mail will (in theory) be sent to the post office you specify, or if you simply specify the city, it will be held at a special desk in the central post office. It's best to use the largest post office, since mail may be sent there regardless. It is usually safer and quicker, though more expensive, to send mail express or registered. Bring your passport (or other photo ID) for pickup; there may be a small fee. If the clerks insist that there is nothing for you, ask them to check under your first name as well. *Let's Go* lists post offices in the **Practicalities** section for each city.

American Express has travel offices throughout the world that offer a free **Client Letter Service** (mail held up to 30 days and forwarded upon request) for cardholders who contact them in advance. Some offices provide these services to non-cardholders (especially AmEx Travelers Cheque holders), but call ahead to make sure. For a complete list of AmEx locations, call ☎+1-800-528-4800 or visit 🖳www.americanexpress.com/travel.

climate

You'd think that Italy was balmy and beautiful, bordering the Mediterranean as it does. And you'd be right—for some places, some of the time. Actually, the country is pretty diverse, climate-wise. Italy definitely has seasons; if you're in Milan in January, you'll need a coat. A thick one. If you're in Rome in July, you'll probably be asking if it's really necessary to wear more than a bikini to the Sistine Chapel (the answer is unfortunately yes). In general, summertime is hot and sometimes extremely so. Heatwaves are not uncommon, so be prepared to hydrate heavily, particularly if you're toward the south of the country. The north gets much cooler in the winter, with snowfall not unheard of, and in the Alps, it obviously never really gets warm. Bear in mind that just a few years ago Turin hosted the Winter Olympics, so there's definitely cold stuff around. But if you visit in the summer, the balmy and beautiful thing will be all you have to worry about (at least when it comes to the weather).

AVG. TEMP.(LOW/ HIGH), PRECIP.	JANUARY			APRIL			JULY			OCTOBER		
	°C	°F	mm	°C	°F	mm	°C	°F	mm	°C	°F	mm
Florence	1/10	34/50	73	8/19	46/66	78	17/31	63/88	40	10/21	50/70	88
Milan	0/5	32/41	44	10/18	50/64	94	20/29	68/84	64	11/17	52/63	125
Rome	5/11	41/52	71	10/19	50/66	51	20/30	68/86	15	13/22	55/72	99
Venice	1/6	41/52	37	10/17	50/63	78	19/27	66/81	52	11/19	52/66	77

To convert from degrees Fahrenheit to degrees Celsius, subtract 32 and multiply by 5/9. To convert from Celsius to Fahrenheit, multiply by 9/5 and add 32. If thinking about that makes your brain hurt, you could just use this handy chart we drew up for you:

°CELSIUS	-5	0	5	10	15	20	25	30	35	40
°FAHRENHEIT	23	32	41	50	59	68	77	86	95	104

measurements

Like the rest of the rational world, Italy uses the metric system. The basic unit of length is the meter (m), which is divided into 100 centimeters (cm) or 1000 millimeters (mm). One thousand meters make up one kilometer (km). Fluids are measured in liters (L), each divided into 1000 milliliters (mL). A liter of pure water weighs one kilogram (kg), the unit of mass that is divided into 1000 grams (g). Italian food stores will sometimes measure by *ettos*, which are equal to 100g. One metric ton is 1000kg. Again, you should probably just use the chart:

MEASUREMENT CONVERSIONS	
1 inch (in.) = 25.4mm	1 millimeter (mm) = 0.039 in.
1 foot (ft.) = 0.305m	1 meter (m) = 3.28 ft.
1 yard (yd.) = 0.914m	1 meter (m) = 1.094 yd.
1 mile (mi.) = 1.609km	1 kilometer (km) = 0.621 mi.
1 ounce (oz.) = 28.35g	1 gram (g) = 0.035 oz.
1 pound (lb.) = 0.454kg	1 kilogram (kg) = 2.205 lb.
1 fluid ounce (fl. oz.) = 29.57mL	1 milliliter (mL) = 0.034 fl. oz.
1 gallon (gal.) = 3.785L	1 liter (L) = 0.264 gal.

language

It is (hopefully) not necessary to inform you that the primary language spoken in Italy is Italian. The prevalence of English-speaking varies wildly. If your trip will focus on major tourist sights, you'll probably be able to get by without speaking a word of Dante's tongue. Once you head away from these hotspots, however, it is much more unusual to encounter English-speakers. To initiate an English conversation, politely ask "Parla inglese?" (PAR-lah een-GLEH-zeh). Try to learn at least a few Italian phrases. For somewhat helpful suggestions, see the **Phrasebook.** Feel free to improvize: your high school French or Spanish knowledge might actually turn out to be much more useful than you thought. And the universal language of point-and-gesture also sometimes does the trick. Whatever the result, end your conversation with a courteous "Grazie" (GRAHT-see-yeh.)

PRONUNCIATION

Vowels

There are seven vowel sounds in standard Italian. **A, i,** and **u** each have one pronunciation. **E** and **o** each have two slightly different pronunciations, one open and one closed, depending on the vowel's placement in the word, the stress placed on it, and the region in which it is spoken. Below are approximate pronunciations.

PHONETIC UNIT	PRONUNCIATION	PHONETIC UNIT	PRONUNCIATION
a	"a" as in "father" (casa)	o (closed)	"o" as in "bone" (sono)
e (closed)	"ay" as in "gray" (sera)	o (open)	"aw" as in "ought" (bocca)
e (open)	"eh" as in "wet" (sette)	u	"oo" as in "moon" (gusto)
i	"ee" as in "cheese" (vino)		

Consonants

C and G

Before a, o, or u, **c** and **g** are hard, as in *candy* and *goose* or as in the Italian *colore* (koh-LOHR-eh; color) and *gatto* (GAHT-toh; cat). Italians soften c and g into **ch** and **j** sounds, respectively, when followed by i or e, as in *cheese* and *jeep* or the Italian *cibo* (CHEE-boh; food) and *gelato* (jeh-LAH-toh; ice cream).

Ch and Gh

H returns **c** and **g** to their "hard" sounds in front of i or e (see above): *chianti* (ky-AHN-tee), the Tuscan wine, and *spaghetti* (spah-GEHT-tee), the pasta.

Gn and Gli

Pronounce **gn** like the **ni** in *onion*, or as in the Italian *bagno* (BAHN-yoh; bath). **Gli** is pronounced like the **lli** in *million*, or as in the Italian *sbagliato* (zbal-YAH-toh; wrong).

Sc and Sch

When followed by **a, o,** or **u, sc** is pronounced as **sk.** *Scusi* (excuse me) yields "SKOO-zee." When followed by an **e** or **i,** sc is pronounced **sh** as in *sciopero* (SHOH-pair-oh; strike). The addition of the letter **h** returns **c** to its hard sound (sk) before **i** or **e,** as in *pesche* (PEHS-keh; peaches).

Double Consonants

When you see a double consonant, stress the preceding vowel; failure to do so can lead to confusion. For example, *penne all'arrabbiata* is "short pasta in a spicy, red sauce," whereas *pene all'arrabbiata* means "penis in a spicy, red sauce."

PHRASEBOOK

ENGLISH	ITALIAN	ENGLISH	ITALIAN
Yes	Si	Is there a bed available tonight?	C'è un posto libero stasera?
No	No	With bath/shower	Con bagno/doccia
Stop	Ferma	With hot bath/shower	Con bagno/doccia caldo/a
Go	Va'	Is there air conditioning?	C'è aria condizionata?
Goodbye	Arrivederci	Does it work?	Funziona
Hello	Buongiorno	Do you think I'm stupid?	Pensi che io sono stupido?
High	Alto	I would like to buy a ticket / pass	Vorrei comprare un biglietto / una tessera
Low	Basso	One-way	Solo andata
Why?	Perché?	Round-trip	Andata e ritorno
I Don't Know	Non lo so	I got on the wrong train	Sono salito sul treno sbagliato
Thank You	Grazie	The middle of nowhere	Nel mezzo del nulla
How are you?	Come stai?	Help!	Aiuto!
I am from the US	Sono degli Stati Uniti	I lost my passport/wallet	Ho perso il passaporto/ portafoglio
I have a visa/ID	Ho un visto/ carta d'identità	I've been robbed	Sono stato derubato/a
I have nothing to declare (but my genius)	Non ho nulla da dichiarare (ma il mio genio)	Leave me alone!	Lasciami stare!/Mollami!
I will be here for less than three months	Lo sarò qui per meno di tré mesi	I'm calling the police!	Telefono alla polizia!
No, I swear, I'm not smuggling anything	No giuro, io non ho nulla di contrabbando	You're going to jail	Si sta andando in prigione
Please release me from jail	Vi prego di liberare dal carcere	Go away, moron!	Vattene, cretino!
Could you repeat that?	Potrebbe ripetere?	And now for something completely different	E ora qualcosa di completamente diverso
I don't understand	Non capisco	You're cute	Sei carino/a (bello/a)
Leave me alone!	Lasciami stare!/Mollami!	I have a reservation	Ho una prenotazione
I don't want to buy your souvenirs	Non voglio acquistare il souvenir	I love you, I swear	Ti amo, te lo giuro
Hotel/hostel	Albergo/ostello	I only have safe sex	Pratico solo sesso sicuro

language · phrasebook

let's go online

Plan your next trip on our spiffy website, ▣www.letsgo.com. It features full book content, the latest travel info on your favorite destinations, and tons of interactive features: make your own itinerary, read blogs from our trusty Researcher-Writers, browse our photo library, watch exclusive videos, check out our newsletter, find travel deals, follow us on Facebook, and buy new guides. Plus, if this Essentials wasn't enough for you, we've got even more online. We're always updating and adding new features, so check back often!

essentials

ITALY 101

Somewhere between the Roman Empire, the Venetian Republic, and the Italian Renaissance, a lot of stuff ended up in Italy. Roman sculptures, unimaginably ornate *palazzi*, Roman-*style* sculptures, and dramatic oil paintings fill Italy, and they're all on view for you to enjoy. However, wherever there's a lot to see, there's also a lot to know—from who painted the Sistine Chapel to what the heck a *doge* is and why it had such a nice house. To save you from the oh-so-*gauche* faux pas of confusing a Botticelli with a Bernini, we've included some summaries of the art, architecture, and history that give this cultured country its special seasoning. Think of this chapter as Art History 101 but with fewer lectures and more penis jokes. We've also slipped in tips on how to avoid offending Italians who *aren't* dead, since you'll probably run into a few of them, too. Italy is an amazing country with a seriously incredible collection of artistic and historical goodies, so read up on them ahead of time to make the most of your travels. What else are you going to do on the plane ride, anyway? One can only flip through *SkyMall* magazine so many times...

facts and figures

- **AREA:** 116,400 sq. miles
- **2009 POPULATION:** 58 million
- **REGISTERED CATHOLICS:** 51.6 million
- **ACTIVE VOLCANOES:** 3
- **MONEY THROWN INTO TREVI FOUNTAIN DAILY:** €30,000
- **ANNUAL WINE CONSUMPTION PER CAPITA:** 26 gallons
- **ANNUAL BREAD CONSUMPTION PER CAPITA:** 183 pounds
- **FIFA WORLD CUP WINS:** 4
- **TEENAGE MUTANT NINJA TURTLES NAMESAKES:** 4

history

YES WE (ETRUS)CAN! (BEGINNING OF TIME-753 BCE)

The first evidence of human life in what is now Italy dates back around 50,000 years. However, the most famous Italian remains are somewhat newer: **Ötzi the Iceman,** a naturally formed mummy and archaeological superstar, was found in the frosty Dolomites and dated to 3000 BCE. After Ötzi's tribe, several primitive peoples cycled through the area before **the Etruscans** settled down for good (800 BCE). A relatively advanced society with its own state system (as opposed to a whole lot of chieftains), the Etruscan civilization was only rivaled by the presence of Magna Graecia along the Mediterranean coast. However, it was not long before the **Roman Empire,** that famous kudzu of cultures, overtook both of these early societies.

LITERALLY ANCIENT HISTORY

Kingdom (753-509 BCE)

There are many tales about the founding of Rome, but by far the best known involves two sons of the god Mars, **Romulus** and **Remus.** Their birth was scandalous, seeing as their mother was one of the sacred Vestal Virgins—in fact, a concerned royal uncle ordered that they be killed immediately. However, the man ordered to do so pitied the helpless infants and instead left them in a basket by the Tiber River. Various accounts exist for what happened next, the most common being that an oddly compassionate **she-wolf** rescued and suckled the twins, caring for them into adulthood. She seems to have raised some ambitious young men, for the brothers founded Rome together in 753 BCE. Fraternal rivalry soon brought this partnership to an end when Romulus, understandably offended when Remus dared to jump over a wall he had built, did what any upstanding man-raised-by-she-wolves would do and killed his brother, thereby ensuring their newly established kingdom would bear his name. Rome remained a kingdom for a couple hundred years, with the Etruscans making their way back into power for a while in the form of the **Tarquin Dynasty** (616 BCE). However, after another big **sex scandal,** a man named Lucius Brutus got the gumption to overpower the Tarquins and establish a Republic.

To the Republic (509-27 BCE)

Contrary to the teachings of your eighth-grade history teacher, functional republican government did exist before the United States. Indeed, the Roman Republic had a lot of the staples of a good Republic down—checks and balances, separation of powers, the whole shebang. What it didn't master so well was equality; contention raged between the **aristocracy,** the **patricians,** and the lowest class, the **plebeians.** Despite these tensions, the Roman dominion began to expand way beyond modern-day Italy, northward into what is now England and all the way to Iran in the East. However, this expansion only further weakened the rule of the aristocracy and led to an uprising of slaves, led by ex-gladiator and historical VIP **Spartacus** (73 BCE). When Spartacus was finally stopped by Pompey the Great and Marcus Cressus, another big name decided to throw himself into the mix and quickly overtook these "allies." That's right, **Julius Caesar** emerged as self-declared Dictator for Life in 45 BCE However, we all know that "Life" was not so long—his dear friend **Marcus Brutus** led his assassination on March 15th, 44 BCE. After another struggle for power, Caesar's adopted nephew Octavian came out on top and was granted the honorific title Caesar Augustus in 27 BCE.

Age of Empire (27 BCE-476 CE)

Roman civilization reached its largest size during this Empire period, so called after Caesar Augustus took the title of Emperor. Containing 6,500,000 kilometers of land at its peak, the Empire asserted its influence over a whole lot of cultures, and this influence is still felt today (see Romance languages, republican governments, etc.). In fact, the Empire was so vast that a third-century Roman Emperor named **Diocletian,** known for his hatred and persecution of Christians, saw fit to divide the authority up among four co-emperors. This worked just fine until Diocletian died and passed the severed empire to his less capable (but more tolerant) successor, **Constantine.** Constantine moved the capital to Byzantium, narcissistically renamed it **Constantinople,** and set the stage for one of the most annoying songs of all time. This reshuffling broke up the already divided empire permanently, leaving a large, successful Byzantine Empire in the East and a relatively puny Roman Empire in modern day Italy. It was all pretty much downhill from there, with Rome's final blow being dealt when a German chief, **Odoacer,** crowned himself king and put the last Roman Emperor, ironically named Romulus, under house arrest.

MEDIEVAL TIMES (476-1375)

Often called the **Dark Ages,** this time period in Italy is probably best defined by religious contention: with the Roman Empire out, the Roman Catholic papacy saw an opportunity to extend its power, even beginning to take action without the emperor's blessing. In fact, Pope Gregory I independently decided to add Italy to the Holy Roman Empire with the help of a barbarian chieftain named **Charlemagne.** This famous crusader went on to have an illustrious career as Holy Roman Emperor. However, his disappointing descendants did not—Italy was subject to small but numerous wars for centuries after. This led to Italy's division into rival city-states, causing cultural and mental divisions that are obvious even today. Division seems to be a theme of the period, in fact, because the Middle Ages simply wouldn't be the Middle Ages without the next big event: **The Great Schism.** It all started with a rebellious Emperor, Henry IV, who started a name-calling war with the then-pope, Gregory VII. The conflict escalated until the papacy huffily moved from Rome to Avignon, France, ushering in a period known as the **Babylonian Captivity** (1309-1377). To top off all the confusion, three popes simultaneously claimed holiness and gave history one of the most unpronounceable periods of all time: The Great Schism! (1378-1417) Meanwhile, as if that weren't enough, the tragedy that was the **Bubonic Plague** swept through Europe, killing a third of the total population.

RINASCIMENTO (1375-1540)

The more secular humanism of the Italian Renaissance can be, in part, attributed to the political shifts that accompanied it. These shifts took place as a number of ancient Italian families who exercised a positively papal power over their respective city-states rose to rival the Holy Roman Emperor. The most famous of these families, the **Medici** of Florence, set the standard for Renaissance rule, shifting their focus from banking and stabbing people to patronizing the arts. In fact, they even fought with the pope himself (Julius II) to bring the artist **Michelangelo** to Florence. However, just as humanitarianism was beginning to flourish, a wet blanket of a friar named **Girolamo Savonarola** stepped up and fought ferociously against what he considered "excesses of the church." In 1497, he and his followers burned thousands of "blasphemous" books, works of art, musical instruments and othertools of sin in what became known as **The Bonfire of the Vanities.** Boticelli even got in on the action, apparently realizing the error of his myth-painting ways. Savonarola was a controversial hero until the Pope realized what a threat he had become and excommunicated him. Ironically, Savonarola was eventually executed by the very same Florentines who had previously been his partners in arson. Meanwhile, the feuding Italian princes left the country open to more petty wars, and Spanish armies quickly jumped at the opportunity to invade. By 1540, Spain controlled all of the Italian cities except Venice.

DIVIDED AND CONQUERED (1540-1815)

Divided and under the rule of the Spanish Hapsburgs, Italy had fallen a long way from its powerful beginnings. When the last Hapsburg ruler, Charles II, died in 1700, the country was so weak that the game of **tug-of-war** that ensued as Austria, France, and Spain all vied for possession of the decentralized peninsula was inevitable. After a hundred years of this back and forth, a Frenchman named **Napoleon Bonaparte** came along and settled things pretty quickly: he took Italy for himself. By uniting many of the cities into the **Kingdom of Italy** in 1804, he brought unity back to the broken country and positioned himself as its monarch. After his final battle at **Waterloo** in 1815, however, the Congress of Vienna re-divided poor Italy and gave much of the power, unsurprisingly, to Austria.

FORZA ITALIA (1815-PRESENT)

With newfound national spirit, the Italians revolted against this latest injustice: the Risorgimiento, a nationalist movement, was born. Superstars of this rebellion included Giuseppe Mazzini, Giuseppe Garibaldi, and Camillo Cavour, whose efforts culminated with the political unification of Italy in 1860. Despite persistent intra-country conflicts, Italy remained unified throughout the centuries to come, with World War I only adding to the country's nationalistic spirit. A slight stumbling block came along in the form of World War II: a gifted orator named **Benito Mussolini** promised order and stability. Unfortunately, his idea of order and stability included the establishment of the world's first fascist regime in 1919. Not all Italians were thrilled with this development—sentiment towards Mussolini ran the gamut from total loyalty to fierce opposition. Debate over Mussolini became a moot point, however, as Italy entered the war on the side of the Axis, and **Nazi occupation** redefined Italy's political reality.

In 1945 the occupation ended, ushering in the modern era of Italian politics. The current constitution, instituted in 1948, allows for a democratic Republic, with a president, a prime minister, a bicameral parliament, and an independent judiciary. Though the government has changed nearly 60 times since, one element remains consistent: powerful, bold leaders. Self-made tycoon **Silvio Berlusconi** is the latest in this colorful lineup, elected as prime minister in 1994...and 2001...and 2008, with plenty of corruption scandals as well as two resignations in between. Berlusconi's middle-right stance aligned him with American President George Bush and the Iraq war. Though the unpopularity of this decision opened the doors for the more liberal Romano Prodi to move into power, Italians have proven themselves to be more forgiving than the once-divorced Berlusconi's ex- and estranged wives, as this philanderer now once again serves as Prime Minister of Italy.

customs and etiquette

Undeniably a friendly bunch, Italians do have their own ways of doing things, and if you want to fit in, you might need a small course in Italian etiquette. Chances are, with four million visitors each year, they'll still know you're a tourist, but at least they'll think you're a polite one.

AT THE CLUB

Italians place a lot of emphasis on first impressions, so don't get yourself into a *mi scusi* situation. When meeting someone for the first time, a handshake is the way to go—**air kissing** (left side first!) generally comes with a little more familiarity. The Italian people are known to stand pretty close, so get ready to readjust your personal space boundaries. When it comes to clothing, Italians find having *bella figura*, or a good image, very important and tend to value quality over quantity. They dress more formally more frequently than Americans. Women should be warned that short skirts and shorts are slightly more risqué in Italy than America—revealing tops are a little less so.

AT THE TABLE

Italian mealtime etiquette is not so very different from the American—at home, courses are served one by one and passed around the table, and at restaurants, the waiter should bring all dishes at once. What you may not be used to are the meal*times:* lunch is usually served anywhere from 1 to 3pm, and dinner can be as late as 10pm! As for formal table manners, if you're concerned about looking like a foreigner, then remember to keep your fork in your left hand and your knife in your right hand at all times, **Continental-style.** It isn't offensive to switch the fork hand, but it is conspicuous. Finger food is rare—even fruit is generally eaten with a fork and knife at the table. Finally, be sure to ask for seconds when they're available. Not only will you most likely want them, you'll also win brownie points for your *buone maniere!*

art and architecture

REALLY REALLY OLD ART

The Estruscans created the first native Italian artwork, placing an **emphasis on aesthetics** that is noticeable even in Italy today. Though their artwork was largely destroyed by Roman conquerers, evidence of ornate Estruscan funeral statues, tomb paintings, and burial urns still exists today. While these artifacts may give Etruscan culture a **morbid reputation,** they are simply the only aspects of Etruscan culture left to study. When the Romans came a-conquering, they brought with them their own iconic style of art and architecture. Given their buzzing political scene, the Romans found it necessary to divide art into two categories: household art and art in homage to the state. The Roman taste for flair made its way into household art: sumptuous **frescoes** of mythical stories covered wealthy Roman's walls, while **mosaics** (artwork formed by carefully pressing small colorful shards of pottery into mortar) decorated the floor. When it came to the state, however, art was somewhat more realistic. Around every corner there was another statue or painting glorifying a great battle, general, or, most likely, emperor.

MIDDLE-AGED ART

The Middle Ages started out pretty unoriginally, as far as architecture goes: the "in" style, **Romanesque,** mimicked the Romans' rounded arches, heavy columns, and windowless churches of just a few hundred years earlier. Of course, when the hot new **Gothic** movement brought airy vaulted ceilings and giant stained-glass windows down to Italy from France, the dark and heavy Romanesque style moved to the not list. Despite architecture's new, less gloomy beauty, sculptors and artists continued to depict dead or dying Christians in their art.

REBORN ART

Ninja Turtles Assemble

All that began to change during the Renaissance. **Sandro Botticelli's** *The Birth of Venus*, depicting the goddess rising from a seashell, marked the beginning of a new age for art. *David,* one of the most gawked-at **nude statues** of all time, did the same for sculpture, thanks to artist **Michelangelo Buanarotti.** Michelangelo also painted the ceiling of the Sistine Chapel, arguably one of the greatest works of all time, then declared to Pope Julius II, "I am not a painter!" Painter, sculptor, or Queen of England, the guy was an artistic genius. The other three ninja turtles' namesakes, **Raphael, Donatello,** and **Leonardo** (da Vinci) also left their marks on the Italian art scene. Raphael was a prolific painter, Donatello specialized in relief sculpture, and da Vinci...well, the man merits a whole paragraph to himself. Genius, artist, inventor, sculptor, and author—

he was, in short, the original Renaissance Man. Some of his ingenious sketches have proven themselves to be perfectly viable plans for flying machines, testifying to their creator's visionary imagination.

Let's Talk About Our Feelings.

By the end of the Renaissance, artists had nearly perfected the representation of a scene: the perspective, shadow, and human figures they painted were all completely realistic. Once this got boring, the natural next step forward was to depict how the artist *felt* about the subject. This new approach to painting characterized a style now referred to as **Mannerism**. The most famous painter of this style, **Tintoretto**, gained a reputation for his temper, earning himself the nickname *Il Furioso*. His violent imagery and emotional scenes are said to have inspired **El Greco.**

MODERNITY

No More Order

From this time forward, art began to move and develop in a less uniform fashion as various movements simultaneously formed to both oppose and complement one other. During the 16th century, this fragmentation gave rise to the some of the most famous movements of art history. The **Baroque** and **Rococo** styles were the first two on the scene and became popular in quick succession: the baroque period's combination of the Renaissance's grandeur and the emotional affect of Mannerism made for powerful works that displayed nature at its most raw and realistic. **Caravaggio,** the most famous of the Italian Baroque artists, is even rumored to have used a prostitute's corpse as a model for Mary in his unsettling painting, *Death of the Virgin*. Rococo style evolved towards the tail end of the Baroque period and presented a striking contrast as its light, airy motifs such as **seashells, flowers,** and **clouds** replaced Caravaggio's gritty dynamism.

Inundated with Isms

The 19th century saw the beginning of a flood of famous isms. The first of these, **Impressionism**, developed naturally from Mannerism, as it, too, emphasized the artist's unique perception of the scene depicted. At first harshly criticized for being seemingly unfinished and less-than-realistic, Impressionism is now one of the most widely recognizable artistic styles. Famous Italian Impressionists include Federico Zandomeneghi and Giuseppe De Nittis. Another 19th century movement, **Neoclasicism,** contrasted sharply with the **loosey-goosey** ways of Impressionism. Glorifying ancient Roman and Greek architecture, this style emphasized symmetry, geometry, and proportion. Such an artistic revival made sense, since after the excavation of **Herculaneum** and **Pompeii,** Italians found themselves living amidst the beautiful, largely intact ruins of the Roman Empire.

You Say You Want a Revolution

In 1909, writer **Filippo Tommaso Marinetti** burst on to the scene, violently declaring his hatred of anything old and announcing a new movement he would call **Futurism**. He and his followers admired **speed, violence,** and the **industrial city,** and trumpeted the triumph of humanity over nature in their works, which largely consisted of manifestos criticizing the past of anything from architecture to cooking.

After World War II, Futurism made another brief stand when it was revived by its inventor. Otherwise, postwar Italian art lacked unity, but nevertheless included some interesting characters. For example, **Piero Manzoni,** a conceptual artist, shocked the world by sealing an unknown (but often guessed) substance into cans labeled **Artist's Shit** and setting their price at their weight in gold. Amazingly, in 2007, the most recently auctioned can sold for US$80,000. Today, Italian postmodern artists reject the division of art into different categories and isms. Although Italian art may be defined by an artistic history that fits neatly into such categories, these contemporary artists and architects ensure Italy's continued status as a vibrant center of creativity and artistic development.

fashion

As early as the 11th century, Italians understood that the good life not only included beautiful art and architecture, but also a fashionable wardrobe. This culture of style has only grown stronger throughout the centuries, making us wonder if Italian babies are born sporting couture. In 1881, when a couturier named **Cerutti** started his own line, he began a tradition of fashion design that would make Italy a style mecca for, well, forever. His pupils included **Giorgio Armani**, a still-practicing designer known for stylish menswear. **Guccio Gucci**, who started out with a single leather store in 1914, and **Gianni Versace**, whose sister **Donatella** is an icon in her own right are other Italian designers whose brandnames you may recognize. If you want to personally experience what it's like to be on the red carpet, visit Milan, where the majority of these fashion houses have their headquarters. (Just don't expect to stay within a tight budget!)

food and drink

If you're headed to Italy, it is not unlikely that one of the highlights of your trip will come in a culinary form: people have been known to visit Italy just for the food. Whether you're enjoying wine (from the number one exporter in the world) or the internationally famous pasta, you're sure to be impressed by the local fare.

THE THREE SQUARES

The first meal of the day in Italy generally isn't anything too elaborate: *la colazione* may consist simply of coffee and a *cornetto* (croissant). Lunch *(il pranzo)* can go either way: in rural regions you may find it to be a hugely elaborate affair that precedes a nap and separates the two halves of the workday. However, most Italians will just grab a simple panino (sandwich) or salad. The last meal of the day, *la cena*, is generally the most important, and starts at approximately 8pm. It can continue through most of evening, seeing as it may contain any or all of the following courses: an *antipasto* (appetizer), a *primo piatto* (starchy first course like pasta or risotto), a *secondo piatto* (meat or fish), a *contorno* (vegetable side dish), a *dolce* (dessert), a *caffè* (espresso), and often an after-dinner liqueur.

POTENT POTABLES

You can't write about Italian food without acknowledging the drinks that accompany it. Coffee and wine in particular enjoy an unrivaled respect from the Italian people, and therefore come in infinite delicious varieties.

Non-Alcoholic Shots

Italian-style coffee, or *espresso*, is famous, though the blend of coffee beans used is often from **Brazil.** The beans are roasted medium to medium-dark in the north, getting progressively darker as you move toward the south. *Espresso* is commonly thought to contain more caffeine than drip coffee, but in fact, the opposite is true! The modern *espresso* machine uses extremely high pressure to force water through a small amount of finely ground coffee in just **half a minute**, resulting in a more concentrated brew. This can then be mixed with water and milk in various ways, forming several classes of drink: *caffè macchiato* is topped with a bit of steamed milk or foam, *cappuccino* is mixed with steamed, frothy milk, and *caffelatte* is equal parts espresso and steamed milk. Other varieties include the frowned-upon *caffè americano*, watered down and served in a large cup, and *caffè coretto*, a kicked-up version that includes a bit of strong liqueur.

Putting a Cork in It

Leading the world in both wine exports and national wine consumption, Italy is a country that values a good *vino*. Every year over one million vineyards cultivate grapes for *rosso* (red wine) and *bianco* (white wine). The difference? Red wine includes the skins of the grapes in the fermenting process, while white wine does not. The Italians classify their wine under four headings, and bottles are helpfully labeled with the category to which they belong. Your basic table wine, or *Vino de Tavola*, may say VDT; this doesn't necessarily mean it is inferior, but it might not conform to certain wine laws. **Regional wines** may be labeled with an "IGT" *(Indicazione Geografica Tipica)*, which simply denotes which region they come from. If you want a wine of guaranteed quality, you'll need to look for **DOCG** *(Denominazione di Origine Controllata e Garantita)*, which means the wine has undergone a rigorous taste-testing process. A plain old DOC is also an indication of quality: this means the wine has not been tested but does follow a set of strict quality-control regulations. Try such regional beauties as Barolo, a classy (read: expensive) staple of Piedmont made from red grapes that are fermented for over 20 years, or Frascati, a cold, clean Roman white.

music

Producing **Verdi, Vivaldi,** and one of the **three tenors,** Italy has made a name for itself in the field of music. As every musician knows, Italian is the language of sheet music, so there's no better place to hear the **fat lady** sing.

INTRODUCING: POPE GREGORY AND THE MONKS

Monks were the main musical act back in the 6th century, and Italian monks were especially prolific. That's why we here devote a whole section on music to people living the celibate life, starting with the granddaddy of them all, **Pope Gregory I,** inventor of the **Gregorian chant,** a style of song characterized by a repeating note that only occasional deviates. **Guido D'Arezzo** furthered musical development with his invention of modern staff notation and experimentation in **polyphony,** the layering of multiple musical lines.

DIVAS AND CASTRATI: OPERA

Italy's most favored art form (whose name literally means "work") emerged in Florence in the mid-1590s, but soon spread to Venice, Naples, and especially Milan. Dreamt up by a group of Florentine aesthetes called the **Camarata,** opera became a symbol for Italian nationalism and unity, especially in the 19th-century works of iconic composer **Giuseppe Verdi,** whose **La Traviata, Aida,** and **Rigoletto** are some of the best known operas of all time. Though this dramatic art form's popularity declined in the late 20th century, today, a revitalized interest in opera has arisen, with several new composers on the scene. However, the works of three classic Italian operettists, **Verdi, Rossini** and **Puccini,** still dominate the performance repertoire, making up well over a third of the list of the 20 most-performed operas in the world.

italy 101

BEYOND TOURISM

If you are reading this, then you are a member of an elite group—and we don't mean "the literate." You're a student preparing for a semester abroad. You're taking a gap year to save the trees, the whales, or the dates. You're an 80-year-old woman who has devoted her life to egg-laying platypuses and figuring out what the hell is up with that. In short, you're a traveler, not a tourist; like any good spy, you don't observe your surroundings—you become an active part of them.

Your mission, should you choose to accept it, is to study, volunteer, or work in Italy as laid out in the dossier—er, chapter—below. More general wisdom, including international organizations with a presence in many destinations and tips on how to pick the right program, is also accessible by logging onto the Beyond Tourism section of ▇www.letsgo.com. We leave the rest (when to go, whom to bring, and how many changes of underwear to pack) in your hands. This message will ▇**self-destruct** in five seconds. Good luck.

greatest hits

- **FREE WILLY.** Enjoy life on the high seas, sailing in the Bay of Naples while researching the ecology of dolphin and whale habitats (p. 463).

- **BE INDIANA JONES, EXCEPT REAL.** Dig up artifacts dating from the first century with real-life archaeologists (p. 462).

- **PERFECT YOUR PIZZA-TOSSING SKILLS.** Apprentice with an Italian chef while studying at a culinary academy in Florence (p. 462).

- **MASTER A NEW TONGUE.** Perfect your Italian in the morning and your tan in the afternoon on the beautiful shore of Italy's "toe" (p. 461).

- **GET YOUR TILE ON.** Take a five-day crash course in mosaic-making at Ravenna's Mosaic Art School (p. 461).

studying

The best cure for a quarter-life crisis (you know—that moment when, while sitting at your desk attempting to memorize your ten amino acids of the day, you start asking yourself, what's the point of it all?) is some time spent studying abroad. When going to class means walking by the Roman Colosseum, it's hard to become jaded, and being forced to reevaluate your habits and cultural norms in the full-on immersion experience of a homestay can help you find a refreshingly new worldview. Do your research before you go abroad, keeping in mind that different programs will be populated by different kinds of students (summer programs, especially, tend to be filled with lots of Americans likely to slip into English). Where and with whom you choose to live can have a major impact on your experience. If you are a college student, your local study-abroad office is a great place to begin your investigation. Many American universities partner with universities abroad to set up great international opportunities, and some offer foreign campuses staffed by faculty of the home institution.

visa information

All non-EU citizens visiting Italy must obtain a visa for any stay **longer than three months**. You can apply for a student visa at your local Italian embassy or consulate. Make sure to bring a valid passport, visa application form, a passport photo, proof of residency, documentation of the course or program in which you are participating, proof of health insurance coverage, and (if you are under the age of 18) an affidavit of financial support from your parents as well as your parents' most recent bank statement. Within eight days of your arrival in Italy, you will need to obtain a **Permesso di Soggiorno** (residency permit) from your local police station.

UNIVERSITIES

Whether you choose to go through a study-abroad organization or enroll directly in to an Italian institution (possibly a cheaper option), numerous universities will be happy to welcome your smiling English-speaking self to their campus. Most international programs will offer instruction in English and Italian, while Italian institutions are likely to have English programs in more upper-level master's programs. Most schools are in Italy's major cities (Rome, Florence, Venice, and Milan), but you can find more rural areas where less English is likely to be spoken in Siena, Cesena, and Tuscania.

International Programs

AMERICAN INSTITUTE FOR FOREIGN STUDY

College Division, River Plaza, 9 W. Broad St., Stamford, CT ☎800-727-2473 🖳www.aifs.com
Summer, semester, and academic-year programs in Florence and Rome. Programs are taught by faculty from Richmond, an American international university based in London. Internship program available in Florence. Courses available in English, but at least one course must be taken in Italian.
i College students; summer program also open to high school graduates. 2.5 min. GPA. Ⓢ Semester $15,995; summer $6495.

ARCADIA UNIVERSITY

450 S. Easton Rd., Glenside, PA ☎866-927-2234 🖳www.arcadia.edu/abroad
Semester and year-long programs offered in Florence, Lecce, Perugia, Rome,

and Syracuse, Sicily. A special program in Rome has a business concentration. You can spend a winter quarter in modern Mediterranean studies at Syracuse, or if you're not feeling that up-to-date, check out ancient Mediterranean studies in spring quarter. During the summer, Arcadia runs Italian language and culture programs in all of the above cities as well as special design and intensive fashion design programs in Florence.

i 2.7-3.0 min. GPA depending on program. $ Semester $12,500-16,500; full year $21,500-28,850, depending on program; summer $2550-5500, depending on program location and length. Semester and full-year estimates do not include meal costs; summer estimate does not include room and board.

CCIS STUDY ABROAD

2000 NW P St., Ste. 503, Washington, DC ☎800-453-6956 🖥www.ccisstudyabroad.org

Jet to Florence, Rome, Tuscany, or Venice for a summer or a semester, or take advantage of CCIS' three-city program (only available in semester length) and turn your study abroad into a regular sightseeing vacation. You can figure out your own housing or live in a student apartment.

i 18+. 2.5-2.6 min. GPA. $ Semester $4685-8580, depending on program; academic year $14,800; summer $1640-5925, depending on program. Does not include room and board. Non-NY residents should contact the College of Staten Island for cost information.

COUNCIL ON INTERNATIONAL EDUCATIONAL EXCHANGE

300 Fore St., Portland, ME ☎207-553-4000 🖥www.ciee.org

Language and culture program offered in Ferrara and classical studies in Naples. Offers a mix of English- and Italian-language instruction to beginners or complete novices of the language. A liberal arts program is available in both cities but is taught entirely in Italian and targets intermediate to advanced students of the language. All programs available for either semester or the full academic year.

i College students. 2.75 min. GPA. Liberal arts program in Ferrara requires 4 semesters of college-level Italian; Naples requires 5. Classical studies program in Naples only open to students majoring in classical studies. $ Semester $13,900; full year $26,500. Includes 2 meals per day with homestay option.

EXPERIENTIAL LEARNING INTERNATIONAL

1557 Ogden St., Denver, CO ☎303-321-8278 🖥www.eliabroad.org

A smaller study-abroad organization, ELI offers summer, semester, and academic-year programs in Florence. Take your pick of a Studio Art, Intensive Italian Language, or Liberal Arts program of study. You'll likely share an apartment about 20min. away from the main campus with a fellow student unless you arrange your own housing.

$ Semester $12,595-13,595 depending on program; summer $4195-5335, depending on program. Does not include meals.

INTERNATIONAL PARTNERS FOR STUDY ABROAD

13832 N. 32nd St., Ste. 151, Phoenix, AZ ☎602-743-9682 🖥www.studyabroadinternational.com

It may be more difficult to arrange credit transfers for classes taken through International Partners for Study Abroad (IPSA)'s programs, which enroll you directly in Italian institutions, but this direct enrollment also could make studying with IPSA in Florence, Rome, or Tuscania quite the steal.

i 18+. $ Semester €2000-6350; summer €900-2950; Jan term €900-1600. Cost depends on location and academic program. Does not include room and board.

INSTITUTE FOR THE INTERNATIONAL EDUCATION OF STUDENTS

33 N. LaSalle St., 15th fl., Chicago, IL ☎1-800-995-2300 🖥www.iesabroad.org

Semester, academic year, and summer programs offered in Milan, Rome, and Siena. A January term program is also available in Rome. Instruction is given in both English and Italian. Opportunities for enrollment in courses at local universities, term-time and summer internships, "field study activities" (read: field trips), and language improvement. Homestays or apartment housing can be found through the institute.

i *18+ for semester programs. College students 3.0 min. GPA, though graduate students welcomed for summer programs.* Ⓢ *Semester $17,615-18,760, depending on location; summer $6550-6698, depending on location; Jan term $3500. Does not include all meals or food costs. Semester price does not include fees for enrollment in local universities.*

INTERNATIONAL STUDIES ABROAD

1112 W. Ben White Blvd., Austin, TX ☎800-580-8826 🖳www.studiesabroad.com

Studying abroad during the summer, over a semester, or during an academic year in International Studies Abroad (ISA)'s Rome or Florence programs means you'll be in an international university filled largely with other Americans, but trips (included in the program fees) to places like Pompeii, Capri, Cinque Terre, and Orvieto may help you escape your English-speaking peers.

i *2.5-3.3 min. GPA, depending on program.* Ⓢ *Semester $14,500-15,500, depending on program; full year $26,000-29,800, depending on program; summer $4100-8900, depending on program. Does not include meals.*

Italian Programs

UNIVERSITÀ COMMERCIALE LUIGI BOCCONI

V. Sarfatti 25, Milan ☎+39 025 836 3535 🖳www.uni-bocconi.it

Future i-bankers with a taste for the good life might want to consider studying abroad at Bocconi, Italy's first university to award a degree in economics. With a business school ranked among the global top 40, Bocconi is likely to draw a fair share of Enzo Ferrari wannabes. Check to see if your school is one of the 180 with which Bocconi runs an exchange program.

UNIVERSITÀ DEGLI STUDI DI ROMA SAPIENZA

Piazzale Aldo Moro 5, Rome 🖳www.uniroma1.it

As possibly made evident by the less-than-expert English version of Sapienza's website, those looking to study abroad here should probably make sure they are well-schooled in Italian, though higher-level courses taught in English are available. A summer school in Italian language and culture may be more appropriate for students less confident in their command of the language.

UNIVERSITÀ DI BOLOGNA

V. Zamboni 33, Bologna ☎+39 051 208 8101 🖳www.eng.unibo.it

Take your pick of one of Bologna's five campuses, one each in Cesena, Forlì, Ravena, Rimini, and...Bologna! Luckily, no matter where you go, you can still say that you attend the super-cute-sounding "UniBo." The university offers a range of courses taught in English, including some classes created in partnership with other institutions of higher learning. You can also check out Bologna's summer school in Italian language and culture. With great generosity, the school offers free Italian-language instruction to non-Italian EU and other foreign students.

UNIVERSITÀ DI PISA

Lungarno Pacinotti 43, Pisa ☎+39 050 221 2111 🖳www.unipi.it/english

The University of Pisa offers some courses in English (primarily upper-level ones), a sports center, youth orchestra, and choir to its students. Plus, you'll be certain to have the chance to climb up Pisa's famous leaning tower, unlike your friends, who have likely stopped here on a whirlwind tour of Italy only to find the tower filled to capacity.

Ⓢ *Full year €2000. Does not include room and board.*

beyond tourism

POLITECNICO DI MILANO

V. Golgi 42, Milan ☎+39 022 399 2250 ⬛www.english.polimi.it

The largest Italian institution for the study of engineering, architecture, and industrial design, Politecnico di Milano offers English-language courses at the bachelor level in architecture and urban planning and partners with several North American universities to host student exchange programs. Check to see if yours is one of them.

Ⓢ *€800-3300 per year, depending on family income. Does not include room and board.*

LANGUAGE SCHOOLS

As renowned novelist Gustave Flaubert once said, "Language is a cracked kettle on which we beat out tunes for bears to dance to." While we at Let's Go have absolutely no clue what he was talking about, we do know that the following are good resources for learning Italian.

AMERISPAN STUDY ABROAD

1334 Walnut St., 6th fl., Philadelphia, PA ☎800-879-6640 ⬛www.amerispan.com

With a presence on Facebook, Twitter, YouTube, and Skype, Amerispan may be invading all the newfangled social media, but it actually provides helpful information about a bunch of Italian-language schools in Italy and Switzerland.

Ⓢ *$320-3135, depending on program location, length, and choice of accommodations; Switzerland can be considerably more expensive ($6835 more, to be exact). Typical.*

EUROCENTRES

56 Eccleston Sq., London, UK ☎+41 044 485 5040 ⬛www.eurocentres.com

Study Italian in a 16th-century *palazzo* near the Ponte Vecchio while following Eurocentres' basic general language or more intensive language and culture programs, both of which can be enriched with add-on packages of five one-on-one lessons.

i 16+. Ⓢ *Semester €3456-4272; full year €5184-8544. 20-week €378-1812; 25-week €450-2244. Cost depends on number of lessons per week and type of program. Does not include room and board.*

SPRACHCAFFE

Gartenstr. 6, Frankfurt, Germany ☎+356 25 70 1000 ⬛www.sprachcaffe.com/english

While you'll be hitting the books in Sprachcaffe's standard 4-classes-a-day curriculum offered at their schools in Calabria, Florence, and Rome, their suggestively titled "Holiday Courses" in Calabria and Florence cut the workload in half—perfect if your vacation isn't complete without a little homework.

Ⓢ *€210-6555, depending on program location, length (2-5 weeks), number of classes per day (2-6), group or private classes, and choice of accommodations.*

FINE ARTS SCHOOLS

- **AEGEAN CENTER FOR THE FINE ARTS:** Learn how to sing, study Italian art history, or try painting in a bid to rival da Vinci (talk about a losing battle) at this international school for the arts. (☎+30 22840 23 287 ⬛www.aegeancenter.org)

- **MOSAIC ART SCHOOL:** Want a little mo' saic in your life? Then consider taking a five-day class (open to all levels, who knew there were advanced mosaicists these days?) in Ravenna. You'll walk away having completed two original pieces of your own design. (☎+39 349 601 4566 ⬛www.sira.it/mosaic/studio.htm)

- **STUDIO ART CENTERS INTERNATIONAL, FLORENCE:** Advanced students of the arts can embark on a year of self-structured study in Florence with Studio Art Centers International (SACI)'s Post-Baccalaureate Certificate Program in Art, Art History, and Art Conservation, while more casual artists can take classes in the summer for no academic credit. See p. 462 for SACI's archaeological program. (☎+39 055 289948 ⬛www.saci-florence.org)

CULINARY SCHOOLS

- **APICIUS INTERNATIONAL SCHOOL OF HOSPITALITY:** At Apicius' campus in Florence, aspiring chefs, sommeliers, bakers, or extreme foodies can study their hearts out, with one-, two-, and four-year professional programs. Amateurs can also indulge in less intense instruction that may include gastronomic walking tours or visits to local farms and markets. (☎+39 055 265 81.35 ▣www.apicius.it)

- **COOK ITALY:** With short courses (most are five days or less) that focus on the food of specific regions or on particular dishes, Bologna-based Cook Italy's programs in towns like Naxxar, Lucca, and Siracusa are perfect for amateurs interested in getting a literal taste of what it means to cook Italian. One-day classes and culinary vacations are also available. (☎+39 349 007 8298 ▣www.cookitaly.com)

- **LA VECCHIA SCUOLA BOLOGNESE** The cornerstone of Bolognese culture is food. Not theater, not music, but food. Take home a piece of that cultural knowledge by creating fresh pasta under the instruction of the English-speaking staff at this excellent cooking school. By day's end (or after three or five if you really like it), you'll have nothing to show for yourself but a happy belly. Even if your attempts don't succeed, a meal by the pros is guaranteed. (☎051 64 93 627 ▣www.lavecchiascuola.it)

SCHOOLS FOR INDIANA JONES WANNABES

While you may not discover the Temple of Doom, you might just find something even cooler: real artifacts from ancient Etruscan and Roman civilizations.

- **ARCHAEOSPAIN:** Check out the "ancient pottery dump" of Monte Testaccio in Rome. If that doesn't sound super-appealing, maybe knowing that the artifacts you'll be digging up date from the first to third centuries will make the excavation more exciting. Anyone 18+ is welcome, and academic credit is available. (☎866-932-0003 ▣www.archaeospain.com)

- **STUDIO ART CENTERS INTERNATIONAL, FLORENCE:** While offering a comprehensive arts program, SACI also hosts a two-course summer program on archaeology that includes field work at the school's excavation site in Tuscany as well as study of Etruscan art and civilization. (☎+39 055 289948 ▣www.saci-florence.org)

volunteering

If you're that glutton for punishment who can't help feeling a pang of guilt while on vacation (Must offset the carbon emissions of my plane flight! Think of the baby seals I could be saving if I weren't wandering the halls of the Uffizi!), perhaps it's time to consider traveling in Italy as a volunteer. There are loads of opportunities to enjoy the natural beauty of Tuscany, the rich history of Rome, or the gastronomical delights of Umbria as a summer or year-long volunteer. In the listings below, you'll find a mix of organizations, some of which you can contact directly and others that are umbrella organizations with sweet hook-ups to local projects. In some cases, you will pay a fee for this service, but consider what a less altruistic vacation would cost you and then evaluate volunteer prices in that light. When choosing an organization with which to volunteer, always make an effort to speak with past participants, investigate how your participation fee is spent, and check out the group's reputability in order to ensure that your efforts are serving the people, creatures, or issues you signed up to help in the first place. The International Volunteer Programs Association has a user-friendly website (▣www.volunteerinternational.org) that should help you as you plan your volunteering vacation.

ENVIRONMENTAL AND WILDLIFE CONSERVATION

- **ECOVOLUNTEER, COMMON DOLPHINS:** Sleep on a 17.7m cutter in the Bay of Naples, and save the whales (dolphins too!) with this international volunteer organization. (☎31 74 2508250 🖳www.ecovolunteer.org)

- **GLOBAL VISION INTERNATIONAL:** Help research the ecology of the Pelagos Cetacean Sanctuary (Flipper and Free Willy fans wanted) on a 21m 🖳sailing boat in the Ligurian Sea with this company's Italy program. (☎888 653 6028 🖳www.gviusa.com)

ARCHAEOLOGY AND HISTORICAL RESTORATION

- **ARCHEO VENEZIA:** Organizes archaeological summer camps in which participants work to preserve the historical artifacts in Venice's lagoon. Recommended for those comfortable with Italian. (☎041 710515 🖳www.archeove.com)

- **EARTHWATCH:** In the Italy program offered by this international non-profit, you'll have the chance to dig up ancient Roman artifacts in Tuscany's central coast. Oh yeah, and you'll be helping to preserve this region's cultural and archaeological heritage. (☎800-776-0188 🖳www.earthwatch.org)

- **FOOTSTEPS OF MAN:** Accepts volunteers for a min. of 7 days to analyze rock art in the Italian Alps, with over 300,000 samples dating from the Neolithic era to the Middle Ages. (☎+39 036 443 3983 🖳www.rupestre.net/field/index.html)

- **INVOLVEMENT VOLUNTEERS:** Get down and dirty working in this global volunteering company's archaeological workcamp in Sicily, or practice a little extreme home makeover, royalty edition, and help restore a southern Italian palace. (☎+61 3 9646 9392 🖳www.volunteering.org.au)

- **RESPONSIBLETRAVEL.COM:** Lists over 100 "responsible tours" of Italy, such as archaeological volunteering in Tuscany. (🖳www.responsibletravel.com)

COMMUNITY OUTREACH AND ACTIVISM

- **AGAPE CENTRO ECUMENICO:** This ecumenical center in the Alps is a Protestant-run conference area for the peaceful interaction of people from all faith backgrounds, including atheists. The center welcomes volunteers to act as interpreters for its summer camps and will provide food, accommodations, and the cost of travel. (☎+39 012 180 7514 🖳www.agapecentroecumenico.org)

- **MANI TESE:** This organization, committed to the fight against world hunger and with a particular focus on inequities between the northern and southern hemispheres, organizes summer work camps throughout Italy that focus on sustainability and "food sovereignty." (🖳www.manitese.it)

- **PUEBLO INGLÉS:** Volunteer to teach English immersion-style to Italians in rural Umbria. (☎+34 913. 913. 400 🖳www.morethanenglish.com/anglos/index.asp)

- **UNITED PLANET:** This international non-profit organizes "volunteer quests" in partnership with local programs in need of volunteers. Several such projects are available in Italy for lengths of four weeks to three months and offer the opportunity to experience a high level of cultural immersion while assisting disabled people or the elderly. (☎800-292-2316 🖳www.unitedplanet.org)

FOR THE UNDECIDED ALTRUIST

- **SERVICE CIVIL INTERNATIONAL (SCI):** SCI lists a select number of service opportunities (30-40 total in Italy) but includes a wide range of project types, with activities ranging from restoration of a historical agricultural building in Pavia to

volunteering . for the undecided altruist

the staffing of an environmentally friendly youth festival near Bologna. (☎434-336 3545 ▪www.sci-ivs.org)

- **VOLUNTEERS FOR PEACE:** Lists more than 70 volunteer opportunities in Italy, ranging from prepping a puppetry festival in Pinerolo (just hope that none of those puppets turn into real boys) to working at a summer animation camp for Arabic-speaking immigrant children in Turin. (☎802-259-2759 ▪www.vfp.org)

working

While it might seem strange to travel to another country to work, Italy offers many singular experiences that you just can't replicate elsewhere. Consider working as a fashion intern in the world's fashion capital, Milan. Pick grapes in a Tuscan vineyard, or teach people how to ski in the Italian alps. You'll experience cultural immersion like no other and have unique stories to tell when you return home. Work visas are necessary for stays longer than three months, so make sure to determine your plans in advance if you intend to work for an extended period. As these pesky documents can be difficult to obtain, short-term work is easier to come by, especially in agriculture, the service sector, and the tourism industry.

LONG-TERM WORK

If you're serious about finding a job in Italy, make the **Sezione Circoscrizionate per l'Impiego** (government employment agency) your friend and register with the nearest employment office (*ufficio di collocamento*). Be persistent and creative in your job hunt and consider checking out the tips offered on the wealth of expat websites floating around the interwebs. Keep in mind, however, that Italy suffers from a relatively high level of unemployment. For the student working in Italy, an internship or au pair position are probably the most reliable long-term options.

Teaching English

If you are not an EU citizen, getting a job teaching English in Italy will likely be a daunting task. Use the sites listed below to conduct your own investigation into the possibilities available to you. In the end, a long-term position may not be in the cards. Instead, consider a summertime camp counselor gig or dabble in freelance tutoring.

- **ASSOCIAZIONE CULTURALE LINGUISTA EDUCATIONAL (ACLE):** This non-profit brings English to Italian children through the use of games, songs, and drama. Employees can act as counselors for the organization's summer camps and, during the school year, as English tutors, language school staff members, actors in ACLE's traveling theater program, or office assistants. (☎+39 018 450 6070 ▪www.acle.org)

- **ESL BASE:** This site is a helpful resource for those investigating the possibility of traveling through Italy on the strength of their English. (▪www.eslbase.com)

- **INLINGUA:** Another of Italy's major English-language schools has over 55 branches in the country. EU nationals often preferred. (▪www.inlingua.com)

- **OXFORD SEMINARS:** Provides a ton of helpful information, including detailed explanations of how to obtain work visas for citizens of all different countries hoping to teach in Italy. (▪www.oxfordseminars.com)

- **TRANSITIONS ABROAD:** This extensive website's section on teaching English in Italy contains a mother lode of tips on finding teaching positions in Italy, many of them the result of the writers' first-hand experiences. (▪www.transitionsabroad.com/listings/work/esl/index.shtml)

beyond tourism

- **WANTED IN ROME:** A Craigslist-style assortment of listings and adverts for Rome. Sometimes postings looking for English teachers or tutors pop up, and given the difficulty of securing a long-term English-teaching post in Italy, finding more informal positions on this kind of listing service may lead to more job offers. *(💻www.wantedinrome.com)*

Au Pair Work

If you find a family that will take you on for three months or less, you should be free to Mary Poppins your heart out as an au pair in Italy. Non-EU citizens hoping to take a job longer than three months will have to apply for a Long-Stay Au Pair Visa, which requires enrollment in Italian-language courses while working as an au pair. A spoonful of sugar helps the medicine go down, so make sure to indulge in a lot of gelato if you choose this option.

- **AU PAIR.COM:** Families post listings directly to this site. *(💻www.aupair.com)*
- **CHILDCARE INTERNATIONAL:** Lists au pair opportunities throughout Europe, including Italy. *(💻www.childint.co.uk)*
- **GEOVISIONS:** Be an au pair in Italy for two months to one year in this company's program. The site also includes details about how to obtain the Long-Stay Au Pair Visa for jobs of more than three months. *(☎877-949-9998 💻www.geovisions.org)*
- **GREAT AU PAIR:** American website with au pair listings by location and country in English. *(💻www.greataupair.com)*
- **NEW AUPAIR.COM:** This site offers lots of free listings for prospective au pairs as well as information about visas and (out of date, as they will inform you) average au pair salary listings. *(💻www.newaupair.com)*
- **ROMA AU PAIR:** Places young EU citizens with families in Italy. *(💻www.romaaupair.it)*

Internships

Why do one at home when you could pad your resumé in Italy?

- **CENTER FOR CULTURAL INTERCHANGE:** Offers internships in Florence. Min. stay of 3 months, including 4 weeks of intensive language training in preparation for the internship. Positions available in areas such as architecture, finance, and international business. Interns have the option of living in a homestay. *(💻www.cci-exchange.com/abroad/intern.shtml $ $3090-11,850, depending on length of internship and choice of accommodations.)*
- **GLOBAL EXPERIENCES:** Arranges internships with companies in Florence, Rome, and Milan. Programs include intensive language training, accommodation, emergency medical travel insurance, and full-time on-site support. *(💻www.globalexperiences.com $ $6890-8990, depending on location and length of internship.)*
- **INSTITUTE FOR THE INTERNATIONAL EDUCATION OF STUDENTS:** Internships for academic credit in Rome during the summer. Past assignments at the Museo Nazionale Romano, the Explora Children's Museum, Associated Press Italia, Italian NGOs, and think tanks. Includes tuition for six credits, orientation, housing, and medical insurance. *(💻www.iesabroad.org $ $6655)*
- **PEGGY GUGGENHEIM COLLECTION:** Interns assist museum operations such as gallery preparation, tour guidance, workshops with children, and administrative matters for one to three months. Offers a stipend. Italian skills a plus. *(💻www.guggenheim-venice.it/inglese/education/internship.html)*
- **WORLD ENDEAVORS:** Three- to six-month internships in Florence in a wide variety of fields, from handicraft apprenticeships to sports training positions with professional

calcio (a.k.a soccer) teams. Include intensive Italian training and various English-speaking support services. (🖥*www.worldendeavors.com* $ *$4655-7755.)*

Other Long-Term Work

- **BOLLETTINO DEL LAVORO:** A monthly publication available in employment offices and libraries, this Italian job bulletin may be useful to those comfortable with the language and looking for long-term jobs. (🖥*www.bollettinodellavoro.it)*
- **ENGLISH YELLOW PAGES:** Resource for English-speaking expats in Italy founded by an American who relocated to the country in 1984. Includes job listings, classifieds, photos, blogs, and more. (🖥*www.englishyellowpages.it)*
- **EXPAT EXCHANGE:** Includes an Italy forum with articles by Italian expats on everything from having a baby in Italy to where to find the best pizza. Also includes international job listings. (🖥*www.expatexchange.com)*
- **EXPATS IN ITALY:** The subtitle of this website, "for those who dream and those who live the dream," pretty much says it all. (🖥*www.expatsinitaly.com)*
- **WORKAWAY:** Site lists opportunities for work exchange (you work, they provide room and board) that can be searched by region and type of work. Lots of options at bed and breakfasts and farms in Italy. (🖥*www.workaway.info)*

more visa information

Any non-EU citizen traveling in Italy to work must possess a work visa, a *permesso di soggiorno per lavoro* (permission to stay for those with a work visa), and a work permit. Both the permission to stay and an interim work permit (good for 90 days) can be obtained at the police station of the town in which you are residing once you have received your work visa. While there are many types of work visas, it is quite difficult for most **non-EU citizens** to obtain one of any kind because, in order for the visa to be issued, prospective employers must initiate the process by providing evidence that their foreign employee is both an expert in the field and that his or her employment does not take a job away from an EU citizen. As you might imagine, this process involves lots of paperwork and takes time—basically, it's a bureaucratic nightmare. If you want to give it a shot, your best bet is to bring your passport, proof of residency, a letter explaining the purpose and nature of your trip, your round-trip ticket to Italy, proof of financial means in Italy, and the necessary information from your employer to your local Italian embassy or consulate...and grovel. Visit the Italian Ministry of Foreign Affairs website (🖥www.esteri.it) or the US Embassy site (🖥italy.usembassy.gov) for more information.

SHORT-TERM WORK

Illegal working is not necessarily frowned upon in Italy. Indeed, the **black economy** is said to thrive in the south of the country, with conservative estimates placing the amount of southern income withheld from Italian tax authorities at **50%.** Itinerant workers are most commonly employed as bartenders or restaurant staff, construction workers, farmhands, tour guides or souvenir vendors, domestics, or language tutors. However, it's definitely illegal for non-EU citizens to work in Italy without a work permit. If you do so, you are liable to a hefty fine as well as deportation. Let's Go never recommends working illegally. Foreign students can obtain an **autorizzazione di lavoro provvisoria** (temporary work permit) for part-time work during the summer and term-time. As much as we like a little rule-breaking every now and then, Let's Go encourages you to work legally.

- **ALPITOUR ITALIA:** This vacation resort company hires holiday representatives for summer and winter hotels and camps to shepherd guests back and forth from the airport, arrange ski passes and equipment rental, and otherwise take care of clueless tourists. Jobs are competitive and require good people skills and good spoken Italian (fluency in other languages a plus). (■*www.alpitour.it*)

- **CANVAS HOLIDAYS:** Runs camping holidays across Europe, including some in Italy and hires summer staff. Recruitment begins in October and is open to individuals 18+ with customer service experience. (■*www.canvasholidaysrecruitment.com*)

- **IDEALIST.ORG:** Compiles an international listing of volunteer opportunities and public interest jobs. Several opportunities in Italy that offer room and board in exchange for your work can be found on the site. (■*www.idealist.org*)

- **INFORMAGIOVANI:** A great resource for young people (who are fairly fluent in Italian) looking for part-time and temp work, these local information centers found in most towns and cities post opportunities for baby-sitting, tutoring, gardening, and domestic work and also provide information about how to find jobs in Italy. You can post your CV to their website. (■*www.informagiovani.it*)

- **SEASONWORKERS.COM:** Lots of different opportunities including jobs as aerobics instructors and ski resort employees. Site also includes information on work visas and permits. (■*www.seasonworkers.com*)

- **TRANSITIONS ABROAD:** Check out this website for tips on how and where to find short-term work while abroad. (■*www.transitionsabroad.com*)

- **WORLD WIDE OPPORTUNITIES ON ORGANIC FARMS:** As a WWOOFer (there's nothing canine about it, we promise), you'll exchange your time and energy working on an organic farm for room and board. You'll likely undergo a unique cultural immersion, enjoy scrumptious, farm-fresh produce, and have free time to explore the countryside. Two-week trip to Tuscany anyone? (■*www.wwoof.it*)

tell the world

If your friends are tired of hearing about that time you saved a baby orangutan in Indonesia, there's clearly only one thing to do: get new friends. Find them at our website, ■www.letsgo.com, where you can post your study-, volunteer-, or work-abroad stories for other, more appreciative community members to read. There's also a Beyond Tourism section that elaborates on non-destination-specific volunteering, studying, and working opportunities. If you liked this chapter, you'll love it; if you didn't like this chapter, maybe you'll find the website's more general Beyond Tourism tips more likeable, you non-likey person.

INDEX

index

index

index

MAP INDEX

MAP LEGEND

- ■ Sight/Service
- ✈ Airport
- ⊓ Arch/Gate
- 🏦 Bank
- 🏖 Beach
- 🚌 Bus Station
- ⊕ Capital City
- 🏰 Castle
- ⚑ Church
- ⚑ Consulate/Embassy
- ⚑ Convent/Monastery
- ⚓ Ferry Landing
- ☙ Gondola Station
- (347) Highway Sign
- ✚ Hospital
- 💻 Internet Cafe

- 🏛 Library
- Ⓜ M Metro Station
- ▲ Mountain
- 🕌 Mosque
- 🏛 Museum
- ℞ Pharmacy
- 🛡 Police
- ✉ Post Office

- 🎿 Skiing
- ✡ Synagogue
- ☎ Telephone Office
- 🎭 Theater
- ⓘ Tourist Office
- ⓣ Traghetto Stop
- 🚆 Train Station
- Ⓥ Vaporetto Stop

🧭 The Let's Go compass always points NORTH.

- Pedestrian Zone
- Stairs

- Park
- Water
- Beach

map index

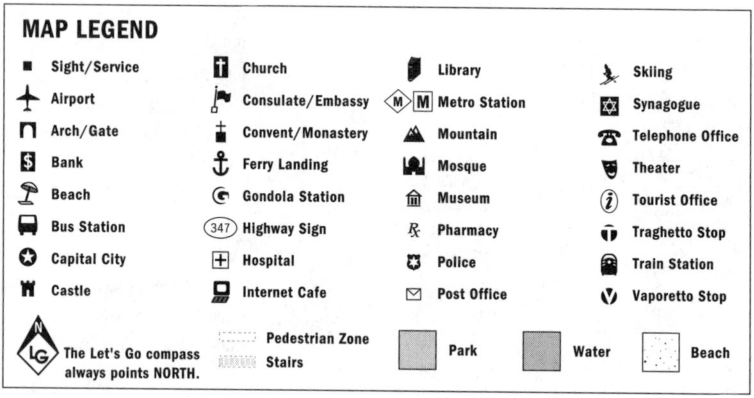

THE STUDENT TRAVEL GUIDE

These Let's Go guidebooks are available at bookstores and through online retailers:

EUROPE
Let's Go Amsterdam & Brussels, 1st ed.
Let's Go Berlin, Prague & Budapest, 2nd ed.
Let's Go France, 32nd ed.
Let's Go Europe 2011, 51st ed.
Let's Go European Riviera, 1st ed.
Let's Go Germany, 16th ed.
Let's Go Great Britain with Belfast and Dublin, 33rd ed.
Let's Go Greece, 10th ed.
Let's Go Istanbul, Athens & the Greek Islands, 1st ed.
Let's Go Italy, 31st ed.
Let's Go London, Oxford, Cambridge & Edinburgh,
    2nd ed.
Let's Go Madrid & Barcelona, 1st ed.
Let's Go Paris, 17th ed.
Let's Go Rome, Venice & Florence, 1st ed.
Let's Go Spain, Portugal & Morocco, 26th ed.
Let's Go Western Europe, 10th ed.

UNITED STATES
Let's Go Boston, 6th ed.
Let's Go New York City, 19th ed.
Let's Go Roadtripping USA, 4th ed.

MEXICO, CENTRAL & SOUTH AMERICA
Let's Go Buenos Aires, 2nd ed.
Let's Go Central America, 10th ed.
Let's Go Costa Rica, 5th ed.
Let's Go Costa Rica, Nicaragua & Panama, 1st ed.
Let's Go Guatemala & Belize, 1st ed.
Let's Go Yucatán Peninsula, 1st ed.

ASIA & THE MIDDLE EAST
Let's Go Israel, 5th ed.
Let's Go Thailand, 5th ed.

Exam and desk copies are available for study-abroad programs and resource centers.
Let's Go guidebooks are distributed to bookstores in the U.S. through Publishers Group West
and through Publishers Group Canada in Canada.
For more information, email letsgo.info@perseusbooks.com.

ACKNOWLEDGMENTS

BRONWEN THANKS: Ursula Brangwen. Lamont and Widener. Conor. The apartment is clean, and I miss you. Tarek and HubSummer, for getting me out of the office. Chris, for your commitment to Tanjore Tuesdays, the boat ikon, orange highlighter, and shots with silly names. You'll get your cannoli when you get it. Our RWs, who transported me to sunny beaches and moonlit *piazze* on rainy Cambridge days. Too many times I wanted to run off to the North End after reading your restaurant write-ups. Rossi and the Masthead team, for all their assists in the P1 and prod process. Mama MK. Hope this one's a winner. Sleep now? Most of all, my mom and dad. I am so lucky to have such wonderful parents. My week at home traversing California's golden hills with you guys was one of the best of the summer, closely rivaled by the week you came to Boston. To future travel together!

CHRIS THANKS: Bronwen, for being the hardest-working person at LGHQ and an awesome person at the same time. Marykate, for remarkable patience in the face of an avalanche of questions. My RWs, for each bringing their own style and personality to this book, for being great at their jobs, and for a whole load of amity. DChoi and all of Prod land, for coming to the rescue countless times. *Let's Go Italy 1982,* for being totally baller. *Gazetta Football Italia,* for teaching me everything I know about this great country. Any product preceded by the letter G, for making everything so much easier. Kirkland House, for being so damn fine. Catan, for the settlers. Tanjore, for feeding me. No thanks to the Nepalese flag, the Social Security Administration, or any and all Florentine purse-snatchers. Finally, the most special thanks to Area 51, for three years of happiness; my family, for 22 years of the same; and PJ, for everything.

DIRECTOR OF PUBLISHING Ashley R. Laporte
EXECUTIVE EDITOR Nathaniel Rakich
PRODUCTION AND DESIGN DIRECTOR Sara Plana
PUBLICITY AND MARKETING DIRECTOR Joseph Molimock
MANAGING EDITORS Charlotte Alter, Daniel C. Barbero, Marykate Jasper, Iya Megre
TECHNOLOGY PROJECT MANAGERS Daniel J. Choi, C. Alexander Tremblay
PRODUCTION ASSOCIATES Rebecca Cooper, Melissa Niu
FINANCIAL ASSOCIATE Louis Caputo

DIRECTOR OF IT Yasha Iravantchi
PRESIDENT Meagan Hill
GENERAL MANAGER Jim McKellar

LET'S GO
masthead

ABOUT LET'S GO

THE STUDENT TRAVEL GUIDE

Let's Go publishes the world's favorite student travel guides, written entirely by Harvard students. Armed with pens, notebooks, and a few changes of clothes stuffed into their backpacks, our student researchers go across continents, through time zones, and above expectations to seek out invaluable travel experiences for our readers. Because we are a completely student-run company, we have a unique perspective on how students travel, where they want to go, and what they're looking to do when they get there. If your dream is to grab a machete and forge through the jungles of Costa Rica, we can take you there. If you'd rather bask in the Riviera sun at a beachside cafe, we'll set you a table. In short, we write for readers who know that there's more to travel than tour buses. To keep up, visit our website, www.letsgo.com, where you can sign up to blog, post photos from your trips, and connect with the Let's Go community.

TRAVELING BEYOND TOURISM

We're on a mission to provide our readers with sharp, fresh coverage packed with socially responsible opportunities to go beyond tourism. Each guide's Beyond Tourism chapter shares ideas about responsible travel, study abroad, and how to give back to the places you visit while on the road. To help you gain a deeper connection with the places you travel, our fearless researchers scour the globe to give you the heads-up on both world-renowned and off-the-beaten-track opportunities. We've also opened our pages to respected writers and scholars to hear their takes on the countries and regions we cover, and asked travelers who have worked, studied, or volunteered abroad to contribute first-person accounts of their experiences.

FIFTY-ONE YEARS OF WISDOM

Let's Go has been on the road for 51 years and counting. We've grown a lot since publishing our first 20-page pamphlet to Europe in 1960, but five decades and 60 titles later, our witty, candid guides are still researched and written entirely by students on shoestring budgets who know that train strikes, stolen luggage, food poisoning, and marriage proposals are all part of a day's work. Meanwhile, we're still bringing readers fresh new features, such as a student-life section with advice on how and where to meet students from around the world; a revamped, user-friendly layout for our listings; and greater emphasis on the experiences that make travel abroad a rite of passage for readers of all ages. And, of course, this year's 16 titles—including five brand-new guides—are still brimming with editorial honesty, a commitment to students, and our irreverent style.

THE LET'S GO COMMUNITY

More than just a travel guide company, Let's Go is a community that reaches from our headquarters in Cambridge, MA, all across the globe. Our small staff of dedicated student editors, writers, and tech nerds comes together because of our shared passion for travel and our desire to help other travelers get the most out of their experience. We love it when our readers become part of the Let's Go community as well—when you travel, drop us a postcard (67 Mt. Auburn St., Cambridge, MA 02138, USA), send us an email (feedback@letsgo.com), or sign up on our website (www.letsgo.com) to tell us about your adventures and discoveries.

For more information, updated travel coverage, and news from our researcher team, visit us online at www.letsgo.com.

- **HOSTELS ALESSANDRO.** ☎39 06-4461958. ▣www.hostelsalessandro.com.
- **ALESSANDRO PALACE AND BAR.** Via Vicenza 42, 00185 Rome, Italy.
- **ALESSANDRO DOWNTOWN.** Via Carlo Cattaneo 23, 00185 Rome, Italy.
- **HOTEL SAN PIETRINO.** Via Giovanni Bettolo, 43 00195 Rome. ☎39 06 37 00 132. ▣www.sanpietrino.it.
- **MARTA GUEST HOUSE.** ☎39 06 6889 2992. ▣www.martaguesthouse.com. ▣marta.hotelinroma.com.
- **HOTEL ABACO.** 1 Via dei Banchi, Santa Maria Novella, 50123 Florence, Italy. ☎39 055 2381919. ▣www.hotelabaco.it.
- **HOTEL ANNABELLA.** Via Fiume 5, 50123 Florence, Italy. ☎39 055 281877. ▣www. hotelannabella.it.
- **HOTEL BIJOU BED AND BREAKFAST.** Via Fiume 5, 50123 Florence, Italy. ☎39 055 214156. ▣www.hotel-bijou.it.
- **HOSTEL OF THE SUN.** Via Melisurgo 15, 80133 Napoli, Italy. ☎39 081 4206393. ▣www.hostelnapoli.com.
- **HOSTELS OF NAPLES.** ▣www.hostelsofnaples.com.
- **HOSTEL AND HOTEL BELLACAPRI.** Via Melisurgo 4, 08133 Napoli, Italy. ☎39 081 5529494. ▣www.bellacapri.it.
- **HOSTEL PENSIONE MANCINI.** Via P.S. Mancini 33, 80139 Napoli, Italy. ☎081 553 6731. ▣www.hostelpensionemancini.com.
- **NAPLES PIZZA HOSTEL.** Via San Paolo ai Tribunali 44, 80138 Naples, Italy. ☎0039 08119323562. ▣www.naplespizzahostel.com.
- **HOTEL BELLINI.** Via San Paolo ai Tribunali 44, 80138 Naples, Italy. ☎0039 08119323562. ▣www.hotelbellini.net.
- **RING HOSTEL.** Via Gaetano Margero 72, Fario, Island of Ischio, Gulf of Naples, Italy. ☎0039 081 987 546; ☎0039 081 997 136. ▣www.ringhostel.com.
- **HOTEL VILLAEVA.** Via Grotta Azzurra, Trav la Fabbrica, n. 8-16, 80071 Anacapri, Naples, Italy. ☎39 0818371549. ▣www.villaeva.com.
- **LE SIRENE.** Via degli Aranci 160, 80065 Sorrento, Naples, Italy. ☎081 807 2925. ▣www.hostellesirene.com.

If you are interested in purchasing advertising space in a Let's Go publication, contact Edman & Company at ☎1-203-656-1000.